VW Transporter (T4) diesel
Owners Workshop Manual

John S. Mead

Models covered

(5711 - 304)

VW Transporter 'T4' variants with front-mounted diesel engines and front-wheel-drive
Diesel: 1.9 litre (1896cc) 4-cyl and 2.4 litre (2370cc) & 2.5 litre (2461cc) 5-cyl

Does NOT cover petrol engined models, all-wheel-drive 'Syncro' models, interior features specific to Westfalia, Caravelle or Multivan, or specialist bodywork/camper conversions
Does NOT cover Transporter 'T5' range introduced July 2003

© Haynes Group Limited 2014

ABCDE
FG

A book in the **Haynes Owners Workshop Manual Series**

ISBN **978 0 85733 711 5**

British Library Cataloguing in Publication Data
A catalogue record for this book is available from the British Library.

Printed in India

Haynes Group Limited
Sparkford, Yeovil, Somerset BA22 7JJ, England

Haynes North America, Inc
2801 Townsgate Road, Suite 340, Thousand Oaks, CA 91361

Disclaimer

There are risks associated with automotive repairs. The ability to make repairs depends on the individual's skill, experience and proper tools. Individuals should act with due care and acknowledge and assume the risk of performing automotive repairs.

The purpose of this manual is to provide comprehensive, useful and accessible automotive repair information, to help you get the best value from your vehicle. However, this manual is not a substitute for a professional certified technician or mechanic.

This repair manual is produced by a third party and is not associated with an individual vehicle manufacturer. If there is any doubt or discrepancy between this manual and the owner's manual or the factory service manual, please refer to the factory service manual or seek assistance from a professional certified technician or mechanic.

Even though we have prepared this manual with extreme care and every attempt is made to ensure that the information in this manual is correct, neither the publisher nor the author can accept responsibility for loss, damage or injury caused by any errors in, or omissions from, the information given.

Contents

LIVING WITH YOUR VW TRANSPORTER

MAINTENANCE

Contents

The VW T4 Transporter covered by this manual was introduced in the UK in December 1990 and continued in production until July 2003. The range was facelifted in May 1996 with significant mechanical revisions also incorporated. Seemingly innumerable variations of body types and styles were available, in either short or long wheelbase configuration.

The Transporter was available with 1.9, 2.4 and 2.5 litre diesel engines, in a wide range of power outputs. 1.8, 2.0, 2.5, and 2.8 litre petrol engines were also available but are not covered by this manual. 1.9 litre diesel engines were of 4-cylinder SOHC 8-valve configuration with indirect diesel injection and were either normally-aspirated or turbocharged. 2.4 and 2.5 litre engines were of 5-cylinder SOHC 10-valve configuration. 2.4 litre engines utilised indirect diesel injection and were all normally-aspirated. 2.5 litre engines utilised direct diesel injection and were all turbocharged. A 5-speed manual transmission was fitted as standard equipment

with a 4-speed automatic transmission being optionally available. The engine was mounted transversely at the front of the vehicle with the transmission mounted on the left-hand side. All models are of front-wheel drive configuration (a 4-wheel drive version was also available but is not covered by this manual).

The front suspension is fully independent using upper and lower transverse wishbones, torsion bars, telescopic shock absorbers and an anti-roll bar. The rear suspension is also fully independent by means of trailing arms, coil springs and telescopic shock absorbers. An anti-roll bar is fitted to certain versions.

The dual-circuit, servo-assisted braking system has discs at the front and self-adjusting drum brakes at the rear on vehicles produced up to May 1996. On later models, disc brakes are fitted at the front and rear. ABS, and on later models, traction control are optionally available, for extra safety when braking in emergency situations.

A wide range of standard and optional equipment is available within the Transporter range, including power steering, air conditioning, remote central locking, electric windows, electronic engine immobiliser and supplemental restraint systems.

For the home mechanic, the Transporter is a relatively straightforward vehicle to maintain, and most of the items requiring frequent attention are easily accessible.

Your VW Transporter Manual

The aim of this manual is to help you get the best value from your vehicle. It can do so in several ways. It can help you decide what work must be done (even should you choose to get it done by a garage). It will also provide information on routine maintenance and servicing, and give a logical course of action and diagnosis when random faults occur. However, it is hoped that you will use the manual by tackling the work yourself. On simpler jobs it may even be quicker than booking the vehicle into a garage and going there twice, to leave and collect it. Perhaps most important, a lot of money can be saved by avoiding the costs a garage must charge to cover its labour and overheads.

The manual has drawings and descriptions to show the function of the various components so that their layout can be understood. Tasks are described and photographed in a clear step-by-step sequence.

References to the 'left' and 'right' of the vehicle are in the sense of a person in the driver's seat facing forward.

Project vehicles

The main vehicle used in the preparation of this manual, and which appears in many of the photographic sequences, was a VW Transporter van with a 2.5 litre engine. Additional work was carried out on a Transporter van with a 2.4 litre engine.

Acknowledgements

Thanks are due to Draper Tools Limited, who provided some of the workshop tools, and to all those people at Sparkford who helped in the production of this manual. Thanks also go to Ryan Waters and John Fownes for the loan of their Transporter T4s for use in the project photography carried out in our workshop

This manual is not a direct reproduction of the vehicle manufacturer's data, and its publication should not be taken as implying any technical approval by the vehicle manufacturers or importers.

We take great pride in the accuracy of information given in this manual, but vehicle manufacturers make alterations and design changes during the production run of a particular vehicle of which they do not inform us. No liability can be accepted by the authors or publishers for loss, damage or injury caused by any errors in, or omissions from, the information given.

Working on your vehicle can be dangerous. This page shows just some of the potential risks and hazards, with the aim of creating a safety-conscious attitude.

General hazards

Scalding

• Don't remove the radiator or expansion tank cap while the engine is hot.
• Engine oil, transmission fluid or power steering fluid may also be dangerously hot if the engine has recently been running.

Burning

• Beware of burns from the exhaust system and from any part of the engine. Brake discs and drums can also be extremely hot immediately after use.

Crushing

• When working under or near a raised vehicle, always supplement the jack with axle stands, or use drive-on ramps.
Never venture under a vehicle which is only supported by a jack.
• Take care if loosening or tightening high-torque nuts when the vehicle is on stands. Initial loosening and final tightening should be done with the wheels on the ground.

Fire

• Fuel is highly flammable; fuel vapour is explosive.
• Don't let fuel spill onto a hot engine.
• Do not smoke or allow naked lights (including pilot lights) anywhere near a vehicle being worked on. Also beware of creating sparks (electrically or by use of tools).
• Fuel vapour is heavier than air, so don't work on the fuel system with the vehicle over an inspection pit.
• Another cause of fire is an electrical overload or short-circuit. Take care when repairing or modifying the vehicle wiring.
• Keep a fire extinguisher handy, of a type suitable for use on fuel and electrical fires.

Electric shock

• Ignition HT and Xenon headlight voltages can be dangerous, especially to people with heart problems or a pacemaker. Don't work on or near these systems with the engine running or the ignition switched on.

• Mains voltage is also dangerous. Make sure that any mains-operated equipment is correctly earthed. Mains power points should be protected by a residual current device (RCD) circuit breaker.

Fume or gas intoxication

• Exhaust fumes are poisonous; they can contain carbon monoxide, which is rapidly fatal if inhaled. Never run the engine in a confined space such as a garage with the doors shut.

• Fuel vapour is also poisonous, as are the vapours from some cleaning solvents and paint thinners.

Poisonous or irritant substances

• Avoid skin contact with battery acid and with any fuel, fluid or lubricant, especially antifreeze, brake hydraulic fluid and Diesel fuel. Don't syphon them by mouth. If such a substance is swallowed or gets into the eyes, seek medical advice.
• Prolonged contact with used engine oil can cause skin cancer. Wear gloves or use a barrier cream if necessary. Change out of oil-soaked clothes and do not keep oily rags in your pocket.
• Air conditioning refrigerant forms a poisonous gas if exposed to a naked flame (including a cigarette). It can also cause skin burns on contact.

Asbestos

• Asbestos dust can cause cancer if inhaled or swallowed. Asbestos may be found in gaskets and in brake and clutch linings. When dealing with such components it is safest to assume that they contain asbestos.

Special hazards

Hydrofluoric acid

• This extremely corrosive acid is formed when certain types of synthetic rubber, found in some O-rings, oil seals, fuel hoses etc, are exposed to temperatures above 4000C. The rubber changes into a charred or sticky substance containing the acid. *Once formed, the acid remains dangerous for years. If it gets onto the skin, it may be necessary to amputate the limb concerned.*
• When dealing with a vehicle which has suffered a fire, or with components salvaged from such a vehicle, wear protective gloves and discard them after use.

The battery

• Batteries contain sulphuric acid, which attacks clothing, eyes and skin. Take care when topping-up or carrying the battery.
• The hydrogen gas given off by the battery is highly explosive. Never cause a spark or allow a naked light nearby. Be careful when connecting and disconnecting battery chargers or jump leads.

Air bags

• Air bags can cause injury if they go off accidentally. Take care when removing the steering wheel and trim panels. Special storage instructions may apply.

Diesel injection equipment

• Diesel injection pumps supply fuel at very high pressure. Take care when working on the fuel injectors and fuel pipes.

⚠ *Warning: Never expose the hands, face or any other part of the body to injector spray; the fuel can penetrate the skin with potentially fatal results.*

Remember...

DO

• Do use eye protection when using power tools, and when working under the vehicle.
• Do wear gloves or use barrier cream to protect your hands when necessary.
• Do get someone to check periodically that all is well when working alone on the vehicle.
• Do keep loose clothing and long hair well out of the way of moving mechanical parts.
• Do remove rings, wristwatch etc, before working on the vehicle – especially the electrical system.
• Do ensure that any lifting or jacking equipment has a safe working load rating adequate for the job.

DON'T

• Don't attempt to lift a heavy component which may be beyond your capability – get assistance.
• Don't rush to finish a job, or take unverified short cuts.
• Don't use ill-fitting tools which may slip and cause injury.
• Don't leave tools or parts lying around where someone can trip over them. Mop up oil and fuel spills at once.
• Don't allow children or pets to play in or near a vehicle being worked on.

The following pages are intended to help in dealing with common roadside emergencies and breakdowns. You will find more detailed fault finding information at the back of the manual, and repair information in the main chapters.

If your vehicle won't start and the starter motor doesn't turn

☐ If it's a model with automatic transmission, make sure the selector lever is in 'P' or 'N'.

☐ Open the bonnet and make sure that the battery terminals are clean and tight.

☐ Switch on the headlights and try to start the engine. If the headlights go very dim when you're trying to start, the battery is probably flat. Get out of trouble by jump starting (see next page) using a friend's car.

If your vehicle won't start even though the starter motor turns as normal

☐ Is there fuel in the tank?

☐ Is there moisture on electrical components under the bonnet? Switch off the ignition, then wipe off any obvious dampness with a dry cloth. Spray a water-repellent aerosol product (WD-40 or equivalent) on engine and fuel system electrical connectors like those shown in the photos.

1 Check the security and condition of the battery connections.

2 Check all multi-plugs and wiring connectors for security.

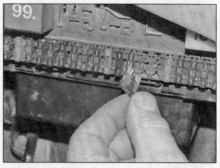

3 Check that all fuses are still in good condition and none have blown.

Check that electrical connections are secure (with the ignition switched off) and spray them with a water-dispersant spray like WD-40 if you suspect a problem due to damp.

Jump starting

Jump starting will get you out of trouble, but you must correct whatever made the battery go flat in the first place. There are three possibilities:

1 *The battery has been drained by repeated attempts to start, or by leaving the lights on.*

2 *The charging system is not working properly (alternator drivebelt slack or broken, alternator wiring fault or alternator itself faulty).*

3 *The battery itself is at fault (electrolyte low, or battery worn out).*

When jump-starting a car, observe the following precautions:

✓ Before connecting the booster battery, make sure that the ignition is switched off.

Caution: Remove the key in case the central locking engages when the jump leads are connected

✓ Ensure that all electrical equipment (lights, heater, wipers, etc) is switched off.

✓ Take note of any special precautions printed on the battery case.

✓ Make sure that the booster battery is the same voltage as the discharged one in the vehicle.

✓ If the battery is being jump-started from the battery in another vehicle, the two vehicles MUST NOT TOUCH each other.

✓ Make sure that the transmission is in neutral (or PARK, in the case of automatic transmission).

Budget jump leads can be a false economy, as they often do not pass enough current to start large capacity or diesel engines. They can also get hot.

1 Connect one end of the red jump lead to the positive (+) terminal of the flat battery.

2 Connect the other end of the red jump lead to the positive (+) terminal of the booster battery.

3 Connect one end of the black jump lead to the negative (-) terminal of the booster battery.

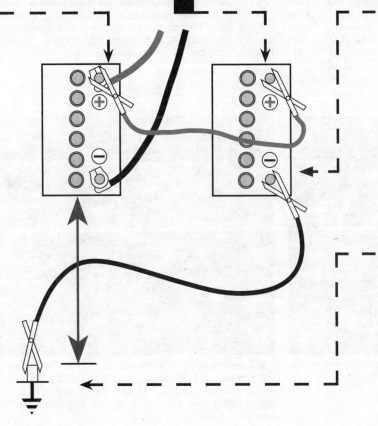

4 Connect the other end of the black jump lead to a bolt or bracket on the engine, well away from the battery, on the vehicle to be started.

5 Make sure that the jump leads will not come into contact with the fan, drive-belts or other moving parts of the engine.

6 Start the engine using the booster battery and run it at idle speed for a minimum of three minutes. Disconnect the jump leads in the reverse order of connection.

Wheel changing

⚠️ **Warning: Do not change a wheel in a situation where you risk being hit by other traffic. On busy roads, try to stop in a lay-by or a gateway. Be wary of passing traffic while changing the wheel – it is easy to become distracted by the job in hand.**

Preparation

- ☐ When a puncture occurs, stop as soon as it is safe to do so.
- ☐ Park on firm level ground, if possible, and well out of the way of other traffic.
- ☐ Use hazard warning lights if necessary.
- ☐ If you have one, use a warning triangle to alert other drivers of your presence.
- ☐ Apply the handbrake and engage first or reverse gear (or P on models with an automatic transmission).
- ☐ Chock the wheel diagonally opposite the one being removed – a couple of large stones will do for this.
- ☐ If the ground is soft, use a flat piece of wood to spread the load under the jack.

Changing the wheel

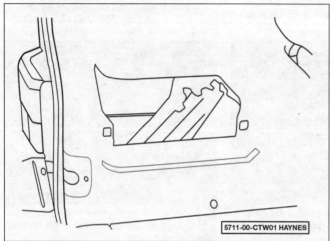

1 On Van and Caravelle models, the jack, wheelbrace and vehicle tools are located in a stowage compartment at the rear left of the luggage compartment. On some models it may be necessary to take off a removable cover for access. On Chassis cab models, the jack, wheelbrace and vehicle tools are located either under the rear seat or behind the driver's seat Release the catches and remove the stowage compartment cover, then unclip the retaining straps and remove the jack, handle and wheelbrace.

2 Depending on vehicle model, the spare wheel is stored at the rear of the passenger compartment, on an exterior bracket mounted at the rear of the vehicle, or under the rear of the vehicle. If the spare wheel is mounted under the rear of the vehicle, slacken the folding bracket safety bolt (arrowed) until it turns freely.

3 Undo the folding bracket retaining bolt and allow the bracket to rest on the safety bolt.

4 Insert the flat end of the wheelbrace into the guide on the folding bracket, up to the stop. Grasp the wheelbrace firmly, lift it slightly and move it to the right until the elongated hole slips over the safety bolt. Lower the folding bracket to the ground. Lift the spare wheel out of the folding bracket.

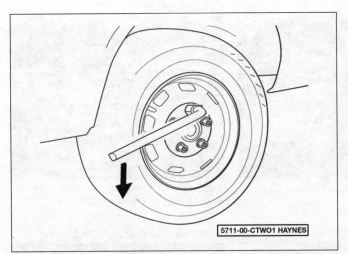

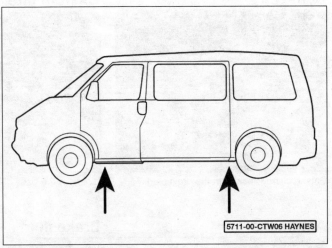

5 Where applicable, prise off the wheel bolt covers or wheel trim, using the flat end of the wheelbrace, for access to the wheel bolts. Slacken each wheel bolt by half a turn.

6 Position the jack under the jacking point nearest the punctured wheel. On Van and Caravelle models, the jacking points are indicated by depressions in the side sills just to the rear of the front wheels and just to the front of the rear wheels. On Chassis cab models, the front jacking points are indicated by depressions in the side sills just to the rear of the front wheels. The rear jacking points are indicated by a triangular mark under the mounting for the trailing arms.

8 Fit the spare wheel and screw on the bolts. Lightly tighten the bolts with the wheelbrace. Lower the vehicle to the ground and fully tighten the wheel bolts in a diagonal sequence. Refit the wheel bolt covers or wheel trim, as applicable.

Finally...

- [ ] Remove the wheel chocks.
- [ ] Secure the punctured wheel back in or under the vehicle, then stow the jack and tools in the stowage compartment.
- [ ] Check the tyre pressure on the wheel just fitted. If it is low, or if you don't have a pressure gauge with you, drive slowly to the next garage and inflate the tyre to the correct pressure.
- [ ] Have the damaged tyre or wheel repaired as soon as possible, or another puncture will leave you stranded.
- [ ] Where applicable, don't leave the spare wheel folding bracket empty and unsecured – it could drop onto the ground while the vehicle is moving.
- [ ] Have the wheel bolts tightened to the correct torque (see Chapter 10) at the earliest opportunity.

7 Engage the head of the jack with the jacking point and turn the jack handle clockwise until the wheel is raised clear of the ground. Unscrew the wheel bolts and remove the wheel.

Identifying leaks

Puddles on the garage floor or drive, or obvious wetness under the bonnet or underneath the car, suggest a leak that needs investigating. It can sometimes be difficult to decide where the leak is coming from, especially if an engine undershield is fitted. Leaking oil or fluid can also be blown rearwards by the passage of air under the car, giving a false impression of where the problem lies.

 Warning: Most automotive oils and fluids are poisonous. Wash them off skin, and change out of contaminated clothing, without delay.

 The smell of a fluid leaking from the vehicle may provide a clue to what's leaking. Some fluids are distinctively coloured. It may help to remove the engine undershield, clean the vehicle carefully and to park it over some clean paper overnight as an aid to locating the source of the leak. Remember that some leaks may only occur while the engine is running.

Sump oil

Engine oil may leak from the drain plug...

Oil from filter

...or from the base of the oil filter.

Gearbox oil

Gearbox oil can leak from the seals at the inboard ends of the driveshafts.

Antifreeze

Leaking antifreeze often leaves a crystalline deposit like this.

Brake fluid

A leak occurring at a wheel is almost certainly brake fluid.

Power steering fluid

Power steering fluid may leak from the pipe connectors on the steering rack.

Towing

When all else fails, you may find yourself having to get a tow home – or of course you may be helping somebody else. Long-distance recovery should only be done by a garage or breakdown service. For shorter distances, DIY towing using another vehicle is easy enough, but observe the following points:

☐ Use a proper tow-rope – they are not expensive. The vehicle being towed must display an ON TOW sign in its rear window.

☐ Always turn the ignition key to the 'on' position when the vehicle is being towed, so that the steering lock is released, and the direction indicator and brake lights work.

☐ Only attach the tow-rope to the towing eyes located below the front and rear bumpers.

☐ Before being towed, release the handbrake and select neutral on the transmission.

☐ On models with automatic transmission, special precautions apply. If in doubt, do not tow, or transmission damage may result.

☐ Note that greater-than-usual pedal pressure will be required to operate the brakes, since the vacuum servo unit is only operational with the engine running.

☐ On models with power steering, greater-than-usual steering effort will also be required.

☐ The driver of the vehicle being towed must keep the tow-rope taut at all times to avoid snatching.

☐ Make sure that both drivers know the route before setting off.

☐ Only drive at moderate speeds and keep the distance towed to a minimum. Drive smoothly and allow plenty of time for slowing down at junctions.

Introduction

There are some very simple checks which need only take a few minutes to carry out, but which could save you a lot of inconvenience and expense.

These checks require no great skill or special tools, and the small amount of time they take to perform could prove to be very well spent, for example:

☐ Keeping an eye on tyre condition and pressures, will not only help to stop them wearing out prematurely, but could also save your life.

☐ Many breakdowns are caused by electrical problems. Battery-related faults are particularly common, and a quick check on a regular basis will often prevent the majority of these.

☐ If your vehicle develops a brake fluid leak, the first time you might know about it is when your brakes don't work properly. Checking the level regularly will give advance warning of this kind of problem.

☐ If the oil or coolant levels run low, the cost of repairing any engine damage will be far greater than fixing the leak, for example.

Underbonnet check points

◀ **2.5 litre models (others similar)**

1 *Engine oil level dipstick*

2 *Engine oil filler cap*

3 *Coolant reservoir (expansion tank)*

4 *Brake and clutch fluid reservoir*

5 *Power steering fluid reservoir*

6 *Screen washer fluid reservoir*

7 *Battery*

Engine oil level

Before you start

✔ Make sure that the vehicle is on level ground.
✔ Check the oil level before the vehicle is driven, or at least 10 minutes after the engine has been switched off.

HAYNES HINT *If the oil is checked immediately after driving the vehicle, some of the oil will remain in the upper engine components, resulting in an inaccurate reading on the dipstick.*

The correct oil

Modern engines place great demands on their oil. It is very important that the correct oil for your vehicle is used (see *Lubricants and fluids*).

Vehicle care

● If you have to add oil frequently, you should check whether you have any oil leaks. Place some clean paper under the vehicle overnight, and check for stains in the morning. If there are no leaks, then the engine may be burning oil.

● Always maintain the level in the dipstick's cross-hatched area (see photo 3). If the level is too low severe engine damage may occur. Oil seal failure may result if the engine is overfilled by adding too much oil.

1 The dipstick is brightly coloured for easy identification (see *Underbonnet check points* on page 0•11 for exact location). Withdraw the dipstick.

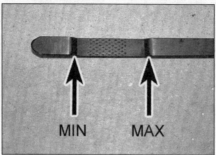
MIN   MAX

3 Note the oil level on the end of the dipstick; it should be in the cross-hatched area - never above the 'MAX' line or below the 'MIN' line. If topping-up is required (only if the level is between the cross-hatched area and the 'MIN' line, or below) add no more than 0.5 litre of oil at a time.

2 Using a clean rag or paper towel remove all oil from the dipstick. Insert the clean dipstick into the tube as far as it will go, then withdraw it again.

4 Oil is added through the filler cap. Unscrew the cap and top-up the level. A funnel may help to reduce spillage. Add the oil slowly, checking the level on the dipstick frequently. Avoid overfilling (see *Vehicle Care*).

Coolant level

Warning: Do not attempt to remove the expansion tank pressure cap when the engine is hot, as there is a very great risk of scalding. Do not leave open containers of coolant about, as it is poisonous.

Vehicle care

● Adding coolant should not be necessary on a regular basis. If frequent topping-up is required, it is likely there is a leak. Check the radiator, all hoses and joint faces for signs of staining or wetness, and rectify as necessary.

● It is important that antifreeze is used in the cooling system all year round, not just during the winter months. Don't top up with water alone, as the antifreeze will become too diluted.

1 The coolant level varies with the temperature of the engine, and is visible through the expansion tank. When the engine is cold, the coolant level should be between the MAX and MIN marks on the side of the tank. When the engine is hot, the level may rise slightly above the MAX mark.

2 If topping-up is necessary, wait until the engine is cold. Slowly unscrew the expansion tank cap, to release any pressure present in the cooling system, and remove it.

3 Add a mixture of water and antifreeze to the expansion tank until the coolant level is halfway between the level marks. Refit the cap and tighten it securely.

Brake and clutch fluid level

Note: *All models have a hydraulically-operated clutch, which uses the same fluid as the braking system.*

Warning:
• *Hydraulic can harm your eyes and damage painted surfaces, so use extreme caution when handling and pouring it.*
• *Do not use fluid that has been standing open for some time, as it absorbs moisture from the air, which can cause a dangerous loss of braking effectiveness.*

Make sure that your vehicle is on level ground.
The fluid level in the reservoir will drop slightly as the brake pads/shoes wear down, but the fluid level must never be allowed to drop below the MIN mark.

Safety first!

● If the reservoir requires repeated topping-up this is an indication of a fluid leak somewhere in the system, which should be investigated immediately.

● If a leak is suspected, the vehicle should not be driven until the braking system has been checked. Never take any risks where brakes are concerned.

1 The MAX and MIN marks are indicated on the side of the reservoir. The fluid level must be kept between the marks at all times.

3 Unscrew the reservoir cap and remove it. Inspect the reservoir, if the fluid is dirty the hydraulic system should be drained and refilled (see Chapter 1, Section 24).

2 If topping-up is necessary, first wipe clean the area around the filler cap to prevent dirt entering the hydraulic system.

4 Carefully add fluid, taking care not to spill it onto the surrounding components. Use only the specified fluid; mixing different types can cause damage to the system. After topping-up to the correct level, securely refit the cap and wipe off any spilt fluid.

Power steering fluid level

Before you start

✔ Park the vehicle on level ground.
✔ Set the steering wheel straight-ahead.
✔ The engine should be turned off.

✔ For the check to be accurate, the steering must not be turned once the engine has been stopped.

Safety first!

● The need for frequent topping-up indicates a leak, which should be investigated immediately.

1 The reservoir is mounted at the front right-hand side of the engine compartment. The fluid level can be viewed through the reservoir body and should be between the MIN and MAX marks when the engine is cold.

2 If topping-up is necessary, first wipe clean the area around the filler cap to prevent dirt entering the system. Unscrew the reservoir cap.

3 When topping-up, use the specified type of fluid and do not overfill the reservoir. When the level is correct, securely refit the cap.

Screen washer fluid level

● Screenwash additives not only keep the windscreen clean during bad weather, they also prevent the washer system freezing in cold weather – which is when you are likely to need it most. Don't top up using plain water, as the screenwash will become diluted, and will freeze in cold weather.

⚠️ *Warning: On no account use engine coolant antifreeze in the screen washer system – this could discolour or damage the paintwork.*

1 The reservoir for the washer systems is located on the front right-hand side of the engine compartment. If topping-up is necessary, open the filler cap.

2 When topping-up the reservoir a screenwash additive should be added in the quantities recommended on the bottle.

Wiper blades

● Only fit good-quality wiper blades.
● When removing an old wiper blade, note how it is fitted. Fitting new blades can sometimes be tricky, and noting how the old blade came off can save time.
● While the wiper blade is removed, take care not to knock the wiper arm from its locked position, or it could strike the glass.
● Offer the new blade into position the same way round as the old one. Ensure that it clicks home securely, otherwise it may come off in use, damaging the glass.

HAYNES HiNT *If smearing is still a problem despite fitting new wiper blades, try cleaning the glass with neat screenwash additive or methylated spirit.*

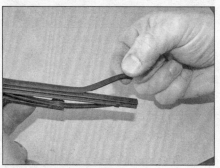

1 Check the condition of the wiper blades; if they are cracked or show any signs of deterioration, or if the glass swept area is smeared, renew them. Wiper blades should be renewed annually.

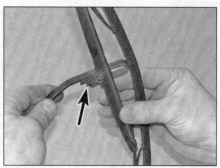

2 To remove a windscreen wiper blade, pull the arm fully away from the windscreen until it locks. Swivel the blade through 90°, then depress the locking tab (arrowed) and push the blade down the arm.

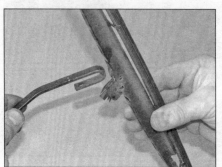

3 Detach the blade from the end fitting on the arm. When fitting the new blade, make sure that the blade locks securely into the arm, and that the blade is orientated correctly.

4 Don't forget to check the rear wiper blade(s) as well (where applicable) which are removed in the same way.

Tyre condition and pressure

It is very important that tyres are in good condition, and at the correct pressure - having a tyre failure at any speed is highly dangerous. Tyre wear is influenced by driving style - harsh braking and acceleration, or fast cornering, will all produce more rapid tyre wear. As a general rule, the front tyres wear out faster than the rears. Interchanging the tyres from front to rear ("rotating" the tyres) may result in more even wear. However, if this is completely effective, you may have the expense of replacing all four tyres at once!

Remove any nails or stones embedded in the tread before they penetrate the tyre to cause deflation. If removal of a nail does reveal that the tyre has been punctured, refit the nail so that its point of penetration is marked. Then immediately change the wheel, and have the tyre repaired by a tyre dealer.

Regularly check the tyres for damage in the form of cuts or bulges, especially in the sidewalls. Periodically remove the wheels, and clean any dirt or mud from the inside and outside surfaces. Examine the wheel rims for signs of rusting, corrosion or other damage. Light alloy wheels are easily damaged by "kerbing" whilst parking; steel wheels may also become dented or buckled. A new wheel is very often the only way to overcome severe damage.

New tyres should be balanced when they are fitted, but it may become necessary to re-balance them as they wear, or if the balance weights fitted to the wheel rim should fall off. Unbalanced tyres will wear more quickly, as will the steering and suspension components. Wheel imbalance is normally signified by vibration, particularly at a certain speed (typically around 50 mph). If this vibration is felt only through the steering, then it is likely that just the front wheels need balancing. If, however, the vibration is felt through the whole car, the rear wheels could be out of balance. Wheel balancing should be carried out by a tyre dealer or garage.

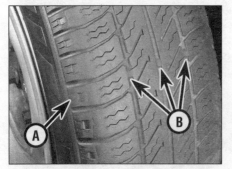

1 Tread Depth - visual check
The original tyres have tread wear safety bands (B), which will appear when the tread depth reaches approximately 1.6 mm. The band positions are indicated by a triangular mark on the tyre sidewall (A).

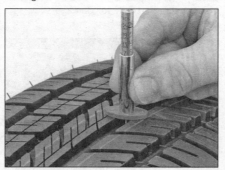

2 Tread Depth - manual check
Alternatively, tread wear can be monitored with a simple, inexpensive device known as a tread depth indicator gauge.

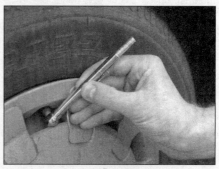

3 Tyre Pressure Check
Check the tyre pressures regularly with the tyres cold. Do not adjust the tyre pressures immediately after the vehicle has been used, or an inaccurate setting will result.

Tyre tread wear patterns

Shoulder Wear

Underinflation (wear on both sides)
Under-inflation will cause overheating of the tyre, because the tyre will flex too much, and the tread will not sit correctly on the road surface. This will cause a loss of grip and excessive wear, not to mention the danger of sudden tyre failure due to heat build-up.
Check and adjust pressures
Incorrect wheel camber (wear on one side)
Repair or renew suspension parts
Hard cornering
Reduce speed!

Centre Wear

Overinflation
Over-inflation will cause rapid wear of the centre part of the tyre tread, coupled with reduced grip, harsher ride, and the danger of shock damage occurring in the tyre casing.
Check and adjust pressures

If you sometimes have to inflate your car's tyres to the higher pressures specified for maximum load or sustained high speed, don't forget to reduce the pressures to normal afterwards.

Uneven Wear

Front tyres may wear unevenly as a result of wheel misalignment. Most tyre dealers and garages can check and adjust the wheel alignment (or "tracking") for a modest charge.
Incorrect camber or castor
Repair or renew suspension parts
Malfunctioning suspension
Repair or renew suspension parts
Unbalanced wheel
Balance tyres
Incorrect toe setting
Adjust front wheel alignment
Note: *The feathered edge of the tread which typifies toe wear is best checked by feel.*

Battery

Caution: Before carrying out any work on the vehicle battery, read the precautions given in 'Safety first!' at the start of this manual. If the battery is to be disconnected, refer to 'Disconnecting the battery' before proceeding.

✔ Make sure that the battery tray is in good condition, and that the clamp is tight. Corrosion on the tray, retaining clamp and the battery itself can be removed with a solution of water and baking soda. Thoroughly rinse all cleaned areas with water. Any metal parts damaged by corrosion should be covered with a zinc-based primer, then painted.

✔ Periodically (approximately every three months), check the charge condition of the battery, as described in Chapter 5, Section 3.

✔ If the battery is flat, and you need to jump start your vehicle, see *Roadside repairs*.

 HAYNES HiNT *Battery corrosion can be kept to a minimum by applying a layer of petroleum jelly to the clamps and terminals after they are reconnected.*

1 The battery is located on the left-hand side of the engine compartment. Where fitted, release the retaining catch, disengage the locating tabs and lift off the cover over the battery. The exterior of the battery should be inspected periodically for damage such as a cracked case or cover.

2 Check the tightness of battery clamps to ensure good electrical connections. You should not be able to move them. Also check each cable for cracks and frayed conductors.

3 If corrosion (white, fluffy deposits) is evident, remove the cables from the battery terminals, clean them with a small wire brush, then refit them. Automotive stores sell a tool for cleaning the battery post . . .

4 . . . as well as the battery cable clamps

Electrical systems

✔ Check all external lights and the horn. Refer to Chapter 12 Section 2 for details if any of the circuits are found to be inoperative.

✔ Visually check all accessible wiring connectors, harnesses and retaining clips for security, and for signs of chafing or damage.

 HAYNES HiNT *If you need to check your brake lights and indicators unaided, back up to a wall or garage door and operate the lights. The reflected light should show if they are working properly.*

1 If a single indicator light, stop-light or headlight has failed, it is likely that a bulb has blown and will need to be replaced. Refer to Chapter 12, Section 5 for details. If both stop-lights have failed, it is possible that the switch has failed (see Chapter 9, Section 22).

2 If more than one indicator light or headlight has failed, it is likely that either a fuse has blown or that there is a fault in the circuit (see Chapter 12, Section 2). The main fuse/relay box is located under the facia on the driver's side. To gain access, turn the retaining catch anti-clockwise and open the stowage box fully. Lift the stowage box out of the lower retainers and remove it from the facia.

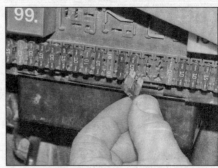
3 To renew a blown fuse, remove it, where applicable, using the plastic tool provided or needle nosed pliers. Fit a new fuse of the same rating, available from car accessory shops. It is important that you find the reason that the fuse blew (see *Electrical fault finding* in Chapter 12, Section 2).

Lubricants and fluids

Engine:

    Diesel . . . .   Multigrade diesel engine oil to VW spec 500 00 (viscosity between SAE 5W/30 and 10W/40) or 505 00 (viscosity between SAE 5W/30 and 20W/50)

    Turbodiesel . . . .   Multigrade diesel engine oil to VW spec 505 00 (viscosity between SAE 5W/30 and 20W/50)

Cooling system . . . .   Mixture of 40% VW coolant G12 (to spec TL-VW 774 F or G) and 60% water

Manual transmission . . . .   VW synthetic gear oil G51 (SAE 75W/90)

Automatic transmission:

    Transmission/torque converter fluid:

      098 type transmissions . . . .   Automatic Transmission Fluid (ATF) to Dexron standard

      01P type transmissions . . . .   VW Automatic Transmission Fluid (ATF)

    Final drive/differential . . . .   VW synthetic gear oil (SAE 75W/90)

Brake and clutch hydraulic system . . . .   Hydraulic fluid to US standard FMVSS 116 DOT 4

Power steering . . . .   VW hydraulic fluid G 002 000

Tyre pressures

Note: *Vehicle specific information on tyre pressures and wheel and tyre data is contained on a sticker attached to the driver's side door pillar. Additional information is also contained in the driver's handbook supplied with the vehicle. The pressures and sizes given are for the original-equipment tyres – the recommended pressures may vary if any other make or type of tyre is fitted. Check with the tyre manufacturer or supplier for latest recommendations. The following pressures are typical.*

Tyre size	Front	Rear
185 x 14	3.3 bar (48 psi)	3.8 bar (55 psi)
195/70 x 15	2.6 bar (38 psi)	3.4 bar (50 psi)
205/65 x 15	2.6 bar (38 psi)	3.4 bar (50 psi)
215/65 x 15	2.4 bar (35 psi)	3.0 bar (44 psi)

Chapter 1
Routine maintenance and servicing

Contents

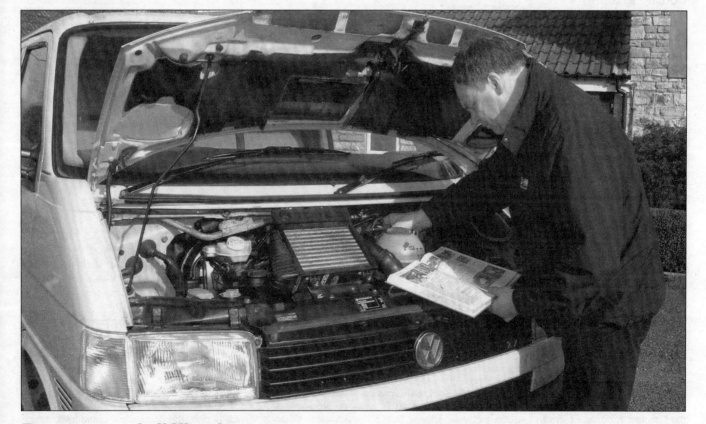

Degrees of difficulty

Easy, suitable for novice with little experience 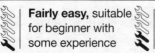	**Fairly easy,** suitable for beginner with some experience 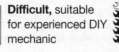	**Fairly difficult,** suitable for competent DIY mechanic
Difficult, suitable for experienced DIY mechanic 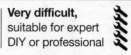	**Very difficult,** suitable for expert DIY or professional	

Lubricants and fluids . . . . Refer to the end of *Weekly checks* on page 0•17

Capacities – approximate

Engine oil (including oil filter):

4-cylinder engines:
   With filter . . . . 5.0 litres
   Without filter . . . . 4.5 litres

5-cylinder engines:
   With filter . . . . 5.5 litres
   Without filter . . . . 5.0 litres

Cooling system . . . . 9.0 litres

Manual transmission:

02B type transmissions . . . . 2.5 litres
02G type transmissions . . . . 2.3 litres

Automatic transmission:

098 type transmissions:
   Transmission/torque converter fluid . . . . 6.1 litres total (3.5 litres at fluid change)
   Final drive/differential . . . . 1.15 litres

01P type transmissions:
   Transmission/torque converter fluid . . . . 5.3 litres total (3.5 litres at fluid change)
   Final drive/differential . . . . 1.15 litres

Power-assisted steering system . . . . 1.0 litre

Fuel tank . . . . 80 litres

Cooling system

Antifreeze mixture:	Antifreeze	Water
Protection down to -25°C	40%	60%
Protection down to -35°C	50%	50%

Note: *Refer to antifreeze manufacturer's instructions for latest recommendations.*

Braking system

Minimum brake pad lining thickness . . . . 2.0 mm
Minimum brake shoe lining thickness . . . . 1.0 mm

Torque wrench settings

	Nm	lbf ft
Roadwheel bolts:		
Up to December 1995	160	118
January 1996 onward	180	133
Sump drain plug:		
4-cylinder engines	30	22
5-cylinder engines	50	37

Maintenance schedule

The maintenance intervals in this manual are provided with the assumption that you, not the dealer, will be carrying out the work. These are the minimum intervals recommended by us for vehicles driven daily. If you wish to keep your vehicle in peak condition at all times, you may wish to perform some of these procedures more often. We encourage frequent maintenance, since it enhances the efficiency, performance and resale value of your vehicle. If the vehicle is driven in dusty areas, used to tow a trailer, or driven frequently at slow speeds (idling in traffic) or on short journeys, more frequent maintenance intervals are recommended. **Note:** *The mileage conversions from kilometres are approximate.*

Later Transporter models are equipped with a service interval display indicator in the instrument panel. Every time the engine is started the panel will illuminate for a short time, displaying one of the following.

In 0 – no service required
service OIL – 15 000 km service required
service INSP – 12 month, 30 000 km or 60 000 km service required, according to mileage completed

This is basically a reminder that a service is due, eg: when the VW technician completes an oil change service, the display indicator is re-programmed to show OIL when another 15 000 km have been covered. When a service is due, the display will begin indicating it sometime beforehand. The indicator is programmed in km, even if the vehicle has mileage indication.

Every 250 miles (400 km) or weekly
☐ Refer to *Weekly checks*

Every 5 000 miles (7 500 km) or 6 months – 'OIL' on interval display*

*Note: This service interval only applies to pre-1999 1.9 litre models with engine code ABL and 2.4 litre models with engine code AJA.

- [ ] Change the engine oil and filter (Section 3).
- [ ] Drain any water from the fuel filter (Section 4).
- [ ] Check the thickness of the front brake pads (Section 5).
- [ ] Check the thickness of the rear brake pads or brake shoes (Sections 6 and 7).
- [ ] Check the condition of the wiper blades and renew if necessary (Weekly Checks).
- [ ] Reset the service interval display – later models (Section 8).

Every 10 000 miles (15 000 km) or 6 months – 'OIL' on interval display

- [ ] Change the engine oil and filter (Section 3).
- [ ] Drain any water from the fuel filter (Section 4).
- [ ] Check the thickness of the front brake pads (Section 5).
- [ ] Check the thickness of the rear brake pads or brake shoes (Sections 6 and 7).
- [ ] Check the condition of the wiper blades and renew if necessary (Weekly Checks).
- [ ] Reset the service interval display – later models (Section 8).

Annual inspection – 'INSP' on interval display

In addition to the relevant items listed in the previous services, carry out the following:

- [ ] Check all underbonnet components and hoses for fluid leaks (Section 9).
- [ ] Check the antifreeze concentration (Section 10).
- [ ] Check the operation of the handbrake (Section 11).
- [ ] Check the steering and suspension components for condition and security (Section 12).
- [ ] Check the condition of the driveshaft gaiters (Section 13).
- [ ] Check the exhaust system for leaks or damage (Section 14).
- [ ] Check the headlight beam adjustment (Section 15).
- [ ] Check the windscreen/rear window/headlight washer system(s) (Section 16).
- [ ] Check the airbag(s) for damage (Section 17).
- [ ] Renew the pollen filter element (Section 18).
- [ ] Lubricate door locks, check straps and securing pins (Section 19).
- [ ] Check, and if necessary adjust, the engine idle speed – SD and TD models (Section 20).
- [ ] Carry out a road test (Section 21).
- [ ] Reset the service interval display – later models (Section 8).

Every 2 years (regardless of mileage)

- [ ] Renew the air filter element (Section 22).
- [ ] Renew the coolant (Section 23).

Note: This is a Haynes recommendation, to be applied if there is any doubt about the quality of antifreeze in the cooling system. If the vehicle is known still to have the original coolant, VW do not specify a renewal interval. Seek the advice of a VW dealer if in doubt on this point.

- [ ] Renew the brake fluid (Section 24).
- [ ] Check the engine management system and exhaust emissions (Section 25).

Every 20 000 miles (30 000 km) – 'INSP' on interval display

In addition to the relevant items listed in the previous services, carry out the following:

- [ ] Check the condition and tension of the timing belt (Section 26).
- [ ] Check the condition and tension of the injection pump drivebelt – 5-cylinder engines (Section 27).
- [ ] Check the condition of the auxiliary drivebelt(s), and renew if necessary (Section 28).
- [ ] Check the manual transmission oil level (Section 29).
- [ ] Check the underbody sealant for damage (Section 30).
- [ ] Check the operation of the sunroof and lubricate the guide rails (Section 31).
- [ ] Reset the service interval display (Section 8).

Every 40 000 miles (60 000 km) – 'INSP' on interval display

In addition to the relevant items listed in the previous services, carry out the following:

- [ ] Renew the fuel filter (Section 32).
- [ ] Check the automatic transmission fluid level (Section 33).
- [ ] Check the automatic transmission final drive oil level (Section 34).

Every 80 000 miles (120 000 km) – 'INSP' on interval display

In addition to the relevant items listed in the previous services, carry out the following:

- [ ] Renew the timing belt and tensioner (Section 35).
- [ ] Renew the injection pump drivebelt – 5-cylinder engines (Section 36).

Underbonnet view of a 2.5 litre model (others similar)

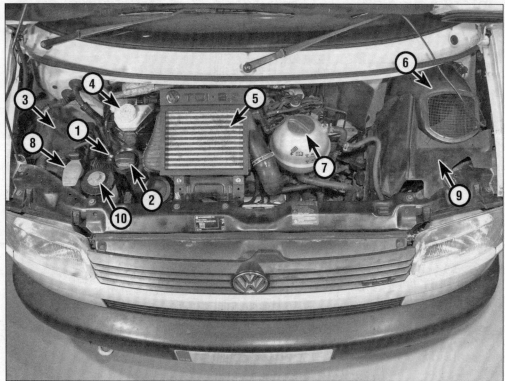

1 Engine oil level dipstick
2 Engine oil filler cap
3 Air cleaner assembly
4 Brake (and clutch) fluid reservoir
5 Intercooler
6 Pollen filter housing
7 Coolant expansion tank
8 Screen washer fluid reservoir
9 Battery (below cover)
10 Power steering fluid reservoir

Front underbody view of a 2.5 litre model (others similar)

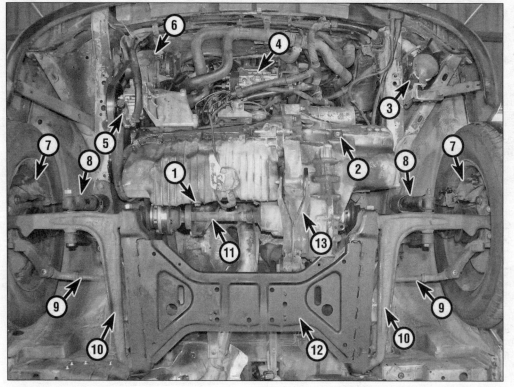

1 Engine oil drain plug
2 Transmission oil filler plug
3 Fuel filter
4 Fuel injection pump
5 Power steering pump
6 Alternator
7 Front brake calipers
8 Front shock absorbers
9 Steering track rods
10 Lower wishbones
11 Right-hand driveshaft
12 Front subframe
13 Rear engine mounting

Rear underbody view

1 Handbrake cables
2 Exhaust tailpipe
3 Shock absorber lower
   mountings
4 Trailing arms
5 Brake hydraulic hoses
6 Spare wheel

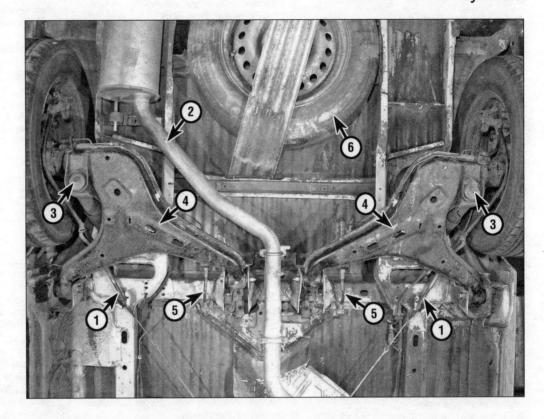

Maintenance procedures

1 General information

This Chapter is designed to help the home mechanic maintain his/her vehicle for safety, economy, long life and peak performance.

The Chapter contains a master maintenance schedule, followed by Sections dealing specifically with each task in the schedule. Visual checks, adjustments, component renewal and other helpful items are included. Refer to the accompanying illustrations of the engine compartment and the underside of the vehicle for the locations of the various components.

Servicing your vehicle in accordance with the mileage/time maintenance schedule and the following Sections will provide a planned maintenance programme, which should result in a long and reliable service life. This is a comprehensive plan, so maintaining some items but not others at the specified service intervals, will not produce the same results.

As you service your vehicle, you will discover that many of the procedures can – and should – be grouped together, because of the particular procedure being performed, or because of the proximity of two otherwise-unrelated components to one another. For example, if the vehicle is raised for any reason, the exhaust can be inspected at the same time as the suspension and steering components.

The first step in this maintenance programme is to prepare yourself before the actual work begins. Read through all the Sections relevant to the work to be carried out, then make a list and gather all the parts and tools required. If a problem is encountered, seek advice from a parts specialist, or a dealer service department.

2 Regular maintenance

1 If, from the time the vehicle is new, the routine maintenance schedule is followed closely, and frequent checks are made of fluid levels and high-wear items, as suggested throughout this manual, the engine will be kept in relatively good running condition, and the need for additional work will be minimised.

2 It is possible that there will be times when the engine is running poorly due to the lack of regular maintenance. This is even more likely if a used vehicle, which has not received regular and frequent maintenance checks, is purchased. In such cases, additional work may need to be carried out, outside of the regular maintenance intervals.

3 If engine wear is suspected, a compression test or leak-down test will provide valuable information regarding the overall performance of the main internal components. Such a test can be used as a basis to decide on the extent of the work to be carried out. If, for example, a compression or leak-down test indicates serious internal engine wear, conventional maintenance as described in this Chapter will not greatly improve the performance of the engine, and may prove a waste of time and money, unless extensive overhaul work is carried out first.

4 The following series of operations are those most often required to improve the

performance of a generally poor-running engine:

Primary operations

a) *Clean, inspect and test the battery (See Weekly checks).*
b) *Check all the engine-related fluids (See Weekly checks).*
c) *Drain the water from the fuel filter (Section 4).*
d) *Check the condition and tension of the auxiliary drivebelt(s) (Section 28).*

e) *Check the condition of the air filter, and renew if necessary (Section 22).*
f) *Check the condition of all hoses, and check for fluid leaks (Section 9).*
g) *Check the engine idle speed setting – SD and TD models (Section 20).*
h) *Check the exhaust gas emissions (Section 25).*

5 If the above operations do not prove fully effective, carry out the following secondary operations:

Secondary operations

All items listed under 'Primary operations', plus the following:

a) *Check the charging system (see Chapter 5, Section 5).*
b) *Check the preheating system (see Chapter 5, Section 12).*
c) *Renew the fuel filter (Section 32) and check the fuel and emission control systems (see Chapter 4A and Chapter 4B).*

Oil change service – 'OIL' on interval display

3 Engine oil and filter renewal

1 Frequent oil and filter changes are the most important preventative maintenance procedures which can be undertaken by the DIY owner. As engine oil ages, it becomes diluted and contaminated, which leads to premature engine wear.
2 Before starting this procedure, gather all the necessary tools and materials. Also make sure that you have plenty of clean rags and newspapers handy, to mop up any spills. Ideally, the engine oil should be warm, as it will drain better, and more built-up sludge will be removed with it. Take care, however, not to touch the exhaust or any other hot parts of the engine when working under the vehicle. To avoid any possibility of scalding, and to protect yourself from possible skin irritants and other harmful contaminants in used engine oils, it is

advisable to wear gloves when carrying out this work.
3 Access to the underside of the vehicle will be greatly improved if it can be raised on a lift, driven onto ramps, or jacked up and supported on axle stands (see *Jacking and vehicle support*). Whichever method is chosen, make sure that the vehicle remains level, or if it is at an angle, that the drain plug is at the lowest point.
4 Remove the engine undertray as described in Chapter 11, Section 25.
5 Slacken the sump drain plug about half a turn **(see illustration).** Position the draining container under the drain plug, then remove the plug completely. Recover the sealing ring from the drain plug.
6 Allow some time for the old oil to drain, noting that it may be necessary to reposition the container as the oil flow slows to a trickle.
7 After all the oil has drained, wipe off the drain plug with a clean rag, and fit a new sealing washer. Clean the area around the

drain plug opening, and refit the plug. Tighten the plug to the specified torque.
8 If the filter is also to be renewed, move the container into position under the oil filter, which is located on the front side of the cylinder block on 4-cylinder engines and at the rear of the cylinder block on 5-cylinder engines **(see illustration).**
9 Using an oil filter removal tool if necessary, slacken the filter initially, then unscrew it by hand the rest of the way. Empty the oil in the old filter into the container – puncture holes in the filter to ensure it drains completely, then dispose properly of the empty filter.
10 Use a clean rag to remove all oil, dirt and sludge from the filter sealing area on the engine. Check the old filter to make sure that the rubber sealing ring has not stuck to the engine. If it has, carefully remove it.
11 Apply a light coating of clean engine oil to the sealing ring on the new filter, then screw it into position on the engine. Tighten the filter firmly by hand only – **do not** use any tools.

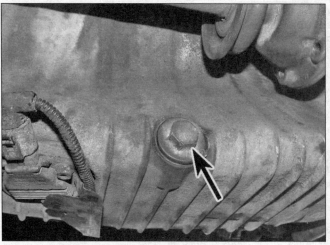

3.5 Engine oil drain plug (arrowed)

3.8 Engine oil filter location on 5-cylinder engines

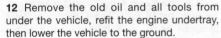
3.13 Unscrew the cap from the oil filler pipe on the camshaft cover

4.2a To gain access to the fuel filter, turn the plastic retainer half a turn...

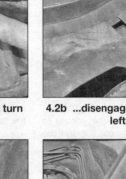
4.2b ...disengage the locating tabs on the left-hand side...

12 Remove the old oil and all tools from under the vehicle, refit the engine undertray, then lower the vehicle to the ground.

13 Remove the dipstick, then unscrew the cap from the oil filler pipe on the camshaft cover **(see illustration)**. Fill the engine, using the correct grade and type of oil (see *Lubricants and fluids*). An oil can spout or funnel may help to reduce spillage. Pour in half the specified quantity of oil first, then wait a few minutes for the oil to fall to the sump. Continue adding oil a small quantity at a time until the level is up to the cross-hatched area on the dipstick. Refit the filler cap.

14 Start the engine and run it for a few minutes; check for leaks around the oil filter seal and the sump drain plug. Note that there may be a few seconds delay before the oil pressure warning light goes out when the engine is started, as the oil circulates through the engine oil galleries and the new oil filter (where fitted) before the pressure builds up.

15 Switch off the engine, and wait a few minutes for the oil to settle in the sump once more. With the new oil circulated and the filter completely full, recheck the level on the dipstick, and add more oil as necessary.

16 Dispose of the used engine oil and filter safely, with reference to *General repair procedures*. Do not discard the old filter with

4.2c ...and right-hand side (arrowed)...

4.2d ...then lift off the cover over the battery

domestic household waste. The facility for waste oil disposal provided by many local council refuse tips and/or recycling centres generally has a filter receptacle alongside.

4 Fuel filter water draining

Caution: Before starting any work on the fuel filter, wipe clean the filter assembly and the area around it; it is essential that no dirt or other foreign matter is allowed into the system. Obtain a suitable container

into which the filter can be drained and place rags or similar material under the filter assembly to catch any spillages.

1 The fuel filter is located at the left-hand side of the engine compartment, in front of the battery.

2 To gain access to the filter, turn the plastic retainer half a turn, disengage the locating tabs and lift off the cover over the battery **(see illustrations)**.

3 At the top of the filter unit, pull off the retaining clip and lift out the fuel control valve, leaving the fuel hoses attached **(see illustrations)**.

4.3a Pull off the retaining clip...

4.3b ...and lift out the fuel control valve, leaving the fuel hoses attached

4 Position a suitable container under the front of the vehicle below the filter.
5 Unscrew the drain valve at the base of the filter unit, until water and fuel starts to run out into the container **(see illustration)**. Keep the valve open until about 100 cc of water/fuel has been collected. Close the drain valve and wipe off any surplus fuel from the nozzle.
6 Using a new O-ring, refit the fuel control valve to the top of the filter and insert the retaining clip.
7 Start the engine, allow it to idle and check around the fuel filter for fuel leaks.
8 Raise the engine speed to about 2000 rpm several times, then allow the engine to idle again. Observe the fuel flow through the transparent hose leading to the fuel injection pump and check that it is free of air bubbles.
9 On completion, dispose of the drained fuel safely.

4.5 Unscrew the drain valve at the base of the filter unit, until water and fuel emerges

5 Front brake pad wear check

1 Firmly apply the handbrake, then jack up the front of the vehicle and support it securely on axle stands (see *Jacking and vehicle support*). Remove the front roadwheels.
2 For a quick check, the brake pads can be observed through the opening on the front of the caliper. This will provide a rough guide as to the amount of friction material remaining on the pads **(see Haynes Hint 1)**. For a comprehensive check, the brake pads should be removed and cleaned and the thickness of the friction material measured. The operation of the caliper can then also be checked, and the condition of the brake disc itself can be fully examined on both sides. Chapter 9, Section 7 contains a detailed description of how the brake disc should be checked for wear and/or damage.
3 If any pad's friction material is worn to the specified thickness or less, *all four pads must be renewed as a set*. Refer to Chapter 9, Sections 5 or 6 for details.
4 On completion, refit the roadwheels and lower the vehicle to the ground.

6 Rear brake pad wear check
– models with rear disc brakes

1 Firmly apply the handbrake, then jack up the rear of the vehicle and support it securely on axle stands (see *Jacking and vehicle support*). Remove the rear roadwheels.
2 For a quick check, the brake pads can be observed through the opening on the rear of the caliper. This will provide a rough guide as to the amount of friction material remaining on the pads **(see Haynes Hint 2)**. For a comprehensive check, the brake pads should be removed and cleaned and the thickness of the friction material measured. The operation of the caliper can then also be checked, and the condition of the brake disc itself can be fully examined on both sides. Chapter 9, Section 12 contains a detailed description of how the brake disc should be checked for wear and/or damage.
3 If any pad's friction material is worn to the specified thickness or less, *all four pads must be renewed as a set*. Refer to Chapter 9, Section 11 for details.
4 On completion, refit the roadwheels and lower the vehicle to the ground.

7 Rear brake shoe wear check
– models with rear drum brakes

1 Firmly apply the handbrake, then jack up the rear of the vehicle and support it securely on axle stands (see *Jacking and vehicle support*).
2 For a quick check, the thickness of friction material remaining on one of the brake shoes can be observed through the hole in the brake backplate which is exposed by prising out the sealing grommet **(see illustration)**. If a rod of the same diameter as the specified minimum friction material thickness is placed against the shoe friction material, the amount of wear can be assessed. A torch or inspection light will probably be required. If the friction material on any shoe is worn down to the specified minimum thickness or less, *all four shoes must be renewed as a set*. Refer to Chapter 9, Section 10 for details.
3 For a comprehensive check, the brake drum should be removed and cleaned. This will allow the wheel cylinders to be checked, and the condition of the brake drum itself to be fully examined (see Chapter 9, Section 9).

8 Resetting the service interval display

1 On later models, after all necessary maintenance work has been completed, the relevant service interval display code must be reset. If more than one service schedule is carried out, note that the relevant display intervals must be reset individually.
2 The display is reset using the trip reset button on the right-hand side of the instrument panel (below the speedometer) and the clock setting button on the left-hand side of the panel (below the clock/tachometer); on models with a digital clock the lower (minute) button is used. Resetting is carried out as follows.
3 With the ignition switched off, press and hold the trip reset button. Keeping the button depressed, turn the ignition on (turn the key

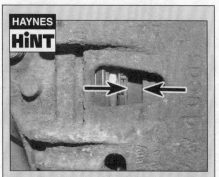

Hint 1: For a quick check, the front brake pads can be observed through the aperture in the caliper body

Hint 2: For a quick check, the rear brake pads can be observed through the aperture in the caliper body

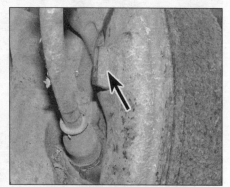

7.2 Prise out the sealing grommet (arrowed) from the inspection hole in the brake backplate

two clicks, but don't start the engine). Now release the trip reset button and turn the clock setting button to the right (or press the minute button). The service shown on the display should now be reset and the ignition can be switched off.

4 Depending on what is now shown on the display (it may be 'OIL' or 'INSP') it may be necessary to repeat the procedure to fully reset the display. Note that this is the general procedure and should work with the majority of vehicles. There may be instances where an

alternative instrument panel from a different VW vehicle has been fitted. In this case modify the procedure slightly by depressing/ turning both buttons with the ignition switched off, then turn the ignition on, or try various combinations of the above.

Annual inspection – 'INSP' on interval display

9 Hose and fluid leak check

1 Visually inspect the engine joint faces, gaskets and seals for any signs of water or oil leaks. Pay particular attention to the areas around the camshaft cover, cylinder head, oil filter and sump joint faces. Bear in mind that, over a period of time, some very slight seepage from these areas is to be expected – what you are really looking for is any indication of a serious leak. Should a leak be found, renew the offending gasket or oil seal by referring to the appropriate Chapters in this manual.

2 Also check the security and condition of all the engine-related pipes and hoses. Ensure that all cable-ties or securing clips are in place and in good condition. Clips which are broken or missing can lead to chafing of the hoses, pipes or wiring, which could cause more serious problems in the future.

3 Carefully check the radiator hoses and heater hoses along their entire length. Renew any hose which is cracked, swollen or deteriorated. Cracks will show up better if the hose is squeezed. Pay close attention to the hose clips that secure the hoses to the cooling system components. Hose clips can pinch and puncture hoses, resulting in cooling system leaks.

4 Inspect all the cooling system components (hoses, joint faces etc.) for leaks. A leak in the cooling system will usually show up as white or rust coloured deposits on the area adjoining the leak (see Haynes Hint). Where any problems of this nature are found on system components, renew the component or gasket with reference to Chapter 3.

5 Where applicable, inspect the automatic transmission fluid cooler hoses for leaks or deterioration.

6 With the vehicle raised, inspect the fuel tank and filler neck for punctures, cracks and other damage. The connection between the filler neck and tank is especially critical. Sometimes a rubber filler neck or connecting hose will leak due to loose retaining clamps or deteriorated rubber.

7 Carefully check all rubber hoses and metal fuel lines leading away from the fuel tank. Check for loose connections, deteriorated hoses, crimped lines, and other damage. Pay particular attention to the vent pipes and hoses, which often loop up around the filler neck and can become blocked or crimped.

Follow the lines to the front of the vehicle, carefully inspecting them all the way. Renew damaged sections as necessary.

8 From within the engine compartment, check the security of all fuel hose attachments and pipe unions, and inspect the fuel hoses and vacuum hoses for kinks, chafing and deterioration.

9 Where applicable, check the condition of the power steering fluid hoses and pipes.

10 Antifreeze concentration check

1 The cooling system should be filled with the recommended antifreeze and maintained at the correct concentration all year round. Over a period of time, the concentration of fluid may be reduced due to topping-up (this can be avoided by topping-up with the correct antifreeze mixture) or fluid loss. If loss of coolant has been evident, it is important to make the necessary repair before adding fresh fluid. The exact mixture of antifreeze-to-water which you should use depends on the relative weather conditions. The mixture should contain at least 40% antifreeze, but not more than 60%. Consult the mixture ratio chart on the antifreeze container before adding coolant. Use antifreeze which meets the vehicle manufacturer's specifications.

2 With the engine cold, carefully remove the cap from the expansion tank. If the engine is not completely cold, place a cloth rag over the cap before removing it, and remove it slowly to allow any pressure to escape.

3 Antifreeze checkers are available from car accessory shops. Draw some coolant from the expansion tank and observe how

many plastic balls are floating in the checker. Usually, 2 or 3 balls must be floating for the correct concentration of antifreeze, but follow the manufacturer's instructions.

4 If the concentration is incorrect, it will be necessary to either withdraw some coolant and add antifreeze, or alternatively drain the old coolant and add fresh coolant of the correct concentration.

11 Handbrake check and adjustment

Refer to Chapter 9, Section 17.

12 Steering, suspension and roadwheel check

Front suspension and steering

1 Firmly apply the handbrake, then jack up the front of the vehicle and support it securely on axle stands (see Jacking and vehicle support).

2 Visually inspect the balljoint dust covers and the steering rack-and-pinion gaiters for splits, chafing or deterioration (see illustration). Any wear of these components will cause loss of lubricant, together with dirt and water entry, resulting in rapid deterioration of the balljoints or steering gear.

3 On vehicles with power steering, check the fluid hoses for chafing or deterioration, and the pipe and hose unions for fluid leaks. Also check for signs of fluid leakage under pressure from the steering gear rubber gaiters, which would indicate failed fluid seals within the steering gear.

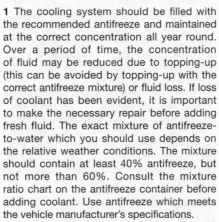

A leak in the cooling system will usually show up as white- or rust-coloured deposits on the area adjoining the leak.

12.2 Visually inspect the steering rack-and-pinion gaiters for splits, chafing or deterioration

12.4 Checking for wear in the front suspension and hub bearings

4 Grasp the roadwheel at the 12 o'clock and 6 o'clock positions, and try to rock it **(see illustration)**. Very slight free play may be felt, but if the movement is appreciable, further investigation is necessary to determine the source. Continue rocking the wheel while an assistant depresses the footbrake. If the movement is now eliminated or significantly reduced, it is likely that the hub bearings are at fault. If the free play is still evident with the footbrake depressed, then there is wear in the suspension joints or mountings.

5 Now grasp the wheel at the 9 o'clock and 3 o'clock positions, and try to rock it as before. Any movement felt now may again be caused by wear in the hub bearings or the steering track-rod balljoints. If the inner or outer balljoint is worn, the visual movement will be obvious.

6 Using a large screwdriver or flat bar, check for wear in the suspension mounting bushes by levering between the relevant suspension component and its attachment point. Some movement is to be expected as the mountings are made of rubber, but excessive wear should be obvious. Also check the condition of any visible rubber bushes, looking for splits, cracks or contamination of the rubber.

7 With the vehicle standing on its wheels, have an assistant turn the steering wheel back and forth about an eighth of a turn each way. There should be very little, if any, lost movement between the steering wheel and roadwheels. If this is not the case, closely observe the joints and mountings previously described, but in addition, check the steering column universal joints for wear, and the rack-and-pinion steering gear itself.

14.2a Check the exhaust pipes and connections for evidence of leaks, severe corrosion, and damage...

13.2 Check the driveshaft gaiters by hand for cracks and/or leaking grease

Rear suspension

8 Chock the front wheels, then jack up the rear of the vehicle and support securely on axle stands (see *Jacking and vehicle support*).

9 Working as described previously for the front suspension, check the rear hub bearings, the trailing arm mounting bushes and the shock absorber mountings for wear.

Shock absorbers

10 Check for any signs of fluid leakage around the shock absorber body. Should any fluid be noticed, the shock absorber is defective internally, and should be renewed. **Note:** *Shock absorbers should always be renewed in pairs on the same axle.*

11 The efficiency of the shock absorber may be checked by bouncing the vehicle at each corner. Generally speaking, the body will return to its normal position and stop after being depressed. If it rises and returns on a rebound, the shock absorber is probably suspect. Examine also the shock absorber upper and lower mountings for any signs of wear.

Roadwheels

12 Periodically remove the roadwheels, and clean any dirt or mud from the inside and outside surfaces. Examine the wheel rims for signs of rusting, corrosion or other damage. Light alloy wheels are easily damaged by 'kerbing' whilst parking, and similarly, steel wheels may become dented or buckled. Renewal of the wheel is very often the only course of remedial action possible.

13 The balance of each wheel and tyre assembly should be maintained, not only to avoid

14.2b ...and make sure that all brackets and mountings are in good condition

excessive tyre wear, but also to avoid wear in the steering and suspension components. Wheel imbalance is normally signified by vibration through the vehicle's bodyshell, although in many cases it is particularly noticeable through the steering wheel. Conversely, it should be noted that wear or damage in suspension or steering components may cause excessive tyre wear. Out-of-round or out-of-true tyres, damaged wheels and hub bearing wear also fall into this category. Balancing will not usually cure vibration caused by such wear.

13 Driveshaft gaiter check

1 The driveshaft rubber gaiters are very important, because they prevent dirt, water and foreign material from entering and damaging the constant velocity (CV) joints. External contamination can cause the gaiter material to deteriorate prematurely, so it's a good idea to wash the gaiters with soap and water occasionally.

2 With the vehicle raised and securely supported on axle stands (see *Jacking and vehicle support*), turn the steering onto full-lock, then slowly rotate each front wheel in turn. Inspect the condition of the outer constant velocity (CV) joint rubber gaiters, squeezing the gaiters to open out the folds **(see illustration)**. Check for signs of cracking, splits, or deterioration of the rubber, which may allow the escape of grease, and lead to the ingress of water and grit into the joint. Also check the security and condition of the retaining clips. Repeat these checks on the inner CV joints. If any damage or deterioration is found, the gaiters should be renewed as described in Chapter 8, Section 3.

3 At the same time, check the general condition of the outer CV joints themselves, by first holding the driveshaft and attempting to rotate the wheels. Repeat this check on the inner joints, by holding the inner joint yoke and attempting to rotate the driveshaft.

4 Any appreciable movement in the CV joint indicates wear in the joint, wear in the driveshaft splines, or a loose driveshaft retaining bolt.

14 Exhaust system check

1 With the engine cold, check the complete exhaust system, from its starting point at the engine to the end of the tailpipe. If necessary, raise the front and rear of the vehicle and support it on axle stands (see *Jacking and vehicle support*).

2 Check the exhaust pipes and connections for evidence of leaks, severe corrosion, and damage. Make sure that all brackets and mountings are in good condition and that all relevant nuts and bolts are tight **(see illustrations)**. Leakage at

18.2 Disengage the bonnet release cable from the clip on the pollen filter housing

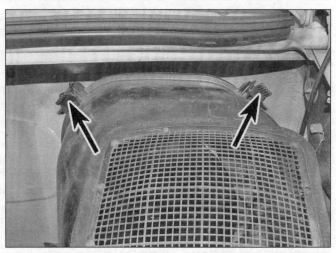

18.3a Open the upper retaining catches (arrowed)...

any of the joints or in other parts of the system will usually show up as a black sooty stain in the vicinity of the leak.

3 Rattles and other noises can often be traced to the exhaust system, especially the brackets and rubber mountings. Try to move the pipes and silencers. If the components are able to come into contact with the body or suspension parts, secure the system with new mountings. Otherwise separate the joints (if possible) and twist the pipes as necessary to provide additional clearance.

15 Headlight beam alignment check
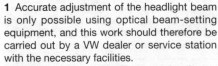

1 Accurate adjustment of the headlight beam is only possible using optical beam-setting equipment, and this work should therefore be carried out by a VW dealer or service station with the necessary facilities.

2 Refer to Chapter 12, Section 8 for further information.

16 Windscreen/rear window/ headlight washer system(s) check

Check that each of the washer jet nozzles are clear and that each nozzle provides a strong jet of washer fluid. The jets should be aimed to spray at a point slightly above the centre of the windscreen/rear window/ headlight. If necessary, adjust the jets using a pin. Note that on vehicles where the water is sprayed across the windscreen in the shape of a fan, it is not possible to adjust the position of the jets.

17 Airbag unit check

Where fitted, inspect the airbag(s) exterior condition checking for signs of damage or deterioration. If an airbag shows signs of

damage, it must be renewed (see Chapter 12, Section 20).

18 Pollen filter renewal

1 Where fitted, turn the plastic retainer half a turn, disengage the locating tabs and lift off the cover over the battery **(see illustrations 4.2a to 4.2d)**.

2 Disengage the bonnet release cable from the clip on the side of the pollen filter housing **(see illustration)**.

3 Open the upper retaining catches, disengage the lower lugs and lift off the pollen filter cover **(see illustrations)**.

4 Squeeze together the retaining tabs and pull the pollen filter from its location **(see illustration)**.

5 Fit the new filter using the reverse sequence to removal, ensuring that the filter audibly engages as it is pushed into position.

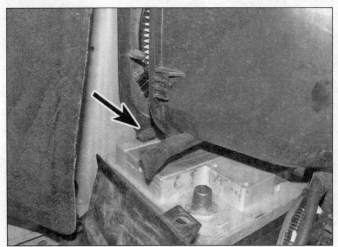

18.3b ...then disengage the lower lugs (arrowed) and lift off the pollen filter cover

18.4 Squeeze together the retaining tabs (arrowed) and pull the pollen filter from its location

20.3a **Idle speed adjustment screw (arrowed) on 4-cylinder engines**

19 Hinge and lock lubrication

1 Lubricate the hinges of the bonnet, doors and, where fitted, the tailgate with a light general-purpose oil. Similarly, lubricate all latches, locks and lock strikers.

2 Lightly lubricate the bonnet release mechanism and cable with a suitable grease.

20 Idle speed check and adjustment – SD and TD models

1 Start the engine and run it until it reaches its normal operating temperature. With the handbrake applied and the transmission in neutral, allow the engine to idle. Check that the cold start knob is pushed in to the fully 'off' position.

2 Using a diesel tachometer, check the idle speed against Chapter 4A Specifications.

3 If necessary, adjust the engine idle speed by rotating the adjustment screw at the fuel injection pump (see illustrations).

21 Road test

Instruments and electrical equipment

1 Check the operation of all instruments and electrical equipment.

2 Make sure all instruments read correctly, and switch on all electrical equipment in turn, to check that it functions properly.

Steering and suspension

3 Check for any abnormalities in the steering, suspension, handling or road 'feel'.

4 Drive the vehicle, and check that there are no unusual vibrations or noises.

5 Check that the steering feels positive, with no excessive 'sloppiness', or roughness, and check for any suspension noises when cornering and driving over bumps.

Drivetrain

6 Check the performance of the engine, clutch (where applicable), gearbox/transmission and driveshafts.

7 Listen for any unusual noises from the engine, clutch and gearbox/transmission.

8 Make sure that the engine runs smoothly when idling, and that there is no hesitation when accelerating.

9 Check that, where applicable, the clutch action is smooth and progressive, that the drive is taken up smoothly, and that the pedal travel is not excessive. Also listen for any noises when the clutch pedal is depressed.

10 On manual gearbox models, check that all gears can be engaged smoothly without noise, and that the gear lever action is not abnormally vague or 'notchy'.

11 On automatic transmission models, make sure that all gearchanges occur smoothly, without snatching, and without an increase in engine speed between changes. Check that all the gear positions can be selected with the vehicle at rest. If any problems are found, they should be referred to a VW dealer or automatic transmission specialist.

12 Listen for a metallic clicking sound from the front of the vehicle, as the vehicle is driven slowly in a circle with the steering on full-lock. Carry out this check in both directions. If a clicking noise is heard, this indicates wear in a driveshaft joint (see Chapter 8, Section 4).

Check the operation and performance of the braking system

13 Make sure that the vehicle does not pull to one side when braking, and that the wheels do not lock prematurely when braking hard.

14 Check that there is no vibration through the steering when braking.

15 Check that the handbrake operates correctly without excessive movement of the lever, and that it holds the vehicle stationary on a slope.

16 Test the operation of the brake servo unit as follows. With the engine off, depress the footbrake four or five times to exhaust the vacuum. Hold the brake pedal depressed, then start the engine. As the engine starts, there should be a noticeable 'give' in the brake pedal as vacuum builds up. Allow the engine to run for at least two minutes, and then switch it off. If the brake pedal is depressed now, it should be possible to detect a hiss from the servo as the pedal is depressed. After about four or five applications, no further hissing should be heard, and the pedal should feel much harder.

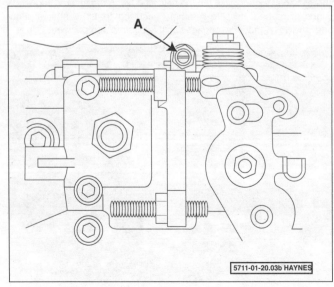

20.3b **Idle speed adjustment screw (A) on early 5-cylinder engines...**

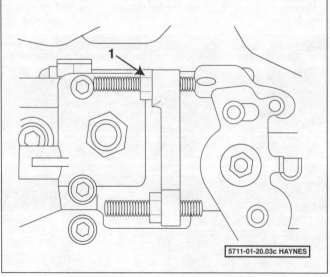

20.3c **...and (1) on later 5-cylinder engines**

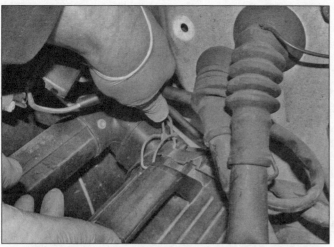

22.2 Release the upper air cleaner housing retaining clip

22.3 Push the locking handle down and unhook it from the air cleaner housing

22.4 Lift the air cleaner housing up and manipulate it out from its location

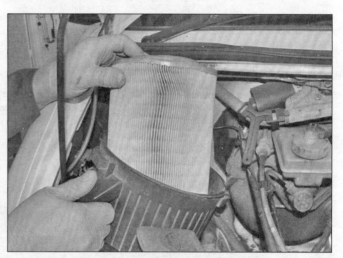

22.5 Lift out the element and wipe out the housing

Every 2 years (regardless of mileage)

22 Air filter element renewal

Circular-type air cleaner housing

1 The air filter element is located in the air cleaner housing, which is situated on the right-hand side of the engine compartment.
2 Release the upper air cleaner housing retaining clip **(see illustration)**.
3 Push the locking handle down and unhook it from the air cleaner housing **(see illustration)**.
4 Lift the air cleaner housing up and manipulate it out from its location **(see illustration)**.
5 Lift out the element, noting its direction of fitting, and wipe out the housing **(see illustration)**.

6 If carrying out a routine service, the element must be renewed regardless of its apparent condition.
7 If you are checking the element for any other reason, inspect its lower surface; if it is oily or very dirty, renew the element. If it is only moderately dusty, it can be re-used by blowing it clean with compressed air.
8 Fit the new element using a reversal of the removal procedure. Ensure that the plastic lug on the end of the filter element locates in the retainer element. With the housing in position, pull the locking handle up until it engages.

Square-type air cleaner housing

9 The air filter element is located in the air cleaner housing, which is situated on the right-hand side of the engine compartment.
10 Release the hose clip and disconnect the air outlet duct from the air cleaner cover **(see illustration)**.

22.10 Release the hose clip and disconnect the air outlet duct from the air cleaner cover

22.11 Disconnect the wiring connector from the airflow meter located on the air cleaner cover

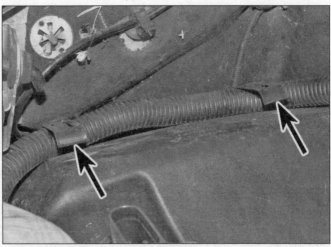

22.12 Lift the two clips (arrowed) and release the wiring harness from the air cleaner cover

11 On TDi engines, disconnect the wiring connector from the airflow meter located on the air cleaner cover **(see illustration)**.

12 Lift the two clips and release the wiring harness from the air cleaner cover **(see illustration)**.

13 Release the two catches securing the air cleaner cover to the housing. Lift the cover up, disengage it from the housing and manipulate it out from the engine compartment **(see illustrations)**.

14 Lift out the element, noting its direction of fitting, and wipe out the housing **(see illustration)**.

15 If carrying out a routine service, the element must be renewed regardless of its apparent condition.

16 If you are checking the element for any other reason, inspect its lower surface; if it is oily or very dirty, renew the element. If it is only moderately dusty, it can be re-used by blowing it clean with compressed air.

17 Fit the new element using a reversal of the removal procedure.

22.13a Release the front catch (arrowed)...

22.13b ...and the rear catch...

22.13c ...then lift the cover up and manipulate it out from the engine compartment

22.14 Lift out the element and wipe out the housing

23 Coolant renewal

⚠️ *Warning: Do not allow antifreeze to come in contact with your skin or painted surfaces of the vehicle. Flush contaminated areas immediately with plenty of water. Don't store new coolant, or leave old coolant lying around, where it's accessible to children or pets – they're attracted by its sweet smell. Ingestion of even a small amount of coolant can be fatal. Wipe up garage-floor and drip-pan spills immediately. Keep antifreeze containers covered, and repair cooling system leaks as soon as they're noticed.*

⚠️ *Warning: Never remove the expansion tank filler cap when the engine is running, or has just been switched off, as the cooling system will be hot, and the consequent escaping steam and scalding coolant could cause serious injury.*

⚠️ *Warning: Wait until the engine is cold before starting these procedures.*

Cooling system draining

1 Remove the engine undertray as described in Chapter 11, Section 25.

2 Cover the expansion tank cap with a wad of rag, and slowly turn the cap anti-clockwise to relieve the pressure in the cooling system (a hissing sound will normally be heard). Wait until any pressure remaining in the system is released, then continue to turn the cap until it can be removed.

3 Place a large drain tray underneath the front facing side of the engine, towards the transmission end. Unscrew the coolant drain plug from the metal coolant pipe and allow the coolant to drain into the tray **(see illustrations)**. To speed up the draining process, release

23.3a Unscrew the coolant drain plug from the metal coolant pipe...

23.3b ...and allow the coolant to drain

the retaining clip and disconnect the radiator bottom hose from the thermostat housing.

4 On completion, check the condition of the drain plug sealing washer and renew it if necessary **(see illustration)**. Refit the drain plug and tighten it securely. Where applicable, reconnect the radiator bottom hose to the thermostat housing, then refit the engine undertray.

Cooling system flushing

5 If coolant renewal has been neglected, or if the antifreeze mixture has become diluted, then in time, the cooling system may gradually lose efficiency, as the coolant passages become restricted due to rust, scale deposits, and other sediment. The cooling system efficiency can be restored by flushing the system clean.

6 The radiator should be flushed independently of the engine, to avoid unnecessary contamination.

Radiator flushing

7 Disconnect the top and bottom hoses and any other relevant hoses from the radiator.

8 Insert a garden hose into the radiator top inlet. Direct a flow of clean water through the radiator, and keep flushing until clean water emerges from the radiator bottom outlet.

9 If after a reasonable period, the water still does not run clear, the radiator can be flushed with a good proprietary cooling system cleaning agent. It is important that their manufacturer's instructions are followed carefully. If the contamination is particularly bad, insert the hose in the radiator bottom outlet, and reverse-flush the radiator.

Engine flushing

10 Remove the thermostat as described in Chapter 3, Section 5, then temporarily refit the thermostat cover.

11 With the top and bottom hoses disconnected from the radiator, insert a garden hose into the radiator top hose. Direct a clean flow of water through the engine, and

continue flushing until clean water emerges from the radiator bottom hose.

12 On completion, refit the thermostat and reconnect the hoses with reference to Chapter 3, Section 5.

Antifreeze mixture

Note: *From the start of production, Transporters were filled at the factory with VW G11 coolant (coloured blue). During the mid-1990's this was changed to G12 (coloured red), then later to G12 Plus, G12 Plus Plus and G13 which are all coloured purple. VW state that the red and blue coolant must not be mixed, but the purple coolant can be mixed with the blue or the red. Unless you are absolutely sure which coolant has been used previously, it is advisable to thoroughly flush the system before filling with fresh purple coolant.*

13 VW state that, if the only antifreeze (coolant) used is VW's own G12 or G13, then it does not need to be renewed. This is subject to it being used in the recommended concentration, unmixed with any other type of antifreeze or additive, and topped-up when necessary using only that antifreeze type, mixed with clean water. If any other type of antifreeze is (or has been) added, the above no longer applies; in this case, the system must be drained and thoroughly flushed before fresh coolant mixture is poured in.

14 If any antifreeze other than VW's is to be used, the coolant must be renewed at regular intervals to provide an equivalent degree of protection. The conventional recommendation is to renew the coolant every two years.

15 If the antifreeze used is to VW's specification, the levels of protection it affords are indicated in the Specifications Section of this Chapter. To give the recommended standard mixture ratio for this antifreeze, 40% (by volume) of antifreeze must be mixed with 60% of clean, soft water. If you are using any other type of antifreeze, follow its manufacturer's instructions to achieve the correct ratio.

16 It is best to make up slightly more than the system's specified capacity, so that a supply is available for subsequent topping-up. However, note that you are unlikely to fully drain the system at any one time (unless the engine is being completely stripped), and the capacities quoted are therefore slightly academic for routine coolant renewal.

17 Before adding antifreeze, the cooling system should be completely drained, preferably flushed, and all hoses checked for condition and security. Fresh antifreeze will rapidly find any weaknesses in the system.

18 After filling with antifreeze, a label should be attached to the expansion tank, stating the type and concentration of antifreeze used, and the date installed. Any subsequent topping-up should be made with the same type and concentration of antifreeze.

19 Do not use engine antifreeze in the washer system, as it will damage the vehicle's paintwork. A screen wash additive should be added to the washer system in its maker's recommended quantities.

Cooling system filling

20 Before attempting to fill the cooling system, make sure that all hoses and clips are in good condition, and that the clips are tight.

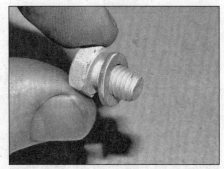

23.4 Check the condition of the drain plug sealing washer and renew it if necessary

23.21 On 5-cylinder engines, open the bleed screw (arrowed) located in the heater matrix coolant hose

Note that an antifreeze mixture must be used all year round, to prevent corrosion of the engine components.

21 On 5-cylinder engines, open the bleed screw (if fitted) located in the heater matrix coolant hose **(see illustration)**.

22 Remove the expansion tank filler cap, and fill the system by slowly pouring the coolant mixture into the expansion tank. On engines with a bleed screw, close the screw as soon as coolant is seen to emerge.

23 Once the level in the expansion tank starts to rise, squeeze the radiator top and bottom hoses to help expel any trapped air in the system. Once all the air is expelled, top-up the coolant level to the 'MAX' mark and refit the expansion tank cap.

24 Start the engine and run it until it reaches normal operating temperature, then stop the engine and allow it to cool.

25 Check for leaks, particularly around disturbed components. Check the coolant level in the expansion tank, and top-up if necessary. Note that the system must be cold before an accurate level is indicated in the expansion tank. If the expansion tank cap is removed while the engine is still warm, cover the cap with a thick cloth, and unscrew the cap slowly to gradually relieve the system pressure (a hissing sound will normally be heard). Wait until any pressure remaining in the system is released, then continue to turn the cap until it can be removed.

Airlocks

26 If, after draining and refilling the system, symptoms of overheating are found which did not occur previously, then the fault is almost certainly due to trapped air at some point in the system, causing an airlock and restricting the flow of coolant; usually, the air is trapped because the system was refilled too quickly.

27 If an airlock is suspected, first try gently squeezing all visible coolant hoses. A coolant hose which is full of air feels quite different to one full of coolant when squeezed. After refilling the system, most airlocks will clear once the system has cooled, and been topped-up.

28 While the engine is running at operating temperature, switch on the heater and heater fan, and check for heat output. Provided there is sufficient coolant in the system, lack of heat output could be due to an airlock in the system.

29 Airlocks can have more serious effects than simply reducing heater output – a severe airlock could reduce coolant flow around the engine. Check that the radiator top hose is hot when the engine is at operating temperature – a top hose which stays cold could be the result of an airlock (or a non-opening thermostat).

30 If the problem persists, stop the engine and allow it to cool down **completely**, before unscrewing the expansion tank filler cap or loosening the hose clips and squeezing the hoses to bleed out the trapped air. In the worst case, the system will have to be at least partially drained (this time, the coolant can be saved for re-use) and flushed to clear the problem. If all else fails, have the system evacuated and vacuum filled by a suitably-equipped garage.

24 Brake fluid renewal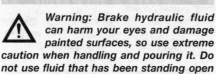

⚠ *Warning: Brake hydraulic fluid can harm your eyes and damage painted surfaces, so use extreme caution when handling and pouring it. Do not use fluid that has been standing open for some time, as it absorbs moisture from the air. Excess moisture can cause a dangerous loss of braking effectiveness.*

1 The procedure is similar to that for the bleeding of the hydraulic system as described in Chapter 9, Section 2, except that the brake fluid reservoir should be emptied by siphoning, using a clean poultry baster or similar before starting, and allowance should be made for the old fluid to be expelled when bleeding a section of the circuit.

2 Working as described in Chapter 9, Section 2, open the first bleed screw in the sequence, and pump the brake pedal gently until nearly all the old fluid has been emptied from the master cylinder reservoir.

3 Top-up to the 'MAX' level with new fluid, and continue pumping until only the new fluid remains in the reservoir, and new fluid can be seen emerging from the bleed screw. Tighten the screw, and top the reservoir level up to the 'MAX' level line.

4 Work through all the remaining bleed screws in the sequence until new fluid can be seen at all of them. Be careful to keep the master cylinder reservoir topped-up to above the 'MIN' level at all times, or air may enter the system and greatly increase the length of the task.

5 When the operation is complete, check that all bleed screws are securely tightened, and that their dust caps are refitted. Wash off all traces of spilt fluid, and recheck the master cylinder reservoir fluid level.

6 Check the operation of the brakes before taking the vehicle on the road.

25 Exhaust gas emissions check

1 This check is part of the manufacturer's maintenance schedule, and involves checking exhaust gas emissions and testing the engine management system (TDi models only) using special dedicated test equipment. Such testing will allow the test equipment to read any fault codes stored in the electronic control unit memory.

2 Unless a fault is suspected, this test is not essential, although it should be noted that it is recommended by the manufacturers. Diesel exhaust gas emissions can be tested only by a VW dealer or diesel specialist who has the necessary test equipment.

3 If access to suitable test equipment is not possible, make a thorough check of all fuel and emissions control system components, hoses and wiring, for security and obvious signs of damage. Further details of the fuel system and emissions control systems can be found in Chapters 4A and 4B.

Every 20 000 miles (30 000 km) – 'INSP' on interval display

26 Timing belt check and adjustment

Note: For early SD and TD models with a manual timing belt tensioner, VW specify a timing belt inspection every 20 000 miles (30 000 km). A belt thought to be defective as a result of any of these inspections must be renewed immediately; no particular renewal interval is specified.

For all later models with the semi-automatic timing belt tensioner, VW specify an annual inspection of the timing belt and a check of the tensioner's operation; a belt or tensioner thought to be defective as a result of any of these inspections must be renewed immediately. For these later models, VW specify that the timing belt and its semi-automatic tensioner MUST be renewed as a matter of course every 80 000 miles (120 000 km).

1 Remove the timing belt upper cover as

described in Chapter 2A, Section 4 (4-cylinder engines) or Chapter 2B, Section 4 or 5 (5-cylinder engines).

2 Using a spanner or socket on the crankshaft pulley bolt, turn the engine slowly in a clockwise direction. Do not turn the engine on the camshaft pulley bolt.

3 Check the complete length of the timing belt for signs of cracking, tooth separation, fraying, side glazing, and oil or grease contamination. Use a torch and mirror to check the underside of the belt; it is especially important to check for any signs of cracks in the belt's coating, of side contact, of fraying and of cracks in the roots of the teeth.

4 If there is any evidence of wear or damage the timing belt must be renewed. A broken belt will cause major damage to the engine.

5 On early engines without the semi-automatic tensioner, test the belt tension by grasping it between the fingers mid-way between the camshaft and fuel injection pump sprockets and twisting it; the belt tension is correct when it can just be twisted through 45° (one-eighth of a turn) and no further. Re-tension the belt if required as described in Chapter 2A, Section 4 (4-cylinder engines) or Chapter 2B, Section 4 or 5 (5-cylinder engines).

6 On engines with the semi-automatic tensioner, test the operation of the tensioner by pressing down on it firmly with the thumb mid-way between the camshaft and fuel injection pump sprockets; if the tensioner is operating correctly the notch in the tensioner's centre will move away from the raised rib on the outer part as pressure is applied – as pressure is released, the notch and raised rib will move back into alignment again. If there is any doubt at all about the tensioner's operation, it must be renewed immediately, as described in Chapter 2A, Section 5 (4-cylinder engines) or Chapter 2B, Section 7 (5-cylinder engines).

7 After making the check, refit the timing belt cover and remove the spanner/socket from the crankshaft pulley bolt.

27 Injection pump drivebelt check and adjustment – 5-cylinder engines

1 Remove the injection pump drivebelt cover for access to the drivebelt.

2 Inspect the drivebelt for signs of excessive wear, fraying, cracking and damage. Also check for traces of oil which may have come from a faulty oil seal. The full length of the drivebelt should be checked by turning the engine with a spanner on the crankshaft pulley bolt.

3 Ideally, the drivebelt tension should be checked as described in Chapter 2B, Section 6).

28 Auxiliary drivebelt check and renewal

Checking

1 Disconnect the battery negative terminal (refer to *Disconnecting the battery*).

2 Firmly apply the handbrake, then jack up the front of the vehicle and support it securely on axle stands (see *Jacking and vehicle support*).

3 Remove the engine undertray as described in Chapter 11, Section 25.

4 Using a socket or spanner on the crankshaft sprocket bolt, rotate the crankshaft so that the full length of the auxiliary drivebelts can be examined. Look for cracks, splitting and fraying on the surface of the belt; check also for signs of glazing (shiny patches) and separation of the belt plies. If damage or wear is visible, the belt should be renewed.

5 Where the drivebelt tension is adjusted manually (engines without an automatic tension adjuster) check the belt tension as described in Chapter 2A, Section 6 (4-cylinder engines) or Chapter 2B, Section 8 (5-cylinder engines).

6 On completion, refit the engine undertray,

lower the vehicle to the ground and reconnect the battery negative terminal.

Renewal

7 For details of auxiliary drivebelt renewal, refer to Chapter 2A, Section 6 (4-cylinder engines) or Chapter 2B, Section 8 (5-cylinder engines).

29 Manual transmission oil level check

1 Park the vehicle on a level surface. The oil level must be checked before the vehicle is driven, or at least 5 minutes after the engine has been switched off. If the oil is checked just after driving the vehicle, some of the oil will remain distributed around the transmission, resulting in an inaccurate level reading.

2 Remove the engine undertray as described in Chapter 11, Section 25.

3 A 17 mm male hexagon key is required to unscrew and tighten the manual transmission oil filler/level and drain plugs. Wipe clean the area around the filler/level plug, which is situated on the front of the gearbox, then unscrew the plug and clean it (see illustrations).

4 The oil level should reach the lower edge of the filler/level hole. A certain amount of oil will have gathered behind the filler/level plug, and will trickle out when it is removed; this does not necessarily indicate that the level is correct. To ensure that a true level is established, wait until the initial trickle has stopped, then add oil as necessary until a trickle of new oil can be seen emerging. The level will be correct when the flow ceases. When topping-up, use only good-quality oil of the specified type (refer to *Lubricants and fluids*).

5 Filling the transmission with oil is an extremely awkward operation; above all, allow plenty of time for the oil level to settle properly before checking it. If a large amount is added to the transmission, and a large amount flows out on checking the level, refit the filler/level plug and take the vehicle on a short journey

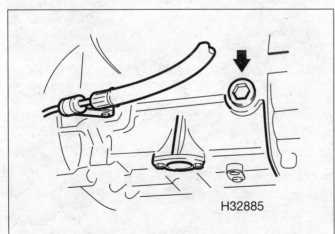

29.3a Manual transmission oil filler/level plug (arrowed) on the 02B transmission...

29.3b ...and on the 02G transmission

so that the new oil is distributed fully around the transmission components, then recheck the level when it has settled again.

6 If the transmission has been overfilled so that oil flows out when the filler/level plug is removed, check that the vehicle is completely level (front-to-rear and side-to-side), and allow the surplus to drain off into a suitable container.

7 When the level is correct, refit the plug, tightening it securely. Wash off any spilt oil, refit the engine undertray and lower the vehicle to the ground.

30 Underbody sealant check

With the vehicle raised and securely supported, carry out a thorough check of the vehicle underbody sealant for signs of damage. If any area of the underbody sealant shows visible damage, the affected area should be repaired to prevent possible problems with corrosion occurring at a later date.

31 Sunroof check and lubrication

1 Slide the sunroof fully backwards to expose the slider rails on either side.
2 Remove all dirt and grime from each slider then lubricate both mechanisms with a silicone-spray type lubricant.
3 Wipe off any excess lubricant then close the sunroof.

Every 40 000 miles (60 000 km) – 'INSP' on interval display

32 Fuel filter renewal

Caution: Before starting any work on the fuel filter, wipe clean the filter assembly and the area around it; it is essential that no dirt or other foreign matter is allowed into the system. Obtain a suitable container into which the filter can be drained and place rags or similar material under the filter assembly to catch any spillages.

1 The fuel filter is located at the left-hand side of the engine compartment, in front of the battery.
2 To gain access to the filter, turn the plastic retainer half a turn, disengage the locating tabs and lift off the cover over the battery **(see illustrations 4.2a to 4.2d)**.
3 At the top of the filter unit, pull off the retaining clip and lift out the fuel control valve, leaving the fuel hoses attached **(see illustrations 4.3a and 4.3b)**.
4 Slacken the hose clips and pull the fuel supply and return hoses from the ports on the top of the filter unit **(see illustration)**. If crimp-type clips are fitted, cut them off using

snips, and use equivalent size worm-drive clips on refitting. Note the fitted position of each hose, to aid correct refitting later.
5 Push the filter up from below and lift it from its location **(see illustration)**.
6 Fill the new filter with clean diesel fuel, then push it back into position in the engine compartment.
7 Reconnect the fuel supply and return hoses, using the notes made during removal – note the fuel flow arrow markings next to each port. Where crimp-type hoses were originally fitted, use equivalent size worm-drive clips on refitting.
8 Using a new O-ring, refit the control valve to the top of the filter and insert the retaining clip.
9 Start and run the engine at idle, then check around the fuel filter for fuel leaks. **Note:** *It may take a few seconds of cranking before the engine starts.*
10 Raise the engine speed to about 2000 rpm several times, then allow the engine to idle again. Observe the fuel flow through the transparent hose leading to the fuel injection pump and check that it is free of air bubbles.
11 On completion, dispose of the old filter safely.

33 Automatic transmission fluid level check

01P type automatic transmission

Note: *An accurate fluid level check can only be made with the transmission fluid at a temperature of between 35°C and 45°C; if it is not possible to ascertain this temperature, it is strongly recommended that the check be made by a VW dealer who will have the instrumentation to check the temperature and to check the transmission electronics for fault codes. Overfilling or underfilling adversely affects the function of the transmission.*

1 Take the vehicle on a short journey to warm the transmission slightly (see Note above), then park the vehicle on level ground and engage P with the selector lever.
2 Raise the front and rear of the vehicle and support it on axle stands (see *Jacking and vehicle support*), ensuring the vehicle is kept level.
3 Remove the engine undertray as described in Chapter 11, Section 25.

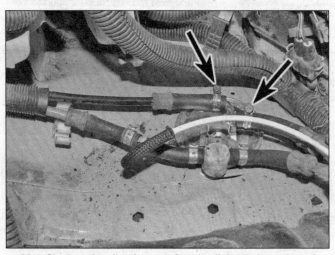

32.4 Slacken the clips (arrowed) and pull the fuel supply and return hoses from the ports on the top of the filter unit

32.5 Push the filter up from below and lift it from its location

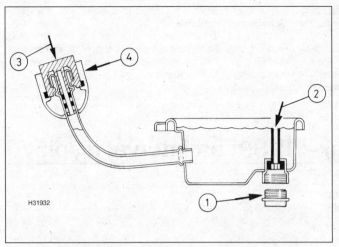

33.5 01P type automatic transmission fluid level check

1	*Level plug*	*3*	*Filler cap*
2	*Level tube*	*4*	*Retaining clip*

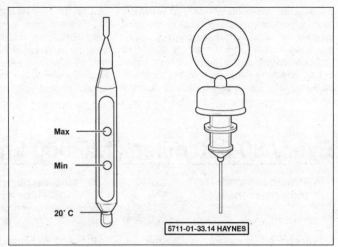

33.14 Fluid level dipstick markings on the 098 type automatic transmission

4 Start the engine and run it at idle speed until the transmission fluid temperature reaches 35°C.

5 Unscrew the fluid level plug from the bottom of the transmission sump **(see illustration)**.

6 If fluid **continually** drips from the level tube as the fluid temperature increases, the fluid level is correct and does not need to be topped-up. Note that there will be some fluid already present in the level tube, and it will be necessary to observe when this amount has drained before making the level check. Make sure that the check is made before the fluid temperature reaches 45°C. Check the condition of the seal on the level plug and renew it if necessary by cutting off the old seal and fitting a new one. Refit the plug and tighten to the specified torque.

7 If no fluid drips from the level tube, even when the fluid temperature has reached 45°C, it will be necessary to add fluid as follows while the engine is still running.

8 Using a screwdriver, lever off the cap from the filler tube on the side of the transmission sump. **Note:** *On some models the locking device will be permanently damaged and a new cap must be obtained. On other models, the cap securing clip must be renewed.*

9 With the cap removed, pull out the filler tube plug then add the specified fluid until it drips out of the level tube. Check the condition of the seal on the level plug and renew it if necessary by cutting off the old seal and fitting a new one. Refit the plug and tighten to the specified torque.

10 Refit the filler tube plug and the new cap or cap securing clip.

11 Switch off the ignition then refit the engine undertray and lower the vehicle to the ground.

12 Frequent need for topping-up indicates that there is a leak, which should be found and corrected before it becomes serious.

098 type automatic transmission

13 Take the vehicle on a short journey, to warm the transmission up to normal operating temperature, then park the vehicle on level ground. The fluid level is checked using the dipstick located at the front of the transmission.

14 With the engine idling, the handbrake applied and the selector lever in the P (Park) position, withdraw the dipstick from the tube, and wipe all the fluid from its end with a clean rag or paper towel. Insert the clean dipstick back into the tube as far as it will go, then withdraw it once more. Note the fluid level on the end of the dipstick; it should be between the MAX and MIN marks **(see illustration)**.

15 If topping-up is necessary, add the required quantity of the specified fluid to the transmission through the dipstick tube. Use a funnel with a fine mesh gauze, to avoid spillage, and to ensure that no foreign matter enters the transmission. **Note:** *Never overfill the transmission so that the fluid level is above the upper mark.*

16 After topping-up, take the vehicle on a short run to distribute the fresh fluid,

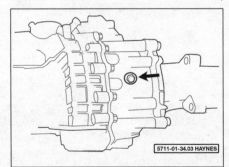

34.3 Automatic transmission final drive oil filler/level plug (arrowed)

then recheck the level again, topping-up if necessary.

17 Always maintain the level between the two dipstick marks. If the level is allowed to fall below the lower mark, fluid starvation may result, which could lead to severe transmission damage. If the level is too high, the excess fluid may be ejected. In either case, an incorrect level will adversely affect the operation of the transmission.

18 Frequent need for topping-up indicates that there is a leak, which should be found and corrected before it becomes serious.

34 Automatic transmission final drive oil level check

1 Apply the handbrake, then jack up the front of the vehicle and support it on axle stands (see *Jacking and vehicle support*), but note that the rear of the vehicle should also be raised to ensure an accurate level check.

2 Remove the engine undertray as described in Chapter 11, Section 25.

3 Working through the opening in the front subframe, wipe clean the area around the filler/level plug, which is situated on the rear of the final drive/differential housing, then unscrew the plug and clean it **(see illustration)**.

4 The oil level should reach the lower edge of the filler/level hole. A certain amount of oil will have gathered behind the filler/level plug, and will trickle out when it is removed; this does **not** necessarily indicate that the level is correct. To ensure that a true level is established, wait until the initial trickle has stopped, then add oil as necessary until a trickle of new oil can be seen emerging. The level will be correct when the flow ceases. When topping-up, use only good-quality oil of the specified type (refer to *Lubricants and fluids*).

5 Filling the differential with oil is an extremely awkward operation; above all, allow plenty of time for the oil level to settle properly before checking it. If a large amount is added to the differential, and a large amount flows out on checking the level, refit the filler/level plug and take the vehicle on a short journey so that the new oil is distributed fully around the differential components, then recheck the level when it has settled again.

6 If the differential has been overfilled so that oil flows out when the filler/level plug is removed, check that the vehicle is completely level (front-to-rear and side-to-side), and allow the surplus to drain off into a suitable container.

7 When the level is correct, refit the plug, tightening it securely. Wash off any spilt oil, refit the engine undertray and lower the vehicle to the ground.

Every 80 000 miles (120 000 km) – 'INSP' on interval display

35 Timing belt and tensioner renewal

Proceed as described in Chapter 2A, Section 4 and 5 (4-cylinder engines) or Chapter 2B, Section 4, 5 or 7 (5-cylinder engines).

36 Injection pump drivebelt renewal – 5-cylinder engines

Proceed as described in Chapter 2B, Section 6.

Chapter 2 Part A:
4-cylinder engine in-vehicle repair procedures

Contents

Degrees of difficulty

Easy, suitable for novice with little experience	**Fairly easy,** suitable for beginner with some experience	**Fairly difficult,** suitable for competent DIY mechanic	**Difficult,** suitable for experienced DIY mechanic	**Very difficult,** suitable for expert DIY or professional

Specifications

General

Engine type	4-cylinder, in-line, single overhead camshaft
Engine codes:	
45 kW (normally aspirated) engines	1X
50 kW (turbocharged) engines	ABL
Capacity	1896 cc
Bore	79.5 mm
Stroke	95.5 mm
Compression ratio	22.5 : 1
Compression pressures – minimum	26 bar
Firing order	1-3-4-2 (No 1 cylinder at timing belt end)
Direction of crankshaft rotation	Clockwise (seen from right-hand side of vehicle)
Auxiliary drivebelt tension:	
Alternator and coolant pump V-belt adjustment arm nut:	
New V-belt	8 Nm (6 lbf ft)
Used V-belt	4 Nm (3 lbf ft)
Timing belt tension:	
Early engines only – without semi-automatic tensioner	Scale reading of 12-13 units measured using Volkswagen tool VW 210

Lubrication system

Oil pump type	Sump-mounted, driven indirectly from intermediate shaft
Normal operating oil pressure	2.0 bar minimum (at 2000 rpm, oil temperature 80°C)
Oil pump backlash	0.2 mm (wear limit)
Oil pump axial clearance	0.15 mm (wear limit)

Torque wrench settings

	Nm	lbf ft
Alternator mountings:		
With auxiliary V-belt drive:		
Adjustment arm nut locking bolt	35	26
Adjustment arm-to-mounting bracket bolt	23	17
Mounting bolts	35	26
With ribbed auxiliary belt drive:		
Mounting bolts	23	17
Big-end bearing caps bolts:*		
Stage 1	30	22
Stage 2	Angle-tighten a further 90°	
Camshaft cover nuts	10	7
Camshaft bearing cap nuts	20	15
Camshaft sprocket bolt	45	33
Coolant pump pulley bolts	20	15
Crankshaft auxiliary belt pulley bolts	25	18
Crankshaft front oil seal housing bolts	20	15
Crankshaft rear oil seal housing bolts	10	7
Crankshaft pulley-to-sprocket bolts	25	18
Crankshaft sprocket bolt:*		
Stage 1	90	66
Stage 2	Angle-tighten a further 90°	
Cylinder head bolts:*		
Stage 1	40	30
Stage 2	60	44
Stage 3	Angle-tighten a further 90°	
Stage 4	Angle-tighten a further 90°	
Engine mountings:		
Left-hand mounting-to-body through bolt	65	48
Left-hand mounting-to-body nuts	55	41
Left-hand mounting transmission bracket-to-transmission	65	48
Rear mounting-to-subframe (early models)	45	33
Rear mounting-to-subframe through bolt (later models)*	200	148
Rear mounting-to-transmission through bolt (later models):*		
Stage 1	80	59
Stage 2	Angle-tighten a further 90°	
Rear mounting-to-transmission rear bolts (later models)	40	30
Rear mounting-to-transmission right-hand bolts (later models)	100	74
Right-hand mounting-to-body through bolt	65	48
Right-hand mounting-to-body nuts	55	41
Exhaust manifold nuts:		
M6 nuts	5	5
M8 nuts	23	17
M10 nuts	40	30
Flywheel bolts:*		
Stage 1	30	22
Stage 2	Angle-tighten a further 90°	
Fuel injection pump sprocket outer bolts (two-part sprocket)	25	18
Inlet manifold bolts	25	18
Intermediate shaft flange bolts	25	18
Intermediate shaft sprocket bolt	45	33
Main bearing cap bolts	65	48
Oil pump cover bolts	10	7
Oil pump mounting bolts	20	15
Oil pump pickup tube screws	10	7
Power steering pump mounting bolts	20	15
Power steering pump pulley bolts	20	15
Roadwheel bolts:		
Up to December 1995	160	118
January 1996 onward	180	133
Sump retaining bolts	20	15
Timing belt tensioner locknut	20	15
Transmission bellhousing to engine:		
M8 bolts	20	15
M10 bolts	60	44
M12 bolts	80	59

*Use new nuts/bolts

1 General information

Using this Chapter

Chapter 2 is divided into three parts; A, B and C. Repair operations that can be carried out with the engine in the vehicle are described in Parts A (4-cylinder engines) and B (5-cylinder engines). Part C covers the removal and refitting of the engine/transmission as a unit and describes the engine dismantling and overhaul procedures.

In Parts A and B, the assumption is made that the engine is installed in the vehicle, with all ancillaries connected. If the engine has been removed for overhaul, the preliminary dismantling information which precedes each operation may be ignored.

Engine description

The engines are water-cooled, single overhead camshaft, in-line four cylinder units with cast-iron cylinder blocks and aluminium-alloy cylinder heads. All are mounted transversely at the front of the vehicle, with the transmission bolted to the left-hand side of the engine.

The cylinder head carries the camshaft, which is driven by a toothed timing belt. It also houses the inlet and exhaust valves, which are closed by double coil springs, and which run in guides pressed into the cylinder head. The camshaft actuates the valves directly via hydraulic tappets, mounted in the cylinder head. The cylinder head contains integral oilways which supply and lubricate the tappets.

The crankshaft is supported by five main bearings, and endfloat is controlled by a thrust bearing fitted between cylinders No 2 and 3.

The engines are fitted with a timing belt-driven intermediate shaft, which provides drive for the brake servo vacuum pump and the oil pump.

Engine coolant is circulated by a pump, driven by the auxiliary drivebelt. For details of the cooling system, refer to Chapter 3.

Lubricant is circulated under pressure by a gear-type. Oil is drawn from the sump through a strainer, and then forced through an externally-mounted, replaceable screw-on filter. From there, it is distributed to the cylinder head, where it lubricates the camshaft journals and hydraulic tappets, and also to the crankcase, where it lubricates the main bearings, connecting rod big- and small-ends, gudgeon pins and cylinder bores. Oil jets are fitted to the base of each cylinder – these spray oil onto the underside of the pistons, to improve cooling. An oil cooler, supplied with engine coolant, reduces the temperature of the oil before it re-enters the engine.

Repairs possible with the engine installed in the vehicle

The following operations can be performed without removing the engine:

a) *Compression pressure – testing.*
b) *Auxiliary drivebelts – removal and refitting.*
c) *Camshaft cover – removal and refitting.*
d) *Timing belt, sprockets and cover – removal, inspection and refitting.*
e) *Camshaft – removal and refitting.**
f) *Camshaft oil seal – renewal.*
g) *Camshaft sprocket – removal and refitting.*
h) *Coolant pump – removal and refitting (refer to Chapter 3, Section 8).*
i) *Crankshaft oil seals – renewal.*
j) *Crankshaft sprocket – removal and refitting.*
k) *Cylinder head – removal and refitting.**
l) *Flywheel – removal and refitting.*
m) *Intermediate shaft oil seal – renewal.*
n) *Sump – removal and refitting.*
o) *Oil pump and pickup assembly – removal and refitting.*
p) *Pistons, connecting rods and big-end bearings – removal and refitting.*
q) *Engine mountings – inspection and renewal.*

Cylinder head dismantling procedures are given in Chapter 2C, Section 6 and also contain details of camshaft and hydraulic tappet removal.
Note: *It is possible to remove the pistons and connecting rods (after removing the cylinder head and sump) without removing the engine from the vehicle. However, this procedure is not recommended. Work of this nature is more easily and thoroughly completed with the engine on the bench.*

2 Location of TDC on No 1 cylinder

General information

1 The crankshaft, camshaft and intermediate shaft sprockets are driven by the timing belt. The crankshaft and camshaft sprockets move in phase with each other to ensure correct valve timing.
2 The design of the engines covered in this Chapter is such that piston-to-valve contact will occur if the crankshaft is turned with the timing belt removed. For this reason, it is important that the correct phasing between the camshaft and crankshaft is preserved whilst the timing belt is off the engine. This is achieved by setting the engine in a reference condition (known as Top Dead Centre or TDC) before the timing belt is removed, and then preventing the shafts from rotating until the belt is refitted. Similarly, if the engine

2.6 Removing the press-stud fixings from the timing belt upper cover

has been dismantled for overhaul, the engine can be set to TDC during reassembly to ensure that the correct shaft phasing is restored.
3 TDC is the highest position a piston reaches within its respective cylinder – in a four-stroke engine, each piston reaches TDC twice per cycle; once on the compression stroke, and once on the exhaust stroke. In general, TDC normally refers to No 1 cylinder on the compression stroke. Note that the cylinders are numbered one to four, starting from the timing belt end of the engine.

Setting TDC on No 1 cylinder

4 Remove the auxiliary drivebelts as described in Section 6.
5 Remove the camshaft cover as described in Section 7.
6 Release the uppermost part of the timing belt outer cover by prising open the metal spring clips and where applicable, removing the press-stud fixings **(see illustration)**. Lift the cover away from the engine
7 Where fitted, remove the inspection bung from the transmission bellhousing, if necessary using a large nut to unscrew it. Rotate the crankshaft clockwise with a wrench and socket, or a spanner, until the timing mark machined onto the edge of the flywheel lines up with the pointer on the bellhousing casting **(see illustrations)**.
8 To lock the engine in the TDC position, the camshaft (not the sprocket) and fuel injection pump sprocket must be secured in a reference position, using special locking tools.

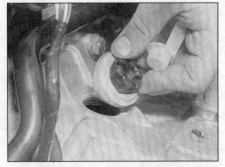

2.7a Use a large nut to remove the bung from the transmission bellhousing...

2.7b ...then turn the crankshaft until the timing mark (arrowed) machined onto the edge of the flywheel...

2.7c ...lines up with the pointer (arrowed) on the bellhousing casting

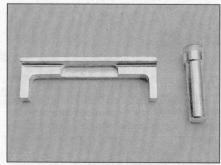

2.8 Engine locking tools

2.9 Engage the locking bar with the slot in the camshaft

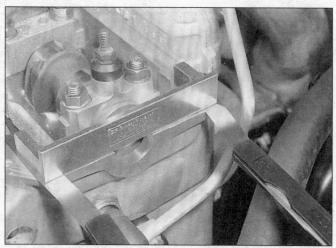

2.11 Camshaft centred and locked using locking bar and feeler gauges

Improvised tools may be fabricated, but due to the exact measurements and machining involved, it is strongly recommended that a kit of locking tools is either borrowed or hired, or purchased from a reputable tool manufacturer (see illustration).
Caution: Do not use these locking tools to prevent the rotation of the crankshaft, camshaft, etc. while slackening or tightening fasteners – they are not intended for this purpose and may break if over-stressed in such a way; use only the method described at the relevant point in this manual

2.12 Injection pump sprocket locked using locking pin (arrowed)

9 Engage the edge of the locking bar with the slot in the end of the camshaft (see illustration).
10 With the locking bar still inserted, turn the camshaft slightly (by turning the crankshaft clockwise, as before), so that the locking bar rocks to one side, allowing one end of the bar to contact the cylinder head surface. At the other side of the locking bar, measure the gap between the end of the bar and the cylinder head using a feeler blade.
11 Turn the camshaft back slightly, then pull out the feeler blade. The idea now is to level the locking bar by inserting two feeler blades, each with a thickness equal to *half* the originally measured gap, on either side of the camshaft between each end of the locking bar and the cylinder head. This centres the camshaft, and sets the valve timing in the reference condition (see illustration).
12 Insert the locking pin through the fuel injection pump sprocket alignment hole, and thread it into the support bracket behind the sprocket. This locks the fuel injection pump in the reference condition (see illustration).
13 The engine is now set to TDC on No 1 cylinder.

3 Compression and leakdown tests – description and interpretation

Compression test

Note: *A compression tester specifically designed for diesel engines must be used for this test.*

1 When engine performance is down, or if misfiring occurs, a compression test can provide diagnostic clues as to the engine's condition. If the test is performed regularly, it can give warning of trouble before any other symptoms become apparent.
2 A compression tester specifically intended for diesel engines must be used, because of the higher pressures involved. The tester is connected to an adapter which screws into the fuel injector hole. It is unlikely to be worthwhile buying such a tester for occasional use, but it may be possible to borrow or hire one – if not, have the test performed by a garage.
3 Unless specific instructions to the contrary are supplied with the tester, observe the following points:
a) *The battery must be in a good state of charge, the air filter must be clean, and*

the engine should be at normal operating temperature.

b) *All the injectors must be removed as described in Chapter 4A, Section 11 before starting the test.*

c) *The injection pump stop solenoid must be disconnected, to prevent the engine from running or fuel from being discharged.*

4 Fit a compression tester to the No 1 cylinder injector hole.

5 Crank the engine for several seconds on the starter motor. After one or two revolutions, the compression pressure should build up to a maximum figure and then stabilise. Record the highest reading obtained.

6 Repeat the test on the remaining cylinders, recording the pressure in each.

7 VW specify wear limits for compression pressures – refer to the Specifications. Seek the advice of a VW dealer or other diesel specialist if in doubt as to whether a particular pressure reading is acceptable.

8 The cause of poor compression is less easy to establish on a diesel engine than on a petrol one. The effect of introducing oil into the cylinders ('wet' testing) is not conclusive, because there is a risk that the oil will sit in the swirl chamber, instead of passing to the rings. However, the following can be used as a rough guide to diagnosis.

9 All cylinders should produce very similar pressures; a difference of more than 5 bars between any two cylinders indicates the existence of a fault. Note that the compression should build up quickly in a healthy engine; low compression on the first stroke, followed by gradually-increasing pressure on successive strokes, indicates worn piston rings. A low compression reading on the first stroke, which does not build up during successive strokes, indicates leaking valves or a blown head gasket (a cracked head could also be the cause).

10 A low reading from two adjacent cylinders is almost certainly due to the head gasket having blown between them; the presence of coolant in the engine oil will confirm this.

11 If the compression reading is unusually high, the cylinder head surfaces, valves and pistons are probably coated with carbon deposits. If this is the case, the cylinder head should be removed and decarbonised (refer to Chapter 2C, Section 6).

12 On completion, remove the compression tester, and refit the injectors as described in Chapter 4A, Section 11. Reconnect the wiring to the injection pump stop solenoid.

Leakdown test

13 A leakdown test measures the rate at which compressed air fed into the cylinder is lost. It is an alternative to a compression test, and in many ways it is better, since the escaping air provides easy identification of where pressure loss is occurring (piston rings, valves or head gasket).

14 The equipment needed for leakdown testing is unlikely to be available to the home mechanic. If poor compression is suspected, have the test performed by a suitably-equipped garage.

4 Timing belt and outer covers – removal and refitting

General information

1 The primary function of the toothed timing belt is to drive the camshaft, but it is also used to drive the fuel injection pump, intermediate shaft and coolant pump. Should the belt slip or break in service, the valve timing will be disturbed and piston-to-valve contact will occur, resulting in serious engine damage.

2 For this reason, it is important that the timing belt is tensioned correctly, and inspected regularly for signs of wear or deterioration.

3 Note that the removal of the *inner* section of the timing belt cover is described as part of the cylinder head removal procedure; see Section 11 later in this Chapter.

Removal

4 Disconnect the battery negative terminal (refer to *Disconnecting the battery*).

5 For improved access, move the radiator to the service position as described in Chapter 3, Section 3.

6 Remove the air cleaner housing as described in Chapter 4A, Section 2.

7 Disconnect the wiring at the fuel injection pump stop solenoid.

8 Release the uppermost part of the timing belt outer cover by prising open the metal spring clips and where applicable, removing the press-stud fixings **(see illustration 2.6)**. Lift the cover away from the engine

9 With reference to Section 6, remove the auxiliary drivebelt(s). Slacken and withdraw the screws, and lift off the coolant pump pulley.

10 Refer to Section 2, and using the engine alignment markings, set the engine to TDC on No 1 cylinder.

11 Slacken and withdraw the retaining bolts, then remove the pulley for the ribbed auxiliary

4.11 Removing the crankshaft auxiliary belt pulleys

belt (together with the V-belt pulley, where fitted) from the crankshaft sprocket **(see illustration)**. On completion, check that the engine is still set to TDC.

12 Remove the retaining screws and clips, and lift off the timing belt lower cover.

13 On engines with a two-part fuel injection pump sprocket, ensure that the sprocket locking pin is firmly in position (see Section 2), then loosen the outer sprocket securing bolts by half a turn.

Caution: Do not loosen the sprocket centre bolt, as this will alter the fuel injection pump's basic timing setting.

14 With reference to Section 5, relieve the tension on the timing belt by slackening the tensioner mounting nut slightly, allowing it to pivot away from the belt.

15 Examine the timing belt for manufacturer's markings that indicate the direction of rotation. If none are present, make your own using typist's correction fluid or a dab of paint – do not cut or score the belt in any way.

Caution: If the belt appears to be in good condition and can be re-used, it is essential that it is refitted the same way around, otherwise accelerated wear will result, leading to premature failure.

16 Slide the belt off the sprockets, taking care to avoid twisting or kinking it excessively.

Inspection

17 Examine the belt for evidence of contamination by coolant or lubricant. If this is the case, find the source of the contamination before progressing any further. Check the belt for signs of wear or damage, particularly around the leading edges of the belt teeth. Renew the belt if its condition is in any doubt; the cost of belt renewal is negligible compared with potential cost of the engine repairs, should the belt fail in service. Where fitted, the semi-automatic tensioner should be renewed as a matter of course at the same time as the timing belt.

18 If the timing belt is not going to be refitted for some time, it is a wise precaution to hang a warning label on the steering wheel, to remind yourself (and others) not to attempt to start the engine.

Refitting

19 Ensure that the crankshaft is still set to TDC on No 1 cylinder, as described in Section 2.

20 Refer to Section 5 and slacken the camshaft sprocket bolt by half a turn. Release the sprocket from the camshaft taper mounting by carefully tapping it with a pin punch, inserted through the hole provided in the timing belt inner cover **(see illustration)**.

21 Loop the timing belt loosely under the crankshaft sprocket.

Caution: Observe the direction of rotation markings on the belt.

22 Engage the timing belt teeth with the crankshaft sprocket, then manoeuvre it into

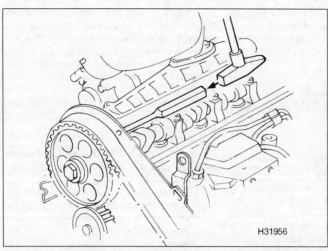

4.20 Releasing the camshaft sprocket from the taper using a pin punch

4.26 Tensioning the timing belt using a pair of circlip pliers in the belt tensioner

position over the camshaft and injection pump sprockets. Ensure the belt teeth seat correctly on the sprockets. **Note:** *Slight adjustments to the position of the camshaft sprocket (and where applicable, injection pump sprocket) may be necessary to achieve this.*

23 Pass the flat side of the belt over the intermediate shaft pulley and tensioner roller – avoid bending the belt back on itself or twisting it excessively as you do this.

24 On engines with a single-part fuel injection pump sprocket, remove the locking pin from the fuel injection pump sprocket (see Section 2).

25 Ensure that the 'front run' of the belt is taut – ie all the slack should be in the section of the belt that passes over the tensioner roller.

26 Tension the belt by turning the eccentrically-mounted tensioner clockwise; two holes are provided in the side of the tensioner hub for this purpose – a pair of sturdy right-angled circlip pliers is a suitable substitute for the correct VW tool **(see illustration)**.

27 On engines with a semi-automatic belt tensioner, turn the tensioner clockwise until the notch in the tensioner's centre aligns with the raised rib on its outer part **(see illustration)**. **Note:** *If the tensioner is turned too far, it must be rotated fully anticlockwise to release the pressure **completely** before turning it clockwise again; if excessive pressure has been applied, **do not** merely relax that pressure to bring the notch and raised rib into alignment.*

28 Test the timing belt tension by grasping it between the fingers at a point mid-way between the injection pump and camshaft sprockets, and twisting it. The belt tension is correct when the belt can just be twisted through 45° (1/8 of a turn) and no further.

29 When the correct belt tension has been achieved, tighten the tensioner locknut to the specified torque.

30 On engines without a semi-automatic tensioner, the belt tension must be accurately checked, and if necessary adjusted – this involves the use of a dedicated belt tension measuring device (Volkswagen tool VW 210), and it is advisable to have this operation carried out by a VW dealer.

31 At this point, check the crankshaft is still set to TDC on No 1 cylinder (see Section 2).

32 Refer to Section 5 and tighten the camshaft sprocket bolt to the specified torque.

33 On engines with a two-part fuel injection pump sprocket, tighten the outer sprocket bolts, then remove the sprocket locking pin.

34 With reference to Section 2, remove the camshaft locking bar.

35 Using a spanner or wrench and socket on the crankshaft pulley centre bolt, rotate the crankshaft through two complete revolutions. Reset the engine to TDC on No 1 cylinder, with reference to Section 2 and check that the fuel injection pump sprocket locking pin can be inserted. Re-check the timing belt tension and adjust it, if necessary.

36 Refit the upper and lower sections of the timing belt outer cover, tightening the retaining screws securely.

37 Refit the coolant pump pulley and tighten the retaining screws to the specified torque.

38 Refit the crankshaft auxiliary belt pulley and tighten the retaining screws to the specified torque, using the method employed during removal. Note that the offset of the pulley mounting holes allows only one fitting position.

39 With reference to Section 6, refit and tension the auxiliary drivebelt(s).

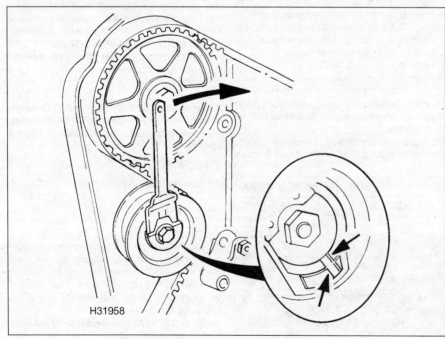

4.27 Notch must align with raised rib – engines with semi-automatic tensioner

40 Refit the camshaft cover as described in Section 7.
41 Reconnect the fuel injection pump stop solenoid wiring.
42 Refit the air cleaner housing as described in Chapter 4A, Section 2.
43 Move the radiator back to its normal position as described in Chapter 3, Section 3, then reconnect the battery negative terminal.
44 On completion, refer to Chapter 4A, Section 8 and check the fuel injection pump timing.

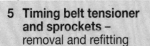

5 Timing belt tensioner and sprockets –
removal and refitting

1 Disconnect the battery negative terminal (refer to *Disconnecting the battery*).
2 For improved access, move the radiator to the service position as described in Chapter 3, Section 3.
3 Remove the air cleaner housing as described in Chapter 4A, Section 2.
4 Remove the auxiliary drivebelt(s) as described in Section 6.

Timing belt tensioner

Removal

5 With reference to the relevant paragraphs of Sections 2 and 4, set the engine to TDC on No 1 cylinder, then remove the upper section of the timing belt outer cover.
6 Slacken the retaining nut at the hub of the tensioner pulley and allow the assembly to rotate anti-clockwise, relieving the tension on the timing belt. Remove the nut and recover the washer **(see illustration)**.
7 Slide the tensioner off its mounting stud **(see illustration)**.
8 Wipe the tensioner clean, but do not use solvents that may contaminate the bearings. Spin the tensioner pulley on its hub by hand. Stiff movement or excessive freeplay is an indication of severe wear; the tensioner is

5.6 Remove the tensioner nut and recover the washer

not a serviceable component, and should be renewed. Where fitted, the semi-automatic tensioner should be renewed as a matter of course at the same interval as the timing belt.

Refitting

9 Slide the tensioner pulley over the mounting stud. On engines with a semi-automatic tensioner, engage the forked end of the backplate with the timing belt pillar.
10 Refit the tensioner washer and retaining nut – do not fully tighten the nut at this stage.
11 With reference to Section 4, refit and tension the timing belt.
12 On engines with a semi-automatic tensioner, the operation of the tensioner can be tested as follows: apply firm thumb pressure to the timing belt at a point mid-way between the camshaft and fuel injection pump sprockets. The notch in the tensioner's centre will move away from the raised rib on the outer part as pressure is applied, and then move back into alignment again as the pressure is released **(see illustration 4.26)**.
13 Refit the camshaft cover as described in Section 7.
14 Refer to Section 4 and refit the timing belt cover.
15 With reference to Section 6, refit and tension the auxiliary drivebelt(s).

5.7 Slide the tensioner off its mounting stud

16 Refit the air cleaner housing as described in Chapter 4A, Section 2.
17 Move the radiator back to its normal position as described in Chapter 3, Section 3, then reconnect the battery negative terminal.

Camshaft timing belt sprocket

Removal

18 Refer to the relevant paragraphs of Section 2 and 4, set the engine to TDC on No 1 cylinder, then remove the timing belt upper outer cover.
19 Slacken the timing belt tensioner centre nut and allow it to rotate anti-clockwise, to relieve the tension on the timing belt. Carefully slide the timing belt off the camshaft sprocket.
20 The camshaft sprocket must be held stationary whilst its retaining bolt is slackened; if access to the correct VW special tool is not possible, a simple home-made tool using basic materials may be fabricated **(see Tool Tip)**.
21 Using the holding tool, brace the support the camshaft sprocket then slacken and remove the retaining bolt; recover the washer where fitted.
22 Slide the camshaft sprocket from the end of the camshaft **(see illustration)**.
23 With the sprocket removed, examine

To make a camshaft sprocket holding tool, obtain two lengths of steel strip about 6 mm thick by 30 mm wide or similar, one 600 mm long, the other 200 mm long (all dimensions approximate). Bolt the two strips together to form a forked end, leaving the bolt slack so that the shorter strip can pivot freely. At the end of each 'prong' of the fork, secure a bolt with a nut and a locknut, to act as the fulcrums; these will engage with the cut-outs in the sprocket, and should protrude by about 30mm

5.22 Removing the camshaft sprocket

5.37a Insert the crankshaft sprocket bolt...

5.37b ...tighten it to the Stage 1 torque...

5.37c ...then through the Stage 2 angle

the camshaft oil seal for signs of leaking. If necessary, refer to Section 8 and renew it.

24 Wipe the sprocket and camshaft mating surfaces clean.

Refitting

25 Locate the sprocket on the camshaft, then insert the retaining bolt hand-tight at this stage.

26 With reference to Sections 2 and 4, check that the engine is still set to TDC on No 1 cylinder, then refit and tension the timing belt.

27 Refit the camshaft cover as described in Section 7.

28 Refer to Section 4 and refit the timing belt cover.

29 With reference to Section 6, refit and tension the auxiliary drivebelt(s).

30 Refit the air cleaner housing as described in Chapter 4A, Section 2.

31 Move the radiator back to its normal position as described in Chapter 3, Section 3, then reconnect the battery negative terminal.

Crankshaft timing belt sprocket

Removal

32 Remove the timing belt as described in Section 4. If the timing belt is to be re-used, make sure it is marked for direction of rotation.

33 The crankshaft sprocket must be held stationary whilst its retaining bolt is slackened. If access to the correct VW flywheel locking tool is not available, lock the crankshaft in position by removing the starter motor, as described in Chapter 5, Section 10 to expose the flywheel ring gear. Have an assistant insert a stout lever between the ring gear teeth

5.45 Brace the intermediate shaft sprocket, then remove the retaining bolt

and the transmission bellhousing whilst the sprocket retaining bolt is slackened.

34 Withdraw the bolt, recover the washer and lift off the sprocket.

35 With the sprocket removed, examine the crankshaft oil seal for signs of leaking. If necessary, refer to Section 10 and renew it.

36 Wipe the sprocket and crankshaft mating surfaces clean.

Refitting

37 Offer up the sprocket to the crankshaft, engaging the lug on the inside of the sprocket with the recess in the end of the crankshaft. Insert the retaining bolt and washer and tighten it to the specified torque (see illustrations).

38 Refit and tension the timing belt as described in Section 4.

Intermediate shaft sprocket

Removal

39 Remove the timing belt as described in Section 4. If the timing belt is to be re-used, make sure it is marked for direction of rotation.

40 The intermediate shaft sprocket must be held stationary whilst its retaining bolt is slackened; if access to the VW special tool is not possible, a simple home-made tool may be fabricated as described in the camshaft sprocket removal sub-Section. Alternatively, insert a metal dowel rod or socket wrench through one of the holes in the sprocket to hold it stationary.

41 Slacken and remove the retaining bolt, then slide the sprocket from the end of the intermediate shaft. Recover the Woodruff key from the keyway.

42 With the sprocket removed, examine the intermediate shaft oil seal for signs of leaking. If necessary, refer to Section 9 and renew it.

43 Wipe the sprocket and shaft mating surfaces clean.

Refitting

44 Fit the Woodruff key into the keyway with the plain surface facing upwards. Offer up the sprocket to the intermediate shaft, engaging the slot in the sprocket with the Woodruff key.

45 Insert and tighten the sprocket retaining bolt to the specified torque while holding the sprocket using the method employed during removal (see illustration).

46 Refit and tension the timing belt as described in Section 4.

Fuel injection pump sprocket

47 Refer to Chapter 4A, Section 8.

6 Auxiliary drivebelts – removal and refitting

General information

1 Depending on the vehicle specification and engine type, one or two auxiliary drivebelts may be fitted. Both are driven from pulleys mounted on the crankshaft, and provide drive for the alternator, coolant pump and, where fitted, the power steering pump.

2 The run of the belts and the components they drive are also dependent on vehicle specification and engine type. Because of this, the alternator and coolant pump may have pulleys to suit either a ribbed belt or a V-belt.

3 The V-belt driving the alternator and coolant pump is tensioned manually by means of a tensioning nut incorporated in the alternator adjustment arm. The V-belt driving the power steering pump is tensioned by adding shims between the front half and rear half of the two-piece power steering pump pulley. This effectively increases or decreases the diameter of the pulley depending whether shims are added or removed.

4 The ribbed auxiliary belt may have an automatic tensioner or it may be tensioned by the alternator mountings, which have an in-built tensioning spring.

5 On refitting, the auxiliary belt must be tensioned correctly to ensure correct operation and prolonged service life.

Power steering pump V-belt

Removal

6 Firmly apply the handbrake, then jack up the front of the vehicle and support it securely on axle stands (see Jacking and vehicle support). Remove the right-hand front roadwheel.

7 Remove the engine undertray as described in Chapter 11, Section 25.

8 Disconnect the wiring at the fuel injection pump stop solenoid.

9 Undo the three bolts securing the two halves of the power steering pump pulley together. Use the shank of a screwdriver against two of the bolts to hold the pulley stationary while slackening the third bolt, then repeat for the other bolts. Lift off the front half and collect the spacer shims. You are likely to find about six or seven shims fitted.
10 Slip the V-belt off the crankshaft pulley and remove the belt from under the vehicle.
11 Examine the belt for signs or wear or damage, and renew it if necessary.

Refitting and tensioning

12 Locate the belt over the crankshaft pulley then place it in position against the rear half of the power steering pump pulley.
13 The spacer shims are used to tension the V-belt. Removing shims increases the tension of the belt and adding shims decreases the tension. Using a trial and error process, fit the existing shims and the pulley front half and secure the assembly with the three retaining bolts.
14 Crank the engine over two or three turns on the starter motor to settle the V-belt then check the tension. The belt should be a snug fit on the pulleys with very little deflection (about 5 mm under moderate thumb pressure). Remove shims or add additional shims as necessary, cranking the engine over each time, until the correct tension is achieved. When the adjustment is correct, finally tighten the three pulley retaining bolts to the specified torque.
15 Reconnect the wiring at the fuel injection pump stop solenoid and refit the engine undertray.
16 Refit the roadwheel and lower the vehicle to the ground.

Alternator and coolant pump V-belt

Removal

17 Firmly apply the handbrake, then jack up the front of the vehicle and support it securely on axle stands (see *Jacking and vehicle support*). Remove the right-hand front roadwheel.
18 Remove the engine undertray as described in Chapter 11, Section 25.
19 Where fitted, remove the power steering pump V-belt as described previously.
20 Slacken the alternator mounting bolts and the adjustment arm bolts at least one turn.
21 Using a socket or spanner on the adjustment arm nut, turn the nut to pivot the alternator toward the engine, then slip the V-belt off the three pulleys **(see illustration)**.
22 Examine the belt for signs or wear or damage, and renew it if necessary.

Refitting and tensioning

23 Locate the belt over the crankshaft, coolant pump and alternator pulleys, then turn the adjustment arm nut to pivot the alternator away from the engine.
24 Tension the V-belt by tightening the adjustment arm nut to the specified torque, then tightening the adjustment arm nut locking bolt to the specified torque.
25 Where applicable, refit and tension the power steering pump V-belt as described previously.
26 Refit the engine undertray as described in Chapter 11, Section 25.
27 Refit the roadwheel and lower the vehicle to the ground.

Ribbed auxiliary belt

Removal

28 Firmly apply the handbrake, then jack up the front of the vehicle and support it securely on axle stands (see *Jacking and vehicle support*). Remove the right-hand front roadwheel.
29 Remove the engine undertray as described in Chapter 11, Section 25.
30 Remove the power steering pump V-belt as described previously.
31 Examine the ribbed belt for manufacturer's markings, indicating the direction of rotation. If none are present, make some using typist's correction fluid or a dab of paint.

Vehicles without an automatic tensioning roller

32 Slacken the alternator upper and lower mounting bolts at least one turn.
33 Push the alternator down to its stop against the spring tension, so that it rotates around its uppermost mounting.

Vehicles with an automatic tensioning roller

34 Rotate the tensioning roller arm clockwise against its spring tension so that the roller is forced away from the belt – use an adjustable spanner as a lever **(see illustration)**.

All vehicles

35 Pull the belt off the alternator pulley, then release it from the remaining pulleys.

Refitting and tensioning

Caution: Observe the manufacturer's direction of rotation markings on the belt, when refitting.
36 Pass the ribbed belt underneath the crankshaft pulley, ensuring that the ribs seat securely in the channels on the surface of the pulley.

Vehicles without an automatic tensioning roller

37 Repeatedly push the alternator down to its stop against the spring tension, so that it rotates around its uppermost mounting and check that it moves back freely when released. If necessary, slacken the alternator mounting bolts by a further half a turn.
38 Keep the alternator pushed down against its stop, pass the belt over the alternator pulley, then release the alternator and allow it to tension the belt.
39 Start the engine and allow it to idle for approximately ten seconds.

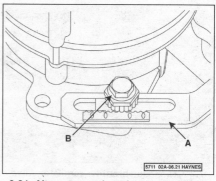

6.21 Alternator and coolant pump V-belt adjustment

A Adjustment arm
B Adjustment arm nut

40 Switch the engine off, then tighten first the lower, then the alternator upper mounting bolts to the specified torque.

Vehicles with an automatic tensioning roller

41 Rotate the tensioning roller arm clockwise against its spring tension – use an adjustable spanner as a lever **(see illustration 6.34)**.
42 Pass the belt around the coolant pump pulley then fit it over the alternator pulley.
43 Release the tensioner pulley arm and allow the roller to bear against the flat surface of the belt.

All vehicles

44 Refit the power steering pump V-belt as described previously.
45 Refit the engine undertray as described in Chapter 11, Section 25.
46 Refit the roadwheel and lower the vehicle to the ground.

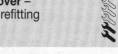

7 Camshaft cover –
removal and refitting

Removal

1 Disconnect the battery negative terminal (refer to *Disconnecting the battery*).
2 Disconnect the wiring at the fuel injection pump stop solenoid.

6.34 Rotate the tensioner roller arm clockwise – use an adjustable spanner – and remove the belt

7.3 Crankcase breather regulator valve

7.4 Camshaft cover retaining nut

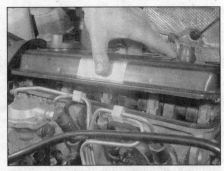

7.5 Lift the camshaft cover away from the cylinder head

7.6 Recover the camshaft cover gasket

7.8 Ensure that the camshaft cover gasket is correctly seated on the cylinder head

3 Disconnect the crankcase breather hose and regulator valve from the camshaft cover **(see illustration)**.

4 Remove the caps, then unscrew and remove the three camshaft cover retaining nuts – recover the washers and seals **(see illustration)**.

5 Lift the cover away from the cylinder head **(see illustration)**; if it sticks, do not attempt to lever it off – instead free it by working around the cover and tapping it lightly with a soft-faced mallet.

6 Recover the camshaft cover gasket **(see illustration)**. Inspect the gasket carefully, and renew it if damage or deterioration is evident.

7 Clean the mating surfaces of the cylinder head and camshaft cover thoroughly, removing all traces of oil and old gasket – take care to avoid damaging the surfaces as you do this.

Refitting

8 Refitting is the reverse of the removal procedure, noting the following points:

a) *Ensure that the gasket is correctly seated on the cylinder head, and take care to avoid displacing it as the camshaft cover is lowered into position* **(see illustration)**.

b) *Tighten the camshaft cover retaining nuts to the specified torque.*

c) *When refitting hoses that were originally secured with crimp-type clips, use standard worm-drive clips in their place on refitting.*

8 Camshaft oil seal – renewal

1 Disconnect the battery negative terminal (refer to *Disconnecting the battery*).

2 Refer to Section 6 and remove the auxiliary drivebelt(s).

3 Refer to Section 5 and remove the timing belt tensioner, and the camshaft and injection pump sprockets.

4 Unbolt and remove the timing belt inner cover.

5 Remove the camshaft cover as described in Section 7.

6 Unbolt the camshaft No 1 bearing cap, and slide off the camshaft oil seal **(see illustration)**.

7 Lubricate the surface of a new camshaft oil seal with clean engine oil, and fit it over the end of the camshaft.

8 Apply a thin film of suitable sealant to the mating surface of the bearing cap, then refit it making sure that the oil seal is located fully against the seating in the head and cap. Tighten the mounting nuts progressively to the specified torque.

9 Refit the camshaft cover as described in Section 7.

10 Refit the timing belt inner cover and tighten the bolts.

11 Refit the camshaft and injection pump sprockets and the timing belt tensioner with reference to Section 5.

12 Refit the auxiliary drivebelts with reference to Section 6.

13 On completion, reconnect the battery negative terminal.

9 Intermediate shaft oil seal – renewal

1 Disconnect the battery negative terminal (refer to *Disconnecting the battery*).

2 Refer to Section 6 and remove the auxiliary drivebelt(s).

3 Refer to Section 5 and remove the timing belt tensioner, and the camshaft, intermediate shaft and injection pump sprockets.

4 Unbolt and remove the timing belt inner cover.

5 Slacken the retaining bolts and withdraw the intermediate shaft flange. Recover the O-ring seal, then press out the oil seal **(see illustrations)**.

6 Press a new shaft oil seal into its housing

8.6 Unbolt the camshaft No 1 bearing cap, and slide off the camshaft oil seal

9.5a Slacken the retaining bolts (arrowed)...

9.5b ...and withdraw the intermediate shaft flange

9.5c Press out the oil seal...

9.5d ...then recover the O-ring seal

in the intermediate shaft flange and fit a new O-ring seal to the inner sealing surface of the flange.

7 Lubricate the inner lip of the seal with clean engine oil, and slide the flange and seal over the end of the intermediate shaft. Ensure that the O-ring is correctly seated, then fit the flange retaining bolts and tighten them to the specified torque. Check that the intermediate shaft can rotate freely.

8 Refit the timing belt inner cover.

9 Refer to Section 5 and refit the timing belt tensioner, and the camshaft, intermediate shaft and injection pump sprockets.

10 Refer to Section 6 and refit the auxiliary drivebelt(s).

11 On completion, reconnect the battery negative terminal.

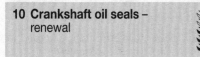

10 Crankshaft oil seals – renewal

Crankshaft front oil seal

1 Remove the crankshaft timing belt sprocket as described in Section 5.

2 Drill two small holes into the existing oil seal, diagonally opposite each other. Thread two self-tapping screws into the holes and using two pairs of pliers, pull on the heads of the screws to extract the oil seal **(see illustration)**. Take great care to avoid drilling through into the seal housing or crankshaft sealing surface.

3 Clean out the seal housing and sealing surface of the crankshaft by wiping it with a lint-free cloth – avoid using solvents that may enter the crankcase and affect component lubrication. Remove any swarf or burrs that could cause the seal to leak.

4 Smear the lip of the new oil seal with clean engine oil, and position it over the housing.

5 Using a hammer and a socket of suitable diameter, drive the seal squarely into its housing. **Note:** *Select a socket that bears only on the hard outer surface of the seal, not the inner lip, which can easily be damaged.*

6 Refit the crankshaft timing belt sprocket with reference to Section 5.

Crankshaft front oil seal housing – gasket renewal

7 Remove the crankshaft timing belt sprocket as described in Section 5.

8 Remove the sump as described in Section 15.

9 Progressively slacken and then remove the oil seal housing retaining bolts.

10 Lift the housing away from the cylinder block, together with the crankshaft oil seal, using a twisting motion to ease the seal along the shaft.

11 Recover the old gasket from the seal housing and cylinder block. Clean the housing and block surfaces.

12 If necessary, prise the old oil seal from the housing using a screwdriver **(see illustration)**.

13 Wipe the oil seal housing clean, and check it visually for signs of distortion or cracking. Lay the housing on a work surface, with the mating surface face down. If removed, press

in a new oil seal, using a block of wood as a press to ensure that the seal enters the housing squarely.

14 Smear the crankcase mating surface with multi-purpose grease, and lay the new gasket in position **(see illustration)**.

15 Wrap the end of the crankshaft with tape to protect the oil seal as the housing is being refitted.

16 Lubricate the inner lip of the crankshaft oil seal with clean engine oil, then offer up the seal and its housing to the end of the crankshaft. Ease the seal along the shaft using a twisting motion, until the housing is flush with the crankcase **(see illustration)**.

17 Insert the bolts and tighten them progressively to the specified torque.

18 Refer to Section 15 and refit the sump.

19 Refit the crankshaft timing belt sprocket with reference to Section 5.

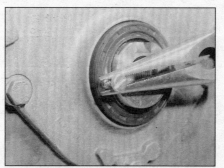

10.2 Removing the crankshaft front oil seal using self-tapping screws

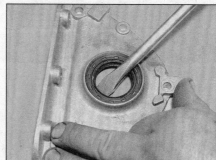

10.12 Prise the old oil seal from the housing

10.14 Locate the new crankshaft front oil seal housing gasket in position

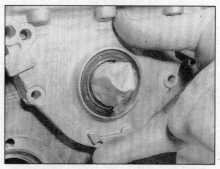

10.16 Offer up the seal and its housing to the end of the crankshaft

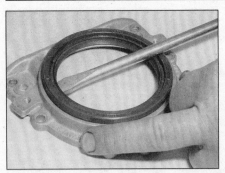

10.36 Prise the crankshaft rear oil seal from the housing

Crankshaft rear oil seal

20 Remove the transmission as described in Chapter 7A, Section 6.

21 Refer to Section 13 of this Chapter and remove the flywheel.

22 Drill a small hole into the existing oil seal and thread a self-tapping screw into the hole. Using a pair of pliers, pull on the head of the screw to extract the oil seal. Take great care to avoid drilling through into the seal housing or crankshaft sealing surface.

23 Clean out the seal housing and sealing surface of the crankshaft by wiping it with a lint-free cloth – avoid using solvents that may enter the crankcase and affect component lubrication. Remove any swarf or burrs that could cause the seal to leak.

24 If available, fit a protector sleeve over the end of the crankshaft to protect the oil seal lips as the seal is initially fitted.

25 Lubricate the lips of the new oil seal and

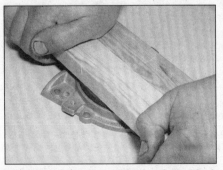

10.37 Press in a new oil seal, using a block of wood

10.39 A protective plastic cap is supplied with genuine VW crankshaft oil seals

locate it over the protector sleeve. If a protector sleeve is not being used, carefully guide the oil seal lips over the crankshaft. Push the seal into the recess in the seal housing. Where applicable, remove the protector sleeve.

26 Tap the seal into position using a suitable large diameter tube, or a wooden block, until it is flush with the outer faces of the oil seal housing.

27 Refit the flywheel with reference to Section 13 of this Chapter.

28 Refit the transmission as described in Chapter 7A, Section 6.

Crankshaft rear oil seal housing – gasket renewal

29 Remove the transmission as described in Chapter 7A, Section 6.

30 Refer to Section 13 of this Chapter and remove the flywheel.

31 Remove the retaining bolts and lift the intermediate plate away from the cylinder block.

32 Remove the sump as described in Section 15.

33 Progressively slacken then remove the oil seal housing retaining bolts.

34 Lift the housing away from the cylinder block, together with the crankshaft oil seal, using a twisting motion to ease the seal off the shaft.

35 Recover the old gasket from the cylinder block, then wipe clean the block before fitting the new oil seal and housing.

36 Prise the old oil seal from the housing using a stout screwdriver **(see illustration)**.

37 Wipe the oil seal housing clean, and

10.38 Locate the new crankshaft rear oil seal housing gasket in position

10.40 Fitting the crankshaft rear oil seal and housing

check it visually for signs of distortion or cracking. Lay the housing on a work surface, with the mating surface face down. Press in a new oil seal, using a block of wood as a press to ensure that the seal enters the housing squarely **(see illustration)**.

38 Smear the crankcase mating surface with multi-purpose grease, and lay the new gasket in position **(see illustration)**.

39 A protective plastic cap is supplied with genuine VW crankshaft oil seals; when fitted over the end of the crankshaft, the cap prevents damage to the inner lip of the oil seal as it is being fitted **(see illustration)**. Use PVC tape to pad the end of the crankshaft if a cap is not available.

40 Lubricate the inner lip of the crankshaft oil seal with clean engine oil, then offer up the seal and its housing to the end of the crankshaft. Ease the seal along the shaft using a twisting motion, until the housing is flush with the crankcase **(see illustration)**.

41 Insert the retaining bolts and tighten them progressively to the specified torque.

42 Refit the sump with reference to Section 15.

43 Refit the intermediate plate to the cylinder block, then insert and tighten the retaining bolts.

44 Refit the flywheel with reference to Section 13 of this Chapter.

45 Refit the transmission as described in Chapter 7A, Section 6.

---

11 Cylinder head – removal and refitting

Note: *Cylinder head dismantling and overhaul is covered in Chapter 2C, Section 6.*

Removal

1 Disconnect the battery negative terminal (refer to *Disconnecting the battery*).

2 Drain the engine oil with reference to Chapter 1, Section 3.

3 Drain the cooling system with reference to Chapter 1, Section 23.

4 Refer to Section 6 and remove the auxiliary drivebelts.

5 Refer to Section 7 and remove the camshaft cover.

6 With reference to Section 2, set the engine to TDC on No 1 cylinder.

7 Refer to Section 5 and remove the timing belt tensioner, and the camshaft, intermediate shaft and injection pump sprockets.

8 Unbolt and remove the timing belt inner cover from the engine block **(see illustrations)**.

9 Loosen the clips and disconnect the radiator hoses from the cylinder head.

10 Loosen the clips and disconnect the expansion tank hose, and the heater inlet and outlet coolant hoses, from the cylinder head.

11 Disconnect and remove the injector fuel supply pipes from the injectors and the injection pump as described in Chapter 4A, Section 8. Also disconnect the leak-off hoses from the injectors.

11.8a Slacken and withdraw the retaining screws...

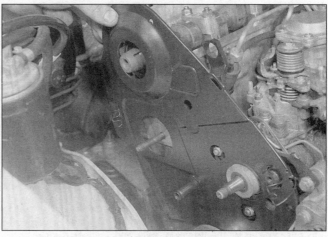

11.8b ...and lift off the timing belt inner covers

12 Disconnect the injector bleed hose from the injection pump fuel return port.

13 Unplug all fuel system electrical cabling at the relevant connectors, labelling each cable to aid refitting later.

14 Disconnect the wiring plug from the coolant temperature sensor **(see illustration)**.

15 Separate the exhaust downpipe from the exhaust manifold or turbocharger as described in Chapter 4A, Section 19.

16 Where fitted, remove the turbocharger together with the exhaust manifold as described in Chapter 4A, Section 16.

17 Where applicable, remove the EGR valve and its connecting pipework from the inlet and exhaust manifolds.

18 Disconnect the supply cable from the glow plug in cylinder No 4.

19 Remove the retaining screw and detach the engine harness connector bracket from the cylinder head.

20 Following the reverse of the tightening sequence **(see illustration 11.42a)**, progressively slacken the cylinder head bolts, by half a turn at a time, until all bolts can be unscrewed by hand. Discard the bolts – new ones must be fitted on reassembly.

21 Check that nothing remains connected to the cylinder head, then lift the head away from the cylinder block; seek assistance if possible, as it is a heavy assembly, especially as it is being removed complete with the manifolds **(see illustration)**.

22 Remove the gasket from the top of the block, noting the locating dowels. If the dowels are a loose fit, remove them and store them with the head for safe-keeping. Do not discard the gasket yet – it will be needed for identification purposes.

23 If the cylinder head is to be dismantled for overhaul, refer to Chapter 2C, Section 6.

Manifold separation and reassembly

Note: *On turbocharged engines, refitting of the exhaust manifold should be carried out as described in Chapter 4A, Section 16, after the cylinder head has been refitted.*

24 With the cylinder head on a work surface, unscrew and remove the inlet manifold

11.14 Disconnect the wiring plug from the coolant temperature sensor

securing bolts. Lift the manifold away, and recover the gasket.

25 Unbolt the heat shield **(see illustration)**, then progressively slacken and remove the exhaust manifold retaining nuts. Lift the manifold away from the cylinder head, and recover the gaskets.

26 Ensure that the inlet and exhaust manifold mating surfaces are completely clean. Refit the exhaust manifold, using new gaskets. Ensure that the gaskets are fitted the correct way around, otherwise they will obstruct the inlet manifold gasket. Tighten the exhaust manifold retaining nuts to the specified torque **(see illustrations)**.

27 Refit the heat shield to the studs on the exhaust manifold, then fit and tighten the retaining nuts.

11.21 Lifting the cylinder head away from the engine

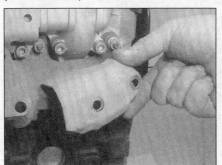

11.25 Unbolt and remove the exhaust manifold heat shield

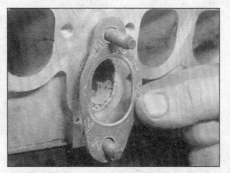

11.26a Fit the exhaust manifold gaskets...

11.26b ...then refit the exhaust manifold. Tighten the nuts to the specified torque

11.28a Fit a new inlet manifold gasket to the cylinder head...

11.28b ...then lift the inlet manifold into position

11.28c Insert the retaining bolts and tighten them to the specified toque

28 Fit a new inlet manifold gasket to the cylinder head, then lift the inlet manifold into position. Insert the retaining bolts and tighten them to the specified torque **(see illustrations)**.

Preparation for refitting

29 The mating faces of the cylinder head and cylinder block/crankcase must be perfectly clean before refitting the head. Use a hard plastic or wood scraper to remove all traces of gasket and carbon; also clean the piston crowns. Take particular care during the cleaning operations, as aluminium alloy is easily damaged. Also, make sure that the carbon is not allowed to enter the oil and water passages – this is particularly important for the lubrication system, as carbon could block the oil supply to the engine's components. Using adhesive tape and paper, seal the water, oil and bolt holes in the cylinder block/crankcase.

30 Check the mating surfaces of the cylinder block/crankcase and the cylinder head for nicks, deep scratches and other damage. If slight, they may be removed carefully with abrasive paper, but note that head machining will not be possible – refer to Chapter 2C, Section 6.

31 If warpage of the cylinder head gasket surface is suspected, use a straight-edge to check it for distortion. Refer to Chapter 2C, Section 6 if necessary.

32 Clean out the cylinder head bolt drillings using a suitable tap. If a tap is not available, make a home-made substitute **(see Tool Tip)**.

33 On the engines covered in this Chapter, it is possible for the piston crowns to strike and damage the valve heads, if the camshaft is rotated with the timing belt removed and the crankshaft set to TDC. For this reason, the crankshaft must be set to a position other than TDC on No 1 cylinder, before the cylinder head is refitted. Use a wrench and socket on the crankshaft pulley centre bolt to turn the crankshaft in its normal direction of rotation, until all four pistons are positioned halfway down their bores, with No 1 piston on its upstroke – approximately 90° before TDC.

Refitting

34 Examine the old cylinder head gasket for manufacturer's identification markings. These will either be in the form of notches or holes, and a part number, on the edge of the gasket. Unless new pistons have been fitted, the new cylinder head gasket must be the same type as the old one.

35 If new piston assemblies have been fitted as part of an engine overhaul, before purchasing the new cylinder head gasket, refer to Chapter 2C, Section 15 and measure the piston projection. Purchase a new gasket according to the results of the measurement (see Chapter 2C Specifications).

36 Lay the new head gasket on the cylinder block, engaging it with the locating dowels. Ensure that the manufacturer's TOP and part number markings are facing upwards.

37 Cut the heads from two of the old cylinder head bolts. Cut a slot, big enough for a screw-driver blade, in the end of each bolt. These can be used as alignment dowels to assist in cylinder head refitting **(see illustration)**.

38 With the help of an assistant, place the cylinder head and manifolds centrally on the cylinder block, ensuring that the locating dowels engage with the recesses in the cylinder head. Check that the head gasket is correctly seated before allowing the full weight of the cylinder head to rest on it.

39 Unscrew the home-made alignment dowels using a screwdriver.

40 Apply a smear of grease to the threads, and to the underside of the heads, of the new cylinder head bolts.

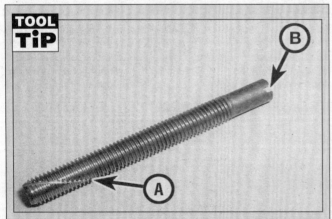

TOOL TiP

If a tap is not available, make a substitute by cutting a slot (A) down the threads of one of the old cylinder head bolts. After use, the bolt head can be cut off, and the shank can then be used as an alignment dowel to assist cylinder head refitting. Cut a screwdriver slot (B) in the top of the bolt, to allow it to be unscrewed

11.37 Two of the old head bolts (arrowed) used as cylinder head alignment dowels

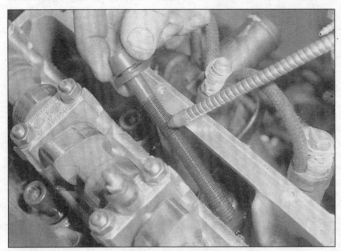

11.41 Oil the cylinder head bolt threads, then place each bolt into its relevant hole

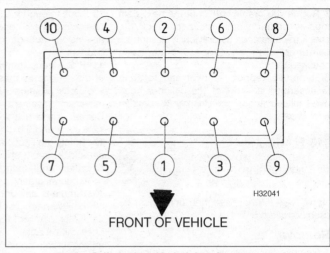

11.42a Cylinder head bolt tightening sequence

41 Oil the bolt threads, then carefully enter each bolt into its relevant hole (*do not drop them in*) and screw in, by hand only, until finger-tight **(see illustration)**.

42 Working progressively and in the sequence shown, tighten the cylinder head bolts to their Stage 1 torque setting, using a torque wrench and suitable socket **(see illustrations)**. Repeat the exercise in the same sequence for the Stage 2 torque setting.

43 Once all the bolts have been tightened to their Stage 2 settings, working again in the given sequence, angle-tighten the bolts through the specified Stage 3 angle, using a socket and extension bar. It is recommended that an angle-measuring gauge is used during this stage of the tightening, to ensure accuracy. If a gauge is not available, use white paint to make alignment marks between the bolt head and cylinder head prior to tightening; the marks can then be used to check the bolt has been rotated through the correct angle during tightening. Repeat for the Stage 4 setting **(see illustration)**. **Note:** *No further tightening of the cylinder head bolts is required after the engine has been started.*

44 Refer to Section 2 and set the engine to TDC on No 1 cylinder.

45 The remainder of refitting is a reversal of the removal procedure, but on completion carry out the following:

a) *Refill the cooling system with the correct quantity of new coolant with reference to Chapter 1, Section 23.*

b) *Refill the engine with the correct grade and quantity of oil with reference to Chapter 1, Section 3.*

12 Hydraulic tappets – operation check

⚠ **Warning: After fitting hydraulic tappets, wait a minimum of 30 minutes (or preferably, leave**

overnight) before starting the engine, to allow the tappets time to settle, otherwise the valve heads will strike the pistons.

1 The hydraulic tappets are self-adjusting, and require no attention whilst in service.

2 If the hydraulic tappets become excessively noisy, their operation can be checked as described below.

3 Run the engine until it reaches its normal operating temperature, then increase the engine speed to approximately 2500 rpm for 2 minutes.

4 Switch off the engine and remove the camshaft cover as described in Section 7.

5 Rotate the camshaft by turning the crankshaft with a socket, until the first cam lobe over No 1 cylinder is pointing upwards.

6 Using a non-metallic tool, press the tappet downwards then use a feeler blade to check the clearance between the base of the cam lobe and the top of the tappet. If this is more than 0.1 mm, the tappet should be renewed.

11.42b Tightening the cylinder head bolts using a torque wrench and socket

11.43 Angle-tightening a cylinder head bolt

7 Rotate the crankshaft until the next cam lobe is pointing upwards and check the check the clearance as previously described. Continue until all tappets have been checked.

8 Hydraulic tappet removal and refitting is described as part of the cylinder head overhaul sequence – see Chapter 2C, Section 6 for details.

13 Flywheel – removal, inspection and refitting

Note: *New flywheel securing bolts must be used on refitting.*

Removal

1 Remove the transmission as described in Chapter 7A, Section 6.

2 Remove the clutch assembly as described in Chapter 6, Section 7.

3 The flywheel bolts are offset to ensure correct fitment. Temporarily insert a bolt in the cylinder block, and use a screwdriver to hold the flywheel, or make up a holding tool. Unscrew the retaining bolts, and remove the flywheel.

Caution: Take care, as the flywheel is heavy.

Inspection

Single-mass (solid) flywheel

4 Either a conventional solid flywheel or a dual-mass flywheel may be fitted according to engine and year of manufacture.

5 Examine the flywheel for wear or chipping of the ring gear teeth. Renewal of the ring gear is not possible and if the wear or chipping is significant, a new flywheel will be required.

6 Examine the flywheel for scoring of the clutch face. If the clutch face is scored significantly, a new flywheel will be required.

7 If there is any doubt about the condition of the flywheel, seek the advice of a VW dealer or engine reconditioning specialist.

Dual-mass flywheel

8 Either a conventional solid flywheel or a dual-mass flywheel may be fitted according to engine and year of manufacture. A dual-mass flywheel has the effect of reducing engine and transmission vibrations and harshness. The flywheel consists of a primary mass and a secondary mass constructed in such a way that the secondary mass is allowed to rotate slightly in relation to the primary mass. Springs within the assembly restrict this movement to set limits.

9 Dual-mass flywheels have earned an unenviable reputation for unreliability and have been known to fail at quite low mileages (sometimes as low as 20 000 miles). As well as the checks described above in paragraphs 5 and 6, some additional checks should be performed as follows.

10 Look through the bolt hole and inspection openings in the secondary mass and check for any visible damage in the area of the centre bearing.

11 Place your thumbs on the clutch face of the secondary mass at the 3 o'clock and 9 o'clock positions and try to rock it. The maximum movement should not exceed 3 mm. Repeat this check with your thumbs at the 12 o'clock and 6 o'clock positions.

12 Rotate the secondary mass clockwise and anti-clockwise. It should move freely in both directions until spring resistance is felt, with no abnormal grating or rattling noises.

13 If there is any doubt about the condition of the flywheel, seek the advice of a VW dealer or engine reconditioning specialist. They will be able to advise if the flywheel is an acceptable condition, or whether renewal is necessary.

Refitting

14 Offer the flywheel to the end of the crankshaft, and align the bolt holes in the crankshaft and flywheel.

15 Coat the threads of the new flywheel bolts with thread-locking compound (note that new bolts may be supplied ready-coated), then fit the bolts and tighten them to the specified torque, then through the specified angle whilst preventing the flywheel from turning as during removal.

16 Refit the clutch as described in Chapter 6, Section 7 then refit the transmission as described in Chapter 7A, Section 6.

14 Engine mountings – inspection and renewal

Inspection

1 To improve access, firmly apply the handbrake, then jack up the front of the vehicle and support it on axle stands (see *Jacking and vehicle support*). Remove the engine undertray as described in Chapter 11, Section 25.

2 Check the mounting blocks (rubbers) to see if they are cracked, hardened or separated from the metal at any point. Renew the mounting block if any such damage or deterioration is evident.

3 Check that all the mounting securing nuts and bolts are securely tightened, using a torque wrench to check if possible.

4 Using a large screwdriver, or a similar tool, check for wear in the mounting blocks by carefully levering against them to check for free play. Where this is not possible, enlist the aid of an assistant to move the engine/transmission unit back-and-forth, and from side-to-side, while you observe the mountings. While some free play is to be expected, even from new components, excessive wear should be obvious. If excessive free play is found, check first to

see that the securing nuts and bolts are correctly tightened, then renew any worn components as described in the following paragraphs.

Renewal

Right-hand mounting

5 Disconnect the battery negative terminal (refer to *Disconnecting the battery*).

6 Firmly apply the handbrake, then jack up the front of the vehicle and support it securely on axle stands (see *Jacking and vehicle support*).

7 Remove the engine undertray as described in Chapter 11, Section 25.

8 Position a trolley jack underneath the sump with an interposed block of wood between the jack head and the sump.

9 Raise the jack until it just takes the weight of the engine off the right-hand mounting.

10 From above, undo the through bolt or the two nuts securing the mounting to the body.

11 From below undo the bolt securing the mounting to the engine bracket.

12 Carefully lower the jack until the mounting can be withdrawn.

13 Refitting is a reversal of removal, tightening all fastenings to the specified torque.

Left-hand mounting

14 Disconnect the battery negative terminal (refer to *Disconnecting the battery*).

15 Turn the plastic retainer half a turn, disengage the locating tabs and lift off the cover over the battery.

16 Firmly apply the handbrake, then jack up the front of the vehicle and support it securely on axle stands (see *Jacking and vehicle support*).

17 Remove the engine undertray as described in Chapter 11, Section 25.

18 Position a trolley jack underneath the transmission with an interposed block of wood between the jack head and the transmission casing.

19 Raise the jack until it just takes the weight of the engine off the left-hand mounting.

20 From above undo the through bolt or the two nuts securing the mounting to the body.

21 From below undo the bolts securing the mounting to the transmission bracket and the bolts securing the transmission bracket to the transmission.

22 Carefully lower the jack until sufficient clearance exists to allow removal of the mounting together with the transmission bracket.

23 Refitting is a reversal of removal, tightening all fastenings to the specified torque.

Rear mounting

24 Disconnect the battery negative terminal (refer to *Disconnecting the battery*).

25 Firmly apply the handbrake, then jack up the front of the vehicle and support it securely on axle stands (see *Jacking and vehicle support*).

26 Remove the engine undertray as described in Chapter 11, Section 25.

27 On early models, undo the two bolts securing the mounting to the subframe and the centre bolt securing the mounting to the transmission. Manipulate the mounting from its location and remove it from under the vehicle.

28 On later models, undo the four bolts securing the mounting to the transmission and the through bolt securing the subframe bracket to the mounting. Manipulate the mounting from its location and remove it from under the vehicle.

29 Refitting is a reversal of removal, tightening all fastenings to the specified torque.

15 Sump – removal and refitting

Removal

1 Disconnect the battery negative terminal (refer to *Disconnecting the battery*).

2 Firmly apply the handbrake, then jack up the front of the vehicle and support it securely on axle stands (see *Jacking and vehicle support*).

3 Remove the engine undertray as described in Chapter 11, Section 25.

4 Drain the engine oil as described in Chapter 1, Section 3.

5 To improve access to the sump, refer to Chapter 8, Section 2 and disconnect the right-hand driveshaft from the transmission output flange.

6 Working around the outside of the sump, progressively slacken and withdraw the sump retaining bolts. Where applicable, unbolt and remove the flywheel cover plate from the transmission to gain access to the left-hand sump fixings.

7 Break the joint by striking the sump with the palm of your hand, then lower the sump and withdraw it from underneath the vehicle. Recover and discard the sump gasket. Where a baffle plate is fitted, note that it can only be removed once the oil pump has been unbolted (see Section 16).

8 While the sump is removed, take the opportunity to check the oil pump pickup/strainer for signs of clogging or disintegration. If necessary, remove the pump as described in Section 16, and clean or renew the strainer.

Refitting

9 Clean all traces of sealant from the mating surfaces of the cylinder block/crankcase and sump, then use a piece of clean rag to wipe out the sump.

10 Ensure that the sump and cylinder block/crankcase mating surfaces are clean and dry, then apply a coating of suitable sealant to the sump and crankcase mating surfaces.

11 Lay a new sump gasket in position on the sump mating surface, then offer up the sump and refit the retaining bolts. Tighten the nuts and bolts evenly and progressively to the specified torque.

12 Reconnect the right-hand driveshaft to the transmission output flange with reference to Chapter 8, Section 2.

13 Refit the engine undertray, then lower the vehicle to the ground.

14 Refer to Chapter 1, Section 3 and refill the engine with the specified grade and quantity of oil.

15 On completion, reconnect the battery negative terminal.

16 Oil pump and pickup – removal, inspection and refitting

Removal

1 Remove the sump as described in Section 15.

2 Unscrew and remove the large oil pump mounting bolts, then withdraw the pump from the block.

3 With the pump on the bench, unscrew the bolts and remove the suction tube from the oil pump. Recover the O-ring.

4 Unscrew the two bolts, and lift off the cover.

Inspection

5 Clean the components, and check them for wear and damage.

6 Using a feeler blade as shown, check the backlash between the gears, and compare with that given in the Specifications. Similarly check the endfloat of the gears, using a straight edge across the end face of the pump. If outside the specified limits, the pump should be renewed, otherwise refit the cover and tighten the bolts.

Refitting

7 Prime the pump with oil by immersing it in oil and turning the driveshaft.

8 Clean the contact faces, then fit the oil pump to the block, insert the mounting bolts, and tighten them to the specified torque.

9 Locate a new O-ring seal on the end of the suction tube. Fit the tube to the oil pump, insert the bolts and tighten them to the specified torque.

10 Refit the sump with reference to Section 15.

Chapter 2 Part B:
5-cylinder engine in-vehicle repair procedures

Contents

Section number (left column)   **Section number** (right column)

Degrees of difficulty

Easy, suitable for novice with little experience	Fairly easy, suitable for beginner with some experience	Fairly difficult, suitable for competent DIY mechanic	Difficult, suitable for experienced DIY mechanic	Very difficult, suitable for expert DIY or professional

Specifications

General

Engine type.	5-cylinder, in-line, single overhead camshaft
Engine codes:	
2.4 litre engines:	
57 kW engines	AAB
55 kW engines	AJA
2.5 litre engines:	
75 kW engines	ACV, AUF, AYC, AXL
111 kW engines	AHY, AXG
65 kW engines	AJT, AYY
Capacity:	
2.4 litre engines	2370 cc
2.5 litre engines	2461 cc
Bore:	
2.4 litre engines	79.5 mm
2.5 litre engines	81.0 mm
Stroke.	95.5 mm
Compression ratio:	
2.4 litre engines	23.0 : 1
2.5 litre engines:	
Engine code ACV (up to May 1999)	20.5 : 1
Engine code ACV (May 1999 onward)	19.5 : 1
Engine codes AHY, AJT	19.5 : 1
Engine codes AUF, AXG, AYC, AXL, AYY.	19.0 : 1
Compression pressures – minimum:	
2.4 litre engines	26 bar
2.5 litre engines	24 bar
Firing order	1-2-4-5-3 (No 1 cylinder at timing belt end)
Direction of crankshaft rotation	Clockwise (seen from right-hand side of vehicle)
Auxiliary drivebelt tension (pre-February 1995 models):	
Alternator V-belt adjustment arm nut:	
New V-belt	8 Nm (6 lbf ft)
Used V-belt.	4 Nm (3 lbf ft)
Timing belt tension (pre-february 1995 models).	Scale reading of 12-13 units measured using Volkswagen tool VW 210
Fuel injection pump drivebelt tension (2.4 litre engines)	Scale reading of 12-13 units measured using Volkswagen tool VW 210

Lubrication system

Oil pump type.	Mounted on front of cylinder block and driven directly from crankshaft
Normal operating oil pressure	2.0 bars minimum (at 2000 rpm, oil temperature 80°C)

Torque wrench settings

	Nm	lbf ft
Alternator mountings:		
With auxiliary V-belt drive:		
Adjustment arm nut locking bolt.	35	26
Adjustment arm-to-mounting bracket bolt.	23	17
Mounting bolts.	35	26
With ribbed auxiliary belt drive:		
Mounting bolts.	25	18
Auxiliary drivebelt idler pulley.	20	15
Auxiliary drivebelt tensioner	20	15
Big-end bearing caps bolts/nuts:*		
Stage 1.	30	22
Stage 2.	Angle-tighten a further 90°	
Camshaft bearing cap nuts	20	15
Camshaft cover nuts/bolts.	10	7
Camshaft sprocket bolt (injection pump drivebelt end):		
2.4 litre engines	100	74
2.5 litre engines	160	118
Camshaft sprocket bolt (timing belt end):		
Bolt strength classification 8.8	85	63
Bolt strength classification 10.9	100	74
Coolant pump bolts	20	15
Crankshaft oil seal housing (flywheel/driveplate end)	10	7
Cylinder bore oil spray jet.	10	7
Cylinder head bolts:*		
Stage 1	40	30
Stage 2	60	44
Stage 3	Angle-tighten a further 90°	
Stage 4	Angle-tighten a further 90°	
Flywheel/driveplate bolts:*		
Stage 1	60	44
Stage 2	Angle-tighten a further 90°	
Fuel injection pump drivebelt idler pulley nut.	20	15
Fuel injection pump drivebelt tensioner bolt	15	11
Fuel injection pump mounting bracket to block.	50	37
Main bearing cap bolts.	65	48
Oil pressure relief valve to pump body.	40	30
Oil pump to block:		
Long bolts.	20	15
Short bolts	10	7
Oil pump pickup tube bolts	10	7
Roadwheel bolts:		
Up to December 1995	160	118
January 1996 onward.	180	133
Sump bolts.	20	15
Timing belt idler pulley bolt	10	7
Timing belt tensioner bolt.	20	15
Vibration damper-to-crankshaft sprocket bolts:		
Pre-February 1995 models.	20	15
February 1995 models onward:		
Stage 1	20	15
Stage 2	Angle-tighten a further 90°	
Vibration damper central bolt:		
Pre-February 1995 models.	460	339
February 1995 models onward:*		
Stage 1	160	118
Stage 2	Angle-tighten a further 180°	

*Use new nuts/bolts

1 General information

Using this Chapter

Chapter 2 is divided into three parts; A, B and C. Repair operations that can be carried out with the engine in the vehicle are described in Parts A (4-cylinder engines) and B (5-cylinder engines). Part C covers the removal and refitting of the engine/transmission as a unit and describes the engine dismantling and overhaul procedures.

In Parts A and B, the assumption is made that the engine is installed in the vehicle, with all ancillaries connected. If the engine has been removed for overhaul, the preliminary dismantling information which precedes each operation may be ignored.

Engine description

Throughout this Chapter, the engines are often identified and referred to by manufacturer's code letters, rather than capacity. A listing of the engines covered, together with their code letters, is given in the Specifications at the start of this Chapter.

The engines are water-cooled, single overhead camshaft, in-line five cylinder units with cast-iron cylinder blocks and aluminium-alloy cylinder heads. All are mounted transversely at the front of the vehicle, with the transmission bolted to the left-hand side of the engine.

The cylinder head carries the camshaft, which is driven by a toothed timing belt. It also houses the inlet and exhaust valves, which are closed by double coil springs, and which run in guides pressed into the cylinder head. The camshaft actuates the valves directly via hydraulic tappets, mounted in the cylinder head. The cylinder head contains integral oilways which supply and lubricate the tappets.

The crankshaft is of six-bearing type, and the No 4 main bearing shells incorporate separate thrustwashers to control crankshaft endfloat. The camshaft is driven by a toothed timing belt from the crankshaft sprocket, and the belt also drives the coolant pump.

The valves are operated by the camshaft through hydraulic bucket type tappets. The fuel injection pump is belt-driven from a sprocket on the rear of the camshaft. The brake vacuum pump is located on the front facing side of the cylinder head and is driven by a plunger from an eccentric on the camshaft.

The engine has a full-flow lubrication system. A gear-and-crescent type oil pump is mounted on the front of the crankshaft. The oil filter is of the cartridge type, mounted on the rear facing side of the cylinder block.

Repairs possible with the engine installed in the vehicle

The following operations can be performed without removing the engine:

a) Compression pressure – testing.
b) Timing belt, sprockets and cover – removal, inspection and refitting.
c) Auxiliary drivebelt – removal and refitting.
d) Camshaft cover – removal and refitting.
e) Camshaft – removal and refitting.*
f) Camshaft oil seals – renewal.
g) Camshaft sprockets – removal and refitting.
h) Coolant pump – removal and refitting (refer to Chapter 3, Section 8).
i) Crankshaft oil seals – renewal.
j) Crankshaft sprocket – removal and refitting.
k) Cylinder head – removal and refitting.*
l) Flywheel/driveplate – removal and refitting.
m) Sump – removal and refitting.
n) Oil pump and pickup assembly – removal, inspection and refitting.
o) Pistons, connecting rods and big-end bearings – removal and refitting.
p) Engine mountings – inspection and renewal.

*Cylinder head dismantling procedures are given in Chapter 2C, Section 6 and also contain details of camshaft and hydraulic tappet removal.

Note: *It is possible to remove the pistons and connecting rods (after removing the cylinder head and sump) without removing the engine from the vehicle. However, this procedure is not recommended. Work of this nature is more easily and thoroughly completed with the engine on the bench.*

2 Location of TDC on No 1 cylinder

General information

1 The camshaft and coolant pump sprockets are driven by the timing belt from the crankshaft sprocket. The crankshaft and camshaft sprockets move in phase with each other to ensure correct valve timing.

2 The design of the engines covered in this Chapter is such that piston-to-valve contact will occur if the crankshaft is turned with the timing belt removed. For this reason, it is important that the correct phasing between the camshaft and crankshaft is preserved whilst the timing belt is off the engine. This is achieved by setting the engine in a reference condition (known as Top Dead Centre or TDC) before the timing belt is removed, and then preventing the shafts from rotating until the belt is refitted. Similarly, if the engine has

2.6 Unbolt and remove the cover over the fuel injection pump sprocket and camshaft sprocket

been dismantled for overhaul, the engine must be set to TDC during reassembly to ensure that the correct shaft phasing is restored.

3 TDC is the highest position a piston reaches within its respective cylinder – in a four-stroke engine, each piston reaches TDC twice per cycle, once on the compression stroke and once on the exhaust stroke. In general, TDC normally refers to No 1 cylinder on the compression stroke. Note that the cylinders are numbered one to five, starting from the timing belt end of the engine.

Setting TDC on No 1 cylinder

4 Remove the glow plugs as described in Chapter 5, Section 13 as an aid to turning the engine.

5 Remove the camshaft cover as described in Section 9.

6 Unbolt and remove the cover over the fuel injection pump sprocket and camshaft sprocket **(see illustration)**.

7 Where fitted, remove the inspection bung from the transmission bellhousing, if necessary using a large nut to unscrew it **(see illustration)**.

8 Using a socket on the crankshaft sprocket bolt, rotate the crankshaft slowly clockwise until the TDC timing mark machined on the edge of the flywheel/driveplate lines up with the pointer on the bellhousing casting and the TDC timing mark on the fuel injection pump sprocket aligns with the mark on the pump

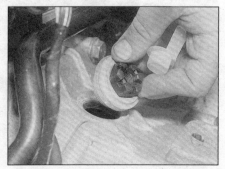

2.7 Use a large nut to remove the bung from the transmission bellhousing

2.8a Turn the crankshaft until the timing mark (arrowed) machined onto the edge of the flywheel...

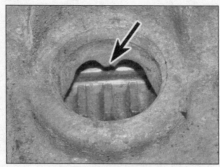

2.8b ...lines up with the pointer (arrowed) on the bellhousing casting...

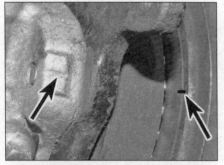

2.8c ...and the TDC timing mark on the fuel injection pump sprocket aligns with the mark on the pump body (arrowed)

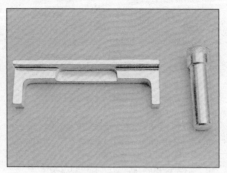

2.10 Engine locking tools

body **(see illustrations)**. The point when No 1 piston commences to move up the cylinder can be determined when air is heard coming from the No 1 glowplug aperture. Also, note the the position of the No 1 cylinder camshaft lobes; when they are both pointing upwards No 1 piston will be at the top of its stroke.
Note: *Due to the method of setting the injection pump timing dynamically, the TDC mark on the pump sprocket may not align exactly with the mark on the pump housing. This occurs because the pump is physically turned on its mounting to make any fine adjustments to the timing.*
9 If the engine is being set to TDC in order to remove the timing belt, the camshaft must be locked in its TDC position, however this means that the drivebelt sprocket at the flywheel end of the camshaft must first be removed as described in Section 7 in order to fit the locking tool to the slot in the camshaft. On engines produced up to January 1995, the fuel injection pump sprocket must also be locked in the TDC position using a special locking pin.
10 To lock the engine in the TDC position, the camshaft (not the sprocket) must be secured in a reference position, using special locking tools. Improvised tools may be fabricated, but due to the exact measurements and machining involved, it is strongly recommended that a kit of locking tools is either borrowed or hired, or purchased from a reputable tool manufacturer **(see illustration)**.
Caution: Do not use these locking tools to prevent the rotation of the crankshaft, camshaft, etc. while slackening or tightening fasteners – they are not intended for this purpose and may break if over-stressed in such a way; use only the method described at the relevant point in this manual
11 With the sprocket removed, engage the edge of the locking bar with the slot in the end of the camshaft **(see illustration)**.
12 If there is any small movement of the locking bar on the cylinder head, turn the camshaft slightly (by turning the crankshaft clockwise, as before) so that the locking bar rocks to one side, allowing one end of the bar to contact the cylinder head surface. At the other side of the locking bar, measure the gap between the end of the bar and the cylinder head using a feeler blade. Now turn the camshaft back slightly and remove the feeler blade. The idea now is to level the locking bar by inserting two feeler blades, each with a thickness equal to *half* the originally measured gap, between each end of the locking bar and the cylinder head. This centres the camshaft, and sets the valve timing in the TDC reference condition **(see illustration)**.
13 The engine is now set to TDC on No 1 cylinder.

3 Compression and leakdown tests –
description and interpretation

Compression test

Note: *A compression tester specifically designed for diesel engines must be used for this test.*
1 When engine performance is down, or if misfiring occurs, a compression test can provide diagnostic clues as to the engine's

2.11 Engage the locking bar with the slot in the camshaft

2.12 Camshaft centred and locked using locking bar and feeler gauges

condition. If the test is performed regularly, it can give warning of trouble before any other symptoms become apparent.

2 A compression tester specifically intended for diesel engines must be used, because of the higher pressures involved. The tester is connected to an adapter which screws into the glow plug or injector hole. It is unlikely to be worthwhile buying such a tester for occasional use, but it may be possible to borrow or hire one – if not, have the test performed by a garage.

3 Unless specific instructions to the contrary are supplied with the tester, observe the following points:

a) *The battery must be in a good state of charge, the air filter must be clean, and the engine should be at normal operating temperature.*

b) *On 2.4 litre engines, remove the fuel injectors as described in Chapter 4A, Section 11.*

c) *On 2.4 litre engines, the injection pump stop solenoid must be disconnected, to prevent the engine from running or fuel from being discharged (see illustration).*

d) *On 2.5 litre engines, remove the glow plugs as described in Chapter 5, Section 13.*

e) *On 2.5 litre engines, the stop solenoid and fuel metering control wiring must be disconnected, to prevent the engine from running or fuel from being discharged.* **Note:** *As a result of the wiring being disconnected, faults will be stored in the ECU memory. These must be erased after the compression test.*

4 Fit a compression tester to the No 1 cylinder injector or glow plug hole.

5 Crank the engine for several seconds on the starter motor. After one or two revolutions, the compression pressure should build up to a maximum figure and then stabilise. Record the highest reading obtained.

6 Repeat the test on the remaining cylinders, recording the pressure in each.

7 VW specify wear limits for compression pressures – refer to the Specifications. Seek the advice of a VW dealer or other diesel specialist if in doubt as to whether a particular pressure reading is acceptable.

8 The cause of poor compression is less easy to establish on a diesel engine than on a petrol one. The effect of introducing oil into the cylinders ('wet' testing) is not conclusive, because there is a risk that the oil will sit in the swirl chamber, instead of passing to the rings. However, the following can be used as a rough guide to diagnosis.

9 All cylinders should produce very similar pressures; a difference of more than 5 bars between any two cylinders indicates the existence of a fault. Note that the compression should build up quickly in a healthy engine; low compression on the first stroke, followed by gradually-increasing pressure on successive strokes, indicates worn piston rings. A low compression reading on the first stroke, which does not build up during successive strokes, indicates leaking valves or a blown head gasket (a cracked head could also be the cause).

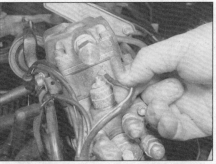

3.3 Disconnecting the wiring at the injection pump stop solenoid

10 A low reading from two adjacent cylinders is almost certainly due to the head gasket having blown between them; the presence of coolant in the engine oil will confirm this.

11 If the compression reading is unusually high, the cylinder head surfaces, valves and pistons are probably coated with carbon deposits. If this is the case, the cylinder head should be removed and decarbonised (refer to Chapter 2C, Section 6).

12 On completion, remove the compression tester, and refit or reconnect the disturbed components.

Leakdown test

13 A leakdown test measures the rate at which compressed air fed into the cylinder is lost. It is an alternative to a compression test, and in many ways it is better, since the escaping air provides easy identification of where pressure loss is occurring (piston rings, valves or head gasket).

14 The equipment needed for leakdown testing is unlikely to be available to the home mechanic. If poor compression is suspected, have the test performed by a suitably-equipped garage.

---

4 Timing belt (pre-February 1995 models) – removal, inspection and refitting

General information

1 The primary function of the toothed timing belt is to drive the camshaft, but it is also used to drive the coolant pump. The injection pump

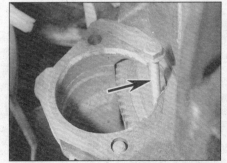

4.12a Using a bolt in one of the holes in the flywheel to hold the crankshaft stationary while the vibration damper bolt is loosened

is driven from the rear of the camshaft by an additional drivebelt. Should the timing belt slip or break in service, the valve timing will be disturbed and piston-to-valve contact will occur, resulting in serious engine damage.

2 For this reason, it is important that the timing belt is tensioned correctly, and inspected regularly for signs of wear or deterioration.

3 Note that the removal of the *inner* section of the timing belt cover is described as part of the cylinder head removal procedure; see Section 12 later in this Chapter.

Removal

4 Disconnect the battery negative terminal (refer to *Disconnecting the battery*).

5 Remove the engine undertray as described in Chapter 11, Section 25.

6 For improved access, move the radiator to the service position as described in Chapter 3, Section 3.

7 Remove the air cleaner housing as described in Chapter 4A, Section 2.

8 Disconnect the wiring at the fuel injection pump stop solenoid.

9 Remove the auxiliary drivebelts as described in Section 8.

10 Release the spring clips and remove the timing belt front upper cover.

11 Set the engine to TDC on No 1 cylinder as described in Section 2 and secure the camshaft and the fuel injection pump sprocket with the locking tools.

12 Hold the crankshaft stationary while loosening the vibration damper central bolt. VW technicians use a special tool which locates inside the vibration damper, however on manual transmission models it may be sufficient to engage 4th gear and have an assistant firmly apply the footbrake pedal. This method cannot be used on automatic transmission models, so it will be necessary to unbolt the cover from the torque converter bellhousing and have an assistant engage a wide-bladed screwdriver with the starter ring gear teeth. On manual transmission models, remove the starter motor as described in Chapter 5, Section 10 and either engage a screwdriver with the starter ring gear teeth or alternatively insert a suitable bolt in one of the holes in the face of the flywheel. Remove the vibration damper bolt **(see illustrations)**.

4.12b Removing the vibration damper central bolt

4.13 Unscrew and remove the bolts securing the vibration damper to the crankshaft sprocket

4.21 Unscrew the camshaft sprocket bolt while holding the sprocket stationary using a home-made tool

13 While still holding the crankshaft stationary, unscrew and remove the bolts securing the vibration damper to the crankshaft sprocket **(see illustration)**.

14 Remove the vibration damper from the crankshaft sprocket. If the sprocket attempts to come away with the damper, temporarily insert two bolts a few threads and gently tap them as the damper is being removed in order to keep the sprocket in position.

15 Unbolt and remove the lower timing belt cover from the block.

16 Slacken the three coolant pump retaining bolts. Using a stout screwdriver as a lever, rotate the coolant pump as far as the elongated retaining bolts will allow to relieve the tension on the timing belt.

17 Mark the timing belt with an arrow to indicate its normal direction of rotation. **Note:** *If the timing belt is to be re-used, it must be refitted the same way round.* **Do not** bend the timing belt sharply if it is to be re-used.

18 Release the timing belt from the crankshaft, camshaft and coolant pump sprockets.

Inspection

19 Examine the belt for evidence of contamination by coolant or lubricant. If this is the case, find the source of the contamination before progressing any further. Check the belt for signs of wear or damage, particularly around the leading edges of the belt teeth. Renew the belt if its condition is in doubt; the cost of belt renewal is negligible compared with potential cost of the engine repairs, should the belt fail in service. **Note:** *If the timing belt is not going to be refitted for some time, it is a wise precaution to hang a warning label on the steering wheel, to remind yourself (and others) not to attempt to start the engine.*

Refitting

20 Ensure that the crankshaft and camshaft are still set to TDC on No 1 cylinder, as described in Section 2 and that the camshaft and the fuel injection pump sprocket are secured in position with the locking tools.

21 Unscrew the camshaft sprocket bolt half a turn, while holding the sprocket stationary using a tool which engages the holes in the sprocket **(see illustration and Tool Tip)**.

22 Release the sprocket from the camshaft taper mounting by carefully tapping it with a soft metal drift inserted through the hole provided in the timing belt inner cover **(see illustration)**.

23 Loop the timing belt loosely under the crankshaft sprocket.

Caution: Observe the direction of rotation markings on the belt.

24 Engage the timing belt teeth with the crankshaft sprocket, then manoeuvre it into position over the coolant pump and camshaft sprockets. Ensure the belt teeth seat correctly on the sprockets.

25 Pass the flat side of the belt over the idler roller – avoid bending the belt back on itself or twisting it excessively as you do this.

26 Using a stout screwdriver as a lever, rotate the coolant pump to apply tension to the timing belt.

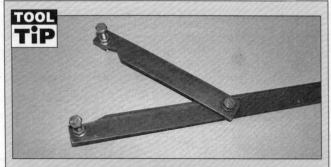

TOOL TiP

To make a camshaft sprocket holding tool, obtain two lengths of steel strip about 6 mm thick by 30 mm wide or similar, one 600 mm long, the other 200 mm long (all dimensions approximate). Bolt the two strips together to form a forked end, leaving the bolt slack so that the shorter strip can pivot freely. At the end of each 'prong' of the fork, secure a bolt with a nut and a locknut, to act as the fulcrums; these will engage with the cut-outs in the sprocket, and should protrude by about 30mm

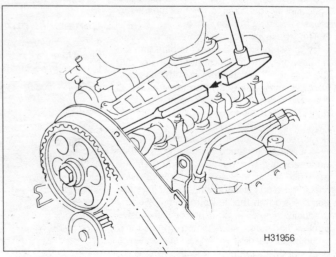

H31956

4.22 Releasing the camshaft sprocket from the taper using a soft metal drift

27 Test the timing belt tension by grasping it between finger and thumb at a point mid-way between the camshaft and coolant pump sprockets, and twisting it. The belt tension is correct when the belt can just be twisted through 90° and no further. If the VW tensioning tool (VW 210) or a suitable alternative is available, set the belt tension to the specified number of tensioning units.

28 When the correct belt tension has been achieved, tighten the three coolant pump retaining bolts to the specified torque.

29 Tighten the camshaft sprocket bolt to the specified torque and angle while holding it stationary with the tool used for removal. Take care not to damage or bend the locking tool while doing this. Note that the torque setting depends on the strength classification of the retaining bolt. The strength classification is stamped on the bolt head and will be either 8.8 or 10.9. Refer to the Specifications for the applicable torque setting.

30 Remove the locking tool from the rear of the camshaft. Turn the crankshaft through two complete turns, then check that the TDC timing marks align correctly as described in Section 2. Check that it is possible to insert the locking tool in the camshaft slot, and also check that the timing belt tension is correct.

31 Refit the lower timing belt cover to the block and tighten the bolts securely.

32 Lubricate the thread and bolt head contact surface of the vibration damper central bolt.

33 Refit the vibration damper to the crankshaft sprocket then insert the damper to sprocket bolts and the damper central bolt and washer. Hold the crankshaft stationary using the method employed on removal, then tighten the damper bolts to the specified torque.

34 Tighten the vibration damper central bolt to the specified torque.

35 Refit the fuel injection pump drivebelt with reference to Sections 2 and 6, then refit the drivebelt cover and tighten the bolts securely.

36 Refit the timing belt upper cover and secure with the spring clips.

37 Refit the camshaft cover with reference to Section 9.

38 If removed, refit the glow plugs as described in Chapter 5, Section 13.

39 Refit the auxiliary drivebelts as described in Section 8.

40 Reconnect the wiring at the fuel injection pump stop solenoid.

41 Refit the air cleaner housing as described in Chapter 4A, Section 2.

42 Move the radiator back to its normal position as described in Chapter 3, Section 3.

43 Refit the engine undertray as described in Chapter 11, Section 25, then reconnect the battery negative terminal.

5.9a Prise off the protective cap from the auxiliary drivebelt idler pulley...

5 Timing belt (February 1995 models onward) – removal, inspection and refitting

General information

1 The primary function of the toothed timing belt is to drive the camshaft, but it is also used to drive the coolant pump. The injection pump is driven from the rear of the camshaft by an additional drivebelt. Should the timing belt slip or break in service, the valve timing will be disturbed and piston-to-valve contact will occur, resulting in serious engine damage.

2 For this reason, it is important that the timing belt is tensioned correctly, and inspected regularly for signs of wear or deterioration.

3 Note that the removal of the inner section of the timing belt cover is described as part of the cylinder head removal procedure; see Section 12 later in this Chapter.

Removal

4 Disconnect the battery negative terminal (refer to Disconnecting the battery).

5 Remove the engine undertray as described in Chapter 11, Section 25.

6 For improved access, move the radiator to the service position as described in Chapter 3, Section 3.

7 Remove the air cleaner housing as described in Chapter 4A, Section 2.

8 Remove the auxiliary drivebelts as described in Section 8.

9 Using a small screwdriver, prise off the protective cap from the centre of the

5.14a Remove the vibration damper from the crankshaft sprocket...

5.9b ...then undo the retaining bolt and remove the idler pulley

auxiliary drivebelt idler pulley. Undo the retaining bolt and remove the idler pulley **(see illustrations)**.

10 Release the spring clips and remove the timing belt front upper cover.

11 Set the engine to TDC on No 1 cylinder as described in Section 2 and secure the camshaft with the locking tool.

12 Hold the crankshaft stationary while loosening the vibration damper central bolt. VW technicians use a special tool which locates inside the vibration damper, however on manual transmission models it may be sufficient to engage 4th gear and have an assistant firmly apply the footbrake pedal. This method cannot be used on automatic transmission models, so it will be necessary to unbolt the cover from the torque converter bellhousing and have an assistant engage a wide-bladed screwdriver with the starter ring gear teeth. On manual transmission models, remove the starter motor as described in Chapter 5, Section 10 and either engage a screwdriver with the starter ring gear teeth or alternatively insert a suitable bolt in one of the holes in the face of the flywheel. Remove the vibration damper bolt – note that the vibration damper central bolt must be renewed whenever removed. **(see illustrations 4.12a and 4.12b)**.

13 While still holding the crankshaft stationary, unscrew and remove the bolts securing the vibration damper to the crankshaft sprocket **(see illustration 4.13)**.

14 Remove the vibration damper from the crankshaft sprocket and collect the diamond coated washer (where fitted) from the end of the sprocket **(see illustrations)**. Note that

5.14b ...and collect the diamond coated washer from the end of the sprocket

5.15 Unbolt and remove the lower timing belt cover from the block

a new washer will be required for refitting. If the sprocket attempts to come away with the damper, temporarily insert two bolts a few threads and gently tap them as the damper is being removed in order to keep the sprocket in position.

15 Unbolt and remove the lower timing belt cover from the block **(see illustration)**.

16 Loosen the bolt on the timing belt tensioner on the front of the engine, then rotate the tensioner anti-clockwise to release the tension on the belt and re-tighten the bolt.

17 Mark the timing belt with an arrow to ~~indi~~cate its normal direction of rotation. **Note:** ~~If~~ timing belt is to be re-used, it must be ~~refitted~~ the same way round. **Do not** bend the ~~timing~~ belt sharply if it is to be re-used.

~~18 R~~elease the timing belt from the crankshaft, camshaft and coolant pump sprockets.

Inspection

19 Examine the belt for evidence of contamination by coolant or lubricant. If this is the case, find the source of the contamination before progressing any further. Check the belt for signs of wear or damage, particularly around the leading edges of the belt teeth. Renew the belt if its condition is in doubt; the cost of belt renewal is negligible compared with potential cost of the engine repairs, should the belt fail in service. **Note:** *If the timing belt is not going to be refitted for some time, it is a wise precaution to hang a warning label on the steering wheel, to remind yourself (and others) not to attempt to start the engine.*

Refitting

20 Ensure that the crankshaft and camshaft

are still set to TDC on No 1 cylinder, as described in Section 2 and that the camshaft is secured in position with the locking tool.

21 Unscrew the camshaft sprocket retaining bolt half a turn, while holding the sprocket stationary using a tool which engages the holes in the sprocket **(see illustration 4.21 and Tool Tip)**.

22 Release the sprocket from the camshaft taper mounting by carefully tapping it with a soft metal drift inserted through the hole provided in the timing belt inner cover **(see illustration 4.22)**.

23 Loop the timing belt loosely under the crankshaft sprocket.

Caution: Observe the direction of rotation markings on the belt.

24 Engage the timing belt teeth with the crankshaft sprocket, then manoeuvre it into position over the coolant pump and camshaft sprockets. Ensure the belt teeth seat correctly on the sprockets.

25 Pass the flat side of the belt over the tensioner roller – avoid bending the belt back on itself or twisting it excessively as you do this.

26 Ensure that the run of the belt is taut between the crankshaft, coolant pump and camshaft sprockets – ie all the slack should be in the section of the belt that passes over the tensioner roller.

27 With the tensioner centre bolt loose, turn the large hexagon clockwise until the lower edge of the tensioner moving pointer is aligned with the lower edge of the tensioner fixed pointer. Hold the hexagon in this position, then tighten the centre bolt to the specified torque **(see illustrations)**.

28 Tighten the camshaft sprocket bolt to the specified torque and angle while holding it stationary with the tool used for removal. Take care not to damage or bend the locking tool while doing this. Note that the torque setting depends on the strength classification of the retaining bolt. The strength classification is stamped on the bolt head and will be either 8.8 or 10.9. Refer to the Specifications for the applicable torque setting.

29 Remove the locking tool from the rear of the camshaft. Turn the crankshaft through two complete turns, then check that the TDC timing marks align correctly as described in Section 2. Check that it is possible to insert

the locking tool in the camshaft slot. Check that the tensioner pointers are still correctly aligned as described in paragraph 27. If not, repeat the adjustment procedure.

30 Refit the lower timing belt cover to the block and tighten the bolts securely.

31 Place a new diamond coated washer in position on the end of the crankshaft sprocket.

32 Lubricate the thread and bolt head contact surface of the new vibration damper central bolt.

33 Refit the vibration damper to the crankshaft sprocket then insert the damper to sprocket bolts and the new damper central bolt and washer. Hold the crankshaft stationary using the method employed on removal, then tighten the damper bolts to the specified torque.

34 Tighten the vibration damper central bolt to the specified torque.

35 Refit the fuel injection pump drivebelt with reference to Sections 2 and 6, then refit the drivebelt cover and tighten the bolts.

36 Refit the timing belt upper cover and secure with the spring clips.

37 Refit the camshaft cover with reference to Section 9.

38 If removed, refit the glow plugs as described in Chapter 5, Section 13.

39 Refit the auxiliary drivebelt idler pulley and secure with the retaining bolt tightened to the specified torque. Refit the protective cap to the centre of the idler pulley.

40 Refit the auxiliary drivebelt as described in Section 8.

41 Refit the air cleaner housing as described in Chapter 4A, Section 2.

42 Move the radiator back to its normal position as described in Chapter 3, Section 3.

43 Refit the engine undertray as described in Chapter 11, Section 25, then reconnect the battery negative terminal.

6 Fuel injection pump drivebelt – removal, inspection and refitting

Removal

1 Disconnect the battery negative terminal (refer to *Disconnecting the battery*).

2 Remove the engine undertray as described in Chapter 11, Section 25.

5.27a Align the lower edge of the tensioner moving pointer (arrowed)...

5.27b ...with the lower edge of the tensioner fixed pointer (arrowed)...

5.27c ...then hold the tensioner in this position and tighten the centre bolt

3 For improved access, move the radiator to the service position as described in Chapter 3, Section 3.

4 Set the engine to TDC on No 1 cylinder as described in Section 2.

2.4 litre engines

5 Mark the drivebelt with an arrow to indicate its normal direction of rotation. **Note:** *If the drivebelt is to be re-used, it must be refitted the same way round.* **Do not** bend the drivebelt sharply if it is to be re-used.

6 Insert a locking pin through the timing hole in the fuel injection pump sprocket and into the pump body to lock the sprocket. Hold the sprocket on the rear of the camshaft stationary using a suitable tool engaged with the holes in the sprocket, then unscrew the retaining bolt and remove the sprocket and drivebelt. Release the drivebelt from the injection pump sprocket.

2.5 litre engines

7 Mark the drivebelt with an arrow to indicate its normal direction of rotation. **Note:** *If the drivebelt is to be re-used, it must be refitted the same way round.* **Do not** bend the drivebelt sharply if it is to be re-used.

8 Slacken the drivebelt tensioner retaining bolt, then turn the tensioner body using an Allen key to release the tension from the drivebelt. Now unscrew the retaining bolt and remove the tensioner.

9 Remove the drivebelt from the idler pulley and the camshaft and injection pump sprockets **(see illustration)**.

Inspection

10 Examine the belt for evidence of contamination by coolant or lubricant. If this is the case, find the source of the contamination before progressing any further. Check the belt for signs of wear or damage, particularly around the leading edges of the belt teeth. Renew the belt if its condition is in doubt.

6.9 Removing the fuel injection pump drivebelt – 2.5 litre engines

Refitting

2.4 litre engines

11 Check that the TDC timing marks are still aligned on the flywheel and on the injection pump.

12 Engage the drivebelt with the injection pump sprocket, then locate the camshaft sprocket in the belt and locate the sprocket on the camshaft.
Caution: Observe the direction of rotation markings on the belt.

13 Insert the bolt and tighten it to 50 Nm while holding the sprocket stationary. The locking pin is still inserted through the injection pump sprocket, and it is important not to strain the drivebelt while tightening the bolt.

14 Loosen the bolt approximately half a turn and make sure that the sprocket is free to turn on the camshaft.

15 The tension of the drivebelt must now be checked. VW technicians use a special tool to do this, however an approximate setting can be made as follows. It should just be possible to twist the belt through 90° at a point midway between the camshaft and injection pump sprockets using the finger and thumb only. If the VW tensioning tool (VW 210) or a suitable alternative is available, set the belt tension to the specified number of tensioning units.

16 Check that the TDC timing marks are

still aligned with each other, then remove the locking pin from the injection pump sprocket. Tighten the camshaft sprocket retaining bolt to the specified torque while holding the sprocket stationary.

17 If the drivebelt tension is incorrect, the injection pump mounting bracket must be repositioned on the cylinder block by loosening the bolts. Tighten the bolts to the specified torque after making the adjustment, then carry out the tensioning procedure again.

18 Check and if necessary adjust the injection pump timing as described in Chapter 4A, Section 9.

19 Refit the glowplugs, then refit the drivebelt cover and tighten the bolts.

20 Refit the camshaft cover as described in Section 9.

21 Move the radiator back to its normal position as described in Chapter 3, Section 3.

22 Refit the engine undertray as described in Chapter 11, Section 25, then reconnect the battery negative terminal.

2.5 litre engines

23 Slacken the camshaft sprocket retaining bolt approximately half a turn and make sure that the sprocket is free to turn on the camshaft.

24 Check that the TDC timing marks are aligned on the flywheel/driveplate and injection pump.

25 Check that the pointer on the idler pulley is aligned with the cylinder head flange contour **(see illustration)**. If not, slacken the retaining nut and turn the pulley using an Allen key until the pointer is correctly positioned. Tighten the retaining nut to the specified torque.

26 Locate the drivebelt over and around the idler pulley.
Caution: Observe the direction of rotation markings on the belt.

27 Place the drivebelt tensioner in position on the cylinder head with the lug on the tensioner body engaged with the slot in the injection pump mounting bracket **(see illustration)**. Fit the retaining bolt and tighten it finger tight.

6.25 Check that the pointer (arrowed) on the idler pulley is aligned with the cylinder head flange contour – 2.5 litre engines

6.27 Engage the lug (arrowed) on the tensioner body with the slot in the injection pump mounting bracket – 2.5 litre engines

6.28a Turn the tensioner using an Allen key...

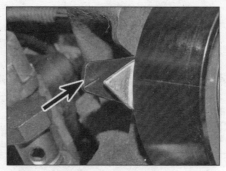

6.28b ...until the moving pointer is aligned with the fixed pointer on the tensioner body (arrowed) – 2.5 litre engines

6.29 Tighten the camshaft sprocket retaining bolt while holding the sprocket stationary – 2.5 litre engines

28 Using an Allen key, turn the tensioner until the moving pointer is aligned with the fixed pointer on the tensioner body (see illustrations). Hold the tensioner in this position and tighten the retaining bolt to the specified torque.

29 Tighten the camshaft sprocket retaining bolt to the specified torque while holding the sprocket stationary (see illustration).

30 Turn the crankshaft through two complete [turns], then check that the TDC timing marks [align] correctly. Check that the tensioner [is still] correctly aligned. As long as [the] pointers are still within the metal backing [plate] the tension is satisfactory. [If] the moving pointer [is not within] the adjustment of the fixed pointer, repeat [the procedure.] If this is not the case, rep[eat the] procedure.

31 Check and if necessary [adjust the injection] pump timing [as described] in Chapter 4A.

32 [Refit the] glowplugs, then refit the drivebelt and tighten the bolts.

33 [Re]fit the camshaft cover as described in Section 9.

34 Move the radiator back to its normal position as described in Chapter 3, Section 3.

35 Refit the engine undertray as described in Chapter 11, Section 25, then reconnect the battery negative terminal.

7 Timing belt tensioner and sprockets – removal and refitting

Timing belt tensioner

Removal

1 A timing belt tensioner is only fitted to February 1995 models onward. On early models, the timing belt is tensioned by repositioning the coolant pump within its elongated mounting bolt holes.

2 Remove the timing belt as described in Section 5.

3 Remove the bolt and withdraw the tensioner from the cylinder block (see illustration).

Refitting

4 Refit the tensioner ensuring that the tensioner arm engages over the peg on the timing belt rear cover (see illustration). Insert the bolt but do not fully tighten it at this stage.

5 Refit and tension the timing belt as described in Section 5.

Timing belt idler pulley

Removal

6 A timing belt idler pulley is only fitted to pre-February 1995 models.

7 Remove the timing belt as described in Section 4.

8 Remove the bolt and withdraw the idler pulley from the cylinder block.

Refitting

9 Refit the idler pulley and tighten the retaining bolt to the specified torque.

10 Refit and tension the timing belt as described in Section 4.

Camshaft sprocket (timing belt end)

Removal

11 Removal and refitting of the camshaft sprocket is part of the timing belt removal, inspection and refitting procedures. Refer to Section 4 (pre-February 1995 models), or Section 5 (February 1995 models onward).

7.3 Remove the bolt and withdraw the timing belt tensioner from the cylinder block

7.4 Refit the tensioner ensuring that the tensioner arm engages over the peg (arrowed) on the timing belt rear cover

Camshaft sprocket (fuel injection pump end)

Removal

12 Remove the fuel injection pump drivebelt as described in Section 6.
13 Hold the camshaft sprocket stationary using a suitable tool engaged with the holes in the sprocket, then loosen the bolt.
14 Remove the bolt and withdraw the sprocket from the end of the camshaft (see illustration).

Refitting

15 Locate the sprocket on the end of the camshaft and insert the bolt loosely.
16 Refit the fuel injection pump drivebelt as described in Section 6.

Crankshaft sprocket

Removal

17 Remove the timing belt as described in Section 4 (pre-February 1995 models), or Section 5 (February 1995 models onward).
18 Slide the crankshaft sprocket from the end of the crankshaft (see illustration). If it is tight, use two screwdrivers or levers to remove it.

Refitting

19 Wipe the sprocket and crankshaft mating surfaces clean.
20 Slide the crankshaft sprocket onto the end of the crankshaft making sure that the lug on the inside of the sprocket engages with the recess in the end of the crankshaft. If it is tight on the crankshaft, tap it on using a block of wood, however do not tap it on so far that it touches the oil pump casing.
21 Refit the timing belt as described in Section 4 (pre-February 1995 models), or Section 5 (February 1995 models onward).

Fuel injection pump sprocket

22 Refer to Chapter 4A, Section 9 (2.4 litre engines) or Chapter 4A, Section 10 (2.5 litre engines).

8 Auxiliary drivebelt – removal, refitting and tensioning

General information

1 Depending on model year and vehicle specification, one or two auxiliary drivebelts may be fitted. Both are driven from a pulley mounted on the crankshaft, and provide drive for the alternator and power steering pump.
2 On pre-February 1995 models, two V-belts are used. One drives the alternator and the other drives the power steering pump. On February 1995 models onward, a single ribbed auxiliary belt is used to drive both the alternator and power steering pump. Where air conditioning is fitted various drivebelt types and layouts may be encountered depending on system type, model year and additional ancillary components that may be fitted.

7.14 Remove the bolt and withdraw the sprocket from the end of the camshaft

3 The V-belt driving the alternator is tensioned manually by means of a tensioning nut incorporated in the alternator adjustment arm. The V-belt driving the power steering pump is tensioned manually by an eccentrically-mounted tensioning pulley.
4 The ribbed auxiliary belt is tensioned by an automatic tensioner.
5 On refitting, the auxiliary belt must be tensioned correctly to ensure correct operation and prolonged service life.

Alternator V-belt

Removal

6 Firmly apply the handbrake, then jack up the front of the vehicle and support it securely on axle stands (see *Jacking and vehicle support*). Remove the right-hand front roadwheel.
7 Remove the engine undertray as described in Chapter 11, Section 25.
8 Slacken the alternator mounting bolts and the adjustment arm bolts at least one turn.
9 Using a socket or spanner on the adjustment arm nut, turn the nut to pivot the alternator toward the engine, then slip the V-belt off the pulleys (see illustration).
10 Examine the belt for signs or wear or damage, and renew it if necessary.

Refitting and tensioning

11 Locate the belt over the crankshaft and alternator pulleys, then turn the adjustment arm nut to pivot the alternator away from the engine.
12 Tension the V-belt by tightening the adjustment arm nut to the specified torque, then tightening the adjustment arm nut locking bolt to the specified torque.
13 Refit the engine undertray as described in Chapter 11, Section 25.
14 Refit the roadwheel and lower the vehicle to the ground.

Power steering pump V-belt

Removal

15 Firmly apply the handbrake, then jack up the front of the vehicle and support it securely on axle stands (see *Jacking and vehicle support*). Remove the right-hand front roadwheel.
16 Remove the engine undertray as described in Chapter 11, Section 25.
17 Remove the alternator V-belt as described previously.

7.18 Slide the crankshaft sprocket from the end of the crankshaft

18 Using an Allen key, slacken the socket-headed bolt in the centre of the tensioning pulley and push the pulley away from the belt. Slip the belt off the crankshaft and power steering pump pulleys.
19 Examine the belt for signs or wear or damage, and renew it if necessary.

Refitting and tensioning

20 Locate the belt over the crankshaft and power steering pump pulleys.
21 Tension the belt by turning the eccentrically-mounted tensioner clockwise; two holes are provided in the side of the tensioner hub for this purpose – a pair of sturdy right-angled circlip pliers is a suitable substitute for the correct VW tool. The tension is correct when it is just possible to deflect the belt by approximately 5 mm under moderate thumb pressure. When the tension is correct, tighten the socket-headed bolt securely.
22 Refit the alternator V-belt as described previously.
23 Refit the engine undertray as described in Chapter 11, Section 25.
24 Refit the roadwheel and lower the vehicle to the ground.

Ribbed auxiliary belt

Removal

25 Firmly apply the handbrake, then jack up the front of the vehicle and support it securely on axle stands (see *Jacking and vehicle support*). Remove the right-hand front roadwheel.

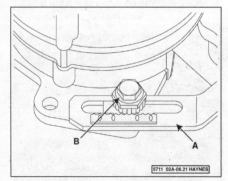

8.9 Alternator V-belt adjustment

A Adjustment arm
B Adjustment arm nut

9.5 Undo the three bolts (arrowed) securing the oil filler tube and crankcase ventilation oil separator to the camshaft cover

26 Remove the engine undertray as described in Chapter 11, Section 25.

27 Examine the ribbed belt for manufacturer's markings, indicating the direction of rotation. If none are present, make some using typist's correction fluid or a dab of paint.

28 Rotate the tensioning roller arm clockwise against its spring tension so that the roller is forced away from the belt – use an adjustable spanner as a lever.

29 Pull the belt off the alternator pulley, then release it from the remaining pulleys.

Refitting and tensioning

Caution: Observe the manufacturer's direction of rotation markings on the belt, when refitting.

30 Pass the ribbed belt underneath the crankshaft pulley, ensuring that the ribs seat securely in the channels on the surface of the pulley.

31 Rotate the tensioning roller arm clockwise against its spring tension – use an adjustable spanner as a lever.

32 Pass the belt around the power steering pump pulley then fit it over the alternator pulley, idler pulley and tensioner pulley.

33 Release the tensioner pulley arm and allow the roller to bear against the flat surface of the belt.

34 Refit the engine undertray as described in Chapter 11, Section 25.

35 Refit the roadwheel and lower the vehicle to the ground.

9 Camshaft cover – removal and refitting

Removal

1 Disconnect the battery negative terminal (refer to *Disconnecting the battery*).

2 For improved access, move the radiator to the service position as described in Chapter 3, Section 3.

3 On engines with an intercooler mounted above the camshaft cover, remove the intercooler as described in Chapter 4A, Section 14.

4 On 2.4 litre engines, remove the inlet manifold as described in Chapter 4A, Section 15.

5 Undo the three bolts securing the oil filler tube and crankcase ventilation oil separator to the camshaft cover **(see illustration)**.

6 Pull the oil separator from its location, undo the remaining oil filler tube retaining bolt and remove the oil filler tube from the camshaft

cover. Recover the two O-ring seals from the base of the filler tube and obtain new O-rings for refitting **(see illustrations)**.

7 Where fitted, disconnect the vacuum hose from the EGR valve **(see illustration)**.

8 On 2.4 litre engines, remove the caps where fitted, then unscrew and remove the four camshaft cover retaining nuts – recover the seals and collars noting the order of removal.

9 On 2.5 litre engines, unscrew and remove the four camshaft cover retaining bolts.

10 Lift the cover away from the cylinder head **(see illustration)**; if it sticks, do not attempt to lever it off – instead free it by working around the cover and tapping it lightly with a soft-faced mallet.

11 Recover the camshaft cover rubber seal. Inspect the seal carefully, and renew it if damage or deterioration is evident **(see illustration)**.

12 Clean the mating surfaces of the cylinder head and camshaft cover thoroughly, removing all traces of oil and dirt – take care to avoid damaging the surfaces as you do this.

Refitting

13 Refitting is the reverse of the removal procedure, noting the following points:
a) *Ensure that the seal is correctly seated in the camshaft cover, and take care to avoid displacing it as the cover is lowered into position.*
b) *Tighten the camshaft cover retaining nuts/bolts to the specified torque.*
c) *On 2.4 litre engines, refit the inlet manifold as described in Chapter 4A, Section 15.*
d) *Move the radiator back to its normal position as described in Chapter 3, Section 3.*

9.6a Pull the oil separator from its location...

9.6b ...undo the remaining retaining bolt and remove the oil filler tube...

9.6c ...and recover the two O-ring seals from the filler tube base

9.7 Disconnect the vacuum hose from the EGR valve

9.10 Lift the camshaft cover off the cylinder head

9.11 Renew the camshaft cover gasket if damage or deterioration is evident

10 Camshaft oil seals – renewal

Timing belt end oil seal

1 Remove the timing belt as described in Section 4 (pre-February 1995 models) or Section 5 (February 1995 models onward).
2 Remove the timing belt idler pulley (pre-February 1995 models) or timing belt tensioner (February 1995 models onward) as described in Section 7.
3 Unscrew the camshaft sprocket retaining bolt half a turn, while holding the sprocket stationary using a tool which engages the holes in the sprocket (see illustration 4.21a).
4 Release the sprocket from the camshaft taper mounting by carefully tapping it with a soft metal drift inserted through the hole provided in the timing belt inner cover (see illustration 4.22).
5 Unbolt and remove the timing belt inner cover.
6 There are two methods of removing the oil seal. Using a screwdriver, carefully prise out the oil seal taking care not to damage the camshaft surface. Clean the seating in the bearing cap, then smear a little oil on the lips of the new oil seal. Wrap adhesive tape around the end of the camshaft, then fit the new oil seal and tap it into position carefully using a tubular bar or socket on the hard outer surface of the seal (see illustrations). Remove the tape on completion.
7 If the oil seal is tight in the bearing cap, the second method should be used. Refer to Chapter 2C, Section 6 and carry out the following:
a) Unscrew the nuts and remove the camshaft No 1 bearing cap, then slide off the old camshaft oil seal.
b) Lubricate the surface of the new camshaft oil seal with clean engine oil, and fit it over the end of the camshaft.
c) Apply a thin film of suitable sealant to the mating surface of the bearing cap, then refit it making sure that the oil seal is located fully against the seating in the head and cap. Tighten the retaining nuts progressively to the specified torque.
8 Refit the timing belt inner cover and securely tighten the bolts.
9 Refit the camshaft sprocket but only tighten the retaining bolt finger tight at this stage.
10 Refit the timing belt idler pulley (pre-February 1995 models) or timing belt tensioner (February 1995 models onward) as described in Section 7.
11 Refit the timing belt as described in Section 4 (pre-February 1995 models) or Section 5 (February 1995 models onward).

Fuel injection pump end oil seal

12 Remove the camshaft cover as described in Section 9.

10.6a Locate the new oil seal over the camshaft...

13 Remove the fuel injection pump drivebelt as described in Section 6. On 2.4 litre engines this procedure also includes the removal of the sprocket from the injection pump drivebelt end of the camshaft.
14 On 2.5 litre engines remove the sprocket from the injection pump end of the camshaft as described in Section 7.
15 Working as described in Chapter 2C, Section 6 carry out the following:
a) Unscrew the nuts and remove the camshaft No 4 bearing cap, then slide off the old camshaft oil seal.
b) Lubricate the surface of the new camshaft oil seal with clean engine oil, and fit it over the end of the camshaft. To prevent damage to the oil seal while fitting, wrap adhesive tape around the end of the camshaft then remove the tape.
c) Apply a thin film of suitable sealant to the mating surface of the bearing cap, then refit it making sure that the oil seal is located fully against the seating in the head and cap. Tighten the mounting nuts progressively to the specified torque.
16 On 2.4 litre engines, refit the fuel injection pump drivebelt as described in Section 6. This procedure also includes the refitting of the drivebelt sprocket.
17 On 2.5 litre engines refit the injection pump drivebelt sprocket to the camshaft as described in Section 7, then refit the fuel injection pump drivebelt as described in Section 6.
18 Refit the camshaft cover as described in Section 9.

11.3 Using a hooked tool to remove the crankshaft oil seal at the timing belt end

10.6b ...and tap it into position using a tubular bar or socket

11 Crankshaft oil seals – renewal

Timing belt end oil seal

1 Remove the timing belt as described in Section 4 (pre-February 1995 models), or Section 5 (February 1995 models onward).
2 Slide the crankshaft sprocket from the end of the crankshaft. If it is tight, use two screwdrivers or levers to remove it.
3 Drill two small holes into the existing oil seal, diagonally opposite each other. Thread two self-tapping screws into the holes and using two pairs of pliers, pull on the heads of the screws to extract the oil seal. Take great care to avoid drilling through into the seal housing or crankshaft sealing surface. Alternatively, prise the old oil seal out using a hooked tool (see illustration).
4 Clean out the seal housing and sealing surface of the crankshaft by wiping it with a lint-free cloth – avoid using solvents that may enter the crankcase and affect component lubrication. Remove any swarf or burrs that could cause the seal to leak.
5 Smear the lip of the new oil seal with clean engine oil, and position it over the crankshaft (see illustration).
6 Using a hammer and a socket of suitable diameter, drive the seal squarely into its housing (see illustration). Note: Select a socket that bears only on the hard oute

11:5 Locate the new oil seal over the crankshaft...

11.6 ...and tap it into position using a tubular bar or socket

11.10 Unscrew the mounting bolts and remove the crankshaft rear oil seal housing

11.12 Locate a new housing gasket on the cylinder block

11.13 Locate the new oil seal and housing onto the crankshaft with the protector...

11.14 ...then remove the protector

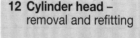

12 Cylinder head – removal and refitting

Note: Cylinder head dismantling and overhaul is covered in Chapter 2C, Section 6.

Removal

1 Disconnect the battery negative terminal (refer to *Disconnecting the battery*).
2 Drain the engine oil with reference to Chapter 1, Section 3.
3 Drain the cooling system with reference to Chapter 1, Section 23.
4 Release the retaining clips and disconnect the coolant hoses at the expansion tank. Disconnect the wiring connector, undo the retaining bolts and remove the expansion tank **(see illustrations)**.
5 Remove the auxiliary drivebelt(s) as described in Section 8.
6 Remove the camshaft cover as described in Section 9.
7 Set the engine to TDC on No 1 cylinder as described in Section 2.
8 Remove the timing belt as described in Section 4 (pre-February 1995 models), or Section 5 (February 1995 models onward).
9 Refer to Section 7 and remove the timing belt tensioner or idler pulley, and the camshaft sprocket.
10 Unbolt and remove the timing belt inner cover from the engine block.
11 Loosen the clips and disconnect the radiator hoses from the cylinder head.

surface of the seal, not the inner lip, which can easily be damaged.
7 Slide the crankshaft sprocket onto the end of the crankshaft making sure that the lug on the inside of the sprocket engages with the recess in the end of the crankshaft. If it is tight on the crankshaft, tap it on using a block of wood, however do not tap it on so far that it touches the oil pump casing.
8 Refit the timing belt as described in Section 4 (pre-February 1995 models), or Section 5 (February 1995 models onward).

Flywheel/driveplate end oil seal

9 The oil seal is integral with the oil seal housing, and it is not possible to renew it separately. First remove the flywheel/driveplate as described in Section 14, then remove the sump as described in Section 16.
10 Unscrew the mounting bolts and remove the housing together with the oil seal from

the cylinder block **(see illustration)**. Recover the gasket from the location dowels on the cylinder block.
11 Clean the surfaces of the block and crankshaft.
12 Locate the new gasket on the cylinder block **(see illustration)**.
13 The new oil seal housing is supplied together with a protector which remains in position until the housing has been fitted. Locate the housing assembly over the end of the crankshaft and press it onto the location dowels **(see illustration)**.
14 Carefully remove the protector making sure that the oil seal lips are seated correctly on the crankshaft **(see illustration)**.
15 Refit the bolts and tighten to the specified torque.
16 Refit the sump as described in Section 16 and flywheel/driveplate as described in Section 14.

12.4a Disconnect the upper...

12.4b ...and lower coolant hoses at the expansion tank...

12.4c ...then disconnect the wiring connector and remove the tank

12 Loosen the clips and disconnect the expansion tank hose, and the heater inlet and outlet coolant hoses, from the cylinder head.

13 Disconnect and remove the injector fuel supply pipes from the injectors and the injection pump as described in Chapter 4A, Section 11.

14 Unplug all fuel and coolant system electrical wiring at the relevant connectors and sensors, labelling each cable to aid refitting later. Also disconnect the supply cable from the glow plug in No 4 cylinder. On 2.5 litre engines, disconnect the wiring from the injector lift sensor on No 4 injector by disconnecting the wiring at the connector.

15 Remove the brake vacuum pump and plunger from the cylinder head as described in Chapter 9, Section 25. Note that the plunger must be removed for access to one of the cylinder head bolts.

16 Following the reverse of the tightening sequence **(see illustration 12.33a)**, progressively slacken the cylinder head bolts, by half a turn at a time, until all bolts can be unscrewed by hand. Discard the bolts – new ones must be fitted on reassembly.

17 Check that nothing remains connected to the cylinder head, then lift the head away from the cylinder block; seek assistance if possible, as it is a heavy assembly.

18 Remove the gasket from the top of the block, noting the locating dowels. If the dowels are a loose fit, remove them and store them with the head for safe-keeping. Do not discard the gasket yet – it will be needed for identification purposes.

19 If the cylinder head is to be dismantled for overhaul, refer to Chapter 2C, Section 6.

Preparation for refitting

20 The mating faces of the cylinder head and cylinder block/crankcase must be perfectly clean before refitting the head. Use a hard plastic or wood scraper to remove all traces of gasket and carbon; also clean the piston crowns. Take particular care during the cleaning operations, as aluminium alloy is easily damaged. Also, make sure that the carbon is not allowed to enter the oil and water passages – this is particularly important for the lubrication system, as carbon could block the oil supply to the engine's components. Using adhesive tape and paper, seal the water, oil and bolt holes in the cylinder block/crankcase.

21 Check the mating surfaces of the cylinder block/crankcase and the cylinder head for nicks, deep scratches and other damage. If slight, they may be removed carefully with abrasive paper, but note that head machining will not be possible - refer to Chapter 2C, Section 6.

22 If warpage of the cylinder head gasket surface is suspected, use a straight-edge to check it for distortion. Refer to Chapter 2C, Section 6 if necessary.

23 Clean out the cylinder head bolt drillings using a suitable tap. If a tap is not available, make a home-made substitute **(see Tool Tip)**.

24 On the engines covered in this Chapter, it is possible for the piston crowns to strike and damage the valve heads, if the camshaft is rotated with the timing belt removed and the crankshaft set to TDC. For this reason, the crankshaft must be set to a position other than TDC on No 1 cylinder, before the cylinder head is refitted. Use a wrench and socket on the crankshaft pulley centre bolt to turn the crankshaft in its normal direction of rotation, until all four pistons are positioned halfway down their bores, with No 1 piston on its upstroke – approximately 90° before TDC.

Refitting

25 Examine the old cylinder head gasket for manufacturer's identification markings. These will be in the form of holes, and a part number, on the edge of the gasket **(see illustration)**. Unless new pistons have been fitted, the new cylinder head gasket must be the same type as the old one.

26 If new piston assemblies have been

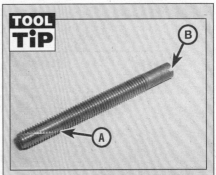

If a tap is not available, make a home-made substitute by cutting a slot (A) down the threads of one of the old cylinder head bolts. After use, the bolt head can be cut off, and the shank can then be used as an alignment dowel to assist cylinder head refitting. Cut a screwdriver slot (B) in the top of the bolt, to allow it to be unscrewed

fitted as part of an engine overhaul, before purchasing the new cylinder head gasket, refer to Chapter 2C, Section 15 and measure the piston projection. Purchase a new gasket according to the results of the measurement (see Chapter 2C Specifications).

27 Lay the new head gasket on the cylinder block, engaging it with the locating dowels **(see illustration)**. Ensure that the manufacturer's TOP and part number markings are facing upwards.

28 Cut the heads from two of the old cylinder head bolts. Cut a slot, big enough for a screw-driver blade, in the end of each bolt. Screw these into opposite end holes in the cylinder block to ensure the cylinder head aligns correctly with the block.

29 With the help of an assistant, place the cylinder head centrally on the cylinder block, ensuring that the locating dowels engage with the recesses in the cylinder head. Check that the head gasket is correctly seated before

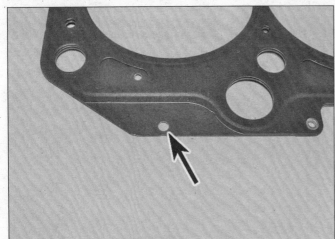

12.25 Cylinder head gasket identification hole (arrowed)

12.27 Lay the new head gasket on the cylinder block, engaging it with the locating dowels

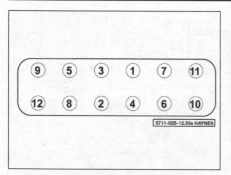

12.33a Cylinder head bolt tightening sequence

12.33b Torque-tightening the cylinder head bolts

12.34 Angle-tightening the cylinder head bolts

allowing the full weight of the cylinder head to rest on it.

30 Unscrew and remove the home-made alignment bolts using a screwdriver.

31 Apply a smear of grease to the threads, and to the underside of the heads, of the new cylinder head bolts.

32 Fit the washers and carefully enter each bolt into its relevant hole (do not drop them in) and screw in, by hand only, until finger-tight.

33 Working progressively and in the sequence shown, tighten the cylinder head bolts to their Stage 1 torque setting, using a torque wrench and socket. Repeat the exercise in the same sequence for the Stage 2 torque setting **(see illustrations)**.

34 Once all the bolts have been tightened to their Stage 2 settings, working again in the given sequence, angle-tighten the bolts through the specified Stage 3 angle, using a socket and extension bar **(see illustration)**. Repeat the exercise in the same sequence for the Stage 4 angle. It is recommended that an angle-measuring gauge is used during these stages of the tightening, to ensure accuracy. If a gauge is not available, use paint to make alignment marks between the bolt head and cylinder head prior to tightening; the marks can then be used to check the bolt has been rotated through the correct angle during tightening. **Note:** *No further tightening of the cylinder head bolts is required after the engine has been started.*

35 The remainder of refitting is a reversal of

the removal procedure, but on completion carry out the following:

a) *Refill the engine with the correct grade and quantity of oil with reference to Chapter 1, Section 3.*

b) *Refill the cooling system with the correct quantity of new coolant with reference to Chapter 1, Section 23.*

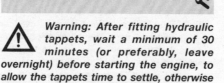

13 Hydraulic tappets – operation check

⚠️ *Warning: After fitting hydraulic tappets, wait a minimum of 30 minutes (or preferably, leave overnight) before starting the engine, to allow the tappets time to settle, otherwise the valve heads will strike the pistons.*

1 The hydraulic tappets are self-adjusting, and require no attention whilst in service.

2 If the hydraulic tappets become excessively noisy, their operation can be checked as described below.

3 Run the engine until it reaches its normal operating temperature, then increase the engine speed to approximately 2500 rpm for 2 minutes.

4 Switch off the engine and remove the camshaft cover as described in Section 9.

5 Rotate the camshaft by turning the crankshaft with a socket, until the first cam lobe over No 1 cylinder is pointing upwards.

6 Using a non-metallic tool, press the tappet downwards then use a feeler blade to check the clearance between the base of the cam lobe and the top of the tappet. If this is more than 0.1 mm, the tappet should be renewed.

7 Rotate the crankshaft until the next cam lobe is pointing upwards and check the check the clearance as previously described. Continue until all tappets have been checked.

8 Hydraulic tappet removal and refitting is described as part of the cylinder head overhaul sequence – see Chapter 2C, Section 6.

14 Flywheel/driveplate – removal, inspection and refitting

Removal

Note: *New flywheel/driveplate retaining bolts will be required on refitting.*

Manual transmission models

1 Remove the transmission as described in Chapter 7A, Section 6 then remove the clutch assembly as described in Chapter 6, Section 7.

2 Prevent the flywheel from turning by locking the ring gear teeth with a similar arrangement to that shown **(see illustration)**.

3 Slacken and remove the retaining bolts and remove the flywheel **(see illustration)**.

Caution: Take care, as the flywheel is heavy.

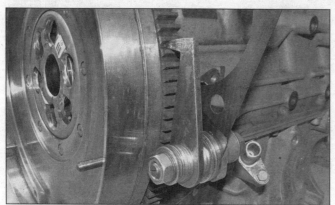

14.2 Prevent the flywheel from turning by locking the ring gear teeth with a suitable tool

14.3 Flywheel retaining bolts

Automatic transmission models

4 Remove the transmission as described in Chapter 7B, Section 3, then remove the driveplate as described in paragraphs 2 and 3 but note the location of the shim and spacer.

Inspection

Flywheel

5 Examine the flywheel for wear or chipping of the ring gear teeth. Renewal of the ring gear is not possible and if the wear or chipping is significant, a new flywheel will be required.
6 Examine the flywheel for scoring of the clutch face. If the clutch face is scored significantly, a new flywheel will be required.
7 The dual-mass flywheel used on these engines has the effect of reducing engine and transmission vibrations and harshness. The flywheel consists of a primary mass and a secondary mass constructed in such a way that the secondary mass is allowed to rotate slightly in relation to the primary mass. Springs within the assembly restrict this movement to set limits.
8 Dual-mass flywheels have earned an unenviable reputation for unreliability and have been known to fail at quite low mileages (sometimes as low as 20 000 miles). As well as the checks described above in paragraphs 5 and 6, some additional checks should be performed as follows.
9 Look through the bolt hole and inspection openings in the secondary mass and check for any visible damage in the area of the centre bearing.
10 Place your thumbs on the clutch face of the secondary mass at the 3 o'clock and 9 o'clock positions and try to rock it. The maximum movement should not exceed 3 mm. Repeat this check with your thumbs at the 12 o'clock and 6 o'clock positions.
11 Rotate the secondary mass clockwise and anti-clockwise. It should move freely in both directions until spring resistance is felt, with no abnormal grating or rattling noises.
12 If there is any doubt about the condition of the flywheel, seek the advice of a VW dealer or engine reconditioning specialist. They will be able to advise if the flywheel is an acceptable condition, or whether renewal is necessary.

Driveplate

13 Closely examine the driveplate and ring gear teeth for signs of wear or damage and check the driveplate surface for any signs of cracks.
14 If there is any doubt about the condition of the driveplate, seek the advice of a VW dealer or engine reconditioning specialist.

Refitting

Manual transmission models

15 Clean the mating surfaces of the flywheel and crankshaft.
16 Offer up the flywheel and engage it on the crankshaft. Apply a drop of locking compound to the threads of each new flywheel retaining bolt (unless they are already precoated) and install the new bolts.
17 Lock the flywheel by the method used on removal then, working in a diagonal sequence, evenly and progressively tighten the retaining bolts to the specified Stage 1 torque, then through the specified Stage 2 angle.
18 Refit the clutch as described in Chapter 6, Section 7, then remove the locking tool and refit the transmission as described in Chapter 7A, Section 6.

Automatic transmission models

19 Clean the mating surfaces of the driveplate and crankshaft.
20 Offer up the driveplate and engage it on the crankshaft. Apply a drop of locking compound to the threads of each new driveplate retaining bolt (unless they are already precoated) and install the new bolts.
21 Lock the driveplate by the method used on removal then, working in a diagonal sequence, evenly and progressively tighten the retaining bolts to the specified Stage 1 torque, then through the specified Stage 2 angle.
22 Remove the locking tool, and refit the transmission as described in Chapter 7B, Section 3.

15 Engine mountings – inspection and renewal

Refer to Chapter 2A, Section 14.

16 Sum p – removal and refitting

Removal

1 Disconnect the battery negative terminal (refer to *Disconnecting the battery*).
2 Firmly apply the handbrake, then jack up the front of the vehicle and support it securely on axle stands (see *Jacking and vehicle support*).
3 Remove the engine undertray as described in Chapter 11, Section 25.
4 Drain the engine oil as described in Chapter 1, Section 3.
5 To improve access to the sump, refer to Chapter 8, Section 2 and disconnect the right-hand driveshaft from the transmission output flange.
6 Where fitted, disconnect the wiring connector at the oil level sender.
7 In order to access the two rear sump bolts the crankshaft must be turned so that the cut-out sections in the sump and flywheel are aligned. Use a spanner on the crankshaft sprocket bolt to do this.
8 Unscrew and remove the sump bolts using a multi-splined key.
9 If the sump is attached to the cylinder block without a gasket, use a wide-bladed scraper or similar tool inserted between the sump and cylinder block, carefully break the joint to release the sump, then manoeuvre the sump out from under the vehicle. If a gasket is used between the sump and cylinder block, break the joint by striking the sump with the palm of your hand, then lower the sump and withdraw it from underneath the vehicle. Recover and discard the sump gasket.

Refitting

10 Clean all traces of sealant or gasket from the mating surfaces of the cylinder block/crankcase and sump, then use a piece of clean rag to wipe out the sump.
11 Ensure that the sump and cylinder block/crankcase mating surfaces are clean and dry then lay a new sump gasket in position on the sump mating surface. Offer up the sump and refit the retaining bolts. Tighten the bolts evenly and progressively to the specified torque.
12 Where fitted, reconnect the wiring connector to the oil level sender.
13 Reconnect the right-hand driveshaft to the transmission output flange with reference to Chapter 8, Section 2.
14 Refit the engine undertray, then lower the vehicle to the ground.
15 Refer to Chapter 1, Section 3 and refill the engine with the specified grade and quantity of oil.
16 On completion, reconnect the battery negative terminal.

17 Oil pump and pickup – removal, inspection and refitting

Removal

1 Remove the crankshaft sprocket as described in Section 7.
2 Remove the sump as described in Section 16.
3 Using a screwdriver or similar tool, knock back the tabs on the lockplate (where fitted). Unscrew the oil pickup tube support bracket bolts on the crankcase, then unbolt the flange from the bottom of the oil pump and recover the lockplate. Withdraw the tube and recover the gasket or O-ring **(see illustrations)**.

17.3a Unscrew the bolts from the oil pump...

17.3b ...and the bolts from the support bracket...

17.3c ...and remove the oil pickup tube

17.3d Removing the O-ring seal from the groove

17.4a The inner timing cover is secured to the oil pump with the long bolts

17.4b Remove the oil pump...

17.4c ...and gasket

4 Unscrew the mounting bolts and withdraw the oil pump over the crankshaft and from the front of the cylinder block. Recover the gasket. Note that the inner timing cover is secured with some of the oil pump mounting bolts (see illustrations).

Inspection

5 Unscrew the countersunk screws securing the pump cover and lift the cover off, exposing the gears.

6 Check that there is a mark on the exposed face of the gears and if not, make a mark to show which side of the gears is towards the engine before removing them.

7 Unscrew the pressure relief valve plug and remove the plug, sealing ring, spring and plunger (see illustrations).

8 Clean all the parts thoroughly and examine the pump casing and cover for signs of wear or scoring. Examine the pressure relief valve plunger and its seating for damage and wear and check that the spring is not damaged or distorted. Check the gears for damage and wear. New gears are not available from the manufacturer's therefore if they are excessively worn, the oil pump must be renewed complete.

9 Using a screwdriver, carefully prise out the oil seal from the front of the pump – this may prove difficult because the lip of the seal is quite weak, and where this is the case a drift should be used from the inner end of the pump. Oil the lip of the new seal, enter the seal with its closed face outwards and use a block of wood to tap the seal in flush. If there is any scoring on the crankshaft in the area on which the lip of the seal bears, the seal may be pushed to the bottom of its recess so that the lip bears on an undamaged part of the crankshaft (see illustration).

10 Reassemble the pump by fitting the gears and cover. The inner gear has its slotted end towards the crankshaft and although the outer gear can be fitted either way round, it should be fitted the same way round as it was before removal. Some gears have a triangle stamped on them and this mark should be towards the

17.7a Remove the oil pump pressure relief valve plug...

17.7b ...spring...

17.7c ...and plunger

17.9 Fitting a new oil seal to the oil pump

pump cover. Before refitting the cover, fill the spaces between the gears with oil to ensure the oil circuit primes itself immediately the engine is started.

11 Tighten the cover countersunk screws securely.

12 Reassemble the pressure relief valve components and tighten the plug to the specified torque.

Refitting

13 Locate a new gasket on the dowels on the front of the cylinder block and retain with a little grease.

14 Locate the oil pump on the block making sure that the slot on the inner gear engages the dog on the crankshaft. As the oil seal is located over the end of the crankshaft make sure it is not damaged.

15 Insert the bolts and tighten them in diagonal sequence to the specified torque.

16 Fit the pickup tube together with a new gasket or O-ring, and tighten the bolts. Where fitted, bend the lock tabs onto the bolts to lock them.

17 Refit the sump as described in Section 16.

18 Refit the crankshaft sprocket as described in Section 7.

Chapter 2 Part C:
Engine removal and overhaul procedures

Contents

Degrees of difficulty

Easy, suitable for novice with little experience 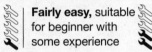 | **Fairly easy,** suitable for beginner with some experience | **Fairly difficult,** suitable for competent DIY mechanic | **Difficult,** suitable for experienced DIY mechanic | **Very difficult,** suitable for expert DIY or professional

Specifications

Engine identification

Engine type	Manufacturer's engine code
4-cylinder engines:	
45 kW (normally aspirated) engines	1X
50 kW (turbocharged) engines	ABL
5-cylinder engines:	
2.4 litre engines:	
57 kW engines	AAB
55 kW engines	AJA
2.5 litre engines:	
75 kW engines	ACV, AUF, AYC, AXL
111 kW engines	AHY, AXG
65 kW engines	AJT, AYY

4-cylinder engines

Cylinder head

Cylinder head gasket surface, maximum distortion.	0.1 mm
Maximum swirl chamber projection	0.07 mm
Cylinder head gasket identification:	
Piston protrusion:	
0.66 to 0.86 mm	1 notch/hole
0.87 to 0.90 mm	2 notches/holes
0.91 to 1.02 mm	3 notches/holes

Valves

Valve stem diameter:	
Inlet.	7.97 mm
Exhaust.	7.95 mm
Valve length	95.0 mm
Valve head diameter:	
Inlet.	36.0 mm
Exhaust.	31.0 mm
Maximum valve head deflection (end of valve stem flush with top of guide)	1.3 mm

4-cylinder engines (continued)

Camshaft

Maximum endfloat	0.15 mm
Maximum runout	0.01 mm
Maximum bearing running clearance	0.11 mm

Intermediate shaft

Maximum endfloat	0.25 mm

Cylinder block

Bore diameter:

Standard	79.51 mm
1st oversize	79.76 mm
2nd oversize	80.01 mm
Maximum bore wear	0.08 mm

Pistons and piston rings

Piston diameter:

Standard	79.48 mm
1st oversize	79.73 mm
2nd oversize	79.98 mm
Maximum deviation	0.04 mm

Piston ring-to-groove clearance:

Top compression ring:

Standard	0.09 to 0.12 mm
Service limit	0.25 mm

2nd compression ring:

Standard	0.05 to 0.08 mm
Service limit	0.25 mm

Oil scraper ring:

Standard	0.03 to 0.06 mm
Service limit	0.15 mm

Piston ring end gaps:*

Top compression ring:

Standard	0.20 to 0.40 mm
Service limit	1.2 mm

2nd compression ring:

Standard	0.20 to 0.40 mm
Service limit	0.6 mm

Oil scraper ring:

Standard	0.25 to 0.50 mm
Service limit	1.2 mm

*Note: Piston ring end gaps should be offset at 120° to each other when fitted

Crankshaft

Endfloat:

Standard	0.07 to 0.17 mm
Service limit	0.37 mm

Main bearing journal diameters:

Standard	54.00 mm
1st undersize	53.75 mm
2nd undersize	53.50 mm
3rd undersize	53.25 mm
Tolerance	-0.022 to -0.042 mm

Main bearing running clearances:

Standard	0.03 to 0.08 mm
Service limit	0.17 mm

Crankpin journal diameters:

Standard	47.80 mm
1st undersize	47.55 mm
2nd undersize	47.30 mm
3rd undersize	47.05 mm
Tolerance	-0.022 to -0.042 mm

Big-end bearing running clearance:

Standard	N/A
Service limit	0.08 mm

Torque wrench settings

Refer to Chapter 2A Specifications

5-cylinder engines

Cylinder head

Cylinder head gasket surface, maximum distortion...............	0.2 mm
Maximum swirl chamber projection (2.4 litre engines).............	0.05 mm

Cylinder head gasket identification:
  2.4 litre engines:
    Piston protrusion:

Up to 0.86 mm	1 hole
0.87 to 0.90 mm	2 holes
Over 0.90 mm	3 holes

  2.5 litre engines:
    Piston protrusion:

Up to 0.96 mm	1 hole
0.97 to 1.01 mm	2 holes
Over 1.01 mm	3 holes

Valves

Valve stem diameter:

Inlet..	7.97 mm
Exhaust.......................................	7.95 mm

Valve length:

2.4 litre engines	95.0 mm
2.5 litre engines	96.85 mm

Valve head diameter:

Inlet..	36.0 mm

  Exhaust:

2.4 litre engines..............................	31.0 mm
2.5 litre engines..............................	31.5 mm
Maximum valve head deflection (end of valve stem flush with top of guide)	1.3 mm

Camshaft

Maximum endfloat	0.15 mm
Maximum runout	0.01 mm
Maximum bearing running clearance......................	0.11 mm

Cylinder block

Bore diameter:
  2.4 litre engines:

Standard.....................................	79.51 mm
1st oversize...................................	79.76 mm
2nd oversize..................................	80.01 mm
Maximum bore wear............................	0.10 mm

  2.5 litre engines:

Standard.....................................	81.01 mm
Oversize.....................................	81.26 mm
Maximum bore wear............................	0.08 mm

Pistons and piston rings

Piston diameter:	2.4 litre engine	2.5 litre engine
Standard.....................................	79.48 mm	80.96 mm
1st oversize...................................	79.73 mm	81.21 mm
2nd oversize..................................	79.98 mm	N/A
Maximum deviation	0.04 mm	0.04 mm
Piston ring-to-groove clearance:	2.4 litre engine	2.5 litre engine
Top compression ring:		
Standard..................................	0.09 to 0.12 mm	0.07 to 0.11 mm
Service limit	0.25 mm	0.25 mm
2nd compression ring:		
Standard..................................	0.05 to 0.08 mm	0.05 to 0.08 mm
Service limit	0.25 mm	0.25 mm
Oil scraper ring:		
Standard..................................	0.03 to 0.06 mm	0.03 to 0.06 mm
Service limit	0.15 mm	0.15 mm

5-cylinder engines (continued)

Pistons and piston rings (continued)

Piston ring end gaps:*	2.4 litre engine	2.5 litre engine
Top compression ring:		
Standard	0.20 to 0.40 mm	0.25 to 0.45 mm
Service limit	1.2 mm	1.0 mm
2nd compression ring:		
Standard	0.20 to 0.40 mm	0.20 to 0.40 mm
Service limit	0.6 mm	1.0 mm
Oil scraper ring:		
Standard	0.25 to 0.50 mm	0.25 to 0.50 mm
Service limit	1.2 mm	1.0 mm

*Note: *Piston ring end gaps should be offset at 120° to each other when fitted*

Crankshaft

Endfloat:	
Standard	0.07 to 0.18 mm
Service limit	0.25 mm
Main bearing journal diameters:	
Standard	58.00 mm
1st undersize	57.75 mm
2nd undersize	57.50 mm
3rd undersize	57.25 mm
Tolerance	-0.022 to -0.042 mm
Main bearing running clearances:	
Standard	0.016 to 0.075 mm
Service limit	0.16 mm
Crankpin journal diameters:	
Standard	47.80 mm
1st undersize	47.55 mm
2nd undersize	47.30 mm
3rd undersize	47.05 mm
Tolerance	-0.022 to -0.042 mm
Big-end bearing running clearance:	
Standard	N/A
Service limit	0.08 mm

Torque wrench settings

Refer to Chapter 2B Specifications

1 General information

This Part of Chapter 2 is devoted to engine/transmission removal and refitting, to those repair procedures requiring the removal of the engine/transmission from the vehicle, and to the overhaul of engine components. It includes only the Specifications relevant to those procedures. Refer to Part A or B (depending on engine type) for additional Specifications and for all torque wrench settings.

The information ranges from advice concerning preparation for an overhaul and the purchase of new parts, to detailed step-by-step procedures covering removal and installation of internal engine components and the inspection of parts.

The following Sections have been written based on the assumption that the engine has been removed from the vehicle. For information concerning in-vehicle engine repair, as well as removal and installation of the external components necessary for the overhaul, see Part A or B of this Chapter.

2 Engine overhaul – general information

It's not always easy to determine when, or if, an engine should be completely overhauled, as a number of factors must be considered.

High mileage is not necessarily an indication that an overhaul is needed, while low mileage doesn't preclude the need for an overhaul. Frequency of servicing is probably the most important consideration. An engine that has had regular and frequent oil and filter changes, as well as other required maintenance, will most likely give many thousands of miles of reliable service. Conversely, a neglected engine may require an overhaul very early in its life.

Excessive oil consumption is an indication that piston rings, valve seals and/or valve guides are in need of attention. Make sure that oil leaks are not responsible before deciding that the rings and/or guides are worn. Perform a cylinder compression test (refer to Part A or B of this Chapter) to determine the likely cause of the problem.

Check the oil pressure with a gauge fitted in place of the oil pressure switch, and compare it with that specified in Chapter 2A or 2B as applicable. If it is extremely low, the main and big-end bearings, and/or the oil pump, are probably worn out.

Loss of power, rough running, knocking or metallic engine noises, excessive valve gear noise, and high fuel consumption may also point to the need for an overhaul, especially if they are all present at the same time. If a complete service does not cure the situation, major mechanical work is the only solution.

A full engine overhaul involves restoring all internal parts to the specification of a new engine. During a complete overhaul, the pistons and the piston rings are renewed, and the cylinder bores are reconditioned. New main and big-end bearings are generally fitted. If necessary, the crankshaft may be reground, to compensate for wear in the journals. The valves are also serviced as well, since they are usually in less-than-perfect condition at this point. Always pay careful attention to the condition of the oil pump when overhauling the engine, and renew it if there is any doubt as to its serviceability. The end result should be an as-new engine that will give many trouble-free miles.

Critical cooling system components such as the hoses, thermostat and coolant pump should be renewed when an engine is overhauled. The radiator should also be checked carefully, to ensure that it is not clogged or leaking.

Before beginning the engine overhaul, read the entire procedure, to familiarise yourself with the scope and requirements of the job. Check on the availability of parts and make sure that any necessary special tools and equipment are obtained in advance. Most work can be done with typical hand tools, although a number of precision measuring tools are required for inspecting parts to determine if they must be renewed.

The services provided by an engineering machine shop or engine reconditioning specialist will almost certainly be required, particularly if major repairs such as crankshaft regrinding or cylinder reboring are necessary. Apart from carrying out machining operations, these establishments will normally handle the inspection of parts, offer advice concerning reconditioning or renewal and supply new components such as pistons, piston rings and bearing shells. It is recommended that the establishment used is a member of the Federation of Engine Re-Manufacturers, or a similar society.

Always wait until the engine has been completely dismantled, and until all components (especially the cylinder block/crankcase and the crankshaft) have been inspected before deciding what service and repair operations must be performed by an engineering works. The condition of these components will be the major factor to consider when determining whether to overhaul the original engine, or to buy a reconditioned unit. Do not, therefore, purchase parts or have overhaul work done on other components until they have been thoroughly inspected. As a general rule, time is the primary cost of an overhaul, so it does not pay to fit worn or sub-standard parts.

As a final note, to ensure maximum life and minimum trouble from a reconditioned engine, everything must be assembled with care, in a spotlessly clean environment.

3 Engine/transmission removal – methods and precautions

If you have decided that the engine must be removed for overhaul or major repair work, several preliminary steps should be taken.

Locating a suitable place to work is extremely important. Adequate work space, along with storage space for the vehicle, will

be needed. If a workshop or garage is not available, at the very least a solid, level, clean work surface is required.

If possible, clear some shelving close to the work area and use it to store the engine components and ancillaries as they are removed and dismantled. In this manner, the components stand a better chance of staying clean and undamaged during the overhaul. Laying out components in groups together with their fixings bolts, screws, etc will save time and avoid confusion when the engine is refitted.

Cleaning the engine compartment and engine/transmission before beginning the removal procedure will help keep tools clean and organised.

An engine hoist will also be necessary. Make sure the equipment is rated in excess of the combined weight of the engine and transmission. Safety is of primary importance, considering the potential hazards involved in removing the engine/transmission from the car.

The help of an assistant is essential. Apart from the safety aspects involved, there are many instances when one person cannot simultaneously perform all of the operations required during engine/transmission removal.

Plan the operation ahead of time. Before starting work, arrange for the hire of or obtain all of the tools and equipment you will need. Some of the equipment necessary to perform engine/transmission removal and installation safely (in addition to an engine hoist) is as follows: a heavy duty trolley jack, complete sets of spanners and sockets as described in the rear of this manual, wooden blocks, and plenty of rags and cleaning solvent for mopping up spilled oil, coolant and fuel. If the hoist must be hired, make sure that you arrange for it in advance, and perform all of the operations possible without it beforehand. This will save you money and time.

Plan for the car to be out of use for quite a while. An engineering machine shop or engine reconditioning specialist will be required to perform some of the work which cannot be accomplished without special equipment. These places often have a busy schedule, so it would be a good idea to consult them before removing the engine, in order to accurately estimate the amount of time required to rebuild or repair components that may need work.

During the engine/transmission removal procedure, it is advisable to make notes of the locations of all brackets, cable ties, earthing points, etc, as well as how the wiring harnesses, hoses and electrical connections are attached and routed around the engine and engine compartment. An effective way of doing this is to take a series of photographs of the various components before they are disconnected or removed; the resulting photographs will prove

invaluable when the engine/transmission is refitted.

Always be extremely careful when removing and refitting the engine/transmission. Serious injury can result from careless actions. Plan ahead and take your time, and a job of this nature, although major, can be accomplished successfully.

On vehicles with 4-cylinder engines, the engine can be removed from below on its own, leaving the transmission in the vehicle, or it can be removed together with the transmission.

On vehicles with 5-cylinder engines, the engine must be removed complete with the transmission as an assembly. There is insufficient clearance in the engine compartment to remove the engine leaving the transmission in the vehicle. The assembly is removed by raising the front of the vehicle, and lowering the assembly from the engine compartment.

4 Engine/transmission – removal, separation and refitting

Note: *Read through the entire Section, as well as reading the advice in Section 3, before beginning this operation.*

Note: *The following procedure describes the removal of the engine and transmission as a unit. On 4-cylinder engine models, the engine can be removed separately leaving the transmission in the vehicle. If this method is being adopted, procedures relating to disconnecting components and attachments at the transmission can be disregarded.*

Removal

1 Disconnect the battery negative terminal (refer to *Disconnecting the battery*).

2 Refer to Chapter 11, Section 6 and remove the bonnet from its hinges.

3 Firmly apply the handbrake, then jack up the front of the vehicle and support it securely on axle stands (see *Jacking and vehicle support*). Remove the front roadwheels.

4 Remove the engine undertray as described in Chapter 11, Section 25.

5 Drain the cooling system as described in Chapter 1, Section 23.

6 If the engine is going to be dismantled, drain the engine oil as described in Chapter 1, Section 3.

7 Remove the auxiliary drivebelt(s) as described in Chapter 2A, Section 6 (4-cylinder engines) or Chapter 2B, Section 8 (5-cylinder engines).

8 Release the retaining clips and disconnect the coolant hoses at the expansion tank. Disconnect the wiring connector, undo the retaining bolts and remove the expansion tank **(see illustrations)**.

9 Remove the radiator as described in Chapter 3, Section 4.

10 Release the retaining clips and disconnect the coolant hoses at the thermostat housing, coolant pump, cylinder head and heater matrix inlet and outlet ports at the bulkhead.

4.8a Disconnect the upper...

4.8b ...and lower coolant hoses at the expansion tank...

4.8c ...then disconnect the wiring connector and remove the tank

4.11 Disconnect the brake servo vacuum hose from the vacuum pump

11 Disconnect the brake servo vacuum hose from the vacuum pump on the cylinder block **(see illustration)**.

12 On vehicles with an Exhaust Gas Recirculation (EGR) system, refer to Chapter 4B and disconnect the vacuum hoses from the connection points on the EGR valve, brake servo vacuum hose, air inlet hose and where applicable, fuel injection pump.

Make a careful note of the order of connection to ensure correct refitting.
13 Slacken and withdraw the banjo bolts, then disconnect the fuel supply and return hoses from the fuel injection pump.
14 Release the clip, then disconnect the injector bleed hose from the port on the fuel return union.
15 Slacken the clips and remove the inlet air hose from the air cleaner, crankcase ventilation

hose and inlet manifold or turbocharger inlet as applicable.
16 Where applicable, disconnect the accelerator cable and the cold start accelerator cable from the fuel injection pump.
17 Remove the exhaust system front pipe as described in Chapter 4A, Section 19.
18 On models with power steering, remove the power steering pump as described in Chapter 10, Section 26.
19 On manual transmission models, carry out the following:
 a) *On models, with the 02B transmission, undo the two bolts and withdraw the clutch slave cylinder from the transmission. Tie the cylinder to one side.* **Note:** *The hydraulic pipe remains connected.*
 b) *On models with the 02G transmission, clamp the clutch hydraulic hose with a suitable hose clamp. Extract the retaining clip and disconnect the hydraulic pipe from the connecting piece above the starter motor. Suitably cover the disconnected unions to prevent dirt entry.*
 c) *Disconnect the wiring connector from the reversing light switch.*
 d) *On early models disconnect the speedometer cable from the speedometer drive. On later models, disconnect the wiring at the speedometer drive transducer.*
 e) *Disconnect the gear selection mechanism from the transmission by first undoing the two bolts and separating the swivel head from the transmission selector lever* **(see illustration)**. *Lever the front selector rod out of the bush in the selector lever. Undo the retaining bolts and release the gate rod mounting bracket from the transmission. Where fitted, unclip the reverse gear detent cable from the reverse gear locking unit. Move the selection mechanism clear of the transmission.*
20 On automatic transmission models, carry out the following:
 a) *Release the selector cable from the selector lever at the top of the transmission casing.*
 b) *Clamp the coolant hoses leading to the transmission fluid cooler, then release the clips and disconnect the hoses from the cooler ports.*
 c) *Unplug the wiring harness from the transmission at the connectors; label each connector to aid refitting later.*
21 On vehicles with air conditioning, unbolt the compressor and suitably support it clear of the engine. Do not disconnect the refrigerant pipes.
22 Working around the engine and transmission, disconnect all remaining electrical wiring, vacuum hoses and fuel connections, labelling each connector carefully to ensure correct refitting.
23 Refer to Chapter 8, Section 2 and remove the left-hand driveshaft. Separate the right-hand driveshaft from the transmission differential output shaft.

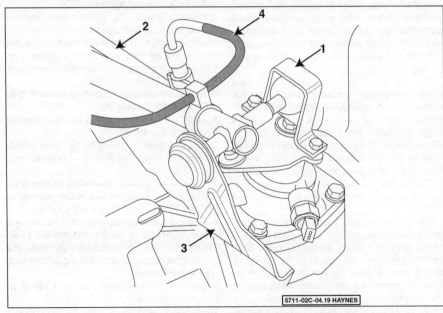

5711-02C-04.19 HAYNES

4.19 Gear selection mechanism components

 1 *Swivel head*
 2 *Front selector rod*
 3 *Gate rod mounting bracket*
 4 *Reverse gear detent cable*

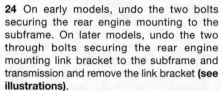

4.24a Undo the through bolt securing the rear engine mounting link bracket to the subframe...

4.24b ...and to the transmission...

4.24c ...and remove the link bracket

24 On early models, undo the two bolts securing the rear engine mounting to the subframe. On later models, undo the two through bolts securing the rear engine mounting link bracket to the subframe and transmission and remove the link bracket **(see illustrations)**.
25 Attach a suitable hoist and lifting tackle to the engine lifting brackets on the cylinder head, and support the weight of the engine/transmission.
26 On 4-cylinder engines, if the engine is being removed leaving the transmission in the vehicle, suitably support the transmission on a trolley jack and undo all the bolts/nuts securing the transmission bellhousing to the engine.
27 Undo the through bolt or the two nuts each side securing the left-hand and right-hand engine/transmission mountings to the body.
28 Make a final check to ensure that all relevant pipes, hoses, wires, etc, have been disconnected, and that they are positioned clear of the engine and transmission.
29 On 4-cylinder engines, if the engine is being removed leaving the transmission in the vehicle, ease the engine away from the transmission until the transmission input shaft is clear of the clutch assembly.
30 With the help of an assistant, carefully lower the engine/transmission assembly to the ground **(see illustration)**. Make sure that the surrounding components in the engine compartment are not damaged. Ideally, the assembly should be lowered onto a trolley jack or low platform with castors, so that it can easily be withdrawn from under the vehicle.
31 Ensure that the assembly is adequately supported, then disconnect the engine hoist and lifting tackle, and withdraw the engine/transmission assembly from under the front of the vehicle.

Separation

32 Rest the engine and transmission assembly on a firm, flat surface, and use wooden blocks as wedges to keep the unit steady.

Manual transmission

33 The transmission is secured to the engine by a combination of bolts and studs

with nuts, threaded into the cylinder block and bellhousing – the total number of fixings depends on the type of transmission and vehicle specification.
34 Starting at the bottom, remove all the bolts and nuts then carefully draw the transmission away from the engine, resting it securely on wooden blocks. Collect the locating dowels if they are loose enough to be extracted.
Caution: Take care to prevent the transmission from tilting, until the input shaft is fully disengaged from the clutch friction plate.

Automatic transmission

35 Unbolt the cover plate from the bottom of the transmission bellhousing, this will expose the rear face of the driveplate.
36 Mark the position of the torque converter with respect to the driveplate, using chalk or a marker pen. Remove the three nuts that secure the driveplate to the torque converter; turn the engine over using a socket and wrench on the crankshaft sprocket to rotate the driveplate and expose each nut in turn.
37 The transmission is secured to the engine by a combination of bolts and studs with nuts, threaded into the cylinder block and bellhousing – the total number of fixings depends on the type of transmission and vehicle specification.
38 Starting at the bottom, remove all the screws and nuts then carefully draw the transmission away from the engine, resting it securely on wooden blocks. Collect the locating dowels if they are loose enough to be extracted.
Caution: Take care to prevent the torque converter from sliding off the transmission input shaft – hold it in place as the transmission is withdrawn.
39 Place a length of batten across the open face of the bellhousing, fastening it with cable ties, to keep the torque converter in place in its housing.

Refitting

40 If the engine and transmission have not been separated, proceed to paragraph 46.

Manual transmission

41 Smear a little high-melting-point grease

on the splines of the transmission input shaft. Do not use an excessive amount as there is the risk of contaminating the clutch friction plate. Carefully offer up the transmission to the cylinder block, guiding the dowels into the mounting holes in cylinder block.
42 Refit the bellhousing bolts and nuts, hand tightening them to secure the transmission in position. **Note:** *Do not tighten them to force the engine and transmission together.* Ensure that the bellhousing and cylinder block mating faces will butt together evenly without obstruction, before tightening the bolts and nuts to their specified torque.

Automatic transmission

43 Remove the torque converter restraint from the face of the bellhousing. Check that the drive lugs on the torque converter hub are correctly engaged with the recesses in the inner wheel of the automatic transmission fluid pump.
44 Carefully offer up the transmission to the cylinder block, guiding the dowels into the mounting holes in cylinder block. Observe the markings made during the removal, to ensure correct alignment between the torque converter and the driveplate.
45 Refit the bellhousing bolts and nuts, hand-tightening them to secure the transmission in position. **Note:** *Do not tighten them to force the engine and transmission together.* Ensure that the bellhousing and cylinder block mating faces will butt together evenly without obstruction, before tightening the bolts and nuts to their specified torque.

4.30 Removing the engine/transmission assembly from the vehicle

All models

46 Manoeuvre the engine or engine/transmission back into position under the front of the vehicle and reconnect the engine hoist and lifting tackle.

47 With the help of an assistant, carefully raise the engine/transmission assembly into position making sure that the surrounding components in the engine compartment are not damaged.

48 On 4-cylinder engines, if the engine is being refitted to the transmission which is still in the vehicle, carry out the operations contained in paragraphs 41 and 42.

49 Refit the through bolt or the two nuts each side securing the left-hand and right-hand engine/transmission mountings to the body. Tighten the bolts/nuts to the specified torque.

50 On early models, refit the two bolts securing the rear engine mounting to the subframe. On later models, refit the two through bolts securing the rear engine mounting link bracket to the subframe and transmission. Tighten the bolts to the specified torque.

51 Disconnect and remove the hoist and lifting tackle from the engine.

52 Refer to Chapter 8, Section 2 and refit the left-hand driveshaft. Reattach the right-hand driveshaft to the transmission differential output shaft.

53 The remainder of the refitting sequence is the direct reverse of the removal procedure, noting the following points:

a) *Ensure that all sections of the wiring harness follow their original routing; use new cable-ties to secure the harness in position, keeping it away from sources of heat and abrasion.*

b) *Where applicable, reconnect the accelerator cable and the cold start accelerator cable to the fuel injection pump as described in Chapter 4A, Section 3 and Chapter 4A, Section 4.*

c) *On vehicles with manual transmission, reconnect the gear shift mechanism to the transmission as described in Chapter 7A, Section 3.*

d) *On vehicles with automatic transmission, reconnect the selector cable to the transmission, then check (and if necessary adjust) the overall operation of the gear selection mechanism as described in Chapter 7B, Section 2.*

e) *On vehicles with the 02G manual transmission, bleed the clutch hydraulic system as described in Chapter 6, Section 2.*

f) *Ensure that all hoses are correctly routed and are secured with the correct hose clips, where applicable.*

g) *Refill the engine with appropriate grade and quantities of oil as described in Chapter 1, Section 3.*

h) *Refill the cooling system as described in Chapter 1, Section 23.*

i) *When the engine is started for the first time, check for air, coolant, lubricant and fuel leaks from manifolds, hoses etc. If the engine has been overhauled, read the notes in Section 16 before attempting to start it.*

5 Engine overhaul – dismantling sequence

1 It is much easier to dismantle and work on the engine if it is mounted on a portable engine stand. These stands can often be hired from a tool hire shop. Before the engine is mounted on a stand, the flywheel should be removed so that the stand bolts can be tightened into the end of the cylinder block/crankcase. **Note:** *Do not measure cylinder bore dimensions with the engine mounted on this type of stand.*

2 If a stand is not available it is possible to dismantle the engine with it mounted on blocks, on a sturdy workbench or on the floor. Be extra careful not to tip or drop the engine when working without a stand.

3 If you are going to obtain a reconditioned engine, all external components must be removed first to be transferred to the new engine (just as they will if you are doing a complete engine overhaul yourself). **Note:** *When removing the external components from the engine, pay close attention to details that may be helpful or important during refitting. Note the fitted position of gaskets, seals, spacers, pins, washers, bolts and other small items. These external components include the following:*

a) *Alternator (including mounting brackets) and starter motor.*

b) *The glow plug/pre-heating system components.*

c) *All fuel system components, including the fuel injection pump, all sensors and actuators.*

d) *Cooling system/thermostat housings.*

e) *The vacuum pump.*

f) *All electrical switches, actuators and sensors, and the engine wiring harness.*

g) *Inlet and exhaust manifolds and where applicable, the turbocharger.*

h) *The engine oil level dipstick and its tube.*

i) *Engine mountings.*

j) *Flywheel/driveplate.*

k) *Clutch components – manual transmission models.*

4 If you are obtaining a short engine (the engine cylinder block/crankcase, crankshaft, pistons and connecting rods, all fully assembled), then the cylinder head, sump, oil pump (4-cylinder engines), timing belt (together with its tensioner and covers), auxiliary belt (together with its tensioner), coolant pump, thermostat housing, coolant outlet elbows, oil filter housing and where applicable oil cooler will also have to be removed.

5 If you are planning a full overhaul, the engine can be dismantled in the order given below:

a) *Inlet manifold (Chapter 4A, Section 15).*

b) *Exhaust manifold (Chapter 4A, Section 16).*

c) *Timing belt, sprockets and tensioner (Chapter 2A, Sections 4 and 5 or Chapter 2B, Sections 4, 5 and 7).*

d) *Cylinder head (Chapter 2A, Section 11 or Chapter 2B, Section 12).*

e) *Flywheel/driveplate (Chapter 2A, Section 13 or Chapter 2B, Section 14).*

f) *Sump (Chapter 2A, Section 15 or Chapter 2B, Section 16).*

g) *Oil pump (Chapter 2A, Section 16 or Chapter 2B, Section 17).*

h) *Piston/connecting rod assemblies (Section 7).*

i) *Crankshaft (Section 8).*

6 Cylinder head – dismantling, cleaning, inspection and reassembly

Note: *New and reconditioned cylinder heads are available from VW, and from engine reconditioning specialists. Specialist tools are required for the dismantling and inspection procedures, and new components may not be readily available. It may, therefore, be more practical for the home mechanic to buy a reconditioned head, rather than to dismantle, inspect and recondition the original head.*

Dismantling

1 Remove the cylinder head as described in Chapter 2A, Section 11 (4-cylinder engines) or Chapter 2B, Section 12 (5-cylinder engines).

2 On 4-cylinder engines, remove the inlet and exhaust manifolds as described in Chapter 2A, Section 11.

3 On 5-cylinder engines, if not already done, remove the inlet manifold as described in Chapter 4A, Section 15, and the exhaust manifold as described in Chapter 4A, Section 16.

4 Remove the fuel injectors as described in Chapter 4A, Section 11.

5 Remove the glow plugs as described in Chapter 5, Section 13.

6 On 5-cylinder engines, remove the camshaft sprockets as described in Chapter 2B, Section 7. Undo the retaining nut and remove the fuel injection pump drivebelt idler pulley.

7 Undo the retaining bolts and remove the coolant outlet elbows together with their gaskets/O-rings.

8 Where applicable, unscrew the coolant sensor and oil pressure switch from the cylinder head.

9 It is important that groups of components are kept together when they are removed and, if still serviceable, refitted in the same groups. If they are refitted randomly, accelerated wear leading to early failure will occur. Stowing groups of components in plastic bags or storage bins will help to keep everything in the right order – label them according to their

fitted location, eg 'No 1 exhaust', 'No 2 inlet', etc **(see illustration)**. (Note that No 1 cylinder is nearest the timing belt end of the engine.)
10 Check that the manufacturer's identification markings are visible on the camshaft bearing caps; if none can be found, make your own using a scriber or centre-punch **(see illustration)**.
11 The camshaft bearing cap nuts must be removed progressively and in sequence to avoid stressing the camshaft, as follows.

4-cylinder engines

12 Slacken the nuts from bearing caps Nos 5, 1 and 3 first, then at bearing caps 2 and 4. Slacken the nuts alternately and diagonally half a turn at a time until they can be removed by hand, then remove the bearing caps. Keep the caps in order and note their fitted positions.
Note: *Camshaft bearing caps are numbered 1 to 5 from the timing belt end.*

5-cylinder engines

13 Slacken the nuts from bearing caps Nos 2 and 4 first, then from bearing caps 1 and 3. Slacken the nuts alternately and diagonally half a turn at a time until they can be removed by hand, then remove the bearing caps. Keep the caps in order and note their fitted positions.
Note: *Camshaft bearing caps are numbered 1 to 4 from the timing belt end.*

All engines

14 Carefully lift the camshaft from the cylinder head, keeping it level and supported at both ends as it is removed so that the journals and lobes are not damaged **(see illustration)**. Remove the oil seal from the front of the camshaft and, on 5-cylinder engines, from the rear of the camshaft also.
15 Lift the hydraulic tappets from their bores and store them with the valve contact surface facing downwards, to prevent the oil from draining out **(see illustration)**. Make a note of the position of each tappet, as they must be fitted to the same valves on reassembly – accelerated wear leading to early failure will result if they are interchanged.
16 Turn the cylinder head over, and rest it on one side. Using a valve spring compressor, compress each valve spring in turn, extracting the split collets when the upper valve spring seat has been pushed far enough down the

valve stem to free them **(see illustrations)**. If the spring seat sticks, tap the upper jaw of the compressor with a hammer to free it.
17 Release the valve spring compressor and remove the upper spring seat, valve spring(s) and lower spring seat **(see illustrations)**. **Note:**

Depending on age and specification, engines may have concentric double valve springs, or single valve springs with no lower spring seat.
18 Withdraw the valve itself from the head gasket side of the cylinder head **(see illustration)**. If the valve sticks in the guide,

6.9 Keep groups of components together in labelled bags or boxes

6.10 Identification markings (arrowed) are visible on the camshaft bearing caps

6.14 Carefully lift the camshaft from the cylinder head

6.15 Lifting the hydraulic tappets from their bores

6.16a Using a valve spring compressor, compress each valve spring in turn...

6.16b ...and extract the split collets

6.17a Remove the upper spring seat...

6.17b ...and valve spring

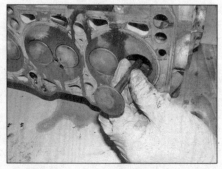
6.18 Withdraw the valve from the head gasket side of the cylinder head

6.19 Extract the valve stem oil seal from the top of the valve guide

carefully debur the end face with fine abrasive paper.

19 Using a pair of pliers, extract the valve stem oil seal from the top of the valve guide **(see illustration)**. Repeat this process and remove the remaining valves.

20 On 1.9 and 2.4 litre engines, if the swirl chambers are badly coked or burned and are in need of renewal, insert a pin punch through each injector hole, and carefully drive out the swirl chambers using a mallet **(see illustration)**. **Note:** *On 1.9 litre engines up to October 1993 with a fibre head gasket, a metal head gasket must be used on reassembly – under these circumstances, new swirl chambers must be fitted to match the new type of gasket.*

Cleaning

21 Using a suitable degreasing agent, remove all traces of oil deposits from the cylinder head, paying particular attention to the journal bearings, hydraulic tappet bores, valve guides and oilways. Scrape off any traces of old gasket from the mating surfaces, taking care not to score or gouge them. If using emery paper, do not use a grade of less than 100. Turn the head over and using a blunt blade, scrape any carbon deposits from the combustion chambers and ports. *Caution: Do not erode the sealing surface of the valve seat. Finally, wash the entire head casting with a suitable solvent to remove the remaining debris.*

22 Clean the valve heads and stems using a fine wire brush. If the valve is heavily coked,

6.20 Carefully drive out the swirl chambers using a pin punch and mallet

scrape off the majority of the deposits with a blunt blade first, then use the wire brush. *Caution: Do not erode the sealing surface of the valve face.*

23 Thoroughly clean the remainder of the components using solvent and allow them to dry completely. Discard the oil seals, as new items must be fitted when the cylinder head is reassembled.

Inspection

Cylinder head casting

Note: *The cylinder heads and valves cannot be reworked (although valves may be lapped in); new or exchange units must be obtained.*

24 Examine the head casting closely to identify any damage sustained or cracks that may have developed **(see illustration)**. Pay particular attention to the areas around the mounting holes and valve seats. If cracking is discovered between the valve seats, Volkswagen state that the cylinder head may be re-used, provided the cracks are no larger than 0.5 mm wide. More serious damage will mean the renewal of the cylinder head casting.

25 Moderately pitted and scorched valve seats can be repaired by lapping the valves in during reassembly, as described later in this Section. Badly worn or damaged valve seats may be restored by recutting; this is a highly specialised operation involving precision machining and accurate angle measurement and as such should be entrusted to an engine reconditioning specialist.

26 Measure any distortion of the gasket surfaces using a straight edge and a set

of feeler blades. Take one measurement longitudinally on both the inlet and exhaust manifold mating surfaces. Take several measurements across the head gasket surface, to assess the level of distortion in all planes **(see illustration)**. Compare the measurements with the figures in the Specifications. If there is any doubt about the condition of the cylinder head, seek the advice of an engine reconditioning specialist.

Camshaft

27 Visually inspect the camshaft for evidence of wear on the surfaces of the lobes and journals. Normally their surfaces should be smooth and have a dull shine; look for scoring, erosion or pitting and areas that appear highly polished – these are signs that wear has begun to occur. Accelerated wear will occur once the hardened exterior of the camshaft has been damaged, so always renew worn items. **Note:** *If these symptoms are visible on the tips of the camshaft lobes, check the corresponding tappet, as it will probably be worn as well.*

28 If the machined surfaces of the camshaft appear discoloured or 'blued', it is likely that it has been overheated at some point, probably due to inadequate lubrication. This may have distorted the shaft, so check the runout as follows: place the camshaft between two V-blocks and using a DTI gauge, measure the runout at the centre journal. If it exceeds the figure quoted in the Specifications at the start of this Chapter, camshaft renewal should be considered.

29 To measure the camshaft endfloat, temporarily refit the camshaft to the cylinder head, then fit the first and last bearing caps and tighten the retaining nuts securely. Anchor a DTI gauge to the timing belt end of the cylinder head and align the gauge probe with the camshaft axis. Push the camshaft to one end of the cylinder head as far as it will travel, then rest the DTI gauge probe on the end of the camshaft, and zero the gauge display. Push the camshaft as far as it will go to the other end of the cylinder head, and record the gauge reading. Verify the reading by pushing the camshaft back to its original position and checking that the gauge indicates zero again **(see illustration)**. **Note:** *The hydraulic tappets must not be fitted to the cylinder whilst this measurement is being taken.*

6.24 Look for cracking between the valve seats

6.26 Measuring the distortion of the cylinder head

6.29 Checking camshaft endfloat using a DTI gauge

30 Check that the camshaft endfloat measurement is within the limit listed in the Specifications. Wear outside of this limit is unlikely to be confined to any one component, so renewal of the camshaft, cylinder head and bearing caps must be considered; seek the advice of an engine reconditioning specialist.

31 The difference between the outside diameters of the camshaft bearing surfaces and the internal diameters formed by the bearing caps and the cylinder head must now be measured, this dimension is known as the camshaft bearing running clearance.

32 The dimensions of the camshaft bearing journals are not quoted by the manufacturer, so running clearance measurement by means of a micrometer and a bore gauge or internal vernier calipers cannot be recommended in this case.

33 Another (more accurate) method of measuring the running clearance involves the use of Plastigauge. This is a soft, plastic material supplied in thin 'sticks' of about the same diameter as a sewing needle. Lengths of Plastigauge are cut to length as required, laid on the camshaft bearing journals and crushed as the bearing caps are temporarily fitted and tightened. The Plastigauge spreads widthways as it is crushed; the running clearance can then be determined by measuring the increase in width using the card gauge supplied with the Plastigauge kit.

34 The following paragraphs describe this measurement procedure step by step, but note that a similar method is used to measure the crankshaft running clearances; refer to the illustrations in Section 13 for further guidance.

35 Ensure that the cylinder head, bearing cap and camshaft bearing surfaces are completely clean and dry. Lay the camshaft in position in the cylinder head.

36 Lay a length of Plastigauge on top of each of the camshaft bearing journals.

37 Lubricate each bearing cap with a little silicone release agent, then place them in position over the camshaft and tighten the retaining nuts down to the specified torque – refer to *Reassembly* later in this Section for guidance. **Note:** *Do not rotate the camshaft whilst the bearing caps are in place, as the measurements will be affected.*

38 Carefully remove the bearing caps again, lifting them vertically away from the camshaft to avoid disturbing the Plastigauge. The Plastigauge should remain on the camshaft bearing surface, squashed into a uniform sausage shape. If it disintegrates as the bearing caps are removed, re-clean the components and repeat the exercise, using a little more release agent on the bearing cap.

39 Hold the scale card supplied with the kit against each bearing journal, and match the width of the crushed Plastigauge with the graduated markings on the card, use this to determine the running clearances.

40 Compare the camshaft running clearance measurements with those listed in the Specifications; if any are outside the specified

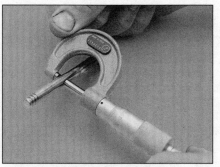

6.42 Measure the diameter of the valve stems with a micrometer

tolerance, the camshaft and cylinder head should be renewed. Note that undersize camshafts with bearing shells may be obtained from VAG dealers, but only as part of an exchange cylinder head package.

41 On completion, remove the bearing caps and camshaft, and clean of all remaining traces of Plastigauge and silicone release agent.

Valves and associated components

Note: *On all engines, the valve heads cannot be re-cut (although they may be lapped in); new or exchange units must be obtained.*

42 Examine each valve closely for signs of wear. Inspect the valve stems for wear ridges, scoring or variations in diameter; measure their diameters at several points along their lengths with a micrometer **(see illustration)**.

43 The valve heads should not be cracked, badly pitted or charred. Note that light pitting of the valve head can be rectified by grinding-in the valves during reassembly, as described later in this Section.

44 Check that the valve stem end face is free from excessive pitting or indentation; this would be caused by defective hydraulic tappets.

45 Place the valves in a V-block and using a DTI gauge, measure the runout at the valve head. A maximum figure is not quoted by the manufacturer, but the valve should be renewed if the runout appears excessive.

46 Insert each valve into its respective guide in the cylinder head and set up a DTI gauge against the edge of the valve head. With the valve end face flush with the top of the valve guide, measure the maximum side to

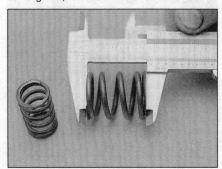

6.48 Measure the free length of each of the valve springs

6.46 Measure the maximum deflection of the valve in its guide, using a DTI gauge

side deflection of the valve in its guide **(see illustration)**.

47 If the measurement is out of tolerance, the valve and valve guide should be renewed as a pair. **Note:** *Valve guides are an interference fit in the cylinder head and their removal requires access to a hydraulic press. For this reason, it would be wise to entrust the job to an engine reconditioning specialist.*

48 Using vernier callipers, measure the free length of each of the valve springs. As a manufacturer's figure is not quoted, the only way to check the length of the springs is by comparison with a new component. Note that valve springs are usually renewed during a major engine overhaul **(see illustration)**.

49 Stand each spring on its end on a flat surface, against an engineer's square **(see illustration)**. Check the squareness of the spring visually; if it appears distorted, renew the spring.

Reassembly

Caution: Unless all new components are to be used, maintain groups when refitting valve train components – do not mix components between cylinders and ensure that components are refitted in their original positions.

50 To achieve a gas-tight seal between the valves and their seats, it will be necessary to grind, or 'lap', the valves in. To complete this process you will need a quantity of fine/coarse grinding paste and a grinding tool – this can either be of the dowel and rubber sucker type, or the automatic type which are driven by a rotary power tool.

6.49 Checking the squareness of a valve spring

2C•12 Engine removal and overhaul procedures

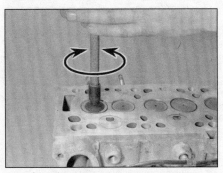

6.51 Grinding-in a valve

6.56a Fitting a swirl chamber

6.56b Swirl chamber locating recess

51 Smear a small quantity of *fine* grinding paste on the sealing face of the valve head. Turn the cylinder head over so that the combustion chambers are facing upwards and insert the valve into the correct guide. Attach the grinding tool to the valve head and using a backward/forward rotary action, grind the valve head into its seat. Periodically lift the valve and rotate it to redistribute the grinding paste **(see illustration)**.
52 Continue this process until the contact between valve and seat produces an unbroken, matt grey ring of uniform width, on both faces. Repeat the operation for the remaining valves.
53 If the valves and seats are so badly pitted that coarse grinding paste must be used, check first that there is enough material left

on both components to make this operation worthwhile – if too little material is left remaining, the valve stems may protrude too far above their guides, impeding the correct operation of the hydraulic tappets. Refer to an engine reconditioning specialist for advice.
54 Assuming the repair is feasible, work as described in the previous paragraphs but use the coarse grinding paste initially, to achieve a dull finish on the valve face and seat. Then, wash off coarse paste with solvent and repeat the process using fine grinding paste to obtain the correct finish.
55 When all the valves have been ground in, remove all traces of grinding paste from the cylinder head and valves with solvent, and allow them to dry completely.

56 Where necessary on 1.9 and 2.4 litre engines, fit new swirl chambers by driving them squarely into their housings with a mallet – use a block of wood to protect the face of the swirl chamber. Note the locating recess on the side of the chamber and the corresponding groove in the housing **(see illustrations)**.
57 On completion, the projection of the swirl chamber from the face of the cylinder head must be measured using a DTI gauge and compared with the limit quoted in the Specifications **(see illustration)**. If this limit is exceeded, there is a risk that the chamber may be struck by the piston, and in this case the advice of an engine reconditioning specialist should be sought.
58 Turn the head over and place it on a stand, or wooden blocks. Where applicable, fit the first lower spring seat into place, with the convex side facing the cylinder head **(see illustration)**.
59 Working on one valve at a time, lubricate the valve stem with clean engine oil, and insert it into the guide. Fit one of the protective plastic sleeves supplied with the new valve stem oil seals over the valve end face – this will protect the oil seal whilst it is being fitted **(see illustrations)**.
60 Dip a new valve stem seal in clean engine oil, and carefully push it over the valve and onto the top of the valve guide – take care not to damage the stem seal as it passes over the valve end face. Use a suitable long reach socket to press it firmly into position **(see illustrations)**.

6.57 Measuring swirl chamber projection using a DTI gauge

6.58 Where applicable, fit the lower spring seat with the convex face facing the cylinder head

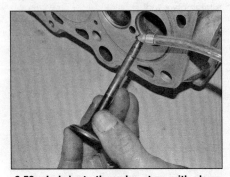

6.59a Lubricate the valve stem with clean engine oil...

6.59b ...and insert it into the guide

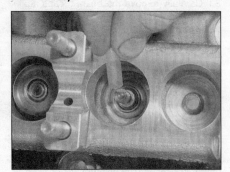

6.59c Fitting a protective plastic sleeve over the valve stem before fitting the stem seal

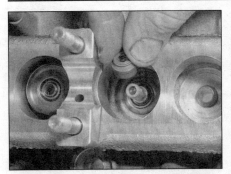

6.60a Fit a new valve stem seal over the valve

6.60b Use a long-reach socket to fit the valve stem seals

6.61 Locate the valve spring over the valve stem

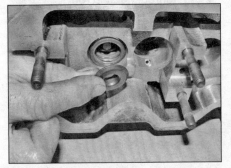

6.62a Fit the upper seat over the top of the valve spring

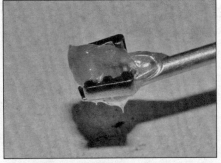

6.62b Use grease to hold the two halves of the split collet in the groove...

6.62c ...then position the collet on the valve stem

61 Locate the valve spring(s) over the valve stem **(see illustration)**. Where a lower spring seat is fitted, ensure that the springs locate squarely on the stepped surface of the seat. **Note:** *Depending on age and specification, engines may have either concentric double valve springs, **or** single valve springs with no lower spring seat.*

62 Fit the upper seat over the top of the spring(s), then using a valve spring compressor, compress the springs until the upper seat is pushed beyond the collet grooves in the valve stem. Refit the split collet, using a dab of grease to hold the two halves in the grooves **(see illustrations)**. Gradually release the spring compressor, checking that the collet remains correctly seated as the spring extends. When correctly seated, the upper seat should force the two halves of the collet together, and hold them

securely in the grooves in the end of the valve.

63 Repeat this process for the remaining sets of valve components. To settle the components after installation, strike the end of each valve stem with a mallet, using a block of wood to protect the stem from damage. Check before progressing any further that the spilt collets remain firmly held in the end of valve stem by the upper spring seat.

64 Smear some clean engine oil onto the sides of the hydraulic tappets, and fit them into position in their bores in the cylinder head. Push them down until they contact the valves, then lubricate the camshaft lobe contact surfaces **(see illustration)**.

65 Lubricate the camshaft and cylinder head bearing journals with clean engine oil, then carefully lower the camshaft into position on the cylinder head **(see illustration)**. Support

the ends of the shaft as it is inserted, to avoid damaging the lobes and journals.

66 Turn the camshaft so that the lobes for No 1 cylinder are pointing upwards.

4-Cylinder engines

67 Lubricate the lip of a new camshaft oil seal with clean engine oil and locate it over the end of the camshaft. Slide the seal along the camshaft until it locates in the lower half of its housing in the cylinder head **(see illustration)**.

68 The bearing cap mounting holes are drilled off-centre; ensure that they are fitted the correct way around **(see illustration)**.

69 Fit caps Nos 2 and 4 over the camshaft, and tighten the retaining nuts alternately and diagonally to the specified torque.

70 Smear the mating surfaces of cap No 1 with sealant then fit it, together with cap Nos 3

6.64 Fit the tappets into their bores in the cylinder head

6.65 Lubricate the camshaft and cylinder head bearing journals with clean engine oil

6.67 Fitting the camshaft oil seal

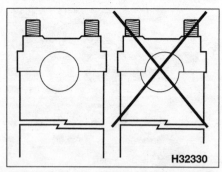

6.68 The camshaft bearing caps are drilled off-centre

6.70 Smear the mating surfaces of cap No 1 with sealant

82 Where applicable, refit the coolant sensor and oil pressure switch to the cylinder head.
83 Refit the coolant outlet elbows using new gaskets/O-rings.
84 Refit the camshaft sprockets as described in Chapter 2B, Section 7.
85 Refit the fuel injection pump drivebelt idler pulley and secure with the retaining nut.
86 Refit the glow plugs as described in Chapter 5, Section 13.
87 Refit the fuel injectors as described in Chapter 4A, Section 11.
88 Refit the cylinder head as described in Chapter 2B, Section 12.

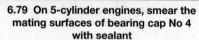

6.79 On 5-cylinder engines, smear the mating surfaces of bearing cap No 4 with sealant

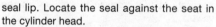
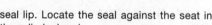
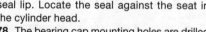

6.80 Fitting No 4 bearing cap

7 Piston/connecting rod assemblies –
removal and inspection

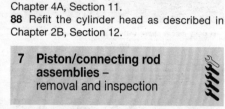

Removal

1 On 4-cylinder engines, remove the cylinder head, sump, baffle plate and oil pump as described in Chapter 2A.
2 On 5-cylinder engines, remove the cylinder head, sump and oil pump pickup as described in Chapter 2B.
3 Inspect the tops of the cylinder bores for ridges at the point where the pistons reach top dead centre. These must be removed otherwise the pistons may be damaged when they are pushed out of their bores. Use a scraper or ridge reamer to remove the ridges.
4 Rotate the crankshaft until piston No 1 is at bottom dead centre. On 4-cylinder engines, piston No 4 will also be at bottom dead centre. Unless they are already identified, mark the big-end bearing caps and connecting rods with their respective piston numbers, using a centre-punch or a scribe (see illustration). Note the orientation of the bearing caps in relation to the connecting rod; it may be difficult to see the manufacturer's markings at this stage, so scribe alignment arrows on them both to ensure correct reassembly.
5 Unscrew the bearing cap bolts half a turn at a time, until they can be removed and the cap withdrawn (see illustrations). Recover the bottom shell bearing, and tape it to the cap for safe keeping. Note that if the shell bearings are to be re-used, they must be refitted to the same connecting rod.

and 5, over the camshaft and tighten the nuts to the specified torque (see illustration).
71 Where applicable, refit the coolant sensor and oil pressure switch to the cylinder head.
72 Refit the coolant outlet elbows using new gaskets/O-rings.
73 Refit the glow plugs as described in Chapter 5, Section 13.
74 Refit the fuel injectors as described in Chapter 4A, Section 11.
75 Refit the inlet and exhaust manifolds as described in Chapter 2A, Section 11.
76 Refit the cylinder head as described in Chapter 2A, Section 11.

5-Cylinder engines

77 Lubricate the lips of the new oil seals in engine oil, then locate on the front and rear of the camshaft. Make sure the closed end of the seal faces outwards from the camshaft and take care not to damage the

seal lip. Locate the seal against the seat in the cylinder head.
78 The bearing cap mounting holes are drilled off-centre; ensure they are fitted the correct way round (see illustration 6.68).
79 Smear the mating surfaces of bearing cap No 4 with sealant (see illustration).
80 Oil the upper surfaces of the camshaft bearing journals, then fit Nos 2 and 4 bearing caps (see illustration). Ensure that they are fitted the right way around and in the correct locations, then progressively tighten the retaining bolts to the specified torque. To make sure the camshaft is tightened down evenly, first fit No 2 bearing cap then press down on the camshaft and fit No 4 bearing cap.
81 Smear the mating surfaces of bearing cap No 1 with sealant then fit caps 1 and 3 over the camshaft and progressively tighten the nuts to the specified torque.

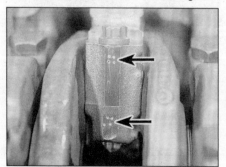

7.4 Mark the big-end caps and connecting rods with their piston numbers (arrowed)

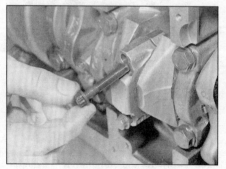

7.5a Unscrew the big-end cap bolts...

7.5b ...and remove the cap

6 Drive the piston out of the top of the bore using a piece of dowel or a hammer handle. As the piston and connecting rod emerge, recover the top shell bearing and tape it to the connecting rod for safekeeping (**see illustration**). Take care not to allow the connecting rod to damage the piston cooling jet as the piston is being removed.

7 On 4-cylinder engines remove No 4 piston and connecting rod in the same manner, then turn the crankshaft through half a turn and remove No 2 and 3 pistons and connecting rods. On 5-cylinder engines turn the crankshaft to bring piston No 2 to bottom dead centre, then remove No 2 piston. Similarly remove pistons 4, 5 and 3. Remember to maintain the components in their cylinder groups, whilst they are in a dismantled state (**see illustration**).

8 Undo the retaining bolts and withdraw the piston cooling jets from the bottom of the cylinder (**see illustrations**).

Inspection

9 Insert a small flat-bladed screwdriver into the removal slot and prise the gudgeon pin circlips from each piston. Push out the gudgeon pin, and separate the piston and connecting rod (**see illustrations**). Discard the circlips as new items must be fitted on reassembly. If the pin proves difficult to remove, heat the piston to 60°C with hot water – the resulting expansion will then allow the two components to be separated.

10 Before an inspection of the pistons can be carried out, the existing piston rings must be removed, using a removal/installation tool, or an old feeler blade if such a tool is not available (**see illustration**). Always remove the upper piston rings first, expanding them to clear the piston crown. The rings are very brittle and will snap if they are stretched too much – sharp edges are produced when this happens, so protect your eyes and hands. Discard the rings on removal, as new items must be fitted when the engine is reassembled.

11 Use a section of old piston ring to scrape the carbon deposits out of the ring grooves, taking care not to score or gouge the edges of the groove.

12 Carefully scrape away all traces of carbon from the tops of the pistons. A hand-held wire brush (or a piece of fine emery cloth) can be

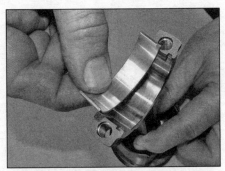
7.6 Removing the top shell bearing from the connecting rod

7.8a Remove the piston cooling jet retaining screws (arrowed)...

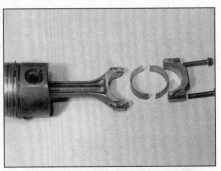
7.7 Keep the piston/connecting rod components in their cylinder groups

7.8b ...and withdraw the jets from their mounting holes

used, once the majority of the deposits have been scraped away. Be careful not to remove any metal from the piston, as it is relatively soft. **Note:** *Make sure each piston is kept identified for position during cleaning.*

13 Once the deposits have been removed, clean the pistons and connecting rods with paraffin or a suitable solvent, and dry thoroughly. Make sure that the oil return holes in the ring grooves are clear.

14 Examine the pistons for signs of excessive wear or damage. Some normal wear will be apparent, in the form of a vertical 'grain' on the piston thrust surfaces and a slight looseness of the top compression ring in its groove. Abnormal wear should be carefully examined, to assess whether the component is still serviceable and what the cause of the wear might be.

15 Scuffing or scoring of the piston skirt may indicate that the engine has been overheating, through inadequate cooling or lubrication.

Scorch marks on the skirt indicate that blow-by has occurred, perhaps caused by worn bores or piston rings. Burnt areas on the piston crown are usually an indication of pre-ignition, pinking or detonation. In extreme cases, the piston crown may be melted by operating under these conditions. Corrosion pit marks in the piston crown indicate that coolant has seeped into the combustion chamber. The faults causing these symptoms must be corrected before the engine is brought back into service, or the same damage will recur.

16 Check the pistons, connecting rods, gudgeon pins and bearing caps for cracks. Lay the connecting rods on a flat surface, and look along the length to see if it appears bent or twisted. If you have doubts about their condition, have them measured by an engine reconditioning specialist. Inspect the small-end bush bearing in the connecting rod for signs of wear or cracking.

7.9a Insert a small screwdriver into the slot and prise off the gudgeon pin circlips

7.9b Push out the gudgeon pin and separate the piston and connecting rod

7.10 Piston rings can be removed using an old feeler blade

7.17 Using a micrometer, measure the diameter of all four pistons

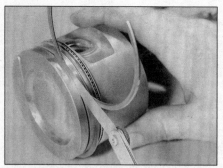

7.18 Measuring the piston ring-to-groove clearance using a feeler blade

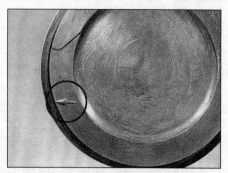

7.20 The piston crown is marked with an arrow which must point towards the timing belt end of the engine

17 Using a micrometer, measure the diameter of all four pistons at a point 10 mm from the bottom of the skirt, at right angles to the gudgeon pin axis **(see illustration)**. Compare the measurements with those listed in the Specifications. If the piston diameter is out of the tolerance band listed for its particular size, then it must be renewed. **Note:** *If the cylinder block was rebored during a previous overhaul, oversize pistons may already have been fitted.* Record all of the measurements and use them to check the piston clearances when the cylinder bores are measured, later in this Chapter.

18 Locate a new piston ring in the appropriate groove and measure the ring-to-groove clearance using a feeler blade **(see illustration)**. Note that the rings are of different widths, so use the correct ring for the groove. Compare the measurements with those listed; if the clearances are outside the tolerance band, then the piston must be renewed. Confirm this by checking the width of the piston ring with a micrometer.

19 Examine the small-end bearing and gudgeon pin for wear and damage. If excessive, the gudgeon pin will have to be renewed and a new bush fitted to the connecting rod. This work must be entrusted to an engine reconditioning specialist.

20 The orientation of the piston with respect to the connecting rod must be correct when the two are reassembled. The piston crown is marked with an arrow (which may be obscured by carbon deposits) **(see illustration)**; this must point towards the timing belt end of the engine when the piston is installed. The

connecting rod and its bearing cap both have recesses machined into them, close to their mating surfaces - these recesses must both face the same way as the arrow on the piston crown (ie towards the timing belt end of the engine) when correctly installed. Reassemble the two components to satisfy this requirement.

21 Lubricate the gudgeon pin and small-end bush with clean engine oil. Slide the pin into the piston, engaging the connecting rod small-end. Fit two new circlips to the piston at either end of the gudgeon pin. Repeat this operation for the remaining pistons.

8 Crankshaft – removal and inspection

Removal

Note: *If no work is to be done on the pistons and connecting rods, then removal of the cylinder head and pistons will not be necessary. Instead, the pistons need only be pushed far enough up the bores so that the connecting rods are positioned clear of the crankpins. The use of an engine stand is strongly recommended.*

1 With reference to Chapter 2A or 2B as applicable, carry out the following:
a) *Remove the timing belt and crankshaft sprocket.*
b) *Remove the clutch components and flywheel or driveplate (as applicable).*

c) *Remove the sump, baffle plate, oil pump and pickup tube.*
d) *Remove the rear crankshaft oil seal and housing. On 4-cylinder engines remove the front oil seal and housing.*

2 Remove the pistons and connecting rods or disconnect them from the crankshaft as described in Section 7 (see Note above).

3 With the cylinder block upside down on the bench, carry out a check of the crankshaft endfloat as follows. **Note:** *This can only be accomplished when the crankshaft is still installed in the cylinder block/crankcase, but is free to move.* Set up a DTI gauge so that the probe is in line with the crankshaft axis and is in contact with a fixed point on the end of the crankshaft. Push the crankshaft along its axis to the end of its travel, and then zero the gauge. Push the crankshaft fully the other way, and record the endfloat indicated on the dial **(see illustration)**. Compare the result with the figure given in the Specifications and establish whether new thrustwashers are required.

4 If a dial gauge is not available, feeler blades can be used. First push the crankshaft fully towards the flywheel end of the engine, then use a feeler blade to measure the gap between cylinder No 3 crankpin web (4-cylinder engines) or No 4 crankpin web (5-cylinder engines) and the main bearing thrustwasher **(see illustration)**. Compare the results with the Specifications.

5 Observe the manufacturer's identification marks on the main bearing caps. The number indicates the cap position in the crankcase, as counted from the timing belt end of the engine **(see illustration)**.

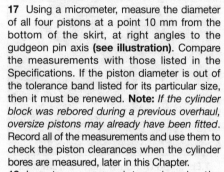

8.3 Measuring crankshaft endfloat using a DTI gauge

8.4 Measuring crankshaft endfloat using feeler blades

8.5 Manufacturer's identification markings on the main bearing caps (arrowed)

8.6 Removing the main bearing cap bolts

8.7 Lifting the crankshaft from the crankcase

8.12 Use a micrometer to measure the diameter of each main bearing journal

6 Loosen the main bearing cap bolts half a turn at a time, until they can be removed **(see illustration)**. Using a soft-faced mallet, strike the caps lightly to free them from the crankcase. Recover the lower main bearing shells, taping them to the cap for safekeeping. Mark them to aid identification, but do not score or scratch them in any way.

7 Carefully lift the crankshaft out, taking care not to dislodge the upper main bearing shells **(see illustration)**.

8 Extract the upper main bearing shells from the crankcase, and tape them to their respective bearing caps. Remove the two thrustwasher bearings from either side of No 3 bearing saddle (4-cylinder engines) or No 4 bearing saddle (5-cylinder engines).

9 With the shell bearings removed, observe the recesses machined into the bearing caps and crankcase – these provide location for the lugs which protrude from the shell bearings

and so prevent them from being fitted incorrectly.

Inspection

10 Wash the crankshaft in a suitable solvent and allow it to dry. Flush the oil holes thoroughly, to ensure they are not blocked – use a pipe cleaner or a needle brush if necessary.

11 Inspect the main bearing and crankpin journals carefully. If uneven wear, cracking, scoring or pitting are evident then the crankshaft should be reground by an engine reconditioning specialist, and refitted to the engine with undersize bearings.

12 Use a micrometer to measure the diameter of each main bearing journal **(see illustration)**. Taking a number of measurements on the surface of each journal will reveal if it is worn unevenly. Differences in diameter measured at 90° intervals indicate that the journal is out of round. Differences in diameter measured

along the length of the journal, indicate that the journal is tapered. Again, if wear is detected, the crankshaft must be reground by an engine reconditioning specialist, and undersize bearings will be needed.

13 Check the oil seal journals at either end of the crankshaft. If they appear excessively scored or damaged, they may cause the new seals to leak when the engine is reassembled. It may be possible to repair the journal; seek the advice of an engine reconditioning specialist.

14 Measure the crankshaft runout by setting up a DTI gauge on the centre main bearing (4-cylinder engines) or 3rd and 4th main bearings (5-cylinder engines) and rotating the shaft in V-blocks. The maximum deflection of the gauge will indicate the runout. Take precautions to protect the bearing journals and oil seal mating surfaces from damage during this procedure. A maximum runout figure is not quoted by the manufacturer, but use the figure of 0.03 mm as a rough guide. If the runout exceeds this figure, crankshaft renewal should be considered – consult an engine reconditioning specialist for advice.

15 Refer to Section 11 for details of main and big-end bearing inspection.

9 Intermediate shaft – removal and refitting

Note: *This Section applies to 4-cylinder engines only.*

Removal

1 Refer to Chapter 2A and remove the timing belt and intermediate shaft sprocket.

2 Before the shaft is removed, the endfloat must be checked. Anchor a DTI gauge to the cylinder block with its probe in line with the intermediate shaft centre axis. Push the shaft into the cylinder block to the end of its travel, zero the DTI gauge and then draw the shaft out to the opposite end of its travel. Record the maximum deflection and compare the figure with that listed in Specifications – renew the shaft if the endfloat exceeds this limit **(see illustration)**.

3 Slacken the retaining bolts and withdraw the intermediate shaft flange. Recover the O-ring seal, then press out the oil seal **(see illustrations)**.

9.2 Check the intermediate shaft endfloat using a DTI gauge

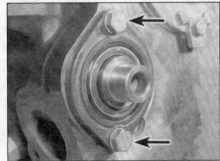
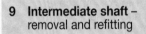

9.3a Slacken the retaining bolts (arrowed)...

9.3b ...and withdraw the intermediate shaft flange

9.3c Press out the oil seal...

9.3d ...then recover the O-ring seal

4 Withdraw the intermediate shaft from the cylinder block and inspect the drive gear at the end of the shaft; if the teeth show signs of excessive wear, or are damaged in any way, the shaft should be renewed.

5 If the oil seal has been leaking, check the shaft mating surface for signs of scoring or damage.

Refitting

6 Liberally oil the intermediate shaft bearing surfaces and drive gear, then carefully guide the shaft into the cylinder block and engage the journal at the leading end with its support bearing.

7 Press a new shaft oil seal into its housing in the intermediate shaft flange and fit a new O-ring seal to the inner sealing surface of the flange.

8 Lubricate the inner lip of the seal with clean engine oil, and slide the flange and seal over the end of the intermediate shaft. Ensure that the O-ring is correctly seated, then fit the flange retaining bolts and tighten them to the specified torque. Check that the intermediate shaft can rotate freely.

9 Refer to Chapter 2A and refit the intermediate shaft sprocket and timing belt.

10 Cylinder block/crankcase – cleaning and inspection

Cleaning

1 Remove all external components as applicable including lifting eyes, mounting

10.6 To clean the cylinder block threads, run a correct-size tap into the holes

brackets, the coolant pump, oil filter mounting housing, fuel injection pump mounting bracket and electrical switches/sensors from the block. For complete cleaning, the core plugs should ideally be removed. Drill a small hole in the plugs, then insert a self-tapping screw into the hole. Extract the plugs by pulling on the screw with a pair of grips, or by using a slide hammer.

2 Scrape all traces of gasket and sealant from the cylinder block/crankcase, taking care not to damage the sealing surfaces.

3 Remove all oil gallery plugs (where fitted). The plugs are usually very tight – they may have to be drilled out, and the holes re-tapped. Use new plugs when the engine is reassembled.

4 If the casting is extremely dirty, it should be steam-cleaned. After this, clean all oil holes and galleries one more time. Flush all internal passages with warm water until the water runs clear. Dry thoroughly, and apply a light film of oil to all mating surfaces and cylinder bores, to prevent rusting. If you have access to compressed air, use it to speed up the drying process, and to blow out all the oil holes and galleries.

 Warning: Wear eye protection when using compressed air!

5 If the castings are not very dirty, you can do an adequate cleaning job with hot, soapy water and a stiff brush. Take plenty of time, and do a thorough job. Regardless of the cleaning method used, be sure to clean all oil holes and galleries very thoroughly, and to dry all components well. Protect the cylinder bores as described above, to prevent rusting.

6 All threaded holes must be clean, to ensure accurate torque readings during reassembly. To clean the threads, run the correct-size tap into each of the holes to remove rust, corrosion, thread sealant or sludge, and to restore damaged threads **(see illustration)**. If possible, use compressed air to clear the holes of debris produced by this operation. **Note:** *Take extra care to exclude all cleaning liquid from blind tapped holes, as the casting may be cracked by hydraulic action if a bolt is threaded into a hole containing liquid.*

7 Apply suitable sealant to the new oil gallery plugs, and insert them into the holes in the block. Tighten them securely.

8 If the engine is not going to be reassembled immediately, cover it with a large plastic bag to keep it clean; protect all mating surfaces and the cylinder bores as described above, to prevent rusting.

Inspection

9 Visually check the casting for cracks and corrosion. Look for stripped threads in the threaded holes. If there has been any history of internal water leakage, it may be worthwhile having an engine reconditioning specialist check the cylinder block/crankcase with professional equipment. If defects are found, have them renewed or if possible, repaired.

10 Check the cylinder bores for scuffing or scoring. Any evidence of this kind of damage should be cross-checked with an inspection of the pistons (see Section 7 of this Chapter). If the damage is in its early stages, it may be possible to repair the block by reboring it. Seek the advice of an engine reconditioning specialist.

11 To allow an accurate assessment of the wear in the cylinder bores to be made, their diameter must be measured at a number of points, as follows. Insert a bore gauge into bore No 1 and take three measurements in line with the crankshaft axis; one at the top of the bore, roughly 10 mm below the top of the bore, one halfway down the bore and one at a point roughly 10 mm above the bottom of the bore **(see illustration)**. **Note:** *Stand the cylinder block squarely on a workbench during this procedure, inaccurate results may be obtained if the measurements are taken when the engine is mounted on a stand.*

12 Rotate the bore gauge through 90°, so that it is at right angles to the crankshaft axis and repeat the measurements detailed in paragraph 11. Record all six measurements, and compare them with the data listed in the Specifications. If the difference in diameter between any two cylinders exceeds the wear limit, or if any one cylinder exceeds its maximum bore diameter, then *all four* cylinders will have to be rebored and oversize pistons will have to be fitted.

13 Use the piston diameter measurements recorded earlier (see Section 7) to calculate the piston-to-bore clearances. Figures are not available from the manufacturer, so seek the advice of an engine reconditioning specialist.

14 Place the cylinder block on a level work surface, crankcase downwards. Use a straight edge and a set of feeler blades to measure the distortion of the cylinder head mating surface in both planes. A maximum figure is not quoted by the manufacturer, but use the figure of 0.05 mm as a rough guide. If the measurement exceeds this figure, repair may be possible by machining – consult an engine reconditioning specialist for advice.

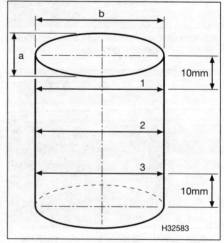

10.11 Bore measurement points

15 Before the engine can be reassembled, the cylinder bores must be honed. This process involves using an abrasive tool to produce a fine, cross-hatch pattern on the inner surface of the bore. This has the effect of seating the piston rings, resulting in a good seal between the piston and cylinder. There are two types of honing tool available to the home mechanic, both are driven by a rotary power tool, such as a drill. The bottle brush hone is a stiff, cylindrical brush with abrasive stones bonded to its bristles. The more conventional surfacing hone has abrasive stones mounted on spring-loaded legs. For the inexperienced home mechanic, satisfactory results will be achieved more easily using the bottle brush hone. **Note:** *If you are unwilling to tackle cylinder bore honing, an engine reconditioning specialist will be able to carry out the job for you at a reasonable cost.*

16 Carry out the honing as follows; you will need one of the honing tools described above, a power drill, a supply of clean rags, some honing oil and a pair of safety glasses.

17 Fit the honing tool in the drill chuck. Lubricate the cylinder bores with honing oil and insert the honing tool into the first bore, compressing the stones to allow it to fit. Turn on the drill and as the tool rotates, move it up and down in the bore at a rate that produces a fine cross-hatch pattern on the surface. The lines of the pattern should ideally cross at about 50 to 60°, although some piston ring manufacturer's may quote a different angle; check the literature supplied with the new rings **(see illustration)**.

 Warning: Wear safety glasses to protect your eyes from debris flying off the honing tool.

18 Use plenty of oil during the honing process. Do not remove any more material than is necessary to produce the required finish. When removing the hone tool from the bore, do not pull it out whilst it is still rotating; maintain the up/down movement until the chuck has stopped, then withdraw the tool whilst rotating the chuck by hand, in the normal direction of rotation.

19 Wipe out the oil and swarf with a rag and proceed to the next bore. When all four bores have been honed, thoroughly clean the whole cylinder block in hot soapy water to remove all traces of honing oil and debris. The block is clean when a clean rag, moistened with new engine oil does not pick up any grey residue when wiped along the bore.

20 Apply a light coating of engine oil to the mating surfaces and cylinder bores to prevent rust forming.

21 Refit all the components removed in paragraph 1.

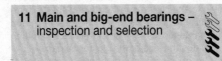

11 Main and big-end bearings – inspection and selection

Inspection

1 Even though the main and big-end bearings

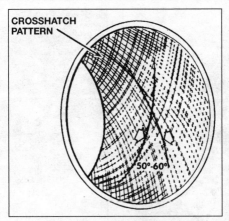

10.17 Cylinder bore honing pattern

should be renewed during the engine overhaul, the old bearings should be retained for close examination, as they may reveal valuable information about the condition of the engine **(see illustration)**.

2 Bearing failure can occur due to lack of lubrication, the presence of dirt or other foreign particles, overloading the engine, or corrosion. Regardless of the cause of bearing failure, the cause must be corrected before the engine is reassembled, to prevent it from happening again.

3 When examining the bearing shells, remove them from the cylinder block/crankcase, the main bearing caps, the connecting rods and the connecting rod big-end bearing caps. Lay them out on a clean surface in the same general position as their location in the engine. This will enable you to match any bearing problems with the corresponding crankshaft journal. *Do not* touch any shell's internal bearing surface with your fingers while checking it, or the delicate surface may be scratched.

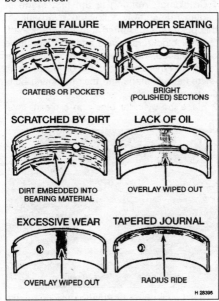

11.1 Typical bearing failures

4 Dirt and other foreign matter gets into the engine in a variety of ways. It may be left in the engine during assembly, or it may pass through filters or the crankcase ventilation system. It may get into the oil, and from there into the bearings. Metal chips from machining operations and normal engine wear are often present. Abrasives are sometimes left in engine components after reconditioning, especially when parts are not thoroughly cleaned using the proper cleaning methods. Whatever the source, these foreign objects often end up embedded in the soft bearing material, and are easily recognised. Large particles will not embed in the bearing, but will score or gouge the bearing and journal. The best prevention for this cause of bearing failure is to clean all parts thoroughly, and keep everything spotlessly-clean during engine assembly. Frequent and regular engine oil and filter changes are also recommended.

5 Lack of lubrication (or lubrication breakdown) has a number of interrelated causes. Excessive heat (which thins the oil), overloading (which squeezes the oil from the bearing face) and oil leakage (from excessive bearing clearances, worn oil pump or high engine speeds) all contribute to lubrication breakdown. Blocked oil passages, which usually are the result of misaligned oil holes in a bearing shell, will also oil-starve a bearing, and destroy it. When lack of lubrication is the cause of bearing failure, the bearing material is wiped or extruded from the steel backing of the bearing. Temperatures may increase to the point where the steel backing turns blue from overheating.

6 Driving habits can have a definite effect on bearing life. Full-throttle, low-speed operation (labouring the engine) puts very high loads on bearings, tending to squeeze out the oil film. These loads cause the bearings to flex, which produces fine cracks in the bearing face (fatigue failure). Eventually, the bearing material will loosen in pieces, and tear away from the steel backing.

7 Short-distance driving leads to corrosion of bearings, because insufficient engine heat is produced to drive off the condensed water and corrosive gases. These products collect in the engine oil, forming acid and sludge. As the oil is carried to the engine bearings, the acid attacks and corrodes the bearing material.

8 Incorrect bearing installation during engine assembly will lead to bearing failure as well. Tight-fitting bearings leave insufficient bearing running clearance, and will result in oil starvation. Dirt or foreign particles trapped behind a bearing shell result in high spots on the bearing, which lead to failure.

9 *Do not* touch any shell's internal bearing surface with your fingers during reassembly as there is a risk of scratching the delicate surface, or of depositing particles of dirt on it.

10 As mentioned at the beginning of this Section, the bearing shells should be renewed as a matter of course during engine overhaul. To do otherwise is false economy.

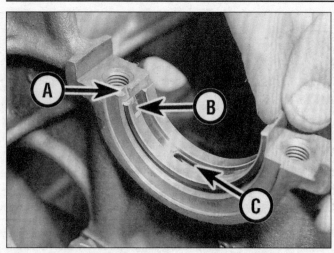

13.3 Bearing shells correctly refitted

A   Recess in bearing   B   Lug on bearing shell
     saddle   C   Oil hole

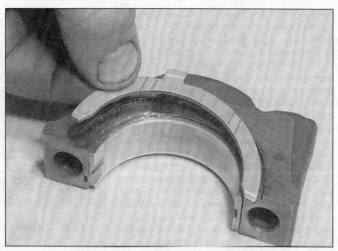

13.4 Fitting the crankshaft thrustwashers

Selection – main and big-end bearings

11 Main and big-end bearings for the engines described in this Chapter are available in standard sizes and a range of undersizes to suit reground crankshafts. Refer to the Specifications for details.

12 The running clearances will need to be checked when the crankshaft is refitted with its new bearings (see Section 13).

12 Engine overhaul – reassembly sequence

1 Before reassembly begins, ensure that all new parts have been obtained, and that all necessary tools are available. Read through the entire procedure to familiarise yourself with the work involved, and to ensure that all items necessary for reassembly of the engine are at hand. In addition to all normal tools and materials, thread-locking compound will be needed. A suitable tube of silicone sealant will also be required for the joint faces that are without gaskets. It is recommended that the manufacturer's own products are used, which are specially formulated for this purpose; the relevant product names are quoted in the text of each Section where they are required.

2 In order to save time and avoid problems, engine reassembly should ideally be carried out in the following order:

a) Crankshaft (see Section 13).
b) Piston/connecting rod assemblies (see Section 15).
c) Oil pump (Chapter 2A, Section 16 or Chapter 2B, Section 17).
d) Sump (Chapter 2A, Section 15 or Chapter 2B, Section 16).
e) Flywheel/driveplate (Chapter 2A, Section 13 or Chapter 2B, Section 14).
f) Cylinder head (Chapter 2A, Section 11 or Chapter 2B, Section 12).

g) Timing belt, sprockets and tensioner (Chapter 2A, Sections 4 and 5 or Chapter 2B, Sections 4, 5 and 7).
h) Exhaust manifold (Chapter 4A, Section 16).
i) Inlet manifold (Chapter 4A, Section 15).
j) Engine external components and ancillaries.
k) Auxiliary drivebelts, pulleys and tensioners.

3 At this stage, all engine components should be absolutely clean and dry, with all faults repaired. The components should be laid out (or in individual containers) on a completely clean work surface.

13 Crankshaft – refitting and running clearance check

1 Crankshaft refitting is the first stage of engine reassembly following overhaul. At this point, it is assumed that the crankshaft, cylinder block/crankcase and bearings have been cleaned, inspected and reconditioned or renewed. Where removed, the oil jets must be refitted at this stage and their mounting bolts tightened securely.

2 Place the cylinder block on a clean, level

13.8 Lay a piece of Plastigauge on each journal, in line with the crankshaft axis

worksurface, with the crankcase facing upwards. Wipe out the inner surfaces of the main bearing caps and crankcase with a clean cloth – they must be kept spotlessly clean.

3 Clean the rear surface of the new bearing shells with a cloth and lay them on the bearing saddles in the crankcase. Ensure that the orientation lugs on the shells engage with the recesses in the saddles, and that the oil holes are correctly aligned **(see illustration)**. Do not hammer or otherwise force the bearing shells into place. It is critically important that the surfaces of the bearings are kept free from damage and contamination.

4 Fit the thrustwashers either side of the No 3 bearing saddle (4-cylinder engines) or No 4 bearing saddle (5-cylinder engines). Use a small quantity of grease to hold them in place. Ensure that they are seated correctly in the machined recesses, with the oil grooves facing outwards **(see illustration)**.

5 Give the newly-fitted main bearing shells and the crankshaft journals a final clean with a cloth. Check that the oil holes in the crankshaft are free from dirt, as any left here will become embedded in the new bearings when the engine is first started.

6 Carefully lay the crankshaft in the crankcase, taking care not to dislodge the bearing shells.

Running clearance check

7 When the crankshaft and bearings are refitted, a clearance must exist between them to allow lubricant to circulate. This clearance is impossible to check using feeler blades, so Plastigauge is used. This is a thin strip of soft plastic that is crushed between the bearing shells and journals when the bearing caps are tightened up. The change in its width then indicates the size of the clearance gap.

8 Cut off pieces of Plastigauge, just shorter than the length of the crankshaft journal. Lay a piece on each journal, in line with its axis **(see illustration)**.

9 Wipe off the rear surfaces of the new lower half main bearing shells and fit them to the main bearing caps, ensuring the locating lugs engage correctly **(see illustration)**.
10 Wipe the front surfaces of the bearing shells and, if available, give them a light coating of silicone release agent – this will prevent the Plastigauge from sticking to the shell. Fit the caps in their correct locations on the bearing saddles, using the manufacturer's markings as a guide. Ensure that they are correctly orientated – the caps should be fitted such that the recesses for the bearing shell locating lugs are on the same side as those in the bearing saddle.
11 Working from the centre bearing cap, tighten the bolts one half turn at a time until they are all correctly tightened to their specified torque. Do not let the crankshaft turn at all whilst the Plastigauge is in place. Progressively unbolt the bearing caps and remove them, taking care not to dislodge the Plastigauge.
12 The width of the crushed Plastigauge can now be measured, using the scale provided **(see illustration)**. Use the correct scale, as both imperial and metric are printed. This measurement indicates the running clearance – compare it with that listed in the Specifications. If the clearance is outside the tolerance, it may be due to dirt or debris trapped under the bearing surface; try cleaning them again and repeat the clearance check. If the results are still unacceptable, re-check the journal diameters and the bearing sizes. If the Plastigauge is thicker at one end, the journals may be tapered, and will require regrinding.
13 When you are satisfied that the clearances are correct, carefully remove the remains of the Plastigauge from the journals and bearings faces. Use a soft, plastic or wooden scraper as anything metallic is likely to damage the surfaces.

Crankshaft – final refitting

14 Lift the crankshaft out of the crankcase. Wipe off the surfaces of the bearings in the crankcase and the bearing caps.
15 Liberally coat the bearing shells in the crankcase with clean engine oil **(see illustration)**.
16 Lower the crankshaft into position so that No 1 cylinder crankpin is at BDC, ready for fitting No 1 piston.
17 Lubricate the lower bearing shells in the

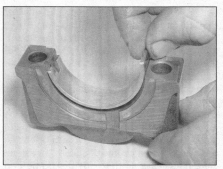
13.9 Fit the new lower half main bearing shells to the main bearing caps

main bearing caps with clean engine oil, then fit the thrustwashers to each side of bearing cap No 3 or No 4 (as applicable), noting that the lugs protruding from the washers engage the recesses in the side of the bearing cap **(see illustrations)**. Make sure that the locating lugs on the shells are still engaged with the corresponding recesses in the caps.
18 Fit the main bearing caps in the correct order and orientation – No 1 bearing cap must be at the timing belt end of the engine and the bearing shell locating recesses in the bearing saddles and caps must be adjacent to each other **(see illustrations)**. Insert the bearing cap bolts and hand tighten them only.
19 Working from the centre bearing cap outwards, tighten the retaining bolts to their specified torque.
20 Check that the crankshaft rotates freely by turning it manually. If resistance is felt, re-check the running clearances, as described above.

13.15 Lubricate the upper bearing shells...

13.12 Measure the width of the crushed Plastigauge using the scale provided

21 Carry out a check of the crankshaft endfloat as described at the beginning of Section 8. If the thrust surfaces of the crankshaft have been checked and new thrust bearings have been fitted, then the endfloat should be within specification.
22 Refit the pistons and connecting rods or reconnect them to the crankshaft as described in Section 15.
23 With reference to Chapter 2A or 2B as applicable, carry out the following:
a) *Refit the crankshaft rear oil seal housing, together with a new oil seal.*
b) *On 4-cylinder engines, refit the front oil seal and housing, together with a new oil seal.*
c) *Refit the oil pump and pick-up tube, baffle plate and sump.*
d) *Refit the flywheel and clutch or driveplate (as applicable).*
e) *Refit the crankshaft sprocket and timing belt.*

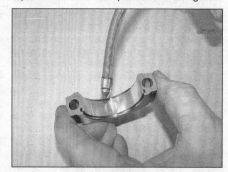
13.17a ...and lower bearing shells with clean engine oil...

13.17b ...then fit the thrustwashers each side of the bearing cap

13.18a Fitting No 4 main bearing cap on a 5-cylinder engine

13.18b Fitting No1 main bearing cap

14.5 Checking a piston ring end gap using a feeler blade

14 Pistons and piston rings – assembly

1 At this point it is assumed that the pistons have been correctly assembled to their respective connecting rods and that the piston ring-to-groove clearances have been checked. If not, refer to the end of Section 7.

2 Before the rings can be fitted to the pistons, the end gaps must be checked with the rings fitted into the cylinder bores.

3 Lay out the piston assemblies and the new ring sets on a clean work surface so that the components are kept together in their groups during and after end gap checking. Place the crankcase on the work surface on its side, allowing access to the top and bottom of the bores.

4 Take the No 1 piston top ring and insert it into the top of the bore. Using the No 1 piston, push the ring close to the bottom of the bore, at the lowest point of the piston travel. Ensure that it is perfectly square in the bore by pushing firmly against the piston crown.

5 Use a set of feeler blades to measure the gap between the ends of the piston ring. The correct blade will just pass through the gap with a minimal amount of resistance **(see illustration)**. Compare this measurement with that listed in Specifications. Check that you have the correct ring before deciding that a gap is incorrect. Repeat the operation for the remaining rings.

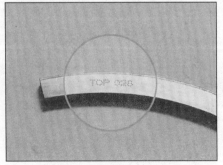

14.7 Piston ring TOP marking

6 If new rings are being fitted, it is unlikely that the end gaps will be too small. If a measurement is found to be undersize, it must be corrected or there is the risk that the ends of the ring may contact each other during operation, possibly resulting in engine damage. This is achieved by gradually filing down the ends of the ring, using a file clamped in a vice. Fit the ring over the file such that both its ends contact opposite faces of the file. Move the ring along the file, removing small amounts of material at a time. Take great care as the rings are brittle and form sharp edges if they fracture. Remember to keep the rings and piston assemblies in the correct order.

7 When all the piston ring end gaps have been verified, they can be fitted to the pistons. Work from the lowest ring groove (oil control ring) upwards. Note that the oil control ring comprises two side rails separated by a expander ring. Note also that the two compression rings are different in cross-section, and so must be fitted in the correct groove and the right way up, using a piston ring fitting tool. Both of the compression rings have marks stamped on one side to indicate the top facing surface. Ensure that these marks face up when the rings are fitted **(see illustration)**.

8 Distribute the end gaps around the piston, spaced at 120° intervals to the each other. *Note: If the piston ring manufacturer supplies specific fitting instructions with the rings, follow these exclusively.*

15 Piston/connecting rod assemblies – refitting and big-end bearing clearance check

Big-end running clearance check

Note: At this point, it is assumed that the crankshaft has been fitted to the engine, as described in Section 13.

1 As with the main bearings, a running clearance must exist between the big-end crankpin and its bearing shells to allow oil to circulate. There are two methods of checking the size of the running clearance, as described in the following paragraphs.

2 Place the cylinder block on a clean, level worksurface, with the crankcase facing upwards. Position the crankshaft such that crankpin No 1 is at BDC.

3 The first method is the least accurate and involves fitting the big-end bearing caps to the connecting rods away from the crankshaft, but with the bearing shells in place. **Note:** *Correct orientation of the bearing caps is critical; refer to the notes in Section 7.* The internal diameter formed by the assembled big-end is then measured using internal vernier callipers. The diameter of the respective crankpin is then subtracted from this measurement and the result is the running clearance.

4 The second method of carrying out this check involves the use of Plastigauge, in the same manner as the main bearing running clearance check (see Section 13) and is much more accurate than the previous method. Clean all crankpins with a cloth. With crankpin No 1 at BDC initially, place a strand of Plastigauge on the crankpin journal.

5 Fit the upper big-end bearing shell to the connecting rod, ensuring that the locating lug and recess engage correctly. Temporarily refit the piston/connecting rod assembly to the crankshaft, then refit the big-end bearing caps, using the manufacturer's markings to ensure that they are fitted the correct way around.

6 Tighten the bearing cap bolts to the Stage 1 torque. Take care not to disturb the Plastigauge or rotate the connecting rod during the tightening process.

7 Dismantle the assembly without rotating the connecting rod. Use the scale printed on the Plastigauge envelope to determine the big-end bearing running clearance and compare it with the figures listed in Specifications.

8 If the clearance is significantly different from that expected, the bearing shells may be the wrong size (or excessively worn, if the original shells are being re-used). Make sure that no dirt or oil was trapped between the bearing shells and the cap or connecting rod when the clearance was measured. Re-check the diameter of the crankpin. Note that if the Plastigauge was wider at one end than at the other, the crankpin may be tapered. When the problem is identified, fit new bearing shells or have the crankpins reground to a listed undersize, as appropriate.

9 Upon completion, carefully scrape away all traces of the Plastigauge material from the crankshaft and bearing shells. Use a plastic or wooden scraper, which will be soft enough to prevent scoring of the bearing surfaces.

Piston and connecting rod assemblies – final refitting

10 Note that the following procedure assumes that the crankshaft main bearing caps are in place (see Section 13).

11 Ensure that the bearing shells are correctly fitted, as described at the beginning of this Section. If new shells are being fitted, ensure that all traces of the protective grease are cleaned off using paraffin. Wipe dry the shells and connecting rods with a lint-free cloth.

12 Lubricate the cylinder bores, the pistons, piston rings and upper bearing shells with clean engine oil **(see illustrations)**. Lay out each piston/connecting rod assembly in order on a worksurface.

13 Start with piston/connecting rod assembly No 1. Make sure that the piston rings are still spaced as described in Section 14, then clamp them in position with a piston ring compressor.

14 Insert the piston/connecting rod assembly into the top of cylinder No 1. Lower the big-end in first, guiding it to protect the cylinder bores.

Where oil jets are located at the bottoms of the bores, take particular care not to break them off when guiding the connecting rods onto the crankpins.

15 Ensure that the orientation of the piston in its cylinder is correct – the piston crown, connecting rods and big-end bearing caps have markings, which must point towards the timing belt end of the engine when the piston is installed in the bore – refer to Section 7 for details.

16 Using a block of wood or hammer handle against the piston crown, tap the assembly into the cylinder until the piston crown is flush with the top of the cylinder **(see illustration)**.

17 Ensure that the bearing shell is still correctly installed. Liberally lubricate the crankpin and both bearing shells with clean engine oil. Taking care not to mark the cylinder bores, tap the piston/connecting rod assembly down the bore and onto the crankpin. Fit the big-end bearing cap, tightening its retaining bolts finger-tight at first **(see illustration)**. Note that the orientation of the bearing cap with respect to the connecting rod must be correct when the two components are reassembled. The connecting rod and its corresponding bearing cap both have recesses machined into them, close to their mating surfaces – these recesses must both face in the same direction as the arrow on the piston crown (ie towards the timing belt end of the engine) when correctly installed.

18 On engines with the combustion chamber in the piston, the piston crowns are specially shaped to improve the engine's combustion characteristics. Because of this, pistons 1 and 2 are different to the remaining pistons. When correctly fitted, the larger inlet valve chambers

15.12a Lubricate the pistons...

15.16 Using a hammer handle to tap the piston into its bore

on pistons 1 and 2 must face the flywheel end of the engine, and the larger inlet valve chambers on the remaining pistons must face the timing belt end of the engine. New pistons have number markings on their crowns to indicate their type – 1/2 denotes piston 1 or 2,

15.12b ...and big-end upper bearing shells with clean engine oil

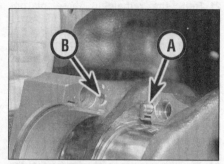

15.17 Fitting a big-end bearing cap

A Dowel   *B Locating hole*

3/4 indicates piston 3 or 4, and 3/4/5 indicated pistons 3, 4 or 5 **(see illustration)**.

19 Tighten the retaining bolts to the specified Stage 1 torque **(see illustration)**.

20 Angle-tighten the retaining bolts to the specified Stage 2 angle **(see illustration)**.

15.19 Tighten the big-end bearing cap bolts to the Stage 1 torque setting...

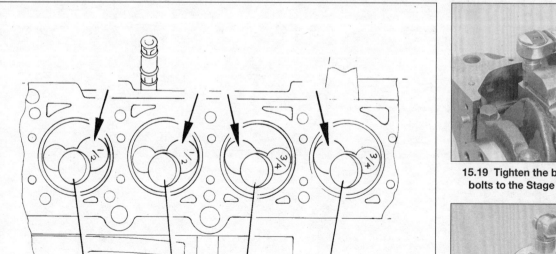

15.18 Piston orientation and fitting order (4-cylinder shown)

H31965

15.20 ...then angle-tighten them to the Stage 2 setting

15.24 Measuring the piston projection with a dial gauge

21 Refit the remaining three piston/connecting rod assemblies in the same way.

22 Rotate the crankshaft by hand. Check that it turns freely; some stiffness is to be expected if new parts have been fitted, but there should be no binding or tight spots.

Checking piston projection

23 If new pistons are fitted or if a new short engine is installed, the projection of the piston crowns above the cylinder head at TDC must be measured, to determine the type of head gasket that should be fitted.

24 Turn the cylinder block over (so that the crankcase is facing downwards) and rest it on a stand or wooden blocks. Anchor a DTI gauge to the cylinder block, and zero it on the head gasket mating surface. Rest the gauge probe on No 1 piston crown and turn the crankshaft slowly by hand so that the piston reaches TDC. Measure and record the maximum projection at TDC **(see illustration)**.

25 Repeat the measurement for the remaining pistons and record.

26 If the measurements differ from piston to piston, take the highest figure and use this to determine the head gasket type that must be used – refer to the Specifications for details.

27 Note that if the original pistons have been refitted, then a new head gasket of the same type as the original item must be fitted.

28 On 4-cylinder engines, refit the cylinder head, sump, baffle plate and oil pump as described in Chapter 2A.

29 On 5-cylinder engines, refit the cylinder head, sump and oil pump pickup as described in Chapter 2B.

16 Engine – initial start-up after overhaul and reassembly

1 Refit the remainder of the engine components in the order listed in Section 12 of this Chapter, referring to Parts A and B where necessary. Refit the engine to the vehicle as described in Section 4 of this Chapter. Double-check the engine oil and coolant levels and make a final check that everything has been reconnected. Make sure that there are no tools or rags left in the engine compartment.

2 Disconnect the stop solenoid and fuel metering control wiring at the fuel injection pump.

3 Turn the engine using the starter motor until the oil pressure warning lamp goes out.

4 If the lamp fails to extinguish after several seconds of cranking, check the engine oil level and oil filter security. Assuming these are correct, check the security of the oil pressure switch cabling – do not progress any further until you are satisfied that oil is being pumped around the engine at sufficient pressure.

5 Reconnect the stop solenoid and fuel metering control wiring.

6 Start the engine, but be aware that as fuel system components have been disturbed, the cranking time may be a little longer than usual.

7 While the engine is idling, check for fuel, water and oil leaks. Don't be alarmed if there are some odd smells and the occasional plume of smoke as components heat up and burn off oil deposits.

8 Assuming all is well, keep the engine idling until hot water is felt circulating through the top hose.

9 After a few minutes, recheck the oil and coolant levels, and top-up as necessary.

10 On all engines described in this Chapter, there is no need to re-tighten the cylinder head bolts once the engine has been run following reassembly.

11 If new pistons, rings or crankshaft bearings have been fitted, the engine must be treated as new, and run-in for the first 600 miles (1000 km). *Do not* operate the engine at full-throttle, or allow it to labour at low engine speeds in any gear. It is recommended that the engine oil and filter are changed at the end of this period.

Chapter 3
Cooling, heating and ventilation systems

Contents

Degrees of difficulty

Easy, suitable for novice with little experience	Fairly easy, suitable for beginner with some experience	Fairly difficult, suitable for competent DIY mechanic	Difficult, suitable for experienced DIY mechanic	Very difficult, suitable for expert DIY or professional

Specifications

General

Maximum system pressure .... 1.3 to 1.5 bar

Thermostat

Starts to open... 87°C
Fully open.. 102°C
Minimum valve lift....................................... 7 mm

Electric cooling fans

Cooling fans cut in:
  Stage 1 speed:
    Switches on .... 84 to 89°C
    Switches off .... 76 to 83°C
  Stage 2 speed:
    Switches on .... 90 to 95°C
    Switches off .... 82 to 89°C

Torque wrench settings	Nm	lbf ft
Alternator/power steering pump bracket	20	15
Cooling fan thermostatic switch	25	18
Coolant pump:		
4-cylinder engines:		
Pump-to-housing bolts	10	7
Pulley bolts	20	15
5-cylinder engines:		
Retaining bolts	20	15
Thermostat housing bolts	10	7

3.4 Undo the radiator upper crossmember retaining bolt on each side

1 General information and precautions

General information

The cooling system is of pressurised type, comprising a coolant pump, an aluminium crossflow radiator, two electric cooling fans, a thermostat, heater matrix, and all associated hoses and switches. On 4-cylinder engines the coolant pump is driven by the auxiliary drivebelt whereas on 5-cylinder engines the coolant pump is driven by the timing belt. Also, on 5-cylinder engines, an additional electrically operated coolant pump is incorporated in the coolant circuit. The system functions as follows.

When the engine is cold, the coolant in the engine is pumped around the cylinder block and head passages, and through the oil cooler. After cooling the cylinder bores, combustion surfaces and valve seats, the coolant passes through the heater, and is returned via the cylinder block to the coolant pump. The thermostat is initially closed, preventing the cold coolant from the radiator entering the engine.

When the coolant in the engine reaches a predetermined temperature, the thermostat opens. The cold coolant from the radiator is then allowed to enter the engine through the bottom hose and the hot coolant from the engine flows through the top hose to the radiator. As the coolant circulates through the

3.5 Pivot the upper crossmember and the radiator forwards and downwards away from the engine

radiator, it is cooled by the inrush of air when the vehicle is in forward motion. The airflow is supplemented by the action of the cooling fans when necessary. Upon reaching the bottom of the radiator, the coolant has now cooled, and the cycle is repeated.

The operation of the cooling fans is controlled by a thermostatic switch. At a predetermined coolant temperature, the switch/sensor actuates the fans.

An expansion tank is fitted to the centre of the engine compartment to accommodate expansion of the coolant when hot.

Precautions

⚠️ *Warning: Do not attempt to remove the expansion tank filler cap, or to disturb any part of the cooling system, while the engine is hot, as there is a high risk of scalding. If the expansion tank filler cap must be removed before the engine and radiator have fully cooled (even though this is not recommended), the pressure in the cooling system must first be relieved. Cover the cap with a thick layer of cloth to avoid scalding, and slowly unscrew the filler cap until a hissing sound is heard. When the hissing has stopped, indicating that the pressure has reduced, slowly unscrew the filler cap until it can be removed; if more hissing sounds are heard, wait until they have stopped before unscrewing the cap completely. At all times, keep well away from the filler cap opening, and protect your hands.*

⚠️ *Warning: Do not allow antifreeze to come into contact with your skin, or with the painted surfaces of the vehicle. Rinse off spills immediately, with plenty of water. Never leave antifreeze lying around in an open container, or in a puddle in the driveway or on the garage floor. Children and pets are attracted by its sweet smell, but antifreeze can be fatal if ingested.*

⚠️ *Warning: If the engine is hot, the electric cooling fans may start rotating even if the engine is not running. Be careful to keep your hands, hair, and any loose clothing well clear when working in the engine compartment.*

⚠️ *Warning: Refer to Section 11 for precautions to be observed when working on models equipped with air conditioning.*

2 Cooling system hoses – disconnection and renewal

Note: *Refer to the warnings given in Section 1 of this Chapter before proceeding. Hoses should only be disconnected once the engine has cooled sufficiently to avoid scalding.*

1 If the checks described in Chapter 1, Section 9 reveal a faulty hose, it must be renewed as follows.

2 First drain the cooling system (see Chapter 1, Section 23). If the coolant is not due for renewal, it may be re-used, providing it is collected in a clean container.

3 Before disconnecting a hose, first note its routing in the engine compartment, and whether it is secured by any additional retaining clips or cable ties. Use a pair of pliers to release the clamp-type clips, or a screwdriver to slacken the screw-type clips, then move the clips along the hose, clear of the relevant inlet/outlet union. Carefully work the hose free.

4 Note that the radiator inlet and outlet unions are fragile; do not use excessive force when attempting to remove the hoses. If a hose proves to be difficult to remove, try to release it by rotating the hose ends before attempting to free it. It may be beneficial to spray an penetrating aerosol lubricant (WD-40 or equivalent) onto the end of the hose to aid its release.

5 When fitting a hose, first slide the clips onto the hose, then work the hose into position. On some hose connections alignment marks are provided on the hose and union; if marks are present, ensure they are correctly aligned.

6 Ensure the hose is correctly routed, then slide each clip back along the hose until it passes over the flared end of the relevant inlet/outlet, before tightening the clip securely.

7 Refill the cooling system as described in Chapter 1, Section 23.

8 Check thoroughly for leaks as soon as possible after disturbing any part of the cooling system.

3 Radiator – moving to the service position

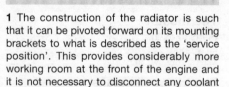

1 The construction of the radiator is such that it can be pivoted forward on its mounting brackets to what is described as the 'service position'. This provides considerably more working room at the front of the engine and it is not necessary to disconnect any coolant hoses to do this.

2 On engines with an intercooler mounted over the top of the camshaft cover, remove the intercooler as described in Chapter 4A, Section 14.

3 Remove the radiator grille as described in Chapter 11, Section 25.

4 Undo the radiator upper crossmember retaining bolt on each side **(see illustration)**. Note that on pre-July 1994 models there are two upper crossmember retaining bolts on each side.

5 Lift the upper crossmember, then pivot the crossmember and the radiator forwards and downwards away from the engine **(see illustration)**.

6 Reverse this procedure to return the radiator to its normal position.

4.7a Release the retaining clips and disconnect the top...

4.7b ...and bottom coolant hoses from the radiator

4.8a Disconnect the power steering fluid hose at the left-hand side...

4.8b ...and right-hand side of the fluid cooler

4.8c Cap or plug the hoses and cooler unions to prevent dirt ingress...

4.8d ...then pull the left-hand hose out through the hole in the fan shroud

4 Radiator –
removal, inspection and refitting

Note: *If leakage is the reason for removing the radiator, bear in mind that minor leaks can often be cured using a radiator sealant with the radiator in situ.*

Removal

1 Disconnect the battery negative terminal (refer to *Disconnecting the battery*).
2 Firmly apply the handbrake, then jack up the front of the vehicle and support it securely on axle stands (see *Jacking and vehicle support*).
3 Remove the engine undertray as described in Chapter 11, Section 25.

4 Drain the cooling system as described in Chapter 1, Section 23.
5 Move the radiator to the service position as described in Section 3.
6 On models equipped with air conditioning, remove the refrigerant pipe retaining clamp, then undo the retaining bolt on each side of the condenser. Lift the condenser out of its mounting bracket and position it to one side. Do not disconnect the refrigerant pipes
7 Release the retaining clips and disconnect the top and bottom coolant hoses from the radiator **(see illustrations)**.
8 On models with power steering, suitably clamp the fluid hoses at each end of the power steering fluid cooler in front of radiator. Extract the retaining clips and disconnect the two hoses from the cooler.

Cap or plug the hoses and cooler unions to prevent dirt ingress. Pull the left-hand hose out through the hole in the fan shroud **(see illustrations)**.
9 Disconnect the wiring connector from the thermostatic switch on the right-hand side of the radiator **(see illustration)**.
10 Disconnect the electric cooling fan wiring at the connectors on the fan shroud **(see illustration)**. Release the wiring harness from the cable tie on the fan shroud.
11 Using a hammer and pin punch, tap out the centre pins from the spreader clips on each side of the radiator **(see illustration)**. Remove the spreader clips from the radiator mounting brackets.
12 Lift the radiator and cooling fan assembly from its location **(see illustration)**.

4.9 Disconnect the wiring connector from the cooling fan thermostatic switch

4.10 Disconnect the cooling fan wiring at the connectors on the fan shroud

4.11 Tap out the centre pins from the spreader clips on each side of the radiator

4.12 Lift the radiator and cooling fan assembly from its location

13 Disengage the radiator upper crossmember from the radiator upper mounting rubbers on each side and lift away the upper crossmember.

14 If necessary, undo the retaining screws and remove the fan shroud from the radiator.

Inspection

15 If the radiator has been removed due to suspected blockage, reverse-flush it as described in Chapter 1, Section 23. Clean dirt and debris from the radiator fins, using an air line (in which case, wear eye protection) or a soft brush. Be careful, as the fins are sharp, and easily damaged.

16 If necessary, a radiator specialist can perform a flow test on the radiator, to establish whether an internal blockage exists.

17 A leaking radiator must be referred to a specialist for permanent repair. Do not attempt to weld or solder a leaking radiator, as damage to the plastic components may result.

18 If the radiator is to be sent for repair or renewed, remove the cooling fan thermostatic switch all remaining attachments.

19 Inspect the condition of the radiator mounting rubbers, and renew them if necessary.

Refitting

20 Refitting is a reversal of removal, bearing in mind the following points.

a) *Make sure all coolant hoses are correctly reconnected and securely retained by their clips.*

b) *Refill the cooling system as described in Chapter 1, Section 23.*

c) *On models equipped with power steering, check and if necessary top-up the power steering fluid level as described in 'Weekly checks'.*

5 Thermostat –
removal, testing and refitting

Removal

1 On 4-cylinder engines, the thermostat is fitted to the base of coolant pump housing. On 5-cylinder engines the thermostat is fitted in the cylinder block, directly behind the coolant pump.

2 Disconnect the battery negative terminal (refer to *Disconnecting the battery*).

3 Firmly apply the handbrake, then jack up the front of the vehicle and support it securely on axle stands (see *Jacking and vehicle support*).

4 Remove the engine undertray as described in Chapter 11, Section 25.

5 Drain the cooling system as described in Chapter 1, Section 23.

6 Move the radiator to the service position as described in Section 3.

7 If necessary, to improve access, unbolt the power steering pump from its bracket as described in Chapter 10, Section 26 and position it clear of the thermostat cover. There is no need to disconnect the hydraulic pipes/hoses from the pump.

4-cylinder engines

8 Release retaining clip and disconnect the coolant hose from the thermostat cover.

9 Unscrew the two retaining bolts and remove the thermostat cover from the coolant pump housing **(see illustration)**.

10 Recover the sealing ring and withdraw the thermostat. Discard the sealing ring; a new one must be used on refitting **(see illustration)**.

5-cylinder engines

11 Release the retaining clip and disconnect the coolant hose from the thermostat cover.

12 Unscrew the two retaining bolts and remove the thermostat housing cover from the engine **(see illustration)**.

13 Remove the thermostat and sealing ring from the housing cover **(see illustrations)**. Discard the sealing ring; a new one must be used on refitting.

Testing

14 A rough test of the thermostat may be made by suspending it with a piece of string in a container full of water. Heat the water to bring it to the boil – the thermostat must open by the time the water boils. If not, renew it.

15 If a thermometer is available, the precise opening temperature of the thermostat may

5.9 Undo the two retaining bolts and remove the thermostat cover – 4-cylinder engines

5.10 Recover the sealing ring, then withdraw the thermostat from its housing, noting its orientation – 4-cylinder engines

5.12 Unscrew the two retaining bolts and remove the thermostat housing cover – 5-cylinder engines

5.13a Remove the thermostat...

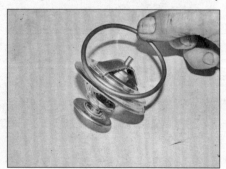

5.13b ...and sealing ring from the housing cover – 5-cylinder engines

be determined; compare with the figures given in the Specifications **(see illustration)**. The opening temperature should also be marked on the thermostat.

16 A thermostat which fails to close as the water cools must also be renewed.

Refitting

17 Refitting is a reversal of removal, bearing in mind the following points.
 a) *Make sure the coolant hose is correctly reconnected and securely retained by its clip.*
 b) *Where removed, refit the power steering pump as described in Chapter 10, Section 26.*
 c) *Refill the cooling system as described in Chapter 1, Section 23.*

6 Electric cooling fans – removal and refitting

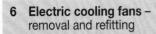

Removal

1 Disconnect the battery negative terminal (refer to *Disconnecting the battery*).
2 Move the radiator to the service position as described in Section 3.
3 Disconnect the cooling fan wiring at the connector on the fan shroud **(see illustration 4.10)**.
4 Unclip the plastic cover over the fan motor wiring on the fan shroud **(see illustration)**.
5 Release the fan wiring connector from the retaining clip on the fan shroud **(see illustration)**.
6 Undo the three retaining bolts and remove the relevant fan and mounting bracket from the fan shroud **(see illustration)**.
7 Undo the three bolts and remove the fan motor from the mounting bracket **(see illustration)**.
8 If required, undo the retaining nut and remove the fan from the motor spindle **(see illustration)**.

Refitting

9 Refitting is a reversal of removal

6.6 Undo the three bolts and remove the relevant fan and mounting bracket from the shroud

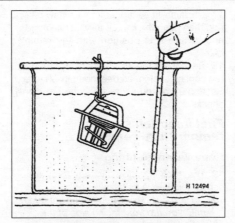

5.15 Method of checking thermostat opening temperature

7 Cooling system electrical switches and sensors – removal and refitting

Electric cooling fan thermostatic switch

Removal

1 The switch is located in the right-hand side of the radiator. The engine and radiator should be cold before removing the switch.
2 Disconnect the battery negative terminal (refer to *Disconnecting the battery*).
3 Drain the cooling system to just below the level of the switch as described in Chapter 1,

6.4 Unclip the plastic cover over the fan motor wiring on the fan shroud

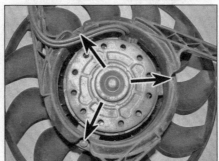

6.7 Undo the three bolts (arrowed) and remove the fan motor from the mounting bracket

Section 23. Alternatively, have ready a suitable bung to plug the switch aperture in the radiator when the switch is removed. If this method is used, take great care not to damage the radiator, and do not use anything which will allow foreign matter to enter the radiator.
4 Disconnect the wiring connector from the switch **(see illustration 4.9)**.
5 Carefully unscrew the switch from the radiator, and recover the sealing washer (where fitted). If the system has not been drained, plug the switch aperture to prevent further coolant loss.

Refitting

6 If the switch was originally fitted using a sealing ring, use a new sealing ring on refitting. Where no sealing ring was fitted, clean the switch threads thoroughly and coat them with fresh sealing compound.
7 Tighten the switch to the specified torque and reconnect the wiring connector.
8 Refill the cooling system as described in Chapter 1, Section 23 or top-up as described in *Weekly checks*.
9 On completion, start the engine and run it until it reaches normal operating temperature. Continue to run the engine, and check that the cooling fan cuts in and out correctly.

Coolant temperature gauge sensor

Removal

10 The coolant temperature gauge sensor location is as follows.

6.5 Release the fan wiring connector from the retaining clip on the shroud

6.8 Undo the retaining nut (arrowed) and remove the fan from the motor spindle

a) *1.9 litre engines – fitted to the left-hand end of the cylinder head.*

b) *2.4 litre engines – fitted to the coolant outlet union on the front facing side of the cylinder head.*

c) *2.5 litre engines – fitted to the bottom of the coolant outlet union on the front facing side of the cylinder head.*

11 Disconnect the battery negative terminal (refer to *Disconnecting the battery*).

12 Drain the cooling system to just below the level of the switch as described in Chapter 1, Section 23. Alternatively, have ready a suitable bung to plug the switch aperture in the radiator when the switch is removed. If this method is used, take great care not to damage the radiator, and do not use anything which will allow foreign matter to enter the radiator.

13 On all engines, disconnect the wiring connector from the sensor and identify whether the sensor is a push-fit or a screw-fit.

14 On screw-fit sensors, unscrew the sensor from the engine and recover its sealing washer.

15 On push-fit sensors, depress the sensor unit and slide out its retaining clip. Withdraw the sensor from the engine and recover its sealing ring.

Refitting

16 On screw-fit sensors, fit a new sealing washer then fit the sensor, tightening it securely.

17 On push-fit sensor units, fit a new sealing ring then push the sensor fully into its aperture and secure it in position with the retaining clip.

18 Reconnect the wiring connector then refill the cooling system as described in Chapter 1, Section 23 or top-up as described in *Weekly checks*.

Fuel injection system temperature sensor

Removal and refitting

19 The fuel injection system temperature sensor location is as follows.

a) *1.9 litre engines - fitted to coolant outlet union on the front facing side of the cylinder head.*

b) *2.5 litre engines - fitted to the top of the coolant outlet union on the front facing side of the cylinder head.*

20 Removal and refitting procedures are the same as for the coolant temperature gauge sensor described in paragraphs 10 to 18

Preheating system temperature sensor – 2.4 litre engines

Removal and refitting

21 On 2.4 litre engines the preheating system temperature sensor occupies the same position as the fuel injection system temperature sensor used by 2.5 litre engines.

22 Removal and refitting procedures are described in paragraphs 10 to 18

8 Coolant pump – removal and refitting

Removal

1 Disconnect the battery negative terminal (refer to *Disconnecting the battery*).

2 Remove the engine undertray as described in Chapter 11, Section 25.

3 Drain the cooling system as described in Chapter 1, Section 23, then proceed as described under the relevant sub-heading.

4-cylinder engines

4 Remove the alternator as described in Chapter 5, Section 7.

5 On models equipped with power steering, remove the power steering pump as described in Chapter 10, Section 26 noting that there is no need to disconnect the hydraulic pipe/hose(s) from the pump. Unbolt the pump from its mountings and position it clear of the coolant pump housing.

6 Slacken and remove the retaining bolts and remove the pulley from the coolant pump **(see illustrations)**.

7 Slacken and remove the nuts securing the alternator mounting bracket assembly to the side of the cylinder block and remove the bracket.

8 Release the retaining clips and disconnect the coolant hoses from the back of the coolant pump housing and the thermostat housing.

9 Unscrew the retaining studs/bolts (as applicable) securing the coolant pump/ thermostat housing to the block and remove the housing assembly from the engine. **Note:** *On some engines it will be necessary to unscrew the bolt(s) that secure the timing belt cover to the housing assembly.* Recover the sealing ring which is fitted between the housing and block and discard it; a new one should be used on refitting **(see illustrations)**.

10 With the assembly on a bench, unscrew the retaining bolts and remove the pump from the housing. Discard the gasket, a new one must be used on refitting

8.6a Undo the retaining bolts...

8.6b ...and remove the pulley from the coolant pump – 4-cylinder engines

8.9a Slacken and remove the retaining bolts/studs...

8.9b ...then remove the coolant pump/ thermostat housing from the block...

8.9c ...and recover its sealing ring – 4-cylinder engines

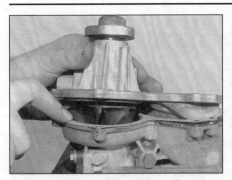

8.10 Undo the retaining bolts and remove the pump and gasket from the housing – 4-cylinder engines

8.14 Undo the retaining bolts and remove the coolant pump from the cylinder block – 5-cylinder engines

8.25 Fit a new sealing ring to the pump prior to refitting – 5-cylinder engines

(see illustration). Note it is not possible to overhaul the pump. If it is faulty, the unit must be renewed.

5-cylinder engines

11 Remove the timing belt and camshaft sprocket as described in Chapter 2B, Section 4 (pre-February 1995 models) or Chapter 2B, Section 5 (February 1995 models onward).
12 Remove the timing belt idler pulley (pre-February 1995 models) or timing belt tensioner (February 1995 models onward) as described in Chapter 2B, Section 7.
13 Unbolt and remove the timing belt inner cover.
14 Slacken and remove the bolts securing the pump to the cylinder block then manoeuvre the pump out of position. Recover the sealing ring and discard it; a new one must be used on refitting **(see illustration)**.

Refitting

4-cylinder engines

15 Ensure that the pump and housing mating surfaces are clean and dry and position a new gasket on the housing.
16 Fit the coolant pump to the housing and evenly tighten its retaining bolts to the specified torque setting.
17 Fit the new sealing ring to the housing assembly recess and refit the housing to the cylinder block. Refit the retaining studs/bolts and tighten them securely.
18 Connect the coolant hoses to the housing and securely tighten their retaining clips.
19 Refit the alternator/power steering pump bracket(s) and tighten the retaining nut/bolts to the specified torque setting (as applicable).
20 Refit the pulley to the coolant pump and tighten its retaining bolts to the specified torque setting (this can be done once the drivebelt is refitted and tensioned).
21 On models equipped with power steering, refit the power steering pump as described in Chapter 10, Section 26.
22 Refit the alternator as described in Chapter 5, Section 7.
23 Refit the engine undertray as described in Chapter 11, Section 25.

24 Reconnect the battery negative terminal, then refill the cooling system as described in Chapter 1, Section 23.

5-cylinder engines

25 Fit a new sealing ring to the pump and locate the pump in the cylinder block **(see illustration)**. Refit the pump retaining bolts and tighten them to the specified torque.
26 Refit the timing belt rear cover and tighten the retaining bolts securely.
27 Refit the timing belt idler pulley (pre-February 1995 models) or timing belt tensioner (February 1995 models onward) as described in Chapter 2B, Section 7.
28 Refit the timing belt and camshaft sprocket as described in Chapter 2B, Section 4 (pre-February 1995 models) or Chapter 2B, Section 5 (February 1995 models onward).
29 Refit the engine undertray as described in Chapter 11, Section 25.
30 Reconnect the battery negative terminal, then refill the cooling system as described in Chapter 1, Section 23.

9 Heating and ventilation system – general information

The heating/ventilation system consists of a four-speed blower motor (housed in the passenger compartment), face-level vents in the centre and at each end of the facia, and air ducts to the footwells.

The control unit is located in the facia, and the controls operate flap valves to deflect and mix the air flowing through the various parts of the heating/ventilation system. The flap valves are contained in the air distribution housing, which acts as a central distribution unit, passing air to the various ducts and vents.

Cold air enters the system through the grille at the rear of the engine compartment. On some models (depending on specification) a pollen filter is fitted to the ventilation inlet to filter out dust, soot, pollen and spores from the air entering the vehicle.

The airflow, which can be boosted by the blower, then flows through the various ducts,

according to the settings of the controls. Stale air is expelled through ducts at the rear of the vehicle. If warm air is required, the cold air is passed through the heater matrix, which is heated by the engine coolant.

If necessary, the outside air supply can be closed off, allowing the air inside the vehicle to be recirculated. This can be useful to prevent unpleasant odours entering from outside the vehicle, but should only be used briefly, as the recirculated air inside the vehicle will soon deteriorate.

10 Heater/ventilation components – removal and refitting

Heater/ventilation control unit

Removal (pre- May 1996 models)

1 Disconnect the battery negative terminal (refer to *Disconnecting the battery*).
2 Pull the knob off the blower motor switch and pull the end fittings off the three control levers.
3 Using a small screwdriver, carefully prise off the heater/ventilation control unit trim panel.
4 Undo the three screws securing the heater/ventilation control unit to the facia.
5 Release the control unit from the facia and twist it around to gain access to the control cable attachments.
6 Unclip the control cables and release each cable from the control unit, noting each cable's correct fitted location and routing; to avoid confusion on refitting, label each cable as it is disconnected. The outer cables are released by simply lifting the retaining clips.

Refitting (pre- May 1996 models)

7 Refitting is reversal of removal. Ensure that the control cables are correctly routed and reconnected to the control panel, as noted before removal. Clip the outer cables in position and check the operation of each knob/lever before refitting the trim panel.

Removal (May 1996 models onward)

8 Disconnect the battery negative terminal (refer to *Disconnecting the battery*).
9 Remove the ashtray, then using a small

10.9 Carefully prise off the ashtray and switch panel trim surround

10.10a Similarly prise free the heater/ventilation control unit trim panel...

10.10b ...and remove the panel from the facia

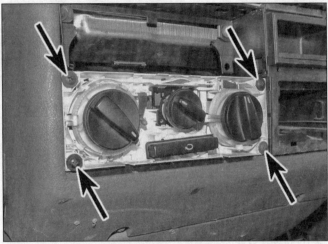

10.11a Undo the four retaining screws (arrowed)...

10.11b ...then pull the control unit from its location and disconnect the wiring connector

screwdriver, carefully prise off the ashtray and switch panel trim surround (see illustration).

10 Similarly prise free and remove the heater/ventilation control unit trim panel (see illustrations).

11 Undo the four retaining screws, pull the control unit from its location and disconnect the wiring connector (see illustrations).

12 Unclip the control cables and release each cable from the control unit, noting each cable's correct fitted location and routing; to avoid confusion on refitting, label each cable as it is disconnected (see illustrations).

Refitting (May 1996 models onward)

13 Refitting is reversal of removal. Ensure that the control cables are correctly routed and reconnected to the control panel, as noted before removal. Clip the outer cables in position and check the operation of each knob before refitting the trim panel.

Blower motor

Removal

14 Disconnect the battery negative terminal (refer to *Disconnecting the battery*).

15 Remove the glovebox as described in Chapter 11, Section 29.

16 Where fitted, remove the passenger's airbag as described in Chapter 12, Section 20.

17 Disconnect the air ducting on the left-hand side, then remove the foam insulation panel.

18 Disconnect the blower motor wiring connector.

19 Using a small screwdriver, lift the blower motor retaining tab and rotate the motor body anti-clockwise. Lift the blower motor out of the air distribution housing (see illustrations).

10.12a Release the control cable from the control unit support...

10.12b ...then disconnect the inner cable from the operating lever

10.19a Lift the blower motor retaining tab and rotate the motor body anti-clockwise...

Refitting

20 Refitting is reversal of removal.

Blower motor resistor

Removal

21 Disconnect the battery negative terminal (refer to *Disconnecting the battery*).
22 Remove the glovebox as described in Chapter 11, Section 29.
23 Where fitted, remove the passenger's airbag as described in Chapter 12, Section 20.
24 Disconnect the air ducting on the left-hand side, then remove the foam insulation panel.
25 Disconnect the blower motor resistor wiring connector **(see illustration)**.
26 Undo the retaining screw and withdraw the resistor from the air distribution housing **(see illustration)**.

Refitting

27 Refitting is reversal of removal.

Air distribution housing

Removal

28 Disconnect the battery negative terminal (refer to *Disconnecting the battery*).
29 Remove the facia as described in Chapter 11, Section 29.
30 Clamp the heater matrix coolant hoses to minimise coolant loss. Position a wad of rag beneath the matrix unions, to catch any spilt coolant, then slacken the retaining clips and disconnect both hoses. Mop up any spilt coolant and rinse off with water. Position absorbent rags around the base of the housing to catch any further coolant spilt as the housing is removed.
31 Disconnect the blower motor and blower motor resistor wiring connectors.
32 Release the retaining clips and remove the centre air duct from the top of the air distribution housing **(see illustration)**.
33 Disconnect the vacuum hose from the recirculating air flap actuator.
34 From within the engine compartment, undo the two air distribution housing retaining bolts. One is visible, the other is behind the bulkhead heat shielding approximately half way down.
35 Ease the air distribution housing away from the bulkhead, detaching the water drain tube when sufficient clearance exists, then remove the housing from the vehicle.

Refitting

36 Refitting is reversal of removal. On completion check, and if necessary top-up, the cooling system as described in *Weekly checks*.

Heater matrix

Removal

Note: *A silicone adhesive sealant will be required to seal up the joint between the matrix and housing.*
37 Remove the air distribution housing as described previously in this Section.
38 Recover the seal which is fitted between the matrix pipe unions and the bulkhead; the

10.19b ...then lift the blower motor out of the air distribution housing

10.26 Undo the retaining screw and withdraw the resistor from the air distribution housing

seal should be renewed if it shows signs of damage or deterioration.
39 Undo the two screws or release the clips and withdraw the matrix from the air distribution housing.
40 Recover the housing gasket.

Refitting

41 Refitting is reversal of removal, bearing in mind the following points:
a) *Apply silicone adhesive sealant to the matrix-to-housing gasket and ensure it is fitted free of gaps all around.*
b) *Refit the air distribution housing as described previously in this Section.*

11 Air conditioning system –
general information and precautions

General information

An air conditioning system is available on certain models. It enables the temperature of incoming air to be lowered, and also dehumidifies the air, which makes for rapid demisting and increased comfort.

The cooling side of the system works in the same way as a domestic refrigerator. Refrigerant gas is drawn into a belt-driven compressor, and passes into a condenser mounted on the front of the radiator, where it loses heat and becomes liquid. The liquid passes through an expansion valve to an evaporator, where it changes from liquid under high pressure to gas under low pressure.

10.25 Disconnect the blower motor resistor wiring connector

10.32 Release the retaining clips and remove the centre air duct from the top of the air distribution housing

This change is accompanied by a drop in temperature, which cools the evaporator. The refrigerant returns to the compressor, and the cycle begins again.

Air blown through the evaporator passes to the air distribution housing, where it is mixed with hot air blown through the heater matrix to achieve the desired temperature in the passenger compartment.

The heating side of the system works in the same way as on models without air conditioning (see Section 9).

There are two different types of air conditioning system available, a manually-controlled system which has a traditional panel with control knobs, and an automatic system which has a push-button control panel with an LCD display. On either system, any problems should be referred to a VW dealer or air conditioning system specialist.

Precautions

When an air conditioning system is fitted, it is necessary to observe special precautions whenever dealing with any part of the system, or its associated components. If for any reason the system must be disconnected, entrust this task to a VW dealer or air conditioning system specialist.

> **Warning: The refrigeration circuit may contain a liquid refrigerant (Freon), and it is therefore dangerous to disconnect any part of the system without specialised knowledge and equipment.**

The refrigerant is potentially dangerous, and should only be handled by qualified persons. If it is splashed onto the skin, it can cause frostbite. It is not itself poisonous, but in the presence of a naked flame (including a cigarette) it forms a poisonous gas. Uncontrolled discharging of the refrigerant is dangerous, and potentially damaging to the environment.

Do not operate the air conditioning system if it is known to be short of refrigerant, as this may damage the compressor.

12 Air conditioning system components – removal and refitting

⚠ Warning: Do not attempt to open the refrigerant circuit. Refer to the precautions given in Section 11.

1 The only operation which can be carried out easily without discharging the refrigerant is the renewal of the compressor drivebelt. All other operations must be referred to a VW dealer or an air conditioning specialist.

2 If necessary, the compressor can be unbolted and moved aside, without disconnecting its flexible hoses, after removing the drivebelt.

Chapter 4 Part A:
Fuel and exhaust systems

Contents

Degrees of difficulty

Easy, suitable for novice with little experience	**Fairly easy,** suitable for beginner with some experience	**Fairly difficult,** suitable for competent DIY mechanic	**Difficult,** suitable for experienced DIY mechanic	**Very difficult,** suitable for expert DIY or professional

Specifications

General

System type:

1.9 litre engines	Indirect injection via mechanical pump. Turbocharger, catalytic converter and exhaust gas recirculation on later models.
2.4 litre engines	Indirect injection via mechanical pump. Catalytic converter on later models
2.5 litre engines	Direct injection via mechanical pump under control of electronic engine management. Turbocharger, catalytic converter and exhaust gas recirculation

Firing order:

4-cylinder engines	1-3-4-2
5-cylinder engines	1-2-4-5-3

Idle speed:

4-cylinder engines	850 ± 30 rpm
5-cylinder (2.4 litre) engines	850 ± 50 rpm
5-cylinder (2.5 litre) engines	Non-adjustable, electronically controlled

Fast idle speed (approximate):

4-cylinder engines	1050 ± 50 rpm
5-cylinder (2.4 litre) engines	1050 ± 50 rpm
5-cylinder (2.5 litre) engines	Non-adjustable, electronically controlled

Fuel injection pump

Injection pump timing, DTI reading:

Test:

1.9 litre engines:*	0.93 to 1.07 mm
2.4 litre engines	0.93 to 1.07 mm
2.5 litre engines	Not applicable

Setting:

1.9 litre engines:*	
Engine code 1X	0.90 ± 0.02 mm
Engine code ABL	0.80 ± 0.02 mm
2.4 litre engines	1.00 ± 0.02 mm
2.5 litre engines	0.55 ± 0.02 mm

Early engines only – refer to a VW dealer or diesel injection specialist for latest information

Torque wrench settings

	Nm	lbf ft
Camshaft sprocket bolt (injection pump drivebelt end):		
2.4 litre engines	100	74
2.5 litre engines	160	118
Exhaust manifold nuts:		
1.9 litre engines:		
M6 nuts	5	5
M8 nuts	23	17
M10 nuts	40	30
2.4 and 2.5 litre engines	25	18
Exhaust system clamp bolt nuts	40	30
Exhaust system front pipe flange joint bolt nuts	25	18
Fuel injection pump blocking bolt (2.5 litre engines)	12	9
Fuel injection pump mounting bolts/nuts	25	18
Fuel injection pump sprocket retaining nut/bolts:		
1.9 litre engines:		
One-piece sprocket retaining nut	45	33
Two-piece sprocket outer bolts	25	18
2.4 litre engines	50	37
2.5 litre engines	90	66
Fuel injection pump stop solenoid	40	30
Fuel injection pump timing plug	20	15
Fuel injector clamp bolts (2.5 litre engines)	23	17
Fuel injector delivery pipe unions	25	18
Fuel injectors (1.9 and 2.4 litre engines)	70	52
Fuel supply and return pipe banjo unions	25	18
Fuel tank support strap bolts	25	18
Turbocharger oil return pipe flange bolts (2.5 litre engines)	30	22
Turbocharger oil return pipe union (1.9 litre engines)	40	30
Turbocharger oil supply pipe cap nut (2.5 litre engines)	15	11
Turbocharger oil supply pipe union (1.9 litre engines)	25	18
Turbocharger outlet elbow retaining bolts/nuts	25	18
Turbocharger retaining bolts/nuts	45	33

1 General information and precautions

General information

1.9 and 2.4 litre engines

The fuel system comprises a fuel tank, a fuel injection pump, a fuel filter with an integral water separator, fuel supply and return lines and four (1.9 litre engines) or five (2.4 litre engines) fuel injectors.

The fuel injection pump is driven at half crankshaft speed by the camshaft timing belt on 1.9 litre engines, and by a separate belt, driven from a sprocket on the rear of the camshaft, on 2.4 litre engines. Fuel is drawn from the fuel tank, through the filter by the injection pump, which then distributes the fuel under very high pressure to the injectors via separate delivery pipes.

The injectors are spring loaded mechanical valves, which open when the pressure of the fuel supplied to them exceeds a specific limit. Fuel is then sprayed from the injector nozzle into the cylinder via a swirl chamber.

The basic injection timing is set by the position of the injection pump on its mounting bracket. When the engine is running, the injection timing is advanced and retarded mechanically by the injection pump itself and is influenced primarily by the accelerator position and engine speed.

The engine is stopped by means of a solenoid operated fuel cut-off valve which interrupts the flow of fuel to the injection pump when de-activated.

When starting from cold, the engine idle speed can be raised manually by means of a cold start accelerator cable, controlled via a knob on the facia.

Later 1.9 litre engines (engine code ABL) are fitted with a turbocharger bolted directly to the exhaust manifold. The turbocharger increases engine efficiency by raising the pressure in the inlet manifold above atmospheric pressure. Instead of the air simply being sucked into the cylinders, it is forced in.

2.5 litre engines

The fuel system comprises a fuel tank, a fuel injection pump, a fuel filter with an integral water separator, fuel supply and return lines and fuel injectors.

The injection pump is driven at half crankshaft speed by a drivebelt from the sprocket on the rear of the camshaft. Fuel is drawn from the fuel tank, through the filter by the injection pump, which then distributes the fuel under very high pressure to the injectors via separate delivery pipes.

The injectors are spring loaded mechanical valves, which open when the pressure of the fuel supplied to them exceeds a specific limit.

Fuel is then sprayed from the injector nozzle into the swirl chambers incorporated in the tops of the pistons.

The direct-injection fuelling system is controlled electronically by a diesel engine management system, comprising an Electronic Control Unit (ECU) and its associated sensors, actuators and wiring.

Basic injection timing is set mechanically by the position of the pump on its mounting bracket. Dynamic timing and injection duration are controlled by the ECU and are dependent on engine speed, throttle position and rate of opening, inlet air flow , inlet air temperature, coolant temperature, fuel temperature, ambient pressure (altitude) and manifold depression information, received from sensors mounted on and around the engine. Closed loop control of the injection timing is achieved by means of an injector needle lift sensor.

Two-stage injectors are used, which improve the engine's combustion characteristics, leading to quieter running and better exhaust emissions.

In addition, the ECU manages the operation of the Exhaust Gas Recirculation (EGR) emission control system, the turbocharger boost pressure control system, and the glow plug control system.

It should be noted that fault diagnosis of the diesel engine management system is only possible with dedicated electronic

2.2 Release the upper air cleaner housing retaining clip

2.3 Push the locking handle down and unhook it from the air cleaner housing

2.4 Lift the air cleaner housing up and manipulate it out from its location

2.5 Lift out the element, noting its direction of fitting, and wipe out the housing

2.6 To remove the air cleaner lid, undo the nut (arrowed) securing the lid to the bulkhead

test equipment. Problems with the system's operation should therefore be referred to an VW dealer or diagnostic specialist for assessment. Once the fault has been identified, the removal/refitting sequences detailed in the following Sections will then allow the appropriate component(s) to be renewed as required.

Precautions

Many of the operations described in this Chapter involve the disconnection of fuel lines, which may cause an amount of fuel spillage. Before commencing work, refer to the warnings below and the information in 'Safety first!' at the beginning of this manual.

⚠️ *Warning: When working on any part of the fuel system, avoid direct contact skin contact with diesel fuel – wear protective clothing and gloves when handling fuel system components. Ensure that the work area is well ventilated to prevent the build up of diesel fuel vapour.*

Fuel injectors operate at extremely high pressures and the jet of fuel produced at the nozzle is capable of piercing skin, with potentially fatal results. When working with pressurised injectors, take great to avoid exposing any part of the body to the fuel spray. It is recommended that any pressure testing of the fuel system components should be carried out by a diesel fuel systems specialist.

Under no circumstances should diesel fuel be allowed to come into contact with coolant hoses - wipe off accidental spillage immediately. Hoses that have been contaminated with fuel for an extended period should be renewed. Diesel fuel systems are particularly sensitive to contamination from dirt, air and water. Pay particular attention to cleanliness when working on any part of the fuel system, to prevent the ingress of dirt. Thoroughly clean the area around fuel unions before disconnecting them. Store dismantled components in sealed containers to prevent contamination and the formation of condensation. Only use lint-free cloths and clean fuel for component cleansing. Avoid using compressed air when cleaning components in situ.

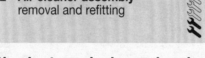

2 Air cleaner assembly – removal and refitting

Circular-type air cleaner housing

Removal

1 The air cleaner housing is situated on the right-hand side of the engine compartment.
2 Release the upper air cleaner housing retaining clip (see illustration).
3 Push the locking handle down and unhook it from the air cleaner housing (see illustration).
4 Lift the air cleaner housing up and manipulate it out from its location (see illustration).
5 If necessary, lift out the element, noting its direction of fitting, and wipe out the housing (see illustration).
6 To remove the air cleaner lid, undo the nut securing the lid to the bulkhead (see

2.10 Disconnect the air outlet duct from the air cleaner cover

illustration). Lift the wiring harness support off the retaining stud.
7 Release the inlet air duct and withdraw the air cleaner lid.

Refitting

8 Refitting is a reverse of the removal procedure. Ensure that the plastic lug on the end of the filter element locates in the recess in the mounting. With the housing in position, pull the locking handle up until it engages.

Square-type air cleaner housing

Removal

9 The air cleaner housing is situated on the right-hand side of the engine compartment.
10 Release the hose clip and disconnect the air outlet duct from the air cleaner cover (see illustration).
11 Disconnect the wiring connector from the airflow meter located on the air cleaner cover (see illustration).

2.11 Disconnect the wiring connector from the airflow meter

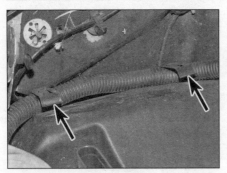

2.12 Lift the two clips (arrowed) and release the wiring harness from the air cleaner cover

2.13a Release the catch at the front (arrowed)...

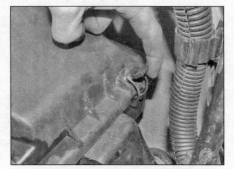

2.13b ...and the catch at the rear...

2.13c ...lift the air cleaner cover up and disengage it from the housing

2.14 Lift out the element, noting its direction of fitting

2.15 Undo the bolt securing the air cleaner housing to the inner wing panel

12 Lift the two clips and release the wiring harness from the air cleaner cover **(see illustration)**.

13 Release the two catches securing the air cleaner cover to the housing. Lift the cover up, disengage it from the housing and manipulate it out from the engine compartment **(see illustrations)**.

14 Lift out the element, noting its direction of fitting, and wipe out the housing **(see illustration)**.

15 Undo the bolt securing the air cleaner housing to the inner wing panel **(see illustration)**.

16 Lift the housing up, disengage the mounting lug and manipulate the housing out of the engine compartment **(see illustrations)**.

Refitting

17 Refitting is a reverse of the removal procedure.

3 Accelerator cable – removal, refitting and adjustment

Note: *This Section only applies to 1.9 and 2.4 litre engines. 2.5 litre engines are fitted with an electronic accelerator pedal position sensor (see Section 5).*

Removal

1 Move the radiator to the service position as described in Chapter 3, Section 3.

2 Remove the steering column shrouds as described in Chapter 11, Section 29.

3 Unclip the accelerator cable end from the top of the accelerator pedal.

4 Working in the engine compartment, remove the clip and detach the end of the

accelerator cable inner from the fuel injection pump lever.

5 Slide back the rubber grommet and extract the accelerator cable outer from the mounting bracket.

6 Release the cable from its securing clips and guide it out through the bulkhead grommet.

Refitting

7 Refit the accelerator cable by following the removal procedure in reverse.

Adjustment

8 At the fuel injection pump, fix the position of the cable outer in its mounting bracket by inserting the metal clip in one of the locating slots, such that when the accelerator is depressed fully, the throttle lever is held wide open to its end stop.

4 Cold Start Accelerator (CSA) cable – removal and refitting

Note: *This Section only applies to 1.9 and 2.4 litre engines.*

1.9 litre engines

Removal

1 Move the radiator to the service position as described in Chapter 3, Section 3.

2 Remove the steering column shrouds as described in Chapter 11, Section 29.

2.16a Disengage the mounting lug (arrowed)...

2.16b ...and manipulate the air cleaner housing out of the engine compartment

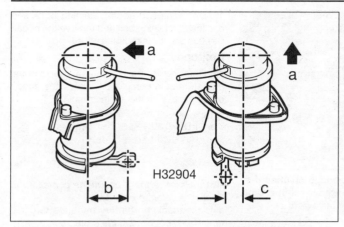

5.7 **Mounting arrangement of accelerator pedal position sensor cable cam plate – early models**

A	Towards front of vehicle	B	41 ± 0.5 mm
		C	22 ± 0.5 mm

5.9 **Disconnect the wiring connector (arrowed) from the accelerator pedal position sensor – later models**

3 Working in the engine compartment, disconnect the inner cable end from the injection pump lever.
4 Prise off the retaining clip and withdraw the outer cable from the mounting bracket on the side of the injection pump. Recover the washer.
5 Pull the lower cable and upper cable apart at the cable connector, then unhook the lower inner cable from the upper inner cable.
6 Release the lower cable from the clips that secure it in position in the engine compartment and remove the lower cable.
7 Pull the cold start knob out to expose its rear surface, then prise off the clip and remove the knob from the upper inner cable.
8 Slacken and remove the retaining nut to release the upper outer cable from the facia.
9 Pull the cable through into the cabin, guiding it through the bulkhead grommet.

Refitting and adjustment

10 Refit the washer to the lower cable, fit the cable to the injection pump mounting bracket and secure with the retaining clip.
11 Connect the inner cable end fitting to the injection pump lever.
12 Set the injection pump lever to the 'on' position.
13 At the other end of the cable screw in the adjusting nut until approximately 15 mm of the inner cable protrudes beyond the end of the cable connector.
14 Feed the upper cable into position, hook the lower inner cable into the upper inner cable and connect the upper and lower cables together.
15 Engage the upper cable with the facia and refit the retaining nut. Refit the knob and secure with the retaining clip.
16 Refit the steering column shrouds as described in Chapter 11, Section 29.
17 Move the radiator back to its normal position as described in Chapter 3, Section 3.

2.4 litre engines

Removal

18 Move the radiator to the service position as described in Chapter 3, Section 3.
19 Remove the steering column shrouds as described in Chapter 11, Section 29.
20 Working in the engine compartment at the fuel injection pump, slacken the locking screw and disconnect the CSA inner cable from the injection pump lever.
21 Prise off the retaining clip and withdraw the outer cable from the mounting bracket on the side of the injection pump. Recover the washer.
22 Release the cable from the clips that secure it in position in the engine compartment.
23 Pull the cold start knob out to expose its rear surface, then prise off the clip and remove the knob from the inner cable.
24 Slacken and remove the retaining nut to release the outer cable from the facia.
25 Pull the cable through into the cabin, guiding it through the bulkhead grommet.

Refitting

26 Refitting is the reverse of the removal procedure.

Adjustment

27 Push the cold start knob into the 'fully off' position.
28 Thread the CSA inner cable through the drilling in the lever on the injection pump. Hold the injection pump cold start lever in the closed position, then pull the inner cable taught to take up the slack and tighten the locking screw.
29 Operate the cold start knob from the cabin and check that it is possible to move the injection pump lever through its full range of travel.
30 Refit the steering column shrouds as described in Chapter 11, Section 29.
31 Move the radiator back to its normal position as described in Chapter 3, Section 3.

5 Accelerator pedal/ position sensor – removal and refitting

Pre-May 1999 models

Removal

1 Remove the steering column shrouds as described in Chapter 11, Section 29.
2 Prise the clip from the end of the accelerator pedal spindle, then withdraw the spindle and recover the bush and spring.
3 Lift the accelerator pedal clear of the pedal bracket, disengaging it from the position sensor cable cam plate.
4 Unplug the position sensor from the wiring harness at the connector.
5 Remove the screw that secures the position sensor to the pedal bracket and remove the sensor.
6 Slacken and remove the spindle nut, then pull the cable cam plate off the spindle.

Refitting

7 Refitting is a reversal of removal, noting the following points:
  a) The cable cam plate must be fitted to the position sensor spindle according to the dimensions shown (see illustration).
  b) On completion, the adjustment of the position sensor must be verified electronically, using dedicated test equipment – refer to a VW dealer or diagnostic specialist for advice.

May 1999 models onward

Removal

8 Remove the steering column shrouds as described in Chapter 11, Section 29.
9 Disconnect the wiring connector from the top of the accelerator pedal position sensor (see illustration).

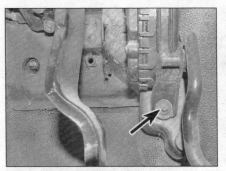

5.10 Accelerator pedal/position sensor lower retaining bolt (arrowed) – later models

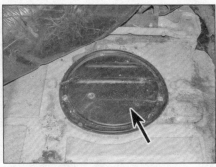

6.3 Lift the floor covering, then undo the retaining screws and remove the fuel tank access cover (arrowed)

6.4 Unplug the wiring harness connector from the sender unit

TOOL TiP

Use a pair of water pump pliers to grip and rotate the fuel tank sender unit plastic securing ring

6.6a Uscrew the plastic securing ring and lift it out

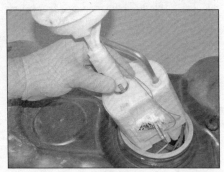

6.6b Lift the sender unit from the tank...

6.6c ...and recover the rubber seal

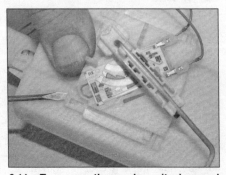

6.11a To remove the sender unit wiper and track, lift the retaining tabs with a small screwdriver...

10 Undo the two upper retaining bolts and one lower retaining bolt and remove the pedal/position sensor **(see illustration)**.

Refitting

11 Refitting is the reverse of the removal procedure. On completion, check the action of the pedal with the engine running.

6 Fuel gauge sender unit – removal and refitting

Note: *Refer to the precautions contained in Section 1 before proceeding.*

1 Disconnect the battery negative terminal (refer to *Disconnecting the battery*).

2 Remove the passenger's front seat as described in Chapter 11, Section 26.

3 Lift the floor covering in the vicinity of the passenger's front seat location, then undo the retaining screws and remove the fuel tank access cover from the floor **(see illustration)**.

4 Unplug the wiring harness connector from the sender unit **(see illustration)**.

5 Pad the area around the supply and return fuel hoses with rags to absorb any spilt fuel, then release the hose clips and remove them from the ports at the sender unit. Observe the supply and return arrows markings on the ports – label the fuel hoses accordingly to ensure correct refitting.

6 Unscrew the plastic securing ring and lift it out **(see Tool Tip)**. Lift the sender unit from the tank, holding it above the level of the fuel in the tank until the excess fuel has drained out. Recover the rubber seal **(see illustrations)**.

7 Remove the sender unit from the vehicle and lay it on an absorbent card or rag. Inspect the float at the end of the swinging arm for punctures and fuel ingress – renew the sender unit if it appears damaged.

8 The fuel pick-up incorporated in the sender unit is spring loaded to ensure that it always draws fuel from the lowest part of the tank. Check that the pick-up is free to move under spring tension with respect to the sender unit body.

9 Inspect the rubber seal for signs of fatigue or other deterioration and renew it if necessary.

10 Inspect the sender unit wiper and track; clean off any dirt and debris that may have accumulated and look for breaks in the track. An electrical specification for the sender unit is not quoted by VW, but the integrity of the wiper and track may be verified by connecting a multimeter, set to the resistance function, across the sender unit connector terminals. The resistance should vary as the float arm is moved up and down, and an open circuit reading indicates that the sender is faulty and should be renewed.

11 To remove the sender unit wiper and track, lift the retaining tabs with a small screwdriver and slide the wiper and track from its location **(see illustrations)**.

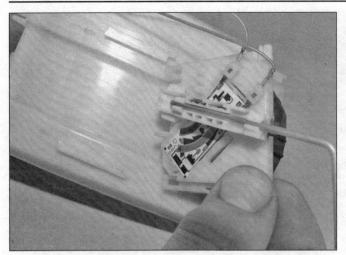

6.11b ...and slide the wiper and track from its location

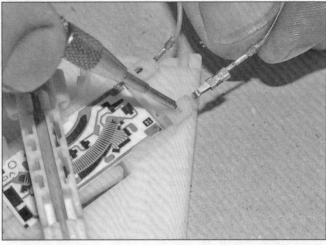

6.12 Depress the tabs on the wiring connectors and disconnect them from the wiper and track contacts

12 Depress the tabs on the wiring connectors and disconnect them from the wiper and track contacts **(see illustration)**.

Refitting

13 Refitting is a reversal of removal, noting the following points:
a) *The arrow markings on the sender unit body and the fuel tank must be aligned (see illustration).*
b) *Smear the tank aperture rubber seal with clean fuel before fitting it in position.*

7 Fuel tank – removal and refitting

Note: *Refer to the precautions contained in Section 1 before proceeding.*

Removal

1 Before removing the fuel tank, all fuel must be drained from the tank. Since a fuel tank drain plug is not provided, it is therefore preferable to carry out the removal operation when the tank is nearly empty. The remaining fuel can then be syphoned or hand-pumped from the tank.
2 Disconnect the battery negative terminal (refer to *Disconnecting the battery*).
3 Remove the fuel tank filler cap then extract the tension ring from the rubber boot. Release the rubber boot from the filler neck and body panel **(see illustrations)**.
4 Slacken the filler neck retaining screw at the top of the filler neck aperture.
5 Firmly apply the handbrake, then jack up the front of the vehicle and support it securely on axle stands (see *Jacking and vehicle support*).
6 Support the weight of the fuel tank on a jack with interposed block of wood.
7 Undo the fuel tank left-hand and centre support strap front retaining bolt and remove the retaining bracket **(see illustration)**.

8 Undo the fuel tank right-hand and centre support strap rear retaining bolts **(see illustration)**.
9 Undo the left-hand support strap rear and right-hand support strap front retaining bolts and remove the support straps **(see illustrations)**.
10 Taking care not to strain the fuel lines and wiring, partially lower the tank until access can be gained to the connections on the top of the tank.
11 Release the hose clips and remove the fuel hoses from the ports at the sender unit

6.13 The arrow markings on the sender unit body and the fuel tank must be aligned when refitting

7.3a Extract the tension ring from the fuel filler neck rubber boot...

7.3b ...then release the rubber boot from the filler neck and body panel

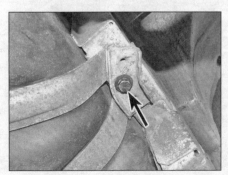

7.7 Fuel tank left-hand and centre support strap front retaining bolt (arrowed)

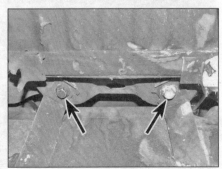

7.8 Fuel tank right-hand and centre support strap rear retaining bolts (arrowed)

7.9a Fuel tank left-hand support strap rear retaining bolt (arrowed)...

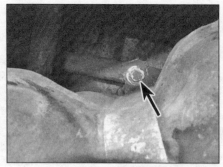

7.9b ...and right-hand support strap front retaining bolt

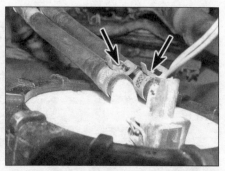

7.11 Release the hose clips (arrowed) and remove the fuel hoses from the ports at the sender unit

(see illustration). Observe the supply and return arrows markings on the ports – label the fuel hoses accordingly to ensure correct refitting.

12 Unplug the wiring harness connector from the sender unit (see illustration 6.4).

13 Lower the tank to the ground and remove it from under the vehicle.

14 If the tank contains sediment or water, it may cleaned out with two or three rinses of clean fuel. Remove the fuel gauge sender unit as described in Section 6. Shake the tank vigorously, and change the fuel as necessary to remove all contamination from the tank.

15 Any repairs to the fuel tank should be carried out by a professional. Do not under any circumstances attempt any form of DIY repair to a fuel tank.

Refitting

16 Refitting is the reverse of the removal procedure, noting the following points:

a) *When raising the tank back into position, take care to ensure that none of the fuel lines become trapped between the tank and vehicle body. Refit the retaining straps and tighten the bolts to the specified torque.*

b) *Ensure all pipes and hoses are correctly routed and all hose unions are securely joined.*

c) *On completion, refill the tank with a small amount of fuel, and check for signs of leakage prior to taking the vehicle out on the road.*

8 Fuel injection pump (1.9 litre engines) – removal, refitting and adjustment

Note: *Observe the precautions in Section 1 before working on any component in the fuel system. A suitable dial gauge and adapter will be required for the initial setting of the injection pump.*

Removal

1 Disconnect the battery negative terminal (refer to *Disconnecting the battery*).

2 Remove the timing belt as described in Chapter 2A, Section 4.

3 Loosen the nut or bolts (as applicable) that secure the timing belt sprocket to the injection pump shaft. The sprocket must be braced whilst its fixings are loosened – a homemade

tool can easily be fabricated for this purpose; refer to Chapter 2A, Section 5.

Caution: On later engines, the sprocket is a two-piece assembly, secured with three bolts – on no account should the shaft centre nut be slackened, as this will alter the basic injection timing.

4 Attach a two-legged puller to the injection pump sprocket, then gradually tighten the puller until the sprocket is under firm tension (see illustration).

Caution: To prevent damage to the injection pump shaft, insert a piece of scrap metal between the end of the shaft and the puller centre bolt.

5 Tap sharply on the puller centre bolt with a hammer – this will free the sprocket from the tapered shaft. Detach the puller, then fully slacken and remove the sprocket fixings, lift off the sprocket and recover the Woodruff key (see illustrations).

6 Using a pair of spanners, slacken the rigid fuel pipe unions at the rear of the injection pump and at each end of the injectors, then lift the fuel pipe assembly away from the engine (see illustrations).

Caution: Be prepared for some fuel leakage during this operation, position a small

8.4 Attach a two-legged puller to the injection pump sprocket

8.5a Lift off the pump sprocket...

container under the union to be slackened and pad the area with old rags, to catch any spilt diesel. Take great care to avoid stressing the rigid fuel pipes as they are removed.

7 Cover the open pipes and ports to prevent the ingress of dirt and excess fuel leakage.

8 Slacken the fuel supply and return banjo bolts at the injection pump ports, again taking precautions to minimise fuel spillage. Cover the open pipes and ports to prevent the ingress of dirt and excess fuel leakage.

9 Disconnect the injector bleed hose from the port on the fuel return union.

10 Disconnect the wiring from the stop solenoid.

11 With reference to Sections 3 and 4, disconnect the cold start accelerator cable and accelerator cable from the injection pump.

12 If the existing injection pump is to be refitted later, use a scriber or a pen to mark the relationship between the injection pump body and the front mounting bracket. This will allow an approximate injection timing setting to be achieved when the pump is refitted.

13 Slacken and withdraw the bolt that secures the injection pump to the rear mounting bracket **(see illustration)**.
Caution: Do not slacken the pump distributor head bolts, as this could cause serious internal damage to the injection pump.

14 Slacken and withdraw the three nuts/bolts that secure the injection pump to the front mounting bracket. Note that where fixing bolts are used, the two outer bolts are held captive with metal brackets. Support the pump body as the last fixing is removed.

15 Check that nothing remains connected to the injection pump, then lift it away from the engine.

Refitting and adjustment

16 Offer up the injection pump to the engine, then insert the injection pump-to-rear support bracket bolt and tighten it to the specified torque.

17 Insert the injection pump-to-front support bracket bolts and tighten them to the specified torque. **Note:** *On certain models, the mounting holes are elongated to allow adjustment – if a new pump is being fitted, then mount it such that the bolts are initially at the centre of the holes to allow the maximum range of pump timing adjustment. Alternatively, if the existing pump is being refitted, use the markings made during removal for alignment.*

18 If a new injection pump is being fitted, prime the new pump by fitting a small funnel to the fuel return pipe union and filling the cavity with clean diesel. Pad the area around the union with clean dry rags to absorb any spillage.

19 Reconnect the fuel injector delivery pipes to the injectors and injection pump head, then tighten the unions to the correct torque using a pair of spanners.

8.5b ...and recover the Woodruff key

8.6b ... then lift the fuel pipe assembly from the engine

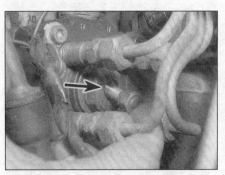

8.26 Unscrew the plug (arrowed) from the pump head and recover the seal

20 Reconnect the fuel supply and return pipes to the pump and tighten the banjo bolts to the specified torque, use new sealing washers. **Note:** *The inside diameter of the banjo bolt for the fuel return pipe is smaller than that of the fuel supply line and is marked 'OUT'.*

21 Push the injector bleed hose onto the port on the return hose union.

22 Fit the timing belt sprocket to the injection pump shaft, ensuring that the Woodruff key is correctly seated. Fit the washer and retaining nut/bolts (as applicable), hand tightening them only at this stage.

23 Lock the injection pump sprocket in position by inserting a bar or bolt through its alignment hole and into the drilling in the pump front mounting bracket. Ensure that there is minimal play in the sprocket, once it has been locked in position.

8.6a Slacken the rigid fuel pipe unions at the rear of the injection pump...

8.13 Withdraw the injection pump rear mounting bolt

24 Refit the timing belt as described in Chapter 2A, Section 4, then check and adjust the injection pump timing as follows.

25 Check that the engine is still set to TDC on No 1 cylinder as described in Chapter 2A, Section 2.

26 At the rear of the injection pump, unscrew the plug from the pump head and recover the seal **(see illustration)**.

27 Using a suitably threaded adapter, screw a DTI gauge into the pump head **(see illustration)**. Pre-load the gauge by a reading of approximately 2.5 mm.

28 Using a socket or spanner on the crankshaft pulley bolt, slowly rotate the crankshaft anti-clockwise; the DTI gauge will indicate movement – keep turning the crankshaft until the movement just ceases.

29 Zero the DTI gauge, with a pre-load of approximately 1.0 mm.

8.27 Screw a DTI gauge into the pump head

30 Now turn the crankshaft clockwise to bring the engine back up to TDC on cylinder No 1. Observe the reading indicated by the DTI gauge and compare it with the Specifications.

31 If the reading is within the 'Test' tolerance quoted in the Specifications, remove the DTI gauge and refit the pump head plug. Use a new seal and tighten the plug to the specified torque.

32 If the reading is out of tolerance, proceed as follows.

33 Slacken the pump securing bolts at the front and rear brackets.

34 Rotate the injection pump body until the 'Setting' reading (see Specifications) is indicated on the DTI gauge.

35 On completion, tighten the pump securing bolts to the specified torque.

36 Remove the DTI gauge and refit the pump head plug. Use a new seal and tighten the plug to the specified torque.

37 Tighten the fuel injection pump sprocket to the specified torque. Refit the timing belt outer cover and camshaft cover, using a new gasket where necessary.

38 The remainder of refitting is the reverse of the removal procedure, noting the following points:

a) *Reconnect all electrical connections to the pump, using the labels made during removal.*

b) *Tighten all nuts and bolts to the specified torque (where given).*

c) *Reconnect the accelerator and cold start accelerator cables to the pump and adjust them as necessary.*

d) *On completion reconnect the battery negative cable.*

9 Fuel injection pump (2.4 litre engines) – removal, refitting and adjustment

Note: *Observe the precautions in Section 1 before working on any component in the fuel system. A suitable dial gauge and adapter will be required for the initial setting of the injection pump.*

Removal

1 Disconnect the battery negative terminal (refer to *Disconnecting the battery*).

2 Remove the fuel injection pump drivebelt as described in Chapter 2B, Section 6.

3 Note and identify the wiring connections on the fuel injection pump, then disconnect them.

4 With reference to Sections 3 and 4, disconnect the cold start accelerator cable and accelerator cable from the injection pump.

5 Using a pair of spanners, slacken the rigid fuel pipe unions at the rear of the injection pump and at each end of the injectors, then lift the fuel pipe assembly away from the engine. *Caution: Be prepared for some fuel leakage during this operation, position a small*

container under the union to be slackened and pad the area with old rags, to catch any spilt diesel. Take great care to avoid stressing the rigid fuel pipes as they are removed.

6 Cover the open pipes and ports to prevent the ingress of dirt and excess fuel leakage.

7 Slacken the fuel supply and return banjo bolts at the injection pump ports, again taking precautions to minimise fuel spillage. Cover the open pipes and ports to prevent the ingress of dirt and excess fuel leakage.

8 Loosen the injection pump sprocket nut approximately one turn, then remove the locking pin.

9 To remove the injection pump sprocket, bolt a suitable puller to it. With the sprocket released from the taper on the driveshaft, fully unscrew the nut and remove the sprocket. Recover the Woodruff key.

10 Mark the position of the injection pump in relation to the mounting bracket as a guide to refitting. Unscrew the pump mounting bolts and withdraw the injection pump from the mounting bracket. Use a long socket bar to access the rear bolt.

Refitting and adjustment

11 Locate the injection pump in the mounting bracket and insert the mounting bolts loosely. Turn the pump as necessary until the mounting bolts are positioned in the centre of the elongated mounting holes, then tighten the bolts to the specified torque.

12 Refit the injection pump sprocket and Woodruff key to the pump shaft and tighten its nut to the specified torque while holding the sprocket stationary using the tool used for removal.

13 Refit and tension the injection pump drivebelt as described in Chapter 2B, Section 6.

14 Reset the engine and injection pump to TDC, then loosen the camshaft rear sprocket bolt by half a turn so that the sprocket is free to turn independent of the camshaft.

15 Unscrew and remove the timing plug from the front of the injection pump, and fit a dial gauge. A suitable adapter will be required.

16 Preload the dial gauge by 2 mm then determine the BDC position of the pump piston by turning the injection pump pulley slowly in both directions. Note that the TDC mark on the pulley is an **engine** TDC mark, but in fact the pump piston is just rising from its BDC position. This can be confusing, so it is important to observe the movement of the dial gauge so that the **pump** BDC position is obtained. The injection pump can be turned using a suitable tool engaged with the holes in the camshaft rear sprocket.

17 With the pump at BDC, zero the gauge then turn the injection pump slowly anticlockwise (viewed from the rear) using the tool on the camshaft rear sprocket until the gauge reads 1.00 ± 0.02 mm. This value is known as the derivative value.

18 Check that the flywheel TDC mark is still

aligned with the transmission aperture, then carefully tighten the bolt securing the sprocket to the rear of the camshaft to the specified torque while holding the sprocket with the tool inserted in the sprocket holes. Take care not to disturb the injection pump setting.

19 Turn the engine two complete turns clockwise and realign the TDC marks on the flywheel/driveplate and transmission. Do not turn the engine beyond the TDC marks.

20 Note the reading on the dial gauge. Due to the induced tension in the timing belt the reading will be slightly less than the derivative value. Note this discrepancy so that it can be added to the derivative value on the second (final) setting procedure. For example, if the reading is 0.94 mm, the discrepancy is 0.06 mm.

21 Repeat the setting procedure by first loosening the camshaft rear sprocket bolt by half a turn so that the sprocket is free to turn independent of the camshaft.

22 Preload the dial gauge by 2 mm then determine the BDC position of the pump piston by turning the injection pump pulley slowly in both directions (see paragraph 16). The injection pump can be turned using a suitable tool engaged with the holes in the camshaft rear sprocket.

23 With the pump at BDC, zero the gauge then turn the injection pump slowly anticlockwise (viewed from the rear) using the tool on the camshaft rear sprocket until the gauge reads 1.00 mm plus the discrepancy noted in paragraph 20 (ie 1.00 + 0.94 mm = 1.94 mm in the example).

24 Check that the flywheel TDC mark is still aligned with the transmission aperture, then carefully tighten the bolt securing the sprocket to the rear of the camshaft to the specified torque while holding the sprocket with the tool inserted in the sprocket holes. Take care not to disturb the injection pump setting.

25 Turn the engine two complete turns clockwise and realign the TDC marks on the flywheel/driveplate and transmission. Do not turn the engine beyond the TDC marks.

26 Note the reading on the dial gauge which should now be 1.00 ± 0.02 mm.

27 Remove the dial gauge and adapter, then refit the timing plug and tighten to the specified torque. Where the plug has a seal, it must be renewed.

28 If a new injection pump is being fitted, prime the new pump by fitting a small funnel to the fuel return pipe union and filling the cavity with clean diesel. Pad the area around the union with clean dry rags to absorb any spillage.

29 Reconnect the fuel injector delivery pipes to the injectors and injection pump head, then tighten the unions to the correct torque using a pair of spanners.

30 Reconnect the fuel supply and return pipes to the pump and tighten the banjo bolts to the specified torque, use new sealing washers.

31 The remainder of refitting is the reverse of

the removal procedure, noting the following points:

a) *Reconnect all electrical connections to the pump, using the labels made during removal.*

b) *Tighten all nuts and bolts to the specified torque (where given).*

c) *Reconnect the accelerator and cold start accelerator cables to the pump and adjust them as necessary.*

d) *On completion reconnect the battery negative cable.*

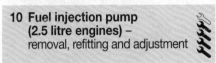

10 Fuel injection pump (2.5 litre engines) – removal, refitting and adjustment

Note: *Observe the precautions in Section 1 before working on any component in the fuel system. A suitable dial gauge and adapter will be required for the initial setting of the injection pump.*

Removal

1 Disconnect the battery negative terminal (refer to *Disconnecting the battery*).

2 Remove the fuel injection pump drivebelt as described in Chapter 2B, Section 6.

3 Note and identify the wiring connections on the fuel injection pump, then disconnect them.

4 Using a pair of spanners, slacken the rigid fuel pipe unions at the rear of the injection pump and at each end of the injectors, then lift the fuel pipe assembly away from the engine. *Caution: Be prepared for some fuel leakage during this operation, position a small container under the union to be slackened and pad the area with old rags, to catch any spilt diesel. Take great care to avoid stressing the rigid fuel pipes as they are removed.*

5 Cover the open pipes and ports to prevent the ingress of dirt and excess fuel leakage.

6 Slacken the fuel supply and return banjo bolts at the injection pump ports, again taking precautions to minimise fuel spillage. Cover the open pipes and ports to prevent the ingress of dirt and excess fuel leakage.

7 Loosen the bolt/nut securing the sprockets to the camshaft and injection pump one or two turns. To do this, hold each sprocket stationary in turn using a suitable tool engaged with the sprocket. For the injection pump sprocket, the tool may be bolted to the sprocket if necessary **(see illustrations)**.

8 To remove the injection pump sprocket, bolt a suitable puller to it. With the sprocket released, fully unscrew the nut and remove the sprocket. Recover the Woodruff key from the driveshaft **(see illustrations)**.

9 Unscrew the pump mounting bolts and mounting nut then withdraw the injection pump from the mounting bracket **(see illustrations)**.

Refitting and adjustment

10 Locate the injection pump in the mounting bracket, fit the retaining bolts and retaining nut then tighten the bolts to the specified torque.

10.7a Using a home-made tool to hold the camshaft sprocket stationary while loosening the bolt

10.8a Unscrew the nut...

11 Refit the injection pump sprocket and Woodruff key to the pump shaft and tighten its nut to the specified torque while holding the sprocket stationary using the tool used for removal.

10.8c ...and recover the Woodruff key

10.9b ...and withdraw the injection pump from the mounting bracket

10.7b Use the special tool to hold the injection pump pulley stationary

10.8b ...remove the sprocket/pulley...

12 Turn the injection pump sprocket so that the TDC timing mark on the pump sprocket aligns with the mark on the pump body **(see illustration)**.

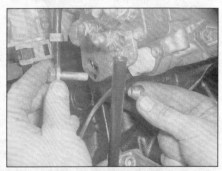

10.9a Unscrew the pump mounting bolts...

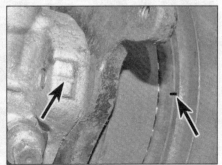

10.12 Align the TDC timing mark on the pump sprocket with the mark on the pump body (arrowed)

10.13 Unscrew the timing plug from the pump head and recover the seal

10.14a Insert a suitable adaptor...

13 At the rear of the injection pump, unscrew the timing plug from the pump head and recover the seal **(see illustration)**.

14 Using a suitable adaptor, fit a DTI gauge to the injection pump **(see illustrations)**. Preload the dial gauge by 2 mm.

15 Slacken the blocking bolt at the sprocket end of the injection pump and remove the intermediate plate **(see illustration)**.

16 Determine the BDC position of the pump piston by turning the injection pump pulley slowly in both directions. Note that the TDC mark on the pulley is an **engine** TDC mark, but in fact the pump piston is just rising from its BDC position. This can be confusing, so it is important to observe the movement of the dial gauge so that the **pump** BDC position is obtained.

17 With the pump piston at BDC, turn the injection pump sprocket slowly in the direction of engine rotation (anti-clockwise) until the DTI gauge reads 0.55 mm. Tighten the blocking bolt on the pump to lock the pump shaft in the timing position.

18 Remove the DTI gauge and refit the pump head plug. Use a new seal and tighten the plug to the specified torque.

19 Refit and tension the injection pump drivebelt as described in Chapter 2B, Section 6. With the drivebelt fitted, but before turning the crankshaft, slacken the blocking bolt, refit the intermediate plate and tighten the blocking bolt to the specified torque.

20 If a new injection pump is being fitted, prime the new pump by fitting a small funnel to the fuel return pipe union and filling the cavity with clean diesel. Pad the area around the union with clean dry rags to absorb any spillage.

21 Reconnect the fuel injector delivery pipes to the injectors and injection pump head, then tighten the unions to the correct torque using a pair of spanners.

22 Reconnect the fuel supply and return pipes to the pump and tighten the banjo bolts to the specified torque, use new sealing washers.

23 The remainder of refitting is the reverse of the removal procedure, noting the following points:

a) *Reconnect all electrical connections to the pump, using the labels made during removal.*

b) *Tighten all nuts and bolts to the specified torque (where given).*

c) *On completion reconnect the battery negative cable.*

11 Injectors – general information, removal and refitting

Note: *Observe the precautions in Section 1 before working on any component in the fuel system.*

⚠ *Warning: Exercise extreme caution when working on the fuel injectors. Never expose the hands or any part of the body to injector spray, as the high working pressure can cause the fuel to penetrate the skin, with possibly fatal results. You are strongly advised to*

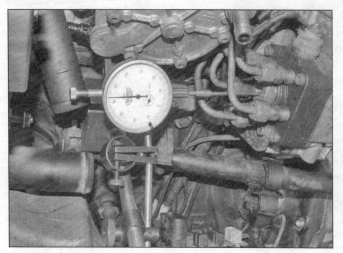

10.14b ...and fit a DTI gauge to the injection pump

10.15 Slacken the blocking bolt and remove the intermediate plate

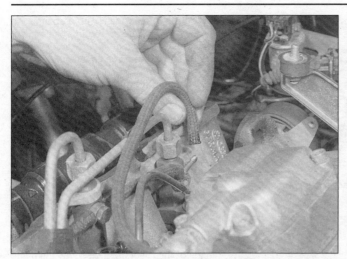

11.5 Disconnecting the leak-off hoses

11.6a Unscrew the fuel pipe union nuts while holding the injector with a further spanner

have any work which involves testing the *injectors under pressure carried out by a dealer or fuel injection specialist. Refer to the precautions given in Section 1 of this Chapter before proceeding.*

General information

1 Injectors do deteriorate with prolonged use and it is reasonable to expect them to need reconditioning or renewal after 60 000 miles or so. Accurate testing, overhaul and calibration of the injectors must be left to a specialist. A defective injector which is causing knocking or smoking can be located without dismantling as follows.
2 Run the engine at a fast idle. Slacken each injector union in turn, placing rag around the union to catch spilt fuel and being careful not to expose the skin to any spray. When the union on the defective injector is slackened, the knocking or smoking will stop.

Removal

Note: *Take great care not to allow dirt into the injectors or fuel pipes during this procedure. Do not drop the injectors or allow the needles at their tips to become damaged. The injectors are precision-made to fine limits and must not be handled roughly.*
3 Disconnect the battery negative terminal (refer to *Disconnecting the battery*).

11.6b Hold the injection pump adapters while unscrewing the union nuts

4 Move the radiator to the service position as described in Chapter 3, Section 3.
5 Carefully clean around the injectors and pipe union nuts and disconnect the leak-off hoses from the injectors (see illustration). On some engines it may be necessary to loosen clips before disconnecting the hoses.
6 Wipe clean the pipe unions then loosen the union nuts securing the injector pipes to each injector and also the union nuts securing the pipes to the rear of the injection pump (pipes are removed as one assembly). As each union nut is slackened, retain the injector or pump adapter with a suitable open-ended spanner to prevent it moving. With the union nuts undone remove

11.6c Removing the fuel pipes

the injector pipes from the engine. Cover the injector and pipe unions to prevent the entry of dirt into the system (see illustrations).

1.9 and 2.4 litre engines

7 Unscrew each injector using a 27 mm deep socket or box spanner, and remove them from the cylinder head (see illustration).
8 Recover the heat shield washers, and discard them – new washers must be used when refitting (see illustration).

2.5 litre engines

9 Disconnect the wiring for the injector needle lift sensor at the connector on the front of the cylinder block (see illustration). On all engines

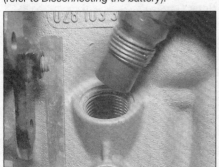

11.7 Removing an injector from the cylinder head – 1.9 and 2.4 litre engines

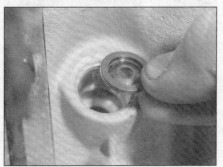

11.8 Recover the heat shield washer – 1.9 and 2.4 litre engines

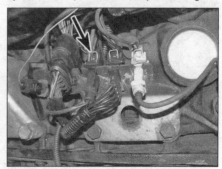

11.9 Injector needle lift sensor wiring connector (arrowed) – 2.5 litre engines

11.10a Unscrew the injector clamp retaining bolts and washers...

11.10b ...then remove the clamps...

11.10c ...and spacers – 2.5 litre engines

11.11 Withdraw the injectors from the cylinder head – 2.5 litre engines

except engine code AJT, the injector with the needle lift sensor is fitted to cylinder No. 5. On engine code AJT it is fitted to cylinder No.4.

10 Unscrew the injector clamp retaining

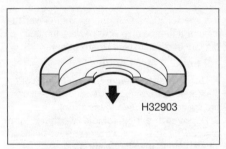

11.14 The heat shield washer must be fitted with the curved side pointing downwards (arrow faces the cylinder head) – 1.9 and 2.4 litre engines

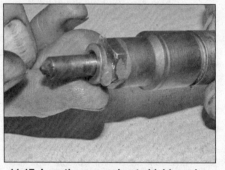

11.17 Locating a new heat shield washer on the injector – 2.5 litre engines

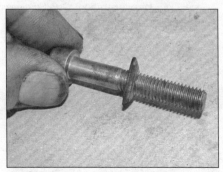

11.19 Fit the washers to the injector clamp retaining bolts with their dished side facing away from the bolt head – 2.5 litre engines

12.4 Disconnect the wiring connector from the top of the stop solenoid

bolts and washers, then remove the clamps and spacers **(see illustrations)**.

11 Withdraw the injectors from the cylinder head **(see illustration)**. If they are tight, ease

them out by turning them with a spanner on their flats. If they are seized in position, VW technicians use a slide hammer tool which is screwed onto the pipe union thread.

12 Using a screwdriver, hook out the heat shield washers from the injector recesses in the cylinder head.

Refitting

1.9 and 2.4 litre engines

13 Clean out the injector location recesses and threads in the cylinder head.

14 Locate new heat shield washers in the cylinder head, making sure that they are fitted the correct way round. The outer rims must face upwards so that the curved sides are pointing downwards **(see illustration)**.

15 Apply a little anti-seize compound to the threads of the injectors, then screw them into the cylinder head and tighten to the specified torque.

2.5 litre engines

16 Clean out the injector location recesses in the cylinder head.

17 Locate new heat shield washers on the injectors **(see illustration)**.

18 Insert each injector making sure that the leak-off hose stubs are pointing away from the engine, and that the needle lift sensing injector is fitted to cylinder No. 4 or 5 as applicable.

19 Fit the washers to the injector clamp retaining bolts with their dished side facing away from the bolt head **(see illustration)**.

20 Refit the spacers and clamps, then fit the bolts and washers and tighten the bolts to the specified torque.

All engines

21 Refit the injector pipes to the injectors and injection pump and tighten the nuts while holding the injectors or pump adapter with a spanner.

22 Reconnect the leak-off hoses and tighten the clips where necessary.

23 Move the radiator back to its normal position as described in Chapter 3, Section 3.

24 Reconnect the battery negative terminal.

12 Fuel injection pump stop solenoid – removal and refitting

Note: *Observe the precautions in Section 1 before working on the fuel system.*

Removal

1 The stop solenoid is located at the rear of the injection pump.

2 For improved access, move the radiator to the service position as described in Chapter 3, Section 3.

3 Disconnect the battery negative terminal (refer to *Disconnecting the battery*).

4 Disconnect the wiring connector from the top of the stop solenoid **(see illustration)**.

5 Slacken and withdraw the solenoid body from the injection pump. Recover the sealing washer, O-ring seal and the plunger.

Refitting

6 Refitting is a reversal of removal. Use a new sealing washer and O-ring seal and tighten the solenoid to the specified torque.

13 Diesel engine management system (2.5 litre engines) – component removal and refitting

Note: *Observe the precautions in Section 1 before working on the fuel system.*

Accelerator pedal position sensor

1 Proceed as described in Section 5.

Coolant temperature sensor

2 Proceed as described in Chapter 3, Section 7.

Engine speed sensor

Removal

3 The engine speed sensor is mounted on the front facing side of the cylinder block, adjacent to the mating surface of the block and transmission bellhousing.
4 Trace the wiring back from the sensor to the adjacent connector and disconnect it.
5 Undo the retaining screw and withdraw the sensor from the cylinder block **(see illustration)**.

Refitting

6 Refitting is a reversal of removal.

Start of injection valve

Removal

7 The start of injection valve is located just below the distributor head on the fuel injection pump. First clean the area around the valve to prevent dust and dirt entering the fuel system.
8 Undo the screw and withdraw the valve from the injection pump. Be prepared for some loss of fuel.
9 Recover the outer O-ring, strainer and inner O-ring.
10 Disconnect the wiring at the connector.

Refitting

11 Refitting is a reversal of removal, but clean all components before fitting and tighten the screw securely.

13.5 Removing the engine speed sensor

Charge pressure control valve

Removal

12 The charge pressure control valve is located on the engine compartment bulkhead, behind the coolant expansion tank.
13 Disconnect the wiring connector.
14 Remove the vacuum hoses, noting their order of connection carefully to aid correct refitting.
15 Unscrew the mounting nuts and withdraw the valve.

Refitting

16 Refitting is a reversal of removal.

Manifold absolute pressure sensor

Removal

17 On pre-May 1999 models the manifold absolute pressure sensor is an integral part of the electronic control unit and cannot be removed separately.
18 On May-1999 models onward, the manifold absolute pressure sensor is located on the side of the intercooler and incorporates the inlet manifold temperature sensor **(see illustration)**.
19 Disconnect the wiring connector from the sensor.
20 Undo the two retaining screws and remove the sensor from the intercooler.

Refitting

21 Refitting is a reversal of removal.

13.18 Manifold absolute pressure sensor (arrowed)

Airflow meter

Removal

22 The airflow meter is located in the air cleaner cover.
23 Remove the air cleaner cover as described in Section 2.
24 Undo the two retaining screws and remove the airflow meter from the air cleaner cover.

Refitting

25 Refitting is a reversal of removal.

Electronic control unit (ECU)

Caution: The unit is coded, and should not be removed without consulting a VW dealer, otherwise it may not function correctly when reconnected. Always wait at least 30 seconds after switching off the ignition before disconnecting the wiring from the ECU. When the wiring is disconnected, all the learned values are erased, although any contents of the fault memory are retained. After reconnecting the wiring, the basic settings must be reinstated by a VW dealer using a special test instrument. Note also that if the ECU is renewed, the identification of the new ECU must be transferred to the immobiliser control unit (where applicable) by a VW dealer.

Removal

26 The ECU is located on the left-hand side of the engine compartment, in front of the battery.
27 Make sure the ignition is switched off.
28 Turn the plastic retainer half a turn, disengage the locating tabs and lift off the cover over the battery **(see illustrations)**.

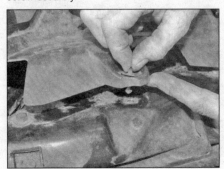

13.28a Turn the plastic retainer half a turn...

13.28b ...disengage the locating tabs on the left-hand side...

13.28c ...and right-hand side (arrowed)...

4A•16 Fuel and exhaust systems

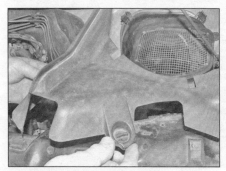

13.28d ...then lift off the cover over the battery

13.29a Lift off the cover over the top of the ECU...

13.29b ...then withdraw the unit from its location

29 Lift off the cover over the top of the ECU then withdraw the unit from its location **(see illustrations)**.

30 Release the locking clip or lever on each ECU wiring connector, and disconnect them with great care. On most models, there is a single large connector but in some cases there are two separate plugs to be disconnected.

Refitting

31 Refitting is a reversal of removal.

Clutch and brake pedal switches

Removal and refitting

32 The clutch and brake pedal switches send signals to the ECU which automatically adjusts the injection pump timing. The switches are located on the clutch and brake pedal mounting bracket in the driver's footwell.

33 Turn the retaining catch anti-clockwise and open the driver's side stowage box fully. Lift the stowage box out of the lower retainers and remove it from the facia **(see illustrations)**.

34 Remove the steering column shrouds as described in Chapter 11, Section 29.

35 Disconnect the wiring connector from the relevant switch **(see illustration)**.

36 Turn the switch 90° and remove it from the mounting bracket **(see illustration)**.

Refitting

37 Refitting is a reversal of removal, but before fitting the switch fully extend the switch plunger, then depress and hold the brake pedal while manoeuvring the switch into position. Turn the switch 90° to secure.

14 Intercooler –
removal and refitting

Removal

1 Lift off the plastic trim cover over the intercooler upper mounting nuts **(see illustration)**.

2 Undo the four nuts securing the intercooler to the rubber mounting blocks **(see illustration)**.

3 Disconnect the wiring connector from the manifold absolute pressure sensor located on the side of the intercooler **(see illustration)**. Where fitted, also disconnect the vacuum hose located adjacent to the pressure sensor.

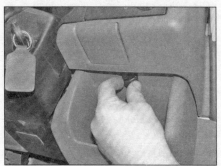

13.33a Open the driver's side stowage box fully...

13.33b ...then lift the stowage box out of the lower retainers and remove it from the facia

13.35 Disconnect the wiring connector (arrowed) from the brake pedal switch

13.36 Turn the switch 90° and remove it from the mounting bracket

14.1 Lift off the plastic trim cover over the intercooler upper mounting nuts

14.2 Undo the four nuts (arrowed) securing the intercooler to the rubber mounting blocks

14.3 Disconnect the wiring connector from the manifold absolute pressure sensor

14.4a Release the right-hand air duct retaining clip...

14.4b ...and left-hand air duct retaining clip...

14.4c ...then disconnect the air ducts from the intercooler

14.5 Lift the intercooler off the rubber mounting blocks and remove it from the engine compartment

14.6 If necessary, undo the retaining bolts and remove the intercooler lower mounting bracket

4 Release the retaining clips and disconnect the air ducts from the intercooler **(see illustrations)**.

5 Lift the intercooler off the rubber mounting blocks and remove it from the engine compartment **(see illustration)**.

6 If the intercooler is being removed to provide access to the engine, undo the two retaining bolts and remove the lower mounting bracket from the radiator upper crossmember **(see illustration)**.

Refitting

7 Refitting is a reversal of removal, but check the condition of the rubber mounting blocks and renew any that show signs of deterioration.

15 Inlet manifold –
removal and refitting

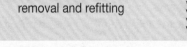

Note: *Observe the precautions in Section 1 before working on fuel system components.*

Removal

1 Disconnect the battery negative terminal (refer to *Disconnecting the battery*).

2 Move the radiator to the service position as described in Chapter 3, Section 3.

3 Remove the air cleaner assembly as described in Section 2.

4 Where applicable, unscrew the nuts and bolts and remove the EGR valve and pipe assembly from the inlet manifold and exhaust manifold. Disconnect the vacuum pipe and recover the gaskets.

5 Loosen the clips and disconnect the vacuum hoses.

6 Where fitted, unbolt and remove the heat shield from the inlet and exhaust manifold **(see illustration)**.

15.6 Undo the retaining bolts and remove the exhaust manifold heat shield (arrowed)

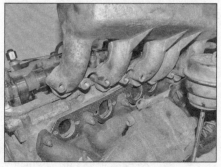

15.7b ...then withdraw the manifold...

7 Using an Allen key, progressively unscrew the bolts securing the inlet manifold to the cylinder head, then withdraw the manifold and remove the gasket **(see illustrations)**.

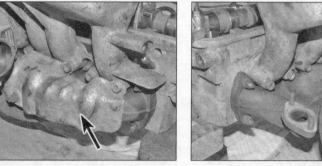

15.7a Unscrew the bolts securing the inlet manifold to the cylinder head...

15.7c ...and remove the gasket

8 Clean the gasket faces of the manifold and cylinder head.

Refitting

9 Refitting is a reversal of removal, but fit a new gasket and tighten the retaining bolts securely.

16 Exhaust manifold – removal and refitting

1.9 litre engines

Removal

1 Remove the inlet manifold as described in Section 15.
2 Remove the engine undertray as described in Chapter 11, Section 25.
3 Slacken the retaining clips and remove the air inlet hoses from the turbocharger.
4 Unscrew the union nuts and disconnect the oil supply and return pipes from the turbocharger.
5 Undo the retaining bolts and separate the exhaust front pipe elbow from the turbocharger. Move the elbow slightly to one side.
6 Progressively unscrew the mounting nuts and remove the washers, then withdraw the exhaust manifold, complete with the turbocharger from the studs on the cylinder head. Recover the gaskets.
7 With the manifold on the bench unscrew the mounting bolts and remove the turbocharger.

Refitting

8 Clean the mating surfaces of the manifold and cylinder head, then locate new gaskets on the studs.
9 Clean the mating surfaces of the turbocharger and manifold, then refit the turbocharger to the manifold. Tighten the mounting bolts to the specified torque.
10 Refit the manifold to the studs on the cylinder head, and tighten the nuts to the specified torque.
11 Refit the exhaust front pipe elbow to the turbocharger and tighten the retaining bolts to the specified torque.
12 Fill the turbocharger with clean engine oil via the oil supply pipe connection.
13 Reconnect the oil supply and return pipes to the turbocharger. Tighten the union nuts to the specified torque.
14 Reconnect the air inlet hoses to the turbocharger.
15 Refit the inlet manifold as described in Section 15.
16 Refit the engine undertray as described in Chapter 11, Section 25, then lower the vehicle to the ground.
17 When the engine is started after refitting, allow it idle for approximately one minute to give the oil time to circulate around the turbine shaft bearings.

2.4 litre engines

Removal

18 Remove the inlet manifold as described in Section 15.
19 Remove the engine undertray as described in Chapter 11, Section 25.
20 Disconnect the exhaust system front pipe from the manifold as described in Section 19.
21 Progressively unscrew the mounting nuts and remove the washers, then withdraw the exhaust manifold from the studs on the cylinder head. Recover the gaskets.

Refitting

22 Refitting is a reversal of removal, but fit new gaskets and tighten the mounting nuts to the specified torque.

2.5 litre engines

Removal

23 Remove the turbocharger as described in Section 18.
24 Progressively unscrew the mounting nuts and remove the washers, then withdraw the exhaust manifold from the studs on the cylinder head. Recover the gaskets.

Refitting

25 Refitting is a reversal of removal, but fit new gaskets and tighten the mounting nuts to the specified torque. On completion, refit the turbocharger as described in Section 18.

17 Turbocharger – general information and precautions

General information

1.9 litre (engine code ABL) and all 2.5 litre engines are equipped with a turbocharger mounted directly on the exhaust manifold.

The turbocharger increases engine efficiency by raising the pressure in the inlet manifold above atmospheric pressure. Instead of the air simply being sucked into the cylinders, it is forced in. Additional fuel is supplied by the injection pump, in proportion to the increased amount of air.

Energy for the operation of the turbocharger comes from the exhaust gases. The gas flows through a specially-shaped housing (the turbine housing) and in so doing, spins the turbine wheel. The turbine wheel is attached to a shaft, at the end of which is another vaned wheel, known as the compressor wheel. The compressor wheel spins in its own housing, and compresses the inducted air on the way to the inlet manifold.

On certain 2.5 litre engines (engine codes ACV, AUF and AYC), between the turbocharger and the inlet manifold, the compressed air passes through an intercooler. The purpose of the intercooler is to remove from the inducted air some of the heat gained in being compressed. Because cooler air is denser, removal of this heat further increases engine efficiency.

The turbo shaft is pressure-lubricated by its own dedicated oil feed pipe. The shaft 'floats' on a cushion of oil. Oil is returned to the sump via a return pipe that connects to the sump.

The turbocharger unit has an integral wastegate valve and vacuum actuator diaphragm, which is used to control the boost pressure applied to the inlet manifold.

Precautions

Caution: Do not operate the engine if any of air intake ducts are disconnected or the filter element is removed. Any debris entering the engine will cause severe damage to the turbocharger.

Caution: To prevent damage to the turbocharger, do not race the engine immediately after start-up, especially if it is cold. Allow it to idle smoothly to give the oil a few seconds to circulate around the turbocharger bearings. Always allow the engine to return to idle speed before switching it off – do not blip the throttle and switch off, as this will leave the turbo spinning without lubrication.

Caution: Observe the recommended intervals for oil and filter changing, and use a reputable oil of the specified quality. Neglect of oil changing, or use of inferior oil, can cause carbon formation on the turbo shaft, leading to subsequent failure.

18 Turbocharger – removal and refitting

Note: *The turbocharger should only be removed with the engine completely cool.*

1.9 litre engines

1 The turbocharger is removed together with the exhaust manifold and the two components are then separated on the bench. Proceed as described in Section 16.

2.5 litre engines

Removal

2 Remove the inlet manifold as described in Section 15.
3 Remove the engine undertray as described in Chapter 11, Section 25.
4 Remove the exhaust system front pipe as described in Section 19.
5 Disconnect the vacuum hoses at the charge pressure control valve and at the turbocharger vacuum actuator and banjo union **(see illustrations)**.
6 Slacken the retaining clip and remove the air inlet hose from the turbocharger air duct **(see illustration)**.
7 Remove the breather hose between the crankcase ventilation valve and the turbocharger air duct, then undo the retaining bolts and remove the air duct.

18.5a Disconnect the vacuum hoses at the turbocharger vacuum actuator...

18.5b ...and banjo union

18.6 Slacken the retaining clip and remove the air inlet hose from the turbocharger air duct

8 Undo the cap nut, disconnect the oil supply pipe from the turbocharger and collect the two washers **(see illustrations)**.
9 Undo the two bolts and disconnect the oil return pipe flange from the turbocharger. Collect the gasket **(see illustrations)**.
10 Undo the bolt and two nuts securing the turbocharger to the manifold **(see illustrations)**. Lift the turbocharger upwards and remove it from the manifold.

Refitting

11 Refitting is a reversal of removal, bearing in mind the following points:
a) Use new gaskets and seals at all disturbed connections.
b) Tighten all fastenings to the specified torque (where given).
c) Before reconnecting the oil supply pipe,

fill the turbocharger with clean engine oil via the oil supply pipe connection.
d) When the engine is started after refitting,

allow it idle for approximately one minute to give the oil time to circulate around the turbine shaft bearings.

18.8a Undo the cap nut...

18.8b ...remove the upper copper washer...

18.8c ....lift off the oil supply pipe...

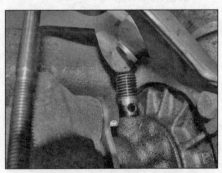

18.8d ...and remove the lower copper washer

18.9a Undo the two bolts (arrowed)...

18.9b ...then disconnect the turbocharger oil return pipe flange and collect the gasket

18.10a Turbocharger mounting bolt (arrowed)...

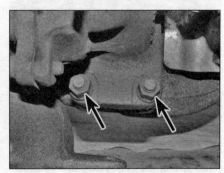

18.10b ...and mounting nuts (arrowed)

TOOL TiP

To make an exhaust system clamping wedge, obtain a strip of steel about 3 mm thick, 100 mm long and 40 mm wide. Cut off approximately 7 mm on each side, leaving a small flange at the bottom of the cut. Use a file to chamfer each side slightly at the top of the cut. You will need to make two of these wedges.

19 Exhaust system – general information and component renewal

⚠️ **Warning: Inspection and repair of exhaust system components should be done only after the system has cooled completely. This applies particularly to the catalytic converter, which runs at very high temperatures.**

General information

1 The exhaust system consists of the front pipe, the front silencer (or catalytic converter, depending on specification), the intermediate silencer and the tail pipe which contains a rear silencer on certain models. A semi-flexible coupling is used in the front pipe attachment at the exhaust manifold or turbocharger elbow.

2 The system is suspended throughout its entire length by rubber mountings, which are secured to the underside of the vehicle by metal brackets.

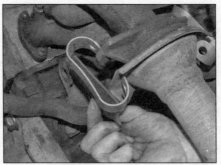

19.8a Push the exhaust system front pipe sideways and insert the clamping wedge

Removal

3 Each exhaust section can be removed individually or, alternatively, the complete system can be removed as a unit.

4 To remove the system or part of the system, first jack up the front or rear of the vehicle and support it on axle stands (see *Jacking and Vehicle Support*). Alternatively position the vehicle over an inspection pit or on car ramps.

Front pipe

5 On models without a catalytic converter, separate the front pipe from the front silencer by undoing the nut and bolt and releasing the clamp. Apply penetrating fluid to the joint and pull the front silencer out of the front pipe if possible. It may be necessary to release part of the system from its mountings so that the joint can be twisted apart.

6 On models with a catalytic converter, undo the three nuts, remove the bolts and separate the flange joint. Recover the gasket.

7 It is now necessary to remove the two clamping springs that secure the front pipe to the exhaust manifold or turbocharger elbow. To do this it will be necessary to obtain two clamping wedges (VW special tool 3140) or make up suitable alternatives **(see Tool Tip)**.

8 Push the bottom of the exhaust system front pipe toward the right-hand side of the vehicle as far as possible to spread the left-hand clamping spring. Insert the VW tool or the home-made alternative into the

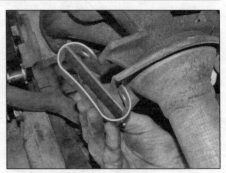

19.8b Push the front pipe the other way and remove the clamping spring and wedge

clamping spring from the front and push it fully into the clamping spring, up to the flange. Move the front pipe toward the left-hand side of the vehicle as far as it will go and withdraw the clamping spring and the tool **(see illustrations)**.

9 Using the same procedure, remove the remaining clamping spring in the same way, then remove the front pipe from under the vehicle **(see illustration)**. Check the condition of the sealing ring and renew it if necessary

10 To remove the tool from the clamping spring after removal, place the clamping spring over the slightly open jaws of a vice and tap the tool out of the clamping spring using a hammer **(see illustration)**.

11 To insert the tool into the clamping springs so they are ready for refitting, secure the clamping spring in the vice. Use two screwdrivers inserted in the holes in the clamping spring and push down on the screwdrivers to spread the spring apart. With the spring fully spread, tap the tool into position with a hammer then remove the screwdrivers **(see illustration)**.

Front silencer

12 Separate the front silencer from the front pipe by undoing the nut and bolt and releasing the clamp. Apply penetrating fluid to the joint and pull the front silencer out of the front pipe if possible. It may be necessary to release part of the system from its mountings so that the joint can be twisted apart.

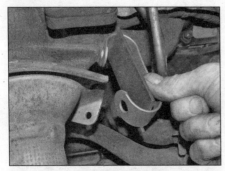

19.9 Using the same procedure, remove the remaining clamping spring in the same way

19.10 Place the clamping spring over the slightly open vice jaws and tap the clamping wedge out of the clamping spring

19.11 Fitting the clamping wedge to the clamping spring

13 Separate the front silencer from the intermediate silencer using the same procedure, release it from the mountings, then remove the front silencer from under the vehicle.

Catalytic converter

14 Slacken and remove the nuts securing the front pipe to the catalytic converter. Remove the bolts and recover the gasket from the flange joint.

15 Separate the catalytic converter from the intermediate pipe by undoing the nut and bolt and releasing the clamp. Apply penetrating fluid to the joint, release it from the mountings, and pull the catalytic converter out of the intermediate silencer using a twisting motion.

Intermediate silencer

16 Undo the nuts and bolts and disengage the clamp at each end if the intermediate silencer.

17 Disengage the intermediate pipe from the tailpipe and the catalytic converter/front pipe, release it from the mountings, and remove it from the vehicle.

Tailpipe

18 Undo the nut and bolt, disengage the tailpipe clamp, then separate the joint.

19 Unhook the tailpipe from its mounting rubbers and remove it from the vehicle.

Complete system

20 Disconnect the front pipe from the manifold – see paragraphs 7 to 11.

21 With the aid of an assistant, free the system from all its mounting rubbers and manoeuvre it out from underneath the vehicle.

Heatshield(s)

22 The heatshields are secured to the underside of the body by a mixture of nuts, bolts and clips. Each shield can be removed once the relevant exhaust section has been removed. Note that if the shield is being removed to gain access to a component located behind it, in some cases it may prove sufficient to remove the retaining nuts and/or bolts and simply lower the shield, removing the need to disturb the exhaust system.

Refitting

23 Each section is refitted by a reverse of the removal sequence, noting the following points.

  a) Ensure that all traces of corrosion have been removed from the flanges and renew all necessary gaskets.

  b) Inspect the rubber mountings for signs of damage or deterioration and renew as necessary.

  c) When reconnecting the front pipe to the manifold or turbocharger elbow, fit the clamping springs so that the flange on the clamping wedge is facing forward, then tap out the clamping wedge using a hammer.

  d) Prior to tightening the exhaust system fasteners, ensure that all rubber mountings are correctly located and that there is adequate clearance between the exhaust system and vehicle underbody.

Chapter 4 Part B:
Emission control systems

Contents

Degrees of difficulty

Easy, suitable for novice with little experience	**Fairly easy,** suitable for beginner with some experience	**Fairly difficult,** suitable for competent DIY mechanic	**Difficult,** suitable for experienced DIY mechanic	**Very difficult,** suitable for expert DIY or professional

Specifications

Torque wrench settings

	Nm	lbf ft
4-cylinder engines:		
EGR valve-to-manifold bolts	25	18
EGR valve semi-flexible pipe nuts/bolts	25	18
5-cylinder engines:		
EGR valve-to-manifold bolts	15	11
EGR valve semi-flexible pipe:		
To EGR valve bolts	15	11
To exhaust manifold nuts	25	18

1 General information

Emission control systems

A number of systems are fitted that help to minimise harmful emissions: a crankcase emission-control system that reduces the release of pollutants from the engines lubrication system is fitted to all models, catalytic converters that reduce exhaust gas pollutants are fitted to most later models. An Exhaust Gas Recirculation (EGR) system may also be fitted to further decrease exhaust emissions.

Crankcase emission control

To reduce the emission of unburned hydrocarbons from the crankcase into the atmosphere, the engine is sealed and the blow-by gases and oil vapour are drawn from inside the crankcase, through a wire mesh oil separator, into the inlet manifold to be burned by the engine during normal combustion.

A pressure regulating valve (on the camshaft cover) controls the flow of gases from the crankcase.

If the engine is worn, the raised crankcase pressure (due to increased blow-by) will cause some of the flow to return through the inlet manifold under all operating conditions.

Exhaust emission control

An oxidation catalyst is fitted in the exhaust system on most models. This has the effect of removing a large proportion of the gaseous hydrocarbons, carbon monoxide and particulates present in the exhaust gas.

The Exhaust Gas Recirculation (EGR) system reduces the level of nitrogen oxides produced during combustion by introducing a proportion of the exhaust gas back into the inlet manifold, under certain engine operating conditions, via a plunger valve. The system is controlled electronically by the glow plug control module (4-cylinder engines) by the diesel engine management ECU (5-cylinder engines).

2 Crankcase emission control system – general information

The crankcase emission control system consists of a series of hoses that connect the crankcase vent to the camshaft cover vent and the air inlet, a pressure regulating valve (where applicable) and an oil separator unit.

The system requires no attention other than to check at regular intervals that the hose(s) are free of blockages and undamaged.

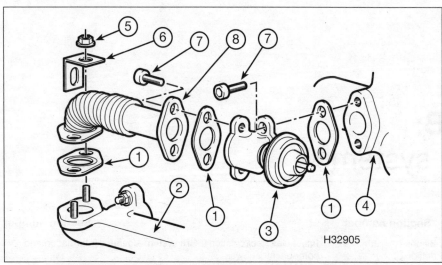

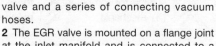

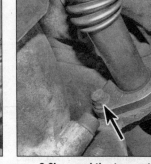

3.5b Disconnect the vacuum hose from the port on the EGR valve – 2.5 litre engines

3.5a Typical arrangement of EGR valve and associated components – 1.9 litre engines

1 Gaskets	4 Inlet manifold	7 Bolts
2 Exhaust manifold	5 Nut	8 Semi-flexible pipe
3 EGR valve	6 Oil supply pipe bracket	

3 Exhaust Gas Recirculation (EGR) system – general information and component renewal

General information

1 The EGR system is only fitted to 1.9 litre and 2.5 litre engines, and consists of an EGR recirculation valve, an EGR modulator valve and a series of connecting vacuum hoses.

2 The EGR valve is mounted on a flange joint at the inlet manifold and is connected to a second flange joint at the exhaust manifold by a semi-flexible pipe.

3 The EGR modulator valve is mounted on the on the engine compartment bulkhead.

Component renewal

EGR valve

4 On engines with an intercooler mounted over the top of the camshaft cover, remove the intercooler as described in Chapter 4A, Section 14.

5 Disconnect the vacuum hose from the port on the EGR valve **(see illustrations)**.

6 Unscrew the two bolts securing the semi-flexible pipe to the EGR valve and the two nuts securing the pipe to the exhaust manifold. Lift off the pipe and collect the two flange gaskets **(see illustrations)**.

7 Unscrew the bolts that secure the EGR valve to the inlet manifold flange. Lift off the EGR valve assembly and collect the gasket **(see illustrations)**.

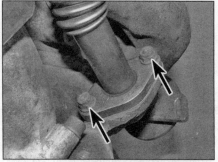

3.6a Unscrew the two bolts (arrowed) securing the semi-flexible pipe to the EGR valve...

3.6b ...and the two nuts (arrowed) securing the pipe to the exhaust manifold – 2.5 litre engines

3.6c Lift off the pipe...

3.6d ...and collect the two flange gaskets – 2.5 litre engines

3.7a Remove the EGR valve assembly from the inlet manifold...

3.7b ...and collect the gasket – 2.5 litre engines

8 Refitting is a reversal of removal, noting the following points:
- a) *Use new flange joint gaskets and self-locking nuts.*
- b) *When reconnecting the semi-flexible pipe, fit the retaining nuts/bolts loosely and ensure that the pipe is unstressed before tightening the nuts/bolts to the specified torque.*

EGR modulator valve

9 Disconnect the wiring connector from the valve **(see illustration)**.
10 Identify the vacuum hoses for position, then disconnect them from the valve.
11 Unscrew the mounting nuts and remove the valve from the bulkhead bracket.
12 Refitting is a reversal of removal.
Caution: Ensure that the vacuum hoses are refitted correctly; combustion and exhaust smoke production can be drastically affected by an incorrectly operating EGR system.

4 Catalytic converter – general information and precautions

General information

1 The catalytic converter reduces harmful exhaust emissions by chemically converting the more poisonous gases to ones which (in theory at least) are less harmful. The chemical reaction is known as an 'oxidising' reaction, or one where oxygen is 'added'.
2 Inside the converter is a honeycomb structure, made of ceramic material and coated with the precious metals palladium, platinum and rhodium (the 'catalyst' which promotes the chemical reaction). The chemical reaction generates heat, which itself promotes the reaction – therefore, once the vehicle has been driven several miles, the body of the converter will be very hot.
3 The ceramic structure contained within the converter is understandably fragile, and will not withstand rough treatment. Since the converter runs at a high temperature, driving through deep standing water (in flood conditions, for example) is to be avoided, since the thermal stresses imposed when plunging the hot converter into cold water may well cause the ceramic internals to fracture, resulting in a 'blocked' converter – a common cause of failure. A converter which has been damaged in this way can be checked by shaking it (do not strike it) – if a rattling noise is heard, this indicates probable failure. **Note:** *Checking the operation of a catalytic converter requires expensive and sophisticated diagnostic equipment, starting with a high-quality exhaust gas analyser. If the level of CO in the exhaust gases is too high, a full check of the engine management system must be carried out to eliminate all other possibilities before the converter is suspected of being faulty. The vehicle should be taken to a VW dealer for this work to be carried out using the correct diagnostic equipment. Do not waste time trying to test the system without such facilities.*

Precautions

4 The catalytic converter is a reliable and simple device which needs no maintenance in itself, but there are some facts of which an

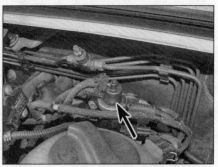

3.9 EGR modulator valve location on the engine compartment bulkhead – 2.5 litre engines

owner should be aware if the converter is to function properly for its full service life.
- a) *DO NOT use fuel or engine oil additives – these may contain substances harmful to the catalytic converter.*
- b) *DO NOT continue to use the vehicle if the engine burns oil to the extent of leaving a visible trail of blue smoke.*
- c) *Remember that the catalytic converter operates at very high temperatures. DO NOT, therefore, park the vehicle in dry undergrowth, over long grass or piles of dead leaves after a long run.*
- d) *Remember that the catalytic converter is FRAGILE – do not strike it with tools during servicing work.*
- e) *The catalytic converter, used on a well-maintained and well-driven vehicle, should last for between 50 000 and 100 000 miles – if the converter is no longer effective it must be renewed. Renewal procedures are contained in Chapter 4A, Section 19.*

Chapter 5
Starting and charging systems

Contents

Degrees of difficulty

Easy, suitable for novice with little experience | **Fairly easy,** suitable for beginner with some experience | **Fairly difficult,** suitable for competent DIY mechanic | **Difficult,** suitable for experienced DIY mechanic | **Very difficult,** suitable for expert DIY or professional

Specifications

General
Electrical system type . . . . 12 volt, negative-earth

Battery
Rating . . . . 44 to 110 Ah (depending on model and market)

Alternator
Type . . . . Bosch or Valeo
Rating . . . . 65, 70, 90 or 120 amp

Starter motor
Type . . . . Pre-engaged

Glow plugs
Current consumption . . . . 10 amps per glow plug

Torque wrench settings

	Nm	lbf ft
Alternator mountings:		
With auxiliary V-belt drive:		
Adjustment arm nut locking bolt.	35	26
Adjustment arm-to-mounting bracket bolt	23	17
Mounting bolts	35	26
With ribbed auxiliary belt drive:		
Mounting bolts	25	18
Glow plugs:		
1.9 litre engines	15	11
2.4 litre engines	25	18
2.5 litre engines	15	11
Starter motor mounting bolts:		
Automatic transmission models	40	30
Manual transmission models	20	15

1 General information, precautions and battery disconnection

General information

The engine electrical system consists mainly of the charging and starting systems, and the engine pre/post-heating system. Because of their engine-related functions, these components are covered separately from the body electrical devices such as the lights, instruments, etc (which are covered in Chapter 12).

The electrical system is of 12-volt negative earth type.

The battery may be of the low-maintenance or maintenance-free (sealed for life) type, and is charged by the alternator, which is belt-driven from the crankshaft pulley.

The starter motor is of pre-engaged type incorporating an integral solenoid. On starting, the solenoid moves the drive pinion into engagement with the flywheel/driveplate ring gear before the starter motor is energised. Once the engine has started, a one-way clutch prevents the motor armature being driven by the engine until the pinion disengages.

Further details of the various systems are given in the relevant Sections of this Chapter. While some repair procedures are given, the usual course of action is to renew the component concerned.

Precautions

It is necessary to take extra care when working on the electrical system to avoid damage to semi-conductor devices (diodes and transistors), and to avoid the risk of personal injury. In addition to the precautions given in *Safety first!* at the beginning of this manual, observe the following when working on the system:

• *Always remove rings, watches, etc before working on the electrical system. Even with the battery disconnected, capacitive discharge could occur if a component's live terminal is earthed through a metal object. This could cause a shock or nasty burn.*

• *Do not reverse the battery connections. Components such as the alternator, electronic control units, or any other components having semi-conductor circuitry could be irreparably damaged.*

• *If the engine is being started using jump leads and a slave battery, connect the batteries positive-to-positive and negative-to-negative (see 'Jump starting'). This also applies when connecting a battery charger but in this case both of the battery terminals should first be disconnected.*

• *Never disconnect the battery terminals, the alternator, any electrical wiring or any test instruments when the engine is running.*

• *Do not allow the engine to turn the alternator when the alternator is not connected.*

• *Never test for alternator output by flashing the output lead to earth.*

• *Never use an ohmmeter of the type incorporating a hand-cranked generator for circuit or continuity testing.*

• *Always ensure that the battery negative lead is disconnected when working on the electrical system.*

• *Before using electric arc welding equipment on the vehicle, disconnect the battery, alternator and components such as the engine powertrain control module to protect them from the risk of damage.*

Battery disconnection

Refer to the precautions listed in *Disconnecting the battery* in the Reference chapter at the end of this manual.

2 Electrical fault finding – general information

Refer to Chapter 12, Section 2.

3 Battery – testing and charging

Testing

1 The simplest way to test a battery is with a voltmeter (or multimeter set to voltage testing) – connect the voltmeter across the battery terminals, observing the correct polarity. The test is only accurate if the battery has not been subjected to any kind of charge for the previous six hours. If this is not the case, switch on the headlights for 30 seconds, then wait four to five minutes before testing the battery after switching off the headlights. All other electrical circuits must be switched off, so check that the doors and, where applicable, the tailgate are fully shut when making the test.

2 If the voltage reading is less than 12.0 volts, then the battery is less than healthy. Under 11.5 volts and the battery needs charging. However, as little as 11.0 volts will still usually be enough to start the engine, though a battery in this condition could not be relied on. A reading of around 10.0 volts suggests that one of the six battery cells has died – a common way for modern batteries to fail.

3 If the battery is to be charged, remove it from the vehicle (see Section 4) and charge it as described later in this Section.

Low maintenance battery

4 If the vehicle covers a small annual mileage, it is worthwhile checking the specific gravity of the electrolyte every three months to determine the state of charge of the battery. Use a hydrometer to make the check and compare the results with the tool maker's instructions (typically, there will be a colour-coded scale on hydrometers sold for battery testing).

5 If the battery condition is suspect, first check the specific gravity of electrolyte in each cell. A significant variation between any cells indicates loss of electrolyte or deterioration of the internal plates.

6 If the cell variation is satisfactory but the battery is discharged, it should be charged as described later in this Section.

Maintenance-free battery

7 In cases where a 'sealed for life' maintenance-free battery is fitted, topping-up and testing of the electrolyte in each cell is not possible. The condition of the battery can therefore only be tested using a battery condition indicator or a voltmeter.

Charging

Note: *The following is intended as a guide only. Always refer to the manufacturer's recommendations (often printed on a label attached to the battery), and always disconnect both terminal leads (or preferably remove the battery) before charging.*

Low maintenance battery

8 It is advisable to remove the cell caps or covers if possible during charging, but note that the battery will be giving off potentially explosive hydrogen gas while it is being charged. Small amounts of acidic electrolyte may also escape as the battery nears full charge. Removing the cell caps will allow you to check whether all six cells are receiving charge – after a while, the electrolyte should start to bubble. If any cell does not bubble, this may indicate that it has failed, and the battery is no longer fit for use.

9 Charge the battery at a rate of 3.5 to 4 amps and continue to charge the battery at this rate until no further rise in specific gravity is noted over a four hour period.

10 Alternatively, a trickle charger charging at the rate of 1.5 amps can safely be used overnight.

11 Specially rapid 'boost' charges which are claimed to restore the power of the battery in 1 to 2 hours are not recommended, as they can cause serious damage to the battery plates through overheating.

12 While charging the battery, note that the temperature of the electrolyte should never exceed 38°C.

Maintenance-free battery

13 This battery type takes considerably longer to fully recharge than the standard type, the time taken being dependent on the extent of discharge, but it will take anything up to three days.

14 A constant voltage type charger is required, to be set, when connected, to 13.9 to 14.9 volts with a charger current below 25 amps. Using this method, the battery should be usable within three hours, giving a voltage reading of 12.5 volts, but this is for a partially-discharged battery and, as mentioned, full charging can take considerably longer.

15 If the battery is to be charged from a fully discharged state, have it recharged by your dealer or local automotive electrician, as the charge rate is higher and constant supervision during charging is necessary.

4 Battery – removal and refitting

Note: *Refer to 'Disconnecting the battery' before proceeding.*

Removal

1 Turn the plastic retainer half a turn, disengage the locating tabs and lift off the cover over the battery **(see illustrations)**.

2 For improved access to the battery remove the pollen filter as described in Chapter 1, Section 18.

3 Where fitted, lift out the cover at the side of the battery **(see illustration)**.

4 On later models, unclip the electrical junction box in front of the battery location and drop it down to provide additional clearance.

5 Disconnect the lead at the negative (–) terminal by unscrewing the retaining nut and removing the terminal clamp. Note that the battery negative (–) and positive (+) terminal connections are stamped on the battery case.

6 Disconnect the lead at the positive (+) terminal by unscrewing the retaining nut and removing the terminal clamp.

7 Unscrew the retaining bolt and remove the battery retaining clamp.

8 Carefully lift the battery from its location and remove it from the vehicle. Make sure the battery is kept upright at all times.

Refitting

Note: *As a precaution, before refitting the battery check that all doors are unlocked.*

9 Refitting is a reversal of removal, but smear petroleum jelly on the terminals after reconnecting the leads to reduce corrosion, and always reconnect the positive lead(s) first, followed by the negative lead(s).

5 Charging system – testing

Note: *Refer to the precautions given in 'Safety first!' and in Section 1 of this Chapter before starting work.*

1 If a malfunction occurs in the charging circuit, don't automatically assume that the alternator is causing the problem. First check the following items:

a) *Check the tension and condition of the auxiliary drivebelt (see Chapter 1, Section 28) – renew it if it is worn or deteriorated.*

b) *Ensure the alternator mounting bolts are tight.*

c) *Inspect the alternator wiring harness and the electrical connections at the*

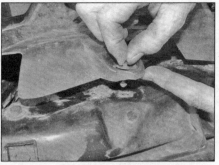

4.1a Turn the plastic retainer half a turn...

4.1b ...disengage the locating tabs on the left-hand side...

4.1c ...and right-hand side (arrowed)...

4.1d ...then lift off the cover over the battery

alternator; they must be in good condition and tight.

d) *Start the engine and check the alternator for abnormal noises – for example, a shrieking or squealing sound may indicate a badly-worn bearing or bush.*

e) *Make sure the battery is fully-charged – one bad cell in a battery can cause overcharging by the alternator.*

f) *Disconnect the battery leads (negative first, then positive). Inspect the battery posts and the lead clamps for corrosion. Clean them thoroughly if necessary (see Weekly checks). Reconnect the lead to the positive terminal.*

g) *With the ignition and all accessories switched off, insert a test light between the battery negative post and the disconnected negative lead clamp:*

1)   If the test light does not come on, re-attach the clamp and proceed to the next step.

2)   If the test light comes on, there is a short in the electrical system of the vehicle. The short must be repaired before the charging system can be checked.

3)   To find the short, disconnect the alternator wiring harness. If the light goes out, the alternator is at fault. If the light stays on, remove each fuse until it goes out – this will tell you which component is short-circuited.

2 Using a voltmeter, check the battery voltage with the engine off. It should be approximately 12.0 volts.

3 Start the engine and check the battery voltage again. Increase the engine speed until the voltmeter remains steady; it should now be approximately 13.5 to 14.6 volts.

4 Switch on as many electrical accessories (eg, the headlights and heater blower) as possible, and check that the alternator maintains the regulated voltage at around 13.0 to 14.0 volts. The voltage may drop and then come back up; it may also be necessary to increase engine speed slightly, even if the charging system is working properly.

5 If the regulated voltage is not as stated, the fault may be due to worn brushes, weak brush springs, a faulty voltage regulator, a faulty diode, a severed phase winding, or worn or damaged slip rings. The alternator should be renewed or taken to a dealer or auto electrician for testing and repair.

4.3 Where fitted, lift out the cover at the side of the battery

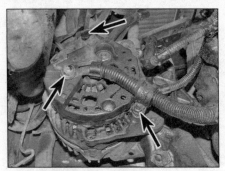

7.6 Wiring attachment points (arrowed) at the rear of the alternator

6 Auxiliary drivebelt – removal and refitting

Refer to Chapter 2A, Section 6 (4-cylinder engines) or Chapter 2B, Section 8 (5-cylinder engines).

7 Alternator – removal and refitting

Removal

1 Disconnect the battery negative terminal (refer to *Disconnecting the battery*).
2 Firmly apply the handbrake, then jack up the front of the vehicle and support it securely on axle stands (see *Jacking and vehicle support*).
3 Remove the engine undertray as described in Chapter 11, Section 25.
4 Remove the auxiliary drivebelt as described in Chapter 2A, Section 6 (4-cylinder engines) or Chapter 2B, Section 8 (5-cylinder engines).
5 Disconnect the charge warning light wiring from the alternator at the connector.
6 Remove the protective cap and unscrew the nut, then disconnect the positive cable from the alternator at the screw terminal. Where applicable, unbolt and remove the cable guide **(see illustration)**.
7 On early models, undo the alternator adjustment arm bolt.
8 Unscrew and remove the lower then upper

10.5 Unscrew the bolt (arrowed) securing the coolant pipe support bracket to the starter motor flange

7.8 Alternator mounting bolts (arrowed)

mounting bolts, then lift the alternator away from its bracket **(see illustration)**.

Refitting

9 Refitting is a reversal of removal, but tighten the mounting bolts to the specified torque.

8 Alternator – testing and overhaul

If the alternator is thought to be suspect, it should be removed from the vehicle and taken to an auto electrician for testing. Most auto electricians will be able to supply and fit brushes at a reasonable cost. However, check on the cost of repairs before proceeding as it may prove more economical to obtain a new or exchange alternator.

9 Starting system – testing

Note: *Refer to the precautions given in 'Safety first!' and in Section 1 of this Chapter before starting work.*
1 If the starter motor fails to operate during the normal starting procedure, the possible causes are as follows:
a) *The engine immobiliser is faulty.*
b) *The battery is faulty.*
c) *The electrical connections between the switch, solenoid, battery and starter motor are somewhere failing to pass the necessary current from the battery through the starter to earth.*
d) *The solenoid is faulty.*
e) *The starter motor is mechanically or electrically defective.*
2 To check the battery, switch on the headlights. If they dim after a few seconds, this indicates that the battery is discharged – recharge (see Section 3) or renew the battery. If the headlights glow brightly, operate the starter switch while watching the headlights. If they dim, then this indicates that current is reaching the starter motor, therefore the fault must lie in the starter motor. If the lights continue to glow brightly (and no clicking sound can be heard from the starter motor

solenoid), this indicates that there is a fault in the circuit or solenoid – see the following paragraphs. If the starter motor turns slowly when operated, but the battery is in good condition, then this indicates either that the starter motor is faulty, or there is considerable resistance somewhere in the circuit.
3 If a fault in the circuit is suspected, disconnect the battery leads (including the earth connection to the body), the starter/solenoid wiring and the engine/transmission earth strap. Thoroughly clean the connections, and reconnect the leads and wiring. Use a voltmeter or test light to check that full battery voltage is available at the battery positive lead connection to the solenoid. Smear petroleum jelly around the battery terminals to prevent corrosion – corroded connections are among the most frequent causes of electrical system faults.
4 If the battery and all connections are in good condition, check the circuit by disconnecting the ignition switch supply wire from the solenoid terminal. Connect a voltmeter or test lamp between the wire end and a good earth (such as the battery negative terminal), and check that the wire is live when the ignition switch is turned to the 'start' position. If it is, then the circuit is sound – if not the circuit wiring can be checked as described in Chapter 12, Section 2.
5 The solenoid contacts can be checked by connecting a voltmeter or test light between the battery positive feed connection on the starter side of the solenoid and earth. When the ignition switch is turned to the 'start' position, there should be a reading or lighted bulb, as applicable. If there is no reading or lighted bulb, the solenoid is faulty.
6 If the circuit and solenoid are proved sound, the fault must lie in the starter motor. In this event, it may be possible to have the starter motor overhauled by a specialist, but check on the cost of spares before proceeding, as it may prove more economical to obtain a new or exchange motor.

10 Starter motor – removal and refitting

Removal

1 Disconnect the battery negative terminal (refer to *Disconnecting the battery*).
2 Firmly apply the handbrake, then jack up the front of the vehicle and support it securely on axle stands (see *Jacking and vehicle support*).
3 Remove the engine undertray as described in Chapter 11, Section 25.
4 Note the location of the two wires on the starter motor. Disconnect the wire from the solenoid, then unscrew the nut and disconnect the battery cable from the main terminal.
5 Unscrew the bolt securing the coolant pipe support bracket to the starter motor flange **(see illustration)**.

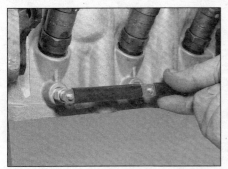

13.11a On early models, remove the nuts and washers from the glow plug terminal, then lift off the bus bar

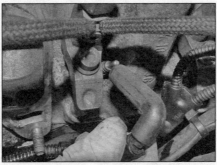

13.11b On later models, pull the glow plug wiring connector off the end of the glow plug

13.12 Slacken and withdraw the glow plug

6 Unscrew the two mounting bolts and withdraw the starter motor downwards from the engine and transmission.

Refitting

7 Refitting is a reversal of removal, but tighten the mounting bolts to the specified torque.

11 Starter motor –
testing and overhaul

If the starter motor is thought to be suspect, it should be removed from the vehicle and taken to an auto electrician for testing. Most auto electricians will be able to supply and fit brushes at a reasonable cost. However, check on the cost of repairs before proceeding as it may prove more economical to obtain a new or exchange motor.

12 Pre/post-heating system –
general information

To assist cold starting, a pre-heating system is fitted, which comprises a glow plug for each cylinder, a glow plug control unit or engine management ECU, a facia mounted warning lamp and the associated electrical wiring.

The glow plugs are miniature electric heating elements, encapsulated in a metal case with a probe at one end and electrical connection at the other. Each swirl chamber/inlet tract has a glow plug threaded into it, the glow plug probe is positioned directly in line with incoming spray of fuel. When the glow plug is energised, the fuel passing over it is heated, allowing its optimum combustion temperature to be achieved more readily when it reaches the cylinder.

The duration of the pre-heating period is governed by the glow plug control unit or engine management ECU, which monitors the temperature of the engine via the coolant temperature sensor and alters the pre-heating time to suit the conditions.

A facia mounted warning lamp informs the driver that pre-heating is taking place. The lamp extinguishes when sufficient pre-heating has taken place to allow the engine to be started, but power will still be supplied to the glow plugs for a further period until the engine is started. If no attempt is made to start the engine, the power supply to the glow plugs is switched off to prevent battery drain and glow plug burn-out.

After the engine has been started, the glow plugs continue to operate for a further period of time. This helps to improve fuel combustion whilst the engine is warming up, resulting in quieter, smoother running and reduced exhaust emissions.

13 Glow plugs –
testing, removal and refitting

Testing

1 If the system malfunctions, testing is ultimately by substitution of known good units, but some preliminary checks may be made as described in the following paragraphs.
2 Connect a voltmeter or 12 volt test lamp between the glow plug supply cable and a good earth point on the engine.
Caution: Make sure that the live connection is kept well clear of the engine and bodywork.
3 Have an assistant activate the pre-heating system with the ignition key and check that battery voltage is applied to the glow plug electrical connection. Note that the voltage will drop to zero when the pre-heating period ends.
4 If no supply voltage can be detected at the glow plug, then either the glow plug relay or the supply cabling must be faulty.
5 To locate a faulty glow plug, first disconnect the battery negative terminal (refer to *Disconnecting the battery*).
6 Remove the supply cabling from the glow plug terminal. Measure the electrical resistance between the glow plug terminal

and the engine earth. A reading of anything more than a few Ohms indicates that the plug is defective.
7 If a suitable ammeter is available, connect it between the glow plug and its supply cable and measure the steady state current consumption (ignore the initial current surge which will be about 50% higher). Compare the result with the Specifications – high current consumption (or no current draw at all) indicates a faulty glow plug.
8 As a final check, remove the glow plugs and inspect them visually, as described in the following paragraphs.

Removal

9 If not already done, disconnect the battery negative terminal (refer to *Disconnecting the battery*).
10 Move the radiator to the service position as described in Chapter 3, Section 3.
11 On early models, remove the nuts and washers from the glow plug terminal. Lift off the bus bar. On later models, pull the glow plug wiring connector off the end of the glow plug **(see illustrations)**.
12 Slacken and withdraw the glow plug **(see illustration)**. If removing No 5 cylinder glow plug on 2.4 litre engines, it may be necessary to remove No 5 fuel injector as described in Chapter 4A, Section 11 to provide additional clearance.
13 Inspect the glow plug probe for signs of damage. A badly burned or charred probe is usually an indication of a faulty fuel injector.

Refitting

14 Refitting is a reversal of removal, noting the following points:
a) Apply a little anti-seize compound (or copper brake grease) to the glow plug threads.
b) Tighten the glow plugs to the specified torque.
c) Make sure when remaking the glow plug wiring connections that the contact surfaces are clean.

Chapter 6
Clutch

Contents

Degrees of difficulty

Easy, suitable for novice with little experience	Fairly easy, suitable for beginner with some experience	Fairly difficult, suitable for competent DIY mechanic	Difficult, suitable for experienced DIY mechanic	Very difficult, suitable for expert DIY or professional

Specifications

General

Type	Single dry plate, hydraulically-operated with automatic adjustment
Disc diameter:	
02B type transmission	215 mm, 219 mm or 228 mm (according to model)
02G type transmission	219 mm or 240 mm (according to model)

Torque wrench settings

	Nm	lbf ft
Clutch pressure plate-to-flywheel:		
02B type transmission:		
With solid (single-mass) flywheel	20	15
With dual-mass flywheel.	13	10
02G type transmission	13	10
Clutch master cylinder retaining bolts	20	15
Clutch slave cylinder retaining bolts:		
02B type transmission	25	18
02G type transmission	12	9
Engine/transmission mountings:		
Left-hand mounting bracket-to-transmission	65	48
Rear mounting-to-subframe (early models)	45	33
Rear mounting-to-subframe through bolt (later models)	200	148
Rear mounting-to-transmission through bolt (later models):		
Stage 1	80	59
Stage 2	Angle-tighten a further 90°	
Gear lever housing mounting bolts	10	7
Hydraulic pipe union nuts.	20	15

2.9a Upper hydraulic system bleed screw (arrowed) on the 02G type transmission

2.9b Lower hydraulic system bleed screw (arrowed) on the 02G type transmission

1 General information

The clutch consists of a friction disc, a pressure plate assembly, and the release mechanism; all of these components are contained in the large cast-aluminium alloy bellhousing, sandwiched between the engine and the transmission.

The friction disc is fitted between the engine flywheel and the clutch pressure plate, and is allowed to slide on the transmission input shaft splines.

The pressure plate assembly is bolted to the engine flywheel. When the engine is running, drive is transmitted from the crankshaft, via the flywheel, to the friction disc (these components being clamped securely together by the pressure plate assembly) and from the friction disc to the transmission input shaft.

To interrupt the drive, the pressure plate spring pressure must be relaxed. This is achieved using a hydraulic release mechanism which consists of a master cylinder, and a slave cylinder and release bearing. On vehicles equipped with the 02B type transmissions, the clutch release bearing is fitted concentrically around the transmission input shaft and the slave cylinder is mounted externally on the side of the bellhousing. The bearing is pushed onto the pressure plate assembly by means of a release lever actuated by the slave cylinder. On vehicles equipped with the 02G type transmissions, the release bearing is integral with the slave cylinder to form a single release assembly fitted concentrically around the transmission input shaft.

The clutch pedal is connected to the clutch master cylinder by a short pushrod. The master cylinder is mounted behind the clutch pedal and receives its hydraulic fluid supply from a separate chamber in the brake master cylinder reservoir. Depressing the clutch pedal moves the piston in the master cylinder forwards, so forcing hydraulic fluid through the clutch hydraulic pipe to the slave cylinder.

On vehicles with an externally mounted slave cylinder, the piston in the slave cylinder moves forward on the entry of the fluid and actuates the clutch release lever by means of a short pushrod. The release lever pivots on its mounting stud and presses the release bearing against the pressure plate spring fingers. This causes the springs to deform and releases the clamping force on the pressure plate. On vehicles with an integral release bearing and slave cylinder assembly, the piston in the slave cylinder moves forward on the entry of the fluid and presses the integral release bearing directly against the pressure plate spring fingers.

On all models, the clutch operating mechanism is self-adjusting and no manual adjustment is required.

2 Hydraulic system – bleeding

⚠️ *Warning: Hydraulic fluid is poisonous; thoroughly wash off spills from bare skin without delay. Seek immediate medical advice if any fluid is swallowed or gets into the eyes. Certain types of hydraulic fluid are inflammable and may ignite when brought into contact with hot components. Hydraulic fluid is also an effective paint stripper. If spillage occurs onto painted bodywork or fittings, it should be washed off immediately, using copious quantities of cold water. It is also hygroscopic (i.e. it can absorb moisture from the air) which then renders it useless. Old fluid may have suffered contamination, and should never be re-used.*

1 If any part of the hydraulic system is dismantled, or if air has accidentally entered the system, the system will need to be bled. The presence of air is characterised by the pedal having a spongy feel and it results in difficulty in changing gear.

2 The design of the clutch hydraulic system does not allow bleeding to be carried out using the conventional method of pumping the clutch pedal. In order to remove all air present in the system, it is necessary to use pressure bleeding equipment. This is available from auto accessory shops at relatively low cost.

3 Begin by removing the engine undertray as described in Chapter 11, Section 25. Proceed as described in the relevant sub-Section according to transmission type.

02B type transmissions

4 The pressure bleeding equipment should be connected to the brake/clutch hydraulic fluid reservoir in accordance with the manufacturer's instructions. The system is bled through the bleed screw of the clutch slave cylinder, which is located at the top of the transmission housing.

5 The system is bled until the fluid being ejected is free from air bubbles. The bleed screw is then closed and the bleeding equipment disconnected and removed.

6 Check the operation of the clutch to see that it is satisfactory. If air still remains in the system, repeat the bleeding operation.

7 Discard any fluid which is bled from the system, even if it looks clean. Hydraulic fluid absorbs water and its re-use can cause internal corrosion of the master and slave cylinders, leading to excessive wear and failure of the seals.

8 On completion, refit the engine undertray as described in Chapter 11, Section 25.

02G type transmissions

9 Proceed as described previously for the 02B transmissions but note that there are two bleed screws on this transmission type. The upper bleed screw is located in the fluid supply pipe on the engine compartment bulkhead and the lower bleed screw is located at the base of the transmission (see illustrations).

10 Bleed the system at the bulkhead mounted bleed screw first. When the fluid being ejected is free from air bubbles, close the bleed screw and continue the bleeding operation at the transmission bleed screw.

11 On completion, refit the engine undertray as described in Chapter 11, Section 25.

3 Clutch master cylinder – removal and refitting

Note: *Refer to the warning in Section 2 concerning the dangers of hydraulic fluid before proceeding.*

Removal

1 The clutch master cylinder is located inside the car, attached to the clutch and brake pedal mounting bracket. Hydraulic fluid for the unit is supplied from the brake master cylinder reservoir.

2 To gain access, turn the retaining catch anti-clockwise and open the driver's side stowage box fully. Lift the stowage box out of the lower retainers and remove it from the facia **(see illustrations)**.

3 Remove the steering column shrouds as described in Chapter 11, Section 29.

4 Extract the clip then withdraw the clevis pin attaching the master cylinder pushrod to the clutch pedal **(see illustration)**.

5 Cover the floor beneath the pedals to protect against hydraulic fluid spillage.

6 Clamp off the flexible hydraulic fluid hose leading from the fluid reservoir to the master cylinder using a brake hose clamp. Clamp off the supply hose to the slave cylinder in the same manner.

7 Carefully pull the hydraulic fluid supply hose from the master cylinder. If necessary, plug the end of the hose with a suitable bolt.

8 Unscrew the hydraulic pipe union at the base of the cylinder, and carefully ease out the pipe **(see illustration)**.

9 Unscrew the two mounting bolts and withdraw the master cylinder from inside the car.

Refitting

10 Refitting is a reversal of removal but tighten the master cylinder mounting bolts and the hydraulic pipe union to the specified torques. Apply a little grease to the clevis pin before refitting it. On completion, bleed the clutch hydraulic system as described in Section 2.

4 Clutch slave cylinder – removal and refitting

Note: *Refer to the warning in Section 2 concerning the dangers of hydraulic fluid before proceeding.*

02B type transmissions

Removal

1 Firmly apply the handbrake, then jack up the front of the vehicle and support it securely on axle stands (see *Jacking and vehicle support*).

2 Remove the engine undertray as described in Chapter 11, Section 25.

3.2a Turn the retaining catch anti-clockwise...

3.2b ...and open the driver's side stowage box fully

3.4 Extract the clip (arrowed) then withdraw the master cylinder pushrod clevis pin

3 Slacken the four bolts securing the gear lever housing to the floor, sufficiently to allow the housing to move.

4 On early models, undo the two bolts securing the engine/transmission rear mounting to the subframe.

5 On later models, undo the through bolt securing the subframe bracket to the engine/transmission rear mounting.

6 Position a trolley jack underneath the transmission with an interposed block of wood between the jack head and the transmission casing.

7 Raise the jack until it just takes the weight of the engine off the left-hand mounting.

8 Undo the two bolts securing the engine/transmission left-hand mounting bracket to the top of the transmission.

9 Carefully lower the trolley jack until sufficient

4.15 Unscrew the hydraulic damper valve from the end of the slave cylinder – 02G type transmission

3.8 Unscrew the hydraulic pipe union (arrowed) at the base of the master cylinder

clearance exists to gain access to the slave cylinder.

10 Clamp off the slave cylinder hydraulic hose using a brake hose clamp.

11 Unscrew the hydraulic pipe union from the slave cylinder, and carefully ease out the pipe.

12 Unscrew the two mounting bolts and withdraw the slave cylinder from the transmission.

Refitting

13 Refitting is a reversal of the removal procedure, noting the following points:
  a) *Ensure that the slave cylinder pushrod correctly engages with the clutch release lever.*
  b) *Tighten all nuts, bolts and pipe unions to the specified torque.*
  c) *On completion, bleed the clutch hydraulic system as described in Section 2.*

02G type transmissions

Removal

14 Unless the complete engine/transmission unit is to be removed from the car and separated for major overhaul (see Chapter 2C, Section 4), the clutch release mechanism can be reached by removing the transmission only, as described in Chapter 7A, Section 6.

15 Unscrew the hydraulic damper valve from the end of the slave cylinder **(see illustration)**.

16 Undo the two retaining bolts and remove

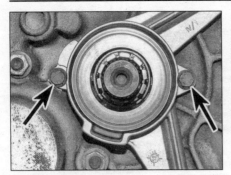

4.16a Undo the two retaining bolts (arrowed)...

4.16b ...and remove the slave cylinder and release bearing assembly from the bellhousing – 02G type transmission

5.4 Unhook the return spring (arrowed) from the clutch pedal

the slave cylinder and release bearing assembly from the transmission bellhousing **(see illustrations)**.

17 Spin the release bearing by hand, and check it for smooth running. Any tendency to seize or run rough will necessitate renewal of the complete assembly. If it is to be re-used, wipe it clean with a dry cloth; on no account should the bearing be washed in a liquid solvent, otherwise the internal grease will be removed.

Refitting

18 Refitting is a reversal of the removal procedure, noting the following points:
  a) *Renew the slave cylinder O-ring prior to refitting.*
  b) *Tighten all nuts, bolts and pipe unions to the specified torque.*
  c) *On completion, bleed the clutch hydraulic system as described in Section 2.*

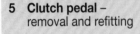

5 Clutch pedal – removal and refitting

Removal

1 Turn the retaining catch anti-clockwise and open the driver's side stowage box fully. Lift the stowage box out of the lower retainers and remove it from the facia **(see illustrations 3.2a and 3.2b)**.

2 Remove the steering column shrouds as described in Chapter 11, Section 29.

3 Extract the clip then withdraw the clevis pin

attaching the master cylinder pushrod to the clutch pedal **(see illustration 3.4)**.

4 Unhook the return spring from the clutch pedal **(see illustration)**.

5 Before removing the over-centre spring (where fitted), a retaining clamp must be fitted to it. This can be made out of a length of metal plate with forked ends bent to fit over the ends of the spring. Fit the clamp, then fully depress the clutch pedal and remove the spring assembly from the pedal and bracket.

6 Extract the retaining clip and remove the washer from the end of the clutch and brake pedal pivot shaft.

7 Using a small drift, tap the pivot shaft out towards the right-hand side of the vehicle until it is possible to remove the clutch pedal.

Refitting

8 Refitting is a reversal of removal, but lightly grease the pivot shaft before assembly.

6 Clutch release bearing and lever – removal, inspection and refitting

Note: *The following procedure is only applicable to the 02B type transmission. On the 02G type transmission, the release bearing is integral with the slave cylinder.*

Removal

1 Unless the complete engine/transmission unit is to be removed from the car and separated for major overhaul (see Chapter 2C,

Section 4), the clutch release mechanism can be reached by removing the transmission only, as described in Chapter 7A, Section 6.

2 Use a screwdriver to prise the release lever from the ball stud inside the transmission bellhousing. If this proves difficult, push the spring clip from the pivot end of the release lever by pushing it through the hole. This will release the pivot end of the lever from the ball stud. Now withdraw the lever together with the release bearing from the guide sleeve.

Inspection

3 Spin the release bearing by hand, and check it for smooth running. Any tendency to seize or run rough will necessitate renewal of the bearing. If it is to be re-used, wipe it clean with a dry cloth; on no account should the bearing be washed in a liquid solvent, otherwise the internal grease will be removed.

Refitting

4 Commence refitting by lubricating the ball stud with a little molybdenum disulphide grease. Smear a little grease on the release bearing surface which contacts the diaphragm spring fingers and the release lever, and also on the guide sleeve.

5 Fit the spring clip onto the release lever. Refit the lever together with the bearing and press the release lever onto the ball stud until the spring holds it in position **(see illustrations)**.

6 Refit the engine/transmission unit as described in Chapter 2C, Section 4, or refit the transmission as described in Chapter 7A, Section 6.

6.5a Locate the spring clip over the end of the release lever...

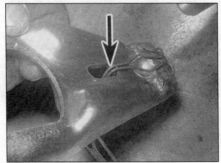

6.5b ...and press the spring into the hole – 02B type transmission

6.5c Press the release lever onto the ball stud until the spring clip holds it in position – 02B type transmission

7.11 GETRIEBESEITE (transmission side) marking on the clutch friction disc (arrowed)

7.12 Placing the clutch pressure plate in position

7 Clutch assembly – removal, inspection and refitting

⚠ *Warning: Dust created by clutch wear and deposited on the clutch components may contain asbestos, which is a health hazard. DO NOT blow it out with compressed air, and do not inhale any of it. DO NOT use petrol or petroleum-based solvents to clean off the dust. Brake system cleaner or methylated spirit should be used to flush the dust into a suitable receptacle. After the clutch components are wiped clean with rags, dispose of the contaminated rags and cleaner in a sealed, marked container.*

Removal

1 Unless the complete engine/transmission unit is to be removed from the vehicle and separated for major overhaul (see Chapter 2C, Section 4), the clutch can be reached by removing the transmission as described in Chapter 7A, Section 6.

2 Before disturbing the clutch, use a marker pen to mark the relationship of the pressure plate assembly to the flywheel.

3 Unscrew and remove the clutch pressure plate retaining bolts, working in a diagonal sequence, and slackening the bolts only a turn at a time. If necessary, the flywheel may be held stationary using a home-made locking tool or a wide-bladed screwdriver, inserted in the teeth of the starter ring gear and resting against part of the cylinder block.

4 Ease the pressure plate off its locating dowels. Be prepared to catch the friction disc, which will drop out as the plate is removed. Note which way round the disc is fitted.

Inspection

5 The most common problem which occurs in the clutch is wear of the friction disc. However, all the clutch components should be inspected at this time, particularly if the engine has covered a high mileage. Unless the clutch components are known to be virtually new, it is worth renewing them all as a set (disc, pressure plate and release bearing). Renewing a worn friction disc by itself is not always satisfactory, especially if the old disc was slipping and causing the pressure plate to overheat.

6 Examine the linings of the friction disc for wear, and the disc hub and rim for distortion, cracks, broken torsion springs, and worn splines. The surface of the friction linings may be highly glazed, but as long as the friction material pattern can be clearly seen, this is satisfactory. The disc must be renewed if the lining thickness has worn down to, or near, the rivets.

7 If there is any sign of oil contamination, indicated by shiny black discoloration, the disc must be renewed, and the source of the contamination traced and rectified. This will be a leaking crankshaft oil seal or transmission input shaft oil seal.

8 Check the machined faces of the flywheel and pressure plate. If either is grooved, or heavily scored, renewal is necessary. The pressure plate must also be renewed if any cracks are apparent, or if the diaphragm spring is damaged or its pressure suspect. Pay particular attention to the tips of the spring fingers, where the release bearing acts upon them.

9 With the transmission removed, it is also advisable to check the condition of the release bearing, as described in Section 6. Having got this far, it is almost certainly worth renewing it.

Refitting

10 It is important that no oil or grease is allowed to come into contact with the friction material of the clutch disc or the pressure plate and flywheel faces. To ensure this, it is advisable to refit the clutch assembly with clean hands, and to wipe down the pressure plate and flywheel faces with a clean dry rag before assembly begins.

11 Place the friction disc against the flywheel, ensuring that it is the right way round (see illustration). It should be marked GETRIEBESEITE (which means transmission side) but if not, position it as follows:
 a) *On engines with a solid (single-mass) flywheel, position the disc with the raised, torsion spring side of the hub facing away from the flywheel.*
 b) *On engines with a dual-mass flywheel, position the disc with the short end of the hub facing away from the flywheel.*

12 Place the clutch pressure plate over the dowels (see illustration). Refit the retaining bolts, and tighten them finger-tight so that the friction disc is gripped lightly, but can still be moved.

13 The friction disc must now be centralised so that when the engine and transmission are mated, the splines of the transmission input shaft will pass through the splines in the centre of the disc hub. To do this, a proprietary tool may be used, or alternatively, use a wooden mandrel made to fit inside the friction disc and into the bush in the centre of the crankshaft. Insert the tool through the friction disc into the bush, and make sure that it is central.

14 Once the clutch is centralised, progressively tighten the cover bolts in a diagonal sequence to the torque setting given in the Specifications.

15 Ensure that the input shaft splines, clutch disc splines and release bearing guide sleeve are clean. Apply a thin smear of high-melting-point grease to the input shaft splines.

16 Refit the transmission to the engine as described in Chapter 7A, Section 6.

Chapter 7 Part A:
Manual transmission

Contents

Degrees of difficulty

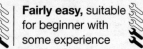

Easy, suitable for novice with little experience	**Fairly easy,** suitable for beginner with some experience	**Fairly difficult,** suitable for competent DIY mechanic	**Difficult,** suitable for experienced DIY mechanic	**Very difficult,** suitable for expert DIY or professional

Specifications

General

Type . . . .   5 forward speeds and reverse. Synchromesh on all forward speeds
Identification code:
   1.9 and 2.4 litre engines 02B
   2.5 litre engines 02G

Lubrication

Lubricant type . . . .   See *Lubricants and fluids* on page 0•17
Lubricant capacity . . . .   See Chapter 1

Torque wrench settings

	Nm	lbf ft
Clutch slave cylinder retaining bolts (02B type transmission)	25	18
Engine/transmission mountings:		
Left-hand mounting support brace bolts (02G type transmission). . .	30	22
Left-hand mounting-to-body through bolt	65	48
Left-hand mounting transmission bracket-to-transmission	65	48
Rear mounting-to-subframe (early models)	45	33
Rear mounting-to-subframe through bolt (later models)*	200	148
Rear mounting-to-transmission through bolt (later models):*		
Stage 1	80	59
Stage 2	Angle-tighten a further 90°	
Rear mounting-to-transmission rear bolts (later models)	40	30
Rear mounting-to-transmission right-hand bolts (later models)	100	74
Intermediate shaft support bearing bolts (02G type transmission)	25	18
Transmission bellhousing to engine:		
M8 bolts	20	15
M10 bolts	60	44
M12 bolts	80	59

* *Use new bolts*

2.3a Unclip the gear lever outer gaiter from the frame...

2.3b ...then unscrew the gear lever knob and remove it together with the outer gaiter

2.4a Lever up the gear lever frame...

2.4b ...and remove it together with the gear lever inner gaiter

1 General information

The transmission is contained in a cast-aluminium alloy casing bolted to the engine's left-hand end, and consists of the gearbox and final drive differential.

Drive is transmitted from the crankshaft via the clutch to the input shaft, which has a splined extension to accept the clutch friction disc and rotates in roller bearings at each end. From the input shaft, drive is transmitted to the output shaft, which also rotates in roller bearings at each end. From the output shaft, the drive is transmitted to the differential crown-wheel, which rotates with the differential case and planetary gears, thus driving the sun gears and driveshafts. The rotation of the planetary gears on their

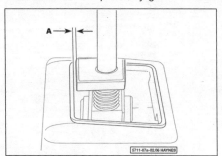

2.6 The distance 'a' between the side of the gear lever stop and the gear lever housing should be approximately 2 mm

shaft allows the inner roadwheel to rotate at a slower speed than the outer roadwheel when the vehicle is cornering.

The input and output shafts are arranged side-by-side, parallel to the crankshaft and driveshafts, so that their gear pinion teeth are in constant mesh. In the neutral position, the output shaft gear pinions rotate freely, so that drive cannot be transmitted to the crownwheel.

Gear selection is via a floor-mounted lever and rod-operated selector linkage. The selector linkage causes the appropriate selector fork to move its respective synchro-sleeve along the shaft, to lock the gear pinion to the synchro-hub. Since the synchro-hubs are splined to the output shaft, this locks the pinion to the shaft, so that drive can be transmitted. To ensure that gearchanging can be made quickly and quietly, a synchromesh system is fitted to all forward gears, consisting of baulk rings and spring-loaded fingers, as well as the gear

2.8 Gate rod clamp retaining nut (arrowed)

pinions and synchro-hubs. The synchromesh cones are formed on the mating faces of the baulk rings and gear pinions.

Because of the complexity, possible unavailability of parts and special tools necessary, internal repair procedures for the transmission are not recommended for the home mechanic. The bulk of the information in this Chapter is therefore devoted to removal and refitting procedures.

The two different transmissions fitted to the models described in this manual can be identified as follows:

a) *02B type transmission – the three-digit type code is marked on the bearing housing which is bolted to the right-hand side of the differential casing.*
b) *02G type transmission – the three-digit type code is marked on the left-hand side of the differential casing, directly below the driveshaft inner CV joint.*

Note: *On all models, the transmission code letters also appear on the vehicle data sticker located below or adjacent to the fuse/relay box in the passenger compartment (see 'Vehicle Identification').*

2 Gearchange linkage – adjustment

1 If a stiff, sloppy or generally imprecise gearchange leads you to suspect that a fault exists within the linkage, dismantle it completely and check it for wear or damage as described in Section 3. Reassemble the linkage, applying a smear of multi-purpose grease to all contact surfaces.
2 Once the linkage has been examined and any wear or damage rectified, adjustment is carried out as follows.
3 Using a small screwdriver, unclip the gear lever outer gaiter from the frame. Unscrew the gear lever knob and remove it together with the outer gaiter **(see illustrations)**.
4 Again, using a small screwdriver lever up the frame and remove it together with the gear lever inner gaiter **(see illustrations)**.
5 Check that with the transmission in neutral, the gear lever should rest in the 3rd/4th gear plane and the lower portion of the gear lever should be vertical.
6 Now move the gear lever into 1st gear. Lightly move the gear lever to the left to take up any free play in the linkage and check that the distance between the side of the gear lever stop and the gear lever housing is approximately 2 mm **(see illustration)**.
7 If any of the conditions described in paragraphs 5 and 6 cannot be met then, if not already done, firmly apply the handbrake, jack up the front of the vehicle and support it securely on axle stands (see *Jacking and vehicle support*).
8 From under the vehicle, slacken the gate rod clamp retaining nut so that the gate rod is free to move **(see illustration)**. Using a trial and

2.10 The V mark (arrowed) on the gear lever inner gaiter and frame must be toward the front of the vehicle

error process reposition the gate rod within the clamp until the conditions described in paragraphs 5 and 6 can be obtained. Hold the gate rod in this position and tighten the clamp retaining nut securely.

9 Check that the gear lever can be moved smoothly through all gear positions and that all gears can be selected. If this is not the case repeat the adjustment procedure.

10 When all is satisfactory, refit the gear lever inner gaiter, together with the frame so that the V mark on the frame is toward the front of the vehicle **(see illustration)**.

11 Refit the gear lever knob and outer gaiter and screw on the knob while holding the gaiter in position. On completion, lower the vehicle to the ground.

3 Gearchange linkage – removal, inspection and refitting

Removal

1 Using a small screwdriver, unclip the gear lever outer gaiter from the frame. Unscrew the gear lever knob and remove it together with the outer gaiter **(see illustrations 2.3a and 2.3b)**.

2 Again, using a small screwdriver lever up the frame and remove it together with gear lever inner gaiter **(see illustrations 2.4a and 2.4b)**.

3 From within the engine compartment, undo the two bolts securing the swivel head to the selector lever on the transmission **(see illustration)**.

4 Using a screwdriver carefully lever the front selector rod out of the bush in the transmission selector lever.

5 Undo the bolts securing the gate rod mounting bracket to the transmission.

6 On models with a reverse gear detent cable, disconnect the cable from the reverse gear locking unit on the transmission.

7 Firmly apply the handbrake, then jack up the front of the vehicle and support it securely on axle stands (see *Jacking and vehicle support*).

8 Undo the nut and withdraw the bolt securing the rear selector rod to the base of the gear lever **(see illustration)**.

9 Undo the gate rod clamp retaining nut and remove the clamp bolt **(see illustration 2.8)**.

Pull the gate rod forward out of the clamp.

10 Undo the four bolts securing the gear lever housing to the floor.

11 Move the gear lever housing and gear lever forward to clear the fuel tank then lower the housing and move it rearwards together with the linkage. Withdraw the linkage assembly from under the vehicle.

Inspection

12 Undo the retaining nut and remove the relay lever with the two selector rods from the gate rod pivot pin.

13 Note the orientation of the selector rods in relation to the relay lever. On the 02B type transmission, use a screwdriver to prise free the selector levers from the ball studs on the relay lever. On the 02G type transmission, simply detach the selector rod ends from the lever **(see illustration)**.

14 Inspect the condition of all the pivot bushes on the complete linkage assembly. Most of the bushes can be simply prised free with a screwdriver and new bushes tapped in with a drift and small hammer **(see illustration)**. A small puller may be required to remove the circular bushes on the gate rod and the bush in the gate rod mounting bracket.

15 Reassemble the selector rods to the relay lever noting the following:

a) *On the 02B type transmission, the longer arm of the relay lever points toward the left-hand side of the vehicle.*

b) *On the 02G type transmission, the longer arm of the relay lever points toward*

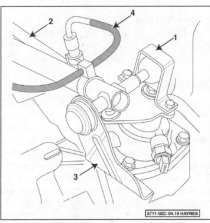

3.3 Gearchange linkage components at the transmission end – 02G type transmission shown

1 *Swivel head*
2 *Front selector rod*
3 *Gate rod mounting bracket*
4 *Reverse gear detent cable (if fitted)*

the right-hand side of the vehicle (see illustration).

16 Refit the relay lever and selector rods to the gate rod pivot and secure with the retaining nut tightened securely.

Refitting

17 Refitting is a reversal of removal. Adjust the gearchange linkage as described in Section 2 before refitting the gear lever inner gaiter and frame.

3.8 Undo the nut and withdraw the bolt securing the rear selector rod to the base of the gear lever

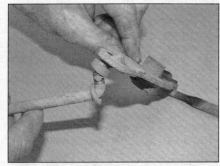

3.13 Detach the selector rod ends from the relay lever – 02G type transmission shown

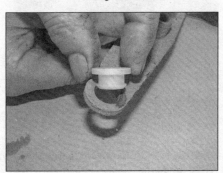

3.14 Renewing a relay lever selector rod bush

3.15 On the 02G transmission, the longer arm of the relay lever (arrowed) points toward the right-hand side of the vehicle

4 Reversing light switch –
testing, removal and refitting

Testing

1 Ensure that the ignition switch is turned to the 'OFF' position.
2 Unplug the wiring harness from the reversing light switch at the connector. The switch is located on the gear selector housing on top of the transmission casing.
3 Connect the probes of a continuity tester, or multimeter set to the resistance measurement function, across the terminals of the reverse light switch.
4 The switch contacts are normally open, so with any gear other than reverse selected, the tester/meter should indicate an open circuit. When reverse gear is then selected, the switch contacts should close, causing the tester/meter to indicate a short circuit.
5 If the switch appears to be constantly open or short circuit, or is intermittent in its operation, it should be renewed.

Removal

6 Ensure that the ignition switch is turned to the 'OFF' position.
7 Unplug the wiring harness from the reversing light switch at the connector.
8 Slacken the switch body using a ring spanner and withdraw it from the transmission casing **(see illustration)**. Recover the sealing ring.

Refitting

9 Refitting is a reversal of removal.

5 Speedometer drive –
removal and refitting

Removal

1 Depending on transmission type and model year, either a cable operated speedometer or an electronic speedometer may be fitted. The driveshaft for the cable operated speedometer is located on the top of the differential housing. Where an electronic speedometer is fitted, an

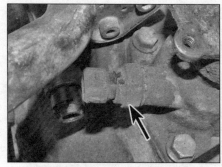

4.8 Reversing light switch location (arrowed) on the gear selector housing

electronic speedometer transducer is located on the left-hand side of the transmission, just above the driveshaft drive flange. This device measures the rotational speed of the transmission final drive and converts the information into an electronic signal, which is then sent to the speedometer module in the instrument panel.
2 Firmly apply the handbrake, then jack up the front of the vehicle and support it securely on axle stands (see *Jacking and vehicle support*).
3 Remove the engine undertray as described in Chapter 11, Section 25.
4 If a cable operated speedometer is fitted, unscrew the end fitting and disconnect the cable from the speedometer drive. Unscrew the speedometer drive body and remove it, together with the driveshaft from the transmission.
5 If an electronic speedometer is fitted, unplug the wiring harness from the transducer at the connector. Remove the transducer retaining screw using an Allen key and withdraw the unit from the transmission casing. Recover sealing ring.

Refitting

6 Refitting is a reversal of removal.

6 Transmission –
removal and refitting

Removal

1 Disconnect the battery negative terminal (refer to *Disconnecting the battery*).

2 Refer to Chapter 11, Section 6 and remove the bonnet from its hinges.
3 Move the radiator to the service position as described in Chapter 3, Section 3.
4 Firmly apply the handbrake, then jack up the front of the vehicle and support it securely on axle stands (see *Jacking and vehicle support*). There must be sufficient clearance below the vehicle for the transmission to be lowered and removed.
5 Remove the engine undertray as described in Chapter 11, Section 25.
6 Remove both driveshafts as described in Chapter 8, Section 2.
7 Remove the exhaust system front pipe as described in Chapter 4A, Section 19.
8 Unbolt the earth strap from the transmission and disconnect any remaining wiring connectors and retaining clips **(see illustration)**.
9 Remove the starter motor as described in Chapter 5, Section 10.
10 On vehicles equipped with air conditioning, remove the auxiliary drivebelt as described in Chapter 2A, Section 6 (4-cylinder engines) or Chapter 2B, Section 8 (5-cylinder engines). Unbolt the air conditioning compressor and secure it to one side. Do not disconnect the refrigerant pipes.
11 On models with the 02G transmission, clamp the clutch hydraulic hose with a suitable hose clamp. Extract the retaining clip and disconnect the hydraulic pipe from the connecting piece above the starter motor location. Suitably cover the disconnected unions to prevent dirt entry.
12 Disconnect the wiring connector from the reversing light switch.
13 On early models disconnect the speedometer cable from the speedometer drive. On later models, disconnect the wiring at the speedometer drive transducer.
14 Disconnect the gear selection mechanism from the transmission as described in Section 3.
15 On models with the 02G type transmission, undo the two bolts securing the intermediate shaft support bearing to the mounting bracket. Pull the intermediate shaft out of the transmission stub shaft.
16 On models with the 02G type transmission, undo the retaining bolts and remove the support brace from the top of the transmission **(see illustrations)**.

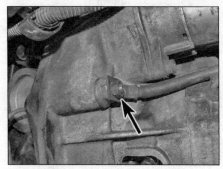

6.8 Engine earth strap attachment (arrowed) on the transmission

6.16a Undo the left-hand bolt (arrowed)...

6.16b ...and the right-hand bolts (arrowed) and remove the support brace from the transmission – 02G type transmission

6.17a On later models, undo the through bolt securing the rear engine mounting link bracket to the subframe...

6.17b ...and to the transmission...

6.17c ...then remove the link bracket

17 On early models, undo the two bolts securing the rear engine mounting to the subframe. On later models, undo the two through bolts securing the rear engine mounting link bracket to the subframe and transmission and remove the link bracket **(see illustrations)**.

18 The engine must now be supported, as the left-hand mounting must be disconnected. Ideally this should be done with an engine hoist connected to the left-hand side of the engine. With an engine hoist, the engine/transmission can be manoeuvred more easily and safely; balancing the engine on a jack is not recommended.

19 Support the transmission with a trolley jack from below, then undo the bolts securing the left-hand mounting to the transmission.

20 Lower the engine/transmission assembly slightly on the left-hand side to provide sufficient clearance for removal of the transmission.

21 On models, with the 02B transmission, undo the two bolts and withdraw the clutch slave cylinder from the transmission. Tie the cylinder to one side. **Note:** *The hydraulic pipe remains connected. Insert a 35 mm M8 bolt through the drilling above the slave cylinder aperture, to hold the clutch release lever in position.*

22 Working your way around the transmission casing, slacken and remove the transmission-to-engine securing bolts. Disconnect any wiring loom brackets, where applicable.

23 With the help of an assistant, withdraw the transmission squarely from the engine, taking care not to allow its weight to hang on the clutch friction disc. Once the transmission is free, lower the transmission on the jack and manoeuvre the unit out from under the vehicle.

Refitting

24 Apply a smear of high-melting-point grease to the transmission input shaft splines.

25 With the transmission secured on the trolley jack as on removal, raise it into position,

and then carefully slide it onto the engine, at the same time engaging the input shaft with the clutch friction disc splines. Do not use excessive force to refit the transmission – if the input shaft does not slide into place easily, readjust the angle of the transmission so that it is level, and/or turn the input shaft so that the splines engage properly with the disc. If problems are still experienced, check that the clutch friction disc is correctly centred (see Chapter 6, Section 7).

26 The remainder of refitting is a reversal of the removal procedure, bearing in mind the following points:

a) *Use new through-bolts when refitting the engine/transmission rear mounting link bracket.*

b) *Tighten all nuts and bolts to the specified torque (where given).*

c) *Reconnect the gear selection mechanism to the transmission as described in Section 3.*

d) *Refit the starter motor as described in Chapter 5, Section 10.*

e) *Refit the exhaust system front pipe as described in Chapter 4A, Section 19.*

f) *Refit the driveshafts as described in Chapter 8, Section 2.*

g) *On models with the 02G transmission, bleed the clutch hydraulic system as described in Chapter 6, Section 2.*

h) *Move the radiator back to its normal position as described in Chapter 3, Section 3.*

i) *Refit the engine undertray as described in Chapter 11, Section 25.*

j) *Refit the bonnet as described in Chapter 11, Section 6.*

27 Make a final check that all connections have been made, and all bolts tightened fully. Road test the vehicle to check for proper transmission operation, then check the transmission visually for leakage of oil.

7 Transmission overhaul – general information

Overhauling a manual transmission unit is a difficult and involved job for the DIY home mechanic. In addition to dismantling and reassembling many small parts, clearances must be precisely measured and, if necessary, changed by selecting shims and spacers. Internal transmission components are also often difficult to obtain, and in many instances, extremely expensive. Because of this, if the transmission develops a fault or becomes noisy, the best course of action is to have the unit overhauled by a specialist repairer, or to obtain an exchange reconditioned unit.

Nevertheless, it is not impossible for the more experienced mechanic to overhaul the transmission, provided the special tools are available, and the job is done in a deliberate step-by-step manner, so that nothing is overlooked.

The tools necessary for an overhaul include internal and external circlip pliers, bearing pullers, a slide hammer, a set of pin punches, a dial test indicator, and possibly a hydraulic press. In addition, a large, sturdy workbench and a vice will be required.

During dismantling of the transmission, make careful notes of how each component is fitted, to make reassembly easier and more accurate.

Before dismantling the transmission, it will help if you have some idea what area is malfunctioning. Certain problems can be closely related to specific areas in the transmission, which can make component examination and replacement easier. Refer to the *Fault finding* Section of this manual for more information.

Chapter 7 Part B:
Automatic transmission

Contents

Degrees of difficulty

Easy, suitable for novice with little experience	Fairly easy, suitable for beginner with some experience	Fairly difficult, suitable for competent DIY mechanic	Difficult, suitable for experienced DIY mechanic	Very difficult, suitable for expert DIY or professional

Specifications

General

Type	Electro-hydraulically controlled planetary gearbox providing four forward speeds and one reverse speed. Drive transmitted through hydrodynamic torque converter

Identification code:

2.4 litre engines	098 or 01P
2.5 litre engines	01P

Lubrication

Lubricant type	See *Lubricants and fluids* on page 0•17
Lubricant capacity	See Chapter 1

Torque wrench settings

	Nm	lbf ft
Engine/transmission mountings:		
Left-hand mounting-to-body through bolt	65	48
Left-hand mounting transmission bracket-to-transmission	65	48
Rear mounting-to-subframe (early models)	45	33
Rear mounting-to-subframe through bolt (later models)*	200	148
Rear mounting-to-transmission through bolt (later models):*		
Stage 1	80	59
Stage 2	Angle-tighten a further 90°	
Rear mounting-to-transmission rear bolts (later models)	40	30
Rear mounting-to-transmission right-hand bolts (later models)	100	74
Torque converter retaining nuts	60	44
Transmission bellhousing to engine:		
M8 bolts	20	15
M10 bolts	60	44
M12 bolts	80	59

* Use new bolts

1 General information

098 type transmission

The VW 098 type automatic transmission fitted up to December 1994 has four forward speeds and one reverse. The automatic gear changes are electronically controlled, rather than hydraulically as with previous conventional types. The advantage of electronic management is to provide a faster gearchange response. A kickdown facility is also provided, to enable a faster acceleration response when required.

The transmission consists of three main assemblies, these being the hydrokinetic torque converter, which is directly coupled to the engine; the final drive unit, which incorporates the differential; and the planetary gearbox, with its multi-disc clutches and brake bands. The final drive is lubricated independently, whilst the transmission is lubricated with automatic transmission fluid (ATF). A transmission fluid cooler is fitted externally for ease of maintenance.

The torque converter incorporates an automatic lock-up feature which eliminates any possibility of converter slip in the top two gears; this aids performance and economy. In addition to the normal alternatives of manual selection of lever positions, the transmission provides for a 'sport' or 'economy' mode as required. In 'sport' mode, upshifts are delayed longer to make full use of engine power, while in 'economy' mode (the default setting), upshifts are taken as soon as possible to permit optimum economy. On early models, the mode is selected via a two-position switch on the facia; on models built after January 1993 this switch was deleted in favour of automatic selection of mode according to accelerator pedal operation – rapid pedal movements cause 'sport' mode to be engaged by the more sohisticated programming of the transmission's electronic control unit acting in conjunction with modified selector components within the transmission. Slower pedal operation causes the transmission to revert back to 'economy' mode.

Another feature of this transmission is the selector lever lock, with which the selector lever can be set in the 'P' or 'N' position when the engine is running, below about 3 mph. Under these conditions, selection from 'P' or 'N' can only be made by depressing the brake pedal.

01P type transmission

The 01P type transmission fitted from January 1995 is very similar to the 098 type in terms of construction, features and general function, but its performance is enhanced by a number of refinements.

The torque converter lock-up facility has been extended to all forward speeds, for greater fuel economy. The electronic control unit now incorporates 'fuzzy logic', allowing infinitely variable gearchange points to be determined in response to driver demands and driving conditions, for maximum performance or economy, as appropriate. The 'sport' and 'economy' modes are determined by throttle position and its rate of change, as described above for the later 098 type units. In this way, gearchanges can be economy-orientated, but full acceleration is always available on demand. A further refinement is the inclusion of a gearchange map for gradients, allowing the control unit to select the most appropriate ratio to match gradient to engine output when climbing hills, and to allow adequate engine braking when descending.

All transmissions

A fault diagnosis system is integrated into the control unit, but analysis can only be undertaken with specialised equipment. If a malfunction should occur in the transmission electrical system, automatic gear selection will continue, but the changes will be noticeably jerky. In the event of automatic selection failure, the selection of gears can be made manually. In either instance, it is important that the transmission fault be identified and rectified at the earliest possible opportunity. Delay in doing so will only cause further problems.

Because of the need for special test equipment, the complexity of some of the parts, and the need for scrupulous cleanliness when servicing automatic transmissions, the amount which the owner can do is limited (this is especially the case with the 01P type transmission). Repairs to the final drive differential are also not recommended. Most major repairs and overhaul operations should be left to a VW dealer or automatic transmission specialist, who will be equipped with the necessary equipment for fault diagnosis and repair. The information in this Chapter is therefore limited to a description of the removal and refitting of the transmission as a complete unit. The removal, refitting and adjustment of the selector cable is also described.

In the event of a transmission problem occurring, consult a VW dealer or transmission specialist before removing the transmission from the vehicle, since the majority of fault diagnosis is carried out with the transmission in situ.

The different transmissions fitted to the models described in this manual can be identified as follows:

a) 098 type transmission – both identifying codes are marked on top of the transmission casing; the three-digit type code underneath the selector lever, and the code letters (alongside a five-digit date code) on the top of the bellhousing, adjacent to the protective cap covering the driveplate TDC marks

b) 01P type transmission – both identifying codes are marked on top of the transmission casing; the three-character type code next to the fluid cooler, and the code letters (alongside a five-digit date code) above the starter motor mounting flange

Note: *On all models, the transmission code letters also appear on the vehicle data sticker located below or adjacent to the fuse/relay box in the passenger compartment (see 'Vehicle Identification').*

2 Selector cable – removal, refitting and adjustment

Removal

1 Disconnect the battery negative terminal (refer to *Disconnecting the battery*).
2 Firmly apply the handbrake, then jack up the front of the vehicle and support it securely on axle stands (see *Jacking and vehicle support*).
3 Remove the engine undertray as described in Chapter 11, Section 25.
4 Move the selector lever to the 'P' position.
5 From below, undo the locking bolt securing the cable end to the selector lever, then detach the outer cable from the housing.
6 Withdraw the cable from the selector lever housing, then working along its length, release the cable from the securing clips. Note the cable routing carefully for refitting.
7 At the transmission end of the cable, extract the retaining clip and detach the selector cable from the lever on the transmission. Extract the outer cable retaining clip and withdraw the selector cable from the support bracket.

Refitting

8 Refit the selector cable by reversing the removal procedure. When fitting the cable to the selector lever, ensure that the recessed side of the cable end is toward the locking bolt. Ensure that the cable is correctly routed, as noted on removal, and that it is securely held by its retaining clips.
9 Before tightening the connection at the selector lever, adjust the selector cable as described below.

Adjustment

10 If not already done, carry out the operations described previously in paragraphs 1 to 4.
11 From below, undo the locking bolt securing the cable end to the selector lever.
12 At the transmission, make sure that the selector shaft lever is also in the 'P' position.
13 Tighten the locking bolt securing the cable end to the selector lever.
14 Verify the operation of the selector lever by shifting through all gear positions and checking that every gear can be selected smoothly and without delay.

3 Automatic transmission –
removed and refitting

Removal

1 Disconnect the battery negative terminal (refer to *Disconnecting the battery*).
2 Refer to Chapter 11, Section 6 and remove the bonnet from its hinges.
3 Move the radiator to the service position as described in Chapter 3, Section 3.
4 Firmly apply the handbrake, then jack up the front of the vehicle and support it securely on axle stands (see *Jacking and vehicle support*). There must be sufficient clearance below the vehicle for the transmission to be lowered and removed.
5 Remove the engine undertray as described in Chapter 11, Section 25.
6 Remove both driveshafts as described in Chapter 8, Section 2.
7 Remove the exhaust system front pipe as described in Chapter 4A, Section 19.
8 Disconnect the wiring connectors at the valve body, road speed sender and multifunction switch. Remove the multifunction switch wiring snd support bracket and place it to one side.
9 Unbolt the earth strap from the transmission and disconnect any remaining wiring connectors and retaining clips.
10 Remove the starter motor as described in Chapter 5, Section 10.
11 On vehicles equipped with air conditioning, remove the auxiliary drivebelt as described in Chapter 2A, Section 6 (4-cylinder engines) or Chapter 2B, Section 8 (5-cylinder engines). Unbolt the air conditioning compressor and secure it to one side. Do not disconnect the refrigerant pipes.
12 On early models disconnect the speedometer cable from the speedometer drive. On later models, disconnect the wiring at the speedometer drive transducer.
13 Position the selector lever in the 'P'

position, then extract the retaining clip and detach the selector cable from the lever on the transmission. Extract the outer cable retaining clip and withdraw the selector cable from the support bracket.
14 Clamp the automatic transmission fluid cooler hoses as close to the cooler as possible, then detach the hoses from the cooler.
15 Unbolt and remove the torque converter housing lower cover plate.
16 Working through the cover plate aperture, slacken and withdraw each torque converter-to-driveplate nut in turn. As each nut is removed, rotate the crankshaft using a wrench and socket on the crankshaft sprocket to expose the next nut. Repeat until all three nuts are removed.
17 On early models, undo the two bolts securing the rear engine mounting to the subframe. On later models, undo the two through bolts securing the rear engine mounting link bracket to the subframe and transmission and remove the link bracket.
18 The engine must now be supported, as the left-hand mounting must be disconnected. Ideally this should be done with an engine hoist connected to the left-hand side of the engine. With an engine hoist, the engine/transmission can be manoeuvred more easily and safely; balancing the engine on a jack is not recommended.
19 Support the transmission with a trolley jack from below, then undo the bolts securing the left-hand mounting to the transmission.
20 Lower the engine/transmission assembly slightly on the left-hand side to provide sufficient clearance for removal of the transmission.
21 Working your way around the transmission casing, slacken and remove the transmission-to-engine securing bolts. Disconnect any wiring loom brackets, where applicable.
22 With the help of an assistant, withdraw the transmission squarely from the engine. Once the transmission is free, lower the transmission on the jack and manoeuvre the unit out from under the vehicle.

Warning: Support the transmission to ensure that it remains steady on the jack head. Ensure that the torque converter remains in position on its shaft in the torque converter housing
23 With the transmission removed, bolt a suitable bar and spacer across the front face of the torque converter housing, to retain the torque converter in position.

Refitting

24 Refitting is a reversal of the removal procedure, but note the following points:
  a) *When reconnecting the transmission to the engine, ensure that the location dowels are in position, and that the transmission is correctly aligned with them before pushing it fully into engagement with the engine. As the torque converter is refitted, ensure that the drive pins at the centre of the torque converter hub engage with the recesses in the automatic transmission fluid pump inner wheel.*
  b) *Tighten all nuts and bolts to the specified torque (where given).*
  c) *Reconnect and adjust the selector cable, as described in Section 2.*

4 Automatic transmission
overhaul –
general information

1 In the event of a fault occurring with the transmission, it is first necessary to determine whether it is of a mechanical, electrical or hydraulic nature, and to do this, special test equipment is required. It is therefore essential to have the work carried out by a VW dealer or suitably equipped specialist if a transmission fault is suspected.
2 Do not remove the transmission from the car for possible repair before professional fault diagnosis has been carried out, since most tests require the transmission to be in the vehicle.

Chapter 8
Driveshafts

Contents

Degrees of difficulty

Easy, suitable for novice with little experience	**Fairly easy,** suitable for beginner with some experience	**Fairly difficult,** suitable for competent DIY mechanic	**Difficult,** suitable for experienced DIY mechanic	**Very difficult,** suitable for expert DIY or professional

Specifications

General
Driveshaft type . . . . Solid steel shafts with ball-and-cage type constant velocity joints at each end

Lubrication (overhaul only – see text)
Lubricant type/specification. . . . . Use only special grease supplied in sachets with gaiter kits – joints are otherwise pre-packed with grease and sealed
Lubricant capacity . . . . 120 g per joint

Torque wrench settings

	Nm	lbf ft
Driveshaft retaining bolt*:		
Stage 1	150	110
Stage 2	Angle-tighten a further 90°	
Engine/transmission rear mounting (automatic transmission models):		
Rear mounting-to-subframe (early models)	45	33
Rear mounting-to-transmission through bolt (later models):*		
Stage 1	80	59
Stage 2	Angle-tighten a further 90°	
Inner constant velocity joint retaining bolts:		
M10 bolts	80	59
M12 bolts	100	74
Lower wishbone balljoint-to-swivel hub bolts*:		
Hexagon head bolts:		
Stage 1	55	41
Stage 2	Angle-tighten through a further 90°	
Multi-point socket head bolts:		
Stage 1	90	66
Stage 2	Angle-tighten through a further 90°	
Roadwheel bolts:		
Up to December 1995	160	118
January 1996 onward	180	133
Shock absorber-to-lower wishbone bolt/nut	160	118

*Use new nuts/bolts.

TOOL TiP

A tool to hold the wheel hub stationary whilst the driveshaft retaining bolt is slackened can be fabricated from two lengths of steel strip (one long, one short) and a nut and bolt; the nut and bolt forming the pivot of a forked tool.

1 General information

Drive is transmitted from the differential to the front wheels by means of two solid steel driveshafts.

Both driveshafts are splined at their outer ends to accept the wheel hubs, and are threaded so that each hub can be fastened by a retaining bolt. The inner end of each driveshaft is bolted to the transmission drive flanges.

2.5 Measure and record the length of exposed thread on the torsion bar adjusting bolt

2.7 Undo the two bolts securing the lower arm balljoint to the swivel hub

2.3 Attach the holding tool to the wheel hub using two wheel bolts

Constant velocity (CV) joints are fitted to each end of the driveshafts, to ensure the smooth and efficient transmission of drive at all the angles possible as the roadwheels move up-and-down with the suspension, and as they turn from side-to-side under steering. Both the inner and outer constant velocity joints are of the ball-and-cage type

2 Driveshaft – removal and refitting

Removal

Note: *The driveshaft outer joint splines may be a tight fit in the hub and it is possible that a puller/extractor will be required to draw the hub assembly off the driveshaft during removal.*

2.6 Unscrew the torsion bar adjusting nut until all load is relieved on the front upper wishbone

2.9 On later automatic transmission models, undo the engine mounting link bracket through bolt

1 Firmly apply the handbrake, then jack up the front of the vehicle and support it securely on axle stands (see *Jacking and vehicle support*). Remove the relevant front roadwheel.

2 Remove the engine undertray as described in Chapter 11, Section 25.

3 To prevent rotation of the wheel hub as the driveshaft retaining bolt is slackened, make up a holding tool and attach the tool to the wheel hub using two wheel bolts **(see Tool Tip and illustration)**.

4 With the holding tool in place, slacken and remove the driveshaft retaining bolt using a socket and long bar. Where necessary, support the socket on an axle stand to prevent it slipping off the nut. This bolt is very tight; make sure that there is no risk of pulling the vehicle off the axle stands as the nut is slackened. Note that a new bolt will be required for refitting.

5 At the torsion bar adjustment bolt, measure and record the length of thread projecting from the underside of the adjusting nut to the end of the bolt **(see illustration)**. This is a critical dimension as it will be needed to determine the vehicle ride height when refitting.

6 Using a spanner or deep socket, unscrew the torsion bar adjusting nut until all load is relieved on the front upper wishbone **(see illustration)**.

7 Undo the two bolts securing the lower wishbone balljoint to the swivel hub **(see illustration)**. On pre-January 1996 vehicles these bolts are conventional hexagon head bolts. On January 1996 vehicles onwards, these bolts are M12 multi-point socket headed bolts and are removed using a 14 mm multi-point key. Note that new bolts (whichever type) will be required for refitting.

8 Undo the nut and remove the bolt securing the anti-roll bar connecting link and the shock absorber to the lower wishbone. Push the lower end of the shock absorber upward as far as it will go.

9 On early models with automatic transmission, undo the two bolts securing the rear engine mounting to the subframe. On later models with automatic transmission, undo the through bolt securing the rear engine mounting link bracket to the transmission **(see illustration)**.

10 Undo and remove the bolts securing the inner driveshaft joint to the transmission flange and recover the retaining plates from underneath the bolts. Support the driveshaft by suspending it with wire or string – do not allow it to hang under its weight, or the joint may be damaged **(see illustrations)**.

11 Carefully pull the swivel hub assembly outwards, and withdraw the driveshaft outer constant velocity joint from the hub assembly **(see illustration)**. The outer joint may be very tight, if so tap the joint out of the hub using a soft-faced mallet. If this fails to free it from the hub, the joint will have to be pressed out using a suitable tool which is bolted to the hub.

2.10a Slacken the inner driveshaft joint retaining bolts...

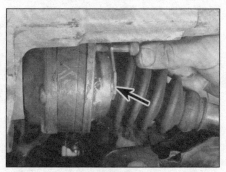

2.10b ...and remove them along with their retaining plates

2.11 Pull the swivel hub assembly outwards, and withdraw the outer constant velocity joint from the hub

12 Manoeuvre the driveshaft out from underneath the vehicle and (where fitted) recover the gasket from the end of the inner constant velocity joint. Discard the gasket – a new one should be used on refitting. On models with automatic transmission, push the engine/transmission forwards slightly to provide the necessary clearance for removal.

13 Do not allow the vehicle to rest on its wheels with one or both driveshaft(s) removed, as damage to the wheel bearing(s) may result. If moving the vehicle is unavoidable, temporarily insert the outer end of the driveshaft(s) in the hub(s), and tighten the driveshaft retaining bolt(s); in this case, the inner end(s) of the driveshaft(s) must be supported, for example by suspending with string from the vehicle underbody. Do not allow the driveshaft to hang down under its weight, or the joint may be damaged.

Refitting

14 Ensure that the transmission flange and inner joint mating surfaces are clean and dry. Fit a new gasket to the joint by peeling off its backing foil and sticking it in position **(see illustrations)**.

15 Ensure that the outer joint and hub splines are clean and dry. Manoeuvre the driveshaft into position, and engage the outer joint with the hub. Ensure that the threads are clean, and apply a smear of oil to the contact face of the new driveshaft retaining bolt. Fit the bolt and use it to draw the joint fully into position.

16 Refit the new lower wishbone balljoint retaining bolts, and tighten them to the specified torque setting, then through the specified angle.

17 Align the driveshaft inner joint with the transmission flange, and refit the retaining bolts and retaining plates. Tighten the retaining bolts to the specified torque.

18 On early models with automatic transmission, refit the two bolts securing the rear engine mounting to the subframe and tighten them to the specified torque. On later models, fit the new through bolt securing the rear engine mounting link bracket to the transmission and tighten it to the specified

2.14a Fit a new gasket to the CV joint by peeling off its backing foil...

2.14b ...and sticking it in position

torque setting, then through the specified angle.

19 Pull the lower end of the shock absorber down and refit the anti-roll bar connecting link and shock absorber retaining bolt. Note that the bolt head is toward the rear of the vehicle. Refit the retaining nut and tighten it to the specified torque.

20 Tighten the torsion bar adjusting nut until the exposed thread dimension recorded during removal is obtained.

21 Refit the engine undertray as described in Chapter 11, Section 25.

22 Using the method employed on removal to prevent the hub from rotating, and tighten the driveshaft retaining bolt to the specified torque setting, then through the specified angle. Check that the hub rotates freely.

23 Refit the roadwheel, lower the vehicle to the ground, and tighten the wheel bolts to specified torque.

3 Driveshaft joint gaiters – renewal

Outer CV joint gaiter

1 Remove the driveshaft from the vehicle as described in Section 2.

2 Release the rubber gaiter retaining clips by cutting off the crimped portion using side cutters **(see illustrations)**. Alternatively cut through them using a junior hacksaw. Spread the clips and remove them from the gaiter.

3.2a Release the rubber gaiter outer retaining clip...

3.2b ...by cutting off the crimped portion using side cutters

3.3 Cut the gaiter open and remove it from the driveshaft

3.5a Screw the driveshaft retaining bolt into the CV joint and tighten it to force the driveshaft out of the joint

3.5b If the driveshaft is difficult to release, drive the joint off by striking the inner member with a hammer and punch

3.6a Withdraw the CV joint from the driveshaft...

3.6b ...followed by the thrustwasher...

3.6c ...dished washer...

3.6d ...and circlip

3.8 Examine the balls and tracks for cracks, flat spots or signs of surface pitting

3.11a Slide the new rubber gaiter...

3.11b ...and small retaining clip onto the driveshaft

3 Cut the gaiter open using a suitable knife and remove it from the driveshaft **(see illustration)**.
4 Using old rags, clean away as much of the old grease as possible from the CV joint. It is advisable to wear disposable rubber gloves during this operation.

5 The outer CV joint is retained on the driveshaft by an internal circlip. Screw the driveshaft retaining bolt into the end of the CV joint and tighten the bolt to force the driveshaft out of the joint. If the driveshaft proves difficult to release, clamp the shaft in a vice and drive the joint off the shaft by striking the inner member with a hammer and punch **(see illustrations)**.
6 Withdraw the joint from the driveshaft followed by the thrustwasher, dished washer and circlip **(see illustrations)**. A new circlip must be fitted on reassembly.
7 Thoroughly clean the constant velocity joint using paraffin, or a suitable solvent, and dry thoroughly. Carry out a visual inspection as follows.
8 Move the inner splined driving member from side to side to expose each ball in turn at the top of its track. Examine the balls for cracks, flat spots or signs of surface pitting **(see illustration)**.
9 Inspect the ball tracks on the inner and outer members. If the tracks have widened, the balls will no longer be a tight fit. At the same time, check the ball cage windows for wear or cracking between the windows.
10 If on inspection any of the constant velocity joint components are found to be worn or damaged, it will be necessary to renew the complete joint assembly. If the joint is in satisfactory condition, obtain a new gaiter and retaining clips, a constant velocity joint circlip and the correct type and quantity of grease. Grease is often supplied with the joint repair kit.
11 Slide the new rubber gaiter and small retaining clip onto the driveshaft **(see illustrations)**.

3.12a Slide on the dished washer...

3.12b ...followed by the thrustwasher

3.12c Correct arrangement of the dished
washer and thrustwasher

12 Slide on the dished washer, making sure its convex side is innermost, followed by the thrustwasher **(see illustrations)**.

13 Fit a new circlip to the driveshaft, then screw the driveshaft retaining bolt into the end of the joint **(see illustrations)**. This will prevent the grease from escaping as the joint is lubricated.

14 Pack the inside of the joint through the inner splines of the ball hub with approximately 80 g of the specified grease **(see illustration)**.

15 Engage the joint with the driveshaft splines. Tap the joint onto the driveshaft until the circlip engages in its groove **(see illustration)**. Make sure that the joint is securely retained, by pulling on the joint, not the shaft.

16 Spread the remaining grease around the inside of the joint. Work the grease well into the bearing tracks whilst twisting the joint **(see illustration)**.

17 Ease the gaiter over the joint, and ensure that the gaiter lips are correctly located on both the driveshaft and constant velocity joint

3.13a Fit a new circlip to the driveshaft...

3.13b ...then screw the driveshaft retaining
bolt into the end of the joint

3.14 Pack the inside of the joint with the
specified grease

3.15a Engage the joint with the driveshaft
splines...

3.15b ...then tap the joint onto the shaft until the circlip engages
in its groove

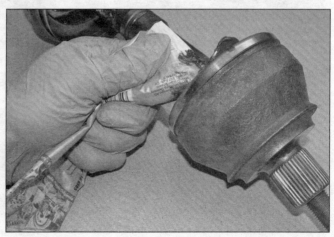

3.16 Spread the remaining grease around the inside of the joint

3.17 Ease the gaiter over the joint, and ensure that the gaiter lips are correctly located

3.18a Fit the large retaining clip, pull it as tight as possible, and locate the hooks on the clip in their slots

3.18b Remove any slack in the gaiter retaining clip by carefully compressing the raised section of the clip

(see illustration). Lift the outer sealing lip of the gaiter to equalise air pressure within the gaiter.

3.18c Secure the small retaining clip using the same procedure

18 Fit the large metal retaining clip to the gaiter. Pull the clip as tight as possible, and locate the hooks on the clip in their slots.

Remove any slack in the gaiter retaining clip by carefully compressing the raised section of the clip. In the absence of the special tool, a pair of side cutters may be used, taking care not to cut the clip. Secure the small retaining clip using the same procedure **(see illustrations)**.

19 Check the constant velocity joint moves freely in all directions, then refit the driveshaft to the vehicle, as described in Section 2.

Inner CV joint gaiter

20 Remove the driveshaft from the car as described in Section 2.

21 Release the rubber gaiter retaining clip by cutting off the crimped portion using side cutters **(see illustration)**.

22 Using circlip pliers, extract the circlip from the end of the driveshaft **(see illustration)**. Note that a new circlip, often supplied with the joint repair kit, will be required for reassembly.

23 Withdraw the CV joint from the driveshaft and remove the gasket from the joint flange **(see illustrations)**.

24 Remove the old gaiter and retaining clip from the driveshaft **(see illustration)**.

25 Thoroughly clean the constant velocity joint using paraffin, or a suitable solvent, and dry thoroughly. Carry out a visual inspection as described previously in paragraphs 8 to 10.

26 Slide the new rubber gaiter onto the driveshaft and locate the small end of the gaiter in the recess in the shaft **(see illustrations)**.

27 Pack both sides of the CV joint with the

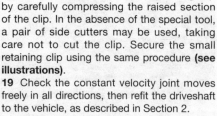

3.21 Release the rubber gaiter retaining clip by cutting off the crimped portion using side cutters

3.22 Extract the circlip from the end of the driveshaft

3.23a Withdraw the CV joint from the driveshaft...

3.23b ...and remove the gasket from the joint flange

3.24 Remove the old gaiter and retaining clip from the driveshaft

3.26a Slide the new rubber gaiter onto the driveshaft...

3.26b ...and locate the small end of the gaiter in the recess in the shaft

3.27a Pack both sides of the CV joint with the specified grease...

3.27b ...working the grease well into the bearing tracks

specified grease. Work the grease well into the bearing tracks whilst twisting the joint **(see illustrations)**.
28 Place the CV joint in position on the driveshaft, then fit the new circlip **(see illustrations)**. Ensure that the circlip is fully seated in the driveshaft groove.
29 Ease the gaiter over the joint, and ensure that the gaiter lips are correctly located on the constant velocity joint **(see illustration)**. Lift the small end of the gaiter to equalise air pressure within the gaiter.
30 Fit the metal retaining clip to the gaiter. Pull the clip as tight as possible, and locate the hooks on the clip in their slots. Remove any slack in the gaiter retaining clip by carefully compressing the raised section of the clip. In the absence of the special tool, a pair of side cutters may be used, taking care not to cut the clip **(see illustration)**.
31 Check the constant velocity joint moves freely in all directions, then refit the driveshaft to the vehicle, as described in Section 2.

4 Driveshaft overhaul – general information

1 If any of the checks described in Chapter 1, Sections 13 and 21 reveal possible wear in any driveshaft joint, carry out the following procedures to identify the source of the problem.
2 Firmly apply the handbrake, then jack up the front of the vehicle and support it securely on axle stands (see *Jacking and vehicle support*).
3 Referring to the information contained in Section 2, make up a tool to hold the wheel hub, and attach the tool to the hub using two wheel bolts. Use a torque wrench to check

3.28a Place the CV joint in position on the driveshaft...

3.29 Ease the gaiter over the joint, and ensure that the gaiter lips are correctly located

that the driveshaft retaining bolt is securely fastened, then repeat this check on the remaining driveshaft bolt.
4 Road test the vehicle, and listen for a metallic clicking from the front as the vehicle is driven slowly in a circle on full-lock. If a clicking noise is heard, this indicates wear in the outer constant velocity joint.

3.28b ...then fit the new circlip

3.30 Remove any slack in the gaiter retaining clip by carefully compressing the raised section

5 If vibration, consistent with road speed, is felt through the vehicle when accelerating, there is a possibility of wear in the inner constant velocity joints.
6 To check the joints for wear, remove the driveshafts, then dismantle them as described in Section 3; if any wear or free play is found, the affected joint must be renewed.

Chapter 9
Braking system

Contents

Degrees of difficulty

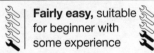

Easy, suitable for novice with little experience	**Fairly easy,** suitable for beginner with some experience	**Fairly difficult,** suitable for competent DIY mechanic	**Difficult,** suitable for experienced DIY mechanic	**Very difficult,** suitable for expert DIY or professional

Specifications

Front brakes

Type . . . .   Solid or ventilated disc, with single-piston calipers
Caliper type:
  With 14 inch wheels . . . .   Lucas C54 floating caliper
  With 15 inch wheels . . . .   Lucas RC54 floating frame caliper or VW FN3 floating caliper
  With 16 inch wheels . . . .   VW FN3 floating caliper or VW FNR floating caliper
Disc diameter:
  Solid disc:
    With 14 inch wheels . . . .   260.0 mm
    With 15 inch wheels . . . .   282.0 mm
  Ventilated disc:
    With 15 inch wheels . . . .   280.0 mm
    With 16 inch wheels . . . .   300.0 mm or 313.0 mm according to model
Disc thickness:
  New:
    Solid disc:
      With 14 inch wheels . . . .   13.0 mm
      With 15 inch wheels . . . .   18.0 mm
    Ventilated disc:
      With 15 inch wheels . . . .   24.0 mm
      With 16 inch wheels . . . .   26.0 mm
  Minimum:
    Solid disc . . . .   15.0 mm
    Ventilated disc:
      With 15 inch wheels . . . .   20.0 mm
      With 16 inch wheels . . . .   22.0 mm
Maximum disc thickness variation . . . .   0.02 mm
Maximum disc run-out . . . .   0.08 mm
Minimum brake pad friction material thickness . . . .   2.0 mm

Rear drum brakes

Type . . . . Drum with leading and trailing shoes and automatic adjusters
Brake shoe friction material minimum thickness . . . . 1.0 mm
Drum diameter (inner):
   New . . . . 268.0 mm
   Maximum . . . . 269.5 mm

Rear disc brakes

Type . . . . Solid disc, with single-piston sliding calipers
Disc thickness:
   New:
      With 15 inch wheels . . . . 12.0 mm
      With 16 inch wheels . . . . 13.5 mm
   Minimum:
      With 15 inch wheels . . . . 10.0 mm
      With 16 inch wheels . . . . 11.5 mm
Minimum brake pad friction material thickness . . . . 2.0 mm

Handbrake

Type . . . . Self-adjusting cable-operated, acting on rear brakes

ABS system type

Up to 1995 . . . . Bosch 2E
1996 to 1997 . . . . Bosch 5.0
1998 onwards. . . . . Bosch 5.3

Torque wrench settings

	Nm	lbf ft
ABS wheel speed sensor retaining bolts	10	7
Front brake calipers:		
Caliper body-to-swivel hub (Lucas floating frame caliper)	280	207
Caliper bridge retaining bolts (Lucas floating frame caliper)	90	66
Caliper mounting bracket-to-swivel hub (except VW FNR caliper)	280	207
Caliper mounting bracket-to-swivel hub (VW FNR caliper)	355	262
Guide pins (VW calipers)	25	18
Guide pin bolts (Lucas floating caliper)*	35	26
Guide pin retaining nuts (Lucas floating frame caliper)	70	52
Handbrake lever retaining nuts	25	19
Master cylinder retaining nuts	20	15
Rear brake caliper guide pin bolts*	35	26
Rear brake caliper mounting bracket-to-trailing arm	170	125
Rear wheel cylinder retaining bolt	20	15
Roadwheel bolts:		
Up to December 1995	160	118
January 1996 onward	180	133
Vacuum servo unit retaining nuts	25	18

*Use new fasteners

1 General information

The braking system is of servo-assisted, dual-circuit hydraulic type split diagonally. The arrangement of the hydraulic system is such that each circuit operates one front and one rear brake from a tandem master cylinder. Under normal circumstances, both circuits operate in unison. However, in the event of hydraulic failure in one circuit, full braking force will still be available at two wheels.

All models are fitted with front disc brakes, with self-adjusting drum brakes at the rear on vehicles produced up to May 1996. On later models, disc brakes are fitted at the front and rear. An Anti-lock Braking System (ABS) is an optional extra on all vehicles covered in this manual. Refer to Section 26 for further information on ABS operation.

The front brake discs are of either the solid or ventilated type and are fitted with single-piston sliding type brake calipers.

The rear drum brakes incorporate leading and trailing shoes, which are actuated by twin-piston wheel cylinders. A self-adjust mechanism is incorporated to automatically compensate for brake shoe wear. As the brake shoe linings wear, the footbrake operation automatically operates the adjuster mechanism, which effectively lengthens the shoe strut, and repositions the brake shoes to maintain the lining-to-drum clearance.

The rear brake discs are of the solid type and are fitted with single-piston sliding pin brake calipers.

The cable-operated handbrake provides an independent mechanical means of rear brake application.

A vacuum servo unit is fitted between the master cylinder and the bulkhead, its function being to reduce the amount of pedal pressure required to operate the brakes. Since there is no throttling as such of the inlet manifold on diesel engines, the manifold is not a suitable source of vacuum to operate the vacuum servo unit. The servo unit is therefore connected to a separate engine-mounted vacuum pump. On 4-cylinder engines, the pump is bolted to the cylinder block and is driven by the intermediate shaft. On 5-cylinder engines, the pump is bolted to the cylinder head and is driven by the camshaft.

On models without ABS, and certain other

models, a brake pressure regulating valve is incorporated in the rear brake hydraulic circuit. The valve function is to regulate the braking force available at each rear wheel, to reduce the possibility of the rear wheels locking up under heavy braking. On later models equipped with ABS, the braking force available at the rear wheels is controlled by the ABS hydraulic modulator under all driving conditions.

⚠️ *Warning: When servicing any part of the system, work carefully and methodically; also observe scrupulous cleanliness when overhauling any part of the hydraulic system. Always renew components (in axle sets, where applicable) if in doubt about their condition, and use only genuine VW replacement parts, or at least those of known good quality. Note the warnings given in 'Safety first!' and at relevant points in this Chapter concerning the dangers of asbestos dust and hydraulic fluid.*

2 Hydraulic system – bleeding

⚠️ *Warning: Hydraulic fluid is poisonous; wash off immediately and thoroughly in the case of skin contact, and seek immediate medical advice if any fluid is swallowed or gets into the eyes. Certain types of hydraulic fluid are inflammable, and may ignite when allowed into contact with hot components; when servicing any hydraulic system, it is safest to assume that the fluid is inflammable, and to take precautions against the risk of fire as though it is petrol that is being handled. Hydraulic fluid is also an effective paint stripper, and will attack plastics; if any is spilt, it should be washed off immediately, using copious quantities of fresh water. Finally, it is hygroscopic (it absorbs moisture from the air) – old fluid may be contaminated and unfit for further use. When topping-up or renewing the fluid, always use the recommended type, and ensure that it comes from a freshly-opened sealed container.*

General

1 The correct operation of any hydraulic system is only possible after removing all air from the components and circuit; this is achieved by bleeding the system.
2 During the bleeding procedure, add only clean, unused hydraulic fluid of the recommended type; never re-use fluid that has already been bled from the system. Ensure that sufficient fluid is available before starting work.
3 If there is any possibility of incorrect fluid being already in the system, the brake components and circuit must be flushed

completely with uncontaminated, correct fluid, and new seals should be fitted to the various components.
4 If hydraulic fluid has been lost from the system, or air has entered because of a leak, ensure that the fault is cured before proceeding further.
5 Park the vehicle over an inspection pit or on car ramps. Alternatively, apply the handbrake then jack up the front and rear of the vehicle and support it on axle stands (see *Jacking and vehicle support*). For improved access with the vehicle jacked up, remove the roadwheels.
6 Check that all pipes and hoses are secure, unions tight and bleed screws closed. Clean any dirt from around the bleed screws.
7 Unscrew the master cylinder reservoir cap, and top the master cylinder reservoir up to the MAX level line; refit the cap loosely, and remember to maintain the fluid level at least above the MIN level line throughout the procedure, otherwise there is a risk of further air entering the system.
8 There are a number of one-man, do-it-yourself brake bleeding kits currently available from motor accessory shops. It is recommended that one of these kits is used whenever possible, as they greatly simplify the bleeding operation, and also reduce the risk of expelled air and fluid being drawn back into the system. If such a kit is not available, the basic (two-man) method must be used, which is described in detail below.
9 If a kit is to be used, prepare the vehicle as described previously, and follow the kit manufacturer's instructions, as the procedure may vary slightly according to the type being used; generally, they are as outlined below in the relevant sub-section.
10 Whichever method is used, the same sequence should be followed (paragraphs 11 and 12) to ensure the removal of all air from the system.

Bleeding sequence

11 If the system has been only partially disconnected, and suitable precautions were taken to minimise fluid loss, it should only be necessary to bleed that part of the system (ie, the primary or secondary circuit). If the master cylinder or main brake lines have been disconnected, then the complete system must be bled.
12 If the complete system is to be bled, then it should be done working in the following sequence:

   a) *Right-hand rear brake.*
   b) *Left-hand rear brake.*
   c) *Right-hand front brake.*
   d) *Left-hand front brake.*

Bleeding

Basic (two-man) method

13 Collect together a clean glass jar or similar container, a suitable length of plastic or rubber

2.14 Remove the dust cap from the brake caliper bleed screw

tubing which is a tight fit over the bleed screw, and a ring spanner to fit the screw. The help of an assistant will also be required.
14 Remove the dust cap from the first bleed screw in the sequence **(see illustration)**. Fit the spanner and tube to the screw, place the other end of the tube in the jar, and pour in sufficient fluid to cover the end of the tube.
15 Ensure that the master cylinder reservoir fluid level is maintained at least above the MIN level line throughout the procedure.
16 Have the assistant fully depress the brake pedal several times to build-up pressure, then maintain it on the final downstroke.
17 While pedal pressure is maintained, unscrew the bleed screw (approximately one turn) and allow the compressed fluid and air to flow into the jar. The assistant should maintain pedal pressure, following it down to the floor if necessary, and should not release it until instructed to do so. When the flow stops, tighten the bleed screw again, have the assistant release the pedal slowly, and recheck the reservoir fluid level.
18 Repeat the steps given in paragraphs 16 and 17 until the fluid emerging from the bleed screw is free from air bubbles. If the master cylinder has been drained and refilled, and air is being bled from the first screw in the sequence, allow approximately five seconds between cycles for the master cylinder passages to refill.
19 When no more air bubbles appear, securely tighten the bleed screw, remove the tube and spanner, and refit the dust cap. Do not overtighten the bleed screw.
20 Repeat the procedure on the remaining screws in the sequence, until all air is removed from the system and the brake pedal feels firm again.

Using a one-way valve kit

21 As the name implies, these kits consist of a length of tubing with a one-way valve fitted, to prevent expelled air and fluid being drawn back into the system; some kits include a translucent container, which can be positioned so that the air bubbles can be more easily seen flowing from the end of the tube.
22 The kit is connected to the bleed screw,

2.22 Bleeding a rear brake caliper using a one-way valve kit

which is then opened **(see illustration)**. The user returns to the driver's seat, depresses the brake pedal with a smooth, steady stroke, and slowly releases it; this is repeated until the expelled fluid is clear of air bubbles.

23 Note that these kits simplify work so much that it is easy to forget the master cylinder reservoir fluid level; ensure that this is maintained at least above the MIN level line at all times.

Using a pressure-bleeding kit

24 These kits are usually operated by a reservoir of pressurised air contained in the spare tyre. However, note that it will probably be necessary to reduce the pressure to a lower level than normal (maximum of 1 bar); refer to the instructions supplied with the kit.

25 By connecting a pressurised, fluid-filled container to the master cylinder reservoir, bleeding can be carried out simply by opening each screw in turn (in the specified sequence), and allowing the fluid to flow out until no more air bubbles can be seen in the expelled fluid.

26 This method has the advantage that the large reservoir of fluid provides an additional safeguard against air being drawn into the system during bleeding.

27 Pressure-bleeding is particularly effective when bleeding 'difficult' systems, or when bleeding the complete system at the time of routine fluid renewal.

All methods

28 When bleeding is complete, and firm pedal feel is restored, wash off any spilt fluid,

3.2 Flexible hydraulic hose retaining spring clip (arrowed)

securely tighten the bleed screws, and refit the dust caps.

29 Check the hydraulic fluid level in the master cylinder reservoir, and top-up if necessary.

30 Discard any hydraulic fluid that has been bled from the system; it will not be fit for re-use.

31 Check the feel of the brake pedal. If it feels at all spongy, air must still be present in the system, and further bleeding is required. Failure to bleed satisfactorily after a reasonable repetition of the bleeding procedure may be due to worn master cylinder seals.

3 Hydraulic pipes and hoses – renewal

Note: *Before starting work, refer to the note at the beginning of Section 2 concerning the dangers of hydraulic fluid.*

1 If any pipe or hose is to be renewed, minimise fluid loss by first removing the master cylinder reservoir cap and screwing it down onto a piece of polythene. Alternatively, flexible hoses can be sealed, if required, using a proprietary brake hose clamp. Metal brake pipe unions can be plugged (if care is taken not to allow dirt into the system) or capped immediately they are disconnected. Place a wad of rag under any union that is to be disconnected, to catch any spilt fluid.

2 If a flexible hose is to be disconnected, unscrew the brake pipe union nut before removing the spring clip which secures the hose to its mounting bracket **(see illustration)**. When removing a front flexible hose, it may be necessary to release the brake pad wear sensor wiring and ABS wheel speed sensor wiring clips from the hose.

3 To unscrew union nuts, it is preferable to obtain a brake pipe spanner of the correct size; these are available from most motor accessory shops. Failing this, a close-fitting open-ended spanner will be required, though if the nuts are tight or corroded, their flats may be rounded-off if the spanner slips. In such a case, a self-locking wrench is often the only way to unscrew a stubborn union, but it follows that the pipe and the damaged nuts must be renewed on reassembly. Always clean a union and surrounding area before disconnecting it. If disconnecting a component with more than one union, make a careful note of the connections before disturbing any of them.

4 If a brake pipe is to be renewed, it can be obtained, cut to length and with the union nuts and end flares in place, from VW dealers. All that is then necessary is to bend it to shape, following the line of the original, before fitting it to the vehicle. Alternatively, most motor accessory shops can make up brake pipes from kits, but this requires very careful

measurement of the original, to ensure that the replacement is of the correct length. The safest answer is usually to take the original to the shop as a pattern.

5 On refitting, do not overtighten the union nuts.

6 When refitting, make sure that the hoses are positioned so that they will not touch surrounding bodywork or the roadwheels.

7 Ensure that the pipes and hoses are correctly routed, with no kinks, and that they are secured in the clips or brackets provided. After fitting, remove the polythene from the reservoir, and bleed the hydraulic system as described in Section 2. Wash off any spilt fluid, and check carefully for fluid leaks.

4 Front brake pads – general information

During the course of production, five different types of front brake calipers have been fitted to Transporter vehicles, depending primarily on model year and wheel size.

The front brake pad renewal procedures will obviously vary somewhat according to the caliper type fitted. Pad renewal procedures for the Lucas RC54 floating frame caliper and the Lucas C54 floating caliper, which are two of the most common caliper types, are contained in Sections 5 and 6.

Pad renewal procedures for the three remaining VW brake calipers are similar to those given in Section 6 for the Lucas C54 caliper.

5 Front brake pad renewal – Lucas RC54 floating frame caliper

⚠ *Warning: Renew BOTH sets of front brake pads at the same time – NEVER renew the pads on only one wheel, as uneven braking may result. Note that the dust created by wear of the pads may contain asbestos, which is a health hazard. Never blow it out with compressed air, and do not inhale any of it. An approved filtering mask should be worn when working on the brakes. DO NOT use petroleum-based solvents to clean brake parts – use brake cleaner or methylated spirit only.*

1 Apply the handbrake, then jack up the front of the vehicle and support it on axle stands (see *Jacking and vehicle support*). Remove the front roadwheels.

2 If the inner brake pad is equipped with a pad wear sensor, disconnect the wiring at the connector on the caliper, then remove the wiring connector from the caliper bracket.

3 Using pliers, extract the brake pad locating pin retaining spring from the caliper **(see illustration)**.

5.3 Extract the brake pad locating pin retaining spring

5.4a Tap free the upper and lower locating pins...

5.4b ...and slide them out of the caliper

5.5a Release the inner brake pad from its location by prising it free with a screwdriver...

5.5b ...then remove the pad using pliers

5.6 Remove the outer brake pad in the same way

4 Using a hammer and punch, tap free the upper and lower locating pins and slide them out of the caliper **(see illustrations)**.

5 Release the inner brake pad from its location by prising it free with a screwdriver, then remove the pad using pliers **(see illustrations)**.

6 Remove the outer brake pad in the same way **(see illustration)**.

7 First measure the thickness of friction material on each brake pad **(see illustration)**. If either pad is worn at any point to the specified minimum thickness or less, all four pads must be renewed. Also, the pads should be renewed if any are fouled with oil or grease; there is no satisfactory way of degreasing friction material, once contaminated. If any of the brake pads are worn unevenly, or are

fouled with oil or grease, trace and rectify the cause before reassembly.

8 If the brake pads are still serviceable, carefully clean them using a clean, fine wire brush or similar, paying particular attention to the sides and back of the metal backing. Clean out the grooves in the friction material (where applicable), and pick out any large embedded particles of dirt or debris.

9 Prior to fitting the pads, check that the caliper body and bridge assembly are free to move in and out and the guide pins are not seized in the caliper bracket. Over time, rust and corrosion can build up on the guide pins restricting movement of the caliper body and bridge assembly. This can lead to binding of the pads on the disc and uneven pad wear. If this condition is evident,

dismantle and clean the guide pins, caliper body and bridge assembly as described in the following paragraphs. If the caliper and bridge movement appears satisfactory, brush the dust and dirt from the caliper and piston, but do not inhale it, as it is injurious to health. Inspect the dust seal around the piston for damage, and the piston for evidence of fluid leaks, corrosion or damage. If attention to any of these components is necessary, refer to Section 8.

10 If attention to the guide pins is necessary, undo the four bolts and lift the bridge off the caliper body **(see illustrations)**.

11 Unscrew the upper and lower guide pin retaining nuts while counter-holding the guide pin with a second spanner. Lift the caliper body off the guide pins and suitably suspend it from

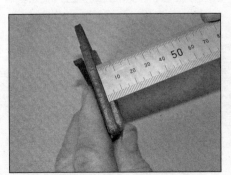

5.7 Measure the thickness of friction material on each brake pad

5.10a Undo the four bolts (arrowed)...

5.10b ...and lift the bridge off the caliper body

5.11a Unscrew the upper and lower guide pin retaining nuts...

5.11b ...then lift the caliper body off the guide pins

5.12a Withdraw the guide pins from the caliper bracket...

5.12b ...followed by the protective rubber gaiters

5.14a Liberally lubricate the guide pins...

5.14b ...and insert them back into the caliper bracket

a convenient location on the underbody using a cable tie or similar **(see illustrations)**. Do not allow the caliper body to hang unsupported from the flexible brake hose.

12 Withdraw the guide pins from the caliper bracket followed by the protective rubber gaiters **(see illustrations)**.

13 Clean the guide pins and inspect the rubber gaiters. If there is any doubt about their condition, obtain new components.

14 Fit the guide pin rubber gaiters to their locations in the caliper bracket. Liberally lubricate the guide pins with high-temperature silicone lubricant and insert them back into the caliper bracket **(see illustrations)**. Make sure that the lips of the rubber gaiters fully engage with the grooves in the guide pins.

15 Locate the caliper body in position on the guide pins. Apply thread locking compound to the guide pin threads then screw on the retaining nuts. Tighten the nuts to the specified torque while counter-holding the guide pins with a second spanner **(see illustrations)**.

16 Place the bridge back in position on the caliper body, insert the four retaining bolts and tighten them to the specified torque **(see illustrations)**.

17 If new brake pads are to be fitted, the caliper piston must be pushed back into the cylinder to allow for the extra pad thickness.

5.15a Apply thread locking compound to the guide pin threads...

5.15b ...screw on the retaining nuts...

5.15c ...and tighten the nuts to the specified torque

5.16a Insert the bridge retaining bolts...

5.16b ...and tighten them to the specified torque

Either use a G-clamp or similar tool, or use suitable pieces of wood or a steel strip as levers (see illustration). Clamp off the flexible brake hose leading to the caliper then connect a brake bleeding kit to the caliper bleed screw. Open the bleed screw as the piston is retracted, the surplus brake fluid will then be collected in the bleed kit vessel. Close the bleed screw just before the caliper piston is pushed fully into the caliper. This should ensure no air enters the hydraulic system.

Note: *On models equipped with ABS, the hydraulic unit contains hydraulic components that are very sensitive to impurities in the brake fluid. Even the smallest particles can cause the system to fail through blockage. The pad retraction method described here prevents any debris in the brake fluid expelled from the caliper from being passed back to the ABS hydraulic unit, as well as preventing any chance of damage to the master cylinder seals.*

18 Where fitted, feed the pad wear sensor wiring connector through the opening in the caliper then place the inner brake pad in position. Locate the wear sensor wiring connector in the caliper bracket and reconnect the wiring (see illustrations).

19 If the outer brake pad contains an anti-squeal pad on the metal backing plate, peel off the protective foil from the pad. Place the brake pad in position then insert the upper pad locating pin. Using a punch tap the locating pin fully into the caliper (see illustration).

5.17 Using a strip of steel as a lever to push back the caliper piston

5.18a Place the inner brake pad in position...

5.18b ...locate the wear sensor wiring connector in the caliper bracket...

5.18c ...and reconnect the wiring

20 Insert the lower pad locating pin into the caliper, then push the tension spring on the inner brake pad inward to allow the locating pin to slide through. Tap the pin fully into the caliper (see illustrations).

21 Hook the brake pad locating pin retaining

5.19a Place the outer brake pad in position...

5.19b ...insert the upper pad locating pin...

5.19c ...and tap the locating pin fully into the caliper using a punch

5.20a Insert the lower pad locating pin...

5.20b ...push the tension spring on the brake pad inward to allow the pin to slide through...

5.20c ...then tap the pin fully into the caliper

5.21a Hook the pad locating pin retaining spring over the lower locating pin...

5.21b ...then push it down at the top and engage it under the upper locating pin

spring over the lower locating pin, then push it down at the top and engage it under the upper locating pin **(see illustrations)**. Ensure that the retaining spring engages with the grooves in the locating pins.

22 With the brake pads installed, depress the brake pedal repeatedly, until normal (non-assisted) pedal pressure is restored, and the pads are pressed into firm contact with the brake disc.

23 Repeat the above procedure on the remaining front brake caliper.

24 Refit the roadwheels, then lower the vehicle to the ground and tighten the roadwheel bolts to the specified torque setting.

25 Check the hydraulic fluid level as described in *Weekly checks*.

Caution: New pads will not give full braking efficiency until they have bedded-in. Be prepared for this, and avoid hard braking as far as possible for the first hundred miles or so after pad renewal.

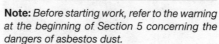

6 Front brake pad renewal – Lucas C54 floating caliper

Note: *Before starting work, refer to the warning at the beginning of Section 5 concerning the dangers of asbestos dust.*

1 Apply the handbrake, then jack up the front of the vehicle and support it on axle stands (see *Jacking and vehicle support*). Remove the front roadwheels.

2 Unscrew and remove the lower guide pin bolt while counter-holding the guide pin with a second spanner **(see illustration)**. Note that a new guide pin bolt will be required for refitting.

3 Lift the caliper upwards to gain access to the brake pads and secure it in the raised position using cable ties **(see illustrations)**.

4 Lift out the outer brake pad followed by the inner brake pad **(see illustrations)**. If the old pads are to be refitted, ensure that they are identified so that they can be returned to their original positions.

5 Measure the thickness of friction material on each brake pad **(see illustration 5.7)**. If either pad is worn at any point to the specified minimum thickness or less, all four pads must be renewed. Also, the pads should be renewed if any are fouled with oil or grease; there is no satisfactory way of degreasing friction material, once contaminated. If any of the brake pads are worn unevenly, or are fouled with oil or grease, trace and rectify the cause before reassembly.

6 Prior to fitting the pads, check that the guide pins are a snug fit in the caliper mounting bracket. Using brake cleaner, clean the dust and dirt from the caliper and piston, but do not inhale it, as it is injurious to health **(see illustration)**. Inspect the dust seal around the piston for damage, and the piston for evidence of fluid leaks, corrosion or damage. If attention to any of these components is necessary, refer to Section 8.

7 If new brake pads are to be fitted, the caliper piston must be pushed back into the cylinder to allow for the extra pad thickness. Either use a G-clamp or similar tool, or use suitable pieces

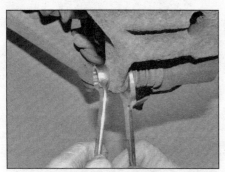

6.2 Unscrew the lower guide pin bolt while counter-holding the guide pin with a second spanner

6.3a Lift the caliper upwards to gain access to the brake pads...

6.3b ...and secure it in the raised position using cable ties

6.4a Lift out the outer brake pad...

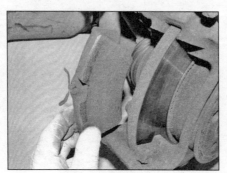

6.4b ...followed by the inner brake pad

6.6 Using brake cleaner, clean the dust and dirt from the caliper and piston

of wood as levers **(see illustration)**. Clamp off the flexible brake hose leading to the caliper then connect a brake bleeding kit to the caliper bleed screw. Open the bleed screw as the piston is retracted, the surplus brake fluid will then be collected in the bleed kit vessel. Close the bleed screw just before the caliper piston is pushed fully into the caliper. This should ensure no air enters the hydraulic system.

Note: *On models equipped with ABS, the hydraulic unit contains hydraulic components that are very sensitive to impurities in the brake fluid. Even the smallest particles can cause the system to fail through blockage. The pad retraction method described here prevents any debris in the brake fluid expelled from the caliper from being passed back to the ABS hydraulic unit, as well as preventing any chance of damage to the master cylinder seals.*

8 Apply a smear of high-temperature silicone lubricant to the contact areas of the caliper mounting bracket and the brake pad backing plate **(see illustrations)**.

9 Place the inner pad in position in the caliper mounting bracket, followed by the outer pad **(see illustrations)**.

10 Lower the caliper back into position over the brake pads **(see illustration)**.

11 Fit the new guide pin bolt and tighten it to the specified torque while counter-holding the guide pin with a spanner **(see illustrations)**.

12 With the brake pads installed, depress the brake pedal repeatedly, until normal (non-assisted) pedal pressure is restored, and the pads are pressed into firm contact with the brake disc.

13 Repeat the above procedure on the remaining front brake caliper.

14 Refit the roadwheels, then lower the vehicle to the ground and tighten the roadwheel bolts to the specified torque setting.

15 Check the hydraulic fluid level as described in *Weekly checks*.

Caution: New pads will not give full braking efficiency until they have bedded-in. Be prepared for this, and avoid hard braking as far as possible for the first hundred miles or so after pad renewal.

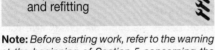

7 Front brake disc – inspection, removal and refitting

Note: *Before starting work, refer to the warning at the beginning of Section 5 concerning the dangers of asbestos dust.*

Inspection

Note: *If either disc requires renewal, BOTH should be renewed at the same time, to ensure even and consistent braking.*

1 Firmly apply the handbrake, then jack up the front of the vehicle and support it securely on axle stands (see *Jacking and vehicle support*). Remove the appropriate front roadwheel.

2 Slowly rotate the brake disc so that the full area of both sides can be checked; remove

6.7 Using a piston retractor tool to push back the caliper piston

6.8b ...and the brake pad backing plate

the brake pads if better access is required to the inner surface. Light scoring is normal in the area swept by the brake pads, but if heavy scoring is found, the disc must be renewed.

3 It is normal to find a lip of rust and brake

6.9b ...followed by the outer pad

6.11a Fit the new guide pin bolt...

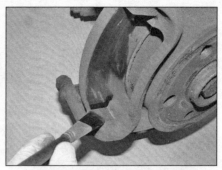

6.8a Apply a high-temperature silicone lubricant to the contact areas of the caliper mounting bracket...

6.9a Place the inner pad in position in the caliper mounting bracket...

dust around the disc's perimeter; this can be scraped off if required. If, however, a lip has formed due to excessive wear of the brake pad swept area, then the disc's thickness must be measured using a micrometer. Take

6.10 Lower the caliper back into position over the brake pads

6.11b ...and tighten it to the specified torque

7.3 Measuring brake disc thickness using a micrometer

7.4 Checking brake disc run-out using a dial gauge

7.7a Undo the two retaining bolts (arrowed)...

7.7b ...and remove the front brake caliper complete with disc pads and mounting bracket

measurements at several places around the disc, at the inside and outside of the pad swept area; if the disc has worn at any point to the specified minimum thickness or less, the disc must be renewed **(see illustration)**.

4 If the disc is thought to be warped, it can be checked for run-out either using a dial gauge mounted on any convenient fixed point, while the disc is slowly rotated, or by using feeler gauges to measure (at several points all around the disc) the clearance between the disc and a fixed point such as the caliper mounting bracket **(see illustration)**.To ensure that the disc is squarely seated on the hub, fit two wheel bolts, complete with spacers approximately 10 mm thick, and tighten them securely. If the measurements obtained are at the specified maximum or beyond, the disc is excessively warped and must be renewed; however, it is worth checking first that the hub bearing is in good condition as described in Chapter 1, Section 12.

5 Check the disc for cracks, especially around the wheel bolt holes, and for any other wear or damage, and renew if necessary.

Removal

6 Where applicable, remove the roadwheel bolts and spacers used when checking the disc.

7 Unbolt and remove the front brake caliper complete with disc pads and mounting bracket and suspend it from a convenient place under the wheel arch using cable ties **(see illustrations)**. Do not allow the caliper to hang unsupported from the flexible brake hose.

8 Remove the securing screw and withdraw the disc from the hub **(see illustrations)**.

Refitting

9 Refitting is the reverse of the removal procedure, noting the following points:

7.8a Remove the securing screw...

7.8b ...and withdraw the disc from the hub

a) Ensure that the mating surfaces of the disc and hub are clean and flat.
b) If a new disc has been fitted, use a suitable solvent to wipe any preservative coating from the disc before refitting the caliper.
c) Tighten the caliper retaining bolts to the specified torque.
d) Refit the roadwheel, then lower the vehicle to the ground and tighten the roadwheel bolts to the specified torque. On completion, repeatedly depress the brake pedal until normal (non-assisted) pedal pressure returns.

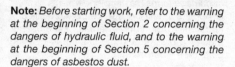

8 Front brake caliper – removal, overhaul and refitting

Note: Before starting work, refer to the warning at the beginning of Section 2 concerning the dangers of hydraulic fluid, and to the warning at the beginning of Section 5 concerning the dangers of asbestos dust.

Removal

1 Firmly apply the handbrake, then jack up the front of the car and support it securely on axle stands (see Jacking and vehicle support). Remove the appropriate roadwheel.

2 Using a brake hose clamp, clamp the flexible hydraulic hose.

3 Unscrew the bolt securing the hydraulic hose support bracket to the brake caliper. Unscrew the brake pipe union nut and remove the brake pipe from the caliper. Plug the brake pipe end and caliper hole, to minimise fluid loss and prevent the ingress of dirt into the hydraulic system.

4 Remove the front brake pads as described in Section 5 or 6 according to caliper type.

5 If working on the Lucas RC54 floating frame caliper unscrew the upper and lower guide pin retaining nuts while counter-holding the guide pin with a second spanner. Slide the caliper off the guide pins and remove it from under the wheel arch.

6 If working on the Lucas C54 floating caliper or the VW calipers, undo and remove the guide pin bolts, or the guide pins themselves (according to caliper type) and remove the brake caliper from the vehicle.

Overhaul

Note: Before starting work, check with your local dealer for the availability of parts to overhaul the caliper.

7 With the caliper on the bench, wipe away all traces of dust and dirt, *but avoid inhaling the dust, as it is a health hazard.*

8 Withdraw the partially-ejected piston from the caliper body, and remove the dust seal. The piston can be withdrawn by hand, or if necessary pushed out by applying compressed air to the brake hose union hole. Only low pressure should be required, such as is generated by a foot pump, and as a precaution a block of wood should be positioned to prevent any damage to the piston.

9 Using a small screwdriver, carefully remove the piston seal from the caliper, taking great care not mark the bore **(see illustration)**.

10 Thoroughly clean all components, using only methylated spirit, isopropyl alcohol or clean hydraulic fluid as a cleaning medium. Never use mineral-based solvents such as petrol or paraffin, which will attack the hydraulic system's rubber components. Dry the components immediately, using compressed air or a clean, lint-free cloth. If compressed air is available, use it to blow through the fluid passages to make sure they are clear

Caution: Always wear eye protection when using compressed air.

11 Check all components, and renew any that are worn or damaged. Check particularly the cylinder bore and piston; these should be renewed (note that this means the renewal of the complete body assembly) if they are scratched, worn or corroded in any way. If there is any doubt about the condition of any component, renew it.

12 If the assembly is fit for further use, obtain the necessary components from your VW dealer. Renew the caliper seals as a matter of course; these should never be re-used.

13 On reassembly, ensure that all components are absolutely clean and dry.

14 Soak the piston and the new piston (fluid) seal in clean hydraulic fluid. Smear clean fluid on the cylinder bore surface.

15 Fit the new piston (fluid) seal, using only the fingers to manipulate it into the cylinder bore groove.

16 Fit the new dust seal to the piston, refit it to the cylinder bore using a twisting motion, and ensure that the piston enters squarely into the bore. Press the dust seal fully into the caliper body, and push the piston fully into the caliper bore.

17 Ease the guide bushes into position in the caliper body.

Refitting

18 If working on the Lucas C54 floating caliper or the VW calipers, refit the brake pads as described in Section 6. Position the caliper on the mounting bracket and fit the guide pins or guide pin bolts, depending on caliper type. Note that new guide pin bolts should be used. Tighten the guide pins or bolts to the specified torque.

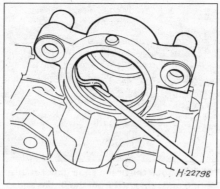
8.9 Removing the piston seal from the caliper body

19 If working on the Lucas RC54 floating frame caliper, slide the caliper over the guide pins and refit the retaining nuts. Tighten the nuts to the specified torque. Refit the brake pads as described in Section 5.

20 Fit the brake pipe union to the caliper, then refit the bolt securing the hydraulic hose support bracket to the brake caliper. Tighten the brake pipe union and support bracket retaining bolt securely. Remove the brake hose clamp from the hose.

21 Bleed the hydraulic system as described in Section 2. Note that, providing the precautions described were taken to minimise brake fluid loss, it should only be necessary to bleed the relevant front brake.

22 Refit the roadwheel, then lower the vehicle to the ground and tighten the roadwheel bolts to the specified torque.

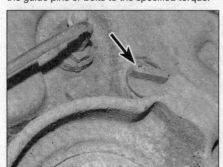
9.3a Remove the plug (arrowed) from the inspection hole in the brake backplate

9.2a Undo the brake drum retaining screw...

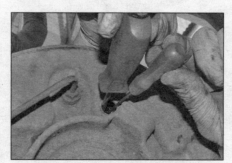
9.3b Push the brake shoe adjusting lever outwards and rotate the adjusting pinion to slacken the brake shoe adjustment

9 Rear brake drum – removal, inspection and refitting

Note: *Before starting work, refer to the warning at the beginning of Section 5 concerning the dangers of asbestos dust.*

Removal

1 Firmly apply the handbrake, then jack up the front of the vehicle and support it securely on axle stands (see *Jacking and vehicle support*).

2 Undo the brake drum retaining screw, then withdraw the brake drum from the rear hub **(see illustrations)**. It may be difficult to remove the drum, due to the brake shoes binding on the inner circumference of the drum. If the brake shoes are binding, first check that the handbrake is fully released, then proceed as follows.

3 Remove the plug from the inspection hole in the brake backplate. Using two screwdrivers, push the brake shoe adjusting lever outwards, so that it is out of engagement with the adjusting pinion. Using the second screwdriver rotate the adjusting pinion as necessary to slacken the brake shoe adjustment **(see illustrations)**. The brake drum can then be withdrawn from the hub.

4 If the brake drum is still difficult to remove, screw three bolts into the holes on the front face of the drum **(see illustration)**. Tighten the bolts while tapping the edge of the drum with a soft-faced mallet until it frees.

9.2b ...then withdraw the brake drum from the rear hub

9.4 Using three bolts to draw off the brake drum

10.2 Remove all traces of brake dust from the brake drum, backplate and shoes

Inspection

Note: *If either drum requires renewal, BOTH should be renewed at the same time, to ensure even and consistent braking.*

5 Working carefully, remove all traces of brake dust from the drum, *but avoid inhaling the dust, as it is a health-hazard.*

6 Scrub clean the outside of the drum, and check it for obvious signs of wear or damage (such as cracks around the roadwheel bolt holes); renew the drum if necessary.

7 Examine the inside of the drum carefully. Light scoring of the friction surface is normal, but if heavy scoring is found, the drum must be renewed. It is usual to find a lip on the drum's inboard edge which consists of a mixture of rust and brake dust; this should be scraped away, to leave a smooth surface which can be polished with fine (120- to 150-grade) emery paper. If, however, the lip is due to the friction surface being recessed by excessive wear, then the drum must be renewed.

8 If the drum is thought to be excessively worn, or oval, its internal diameter must be measured at several points using an internal micrometer. Take measurements in pairs, the second at right-angles to the first, and compare the two to check for signs of ovality. Provided that it does not enlarge the drum to beyond the specified maximum diameter, it

10.5 Unhook the brake shoe upper return spring and remove it from the brake shoes

may be possible to have the drum refinished by skimming or grinding; if this is not possible, the drums on both sides must be renewed. Note that if the drum is to be skimmed, both drums must be refinished, to maintain a consistent internal diameter on both sides.

Refitting

9 If a new brake drum is to be installed, use a suitable solvent to remove any preservative coating that may have been applied to its interior. Note that it may also be necessary to shorten the adjuster strut length by rotating the adjusting pinion, to allow the new drum to pass over the brake shoes.

10 Slide the drum into position, then refit the retaining screw.

11 With the handbrake fully released, adjust the lining-to-drum clearance by repeatedly depressing and releasing the brake pedal. Whilst depressing the pedal, have an assistant listen to the rear drums, to check that the adjuster strut is functioning correctly; if so, a clicking sound will be emitted by the strut as the pedal is depressed.

12 With the lining-to-drum clearance set, check and, if necessary, adjust the handbrake as described in Section 17.

13 Refit the roadwheel, then lower the vehicle to the ground and tighten the roadwheel bolts to the specified torque setting.

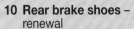

10 Rear brake shoes – renewal

Warning: Brake shoes must be renewed on BOTH rear wheels at the same time – NEVER renew the shoes on only one wheel, as uneven braking may result. The dust created as the shoes wear may contain asbestos, which is a health hazard. Never blow it out with compressed air, and don't inhale any of it. An approved filtering mask should be worn when working on the brakes. DO NOT use petroleum-based solvents to clean brake parts – use brake cleaner or methylated spirit only.

1 Remove the brake drum as described in Section 9.

2 Working carefully and taking the necessary precautions, remove all traces of brake dust from the brake drum, backplate and shoes **(see illustration)**.

3 Measure the thickness of friction material on each brake shoe at several points. If either shoe is worn at any point to the specified minimum thickness or less, all four shoes must be renewed. Also, the shoes should be renewed if any are fouled with oil or grease; there is no satisfactory way of degreasing friction material, once contaminated. If any of the brake shoes are worn unevenly, or are fouled with oil or grease, trace and rectify the cause before reassembly.

4 Note the location and orientation of all components before dismantling as an aid to reassembly.

5 Using pliers, carefully unhook the brake shoe upper return spring and remove it from the brake shoes **(see illustration)**.

6 Lift the upper end of the adjusting lever spring off the adjusting lever, then disengage the lower end of the spring from the brake shoe **(see illustrations)**.

7 Pull the brake shoe adjusting lever

10.6a Lift the upper end of the adjusting lever spring off the adjusting lever...

10.6b ...then disengage the lower end of the spring from the brake shoe

10.7 Pull the adjusting lever outwards, then rotate the adjusting pinion to shorten the length of the adjuster strut

10.8 Disengage the adjuster strut from the brake shoes and remove the strut

10.9a Disengage the leading shoe intermediate return spring...

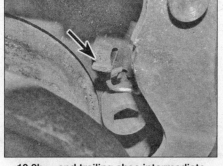

10.9b ...and trailing shoe intermediate return spring from the lugs (arrowed) on the brake backplate

10.10 Depress and turn the trailing shoe retainer spring cup through 90º to remove

outwards, so that it is out of engagement with the adjusting pinion, then rotate the adjusting pinion to shorten the length of the adjuster strut **(see illustration)**.

8 Disengage each end of the adjuster strut from the brake shoes and remove the strut **(see illustration)**.

9 Disengage the leading shoe and trailing shoe intermediate return springs from the lugs on the brake backplate **(see illustrations)**.

10 Using pliers, remove the trailing shoe retainer spring cup by depressing and turning it through 90º **(see illustration)**. As you do this, hold the retainer pin from behind the backplate with your finger. Remove the spring and retainer pin.

11 Disengage the top of the trailing brake shoe from the wheel cylinder piston and swivel it away from the backplate **(see illustration)**.

12 Remove the short lower return spring, then disengage the bottom of the trailing shoe from the lower pivot and remove the long lower return spring **(see illustrations)**.

13 Push back the spring on the handbrake cable and detach the cable end from the handbrake lever on the trailing brake shoe **(see illustration)**. Remove the brake shoe and collect the intermediate return spring from the rear of the shoe web.

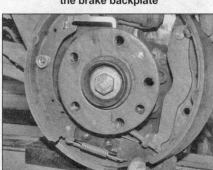

10.11 Disengage the top of the trailing brake shoe from the wheel cylinder piston

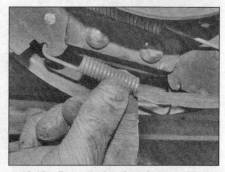

10.12a Remove the short lower return spring...

10.12b ...then disengage the trailing shoe from the lower pivot and remove the long lower return spring

10.13 Push back the spring and detach the handbrake cable end from the lever on the brake shoe

10.14a Remove the leading shoe retainer spring cup, spring and pin...

10.14b ...then remove the shoe

14 Remove the leading shoe retainer spring cup, spring and pin as described in paragraph 10, then remove the shoe and collect the intermediate return spring from the rear of the shoe web **(see illustrations)**.
15 Do not depress the brake pedal until the brake shoes are reassembled. As a precaution, wrap a strong elastic band or a cable tie around the wheel cylinder pistons to retain them.
16 If both brake assemblies are dismantled at the same time, take care not to mix up the adjuster strut components. The adjuster struts are 'handed' – the strut assembly for the left-hand brake has a right-hand thread, and the assembly for the right-hand brake has a left-hand thread.
17 Dismantle and clean the adjuster strut components. Apply a smear of silicone-based grease to the adjuster threads.
18 Examine the return springs. If they are distorted, or if they have seen extensive service, renewal is advisable. Weak springs may cause the brakes to bind.
19 Peel back the rubber protective caps and check the wheel cylinder for fluid leaks or other damage. Ensure that both cylinder pistons are free to move easily. Refer to Section 14 if

necessary for information on wheel cylinder overhaul.
20 Prior to installation, clean the brake backplate thoroughly. Apply a thin smear of high-temperature copper-based brake grease or anti-seize compound to all those surfaces of the backplate which bear on the shoes, particularly the wheel cylinder pistons and lower pivot point **(see illustration)**. Do not allow the lubricant to foul the friction material.
21 Prior to installation, remove the elastic band or cable tie from the wheel cylinder pistons.
22 Engage the intermediate return spring with the leading shoe web, then place the shoe in position on the backplate **(see illustration)**.
23 Install the leading shoe retainer pin and spring and secure it in position with the spring cup **(see illustration)**.
24 Pull the end of the leading shoe intermediate return spring and hook it over the lug on the backplate **(see illustration)**.
25 Push back the spring on the handbrake cable and attach the cable end to the handbrake lever on the trailing brake shoe **(see illustration)**.
26 Engage the intermediate return spring with the trailing shoe web, then fit the long

10.20 Apply a high-temperature copper-based brake grease to the contact surfaces (arrowed) on the backplate

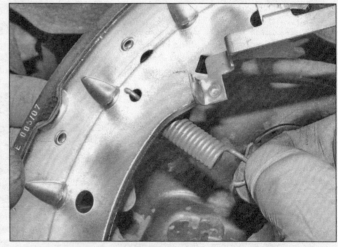

10.22 Engage the intermediate return spring with the leading shoe web, then place the shoe on the backplate

10.23 Install the leading shoe retainer pin, spring and cup

10.24 Hook the end of the leading shoe intermediate return spring over the lug on the backplate

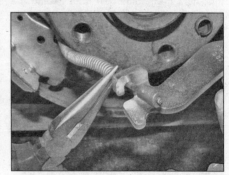

10.25 Push back the spring and attach the handbrake cable end to the lever on the trailing shoe

10.26a Engage the intermediate return spring with the trailing shoe web...

10.26b ...then fit the long lower return spring to both brake shoes

10.27 Fit the short lower return spring to both brake shoes

10.28 Install the trailing shoe retainer pin, spring and cup

10.29 Hook the end of the trailing shoe intermediate return spring over the lug on the backplate

10.31 Manoeuvre the adjuster strut assembly into position between the brake shoes

lower return spring to both brake shoes **(see illustrations)**. Place the trailing shoe in position on the backplate.

27 Fit the short lower return spring to both brake shoes **(see illustration)**.

28 Install the trailing shoe retainer pin and spring and secure it in position with the spring cup **(see illustration)**.

29 Pull the end of the trailing shoe intermediate return spring and hook it over the lug on the backplate **(see illustration)**.

30 Screw the adjuster strut pinion fully onto the forked end of the adjuster so that the adjuster strut is set to its shortest possible length. Back the pinion off half a turn and check that it is free to rotate easily.

31 Manoeuvre the adjuster strut assembly into position between the brake shoes **(see illustration)**. Make sure that both ends of

the strut are correctly engaged with the shoes, noting that the chamfer on the sleeve and the longer strut fork are toward the backplate. Note that it may be necessary to lengthen the adjuster strut by turning the adjusting pinion to retain the assembly in position.

32 Engage the lower end of the adjusting lever spring with the leading brake shoe, then pull the upper end up and hook it over the adjusting lever **(see illustrations)**.

33 Fit the brake shoe upper return spring to the leading brake shoe, then pull the other end into engagement with the trailing brake shoe **(see illustration)**.

34 Centralise the brake shoes on the backplate, then place the brake drum in position. If the drum slides on easily and there appears to be considerable clearance

between the brake shoe linings and the drum, remove the drum and turn the adjusting pinion to lengthen the adjuster strut. Continue doing this on a trial and error basis until there is minimal clearance between the linings and the drum. When all is satisfactory refit and tighten the drum retaining screw.

35 Finally adjust the lining-to-drum clearance by repeatedly depressing and releasing the brake pedal. Whilst depressing the pedal, have an assistant listen to the drum, to check that the adjuster strut is functioning correctly; if so, a clicking sound will be emitted by the strut as the pedal is depressed.

36 Repeat the operation on the remaining brake.

37 Check and, if necessary, adjust the handbrake as described in Section 17.

38 Refit the roadwheels, then lower the vehicle

10.32a Engage the lower end of the adjusting lever spring with the leading brake shoe...

10.32b ...then pull the upper end up and hook it over the adjusting lever

10.33 Fit the upper return spring to both brake shoes

11.2a Lever down the handbrake operating lever and disengage the handbrake cable end fitting from the lever

11.2b Extract the retaining clip and withdraw the handbrake cable from the caliper

11.3 Where applicable, remove the brake pad wear sensor retainer from the brake caliper

to the ground and tighten the roadwheel bolts to the specified torque setting.

39 Check the hydraulic fluid level as described in *Weekly checks*.

Caution: New brake shoes will not give full braking efficiency until they have bedded-in. Be prepared for this, and avoid hard braking as far as possible for the first hundred miles or so after shoe renewal.

11 Rear brake pads – renewal

> ⚠ **Warning: Renew BOTH sets of rear brake pads at the same time – NEVER renew the pads on only one wheel, as uneven braking may result. Note**

that the dust created by wear of the pads may contain asbestos, which is a health hazard. Never blow it out with compressed air, and do not inhale any of it. An approved filtering mask should be worn when working on the brakes. DO NOT use petroleum-based solvents to clean brake parts – use brake cleaner or methylated spirit only.

1 Chock the front wheels, then jack up the rear of the vehicle, and support it securely on axle stands (see *Jacking and vehicle support*). Remove the rear roadwheels.

2 Using a screwdriver, lever down the handbrake operating lever on the brake caliper and disengage the handbrake cable end fitting from the lever. Extract the handbrake outer cable retaining clip and withdraw the handbrake cable from the caliper **(see illustrations)**.

3 Where applicable, remove the brake pad wear sensor retainer from the brake caliper **(see illustration)**.

4 Slacken and remove the caliper upper and lower guide pin bolts, using a slim open-ended spanner to prevent the guide pins from rotating **(see illustrations)**. Discard the guide pin bolts – new bolts must be used on refitting.

5 Where applicable release the brake pad wear sensor wiring from the support bracket, then disconnect the wiring connector **(see illustrations)**.

6 Lift the caliper away from the brake pads, and suspend it from a suitable place under the wheel arch using cable ties or similar **(see illustration)**. Do not allow the caliper to hang unsupported on the flexible brake hose.

7 Withdraw the two brake pads from the caliper mounting bracket. If the old pads are to be refitted, ensure that they are identified so that they can be returned to their original positions. On early models, recover the anti-rattle springs from the mounting bracket, noting their correct fitted locations **(see illustrations)**.

8 Measure the thickness of friction material on each brake pad. If either pad is worn at any point to the specified minimum thickness or less, all four pads must be renewed. Also, the pads should be renewed if any are fouled with oil or grease; there is no satisfactory way of degreasing friction material, once contaminated. If any of the brake pads are worn unevenly, or are fouled with oil or grease, trace and rectify the cause before reassembly.

11.4a Hold the guide pins with an open-ended spanner and slacken the guide pin bolts...

11.4b ...then remove the bolts from the guide pins

11.5a Release the brake pad wear sensor wiring from the support bracket...

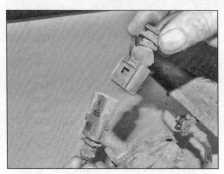

11.5b ...then disconnect the wiring connector

11.6 Lift the caliper off the brake pads

11.7a Withdraw the outer brake pad...

11.7b ...and the inner brake pad...

11.7c ...then, if fitted remove the upper anti-rattle spring...

11.7d ...and lower anti-rattle spring

11.10 Check the condition of the guide pins and rubber gaiters

11.11 Using a caliper retracting tool to retract the caliper piston

9 If the brake pads are still serviceable, carefully clean them using a clean, fine wire brush or similar, paying particular attention to the sides and back of the metal backing. Clean out the grooves in the friction material (where applicable), and pick out any large embedded particles of dirt or debris. Carefully clean the pad locations in the caliper body/ mounting bracket.

10 Prior to fitting the pads, check that the guide pins are free to slide easily in the caliper bracket, and check that the rubber guide pin gaiters are undamaged **(see illustration)**. Brush the dust and dirt from the caliper and piston, but **do not** inhale it, as it is injurious to health. Inspect the dust seal around the piston for damage, and the piston for evidence of fluid leaks, corrosion or damage. If attention

to any of these components is necessary, refer to Section 13.

11 If new brake pads are to be fitted, it will be necessary to retract the piston fully into the caliper bore by rotating it in a clockwise direction. Special tools are readily available at moderate cost to achieve this **(see illustration)**. While the caliper is being retracted, clamp off the flexible brake hose leading to the caliper then connect a brake bleeding kit to the caliper bleed screw. Open the bleed screw as the piston is retracted, the surplus brake fluid will then be collected in the bleed kit vessel. Close the bleed screw just before the caliper piston is pushed fully into the caliper. This should ensure no air enters the hydraulic system.

Note: *On models equipped with ABS, the*

hydraulic unit contains hydraulic components that are very sensitive to impurities in the brake fluid. Even the smallest particles can cause the system to fail through blockage. The pad retraction method described here prevents any debris in the brake fluid expelled from the caliper from being passed back to the ABS hydraulic unit, as well as preventing any chance of damage to the master cylinder seals.

12 Where applicable, fit the anti-rattle springs to the caliper mounting bracket, ensuring that they are correctly located.

13 Apply a smear of high-temperature silicone lubricant to the contact areas of the caliper mounting bracket and the brake pad backing plate, then place the pads in position in the caliper bracket **(see illustrations)**.

11.13a Apply high-temperature silicone lubricant to the contact areas of the caliper mounting bracket and the pad backing plate...

11.13b ...then place the pads in position in the caliper bracket

12.4 Rear brake caliper mounting bracket retaining bolts (arrowed)

12.5a Remove the securing screw (arrowed)...

12.5b ...and withdraw the disc from the hub

14 Where applicable, reconnect the brake pad wear indicator wiring connector.
15 If the threads of the new guide pin bolts are not already pre-coated with locking compound, apply a suitable thread-locking compound to them. Press the caliper into position, then install the bolts, tightening them to the specified torque setting while retaining the guide pin with an open-ended spanner.
16 Where applicable, refit the brake pad wear sensor retainer to the brake caliper.
17 Depress the brake pedal repeatedly, until the pads are pressed into firm contact with the brake disc, and normal (non-assisted) pedal pressure is restored.
18 Repeat the above procedure on the remaining rear brake caliper.
19 Reconnect the handbrake cables to the calipers, and adjust the handbrake as described in Section 17.
20 Refit the roadwheels, then lower the vehicle to the ground and tighten the roadwheel bolts to the specified torque setting.
21 Check the hydraulic fluid level as described in *Weekly Checks*.
Caution: New pads will not give full braking efficiency until they have bedded-in. Be prepared for this, and avoid hard braking as far as possible for the first hundred miles or so after pad renewal.

12 Rear brake disc –
inspection, removal and refitting

Note: *Before starting work, refer to the warning at the beginning of Section 11 concerning the dangers of asbestos dust.*

Inspection

Note: *If either disc requires renewal, BOTH should be renewed at the same time, to ensure even and consistent braking.*
1 Chock the front wheels, then jack up the rear of the vehicle, and support it securely on axle stands (see *Jacking and vehicle support*). Remove the appropriate rear roadwheel.
2 Inspect the disc as described in Section 7.

Removal

3 Where applicable, remove the roadwheel

bolts and spacers used when checking the disc.
4 Unbolt and remove the rear brake caliper complete with disc pads and mounting bracket and suspend it from a convenient place under the wheel arch using cable ties **(see illustration)**. Do not allow the caliper to hang unsupported from the flexible brake hose.
5 Remove the securing screw and withdraw the disc from the hub **(see illustrations)**.

Refitting

6 Refitting is the reverse of the removal procedure, noting the following points:
a) *Ensure that the mating surfaces of the disc and hub are clean and flat.*
b) *If a new disc has been fitted, use a suitable solvent to wipe any preservative coating from the disc before refitting the caliper.*
c) *Tighten the caliper mounting bracket retaining bolts to the specified torque.*
d) *Refit the roadwheel, then lower the vehicle to the ground and tighten the roadwheel bolts to the specified torque. On completion, repeatedly depress the brake pedal until normal (non-assisted) pedal pressure returns.*

13 Rear brake caliper –
removal, overhaul and refitting

Removal

Note: *Before starting work, refer to the note at the beginning of Section 2 concerning the dangers of hydraulic fluid, and to the warning at the beginning of Section 11 concerning the dangers of asbestos dust.*
1 Chock the front wheels, then jack up the rear of the vehicle and support on axle stands (see *Jacking and vehicle support*). Remove the relevant rear roadwheel, then make sure that the handbrake is fully released.
2 Using a screwdriver, lever down the handbrake operating lever on the brake caliper and disengage the handbrake cable end fitting from the lever. Extract the handbrake outer cable retaining clip and withdraw the handbrake cable from the caliper **(see illustrations 11.2a and 11.2b)**.

3 Minimise fluid loss by first removing the master cylinder reservoir cap and screwing it down onto a piece of polythene. Alternatively, use a brake hose clamp to clamp the flexible hose leading to the brake caliper.
4 Clean the area around the caliper brake hose union. Slacken (but do not completely unscrew) the union on the caliper end of the flexible hose.
5 Where applicable, remove the brake pad wear sensor retainer from the brake caliper **(see illustration 11.3)**.
6 Slacken and remove the caliper upper and lower guide pin bolts, using a slim open-ended spanner to prevent the guide pins from rotating **(see illustrations 11.4a and 11.4b)**. Discard the guide pin bolts – new bolts must be used on refitting.
7 Where applicable release the brake pad wear sensor wiring from the support bracket, then disconnect the wiring connector **(see illustrations 11.5a and 11.5b)**.
8 Lift the caliper off the brake pads. Support the caliper in one hand, and prevent the flexible hose from turning with the other hand. Unscrew the caliper from the hose, making sure that the hose is not twisted unduly or strained. Once the caliper is detached, plug the open hydraulic unions in the caliper and hose, to keep out dust and dirt.
9 If necessary, remove the brake pads with reference to Section 11, then undo the two retaining bolts and remove the caliper mounting bracket.

Overhaul

10 No overhaul procedures, or parts, were available at the time of writing. Check the availability of spares before dismantling the caliper. Do not attempt to dismantle the handbrake mechanism inside the caliper; if the mechanism is faulty, the complete caliper assembly must be renewed.

Refitting

11 Refit the caliper by reversing the removal operations. Make sure that the flexible brake hose is not twisted. Tighten the mounting bracket bolts, guide pin bolts and roadwheel bolts to the specified torque.
12 Bleed the brake circuit according to the procedure given in Section 2, remembering

to remove the brake hose clamp (where applicable) from the flexible hose. Make sure there are no leaks from the hose connections. Test the brakes carefully before returning the vehicle to normal service.

14 Rear wheel cylinder – removal, overhaul and refitting

Note: *Before starting work, refer to the warning at the beginning of Section 2 concerning the dangers of hydraulic fluid, and to the warning at the beginning of Section 11 concerning the dangers of asbestos dust.*

Removal

1 Remove the brake drum as described in Section 9.
2 Using pliers, carefully unhook the upper brake shoe return spring, and remove it from both brake shoes. Pull the upper ends of the shoes away from the wheel cylinder to disengage them from the pistons.
3 Minimise fluid loss by first removing the master cylinder reservoir cap, and then tightening it down onto a piece of polythene, to obtain an airtight seal. Alternatively, use a brake hose clamp, a G-clamp or a similar tool to clamp the flexible hose at the nearest convenient point to the wheel cylinder.
4 Wipe away all traces of dirt around the brake pipe union at the rear of the wheel cylinder, and unscrew the union nut. Carefully ease the pipe out of the wheel cylinder, and plug or tape over its end to prevent dirt entry. Wipe off any spilt immediately.
5 Unscrew the wheel cylinder retaining bolt from the rear of the backplate, and remove the cylinder, taking great care not to allow surplus hydraulic fluid to contaminate the brake shoe linings.

Overhaul

6 Brush the dirt and dust from the wheel cylinder, but take care not to inhale it.
7 Pull the rubber dust seals from the ends of the cylinder body.
8 The pistons will normally be ejected by the pressure of the coil spring, but if they are not, tap the end of the cylinder body on a piece of wood, or apply low air pressure – eg, from a foot pump - to the hydraulic fluid union hole to eject the pistons from their bores.
9 Inspect the surfaces of the pistons and their bores in the cylinder body for scoring, or evidence of metal-to-metal contact. If evident, renew the complete wheel cylinder assembly.
10 If the pistons and bores are in good condition, discard the seals and obtain a repair kit, which will contain all the necessary renewable items.
11 Remove the seals from the pistons noting their correct fitted orientation. Lubricate the new piston seals with clean brake fluid, and fit them onto the pistons with their larger diameters innermost.

12 Dip the pistons in clean brake fluid, then fit the spring to the cylinder.
13 Insert the pistons into the cylinder bores using a twisting motion.
14 Fit the dust seals, and check that the pistons can move freely in their bores.

Refitting

15 Ensure that the backplate and wheel cylinder mating surfaces are clean, then spread the brake shoes and manoeuvre the wheel cylinder into position.
16 Engage the brake pipe, and screw in the union nut two or three turns to ensure that the thread has started.
17 Insert the wheel cylinder retaining bolt, and tighten it to the specified torque. Now fully tighten the brake pipe union nut.
18 Remove the clamp from the flexible brake hose, or the polythene from the master cylinder reservoir (as applicable).
19 Ensure that the brake shoes are correctly located in the cylinder pistons, then refit the brake shoe upper return spring, using pliers to stretch the spring into position.
20 Refit the brake drum as described in Section 9.
21 Bleed the brake hydraulic system as described in Section 2. Providing suitable precautions were taken to minimise loss of fluid, it should only be necessary to bleed the relevant rear brake.

15 Master cylinder – removal, overhaul and refitting

Note: *Before starting work, refer to the warning at the beginning of Section 2 concerning the dangers of hydraulic fluid.*

Removal

1 Remove the master cylinder reservoir cap, and syphon the hydraulic fluid from the reservoir. **Note:** *Do not syphon the fluid by mouth, as it is poisonous therefore use a syringe or an old hydrometer.* Alternatively, open the front brake caliper bleed screws, one at a time, and gently pump the brake pedal to expel the fluid through a plastic tube connected to the screw (see Section 2).

15.2 Brake fluid level sensor wiring connector (arrowed) on the master cylinder reservoir

2 Disconnect the wiring connector from the brake fluid level sensor on the reservoir **(see illustration)**.
3 Disconnect the clutch hydraulic hose from the fluid reservoir **(see illustration)**. Tape over or plug the outlet.
4 Place cloth rags beneath the master cylinder to collect escaping brake fluid. Identify the brake pipes for position, then unscrew the union nuts and move the pipes to one side. Plug or tape over the pipe ends to prevent dirt entry.
5 Unscrew the two mounting nuts and withdraw the master cylinder from the vacuum servo unit **(see illustration)**. Take care not to spill fluid on the vehicle paintwork. Recover the master cylinder-to-servo unit seal.
6 If required, the fluid reservoir can be removed from the master cylinder by extracting the retainer pin (where fitted) then pulling the reservoir up and off the mounting seals.

Overhaul

7 If the master cylinder is faulty, it must be renewed. Repair kits are not available from VW dealer, so the cylinder must be treated as a sealed unit.
8 The only items which can be renewed are the mounting seals for the fluid reservoir; if these show signs of deterioration, pull off the reservoir and remove the old seals. Lubricate the new seals with clean brake fluid, and press them into the master cylinder ports. Ease the fluid reservoir into position, and push it fully home.

15.3 Disconnect the clutch hydraulic hose (arrowed) from the reservoir

15.5 Master cylinder mounting nuts (arrowed)

Refitting

9 Place the master cylinder-to-servo unit seal in position, then fit the master cylinder to the servo unit. Ensure that the servo unit pushrod enters the master cylinder piston centrally. Fit the retaining nuts and tighten them to the specified torque.

10 Refit the brake pipes and tighten the union nuts securely.

11 Reconnect the clutch hydraulic hose to the fluid reservoir.

12 Reconnect the wiring connector to the brake fluid level sensor.

13 Remove the reservoir filler cap and polythene, then top-up the reservoir with fresh hydraulic fluid to the MAX mark (see *Weekly checks*).

14 Bleed the brake and clutch hydraulic systems as described in Section 2 and Chapter 6, Section 2 then refit the filler cap. Thoroughly check the operation of the brakes and clutch before using the vehicle on the road.

16 Brake pedal – removal and refitting

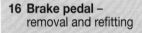

Removal

1 Remove the clutch pedal as described in Chapter 6, Section 5.

2 Disconnect the wiring connector from the stop-light switch located on the brake pedal mounting bracket.

3 Turn the switch 90° anti-clockwise and remove it from the mounting bracket.

4 Extract the retaining clip and pull out the clevis pin securing the vacuum servo unit pushrod to the brake pedal.

5 Using a small drift, tap the pivot shaft out towards the right-hand side of the vehicle until it is possible to remove the brake pedal.

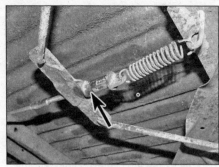

17.5 Handbrake adjusting nut (arrowed)

Refitting

6 Refitting is a reversal of removal, bearing in mind the following points:
a) Lightly grease the pivot shaft before assembly.
b) Before refitting the stop-light switch, fully extend the switch plunger, then depress and hold the brake pedal while manoeuvring the switch into position.
c) Refit the clutch pedal as described in Chapter 6, Section 5.

17 Handbrake – adjustment

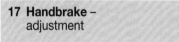

1 Apply the footbrake firmly several times to establish correct shoe-to-drum/pad-to-disc clearance, then apply and release the handbrake several times. Leave the handbrake in the released position.

2 Chock the front wheels, then jack up the rear of the vehicle, and support it securely on axle stands (see *Jacking and vehicle support*). Continue as described under the relevant sub-heading.

Drum brake models

3 Remove the brake drums as described in Section 9.

4 Make sure that the handbrake is in the released position.

5 From underneath the vehicle, locate the handbrake adjusting nut on the end of the front handbrake cable (see illustration).

6 Tighten the handbrake adjusting nut until the handbrake operating levers on the trailing brake shoes lift off the shoes by approximately 2 mm (see illustration).

7 When the adjustment is correct, refit the brake drums as described in Section 9.

8 Apply the footbrake firmly several times to establish correct shoe-to-drum clearance, then apply and release the handbrake several times. With the handbrake released, check that the brake drums are free to rotate without binding.

9 Refit the roadwheels, lower the vehicle to the ground and tighten the roadwheel bolts to the specified torque.

Disc brake models

10 Chock the front wheels, then jack up the rear of the vehicle, and support it securely on axle stands (see *Jacking and vehicle support*).

11 Make sure that the handbrake is in the released position.

12 From underneath the vehicle, locate the handbrake adjusting nut on the end of the front handbrake cable (see illustration 17.5).

13 Tighten the handbrake adjusting nut until the handbrake operating levers on the rear brake calipers lift off their stops by a maximum of 1 mm (see illustration).

14 Apply and release the handbrake several times. With the handbrake released, check that the wheels are free to rotate without binding.

15 On completion, lower the vehicle to the ground.

17.6 Tighten the handbrake adjusting nut until the clearance between the operating levers (arrowed) and brake shoes is approximately 2 mm

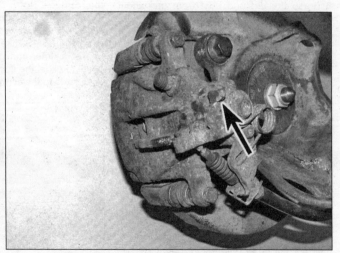

17.13 Tighten the handbrake adjusting nut until the clearance between the operating levers (arrowed) and their stops is a maximum of 1 mm

18.2 Detach the handbrake cable return spring from the bracket on the underbody

18.3 Unscrew the handbrake adjusting nut and remove it from the end of the front handbrake cable

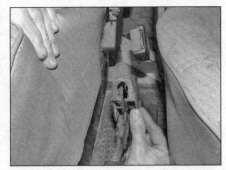

18.4a Remove the handbrake lever upper trim...

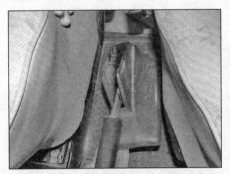

18.4b ...and lower trim

18.5 Handbrake lever retaining nuts (arrowed)

18.7 Disconnect the handbrake warning light switch wiring connector

18 Handbrake lever – removal and refitting

Removal

1 Chock the front wheels, then jack up the rear of the vehicle, and support it securely on axle stands (see *Jacking and vehicle support*).

2 Detach the handbrake cable return spring from the bracket on the underbody, then unscrew the spring holder from the end of the front handbrake cable **(see illustration)**.

3 Unscrew the handbrake adjusting nut and remove it from the end of the front handbrake cable **(see illustration)**.

4 From inside the vehicle, remove the handbrake lever upper trim and lower trim **(see illustrations)**.

5 Undo the two nuts securing the handbrake lever to the floor **(see illustration)**.

6 Lift the handbrake lever off the mounting studs, move it forward and disconnect the front handbrake cable from the lever pawl.

7 Disconnect the warning light switch wiring connector and remove the handbrake lever from the vehicle **(see illustration)**.

Refitting

8 Refitting is a reversal of removal, but adjust the handbrake as described in Section 17 before lowering the vehicle to the ground.

19 Handbrake warning light switch – removal and refitting

Removal

1 From inside the vehicle, remove the handbrake lever upper trim and lower trim **(see illustrations 18.4a and 18.4b)**.

2 Disconnect the wiring connector from the warning light switch on the side of the handbrake lever.

3 Extract the plastic rivet and remove the switch from the handbrake lever bracket.

Refitting

4 Refitting is a reversal of removal.

20 Handbrake cables – removal and refitting

1 The handbrake cable assembly consists of a front cable linking the handbrake lever with the cable compensator, two pull rods linking the compensator with the rear cables and two rear cables linking the pull rods with the relevant rear brake. Each of the handbrake cable components can be removed and refitted individually as described in the following sub-Sections.

Front cable

Removal

2 Chock the front wheels, then jack up the rear of the vehicle, and support it securely on axle stands (see *Jacking and vehicle support*).

3 Detach the handbrake cable return spring from the bracket on the underbody, then unscrew the spring holder from the end of the front handbrake cable **(see illustration 18.2)**.

4 Unscrew the handbrake adjusting nut and remove it from the end of the front handbrake cable **(see illustration 18.3)**.

5 Release the rear cable guide from the bracket on the underbody **(see illustration)**.

20.5 Release the rear handbrake cable guide from the bracket on the underbody

20.6 Prise free the front cable guide from the bracket on the underbody

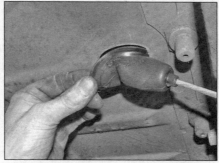

20.7 Release the grommet from the handbrake cable entry point on the floor

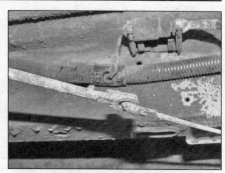

20.14 Unhook the pull rod from the rear handbrake cable

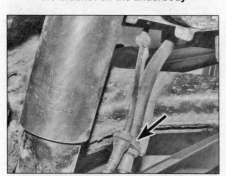

20.19a Release the rear handbrake cable from the brackets on the suspension arm (arrowed)...

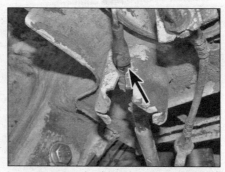

20.19b ...and on the underbody (arrowed)

6 Prise free the front cable guide from the bracket on the underbody **(see illustration)**.

7 Release the grommet from the cable entry point on the floor **(see illustration)**.

8 From inside the vehicle, remove the handbrake lever upper trim and lower trim **(see illustrations 18.4a and 18.4b)**.

9 Pull the handbrake lever up as far as it will go and disconnect the front handbrake cable from the lever pawl.

Refitting

10 Refitting is a reversal of removal, but adjust the handbrake as described in Section 17 before lowering the vehicle to the ground.

Pull rods

Removal

11 Chock the front wheels, then jack up the rear of the vehicle, and support it securely on axle stands (see *Jacking and vehicle support*).

21.1 Brake pressure regulating valve

12 Detach the handbrake cable return spring from the bracket on the underbody, then unscrew the spring holder from the end of the front handbrake cable **(see illustration 18.2)**.

13 Unscrew the handbrake adjusting nut and remove it from the end of the front handbrake cable **(see illustration 18.3)**.

14 Unhook the relevant pull rod from the cable compensator and from the rear handbrake cable and remove it from under the vehicle **(see illustration)**.

Refitting

15 Refitting is a reversal of removal, but adjust the handbrake as described in Section 17 before lowering the vehicle to the ground.

Rear cables

Removal

16 Chock the front wheels, then jack up the rear of the vehicle, and support it securely on axle stands (see *Jacking and vehicle support*).

17 On models with drum brakes, remove the rear brake shoes as described in Section 10. Release the handbrake cable from the brake backplate.

18 On models with disc brakes, lever down the handbrake operating lever on the brake caliper using a screwdriver and disengage the handbrake cable end fitting from the lever. Extract the handbrake outer cable retaining clip and withdraw the handbrake cable from the caliper **(see illustrations 11.2a and 11.2b)**.

19 On all models, release the outer cable from the brackets on the suspension arm and on the underbody **(see illustrations)**.

20 Unhook the handbrake cable from the pull rod and remove it from under the vehicle.

Refitting

21 Refitting is a reversal of removal, bearing in mind the following points:

a) *On models with drum brakes, refit the brake shoes as described in Section 10.*

b) *On all models, adjust the handbrake as described in Section 17 before lowering the vehicle to the ground.*

21 Brake pressure regulating valve – general information

Except on models equipped with Bosch 5.3 ABS and certain special equipment vehicles, a brake pressure regulating valve is incorporated in the hydraulic circuit to the rear brakes **(see illustration)**.

The valve is of the load-dependent-type mounted on the underbody, forward of the rear suspension arms. The valve is attached to a horizontal beam which is in turn connected to each suspension arm by a spring. As the load being carried by the vehicle is altered, the suspension moves in relation to the vehicle body, altering the tension in the springs which is then transmitted to the horizontal beam. The beam then acts on the pressure-regulating valve lever so that the correct pressure is applied to the rear brakes to suit the load being carried.

If the valve position is disturbed, it will require adjustment which entails the use of special setting gauges and reference to several charts depending on the rear coil spring colour code. It is therefore recommended that any work on the brake pressure regulating valve should be entrusted to a VW dealer or suitably equipped garage.

22 Stop-light switch – removal, refitting and adjustment

Removal

1 The stop-light switch is located on the brake pedal mounting bracket in the driver's footwell.

2 Turn the retaining catch anti-clockwise and open the driver's side stowage box fully. Lift the stowage box out of the lower retainers and remove it from the facia **(see illustrations)**.
3 Remove the steering column shrouds as described in Chapter 11, Section 29.
4 Disconnect the wiring connector from the stop-light switch **(see illustration)**.
5 Turn the switch 90° anti-clockwise and remove it from the mounting bracket **(see illustration)**.

Refitting

6 Refitting is a reversal of removal, but before fitting the switch fully extend the switch plunger, then depress and hold the brake pedal while manoeuvring the switch into position. Turn the switch 90° clockwise to secure.

23 Vacuum servo unit –
testing, removal and refitting

Testing

1 To test the operation of the servo unit, with the engine switched off, depress the footbrake pedal several times to exhaust the vacuum. Now start the engine, keeping the pedal firmly depressed. As the engine starts, there should be a noticeable 'give' in the brake pedal as the vacuum builds-up. Allow the engine to run for at least two minutes, then switch it off. The brake pedal should now feel normal, but further applications should result in the pedal feeling firmer, the pedal stroke decreasing with each application.
2 If the servo does not operate as described, first inspect the servo unit check valve as described in Section 24.
3 If the servo unit still fails to operate satisfactorily, the fault lies within the unit itself. Repairs to the unit are not possible; if faulty, the servo unit must be renewed.

Removal

4 Remove the brake master cylinder as described in Section 15.
5 On engines with an intercooler mounted over the top of the camshaft cover, remove the intercooler as described in Chapter 4A, Section 14.
6 For improved access, refer to Chapter 4A, Section 2 and remove the air cleaner assembly and air ducts.
7 Carefully ease the vacuum hose out of the servo unit, taking care not to displace the sealing grommet.
8 Release the wiring harness from the support bracket on the servo.
9 Turn the retaining catch anti-clockwise and open the driver's side stowage box fully. Lift the stowage box out of the lower retainers and remove it from the facia **(see illustrations 22.2a and 22.2b)**.
10 Remove the steering column shrouds as described in Chapter 11, Section 29.

22.2a Open the driver's side stowage box fully...

22.2b ...then lift the stowage box out of the lower retainers and remove it from the facia

22.4 Disconnect the wiring connector (arrowed) from the stop-light switch

11 Extract the retaining clip and pull out the clevis pin securing the vacuum servo unit pushrod to the brake pedal **(see illustration)**.
12 Undo the four nuts securing the servo unit and pedal mounting bracket to the bulkhead.
13 Return to the engine compartment, and lift the servo unit out of position. Recover the servo unit-to-bulkhead gasket.

Refitting

14 Refit the gasket, then locate the vacuum servo unit in position on the bulkhead. Refit the four nuts and tighten them to the specified torque.
15 With the servo unit pushrod engaged with the brake pedal, refit the clevis pin and retaining clip.
16 Refit the steering column shrouds as described in Chapter 11, Section 29, then refit the driver's side stowage box.

23.11 Extract the retaining clip (arrowed) and pull out the servo unit pushrod clevis pin

22.5 Turn the switch 90° anti-clockwise and remove it from the mounting bracket

17 Refit the wiring harness to the support bracket on the servo.
18 Refit the vacuum hose to the servo grommet, ensuring that the hose is correctly seated.
19 Refit the air cleaner assembly and air ducts as described in Chapter 4A, Section 2.
20 Where applicable, refit the intercooler as described in Chapter 4A, Section 14.
21 Refit the brake master cylinder as described in Section 15.

24 Vacuum servo unit
check valve and hose –
removal, testing and refitting

1 The check valve is in the vacuum hose from the vacuum pump to the brake servo **(see illustration)**. If the valve is to be renewed, the complete hose/valve assembly should be replaced.

24.1 Vacuum servo unit check valve (arrowed)

25.5 On 4-cylinder engines ensure the vacuum pump slot (arrowed) aligns correctly with the pump drivegear on refitting

Removal

2 Ease the vacuum hose out of the servo unit, taking care not to displace the grommet.
3 Where applicable, disconnect the secondary vacuum hoses from the main vacuum hose.
4 Note the routing of the hose, then disconnect the opposite end of the hose assembly from the vacuum pump and remove it from the engine compartment.

Testing

5 Examine the check valve and vacuum hose for signs of damage, and renew if necessary.
6 The valve may be tested by blowing through it in both directions, air should flow through the valve in one direction only; when blown through from the servo unit end of the valve. Renew the valve if this is not the case.
7 Examine the servo unit rubber sealing grommet for signs of damage or deterioration, and renew as necessary.

Refitting

8 Ensure that the sealing grommet is correctly fitted to the servo unit.
9 Ease the hose union into position in the servo, taking great care not to displace or damage the grommet.
10 Ensure that the hose is correctly routed, and connect it to the vacuum pump.
11 Where applicable, reconnect the secondary vacuum hoses from the main vacuum hose.
12 On completion, start the engine and check the check valve to servo unit connection for signs of air leaks.

25 Vacuum pump –
removal and refitting

4-cylinder engines

Removal

1 Release the retaining clip, and disconnect the vacuum hose from the top of pump.
2 Slacken and remove the retaining bolt, and remove the pump retaining clamp from the cylinder block.
3 Withdraw the vacuum pump from the cylinder block, and recover the O-ring seal. Discard the O-ring – a new one should be used on refitting.

Refitting

4 Fit the new O-ring to the vacuum pump, and apply a smear of oil to the O-ring to aid installation.
5 Manoeuvre the vacuum pump into position, making sure that the slot in the pump drive gear aligns with the dog on the pump drive gear **(see illustration)**.
6 Refit the retaining clamp and securely tighten its retaining bolt.
7 Reconnect the vacuum hose to the pump, and secure it in position with the retaining clip.

5-cylinder engines

Note: *The vacuum pump on these engines when failing, is known to cause a loud clattering noise and can sound like a failing hydraulic tappet. Often the noise will diminish when you pump the brake pedal many times or disconnect a vacuum hose leading to it.*

Removal

8 The vacuum pump is mounted on the front-facing side of the cylinder head.
9 On engines with an intercooler mounted over the top of the camshaft cover, remove the intercooler as described in Chapter 4A, Section 14.
10 For improved access, move the radiator to the service position as described in Chapter 3, Section 3.
11 Slacken the retaining clip (where fitted) and disconnect the vacuum hose from the pump.
12 Unscrew the retaining nuts and washers then remove the pump from the cylinder head, along with its pushrod. Recover the pump sealing ring and discard it; a new one should be used on refitting **(see illustrations)**.

Refitting

13 Fit a new sealing ring to the pump body and insert the pushrod.
14 Manoeuvre the pump into position, ensuring the pushrod remains correctly positioned. Locate the pump on its studs and refit the washers and retaining nuts, tightening them securely.
15 Reconnect the vacuum hose and secure it in position with the retaining clip (where fitted).
16 Move the radiator back to its normal position as described in Chapter 3, Section 3.
17 Where applicable, refit the intercooler as described in Chapter 4A, Section 14.

26 Anti-lock braking system (ABS) –
general information

Note: *On models equipped with traction control, the ABS unit is a dual function unit, controlling both the anti-lock braking system (ABS) and the electronic differential locking (EDL) and/or anti-slip regulation (ASR) system functions.*

ABS is available as an option on all models covered in this manual. The system comprises a hydraulic modulator and electronic control unit together with four wheel speed sensors. The hydraulic modulator contains the electronic control unit (ECU), the hydraulic solenoid valves (one set for each brake) and the electrically-driven pump. The purpose of the system is to prevent the wheel(s) locking during heavy braking. This is achieved by automatic release of the brake on the relevant wheel, followed by re-application of the brake.

The solenoid valves are controlled by the ECU, which itself receives signals from the four wheel speed sensors which monitor the speed of rotation of each wheel. By comparing these

25.12a On 5-cylinder engines, unscrew the retaining nuts and remove the vacuum pump...

25.12b ...and pushrod from the cylinder head

25.12c Remove the sealing ring from the pump and discard it

signals, the ECU can determine the speed at which the vehicle is travelling. It can then use this speed to determine when a wheel is decelerating at an abnormal rate, compared to the speed of the vehicle, and therefore predicts when a wheel is about to lock. During normal operation, the system functions in the same way as a conventional braking system.

If the ECU senses that a wheel is about to lock, it operates the relevant solenoid valve(s) in the hydraulic unit, which then isolates from the master cylinder the relevant brake(s) on the wheel(s) which is/are about to lock, effectively sealing-in the hydraulic pressure.

If the speed of rotation of the wheel continues to decrease at an abnormal rate, the ECU operates the electrically-driven pump which pumps the hydraulic fluid back into the master cylinder, releasing the brake. Once the speed of rotation of the wheel returns to an acceptable rate, the pump stops, and the solenoid valves switch again, allowing the hydraulic master cylinder pressure to return to the caliper, which then re-applies the brake. This cycle can be carried out many times a second.

The action of the solenoid valves and return pump creates pulses in the hydraulic circuit. When the ABS system is functioning, these pulses can be felt through the brake pedal.

On models with a traction control system, the ABS system also performs the electronic differential lock (EDL)/anti-slip regulation (ASR) functions. If under acceleration the ECU senses that a wheel is spinning, it uses the hydraulic unit to gently apply the brake on that wheel until traction is regained. Once the wheel regains traction, the brake is released. The traction control functions are only available at speeds of up to approximately 25 mph, above this they are disabled.

The operation of the ABS system is entirely dependent on electrical signals. To prevent the system responding to any inaccurate signals, a built-in safety circuit monitors all signals received by the ECU. If an inaccurate signal or low battery voltage is detected, the ABS system is automatically shut down, and the warning light on the instrument panel is illuminated, to inform the driver that the ABS system is not operational. Normal braking should still be available, however.

If a fault does develop in the ABS system, the vehicle must be taken to a VW dealer or diagnostic specialist for fault diagnosis and repair.

27 Anti-lock braking system (ABS) components – removal and refitting

Hydraulic modulator unit

1 Removal and refitting of the hydraulic modulator unit should be entrusted to a VW dealer or suitably equipped garage. Great care has to be taken not to allow any fluid to escape from the unit as the pipes are disconnected. If the fluid is allowed to escape, air can enter the unit, causing air locks which cause the hydraulic unit to malfunction.

Electronic control unit (ECU)

Removal

2 On vehicles manufactured before January 1996, the control unit is situated near the base of the left-hand A-pillar. On vehicles manufactured after January 1996, the control unit is combined with the hydraulic modulator unit and cannot be removed separately.
3 Disconnect the battery negative terminal (refer to *Disconnecting the battery*).
4 Move the floor covering to one side for access to the A-pillar.
5 Disconnect the control unit wiring connector. Unscrew the control unit securing clips and remove the unit from the mounting bracket.

Refitting

6 Refitting is a reversal of removal, ensuring that the ECU wiring connector is correctly and securely reconnected.

Front wheel speed sensor

Removal

7 Firmly apply the handbrake, then jack up the front of the vehicle and support it securely on axle stands (see *Jacking and vehicle support*). Remove the relevant front roadwheel.
8 Trace the wiring back from the sensor to the connector, freeing it from all the relevant retaining clips, and disconnect it from the main loom.
9 Slacken and remove the bolt securing the sensor to the swivel hub, and remove the sensor and lead assembly from the vehicle.

Refitting

10 Prior to refitting, apply a thin coat of multi-purpose grease to the sensor body (VW recommend the use of lubricating paste G 000 650 – available from VW dealers).
11 Ensure that the sensor and swivel hub sealing faces are clean, then fit the sensor to the hub. Refit the retaining bolt and tighten it to the specified torque.
12 Ensure that the sensor wiring is correctly routed and retained by all the necessary clips, and reconnect it to its wiring connector.
13 Refit the roadwheel, then lower the vehicle to the ground and tighten the roadwheel bolts to the specified torque.

Rear wheel speed sensor

Removal

14 Chock the front wheels, then jack up the rear of the vehicle, and support it securely on axle stands (see *Jacking and vehicle support*). Remove the relevant rear roadwheel.
15 Remove the sensor as described above in paragraphs 8 and 9.

Refitting

16 Refit the sensor as described above in paragraphs 10 to 13.

Chapter 10
Suspension and steering

Contents

Degrees of difficulty

Easy, suitable for novice with little experience	**Fairly easy,** suitable for beginner with some experience	**Fairly difficult,** suitable for competent DIY mechanic	**Difficult,** suitable for experienced DIY mechanic	**Very difficult,** suitable for expert DIY or professional

Specifications

Front suspension

Type . . . .   Independent with upper and lower transverse wishbones, torsion bars, telescopic shock absorbers and anti-roll bar

Rear suspension

Type . . . .   Independent with trailing arms, coil springs and telescopic shock absorbers.

Steering

Type . . . .   Rack and pinion with hydraulic power-assistance on later models
Power steering fluid type . . . .   See *Lubricants and fluids* on page 0•17

Torque wrench settings	Nm	lbf ft
Front suspension		
ABS wheel speed sensor retaining bolts	10	7
Anti-roll bar clamp bolts.	55	41
Driveshaft inner constant velocity joint retaining bolts:		
M10 bolts	80	59
M12 bolts	100	74
Driveshaft retaining bolt*:		
Stage 1	150	110
Stage 2	Angle-tighten a further 90°	
Engine/transmission rear mounting:		
Mounting-to-subframe (early models)	45	33
Mounting-to-transmission through bolt (later models):*		
Stage 1	80	59
Stage 2	Angle-tighten a further 90°	
Eccentric bush-to-swivel hub retaining bolt.	60	44
Exhaust system front pipe flange joint nuts.	25	
Front brake caliper mounting bracket bolts (except VW FNR caliper). .	280	207
Front brake caliper mounting bracket bolts (VW FNR caliper).	355	262
Lower wishbone balljoint-to-lower wishbone nut:		
Pre-January 1996 models	110	81
January 1996 models onward*:		
Stage 1	60	44
Stage 2	Angle-tighten through a further 90°	
Lower wishbone balljoint-to-swivel hub bolts*:		
Hexagon head bolts:		
Stage 1	55	41
Stage 2	Angle-tighten through a further 90°	
Multi-point socket head bolts:		
Stage 1	90	66
Stage 2	Angle-tighten through a further 90°	
Lower wishbone front mounting bolt nut	160	118
Lower wishbone rear mounting eccentric bolt nut:		
Early models with M12 bolt*:		
Stage 1	75	55
Stage 2	Angle-tighten through a further 90°	
Later models with M14 bolt	160	118
Shock absorber-to-lower wishbone bolt/nut.	160	118
Shock absorber-to-upper mounting bracket	25	18
Shock absorber upper mounting bracket bolt and nut	100	74
Subframe mounting bolts:		
M12 bolts	100	74
M14 bolts	160	118
Torsion bar-to-upper wishbone upper mounting bolt	160	118
Torsion bar-to-upper wishbone lower mounting bolt nut.	130	96
Upper balljoint-to-swivel hub retaining nut:*		
Stage 1.	60	44
Stage 2	Angle-tighten a further 90°	
Upper wishbone front and rear mounting bolt nuts*	100	74
Rear suspension		
Rear hub flange retaining bolt nut	200	148
Trailing arm inner mounting bolt nut.	100	74
Trailing arm outer mounting bolt nut	160	118
Shock absorber lower mounting bolt.	45	33
Shock absorber upper mounting bolt	100	74
Steering		
Lower steering column shaft-to-steering gear pinion:*		
Stage 1.	30	22
Stage 2	Angle-tighten a further 90°	
Power steering pump mounting bolts	20	15
Power steering pump pulley bolts	20	15
Power steering pump hydraulic pipe union bolts.	40	30
Steering column intermediate shaft-to-lower steering column shaft:*		
Stage 1.	30	22
Stage 2	Angle-tighten a further 90°	

Torque wrench settings (continued)

	Nm	lbf ft
Steering (continued)		
Steering column front mounting bolt	23	17
Steering column rear mounting bolt	50	37
Steering gear-to-front subframe:		
M8 bolts	33	24
M10 bolts	60	44
Steering wheel retaining bolt	70	52
Track rod end balljoint nut*	65	48
Roadwheels		
Roadwheel bolts:		
Up to December 1995	160	118
January 1996 onward	180	133

* Use new nuts/bolts

1 General information

The independent front suspension is of the double wishbone type utilising upper and lower transverse wishbones, torsion bars, telescopic shock absorbers and an anti-roll bar. The front suspension components are mounted on a welded steel subframe bolted to the underside of the bodyshell. The inner ends of the upper and lower wishbones are attached to the subframe via rubber bushes. At their outer ends, the wishbones are attached to the swivel hubs via upper and lower balljoints. The swivel hubs contain the hub bearings which support the outer ends of the driveshafts and also provide mounting points for the disc brake calipers. Springing and damping is catered for by means of two solid steel torsion bars, bolted to the upper wishbones at their forward end and attached to the underbody at their rear end via an adjustable ride height control arm. Telescopic shock absorbers attached to the lower wishbone and subframe provide the damping. An anti-roll bar is also fitted which has connecting links at each end to attach it to the lower wishbone.

The rear suspension is also independent by means of two trailing arms attached to the underbody via rubber pivot bushes. The trailing arms contain the rear brake assemblies and rear hub bearings. Springing and damping is by means of coil springs and telescopic shock absorbers. An anti-roll bar may be fitted as an option on certain models.

The steering column incorporates an upper and lower steering shaft with an intermediate shaft containing universal joints between the two. The upper steering shaft is connected to the steering wheel, while the lower shaft is connected to the steering gear pinion shaft by means of a further universal joint.

The steering gear is mounted on the front subframe. It is connected by two track rods and track rod ends to the steering arms projecting rearwards from the swivel hubs.

The track rod ends are threaded to enable wheel alignment adjustment.

Hydraulic power steering is fitted to later models, with the power steering pump being belt-driven from the crankshaft pulley.

2 Front swivel hub – removal and refitting

Removal

1 Firmly apply the handbrake, then jack up the front of the vehicle and support it securely on axle stands (see *Jacking and vehicle support*). Remove the relevant front roadwheel.

2.3a Undo the front brake caliper mounting bracket retaining bolts (arrowed)...

2.4a Remove the securing screw...

2 Remove the engine undertray as described in Chapter 11, Section 25.
3 Unbolt and remove the front brake caliper complete with disc pads and mounting bracket and suspend it from a convenient place under the wheel arch using cable ties **(see illustrations)**. Do not allow the caliper to hang unsupported from the flexible brake hose.
4 Remove the securing screw and withdraw the disc from the hub **(see illustrations)**.
5 Undo the retaining bolts and remove the brake backplate.
6 To prevent rotation of the wheel hub as the driveshaft retaining bolt is slackened, make up a holding tool and attach the tool to the wheel

2.3b ...then remove the front brake caliper complete with disc pads and mounting bracket

2.4b ...and withdraw the disc from the hub

TOOL
TiP

A tool to hold the wheel hub stationary whilst the driveshaft retaining bolt is slackened can be fabricated from two lengths of steel strip (one long, one short) and a nut and bolt; the nut and bolt forming the pivot of a forked tool.

2.6 Attach the holding tool to the wheel hub using two wheel bolts

2.8 Measure the amount of thread projecting from the underside of the torsion bar adjusting nut to the end of the bolt

hub using two wheel bolts **(see Tool Tip and illustration)**.

7 With the holding tool in place, slacken and remove the driveshaft retaining bolt using a socket and long bar. Where necessary, support the socket on an axle stand to prevent it slipping off the nut. This bolt is very tight; make sure that there is no risk of pulling the vehicle off the axle stands as the nut is slackened. Note that a new bolt will be required for refitting.

8 At the relevant torsion bar adjustment bolt, measure and record the length of thread projecting from the underside of the adjusting nut to the end of the bolt **(see illustration)**.

This is a critical dimension as it will be needed to determine the vehicle ride height when refitting.

9 Using a spanner or deep socket, unscrew the torsion bar adjusting nut until all load is relieved on the front upper wishbone **(see illustration)**.

10 Slacken the track rod end balljoint nut several turns, then use a balljoint separator tool to release the balljoint shank from the steering arm. With the balljoint released, unscrew the nut and disconnect the balljoint from the steering arm. Discard the nut as a new one must be used for refitting.

11 Undo the two bolts securing the lower wishbone balljoint to the swivel hub **(see illustration)**. On pre-January 1996 vehicles these bolts are conventional hexagon head bolts. On January 1996 vehicles onwards,

these bolts are M12 multi-point socket headed bolts and are removed using a 14 mm multi-point key. Note that new bolts (whichever type) will be required for refitting.

12 Undo the nut and remove the bolt securing the anti-roll bar connecting link and the shock absorber to the lower wishbone. Push the lower end of the shock absorber upward as far as it will go.

13 On vehicles with ABS, undo the retaining bolt and withdraw the wheel speed sensor from the swivel hub.

14 Using a permanent marker pen or quick-drying paint, mark the position of the upper wishbone balljoint eccentric bush and eccentric nut in relation to the swivel hub. This will ensure that the camber setting is not lost when reassembling.

15 Undo the nut securing the upper wishbone balljoint to the eccentric bush and lift out the eccentric nut **(see illustrations)**.

16 Undo the bolt securing the eccentric bush to the top of the swivel hub.

17 Carefully pull the swivel hub assembly outwards, and withdraw the driveshaft outer constant velocity joint from the hub assembly. The outer joint may be very tight, if so tap the joint out of the hub using a soft-faced mallet. If this fails to free it from the hub, the joint will have to be pressed out using a suitable tool which is bolted to the hub. Once the driveshaft outer joint is free, remove the swivel hub from the vehicle **(see illustrations)**.

2.9 Unscrew the torsion bar adjusting nut until all load is relieved on the front upper wishbone

2.11 Undo the two bolts securing the lower wishbone balljoint to the swivel hub

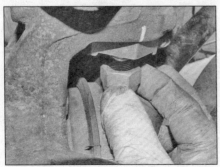

2.15a Undo the nut securing the upper wishbone balljoint to the eccentric bush...

2.15b ...and lift out the eccentric nut

2.17a Withdraw the driveshaft outer joint...

2.17b ...and remove the swivel hub assembly

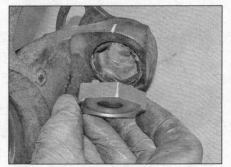

2.19a Place the eccentric nut in place in the eccentric bush and engage the upper wishbone balljoint

2.19b Refit the retaining nut and tighten it while holding the balljoint shank with an Allen key

Refitting

18 Locate the swivel hub in position and engage the hub with the driveshaft outer joint. Ensure that the threads are clean, and apply a smear of oil to the contact face of the new driveshaft retaining bolt. Fit the bolt and use it to draw the joint fully into position.

19 Place the eccentric nut in place in the eccentric bush ensuring the marks made on removal are aligned. Engage the upper wishbone balljoint with the eccentric nut and refit the retaining nut. Tighten the nut to the specified torque while holding the balljoint shank with a 7 mm Allen key **(see illustrations)**.

20 Refit the bolt securing the eccentric bush to the top of the swivel hub and tighten it to the specified torque.

21 Fit the new lower wishbone balljoint retaining bolts, and tighten them to the specified torque setting, then through the specified angle.

22 On vehicles with ABS, refit the wheel speed sensor to the swivel hub and secure with the retaining bolt.

23 Pull the lower end of the shock absorber down and refit the anti-roll bar connecting link and shock absorber retaining bolt. Note that the bolt head is toward the rear of the vehicle. Refit the retaining nut and tighten it to the specified torque.

24 Locate the track rod end balljoint on the steering arm. Screw on a new nut and tighten it to the specified torque. If the balljoint shank is hollow, a 5 mm Allen key can be used to prevent the balljoint from rotating as the nut is tightened. If the shank is solid, use a stout bar to lever down on the top of the track rod end. This will lock the balljoint shank taper in the steering arm and prevent rotation as the nut is tightened.

25 Tighten the torsion bar adjusting nut until the exposed thread dimension recorded during removal is obtained.

26 Using the method employed on removal to prevent the hub from rotating, and tighten the driveshaft retaining bolt to the specified torque setting, then through the specified angle. Check that the hub rotates freely.

27 Refit the brake backplate and tighten the retaining bolts securely.

28 Thoroughly clean the mating surfaces of the brake disc and hub flange ensuring that all traces of dirt and corrosion are removed.

29 Place the disc in position on the hub flange, then refit the retaining screw and tighten it securely.

30 Slide the brake caliper assembly over the disc and into position on the steering knuckle. Refit the two mounting bracket retaining bolts and tighten them to the specified torque.

31 Refit the engine undertray as described in Chapter 11, Section 25.

32 Refit the roadwheel, lower the vehicle to the ground, and tighten the wheel bolts to the specified torque.

33 It is advisable to have the front wheel alignment and steering angles checked and, if necessary, adjusted at the earliest opportunity (see Section 28).

3 Front hub bearings – inspection and renewal

Inspection

1 The front hub bearings are of sealed, pre-adjusted and prelubricated, double-row ball type, and are intended to last the vehicle's entire service life without maintenance or attention.

2 To check the bearings for excessive wear, firmly apply the handbrake, then jack up the front of the vehicle and support it securely on axle stands (see *Jacking and vehicle support*).

3 Grip the front wheel at the top and bottom and attempt to rock it. If excessive movement is noted, it may be that the hub bearings are worn. Do not confuse wear in the upper and lower balljoints with wear in the bearings. Hub bearing wear will show up as roughness or vibration when the wheel is spun; it will also be noticeable as a rumbling or growling noise when driving.

Renewal

Note: *A press will be required to dismantle and rebuild the assembly. The bearing's inner races are an interference fit on the hub flange and the outer bearing inner race will remain on the hub flange when the flange is pressed out of the hub assembly. A knife-edged bearing puller will be required to remove it.*

4 Remove the front hub assembly as described in Section 2.

5 Support the outer face of the hub assembly on the press bed, with the hub flange facing downward. Using a tubular spacer (or suitable socket) which bears only on the inner end of the hub flange, press the hub flange out of the hub assembly **(see illustration)**.

6 With the hub flange removed from hub assembly, remove the outer bearing inner race using a knife-edge bearing puller **(see illustration)**.

3.5 Press the hub flange out of the hub assembly

3.6 Remove the outer bearing inner race from the hub flange using a knife-edge bearing puller

3.7 Extract the bearing retaining circlip from the swivel hub assembly

3.8 Press the bearing assembly out of the swivel hub

3.10 Press the bearing into the swivel hub using spacers and the old bearing outer race

3.11 Secure the bearing in position with a new circlip

3.12 Support the outer face of the hub flange, and press the hub bearing inner race onto the hub flange

12 Support the outer face of the hub flange, and locate the swivel hub bearing inner race over the end of the hub flange. Press the bearing onto the hub, using a tubular spacer which bears only on the inner race of the hub bearing, until it seats against the hub shoulder **(see illustration)**. Check that the hub flange rotates freely, and wipe off any excess oil or grease.

13 Refit the swivel hub assembly as described in Section 2.

4 Front lower wishbone – removal and refitting

Removal

1 Firmly apply the handbrake, then jack up the front of the vehicle and support it securely on axle stands (see *Jacking and vehicle support*). Remove the relevant front roadwheel.

2 Remove the engine undertray as described in Chapter 11, Section 25.

3 At the relevant torsion bar adjustment bolt, measure and record the length of thread projecting from the underside of the adjusting nut to the end of the bolt **(see illustration 2.8)**. This is a critical dimension as it will be needed to determine the vehicle ride height when refitting.

4 Using a spanner or deep socket, unscrew the torsion bar adjusting nut until all load is relieved on the front upper wishbone **(see illustration 2.9)**.

5 Undo the two bolts securing the lower wishbone balljoint to the swivel hub **(see illustration 2.11)**. On pre-January 1996 vehicles these bolts are conventional hexagon head bolts. On January 1996 vehicles onwards, these bolts are M12 multi-point socket headed bolts and are removed using a 14 mm multi-point key. Note that new bolts (whichever type) will be required for refitting.

6 Undo the nut and remove the bolt securing the anti-roll bar connecting link and the shock absorber to the lower wishbone. Push the lower end of the shock absorber upward as far as it will go.

7 Using a permanent marker pen or quick-drying paint, mark the position of the lower wishbone rear mounting eccentric bolt in relation to the subframe **(see illustration)**.

7 Extract the bearing retaining circlip from the swivel hub assembly **(see illustration)**.

8 Securely support the outer face of the swivel hub. Using a tubular spacer, press the

4.7 Make an alignment mark (arrowed) on the lower wishbone eccentric bolt and the subframe

4.8a Undo the retaining nut...

complete bearing assembly out of the swivel hub **(see illustration)**.

9 Thoroughly clean the hub and swivel hub, removing all traces of dirt and grease, and polish away any burrs or raised edges which might hinder reassembly. Check both for cracks or any other signs of wear or damage, and renew them if necessary. Renew the circlip, regardless of its apparent condition.

10 Securely support the inner face of the swivel hub on the press bed, and locate the bearing in the hub. Press the bearing fully into position, ensuring that it enters the hub squarely, using a tubular spacer (such as the old bearing outer race) which bears only on the bearing outer race **(see illustration)**.

11 Once the bearing is correctly seated, secure the bearing in position with the new circlip, ensuring it is correctly located in the groove in the swivel hub **(see illustration)**.

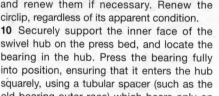
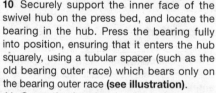

4.8b ...and remove the lower wishbone front mounting bolt

4.9a Undo the retaining nut...

4.9b ...remove the eccentric washer...

4.9c ...then remove the lower wishbone rear mounting eccentric bolt

This will ensure that the castor setting is not lost when reassembling.

8 Undo the retaining nut and remove the lower wishbone front mounting bolt **(see illustrations)**.

9 Undo the retaining nut, remove the eccentric washer, then remove the lower wishbone rear mounting eccentric bolt **(see illustrations)**.

10 Disengage the lower wishbone mounting bushes from their locations in the subframe and remove the wishbone from the vehicle.

11 Thoroughly clean the wishbone and the area around the mounting locations on the subframe, removing all traces of dirt and underseal. Check carefully for cracks, distortion or any other signs of wear or damage, paying particular attention to the mounting bushes. If required, the bushes can be renewed as described in Section 5.

Refitting

12 Place the lower wishbone in position in the subframe and insert the front mounting bolt and the rear mounting eccentric bolt. Note that the front mounting bolt is fitted with its head toward the rear of the vehicle and the rear mounting eccentric bolt is fitted with its head toward the front of the vehicle.

13 Refit the front mounting bolt retaining nut but only tighten it finger tight at this stage.

14 Rotate the rear mounting eccentric bolt until the marks made on removal are aligned. Place the eccentric washer on the bolt then fit the retaining nut but only tighten it finger tight at this stage.

15 Engage the lower wishbone balljoint with the swivel hub, fit the new lower wishbone balljoint retaining bolts, and tighten them to the specified torque setting, then through the specified angle.

16 Pull the lower end of the shock absorber down and refit the anti-roll bar connecting link and shock absorber retaining bolt. Note that the bolt head is toward the rear of the vehicle. Refit the retaining nut and tighten it to the specified torque.

17 Position a trolley jack under the outer end of the lower wishbone and raise the jack and wishbone until the suspension is at its approximate normal running height. Hold the front mounting bolt and tighten the retaining nut to the specified torque.

18 Check that the marking made on the rear mounting eccentric bolt are still aligned, then tighten the retaining nut to the specified torque. Remove the jack under the lower wishbone.

19 Tighten the torsion bar adjusting nut until the exposed thread dimension recorded during removal is obtained.

20 Refit the engine undertray as described in Chapter 11, Section 25.

21 Refit the roadwheel, lower the vehicle to the ground, and tighten the wheel bolts to the specified torque.

22 It is advisable to have the front wheel alignment and steering angles checked and, if necessary, adjusted at the earliest opportunity (see Section 28).

5 Front lower wishbone mounting bushes – renewal

Note: *A press will be required to renew the front and rear mounting bushes.*

Front mounting bush

1 Remove the front lower wishbone as described in Section 4 and securely mount it in a vice.

2 Using a hacksaw, cut off the bush shoulder from the front facing side of the bush **(see illustration)**.

3 Using a hammer and chisel, bend up the metal lip on the rear facing side of the bush **(see illustration)**. It won't be possible to bend the lip up all the way round as the body of the wishbone is in the way, but bend up as much as is accessible.

4 Support the rear facing side of the bush location in the wishbone on the press bed. Using suitable mandrels, press the mounting bush out of the wishbone.

5 Thoroughly clean the bush location in the wishbone, removing all traces of dirt and grease. Polish away any burrs or raised edges which might hinder fitment of the new bush.

6 Lubricate the new bush with liquid soap then place it in position on the pressbed with the metal casing downward. Using a hollow tube or mandrel in contact with the wishbone, press the wishbone down onto the bush up to the metal collar **(see illustration)**.

5.2 Cut off the bush shoulder from the front facing side of the bush

5.3 Using a hammer and chisel, bend up the metal lip on the rear facing side of the bush

5.6 Press the wishbone down onto the new front mounting bush

5.10 Support the wishbone on the press bed and press the rear mounting bush out of the wishbone

5.11 Chisel out the remaining rear bush metal casing from the wishbone

7 Lift up the wishbone and place a small nut under the metal centre sleeve of the bush, then position this arrangement back on the pressbed. Again using the hollow tube or mandrel, continue pressing the wishbone onto the bush until the shoulder on the bush pops out of the wishbone.

8 On completion, refit the wishbone as described in Section 3.

Rear mounting bush

9 Remove the front lower wishbone as described in Section 4.

10 Support the front facing side of the bush location in the wishbone on the press bed. Using suitable mandrels, press the mounting bush out of the wishbone **(see illustration)**.

11 It is quite likely that the centre rubber portion of the bush will press out leaving the metal casing still in the wishbone. If this happens, chisel out the remaining metal casing, taking care not to damage the bush location in the wishbone **(see illustration)**.

12 Thoroughly clean the bush location in the wishbone, removing all traces of dirt and grease. Polish away any burrs or raised edges which might hinder fitment of the new bush.

13 The new bush must be fitted so that it is offset upwards by 11° to the wishbone symmetrical axis. Using a protractor make a mark on the wishbone at the 11° position. Make a similar mark on the bush in the centre of the rubber portion **(see illustrations)**.

14 Support the front facing side of the bush location in the wishbone on the press bed. Place the new bush in position with the positioning marks aligned and press the bush into the wishbone using suitable mandrels **(see illustration)**.

15 When the bush has been pressed in almost to its fully fitted position, measure the distance between the metal centre sleeves on the front and rear mounting bushes. Continue pressing the bush into the wishbone until the distance between the two centre sleeves is 371 ± 1 mm **(see illustrations)**.

16 On completion, refit the wishbone as described in Section 4.

6 Front upper wishbone – removal and refitting

Removal

1 Remove the front subframe as described in Section 14. Note that the upper wishbone can

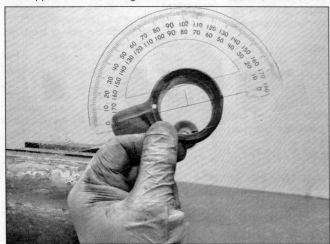

5.13a Mark the wishbone at a point offset upwards by 11° to the wishbone symmetrical axis

5.13b Make a similar mark on the bush in the centre of the rubber portion

5.14 Align the positioning marks and press the bush into the wishbone using suitable mandrels

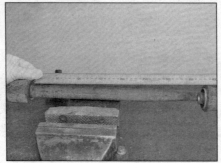

5.15a Measure the distance between the metal centre sleeves on the front and rear mounting bushes

5.15b Continue pressing the bush into the wishbone until the distance between the centre sleeves is 371 ± 1 mm

7.2 Removing the upper wishbone mounting bushes using a bush renewal tool

7.3a Lubricate the relevant bush with liquid soap...

7.3b ...then draw the bush into the wishbone so that the bush shoulders project equally on both sides

only be removed when the front subframe has been removed.

2 Undo the upper bolt and the lower nut and bolt and remove the torsion bar from the upper wishbone.

3 Using a permanent marker pen or quick-drying paint, mark the position of the upper wishbone balljoint eccentric bush and eccentric nut in relation to the swivel hub. This will ensure that the camber setting is not lost when reassembling.

4 Undo the nut securing the upper wishbone balljoint to the eccentric bush and lift out the eccentric nut **(see illustrations 2.15a and 2.15b)**.

5 Undo the bolt securing the eccentric bush to the top of the swivel hub.

6 Undo the retaining nuts and remove the upper wishbone front and rear mounting bolts. Note that new nuts will be required for refitting.

7 Disengage the upper wishbone mounting bushes from their locations in the subframe and remove the wishbone from the subframe.

8 Thoroughly clean the wishbone and the area around the mounting locations on the subframe, removing all traces of dirt and underseal. Check carefully for cracks, distortion or any other signs of wear or damage, paying particular attention to the mounting bushes. If required, the bushes can be renewed as described in Section 7.

Refitting

9 Place the upper wishbone in position in the subframe and insert the front and rear mounting bolts. Note that the front mounting bolt is fitted with its head toward the rear of the vehicle and the rear mounting bolt is fitted with its head toward the front of the vehicle.

10 Refit the new retaining nuts to the mounting bolts, but only tighten the nuts finger tight at this stage.

11· Place the eccentric nut in place in the eccentric bush ensuring the marks made on removal are aligned. Engage the upper wishbone balljoint with the eccentric nut and refit the retaining nut. Tighten the nut to the specified torque while holding the balljoint shank with a 7 mm Allen key **(see illustrations 2.19a and 2.19b)**.

12 Refit the bolt securing the eccentric bush

to the top of the swivel hub and tighten it to the specified torque.

13 Raise the wishbone to approximately its normal running height and support it in this position. Hold the mounting bolts and tighten the front and rear retaining nuts to the specified torque.

14 Locate the torsion bar in position on the wishbone. Refit the upper retaining bolt and the lower retaining bolt and nut and tighten them to the specified torque.

15 Refit the front subframe as described in Section 14.

7 Front upper wishbone mounting bushes – renewal

Note: *A commercially available bush renewal tool will be required for this operation. The renewal procedure is the same for both the front and rear bushes*

1 Remove the front upper wishbone as described in Section 6 and securely mount it in a vice.

2 If the wishbone mounting bushes are worn or perished, they can be withdrawn from the suspension arm using a commercially available bush renewal tool **(see illustration)**. Alternatively (and preferably), if a press is at hand, the bushes can be pushed out using a suitable rod or a length of tube of suitable diameter.

3 To ease the fitting of the new bushes into the wishbone, liberally lubricate the relevant bush and the location in the wishbone with

liquid soap, then press or draw (as applicable) the bush into the wishbone so that the bush shoulders project equally on both sides **(see illustrations)**. It may be necessary to push the bush back slightly after initially fitting it, to achieve equal projection of the shoulders.

4 Wipe off any excess lubricant, then refit the upper wishbone as described in Section 6.

8 Front suspension upper balljoint – renewal

Note: *If balljoint renewal is being undertaken with the upper wishbone installed, a heavy duty hydraulic ram type puller will be required. Alternatively, remove the upper wishbone and use a press for renewal. The latter method is obviously more involved, but considering the difficulties that are likely to be experienced in removing the old balljoint (wear, corrosion etc) it may prove the better option.*

1 If balljoint renewal is being undertaken with the upper wishbone installed, remove the swivel hub as described in Section 2, otherwise remove the upper wishbone as described in Section 6.

2 Using a suitable puller draw the eccentric bush off the upper balljoint tapered shank.

3 Using a screwdriver, extract the balljoint retaining circlip from the top of the upper wishbone **(see illustration)**.

4 Using the hydraulic puller or a press and suitable packing pieces, press the balljoint down and out of the wishbone **(see illustration)**.

8.3 Extract the upper balljoint circlip from the wishbone

8.4 Using a hydraulic puller to press the balljoint out of the wishbone

8.6 Place the new balljoint in position in the wishbone

8.7 Arrange suitable tubes and spacers on the puller and draw the balljoint into the wishbone

8.8 Secure the balljoint in the wishbone using a new circlip

Whichever method is being used, take suitable safety precautions and great care when doing this as the loads being imposed will be quite significant.

5 Clean the balljoint locating area in the wishbone and remove any burrs that might hinder refitting.

6 Lubricate the balljoint locating area in the wishbone with multi-purpose grease and place the balljoint in position **(see illustration)**.

7 Arrange suitable tubes and spacers on the puller or pressbed and draw the new balljoint fully into the wishbone **(see illustration)**.

8 Secure the balljoint in the wishbone using a new circlip (which will be supplied with the balljoint) **(see illustration)**. Ensure that the circlip fully engages with the groove in the balljoint.

9 Refit the swivel hub as described in Section 2, or the upper wishbone as described in Section 6. as applicable.

9 Front suspension lower balljoint – renewal

1 Firmly apply the handbrake, then jack up the front of the vehicle and support it securely on axle stands (see *Jacking and vehicle support*). Remove the relevant front roadwheel.

2 Remove the engine undertray as described in Chapter 11, Section 25.

3 At the relevant torsion bar adjustment bolt, measure and record the length of thread projecting from the underside of the adjusting nut to the end of the bolt **(see illustration 2.8)**. This is a critical dimension as it will be needed to determine the vehicle ride height when refitting.

4 Using a spanner or deep socket, unscrew the torsion bar adjusting nut until all load is relieved on the front upper wishbone **(see illustration 2.9)**.

5 Undo the nut and remove the bolt securing the anti-roll bar connecting link and the shock absorber to the lower wishbone.

6 Undo the two bolts securing the lower wishbone balljoint to the swivel hub **(see illustration 2.11)**. On pre-January 1996 vehicles these bolts are conventional hexagon head bolts. On January 1996 vehicles onwards, these bolts are M12 multi-point

socket headed bolts and are removed using a 14 mm multi-point key. Note that new bolts (whichever type) will be required for refitting.

7 Disengage the balljoint from the base of the swivel hub then move the swivel hub slightly to one side.

8 Slacken the balljoint retaining nut, and unscrew it until it is positioned flush with the end of the balljoint shank threads. Release the balljoint from the swivel hub, using a puller or universal balljoint separator, then unscrew the nut and remove the balljoint from the wishbone. Note that on January 1996 models onward, a new nut will be required for refitting.

9 Clean the balljoint locating area in the swivel hub and lower wishbone and remove any burrs that might hinder refitting.

10 Fit the balljoint to the lower wishbone and fit the new retaining nut (where applicable). Tighten the nut to the specified torque then, on later models, tighten it further through the specified angle. If necessary use an Allen key inserted in the joint shank to prevent rotation as the nut is tightened.

11 Engage the balljoint with the swivel hub, ensuring that it is positioned with the lug on the joint flange toward the centre of the vehicle. Fit the new retaining bolts, and tighten them to the specified torque, then through the specified angle.

12 Pull the lower end of the shock absorber down and refit the anti-roll bar connecting link and shock absorber retaining bolt. Note that the bolt head is toward the rear of the vehicle.

10.7 Unscrew the torsion bar adjusting nut and remove it from the adjusting bolt

Refit the retaining nut and tighten it to the specified torque.

13 Tighten the torsion bar adjusting nut until the exposed thread dimension recorded during removal is obtained.

14 Refit the engine undertray as described in Chapter 11, Section 25.

15 Refit the roadwheel, lower the vehicle to the ground, and tighten the wheel bolts to the specified torque.

10 Front suspension torsion bar – removal and refitting

Removal

1 Firmly apply the handbrake, then jack up the front of the vehicle and support it securely on axle stands (see *Jacking and vehicle support*). Remove the relevant front roadwheel.

2 Remove the engine undertray as described in Chapter 11, Section 25.

3 Remove the fuel tank as described in Chapter 4A, Section 7.

4 If working on the right-hand torsion bar it may be necessary to remove the exhaust system heat shields and release the exhaust system from its mountings, depending on model.

5 At the relevant torsion bar adjustment bolt, measure and record the length of thread projecting from the underside of the adjusting nut to the end of the bolt **(see illustration 2.8)**. This is a critical dimension as it will be needed to determine the vehicle ride height when refitting.

6 Using a spanner or deep socket, unscrew the torsion bar adjusting nut until all load is relieved on the front upper wishbone **(see illustration 2.9)**.

7 Once the load is relieved on the upper wishbone fully unscrew the torsion bar adjusting nut and remove it from the adjusting bolt **(see illustration)**.

8 Turn the adjusting bolt through 90° and remove it from its location in the underbody **(see illustrations)**.

9 Remove the thrust pad located over the torsion bar adjustment arm **(see illustration)**.

10 Undo the upper bolt securing the torsion bar to the upper wishbone **(see illustration)**.

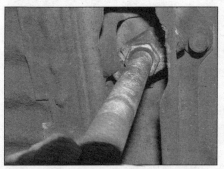

10.8a Turn the adjusting bolt through 90°...

10.8b ...and remove it from its location in the underbody

10.9 Remove the thrust pad located over the torsion bar adjustment arm

10.10 Undo the upper bolt securing the torsion bar to the upper wishbone

10.11a Undo the nut and remove the lower bolt securing the torsion bar to the upper wishbone...

10.11b ...then manipulate the torsion bar out from its location

11 Undo the nut and remove the lower bolt securing the torsion bar to the upper wishbone, then manipulate the torsion bar out from its location **(see illustrations)**.

12 Note that on early models the torsion bars are marked 'R' and 'L' on their end faces to designate right and left. On later models the torsion bars are paint marked on their end faces – blue for right-hand and yellow for left-hand. The torsion bars must not be interchanged.

Refitting

13 Refitting is the reverse of the removal procedure, noting the following points:

a) *Tighten all nuts and bolts to the specified torque.*

b) *Tighten the torsion bar adjusting nut until the exposed thread dimension recorded during removal is obtained.*

c) *Refit the fuel tank as described in Chapter 4A, Section 7.*

d) *Refit the engine undertray as described in Chapter 11, Section 25.*

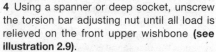

11 Front shock absorber – removal and refitting

Removal

1 Firmly apply the handbrake, then jack up the front of the vehicle and support it securely on axle stands (see *Jacking and vehicle support*). Remove the relevant front roadwheel.

2 Remove the engine undertray as described in Chapter 11, Section 25.

3 At the relevant torsion bar adjustment bolt, measure and record the length of thread projecting from the underside of the adjusting nut to the end of the bolt **(see illustration 2.8)**. This is a critical dimension as it will be needed to determine the vehicle ride height when refitting.

4 Using a spanner or deep socket, unscrew the torsion bar adjusting nut until all load is relieved on the front upper wishbone **(see illustration 2.9)**.

5 Undo the nut and remove the bolt securing the anti-roll bar connecting link and the shock absorber to the lower wishbone.

6 Undo the bolt securing the shock absorber upper mounting bracket to the underbody **(see illustration)**.

7 Undo the nut securing the shock absorber upper mounting bracket to the subframe and remove the shock absorber and mounting bracket from the vehicle **(see illustrations)**.

11.6 Undo the bolt securing the shock absorber upper mounting bracket to the underbody

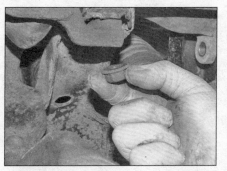

11.7a Undo the nut securing the shock absorber upper mounting bracket to the subframe...

11.7b ...and remove the shock absorber and mounting bracket

11.8 Hold the shock absorber piston rod and unscrew the upper mounting nut

11.9a Lift off the shock absorber mounting plate...

11.9b ...upper mounting rubber...

11.9c ...mounting bracket...

11.9d ...lower mounting rubber...

11.9e ...and the spacer tube

8 Unscrew the shock absorber upper mounting nut, while holding the shock absorber piston rod with a second spanner **(see illustration)**.
9 Lift off the mounting plate, upper mounting rubber, mounting bracket, lower mounting rubber and the spacer tube **(see illustrations)**.
10 To test the shock absorber for efficiency, grip the lower mounting eye in a vice, and then pump the piston repeatedly through its full stroke. If the resistance is weak or is felt to be uneven, the shock absorber is defective and must be renewed. It must also be renewed if it is leaking fluid. It is advisable to renew both front shock absorbers at the same time, or the handling characteristics of the vehicle could be adversely affected. Also check the condition of the mounting rubbers and renew any that are deformed or perished.

Refitting

11 Insert the spacer tube into the lower mounting rubber and fit the mounting rubber to the piston rod.
12 Place the mounting bracket over the lower mounting rubber then refit the upper mounting rubber and mounting plate. Note that the concave side of the mounting plate faces the mounting rubber.
13 Refit the upper mounting nut and tighten it securely while holding the piston rod with a second spanner.
14 Locate the shock absorber and mounting bracket in position on the vehicle and refit the upper mounting bolt and nut. Tighten the bolt and nut to the specified torque.
15 Pull the lower end of the shock absorber down and refit the anti-roll bar connecting link

and shock absorber retaining bolt. Note that the bolt head is toward the rear of the vehicle. Refit the retaining nut and tighten it to the specified torque.
16 Tighten the torsion bar adjusting nut until the exposed thread dimension recorded during removal is obtained.
17 Refit the engine undertray as described in Chapter 11, Section 25.
18 Refit the roadwheel, lower the vehicle to the ground, and tighten the wheel bolts to the specified torque.

12 Anti-roll bar –
removal and refitting

Removal

1 Firmly apply the handbrake, then jack up the

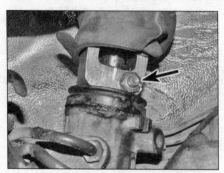

12.8 Unscrew the nut (arrowed) and remove the bolt securing the lower steering column shaft to the steering gear pinion

front of the vehicle and support it securely on axle stands (see *Jacking and vehicle support*). Remove the front roadwheels.
2 Remove the engine undertray as described in Chapter 11, Section 25.
3 At the torsion bar adjustment bolt on each side, measure and record the length of thread projecting from the underside of the adjusting nut to the end of the bolt **(see illustration 2.8)**. This is a critical dimension as it will be needed to determine the vehicle ride height when refitting.
4 Using a spanner or deep socket, unscrew the torsion bar adjusting nut on each side until all load is relieved on the front upper wishbones **(see illustration 2.9)**.
5 Undo the nut and remove the bolt securing the anti-roll bar connecting link and the shock absorber to the lower wishbone on each side. Push the shock absorbers up as far as they will go.
6 Release the rubber gaiters from the steering gear on each side and move them down the track rods slightly.
7 Using a 34 mm AF open ended spanner, unscrew the track rod inner balljoints from the steering gear on each side.
8 Slide up the rubber gaiter, then unscrew the nut and remove the bolt securing the lower steering column shaft to the steering gear pinion **(see illustration)**. Note that a new nut and bolt will be required for refitting. Use paint or a suitable marker pen to make alignment marks between the shaft and the steering gear pinion.
9 Undo the four bolts securing the steering gear to the front subframe, then disengage the

lower steering column shaft from the steering gear pinion.

10 Remove the exhaust system front pipe as described in Chapter 4A, Section 19.

11 Undo the bolt each side securing the anti-roll bar clamps to the subframe. Disengage the upper end of each clamp from the subframe slot and remove both clamps **(see illustrations)**.

12 Turn the anti-roll bar upwards approximately 90° and manipulate it out from the side of the vehicle to remove.

13 With the anti-roll bar removed, check the condition of the mounting bushes and renew as necessary.

Refitting

14 Manipulate the anti-roll bar back into place and refit the two clamps. Tighten the clamp bolts to the specified torque.

15 Refit the exhaust system front pipe as described in Chapter 4A, Section 19.

16 Engage the lower steering column shaft with the steering gear pinion ensuring that the marks made on removal are aligned. Fit the new clamp bolt and nut and tighten to the specified torque.

17 Refit the steering gear retaining bolts and tighten to the specified torque.

18 Screw the track rods onto the steering gear and tighten the inner balljoints to the specified torque. Secure the rubber gaiters back into position.

19 Pull the lower end of each shock absorber down and refit the anti-roll bar connecting link and shock absorber retaining bolt. Note that the bolt head is toward the rear of the vehicle. Refit the retaining nut and tighten it to the specified torque.

20 Tighten the torsion bar adjusting nuts until the exposed thread dimensions recorded during removal are obtained.

21 Refit the engine undertray as described in Chapter 11, Section 25.

22 Refit the roadwheels, lower the vehicle to the ground, and tighten the wheel bolts to the specified torque.

12.11a Undo the bolt securing the anti-roll bar clamp to the subframe...

13 Anti-roll bar mounting and connecting link bushes – renewal

Mounting bushes

1 Firmly apply the handbrake, then jack up the front of the vehicle and support it securely on axle stands (see *Jacking and vehicle support*). Remove the relevant front roadwheel.

2 Undo the bolt securing the anti-roll bar clamp to the subframe. Disengage the upper end of the clamp from the subframe slot and remove the clamp **(see illustrations 12.11a and 12.11b)**.

3 Lift the anti-roll bar slightly, spread open the bush and withdraw it from the anti-roll bar **(see illustration)**.

4 Place the new bush in position on the anti-roll bar with the split in the bush toward the rear of the vehicle.

5 Locate the clamp over the bush, refit the retaining bolt and tighten the bolt to the specified torque.

6 Refit the roadwheel, lower the vehicle to the ground, and tighten the wheel bolts to the specified torque.

Connecting link bushes

7 Firmly apply the handbrake, then jack up the front of the vehicle and support it securely on

12.11b ...then disengage the upper end of the clamp from the subframe slot

axle stands (see *Jacking and vehicle support*). Remove the relevant front roadwheel.

8 Remove the engine undertray as described in Chapter 11, Section 25.

9 At the relevant torsion bar adjustment bolt, measure and record the length of thread projecting from the underside of the adjusting nut to the end of the bolt **(see illustration 2.8)**. This is a critical dimension as it will be needed to determine the vehicle ride height when refitting.

10 Using a spanner or deep socket, unscrew the torsion bar adjusting nut until all load is relieved on the front upper wishbone **(see illustration 2.9)**.

11 On models with a 23 mm diameter anti-roll bar, apply some penetrating oil to the end of the anti-roll bar and the connecting link upper bush. Using a stout bar as a lever, and using the shock absorber as a pivot, lever the connecting link off the anti-roll bar.

12 On models with a 27 mm diameter anti-roll bar, unscrew the connecting link from the end of the anti-roll bar.

13 On all models, undo the nut and remove the bolt securing the anti-roll bar connecting link and the shock absorber to the lower wishbone, and remove the link.

14 To renew the upper rubber bush on models with a 23 mm diameter anti-roll bar, mount the link in a vice and lever the old bush out using a screwdriver **(see illustration)**. Lubricate the

13.3 Spread open the mounting bush and withdraw it from the anti-roll bar

13.14 Lever the anti-roll bar connecting link bush out using a screwdriver

new bush with liquid soap and push it into the connecting link eye.

15 To renew the lower bush, press out the central metal sleeve, then lever out the remaining rubber portion with a screwdriver. Lubricate the new bush with liquid soap and push it into the connecting link eye, then press the metal sleeve back into position.

16 On models with a 27 mm diameter anti-roll bar, screw the connecting link onto the end of the anti-roll bar and tighten it securely.

17 On models with a 23 mm diameter anti-roll bar, thoroughly lubricate the end of the anti-roll bar and the centre of the connecting link bush with liquid soap. Clamp a pair of Mole-grips to the anti-roll bar just inboard of the bush location. Using a suitable puller with its legs engaged behind the Mole-grips, push the connecting link onto the anti-roll bar. Place a strip of metal or similar across the bush for the puller to push on **(see illustration)**. Once the bush is initially in place, remove the puller and grips and push the link on the rest of the way until it fully engages with the depression in the anti-roll bar.

18 Refit the anti-roll bar connecting link and shock absorber retaining bolt. Note that the bolt head is toward the rear of the vehicle. Refit the retaining nut and tighten it to the specified torque.

19 Tighten the torsion bar adjusting nut until the exposed thread dimension recorded during removal is obtained.

20 Refit the engine undertray as described in Chapter 11, Section 25.

21 Refit the roadwheel, lower the vehicle to the ground, and tighten the wheel bolts to the specified torque.

14 Front subframe – removal and refitting

Removal

1 Firmly apply the handbrake, then jack up the front of the vehicle and support it securely on axle stands (see *Jacking and vehicle support*). Remove the front roadwheels.

2 Remove the engine undertray as described in Chapter 11, Section 25.

3 Unbolt and remove the front brake calipers complete with disc pads and mounting brackets and suspend them from a convenient place under the wheel arch using cable ties **(see illustrations 2.3a and 2.3b)**. Do not allow the calipers to hang unsupported from the flexible brake hoses.

4 On vehicles with ABS, disconnect the front wheel speed sensor wiring at the connector.

5 Remove the fuel tank as described in Chapter 4A, Section 7.

6 On later models, undo the three nuts, remove the bolts and disconnect the exhaust system front pipe at the flange joint. Recover the flange gasket. It may be necessary to release the front part of the exhaust system from its mountings so that there is a clearance between the front pipe flange and the rest of the system. When the subframe is lowered, the right-hand torsion bar must pass through at this point.

7 Remove the exhaust system heat shield.

8 At the torsion bar adjustment bolt on each side, measure and record the length of thread projecting from the underside of the adjusting nut to the end of the bolt **(see illustration 2.8)**. This is a critical dimension as it will be needed to determine the vehicle ride height when refitting.

9 Using a spanner or deep socket, unscrew the torsion bar adjusting nut on each side until all load is relieved on the front upper wishbones **(see illustration 2.9)**.

10 Once the load is relieved on the upper wishbones fully unscrew each torsion bar adjusting nut and remove it from the adjusting bolt **(see illustration 10.7)**.

11 Turn each adjusting bolt through 90° and remove it from its location in the underbody **(see illustrations 10.8a and 10.8b)**.

12 Remove the thrust pad located over each torsion bar adjustment arm **(see illustration 10.9)**.

13 Slide up the rubber gaiter, then unscrew the nut and remove the bolt securing the lower steering column shaft to the steering gear pinion **(see illustration 12.8)**. Note that a new nut and bolt will be required for refitting. Use paint or a suitable marker pen to make alignment marks between the shaft and the steering gear pinion.

14 On models with power steering, clamp both the supply and return hoses near the power steering fluid reservoir using brake hose clamps. This will minimise fluid loss during subsequent operations.

15 Mark the unions to ensure that they are correctly positioned on reassembly, then unscrew the feed and return pipe unions from the steering gear assembly; be prepared for fluid spillage, and position a suitable container beneath the pipes whilst unscrewing the unions. Disconnect both pipes and recover the sealing rings; discard the rings new ones must be used on refitting. Plug the pipe ends and steering gear orifices, to prevent fluid leakage and to keep dirt out of the hydraulic system.

16 Undo and remove the bolts securing the inner driveshaft joints to the transmission flanges and recover the retaining plates from underneath the bolts.

17 On early models, undo the two bolts securing the rear engine mounting to the subframe. On later models, undo the through bolt securing the rear engine mounting link bracket to the transmission **(see illustration)**.

18 Support the subframe with a cradle across a trolley jack. Alternatively, two trolley jacks and the help of an assistant will be required.

19 Undo the four bolts each side securing the subframe to the underbody. Slowly and carefully lower the subframe to the ground, guiding the right-hand torsion bar through the exhaust front pipe separation point, where necessary. As the subframe is lowered, make sure there are no cables or wiring still attached.

20 If necessary remove the components attached to the subframe with reference to the relevant Sections of this Chapter.

13.17 Using Mole-grips, a strip of metal and a puller to fit the connecting link to the anti-roll bar

14.17 On later models, undo the through bolt securing the rear engine mounting link bracket to the transmission

Refitting

21 Refitting is a reversal of removal, bearing in mind the following points:
 a) *Tighten all nuts and bolts to the specified torque and, where necessary, through the specified angle.*
 b) *Tighten the torsion bar adjusting nut until the exposed thread dimension recorded during removal is obtained.*
 c) *Refit the fuel tank as described in Chapter 4A, Section 7.*
 d) *Refit the engine undertray as described in Chapter 11, Section 25.*
 e) *On models with power steering, top-up the power steering fluid reservoir as described in 'Weekly checks'.*

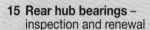

15 Rear hub bearings – inspection and renewal

Inspection

1 The rear hub bearings are of sealed, pre-adjusted and prelubricated, double-row ball type, and are intended to last the vehicle's entire service life without maintenance or attention.
2 To check the bearings for excessive wear, chock the front wheels, then jack up the rear of the vehicle, and support it securely on axle stands (see *Jacking and vehicle support*).
3 Grip the rear wheel at the top and bottom and attempt to rock it. If excessive movement is noted, it is quite likely that the hub bearings are worn. Hub bearing wear will also show up as roughness or vibration when the wheel is spun; it will also be noticeable as a rumbling or growling noise when driving.

Renewal

Note: *A suitable puller arrangement or improvisation will be required for this operation (see text).*
4 If not already done, chock the front wheels, then jack up the rear of the vehicle, and support it securely on axle stands (see *Jacking and vehicle support*). Remove the relevant wheel.
5 On models with rear drum brakes, remove the brake shoes as described in Chapter 9, Section 10, then remove the rear wheel cylinder as described in Chapter 9, Section 14.

15.10 With the tool in place, remove the hub flange from the bearing

15.8a Unscrew the nut from the rear hub flange retaining bolt...

15.8c ...and the bolt and washer

Undo the retaining bolts and remove the brake backplate from the trailing arm.
6 On models with rear disc brakes, remove the brake disc as described in Chapter 9, Section 12. Undo the retaining bolts and remove the brake backplate from the trailing arm.
7 On models with ABS, undo the retaining bolt and remove the rear wheel speed sensor from the trailing arm.
8 Unscrew the nut from the rear hub flange retaining bolt, then remove the tensioning disc and the bolt and washer **(see illustrations)**.
9 It is now necessary to prepare a puller arrangement capable of removing the hub flange from the bearing, then removing the bearing from the trailing arm. Due to the effects of rust and corrosion the hub flange and bearing will be very difficult to remove and even the genuine VW special tool has been

15.11a Remove the bearing front plate...

15.8b ...then remove the tensioning disc...

15.9 Improvised puller arrangement for removal of the rear hub flange from the bearing

known to fail during removal. The arrangement we used consisted of a two-piece gear puller placed against the outer face of the wishbone with a hydraulic ram type puller attached to it. The hydraulic ram puller was positioned behind the bearing in contact with a tube of suitable diameter to enable the hub flange to be pushed out **(see illustration)**. Obviously the method chosen will depend entirely on the tools and materials available and will have to be somewhat of an improvisation. Ensure that adequate safety precautions are taken during the whole removal and refitting procedure.
10 With the improvised tool in place, remove the hub flange from the bearing **(see illustration)**.
11 With the hub flange removed from hub assembly, remove the bearing front plate, then remove the outer bearing inner race using a knife-edge bearing puller **(see illustrations)**.

15.11b ...then remove the outer bearing inner race using a knife-edge bearing puller

15.12 Extract the bearing retaining circlip from the trailing arm

15.13 With the tool in place, remove the bearing from the trailing arm

15.16a Place the fitting tool in the trailing arm...

15.16b ...locate the new bearing in position...

15.16c ...assemble the rest of the fitting tool...

15.16d ...and draw the bearing into position in the trailing arm

15.17 Secure the bearing in position with a new circlip

15.18 Using the bush renewal tool to draw the hub flange into position in the bearing

15.19a Refit the hub flange retaining bolt and washer...

15.19b ...tensioning disc...

15.19c ...and retaining nut

12 Extract the bearing retaining circlip from the trailing arm (see illustration).
13 Using a similar puller arrangement to that just used, push the bearing out of the trailing arm (see illustration).
14 Thoroughly clean the hub flange and trailing arm, removing all traces of dirt, grease and corrosion, then polish away any burrs or raised edges which might hinder reassembly. Check all components for cracks or any other signs of wear or damage, and renew as necessary. Renew the circlip, regardless of its apparent condition.

15 A commercially available bush renewal tool was used to fit the new bearing. Once all the corrosion has been removed from the trailing arm, fitting the new bearing is relatively straightforward, compared to removal.
16 Place the fitting tool in the trailing arm and locate the new bearing in position. Assemble the rest of the fitting tool and draw the bearing into position in the arm (see illustrations).
17 Once the bearing is correctly seated, secure the bearing in position with the new circlip, ensuring it is correctly located in the groove in the trailing arm (see illustration).
18 The bush renewal tool can also be used to draw the hub flange into position in the bearing. Using an attachment that bears only on the inner race of the hub bearing, draw the flange into the bearing until it seats against the bearing (see illustration).
19 Refit the hub flange retaining bolt and washer, tensioning disc and retaining nut,

then tighten the nut to the specified torque **(see illustrations)**.

20 On models with ABS, refit the wheel speed sensor and secure with the retaining bolt tightened securely.

21 On models with rear disc brakes, refit the brake backplate to the trailing arm and tighten the retaining bolts securely. Refit the brake disc as described in Chapter 9, Section 12.

22 On models with rear drum brakes, refit the brake backplate to the trailing arm and tighten the retaining bolts securely. Refit the wheel cylinder as described in Chapter 9, Section 14, then refit the brake shoes as described in Chapter 9, Section 10. On completion bleed the brake hydraulic system as described in Chapter 9, Section 2.

23 Refit the roadwheel, lower the vehicle to the ground, and tighten the wheel bolts to the specified torque.

16 Rear shock absorber – removal and refitting
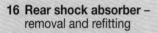

Note: *Always renew shock absorbers in pairs to maintain good road handling.*

Removal

1 Chock the front wheels then jack up the rear of the vehicle and securely support it on axle stands (see *Jacking and vehicle support*). Remove the rear roadwheel.

2 Using a trolley jack, slightly raise the trailing arm on the relevant side.

3 Unscrew and remove the shock absorber upper mounting bolt **(see illustration)**.

4 Using a large open-ended spanner, hold the base of the shock absorber body to prevent rotation, then unscrew and remove the shock absorber lower mounting bolt. Collect the mounting plate and lower mounting rubber.

5 Remove the shock absorber from its location and collect the upper mounting rubber.

6 To test the shock absorber for efficiency, grip the lower mounting eye in a vice, and then pump the piston repeatedly through its full stroke. If the resistance is weak or is felt to be uneven, the shock absorber is defective and must be renewed. It must also be renewed if it is leaking fluid. It is advisable to renew both front shock absorbers at the same time, or the handling characteristics of the vehicle could be adversely affected. Also check the condition of the mounting rubbers and renew any that are deformed or perished.

Refitting

7 Refitting is a reversal of removal, bearing in mind the following points:
 a) *Fit the mounting plate with its concave side towards the shock absorber.*
 b) *Tighten the mounting bolts to the specified torque.*

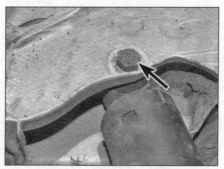

16.3 Shock absorber upper mounting bolt (arrowed)

17 Rear coil spring – removal and refitting
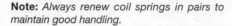

Note: *Always renew coil springs in pairs to maintain good handling.*

Removal

1 Chock the front wheels, then jack up the rear of the vehicle, and support it securely on axle stands (see *Jacking and vehicle support*). Remove the relevant rear roadwheel.

2 Position a trolley jack under the trailing arm and raise the arm slightly.

3 Unscrew and remove the shock absorber upper mounting bolt **(see illustration 16.3)**.

4 Carefully lower the trailing arm until all tension is removed from the coil spring.

18.2 Detach the handbrake cable return spring from the bracket on the underbody

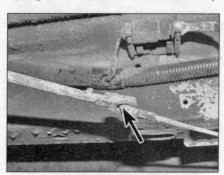

18.4 Unhook the relevant pull rod (arrowed) from the rear handbrake cable

5 Remove the coil spring from the underbody and trailing arm, and withdraw from under the vehicle.

Refitting

6 Refitting is a reversal of removal, but note the following points.
 a) *Fit the spring with the paint mark towards the rear of the vehicle.*
 b) *Ensure that the spring locates correctly on the upper and lower seats.*
 c) *Tighten the shock absorber upper mounting bolt to the specified torque.*

18 Rear suspension trailing arm – removal and refitting

Removal

1 Chock the front wheels, then jack up the rear of the vehicle, and support it securely on axle stands (see *Jacking and vehicle support*). Remove the relevant rear roadwheel.

2 Detach the handbrake cable return spring from the bracket on the underbody, then unscrew the spring holder from the end of the front handbrake cable **(see illustration)**.

3 Unscrew the handbrake adjusting nut and remove it from the end of the front handbrake cable **(see illustration)**.

4 Unhook the relevant pull rod from the rear handbrake cable **(see illustration)**.

5 Release the outer cable from the bracket on the underbody **(see illustration)**.

18.3 Unscrew the handbrake adjusting nut from the end of the front handbrake cable

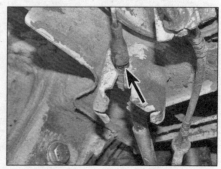

18.5 Release the outer handbrake cable from the bracket on the underbody

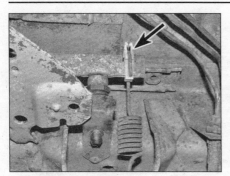

18.11 Unhook the brake pressure regulator tension spring (arrowed) from the horizontal beam

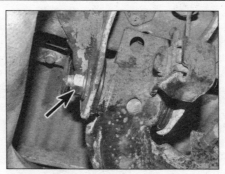

18.14a Trailing arm inner mounting bolt retaining nut (arrowed)...

18.14b ...and outer retaining bolt nut (arrowed)

6 On models with ABS, disconnect the rear wheel speed sensor wiring at the connector on the underbody.

7 Where applicable, disconnect the brake pad wear sensor wiring at the connector on the underbody.

8 Using two brake hose clamps, clamp the flexible hydraulic hoses leading to the rear axle.

9 Unscrew the union nut and disconnect the rear brake hydraulic pipe from the flexible hose at the support bracket on the trailing arm. Be prepared for some loss of brake fluid, and plug or tape over the ends of the pipe and hose to prevent the entry of dust and dirt.

10 Extract the retaining clip and release the brake flexible hose from the support bracket on the trailing arm.

11 Where fitted, unhook the upper end of the brake pressure regulator tension spring from the horizontal beam **(see illustration)**.

12 Remove the rear coil spring as described in Section 17.

13 Mark the fitted position of the trailing arm inner mounting bolt in relation to the mounting bracket. The position of the mounting bolt determines the rear wheel toe-setting and it must be refitted in the same position to preserve the setting.

14 Undo the nuts from the trailing arm inner and outer mounting bolts **(see illustrations)**. Suitably support the trailing arm on a trolley jack, then remove the two mounting bolts. Lower the jack and remove the trailing arm from under the vehicle.

15 If necessary, remove the components remaining on the trailing arm with reference to the relevant Chapters of this manual.

Refitting

16 Refitting is a reversal of removal, but note the following points.

a) *Ensure that the trailing arm inner mounting bolt is fitted in the position marked during removal.*

b) *Raise the trailing arm to approximately its normal running height before tightening the mounting bolts to the specified torque.*

c) *Refit the rear coil spring as described in Section 17.*

d) *Bleed the brake hydraulic system as described in Chapter 9, Section 2.*

e) *Adjust the handbrake as described in Chapter 9, Section 17.*

f) *It is advisable to have the rear wheel alignment checked, and if necessary adjusted, at the earliest opportunity.*

19 Rear suspension trailing arm bushes – renewal

Note: *A commercially available bush renewal tool will be required for this operation. The renewal procedure is the same for both the inner and outer bushes*

1 Remove the relevant trailing arm as described in Section 18.

2 To aid removal of the old bush, cut off the bush shoulder from one end of the bush **(see illustration)**.

3 Assemble the bush renewal tool over the trailing arm and old bush, then use a suitable socket to drive the bush out of the trailing arm **(see illustration)**.

4 Thoroughly clean the bush location area in the trailing arm and polish away any burrs or raised edges which might hinder fitment of the new bush.

5 Liberally lubricate the trailing arm and the new bush with liquid soap, then locate the bush in the trailing arm. Assemble the bush renewal tool and push the bush into the arm until the bush shoulders project equally on both sides **(see illustration)**. It may be necessary to push the bush back slightly after initially fitting it, to achieve equal projection of the shoulders.

6 On completion, refit the trailing arm as described in Section 18.

20 Steering wheel – removal and refitting

Models without airbag

Removal

1 Set the front wheels in the straight-ahead position, and engage the steering lock.

2 Carefully unclip the steering wheel centre pad, and remove it from the wheel.

19.2 Cut off the shoulder from one end of the trailing arm bush

19.3 Using a bush renewal tool to remove a trailing arm bush

19.5 Assemble the bush renewal tool and push the new bush into the trailing arm

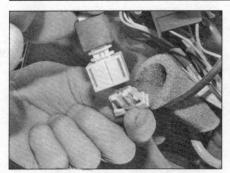
20.9 Disconnect the airbag contact unit wiring connector

20.10a Undo the steering wheel retaining nut...

20.10b ...and remove the washer

20.11a Undo the airbag contact unit locking plate screw (arrowed)...

20.11b ...then remove the locking plate and disconnect the earth lead

20.12 Mark the steering wheel and steering column shaft then lift off the steering wheel

3 Slacken and remove the steering wheel retaining nut.
4 Mark the steering wheel and steering column shaft in relation to each other, then lift the steering wheel off the column splines.

Refitting

5 Refitting is a reversal of removal, bearing in mind the following points:
 a) *Prior to refitting, ensure that the indicator switch stem is in its central position. Failure to do this could lead to the steering wheel lug breaking the switch tab as the steering wheel is refitted.*
 b) *On refitting, align the marks made on removal, and tighten the retaining nut to the specified torque.*

Models with airbag

⚠ *Warning: Make sure that the airbag safety recommendations given in Chapter 12, Section 19 are followed, to prevent personal injury.*

Removal

6 Remove the airbag as described in Chapter 12, Section 20.
7 Remove the steering column shrouds as described in Chapter 11, Section 29.
8 Set the front wheels in the straight-ahead position, then lock the column in position after removing the ignition key.
9 Locate the airbag contact unit wiring connector and disconnect it **(see illustration)**.

10 Undo the steering wheel retaining nut and remove the washer **(see illustrations)**.
11 Where fitted, undo the screw securing the airbag contact unit locking plate to the steering wheel. Remove the locking plate and disconnect the earth lead **(see illustrations)**.
12 Mark the steering wheel and steering column shaft in relation to each other then lift the steering wheel off the column splines, taking care not to damage the contact unit wiring **(see illustration)**.

Refitting

13 Refitting is a reversal of removal. Align the marks made on removal and tighten the retaining nut to the specified torque.

21 Ignition switch/ steering column lock – removal and refitting

Note: *A new lock assembly shear-bolt will be required on refitting.*

Removal

1 Disconnect the battery negative terminal (refer to *Disconnecting the battery*). Insert the key into the lock, and turn it to release the steering lock.
2 Remove the steering wheel as described in Section 20.
3 If not already done, remove the steering column shrouds as described in Chapter 11, Section 29.

4 Disconnect the wiring connectors from the steering column combination switches. Undo the retaining screws, and remove both switch assemblies.
5 Using a puller, carefully draw the splined collar off from the top of the steering column and recover the spring **(see illustration)**.
6 The lock assembly is secured in position with a shear-bolt. The shear-bolt can be extracted using a hammer and suitable chisel to tap the bolt head around until it can be unscrewed by hand. Alternatively, drill a hole in the centre of the bolt head, and extract it using a bolt/stud extractor (sometimes called an 'easy-out').
7 Disconnect the wiring connector, then slide the lock assembly upwards and off the steering column.

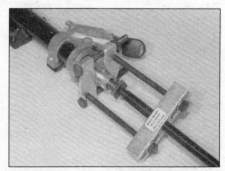
21.5 Draw the splined collar off the steering column using a suitable puller (column removed for clarity)

21.8a Undo the retaining screw...

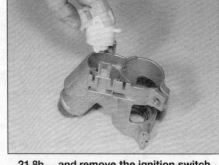

21.8b ...and remove the ignition switch from the steering column lock assembly

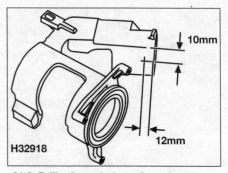

21.9 Drill a 3 mm hole at the point shown to reveal the lock cylinder detent plunger

21.12a Refit the spring and splined collar to the top of the steering column...

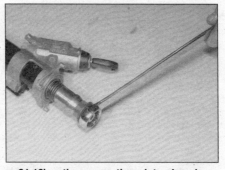

21.12b ...then press them into place by fitting and tightening the steering wheel nut

8 With the lock assembly removed, slacken the retaining screw and remove the ignition switch from the base of the lock assembly **(see illustrations)**.

9 To renew the lock cylinder, carefully drill a 3 mm diameter hole in the side of the lock casting at the point shown in **illustration 21.9**. Depress the lock detent plunger, and withdraw the cylinder from the casting. Slide the new lock cylinder into position, and check it is securely retained by the detent plunger. **Note:** *Renewal of the lock cylinder is a tricky operation, and it is recommended that it is entrusted to a VW dealer. If the hole is not accurately drilled, the lock assembly casting will be ruined, and the complete lock assembly will have to be renewed.*

Refitting

10 Fit the ignition switch (where removed) to the lock assembly, making sure it is correctly

engaged with the lock cylinder, and securely tighten its retaining screw.

11 Slide the lock assembly onto the column, aligning it with the column lug, and fit the new shear-bolt. Tighten the bolt by hand only at this stage, and reconnect the wiring connector.

12 Fit the spring to the top of the column, and fit the splined collar to the shaft. Fit a washer over the end of the collar, then refit the steering wheel retaining nut, and use the nut to press the collar fully onto the steering column shaft **(see illustrations)**. Once the collar is securely seated, unscrew the nut and remove the washer.

13 Check the operation of the steering column lock. If all is well, tighten the shear-bolt until its head breaks off.

14 Reconnect the wiring connectors to the combination switches, and securely tighten the switch retaining screws.

15 Refit the steering wheel as described in Section 20.

16 If not already done, refit the steering column shrouds as described in Chapter 11, Section 29. On completion, reconnect the battery and check the operation of the switches.

22 Steering column – removal and refitting

Removal

Note: *The following information is only applicable to January 1996 models onward. At the time of writing, information relating to pre-January 1996 models was unavailable.*

1 Disconnect the battery negative terminal (refer to *Disconnecting the battery*).

2 Turn the retaining catch anti-clockwise and open the driver's side stowage box fully. Lift the stowage box out of the lower retainers and remove it from the facia **(see illustrations)**.

3 Remove the steering column shrouds as described in Chapter 11, Section 29.

4 Remove the steering wheel as described in Section 20.

5 Remove the steering column combination switches as described in Chapter 12, Section 4.

6 Disconnect the remaining steering column wiring connectors, then release the cable ties securing the wiring harness to the column.

7 Remove the footwell vent console at the base of the facia as described in Chapter 11, Section 29.

8 Unscrew the nut and remove the bolt

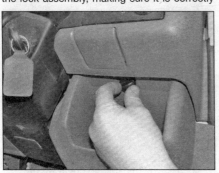

22.2a Turn the retaining catch anti-clockwise...

22.2b ...and open the driver's side stowage box fully

22.8 Unscrew the nut (arrowed) and remove the universal joint clamp bolt securing the steering column intermediate shaft universal joint to the lower steering column shaft **(see illustration)**. Note that a new nut and bolt will be required for refitting. Use paint or a suitable marker pen to make alignment marks between the universal joint and column shaft, then lift the joint off the shaft.

9 Unbolt the support bracket from the steering column **(see illustration)**.

10 Undo the steering column front mounting bolt **(see illustration)**.

11 Undo the steering column rear mounting bolt and manipulate the column assembly out from its location.

Refitting

12 Refitting is a reversal of removal, bearing in mind the following points:
a) *Tighten the steering column mounting bolts to the specified torque.*
b) *Align the mark made on removal when refitting the intermediate shaft universal joint and use a new nut and bolt tightened to the specified torque.*
c) *Refit the footwell vent console as described in Chapter 11, Section 29.*
d) *Refit the steering column combination switches as described in Chapter 12, Section 4.*
e) *Refit the steering wheel as described in Section 20.*
f) *Refit the steering column shrouds as described in Chapter 11, Section 29.*

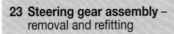

23 Steering gear assembly – removal and refitting

Manual steering gear

Removal

1 Firmly apply the handbrake, then jack up the front of the vehicle and support it securely on axle stands (see *Jacking and vehicle support*). Remove both front roadwheels.

2 Remove the engine undertray as described in Chapter 11, Section 25.

3 Slacken and remove the nuts securing the steering gear track rod end balljoints to the swivel hubs, and release the balljoint tapered shanks using a universal balljoint separator.

4 Undo the retaining nut, remove the washer and separate the steering damper from the mounting bracket on the steering gear. Unbolt the other end of the damper and remove it from under the vehicle.

5 Slide up the rubber gaiter (where fitted), then unscrew the nut and remove the bolt securing the lower steering column shaft to the steering gear pinion. Note that a new nut and bolt will be required for refitting. Use paint or a suitable marker pen to make alignment marks between the shaft and the steering gear pinion.

6 Undo the four bolts securing the steering gear to the front subframe. Disengage the lower steering column shaft from the steering

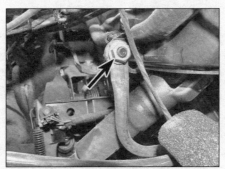

22.9 Unbolt the support bracket (arrowed) from the steering column

gear pinion and manipulate the steering gear out through the opening between the subframe and the underbody.

Refitting

7 Refitting is a reversal of removal, bearing in mind the following points:
a) *Tighten all nuts and bolts to the specified torque.*
b) *Align the mark made on removal when refitting the lower steering column shaft to the steering gear pinion and use a new nut and bolt tightened to the specified torque.*
c) *Refit the engine undertray as described in Chapter 11, Section 25.*

Power-assisted steering gear

Removal

8 Firmly apply the handbrake, then jack up the front of the vehicle and support it securely on axle stands (see *Jacking and vehicle support*). Remove both front roadwheels.

9 Remove the engine undertray as described in Chapter 11, Section 25.

10 At the torsion bar adjustment bolt on each side, measure and record the length of thread projecting from the underside of the adjusting nut to the end of the bolt **(see illustration 2.8)**. This is a critical dimension as it will be needed to determine the vehicle ride height when refitting.

11 Using a spanner or deep socket, unscrew the torsion bar adjusting nut on each side until all load is relieved on the front upper wishbones **(see illustration 2.9)**.

12 Remove the exhaust system front pipe as described in Chapter 4A, Section 19.

13 Release the rubber gaiters from the steering gear on each side and move them down the track rods slightly.

14 Using a 34 mm AF open ended spanner, unscrew the track rod inner balljoints from the steering gear on each side.

15 Slide up the rubber gaiter, then unscrew the nut and remove the bolt securing the lower steering column shaft to the steering gear pinion **(see illustration 12.8)**. Note that a new nut and bolt will be required for refitting. Use paint or a suitable marker pen to make alignment marks between the shaft and the steering gear pinion.

16 Using brake hose clamps, clamp both

22.10 Steering column front mounting bolt (arrowed)

the supply and return hoses near the power steering fluid reservoir. This will minimise fluid loss during subsequent operations.

17 Mark the unions to ensure that they are correctly positioned on reassembly, then unscrew the feed and return pipe union nuts from the steering gear assembly; be prepared for fluid spillage, and position a suitable container beneath the pipes whilst unscrewing the union nuts. Disconnect both pipes, and recover their sealing rings. Plug the pipe ends and steering gear orifices, to prevent fluid leakage and to keep dirt out of the hydraulic system. Release the pipes from the retaining brackets on the steering gear.

18 Undo the bolt each side securing the anti-roll bar clamps to the subframe. Disengage the upper end of each clamp from the subframe slot and remove both clamps **(see illustrations 12.11a and 12.11b)**.

19 Undo the four bolts securing the steering gear to the front subframe.

20 Push the anti-roll bar upwards, then move the steering gear sideways to disengage the lower steering column shaft from the steering gear pinion.

21 Manipulate the steering gear out from its location.

Refitting

22 Place the steering gear in position and engage the lower steering column shaft with the steering gear pinnion. Ensure that the marks made on removal are aligned. Fit the new clamp bolt and nut and tighten to the specified torque.

23 Refit the four steering gear retaining bolts and tighten them to the specified torque.

24 Manipulate the anti-roll bar back into place and refit the two clamps. Tighten the clamp bolts to the specified torque.

25 Wipe clean the feed and return pipe unions, then refit them to their respective positions on the steering gear, and tighten the union nuts to the specified torque. Ensure that the pipes are correctly routed, and are securely held by all the necessary retaining clips and brackets. Remove the brake hose clamps from the supply and return hoses.

26 Screw the track rods onto the steering gear and tighten the inner balljoints to the specified torque. Secure the rubber gaiters back into position.

26.14 Unscrew the retaining bolts (arrowed) and remove the power steering pump pulley

27 Refit the exhaust system front pipe as described in Chapter 4A, Section 19.
28 Tighten the torsion bar adjusting nuts until the exposed thread dimensions recorded during removal are obtained.
29 Refit the engine undertray as described in Chapter 11, Section 25.
30 Refit the roadwheels, lower the vehicle to the ground, and tighten the wheel bolts to the specified torque.
31 Bleed the power steering system as described in Section 25.

24 Steering gear rubber gaiters – renewal

1 Remove the relevant track rod end as described in Section 27.
2 Mark the correct fitted position of the gaiter on the track rod, then release the retaining clip(s) and slide the gaiter off the steering gear housing and track rod.
3 Thoroughly clean the track rod and the steering gear housing, using fine abrasive paper to polish off any corrosion, burrs or sharp edges, which might damage the new gaiter's sealing lips on installation. Scrape off all the grease from the old gaiter, and apply it to the track rod inner balljoint. (This assumes that grease has not been lost or contaminated as a result of damage to the old gaiter. Use fresh grease if in doubt).
4 Carefully slide the new gaiter onto the track rod, and locate it on the steering gear housing. Align the outer edge of the gaiter with the mark made on the track rod prior to removal. Make sure the gaiter is not twisted, then lift the outer sealing lip of the gaiter to equalise air pressure within the gaiter.
5 Secure it in position with new retaining clip(s). Where crimped-type clips are used, pull the clip as tight as possible, and locate the hooks on the clip in their slots. Remove any slack in the gaiter retaining clip by carefully compressing the raised section of the clip. In the absence of the special tool, a pair of side cutters may be used, taking care not to actually cut the clip.
6 Refit the track rod end as described in Section 27.

25 Power steering hydraulic system – bleeding

1 This procedure will only be necessary when any part of the hydraulic system has been disconnected.
2 Referring to *Weekly checks*, remove the fluid reservoir filler cap, and top-up with the specified fluid to the MAX level mark on the dipstick.
3 Firmly apply the handbrake, then jack up the front of the vehicle and support it securely on axle stands (see *Jacking and vehicle support*).
4 With the engine stopped, quickly move the steering from lock-to-lock several times to purge out the trapped air, then top-up the level in the fluid reservoir. Repeat this procedure until the fluid level in the reservoir does not drop any further.
5 Lower the vehicle to the ground again and top-up the fluid level to the MAX level mark.
6 Start the engine and allow it to idle for approximately two minutes with the front wheels in the straight-ahead position. Whilst the engine is running, keep an eye on the fluid level in the reservoir. Once air bubbles stop appearing in the fluid reservoir, switch off the engine.
7 Check that fluid level is up to the upper mark on the power steering fluid reservoir, topping-up if necessary then securely refit the reservoir cap. **Note:** *If an abnormal noise is heard from the fluid lines when the steering wheel is turned, it indicates that there is still air in the system and further bleeding is necessary.*

26 Power steering pump – removal and refitting

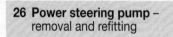

4-cylinder engines

Removal

1 Remove the power steering pump V-belt as described in Chapter 1, Section 28.
2 Using brake hose clamps, clamp both the supply and return hoses near the power steering fluid reservoir. This will minimise fluid loss during subsequent operations.
3 Slacken the retaining clip, and disconnect the fluid supply hose from the pump. Where a crimp-type clip is still fitted, cut the clip and discard it; replace it with a standard worm-drive hose clip on refitting. Slacken the union bolt, and disconnect the feed pipe from the pump, along with its sealing washers; discard the washers – new ones should be used on refitting. Be prepared for some fluid spillage as the pipe and hose are disconnected, and plug the hose/pipe end and pump unions, to minimise fluid loss and prevent the entry of dirt into the system.

4 Slacken and remove the three bolts securing the power steering pump to its mounting bracket, and remove the pump from the engine compartment.
5 If the power steering pump is faulty it must be renewed. The pump is a sealed unit and cannot be overhauled.

Refitting

6 Prior to fitting, ensure that the pump is primed by injecting hydraulic fluid in through the supply hose union and rotating the pump shaft.
7 Manoeuvre the pump into position and refit the mounting bolts, tightening them to the specified torque.
8 Position a new sealing washer on each side of the feed pipe union, then fit the union bolt and tighten it to the specified torque setting. Refit the supply pipe to the pump, and securely tighten its retaining clip. Remove the brake hose clamps used to minimise fluid loss.
9 Refit the drive pulley, making sure it is the correct way around, and fit its retaining bolts.
10 Refit the V-belt to the pump pulley, and tension it as described in Chapter 1, Section 28.
11 On completion, bleed the hydraulic system as described in Section 25.

5-cylinder engines

Removal

12 Remove the power steering pump V-belt or ribbed auxiliary belt (as applicable) as described in Chapter 2B, Section 8
13 Using brake hose clamps, clamp both the supply and return hoses near the power steering fluid reservoir. This will minimise fluid loss during subsequent operations.
14 Unscrew the retaining bolts and remove the pulley from the pump (see illustration).
15 Wipe clean the area around the power steering pump fluid pipe unions.
16 On early models, unscrew the pipe union and disconnect the fluid supply pipe from the pump then slacken the union bolt and disconnect the outlet pipe. Be prepared for some fluid spillage as the pipes are disconnected, and plug the pipe ends and pump unions, to minimise fluid loss and prevent the entry of dirt into the system. Discard the outlet pipe sealing rings; new ones must be used on refitting.
17 On later models, slacken the retaining clip and disconnect the fluid supply hose from the pump then slacken the union bolt and disconnect the outlet pipe. Be prepared for some fluid spillage as the pipe and hose are disconnected, and plug the hose/pipe ends and pump unions, to minimise fluid loss and prevent the entry of dirt into the system. Discard the outlet pipe sealing rings; new ones must be used on refitting.
18 Slacken and remove the pump mounting bolts and withdraw the pump from its bracket (see illustration).

19 If the power steering pump is faulty it must be renewed. The pump is a sealed unit and cannot be overhauled.

Refitting

20 Prior to fitting, ensure that the pump is primed by injecting hydraulic fluid in through the supply hose union and rotating the pump shaft.

21 Manoeuvre the pump into position and refit the mounting bolts, tightening them to the specified torque.

22 Fit a new sealing ring to each side of the hydraulic pipe end fitting then reconnect the pipe to the pump and screw in the union bolt. Ensure the pipe is correctly routed then tighten the union bolt to the specified torque.

23 On early models, fit a new seal to the fluid supply pipe then screw the pipe union into the pump and tighten it securely. On later engines, reconnect the supply hose to the pump and secure it in position with the retaining clip. On all engines, remove the brake hose clamps used to minimise fluid loss.

24 Refit the pulley to the pump then screw in the retaining bolts and tighten them to the specified torque.

25 Refit the power steering pump V-belt or ribbed auxiliary belt (as applicable) as described in Chapter 2B, Section 8.

26 On completion, bleed the hydraulic system as described in Section 25.

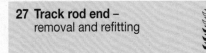

27 Track rod end –
removal and refitting

Removal

1 Firmly apply the handbrake, then jack up the front of the vehicle and support it securely on axle stands (see *Jacking and vehicle support*). Remove the relevant front roadwheel.

2 If the track rod end is to be re-used, use a straight-edge and a scriber, or similar, to mark its relationship to the track rod.

3 Hold the track rod, and unscrew the track rod end locknut by a quarter of a turn. Do not move the locknut from this position, as it will serve as a handy reference mark on refitting.

4 Slacken and remove the nut securing the track rod balljoint to the swivel hub, and release the balljoint tapered shank using a universal balljoint separator.

5 Counting the **exact** number of turns necessary to do so, unscrew the track rod end from the track rod.

26.18 Power steering pump mounting bolts (arrowed)

6 Count the number of exposed threads between the end of the track rod end and the locknut, and record this figure.

7 Carefully clean the track rod end and the threads. Renew the end if its movement is sloppy or too stiff, if excessively worn, or if damaged in any way; carefully check the stud taper and threads. If the gaiter is damaged, the complete track rod end must be renewed; it is not possible to obtain the gaiter separately.

Refitting

8 Screw the track rod end onto the track rod by the number of turns noted on removal. This should bring the track rod end to within a quarter of a turn from the locknut, with the alignment marks that were made on removal (if applicable) lined up.

9 Bring the locknut back into contact with the track rod end and tighten it securely.

10 Refit the track rod end balljoint shank to the swivel hub, then fit a new retaining nut and tighten it to the specified torque.

11 Refit the engine undertray as described in Chapter 11, Section 25.

12 Refit the roadwheel, lower the vehicle to the ground, and tighten the wheel bolts to the specified torque.

13 It is advisable to have the front wheel alignment checked and, if necessary, adjusted at the earliest opportunity (see Section 28).

28 Wheel alignment
and steering angles –
general information

Definitions

1 A vehicle's steering and suspension geometry is defined in three basic settings – all angles are expressed in degrees (toe settings are also expressed as a measurement); the steering axis is defined as an imaginary line drawn through the axis of the wishbone balljoints, extended where necessary to contact the ground.

2 **Camber** is the angle between each roadwheel and a vertical line drawn through its centre and tyre contact patch, when viewed from the front or rear of the vehicle. Positive camber is when the roadwheels are tilted outwards from the vertical at the top; negative camber is when they are tilted inwards.

3 The front wheel camber angle is adjusted by altering the position of the swivel hub eccentric washer located below the front suspension upper balljoint.

4 The rear wheel camber angle is not adjustable.

5 **Castor** is the angle between the steering axis and a vertical line drawn through each roadwheel's centre and tyre contact patch, when viewed from the side of the vehicle. Positive castor is when the steering axis is tilted so that it contacts the ground ahead of the vertical; negative castor is when it contacts the ground behind the vertical.

6 The front wheel castor angle is adjusted by altering the position of the lower wishbone rear mounting eccentric bolt.

7 **Toe** is the difference, viewed from above, between lines drawn through the roadwheel centres and the vehicle's centre-line. 'Toe-in' is when the roadwheels point inwards, towards each other at the front, while 'toe-out' is when they splay outwards from each other at the front.

8 The front wheel toe setting is adjusted by screwing the track rod in or out of its track rod ends, to alter the effective length of the track rod assembly.

9 Rear wheel toe setting is adjusted by slackening the rear trailing arm inner mounting bolt retaining nut and altering the position of the trailing arm at the inner mounting.

Checking and adjustment

10 Due to the special measuring equipment necessary to check the wheel alignment and steering angles, and the skill required to use it properly, the checking and adjustment of these settings is best left to a VW dealer or similar expert. Note that most tyre-fitting shops now possess sophisticated checking equipment.

Chapter 11
Bodywork and fittings

Contents

Degrees of difficulty

Easy, suitable for novice with little experience | **Fairly easy,** suitable for beginner with some experience | **Fairly difficult,** suitable for competent DIY mechanic | **Difficult,** suitable for experienced DIY mechanic | **Very difficult,** suitable for expert DIY or professional

Specifications

Torque wrench setting	Nm	lbf ft
Seat belt mounting bolts	40	30

1 General information

The bodyshell is conventional welded steel unitary construction available in a number of versions according to vehicle application and territory of export. In addition, an extensive list of optional body, interior and exterior is available to suit each version.

Due to the large number of specialist applications of this vehicle range, information contained in this Chapter is given on parts found to be common on the popular factory-produced versions. No information is provided on special body versions.

2 Maintenance – bodywork and underframe

The general condition of a vehicle's bodywork is the one thing that significantly affects its value. Maintenance is easy, but needs to be regular. Neglect, particularly after minor damage, can lead quickly to further deterioration and costly repair bills. It is important also to keep watch on those parts of the vehicle not immediately visible, for instance the underside, inside all the wheel arches, and the lower part of the engine compartment.

The basic maintenance routine for the bodywork is washing – preferably with a lot of water, from a hose. This will remove all the loose solids which may have stuck to the vehicle. It is important to flush these off in such a way as to prevent grit from scratching the finish. The wheel arches and underframe need washing in the same way, to remove any accumulated mud, which will retain moisture and tend to encourage rust. Paradoxically enough, the best time to clean the underframe and wheel arches is in wet weather, when the mud is thoroughly wet and soft. In very wet weather, the underframe is usually cleaned of large accumulations automatically, and this is a good time for inspection.

Periodically, except on vehicles with a wax-based underbody protective coating, it is a good idea to have the whole of the underframe of the vehicle steam-cleaned, engine compartment included, so that a thorough inspection can be carried out to see what minor repairs and renovations are necessary. Steam-cleaning is available at many garages, and is necessary for the removal of the accumulation of oily grime, which sometimes is allowed to become thick in certain areas. If steam-cleaning facilities are not available, there are some excellent grease solvents available which can be brush-applied; the dirt can then be simply hosed off. Note that these methods should not be used on vehicles with wax-based underbody protective coating, or the coating will be removed. Such vehicles should be inspected annually, preferably just prior to Winter, when the underbody should be washed down, and any damage to the wax coating repaired. Ideally, a completely fresh coat should be applied. It would also be worth considering the use of such wax-based protection for injection into door panels, sills, box sections, etc, as an additional safeguard against rust damage, where such protection is not provided by the vehicle manufacturer.

After washing paintwork, wipe off with a chamois leather to give an unspotted clear finish. A coat of clear protective wax polish will give added protection against chemical pollutants in the air. If the paintwork sheen has dulled or oxidised, use a cleaner/polisher combination to restore the brilliance of the shine. This requires a little effort, but such dulling is usually caused because regular washing has been neglected. Care needs to be taken with metallic paintwork, as special non-abrasive cleaner/polisher is required to avoid damage to the finish. Always check that the door and ventilator opening drain holes and pipes are completely clear, so that water can be drained out. Brightwork should be treated in the same way as paintwork. Windscreens and windows can be kept clear of the smeary film which often appears, by the use of proprietary glass cleaner. Never use any form of wax or other body or chromium polish on glass.

3 Maintenance – upholstery and carpets

Mats and carpets should be brushed or vacuum-cleaned regularly, to keep them free of grit. If they are badly stained, remove them from the vehicle for scrubbing or sponging, and make quite sure they are dry before refitting. Seats and interior trim panels can be kept clean by wiping with a damp cloth. If they do become stained (which can be more apparent on light-coloured upholstery), use a little liquid detergent and a soft nail brush to scour the grime out of the grain of the material. Do not forget to keep the headlining clean in the same way as the upholstery. When using liquid cleaners inside the vehicle, do not over-wet the surfaces being cleaned. Excessive damp could get into the seams and padded interior, causing stains, offensive odours or even rot.

4 Minor body damage – repair

Minor scratches

If the scratch is very superficial, and does not penetrate to the metal of the bodywork, repair is very simple. Lightly rub the area of the scratch with a paintwork renovator, or a very fine cutting paste, to remove loose paint from the scratch, and to clear the surrounding bodywork of wax polish. Rinse the area with clean water.

Apply touch-up paint to the scratch using a fine paint brush; continue to apply fine layers of paint until the surface of the paint in the scratch is level with the surrounding paintwork. Allow the new paint at least two weeks to harden, then blend it into the surrounding paintwork by rubbing the scratch area with a paintwork renovator or a very fine cutting paste. Finally, apply wax polish.

Where the scratch has penetrated right through to the metal of the bodywork, causing the metal to rust, a different repair technique is required. Remove any loose rust from the bottom of the scratch with a penknife, then apply rust-inhibiting paint to prevent the formation of rust in the future. Using a rubber or nylon applicator, fill the scratch with bodystopper paste. If required, this paste can be mixed with cellulose thinners to provide a very thin paste which is ideal for filling narrow scratches. Before the stopper-paste in the scratch hardens, wrap a piece of smooth cotton rag around the top of a finger. Dip the finger in cellulose thinners, and quickly sweep it across the surface of the stopper-paste in the scratch; this will ensure that the surface of the stopper-paste is slightly hollowed. The scratch can now be painted over as described earlier in this Section.

Dents

When deep denting of the vehicle's bodywork has taken place, the first task is to pull the dent out, until the affected bodywork almost attains its original shape. There is little point in trying to restore the original shape completely, as the metal in the damaged area will have stretched on impact, and cannot be reshaped fully to its original contour. It is better to bring the level of the dent up to a point which is about 3 mm below the level of the surrounding bodywork. In cases where the dent is very shallow anyway, it is not worth trying to pull it out at all. If the underside of the dent is accessible, it can be hammered out gently from behind, using a mallet with a wooden or plastic head. Whilst doing this, hold a suitable block of wood firmly against the outside of the panel, to absorb the impact from the hammer blows and thus prevent a large area of the bodywork from being 'belled-out'.

Should the dent be in a section of the bodywork which has a double skin, or some other factor making it inaccessible from behind, a different technique is called for. Drill several small holes through the metal inside the area – particularly in the deeper section. Then screw long self-tapping screws into the holes, just sufficiently for them to gain a good purchase in the metal. Now the dent can be pulled out by pulling on the protruding heads of the screws with a pair of pliers.

The next stage of the repair is the removal of the paint from the damaged area, and from an inch or so of the surrounding 'sound' bodywork. This is accomplished most easily by using a wire brush or abrasive pad on a power

drill, although it can be done just as effectively by hand, using sheets of abrasive paper. To complete the preparation for filling, score the surface of the bare metal with a screwdriver or the tang of a file, or alternatively, drill small holes in the affected area. This will provide a really good 'key' for the filler paste.

To complete the repair, see the Section on filling and respraying.

Rust holes or gashes

Remove all paint from the affected area, and from an inch or so of the surrounding 'sound' bodywork, using an abrasive pad or a wire brush on a power drill. If these are not available, a few sheets of abrasive paper will do the job most effectively. With the paint removed, you will be able to judge the severity of the corrosion, and therefore decide whether to renew the whole panel (if this is possible) or to repair the affected area. New body panels are not as expensive as most people think, and it is often quicker and more satisfactory to fit a new panel than to attempt to repair large areas of corrosion.

Remove all fittings from the affected area, except those which will act as a guide to the original shape of the damaged bodywork (eg headlight shells etc). Then, using tin snips or a hacksaw blade, remove all loose metal and any other metal badly affected by corrosion. Hammer the edges of the hole inwards, in order to create a slight depression for the filler paste.

Wire-brush the affected area to remove the powdery rust from the surface of the remaining metal. Paint the affected area with rust-inhibiting paint, if the back of the rusted area is accessible, treat this also.

Before filling can take place, it will be necessary to block the hole in some way. This can be achieved by the use of aluminium or plastic mesh, or aluminium tape.

Aluminium or plastic mesh, or glass-fibre matting, is probably the best material to use for a large hole. Cut a piece to the approximate size and shape of the hole to be filled, then position it in the hole so that its edges are below the level of the surrounding bodywork. It can be retained in position by several blobs of filler paste around its periphery.

Aluminium tape should be used for small or very narrow holes. Pull a piece off the roll, trim it to the approximate size and shape required, then pull off the backing paper (if used) and stick the tape over the hole; it can be overlapped if the thickness of one piece is insufficient. Burnish down the edges of the tape with the handle of a screwdriver or similar, to ensure that the tape is securely attached to the metal underneath.

Filling and respraying

Before using this Section, see the Sections on dent, deep scratch, rust holes and gash repairs.

Many types of bodyfiller are available, but generally speaking, those proprietary kits which contain a tin of filler paste and a tube of resin hardener are best for this type of repair. A wide, flexible plastic or nylon applicator will be found invaluable for imparting a smooth and well-contoured finish to the surface of the filler.

Mix up a little filler on a clean piece of card or board – measure the hardener carefully (follow the maker's instructions on the pack), otherwise the filler will set too rapidly or too slowly. Using the applicator, apply the filler paste to the prepared area; draw the applicator across the surface of the filler to achieve the correct contour and to level the surface. As soon as a contour that approximates to the correct one is achieved, stop working the paste – if you carry on too long, the paste will become sticky and begin to 'pick-up' on the applicator. Continue to add thin layers of filler paste at 20-minute intervals, until the level of the filler is just proud of the surrounding bodywork.

Once the filler has hardened, the excess can be removed using a metal plane or file. From then on, progressively-finer grades of abrasive paper should be used, starting with a 40-grade production paper, and finishing with a 400-grade wet-and-dry paper. Always wrap the abrasive paper around a flat rubber, cork, or wooden block – otherwise the surface of the filler will not be completely flat. During the smoothing of the filler surface, the wet-and-dry paper should be periodically rinsed in water. This will ensure that a very smooth finish is imparted to the filler at the final stage.

At this stage, the 'dent' should be surrounded by a ring of bare metal, which in turn should be encircled by the finely 'feathered' edge of the good paintwork. Rinse the repair area with clean water, until all of the dust produced by the rubbing-down operation has gone.

Spray the whole area with a light coat of primer – this will show up any imperfections in the surface of the filler. Repair these imperfections with fresh filler paste or bodystopper, and once more smooth the surface with abrasive paper. Repeat this spray-and-repair procedure until you are satisfied that the surface of the filler, and the feathered edge of the paintwork, are perfect. Clean the repair area with clean water, and allow to dry fully.

The repair area is now ready for final spraying. Paint spraying must be carried out in a warm, dry, windless and dust-free atmosphere. This condition can be created artificially if you have access to a large indoor working area, but if you are forced to work in the open, you will have to pick your day very carefully. If you are working indoors, dousing the floor in the work area with water will help to settle the dust which would otherwise be in the atmosphere. If the repair area is confined to one body panel, mask off the surrounding panels; this will help to minimise the effects of a slight mis-match in paint colours. Bodywork

fittings (eg chrome strips, door handles etc) will also need to be masked off. Use genuine masking tape, and several thicknesses of newspaper, for the masking operations.

Before commencing to spray, agitate the aerosol can thoroughly, then spray a test area (an old tin, or similar) until the technique is mastered. Cover the repair area with a thick coat of primer; the thickness should be built up using several thin layers of paint, rather than one thick one. Using 400-grade wet-and-dry paper, rub down the surface of the primer until it is really smooth. While doing this, the work area should be thoroughly doused with water, and the wet-and-dry paper periodically rinsed in water. Allow to dry before spraying on more paint.

Spray on the top coat, again building up the thickness by using several thin layers of paint. Start spraying at one edge of the repair area, and then, using a side-to-side motion, work until the whole repair area and about 2 inches of the surrounding original paintwork is covered. Remove all masking material 10 to 15 minutes after spraying on the final coat of paint.

Allow the new paint at least two weeks to harden, then, using a paintwork renovator, or a very fine cutting paste, blend the edges of the paint into the existing paintwork. Finally, apply wax polish.

Plastic components

With the use of more and more plastic body components by the vehicle manufacturers (eg bumpers. spoilers, and in some cases major body panels), rectification of more serious damage to such items has become a matter of either entrusting repair work to a specialist in this field, or renewing complete components. Repair of such damage by the DIY owner is not really feasible, owing to the cost of the equipment and materials required for effecting such repairs. The basic technique involves making a groove along the line of the crack in the plastic, using a rotary burr in a power drill. The damaged part is then welded back together, using a hot-air gun to heat up and fuse a plastic filler rod into the groove. Any excess plastic is then removed, and the area rubbed down to a smooth finish. It is important that a filler rod of the correct plastic is used, as body components can be made of a variety of different types (eg polycarbonate, ABS, polypropylene).

Damage of a less serious nature (abrasions, minor cracks etc) can be repaired by the DIY owner using a two-part epoxy filler repair material. Once mixed in equal proportions, this is used in similar fashion to the bodywork filler used on metal panels. The filler is usually cured in twenty to thirty minutes, ready for sanding and painting.

If the owner is renewing a complete component himself, or if he has repaired it with epoxy filler, he will be left with the problem of finding a suitable paint for finishing which is compatible with the type

of plastic used. At one time, the use of a universal paint was not possible, owing to the complex range of plastics encountered in body component applications. Standard paints, generally speaking, will not bond to plastic or rubber satisfactorily. However, it is now possible to obtain a plastic body parts finishing kit which consists of a pre-primer treatment, a primer and coloured top coat. Full instructions are normally supplied with a kit, but basically, the method of use is to first apply the pre-primer to the component concerned, and allow it to dry for up to 30 minutes. Then the primer is applied, and left to dry for about an hour before finally applying the special-coloured top coat. The result is a correctly-coloured component, where the paint will flex with the plastic or rubber, a property that standard paint does not normally possess.

5 Major body damage – repair

With the exception of Chassis Cab versions, the chassis members are spot-welded to the underbody, and in this respect can be termed of being monocoque or unit construction. Major damage repairs to this type of body combination must of necessity be carried out by body shops with welding and hydraulic straightening facilities.

Extensive damage to the body may distort the chassis, and result in unstable and dangerous handling, as well as excessive wear to tyres and suspension or steering components. It is recommended that checking of the chassis alignment be entrusted to a VW agent or accident repair specialist with special checking jigs.

6 Bonnet – removal, refitting and adjustment

Removal

1 Undo the three screws securing the air intake grille to the bonnet (see illustration).

6.1 Undo the three screws securing the air intake grille to the bonnet

6.2a Carefully release the retaining tabs...

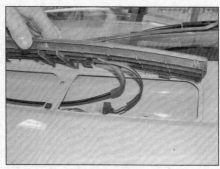

6.2b ...and lift the air intake grille from its location

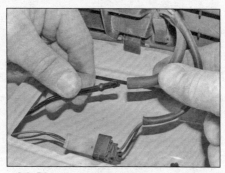

6.3 Disconnect the windscreen washer hose at the rubber connector

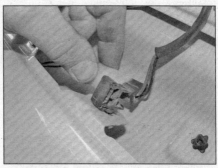

6.4a Where applicable, release the washer jet wiring from the retaining clips...

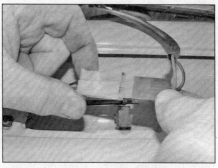

6.4b ...and disconnect the connectors

2 Using a plastic spatula or similar tool carefully release the retaining tabs and lift the air intake grille from its location (see illustrations).
3 Disconnect the windscreen washer hose at the rubber connector (see illustration).
4 If the vehicle is equipped with heated windscreen washer jets, release the washer jet wiring from the retaining clips and disconnect the connectors (see illustrations). Remove the air intake grille.
5 Remove the bonnet lock as described in Section 7.

6 Unclip the windscreen washer hose and release it from the bonnet.
7 Unclip the bonnet release cable from the plastic retainers on the bonnet (see illustration).
8 Mark around the bonnet hinges, to show the outline of their fitted positions for correct realignment on assembly.
9 Have an assistant support the bonnet whilst you unscrew and remove the four bonnet-to-hinge retaining bolts each side, then lift the bonnet clear (see illustration).

Refitting
10 Refitting is a reversal of removal. Tighten the hinge bolts fully when bonnet alignment is satisfactory.

Adjustment
11 Adjustment of the bonnet fit is carried out by slackening the bonnet-to-hinge retaining bolts and repositioning the bonnet as necessary. Adjust the front bump stops so that the bonnet aligns with the front wings on each side. Adjust the striker hoop so that the bonnet locks properly when allowed to fall from approximately 30 cm without having to be pressed down.

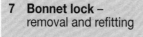

7 Bonnet lock – removal and refitting

Removal
1 Open the bonnet, and support it with its stay rod.
2 Where fitted, release the retainers by turning them through 60° and remove the sound deadening material from inside the bonnet (see illustration).

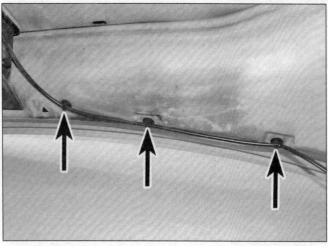

6.7 Unclip the bonnet release cable from the plastic retainers (arrowed) on the bonnet

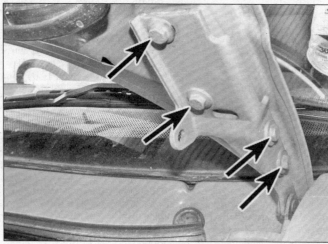

6.9 Bonnet-to-hinge retaining bolts

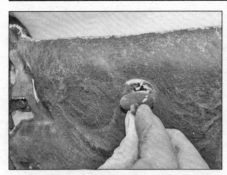

7.2 Turn the retainers through 60º and remove the sound deadening material from the bonnet

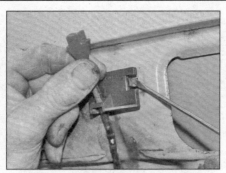

7.3a Depress the retaining tab...

7.3b ...and release the bonnet safety catch lever from its location

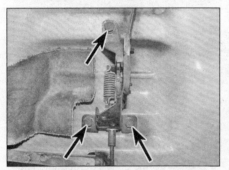

7.4 Undo the three bolts (arrowed) and withdraw the bonnet lock from the bonnet

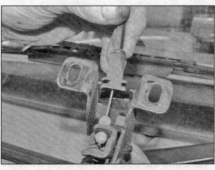

7.5a Lift the bonnet release outer cable out of the bonnet lock...

7.5b ...then disengage the inner cable end fitting from the release lever

3 Depress the retaining tab and release the bonnet safety catch lever from its location **(see illustrations)**.
4 Undo the three bolts and withdraw the bonnet lock from the bonnet **(see illustration)**.
5 Lift the bonnet release outer cable out of the bonnet lock then disengage the inner cable end fitting from the release lever **(see illustrations)**.

Refitting

6 Refitting is a reversal of removal.

8 Bonnet release cable –
removal and refitting

Removal

1 Remove the bonnet lock as described in Section 7.
2 Unclip the bonnet release cable from the plastic retainers on the bonnet **(see illustration 6.7)**.

3 Disengage the bonnet release cable from the clip on the side of the pollen filter housing **(see illustration)**.
4 Undo the two retaining screws securing the bonnet release handle to the A-pillar **(see illustration)**.
5 Release the sealing grommet from the bulkhead, pull the cable into the passenger compartment and remove the cable and handle assembly from the vehicle.

Refitting

6 Refitting is a reversal of removal.

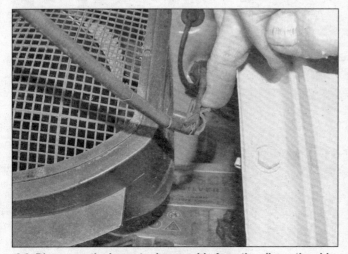

8.3 Disengage the bonnet release cable from the clip on the side of the pollen filter housing

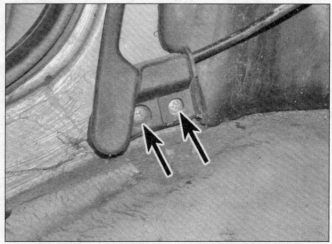

8.4 Undo the two retaining screws (arrowed) securing the bonnet release handle to the A-pillar

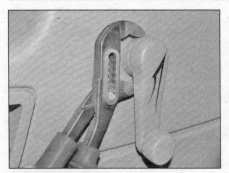

9.1a Squeeze together the top and bottom of the regulator handle inner collar...

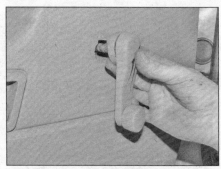

9.1b ...and pull the handle off the regulator shaft

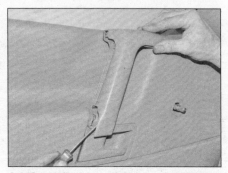

9.4 Carefully prise off the door handle trim panel

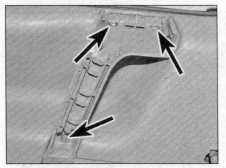

9.5 Undo the three retaining screws (arrowed) and remove the door handle

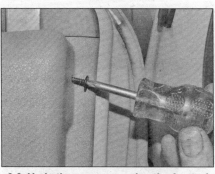

9.6 Undo the screw securing the front of the trim panel to the door

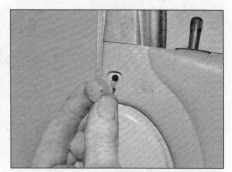

9.7 Unscrew the centre portion, then pull out the expanding plastic rivet

9 Door/tailgate trim panels – removal and refitting

Front doors

1 On models with manual window regulators, observe the window regulator handle. If the handle has a removable trim cover, carefully prise off the trim cover, undo and remove the retaining screw and washer, then pull the handle off the regulator shaft. If there is no removable trim cover on the handle, gently squeeze together the top and bottom of the handle inner collar using adjustable grips and pull the handle off the regulator shaft **(see illustrations)**.

2 On models with electric window regulators, remove the door loudspeaker as described in Chapter 12, Section 17. Undo the three screws in the loudspeaker aperture, then release the speaker wiring grommet from the door trim panel.

3 On models with electric window regulators, carefully prise free the electric window and mirror adjustment switch from the top of the door trim panel, disconnect the switch wiring and remove the switch.

4 Using a small screwdriver, carefully prise off the door handle trim panel **(see illustration)**.

5 Undo the three retaining screws and remove the door handle **(see illustration)**.

6 Undo the screw securing the front of the trim panel to the door **(see illustration)**.

7 Using an Allen key, unscrew the centre

portion, then pull out the expanding plastic rivet securing the rear of the trim panel to the door **(see illustration)**.

8 Unscrew the interior locking button from the locking rod **(see illustration)**.

9.8 Unscrew the interior locking button from the locking rod

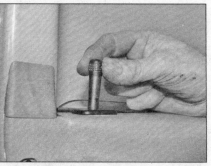

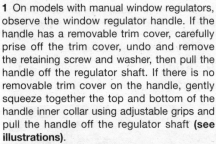

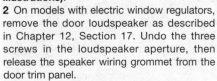

9 Push the trim panel upward to disengage the inner locating lugs from the slots in the door, then withdraw the trim panel from the door (see illustrations).

10 Refitting is a reversal of removal. On

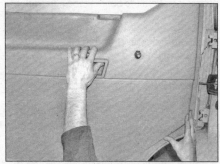

9.9a Push the trim panel upward...

9.9b ...to disengage the inner locating lugs (arrowed) from the slots in the door...

9.9c ...then withdraw the trim panel from the door

models with manual window regulators, with the window closed, position the handle 25° forward of the vertical when refitting.

Sliding side door

11 Undo the retaining screw and remove the centre stop buffer.
12 Undo the trim panel retaining screw and remove the conical washer.
13 Using an Allen key, unscrew the centre portion, then pull out the expanding plastic rivets securing the trim panel to the door. Remove the panel from the door.
14 Refitting is a reversal of removal.

Rear doors

15 Using an Allen key, unscrew the centre portion, then pull out the expanding plastic rivets securing the trim panel to the door. Remove the panel from the door.
16 Refitting is a reversal of removal.

Tailgate

17 Undo the two retaining screws, disengage the locating lug and remove the pull strap from the tailgate (see illustrations).
18 Using an Allen key, unscrew the centre portion, then pull out the expanding plastic rivets securing the trim panel to the tailgate. Remove the panel from the tailgate (see illustrations).
19 Refitting is a reversal of removal.

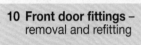

10 Front door fittings – removal and refitting

Exterior handle

Removal

1 Undo the two retaining screws and remove the exterior handle from the door (see illustrations).

Refitting

2 Refitting is a reversal of removal.

Door lock

Removal

3 Remove the front door trim panel as described in Section 9.

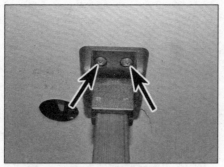

9.17a Undo the two retaining screws (arrowed)...

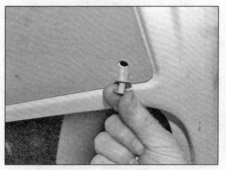

9.18a Pull out the expanding plastic rivets...

4 Remove the exterior handle as described previously.
5 Raise the door window fully.
6 Unclip the interior handle operating rod from the retaining clips and the

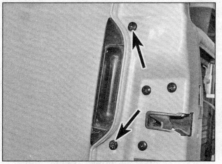

10.1a Undo the two retaining screws (arrowed)...

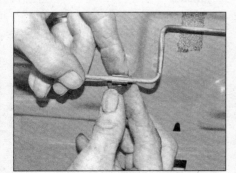

10.6a Unclip the interior handle operating rod from the retaining clips...

9.17b ...then disengage the locating lug and remove the pull strap from the tailgate

9.18b ...and remove the trim panel from the tailgate

guides on the inner door panel (see illustrations).
7 Pull out the door window rear guide channel from the base of the door up to the door lock (see illustration).

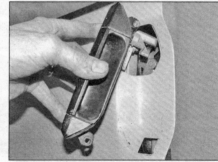

10.1b ...and remove the exterior handle from the door

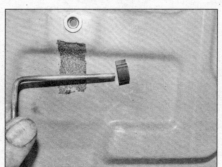

10.6b ...and guides on the inner door panel

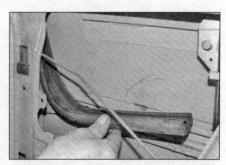

10.7 Pull out the door window rear guide channel from the base of the door up to the door lock

10.8 Undo the three screws (arrowed) securing the lock to the edge of the door

8 Undo the three screws securing the lock to the edge of the door **(see illustration)**.
9 Remove the door lock, together with the interior handle operating rod and the interior locking button operating rod out through the aperture in the inner door panel **(see illustration)**.

Refitting
10 Refitting is a reversal of removal.

Door lock cylinder
Removal
11 Remove the exterior handle as described previously.
12 Insert the key into the lock cylinder.
13 Using a small punch, tap out the tensioning pin and remove the lever from the rear of the lock cylinder.
14 Take off the spring then withdraw the key and lock cylinder from the handle.

11.3 Undo the retaining nut, withdraw the bolt and release the door check strap from the body pillar

12.2a Undo the two retaining screws (arrowed)...

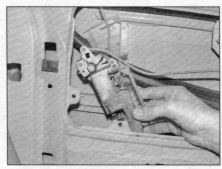

10.9 Remove the door lock out through the aperture in the inner door panel

Refitting
15 Refitting is a reversal of removal.

11 Front door – removal, refitting and adjustment

Removal
1 On models with electric window regulators, central locking, heated exterior mirrors or door mounted loudspeakers, remove the front door trim panel as described in Section 9. Disconnect the wiring connectors at the door electrical components as applicable, then withdraw the wiring harness from the door.
2 Position a suitable padded jack or support blocks underneath the door; don't lift the door, just take its weight.

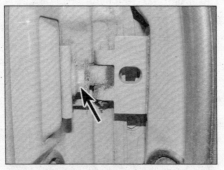

11.4 Front door hinge retaining bolt (arrowed)

12.2b ...and remove the interior release handle from the sliding side door

3 Undo the retaining nut, withdraw the bolt and release the door check strap from the body pillar **(see illustration)**.
4 Have an assistant support the door, then undo the bolts securing the upper and lower hinges to the door **(see illustration)**.

Refitting and adjustment
5 Refitting is a reversal of removal.
6 Close the door and check the door alignment with surrounding body panels. On pre-January 1996 models, slight adjustment of the door position can be made by slackening the door-to-hinge retaining bolts and repositioning the door as necessary within the movement afforded by the elongated bolt holes. On January 1996 models onward, the adjustment is carried out by slackening the hinge-to-body retaining bolts and altering the position of the hinge. To gain access to the hinge-to-body retaining bolts it will be necessary to remove the door, alter the position of the hinge, then refit the door on a trial and error basis.
7 On all models, if necessary, adjust the position of the door striker plate so that the lock engages the striker plate centrally without having to lift or push down the door. The door must not have any play when it is closed.

12 Sliding side door fittings – removal and refitting

Interior release handle
Removal
1 Remove the door inner trim panel as described in Section 9.
2 Undo the two retaining screws and remove the interior release handle from the door **(see illustrations)**.
Refitting
3 Refitting is a reversal of removal.

Remote door release mechanism
Removal
4 Remove the interior release handle as described previously.
5 Disconnect the door lock pull rod from the remote door release mechanism **(see illustration)**.

12.5 Disconnect the door lock pull rod from the remote door release mechanism

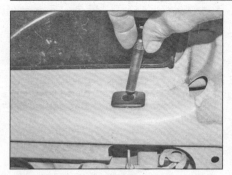

12.6 Unscrew the interior locking button from the locking rod

12.7a Undo the two retaining screws (arrowed)...

12.7b ...and remove the remote door release mechanism from the door

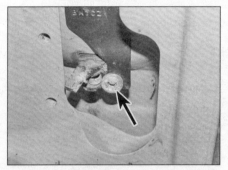

12.10a Undo the retaining screw (arrowed)...

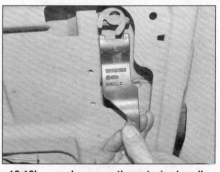

12.10b ...and remove the exterior handle tensioning spring

12.11 Remove the exterior handle from the door

6 Unscrew the interior locking button from the locking rod **(see illustration)**.
7 Undo the two retaining screws and remove the remote door release mechanism from the door **(see illustrations)**.

Refitting

8 Refitting is a reversal of removal.

Exterior handle

Removal

9 Remove the remote door release mechanism as described previously.
10 Undo the retaining screw and remove the exterior handle tensioning spring **(see illustrations)**.
11 Remove the exterior handle from the door **(see illustration)**.

Refitting

12 Refitting is a reversal of removal.

Door lock cylinder

Removal and refitting

13 Proceed as described in Section 10, paragraphs 11 to 15.

Door lock unit

Removal

14 Remove the door inner trim panel as described in Section 9.
15 Disconnect the door lock pull rod from the remote door release mechanism **(see illustration 12.5)**.
16 Undo the two screws securing the lock unit to the edge of the door **(see illustration)**.

17 Withdraw the lock unit from the door, disconnect the door lock pull rod and remove the lock unit **(see illustration)**.

Refitting

18 Refitting is a reversal of removal.

13 Sliding side door –
removal, refitting and adjustment

Removal

Note: *Before slackening any retaining bolts, make alignment marks on the guide supports to aid alignment when refitting.*
1 Undo the retaining screw and remove the end stop from the centre rail **(see illustrations)**.

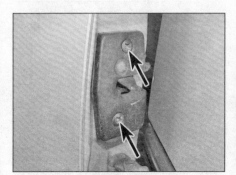

12.16 Undo the two screws (arrowed) securing the lock unit to the edge of the door

12.17 Withdraw the lock unit from the door and disconnect the door lock pull rod

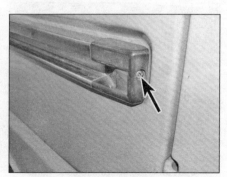

13.1a Undo the retaining screw (arrowed)...

13.1b ...and remove the end stop from the centre rail

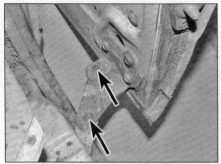

13.2 Unscrew the two screws (arrowed) securing the door bracket to the lower guide roller

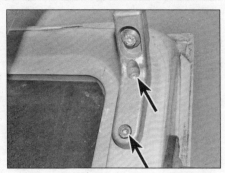

13.3 Undo the two bolts securing the upper guide roller to the door

2 Slide the door open, and unscrew the two screws securing the door bracket to the lower guide roller **(see illustration)**.

3 Enlist the aid of an assistant to support the weight of the door on the centre rail, then undo the two bolts securing the upper guide roller to the door **(see illustration)**.

4 Support the door at each end, slide it to the rear, and remove it from the vehicle.

Refitting

5 Refitting is a reversal of removal. Align the door and engage it onto the centre track, then reconnect the fittings.

Adjustment

6 Check the door for satisfactory flush-fitting adjustment. Adjust if necessary by loosening off the screws securing the door bracket to the door and to the lower guide roller. Reposition the door as required, then tighten them and recheck the fitting. Further adjustment can be obtained by slackening the upper guide roller retaining bolt and repositioning the guide roller on its bracket and by repositioning the centre rail hinge link.

7 When fitted, and in the closed position, the door should be aligned flush to the surrounding body, and should close securely. If required, adjust the striker plate position to suit.

14 Rear door fittings – removal and refitting

Exterior handle (right-hand door)

Removal

1 Open the door and undo the two screws securing the exterior handle to the edge of the door **(see illustration)**.

2 Remove the exterior handle from the outside of the door **(see illustration)**.

Refitting

3 Refitting is a reversal of removal.

Door lock cylinder

Removal and refitting

4 Proceed as described in Section 10, paragraphs 11 to 15.

Interior release handle (right-hand door)

Removal

5 Remove the door inner trim panel as described in Section 9.

6 Detach the release handle operating rod at the lock unit lever **(see illustration)**.

7 Lift the inner edge of the release handle and slide it toward the centre of the door. Lift the handle up and remove it from the door **(see illustrations)**.

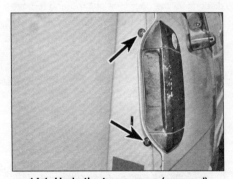

14.1 Undo the two screws (arrowed) securing the exterior handle to the edge of the rear door

14.2 Remove the exterior handle from the outside of the door

14.6 Detach the interior release handle operating rod at the lock unit lever

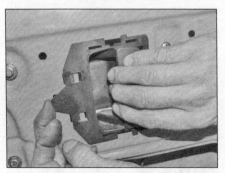

14.7a Lift the inner edge of the release handle and slide it toward the centre of the door...

14.7b ...then lift the handle up and remove it from the door

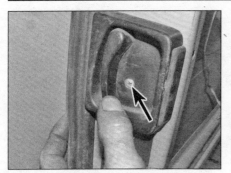

14.11a Undo the retaining screw
(arrowed)...

14.11b ...and remove the interior release
handle from the left-hand door

14.16 Detach the operating rods for the
lock upper and lower latches at the lock
levers

Refitting

8 Refitting is a reversal of removal.

Interior release handle (left-hand door)

9 Remove the door inner trim panel as described in Section 9.
10 Detach the release handle operating rod at the lock lower latch.
11 Undo the retaining screw and remove the release handle from the door (see illustrations).

Refitting

12 Refitting is a reversal of removal.

Door lock unit

Removal

13 Remove the door inner trim panel as described in Section 9.
14 Remove the exterior handle as described previously.
15 Detach the interior release handle operating rod at the lock unit lever (see illustration 14.6).
16 Detach the operating rods for the lock upper and lower latches at the lock levers (see illustration).

14.17a Lift the lock unit up to disengage it
from the door...

17 Lift the lock unit up to disengage it from the door, then lower it down and remove it through the large aperture in the door (see illustrations).

Refitting and adjustment

18 Refitting is a reversal of removal. Check that the upper and lower latches both unlock simultaneously when the lock is operated. If one latch operates before the other, detach the operating rods at the lock unit. Turn the end fittings as necessary to increase or decrease the length of the operating rods, until both latches operate simultaneously.

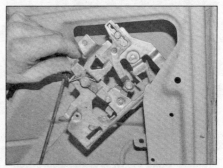

14.17b ...then lower it down and remove it
through the large aperture in the door

Lock upper latch

Removal

19 Remove the door inner trim panel as described in Section 9.
20 Detach the upper latch operating rod from the door lock unit lever (see illustration 14.16).
21 Undo the three screws securing the upper latch to the door (see illustration).
22 Withdraw the latch upward, together with the operating rod and remove it from the door (see illustration).

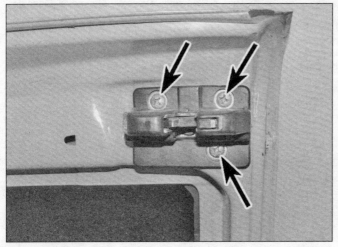

14.21 Undo the three screws (arrowed) securing the upper latch
to the door

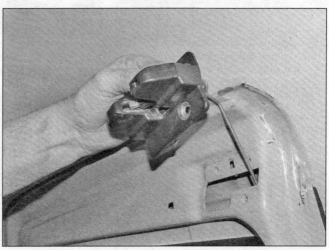

14.22 Withdraw the latch upward, together with the operating rod
and remove it from the door

14.25a Detach the lower latch operating rod (arrowed) from the latch lever...

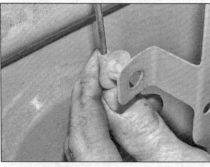

14.25b ...then release the operating rod guide from the door panel

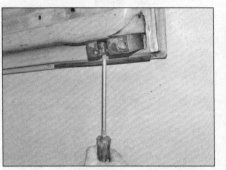

14.26a Undo the two retaining screws...

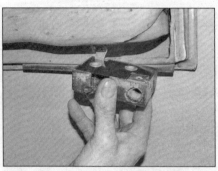

14.26b ...and remove the lock lower latch from the door

Refitting

23 Refitting is a reversal of removal. Check the operation of the upper latch and if necessary adjust the operating rod as described in paragraph 18.

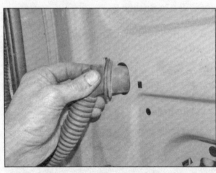

15.2 Release the grommet from the door and withdraw the wiring harness

Lock lower latch

Removal

24 Remove the door inner trim panel as described in Section 9.

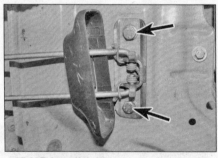

15.3 Prise off the trim cover, then undo the two bolts (arrowed) securing the check strap to the door

25 Detach the lower latch operating rod from the latch lever, then release the operating rod guide (where fitted) from the door panel **(see illustrations)**.
26 Undo the two retaining screws and remove the lock lower latch from the door **(see illustrations)**.

Refitting

27 Refitting is a reversal of removal. Check the operation of the lower latch and if necessary adjust the operating rod as described in paragraph 18.

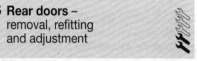

15 Rear doors – removal, refitting and adjustment

Removal

1 Remove the door inner trim panel as described in Section 9.
2 Disconnect the wiring connectors for the rear door wiper motor, heated rear window, central locking motor and high-level stop-light according to equipment fitted. Release the grommet from the door and withdraw the wiring harness **(see illustration)**.
3 Carefully prise off the trim cover, then undo the two bolts securing the check strap to the door **(see illustration)**.
4 Position a suitable padded jack or support blocks underneath the door; don't lift the door, just take its weight.
5 Using a small screwdriver, carefully prise out the plastic covers over the two lower hinge retaining bolts **(see illustration)**.
6 Have an assistant support the door, then undo the bolts securing the upper and lower hinges to the door and carefully lift away the door **(see illustrations)**.

Refitting and adjustment

7 Refitting is a reversal of removal. Open and shut the doors, and ensure that they don't bind with the body aperture at any point. Where necessary, adjust the position of the upper and lower locking wedges to provide an even clearance all round.

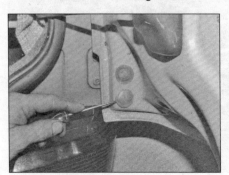

15.5 Carefully prise out the plastic covers over the two lower hinge retaining bolts

15.6a Rear door upper retaining bolts (arrowed)...

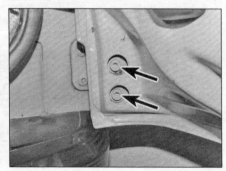

15.6b ...and lower retaining bolts (arrowed)

16.2 Disconnect the operating rods from the tailgate lock unit

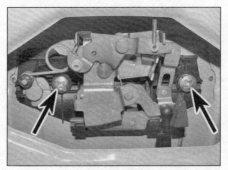

16.3a Undo the two retaining screws (arrowed)...

16.3b ...and remove the lock unit from the tailgate

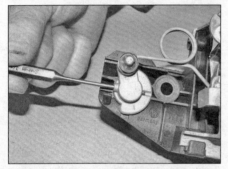

16.7 Tap out the tensioning pin and remove the lever from the rear of the lock cylinder

16.11 Undo the two screws (arrowed) securing the latch to the tailgate

16.12 Withdraw the latch, then reach through the tailgate opening and disconnect the operating rod

16 Tailgate fittings –
removal and refitting

Tailgate lock unit

Removal

1 Remove the tailgate inner trim panel as described in Section 9.
2 Disconnect the tailgate latch, interior release handle and, where fitted, the central locking operating rods from the lock unit (see illustration).
3 Undo the two retaining screws and remove the lock unit from the tailgate (see illustrations).

Refitting

4 Refitting is a reversal of removal.

Tailgate lock cylinder

Removal

5 Remove the tailgate lock unit as described previously.
6 Insert the key into the lock cylinder.
7 Using a small punch, tap out the tensioning pin and remove the lever from the rear of the lock cylinder (see illustration).
8 Take off the spring then withdraw the key and lock cylinder from the lock unit.

Refitting

9 Refitting is a reversal of removal.

Lock latch

Removal

10 Remove the tailgate inner trim panel as described in Section 9.

11 Undo the two screws securing the latch to the tailgate (see illustration).
12 Withdraw the latch, then reach through the tailgate opening and disconnect the latch operating rod (see illustration).
13 Disconnect the wiring connector and remove the latch (see illustration).

Refitting

14 Refitting is a reversal of removal.

Interior opener

Removal

15 Remove the tailgate inner trim panel as described in Section 9.
16 Disconnect the interior opener operating rod at the tailgate lock unit (see illustration).
17 Using a small screwdriver, carefully prise up the retaining tabs and release the interior opener from the tailgate inner panel (see illustration).

16.13 Disconnect the wiring connector and remove the latch

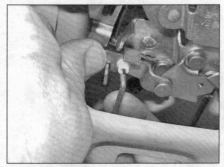

16.16 Disconnect the interior opener operating rod at the tailgate lock unit

16.17 Carefully prise up the retaining tabs and release the interior opener from the tailgate inner panel

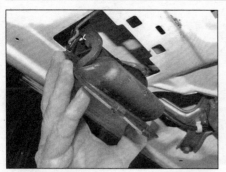

16.18 Remove the interior opener and operating rod from the tailgate aperture

18 Remove the interior opener and operating rod from the tailgate aperture **(see illustration).**

Refitting

19 Refitting is a reversal of removal.

17 Tailgate –
removal, refitting and adjustment

Removal

1 The aid of two assistants will be required to support the tailgate as it is removed.
2 Remove the tailgate inner trim panel as described in Section 9.
3 Disconnect the wiring connectors for the tailgate wiper motor, heated rear window, number plate lights and, where fitted, the central locking motor. Release the grommet from the tailgate and withdraw the wiring harness.
4 Have the two assistants support the weight of the tailgate. Prise up the retaining clips securing the tailgate strut balljoints, and detach the balljoint from the stud each side. Take care not to lift the clips by more than 4 mm.

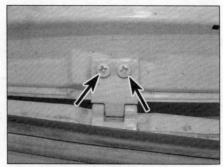

17.5 Tailgate-to-hinge retaining bolts (arrowed)

5 Undo the two screws each side securing the tailgate to the hinges and lift away the tailgate **(see illustration).**

Refitting

6 Refit the tailgate in the reverse order of removal. Press the strut balljoints onto their studs, using hand pressure only. Note that the struts are gas-filled, and therefore cannot be repaired. If renewing them, be sure to obtain the correct replacements.

Adjustment

7 When the tailgate is refitted, check its adjustment and if necessary re-adjust as follows.

Height adjustment

8 Tailgate height adjustment is carried out by altering the position of the hinges at their attachments to the vehicle roof. To gain access to the hinge retaining nuts it will be necessary to remove the passenger compartment headlining. Note that headlining removal requires considerable skill and experience if it is to be carried out without damage, and is therefore best entrusted to an expert.

Guide pin adjustment

9 Undo the retaining screw and remove the trim cover from the guide wedge on each side.
10 With an assistant slowly closing the tailgate, check from inside the vehicle that the guide wedges are pressed evenly by the guide pins approximately 10 to 15 mm each side. If necessary, slacken the retaining screws and reposition the guide pins.

Striker plate adjustment

11 When fitted, and in the closed position, the tailgate should be aligned flush to the surrounding body, and should close securely. If required, adjust the striker plate position to suit.

18 Front door window glass –
removal and refitting

Removal

1 Remove the door inner trim panel as described in Section 9.
2 Temporarily refit the window regulator handle, or reconnect the wiring connector at the electric window switch, as applicable and lower the window fully.
3 Undo the two bolts securing the window glass to the regulator lifting channel **(see illustration).**
4 Tilt the window glass down at the front then lift it up and out towards the outside of the door **(see illustration).**

Refitting

5 Fit the window glass back into the door and refit the two bolts securing the glass to the regulator lifting channel. Only tighten the bolts finger tight at this stage.
6 Raise the window fully by means of the regulator. With the window closed, tighten the two retaining bolts securely.
7 Refit the door inner trim panel as described in Section 9.

18.3 Undo the two bolts (arrowed) securing the window glass to the regulator lifting channel

18.4 Tilt the glass down at the front then lift it out towards the outside of the door

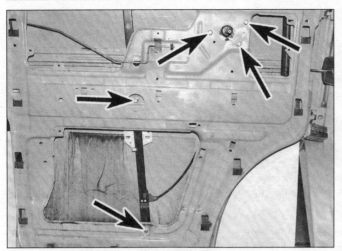

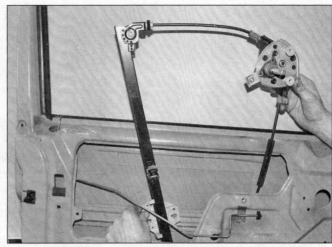

19.6 Undo the bolts (arrowed) securing the window regulator to the door

19.7 Disengage the regulator from the door and manipulate it out through the upper aperture

19 Front door window regulator – removal and refitting

Removal

1 Remove the door inner trim panel as described in Section 9.
2 Temporarily refit the window regulator handle, or reconnect the wiring connector at the electric window switch, as applicable and lower the window fully.
3 Undo the two bolts securing the window glass to the regulator lifting channel (see illustration 18.3).
4 Slide the window glass to the fully closed position. Retain the window glass in the closed position using adhesive tape over the top of the door frame.
5 On vehicles with electric windows, disconnect the regulator motor wiring connector.
6 Undo the bolts securing the regulator to the door (see illustration). On vehicles with electric windows, release the regulator securing clip at the top of the door upper aperture.
7 Disengage the regulator from the door and manipulate it out through the upper door aperture (see illustration).

Refitting

8 Refitting is a reversal of removal.

20 Windscreen/tailgate/door and fixed/sliding windows – removal and refitting

The windscreen, tailgate and fixed/sliding side window assemblies are direct-glazed to the body, using special adhesive. Purpose-made tools are required to remove the old glass and fit the new glass, and therefore this work is best entrusted to a specialist.

21 Exterior mirrors – removal and refitting

Exterior mirror

Removal

1 Undo the three screws securing the mirror to the door and withdraw the mirror. If electric mirrors are fitted, disconnect the wiring connector and remove the mirror.

Refitting

2 Refitting is a reversal of removal.

Mirror glass

Removal

3 If the mirror glass is broken it is advisable to cover it with masking tape prior to removal (see illustration).
4 Using a plastic wedge, prise the upper edge of the glass outwards to release the internal retaining clips, then remove the glass (see illustrations).

Refitting

5 Refitting is a reversal of removal. Carefully press the mirror glass into the housing until the centre retainer clips are engaged.

22 Front bumper – removal and refitting

Pre-January 1996 models

Removal

1 Undo the retaining screws and remove the front number plate.
2 Remove the trim caps then undo the two bolts in the number plate aperture.
3 On vehicles equipped with front foglights, reach under the bumper and disconnect the foglight wiring connector on each side.

21.3 If the mirror glass is broken, cover it with masking tape prior to removal

21.4a Prise the upper edge of the mirror glass outwards to release the internal clips...

21.4b ...then remove the glass

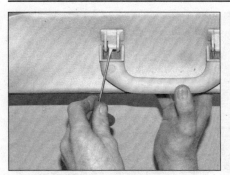

24.2a Lift up the cover flaps...

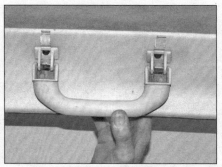

24.2b ...then undo the two screws securing the grab handle to the roof panel

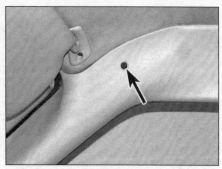

24.3 Undo the A-pillar trim retaining screw (arrowed)

4 Pull out the two pins each side securing the rear of the bumper to the guides.
5 Pull the bumper out of the guides and remove it from the vehicle.

Refitting

6 Refitting is a reversal of removal. Secure the bumper to the guides by knocking the two pins each side back into position.

January 1996 models onward

Removal

7 Undo the retaining screws and remove the front number plate.
8 Remove the trim caps then undo the two bolts in the number plate aperture.
9 On vehicles equipped with front foglights, reach under the bumper and disconnect the foglight wiring connector on each side.
10 Undo the screw each side securing the upper rear corners of the bumper to the body.
11 Undo the screw each side securing the lower rear edges of the bumper to the support struts.
12 Pull the bumper out of the guides and remove it from the vehicle.

Refitting

13 Refitting is a reversal of removal.

23 Rear bumper – removal and refitting

Pre-January 1996 models

Removal

1 Remove the trim caps then undo the two retaining bolts in the loadspace aperture.
2 From below undo the two bolts securing the centre part of the bumper to the support brackets.
3 Reach under the bumper and disconnect the foglight wiring connector.
4 Tap out the centre pins and remove the two plastic rivets from the sides of the loadspace aperture.
5 Pull out the two pins each side securing the front of the bumper to the guides.
6 Pull the bumper out of the guides and remove it from the vehicle.

Refitting

7 Refitting is a reversal of removal. Secure the bumper to the guides by knocking the two pins each side back into position.

January 1996 models onward

Removal

8 Reach under the bumper and disconnect the foglight wiring connector.
9 Undo the screw each side securing the upper front corner of the bumper to the wheel arch.
10 Undo the bolts securing the bumper carrier to the underbody.
11 Undo the screws securing the lower side edges of the bumper to the underbody.
12 Pull the bumper out of the guides and remove it from the vehicle.

Refitting

13 Refitting is a reversal of removal.

24 Interior trim – removal and refitting

Door/tailgate trim panels

1 Refer to the procedures contained in Section 9.

A-pillar trim

Removal

2 Lift up the cover flaps, then undo the two

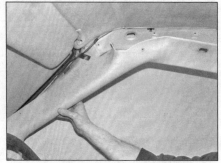

24.4 Pull the trim away to disengage the retaining clips, then unhook the lower end from the bush behind the facia

screws securing the grab handle to the roof panel (see illustrations). Remove the grab handle.
3 Undo the A-pillar trim retaining screw (see illustration).
4 Pull the trim away from the pillar to disengage the retaining clips, then unhook the lower end of the trim from the bonded rubber bush behind the facia (see illustration).

Refitting

5 Refitting is a reversal of removal.

Side and rear trim panels

Removal and refitting – general

6 Numerous variations of interior trim panels are fitted as standard according to vehicle specification and model type. Additionally, there is an extensive assortment of non-standard trim panels fitted to specialist conversions. As it is impossible to provide removal and refitting procedures for all the panels available, the following information can be used as a general guide.

a) The interior trim panels are secured either by screws or by various types of trim fasteners, usually studs or clips.
b) Check that there are no other panels overlapping the one to be removed. Usually there is a sequence that has to be followed that will become obvious on close inspection.
c) Remove all obvious fasteners, such as screws. If the panel will not come free then it is held by hidden clips or fasteners. These are usually situated around the edge of the panel and can be prised up to release them. Note, however, that they can break quite easily, so care should be exercised. The best way of releasing such clips in the absence of the correct type of tool, is to use a large flat-bladed screwdriver. Pad the screwdriver blade by wrapping insulating tape around it, to avoid scratching paintwork. Note that in many cases, rubber sealing strips (such as those fitted to door or tailgate apertures) may need to be prised back when releasing a panel.
d) When removing a panel, never use excessive force or the panel may be damaged. Always check carefully that all

fasteners have been removed or released
before attempting to withdraw a panel.
e) When refitting a panel, secure the
fasteners by pressing them firmly into
place and ensure that all disturbed
components are correctly secured to
prevent rattles.

25 Body exterior fittings – removal and refitting

Radiator grille

Removal – pre-August 1994 models

1 Undo the three screws securing the top
of the radiator grille to the radiator upper
crossmember.
2 Tip the grille forward at the top, then lift it
up to disengage the lower mounting lugs.

Removal – August 1994 models onward

3 Undo the three screws securing the top
of the radiator grille to the radiator upper
crossmember **(see illustration)**.
4 Where fitted, pull out and disconnect the
headlight washer jets.
5 Undo the screw each side securing the
lower radiator grille to the front body panel
(see illustration).
6 Pull the radiator grille assembly forward to
disengage the securing clips from the T-studs
on each side **(see illustrations)**. A VW special
tool (3370) is available to hook over the side of
the grille assembly in the vicinity of the T-studs
enabling it to be pulled forward off the studs.
A suitable alternative can be fabricated out of
2 mm diameter rod (ie welding rod) inserted
through the gap between the headlight and
the grille assembly. In practice, it is usually
possible to release the grille assembly with
gentle persuasion from a suitably padded
screwdriver. Once the securing clips are free,
remove the radiator grille assembly.
7 Prior to refitting, check the condition of the
securing clips and renew as necessary.

Refitting – all models

8 Refitting is a reversal of removal.

Engine undertray

Removal

9 Firmly apply the handbrake, then jack up the
front of the vehicle and support it securely on
axle stands (see *Jacking and vehicle support*).
10 Undo the two retaining bolts at the front
(if fitted), two bolts (or a bolt and nut) each
side, and two bolts at the rear securing the
undertray to the underbody and subframe
(see illustrations).
11 Suitably support the undertray and release
the front locking hook. Lower the front of the
undertray, disengage the rear brackets from
the subframe and remove the undertray from
under the vehicle.

**25.3 Undo the three screws securing the
top of the radiator grille to the radiator
upper crossmember**

**25.6a Pull the radiator grille assembly
forward...**

Refitting

12 Refitting is a reversal of removal.

26 Seats – removal and refitting

Driver's seat

Removal – fixed seat

1 If the seat incorporates a seat heating element,
disconnect the element wiring connector.
2 Undo the two bolts securing the rear of the
seat frame to the floor.
3 Slide the seat to the rear to disengage the
front mountings, then lift the seat up and
remove it from the vehicle.

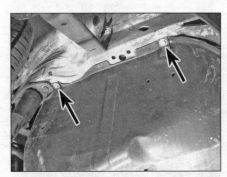

**25.10a Undo the two bolts each side
(arrowed)...**

**25.5 Undo the screw each side securing
the lower radiator grille to the front body
panel**

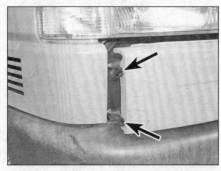

**25.6b ...to disengage the securing clips
(arrowed) from the T-studs on each side**

Removal – swivel seat

4 If the seat incorporates a seat heating
element, disconnect the element wiring
connector.
5 Undo the four bolts securing the seat frame
to the floor.
6 Lift the seat up and remove it from the
vehicle.

Refitting – all seats

7 Refitting is a reversal of removal, tightening
the seat mounting bolts securely.

Front passenger's seat

Removal

8 If the seat incorporates a seat heating
element, disconnect the element wiring
connector.

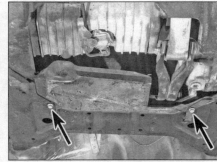

**25.10b ...and two bolts at the rear
(arrowed) securing the undertray to the
underbody and subframe**

26.9 Front passenger's seat frame rear retaining nuts (arrowed)

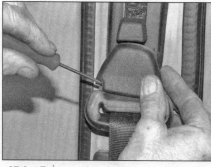

27.2a Remove the plastic cover from the seat belt upper mounting...

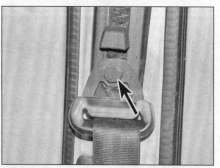

27.2b ...then unscrew the upper mounting bolt (arrowed)

27.3 Remove the trim cap then undo the seat belt lower mounting bolt

9 Undo the nuts securing the seat frame to the floor at the front and rear **(see illustration)**.
10 Lift the seat up and remove it from the vehicle.

Refitting

11 Refitting is a reversal of removal, tightening the seat mounting bolts securely.

27.4a Lift off the trim cover...

27.4b ...then unscrew the inertia reel mounting bolt

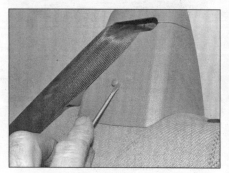

27.6a Extract the plastic retaining pin...

27.6b ...then remove the centre seat belt inertia reel front trim cover

Rear seats

12 Various combinations of rear seats may be fitted, according to vehicle type and specification. The removal and refitting procedures are essentially the same as those described previously for the front seats.

27 Seat belt components – removal and refitting

Note: *Various combinations of seat belts may be fitted, according to vehicle type and specification. The following removal and refitting procedures can be used as a guide for most seat belt installations.*

Front seat belt

Removal

1 Disconnect the battery negative terminal (refer to *Disconnecting the battery*).

⚠️ *Warning: On later models, seat belt tensioners may be incorporated in the inertia reel of the seat belts. Before proceeding, wait a minimum of 3 minutes, as a precaution against accidental firing of the seat belt tensioners. This period ensures that any residual electrical energy is dissipated.*

⚠️ *Warning: There is a potential risk of the seat belt tensioning device firing during removal, so it should be handled carefully. Once removed, treat it with care – do not use chemicals on or near it, and do not expose it to high temperatures, or it may detonate.*

2 Remove the plastic cover from the seat belt upper mounting, then unscrew the upper mounting bolt **(see illustrations)**.
3 Remove the trim cap then undo the seat belt lower mounting bolt from the B-pillar **(see illustration)**. Collect the spacer bush and spacer ring.
4 Lift off the trim cover, then unscrew the mounting bolt, and lift seat belt inertia reel unit to remove it from the base of the pillar **(see illustrations)**.

Refitting

5 Refitting is a reversal of removal, tightening the retaining bolts to the specified torque.

Front centre seat belt

6 Using a small screwdriver, extract the plastic retaining pin, then remove the inertia reel front trim cover **(see illustrations)**.
7 Similarly extract the two inertia reel rear trim cover retaining pins and remove the rear cover **(see illustrations)**.
8 Undo the seat belt lower mounting bolt from the base of the seat **(see illustration)**.
9 Unscrew the mounting bolt, and remove the inertia reel and seat belt from the seat **(see illustration)**.

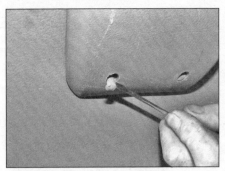

27.7a Extract the two inertia reel rear trim cover retaining pins...

27.7b ...and remove the rear cover

27.8 Undo the seat belt lower mounting bolt (arrowed) from the base of the seat

Refitting

10 Refitting is a reversal of removal, tightening the retaining bolts to the specified torque.

Rear seat belt

Removal and refitting

11 The general procedures for removal and refitting of the rear seat belts are similar to those given for the front seat belts earlier in this Section, but it may be necessary in some instances to remove certain interior trim panels for access.

Seat belt stalks

12 Various combinations of seat belt stalks may be fitted, according to vehicle type and specification **(see illustration)**. The removal and refitting procedures are essentially self-explanatory, but it may be necessary in some instances to remove certain interior trim panels for access. Ensure that all attachment bolts are tightened to the specified torque when refitting.

27.9 Unscrew the mounting bolt (arrowed), and remove the inertia reel and seat belt

(see illustrations). Where fitted, disconnect the wiring connector for the glovebox light.

Refitting

3 Refitting is a reversal of removal.

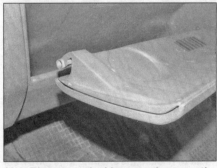

29.1 Disengage the hinges and remove the glovebox lid

29.2b ...and lift the glovebox from its location

27.12 Typical seat belt stalk attachment

Driver's side stowage box

Removal

4 Turn the retaining catch anti-clockwise and open the stowage box fully **(see illustration)**.

29.2a Undo the screws securing the glovebox to the facia...

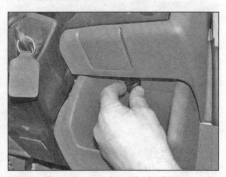

29.4a Turn the catch anti-clockwise and open the stowage box fully

28 Sunroof –
general information

An electric sunroof was offered as an optional extra on certain models. Due to the complexity of the sunroof mechanism, considerable expertise is needed to repair, renew or adjust the sunroof components successfully. Removal of the roof first requires the headlining to be removed, which is a complex and tedious operation in itself, and not a task to be undertaken lightly. Therefore, any problems with the sunroof should be referred to a VW dealer.

29 Facia panel components –
removal and refitting

Glovebox

Removal

1 Open the glovebox lid, disengage the hinges and remove the lid **(see illustration)**.
2 Undo the screws securing the glovebox to the facia and lift the glovebox from its location

29.4b Lift the stowage box out of the lower retainers and remove it from the facia

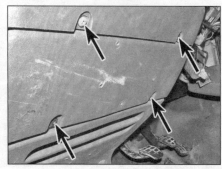

29.6a Undo the retaining screws (arrowed)...

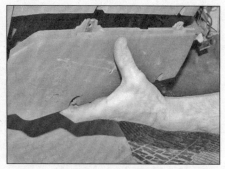

29.6b ...and remove the trim panel over the vent console

29.7a Footwell vent console lower left-hand retaining screw (arrowed)...

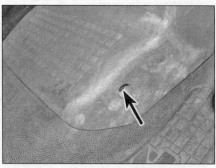

29.7b ...and lower right-hand retaining screw

Lift the stowage box out of the lower retainers and remove it from the facia (see illustration).

Refitting

5 Refitting is a reversal of removal.

Footwell vent console

Removal

6 Undo the retaining screws and remove the trim panel over the vent console (see illustrations).
7 Undo the upper screws and the lower screw each side and remove the footwell vent console (see illustrations).

Refitting

8 Refitting is a reversal of removal.

Instrument panel surround

Removal

9 Undo the two upper screws securing the surround to the facia (see illustration).
10 Pull the surround away from the facia to release the locating lugs from the retaining clips each side, then remove the surround (see illustration).

Refitting

11 Refitting is a reversal of removal.

Side air vents

Removal

12 Insert a small screwdriver into the side of the rotating insert furthest away from the adjuster wheel. Carefully prise out the side of the rotating insert and remove the insert from the air outlet (see illustration).
13 Undo the retaining screw at the base of the air outlet (see illustration).
14 Carefully prise free the air outlet and remove it from the facia (see illustration).

29.9 Undo the two upper screws (arrowed) securing the instrument panel surround to the facia

29.10 Pull the surround away from the facia to release the locating lugs (arrowed) each side

29.12 Carefully prise out the side of the rotating insert and remove the insert from the air outlet

29.13 Undo the retaining screw (arrowed) at the base of the air outlet

29.14 Carefully prise free the air outlet and remove it from the facia

29.15 Release the air duct from the lug on the facia surround

15 If the air vent is being removed as part of the complete facia removal procedure, release the air duct from the lug on the facia surround **(see illustration)**.

Refitting

16 Refitting is a reversal of removal.

Centre air vents

Removal

17 Insert a small screwdriver into the side of the rotating inserts furthest away from the adjuster wheels. Carefully prise out the side of each rotating insert and remove the insert from the air outlet **(see illustrations)**.
18 Undo the two retaining screws at the base of the air outlet **(see illustration)**.
19 Carefully prise free the air outlet and remove it from the facia **(see illustration)**.

Refitting

20 Refitting is a reversal of removal.

Steering column shrouds

Removal

21 Undo the three screws securing the lower shroud to the upper shroud and remove the upper shroud **(see illustrations)**.
22 Disengage the lower shroud from the steering column, then pivot it down and release it from the lower support bar **(see illustrations)**.
23 On later models, disconnect the diagnostic socket wiring connector, then remove the lower shroud **(see illustration)**.

Refitting

24 Refitting is a reversal of removal.

29.17a Carefully prise out the side of each rotating centre insert...

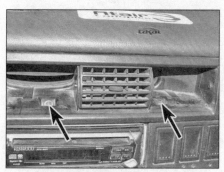

29.18 Undo the two retaining screws (arrowed) at the base of the air outlet

Complete facia assembly

Removal

25 Disconnect the battery negative terminal (refer to *Disconnecting the battery*).

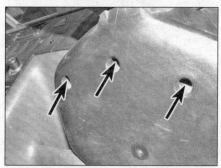

29.21a Undo the three screws securing the lower shroud to the upper shroud...

29.22a Disengage the lower shroud from the steering column...

29.22b ...then pivot it down and release it from the lower support bar (arrowed)

29.17b ...and remove the insert from the air outlet

29.19 Carefully prise free the air outlet and remove it from the facia

26 On later models, remove the A-pillar trim panels on both sides as described in Section 24.
27 Remove the following facia panels as described previously in this Section:

29.21b ...and remove the upper shroud

29.23 On later models, disconnect the diagnostic socket wiring connector

29.38 Undo the bolt (arrowed) securing the centre of the facia to the bulkhead

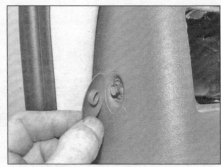

29.39a Extract the cover caps...

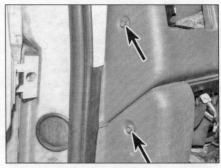

29.39b ...then undo the left-hand retaining bolts (arrowed)...

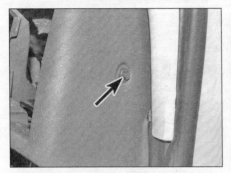

29.39c ...and right-hand retaining bolt (arrowed)

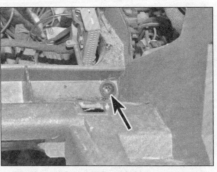

29.40a In the vicinity of the instrument panel aperture undo the upper right-hand retaining screw (arrowed)...

29.40b ...upper left-hand retaining screw (arrowed)...

a) *Glovebox.*
b) *Driver's side stowage box.*
c) *Footwell vent console.*
d) *Instrument panel surround.*
e) *Side air vents.*
f) *Centre air vents.*
g) *Steering column shrouds.*

28 Remove the exterior light switch as described in Chapter 12, Section 4.
29 Remove the instrument panel as described in Chapter 12, Section 9.
30 Where fitted, remove the passenger's airbag as described in Chapter 12, Section 20.
31 Remove the steering column combination switches as described in Chapter 12, Section 4.
32 Remove the steering wheel as described in Chapter 10, Section 20.

33 Remove the heater/ventilation control unit as described in Chapter 3, Section 10.
34 Remove the audio unit as described in Chapter 12, Section 16.
35 Remove the loudspeakers from the top of the facia as described in Chapter 12, Section 17.
36 Disconnect the wiring connectors at the switches in the centre section of the facia.
37 On models with a cold start accelerator cable, pull the cold start knob out to expose its rear surface, then prise off the clip and remove the knob from the upper inner cable. Slacken and remove the retaining nut to release the upper outer cable from the facia.
38 From within the engine compartment, undo the bolt securing the centre of the facia to the bulkhead **(see illustration)**.

39 Extract the cover caps and undo the facia retaining bolts at both ends **(see illustrations)**.
40 Undo the facia upper and lower retaining screws in the vicinity of the instrument panel aperture **(see illustrations)**.
41 With the help of an assistant, carefully lift the facia from its location. Detach the remaining air ducts from the facia and air distribution housing, check that all wiring has been disconnected, then remove the facia from the vehicle **(see illustration)**.

Refitting

42 Refitting is a reversal of removal ensuring that all air ducts and wiring are correctly reconnected and all mountings securely tightened.

29.40c ...lower left-hand retaining screw (arrowed)...

29.40d ...and lower right-hand retaining screw (arrowed)

29.41 Carefully lift the facia from its location

Chapter 12
Body electrical systems

Contents

Degrees of difficulty

| Easy, suitable for novice with little experience | | Fairly easy, suitable for beginner with some experience | | Fairly difficult, suitable for competent DIY mechanic | | Difficult, suitable for experienced DIY mechanic | | Very difficult, suitable for expert DIY or professional | |

Specifications

System type...	12-volt negative earth	
Fuses...	See Wiring diagrams at the end of this Chapter	
Torque wrench settings	**Nm**	**lbf ft**
Tailgate/rear window wiper arm nut............................	16	12
Windscreen wiper arm nuts	19	14

1 General information and precautions

⚠️ **Warning: Before carrying out any work on the electrical system, read through the precautions given in 'Safety first!' at the beginning of this manual, and in Chapter 5, Section 1.**

1 The electrical system is of the 12 volt negative earth type. Power for the lights and all electrical accessories is supplied by a lead-acid type battery, which is charged by the engine-driven alternator.

2 This Chapter covers repair and service procedures for the various electrical components not associated with the engine. Information on the battery, alternator and starter motor can be found in Chapter 5.

3 It should be noted that, prior to working on any component in the electrical system, the battery negative terminal should first be disconnected, to prevent the possibility of electrical short-circuits and/or fires.

Caution: Before proceeding, refer to 'Disconnecting the battery' in the Reference Chapter.

2 Electrical fault finding – general information

Note: *Refer to the precautions given in 'Safety first!' at the beginning of this manual and in Chapter 5, Section 1 before starting work. The following tests relate to testing of the main electrical circuits, and should not be used to test delicate electronic circuits, particularly where an electronic control unit is used.*

General

1 A typical electrical circuit consists of an electrical component, any switches, relays, motors, fuses, fusible links or circuit breakers related to that component, and the wiring and connectors which link the component to both the battery and the chassis. To help to pinpoint a problem in an electrical circuit, wiring diagrams are included at the end of this Chapter.

2 Before attempting to diagnose an electrical fault, first study the appropriate wiring diagram, to obtain a complete understanding of the components included in the particular circuit concerned. The possible sources of a fault can be narrowed down by noting if other components related to the circuit are operating properly. If several components or circuits fail at one time, the problem is likely to be related to a shared fuse or earth connection.

3 Electrical problems usually stem from simple causes, such as loose or corroded connections, a faulty earth connection, a blown fuse, a melted fusible link, or a faulty relay (refer to Section 3 for details of testing relays). Visually inspect the condition of all fuses, wires and connections in a problem circuit before testing the components. Use the wiring diagrams to determine which terminal connections will need to be checked in order to pinpoint the trouble-spot.

4 The basic tools required for electrical fault-finding include a circuit tester or voltmeter (a 12-volt bulb with a set of test leads can also be used for certain tests); an ohmmeter (to measure resistance and check for continuity); a battery and set of test leads; and a jumper wire, preferably with a circuit breaker or fuse incorporated, which can be used to bypass suspect wires or electrical components. Before attempting to locate a problem with test instruments, use the wiring diagram to determine where to make the connections.

5 To find the source of an intermittent wiring fault (usually due to a poor or dirty connection, or damaged wiring insulation), a 'wiggle' test can be performed on the wiring. This involves wiggling the wiring by hand to see if the fault occurs as the wiring is moved. It should be possible to narrow down the source of the fault to a particular section of wiring. This method of testing can be used in conjunction with any of the tests described in the following sub-Sections.

6 Apart from problems due to poor connections, two basic types of fault can occur in an electrical circuit – open-circuit, or short-circuit.

7 Open-circuit faults are caused by a break somewhere in the circuit, which prevents current from flowing. An open-circuit fault will prevent a component from working.

8 Short-circuit faults are caused by a 'short' somewhere in the circuit, which allows the current flowing in the circuit to 'escape' along an alternative route, usually to earth. Short-circuit faults are normally caused by a breakdown in wiring insulation, which allows a feed wire to touch either another wire, or an earthed component such as the bodyshell. A short-circuit fault will normally cause the relevant circuit fuse to blow.

Finding an open-circuit

9 To check for an open-circuit, connect one lead of a circuit tester or the negative lead of a voltmeter either to the battery negative terminal or to a known good earth.

10 Connect the other lead to a connector in the circuit being tested, preferably nearest to the battery or fuse. At this point, battery voltage should be present, unless the lead from the battery or the fuse itself is faulty (bearing in mind that some circuits are live only when the ignition switch is moved to a particular position).

11 Switch on the circuit, then connect the tester lead to the connector nearest the circuit switch on the component side.

12 If voltage is present (indicated either by the tester bulb lighting or a voltmeter reading, as applicable), this means that the section of the circuit between the relevant connector and the switch is problem-free.

13 Continue to check the remainder of the circuit in the same fashion.

14 When a point is reached at which no voltage is present, the problem must lie between that point and the previous test point with voltage. Most problems can be traced to a broken, corroded or loose connection.

Finding a short-circuit

15 To check for a short-circuit, first disconnect the load(s) from the circuit (loads are the components which draw current from a circuit, such as bulbs, motors, heating elements, etc).

16 Remove the relevant fuse from the circuit, and connect a circuit tester or voltmeter to the fuse connections.

17 Switch on the circuit, bearing in mind that some circuits are live only when the ignition switch is moved to a particular position.

18 If voltage is present (indicated either by the tester bulb lighting or a voltmeter reading, as applicable), this means that there is a short-circuit.

19 If no voltage is present during this test, but the fuse still blows with the load(s) reconnected, this indicates an internal fault in the load(s).

Finding an earth fault

20 The battery negative terminal is connected to 'earth' – the metal of the engine/transmission and the vehicle body – and many systems are wired so that they only receive a positive feed, the current returning via the metal of the car body. This means that the component mounting and the body form part of that circuit. Loose or corroded mountings can therefore cause a range of electrical faults, ranging from total failure of a circuit, to a puzzling partial failure. In particular, lights may shine dimly (especially when another circuit sharing the same earth point is in operation), motors (eg wiper motors or the heater blower motor) may run slowly, and the operation of one circuit may have an apparently-unrelated effect on another. Note that on many vehicles, earth straps are used between certain components, such as the engine/transmission and the body, usually where there is no metal-to-metal contact between components, due to flexible rubber mountings, etc.

21 To check whether a component is properly earthed, disconnect the battery and connect one lead of an ohmmeter to a known good earth point. Connect the other lead to the wire or earth connection being tested. The resistance reading should be zero; if not, check the connection as follows.

22 If an earth connection is thought to be faulty, dismantle the connection, and clean both the bodyshell and the wire terminal (or the component earth connection mating surface) back to bare metal. Be careful to remove all

traces of dirt and corrosion, then use a knife to trim away any paint, so that a clean metal-to-metal joint is made. On reassembly, tighten the joint fasteners securely; if a wire terminal is being refitted, use serrated washers between the terminal and the bodyshell, to ensure a clean and secure connection. When the connection is remade, prevent the onset of corrosion in the future by applying a coat of petroleum jelly or silicone-based grease, or by spraying on (at regular intervals) a proprietary water-dispersant lubricant.

3 Fuses and relays – general information

Fuses

1 The main fuse/relay box is located under the facia on the driver's side. To gain access, turn the retaining catch anti-clockwise and open the stowage box fully (see illustrations). Lift the stowage box out of the lower retainers and remove it from the facia.

2 The main fuses are located in a row below the relays. A list of the circuits each fuse protects is contained in the vehicle handbook and in the wiring diagrams at the end of this Chapter. On some models (depending on specification), some additional fuses are located under the driver's seat and in separate holders which can be found in the engine compartment.

3 To remove a fuse, pull it out of its location in the holder. The wire within the fuse is clearly visible, and it will be broken if the fuse is blown (see illustrations).

4 Always renew a fuse with one of an identical rating; never use a fuse with a different rating from the original, nor substitute anything else. Never renew a fuse more than once without tracing the source of the trouble. The fuse rating is stamped on top of the fuse; note that the fuses are also colour-coded for easy recognition.

5 If a new fuse blows immediately, find the cause before renewing it again; a short to earth as a result of faulty insulation is most likely. Where a fuse protects more than one circuit, try to isolate the defect by switching on each circuit in turn (if possible) until the fuse blows again. Always carry a supply of spare fuses of each relevant rating on the vehicle, a spare of each rating should be clipped into the fuse/relay box cover.

Relays

6 The relays are all located in the main fuse/relay box.

7 If a circuit or system controlled by a relay develops a fault and the relay is suspect, operate the system; if the relay is functioning, it should be possible to hear it click as it is energised. If this is the case, the fault lies with the components or wiring of the system. If the relay is not being energised, then either

3.1a Turn the retaining catch anti-clockwise...

3.3a To remove a fuse, pull it out of its location in the holder

4.5 Disconnect the wiring connector for the left-hand combination switch

3.1b ...and open the driver's side stowage box fully

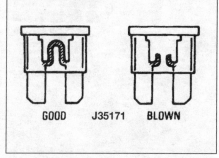
3.3b The fuses can be checked visually to determine if they are blown

the relay is not receiving a main supply or a switching voltage, or the relay itself is faulty. Testing is by the substitution of a known good unit, but be careful; while some relays are identical in appearance and in operation, others look similar but perform different functions.

8 To renew a relay, first ensure that the ignition switch is off. The relay can then simply be pulled out from the socket and the new relay pressed in.

4 Switches – removal and refitting

Note: Disconnect the battery negative terminal (refer to Disconnecting the battery) before removing any switch, and reconnect the terminal after refitting.

Ignition switch/ steering column lock

1 Refer to Chapter 10, Section 21.

Steering column combination switch

2 The steering column combination switch consists of left-hand and right-hand assemblies. The left-hand switch assembly comprises the headlight dip/flasher switch and the direction indicator switch; the right-hand switch assembly comprises the wiper/washer switch.

3 Remove the steering wheel as described in Chapter 10, Section 20.

4 Remove the steering column shrouds as described in Chapter 11, Section 29.

5 Disconnect the wiring connector for the left-hand switch (see illustration).

6 Undo the three retaining screws, and remove the left-hand switch assembly (see illustrations).

4.6a Undo the three retaining screws (arrowed)...

4.7a Disconnect the wiring connector...

4.7b ...and remove the right-hand combination switch

4.6b ...and remove the left-hand combination switch

4.9a Insert a feeler blade into the gap between the exterior light switch and the fresh air vent...

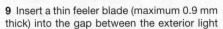

4.9b ...then slide the blade to the left to depress the retaining catch (arrowed) – shown with switch removed

switch and the fresh air vent at a point midway along the switch. Slide the feeler blade to the left to depress the retaining catch and at the same time pull the switch out of the facia by means of the rotary knob (see illustrations).

10 Disconnect the wiring connectors and remove the light switch (see illustrations).

11 Refitting is a reversal of removal.

Facia centre panel switches

12 Remove the ashtray from its location in the facia.

13 Starting at the bottom of the ashtray aperture and working up, carefully prise free the switch panel trim surround (see illustration).

14 Using a small screwdriver, depress the retaining tab and pull the relevant switch from its location. Disconnect the wiring connector and remove the switch (see illustrations).

15 Refitting is a reversal of removal.

Hazard warning light switch

16 On early models the hazard warning light switch is incorporated in the steering column combination switch. Combination switch removal and refitting procedures are contained in paragraphs 2 to 8.

17 On later models the hazard warning light switch is situated adjacent to the facia centre air vents. Begin by removing the centre air vents and air outlet as described in Chapter 11, Section 29.

18 Insert two screwdrivers under the base of the switch to release the retaining tabs, while at the same time reach behind the switch and

7 Disconnect the wiring connector for the right-hand switch and remove the switch (see illustrations).

8 Refitting is a reversal of removal.

Exterior light switch

9 Insert a thin feeler blade (maximum 0.9 mm thick) into the gap between the exterior light

4.10a Disconnect the light switch main wiring connector...

4.10b ...and secondary wiring connector

4.13 Carefully prise free the centre switch panel trim surround

4.14a Depress the retaining tab and pull the relevant switch from its location

4.14b Disconnect the wiring connector and remove the switch

pull it forward, into the facia. Disconnect the wiring connector and remove the switch (see illustrations).

19 Refitting is a reversal of removal.

Stop-light switch

20 Refer to Chapter 9, Section 22.

Handbrake warning light switch

21 Refer to Chapter 9, Section 19.

Electric window/mirror adjustment switch

22 Carefully prise free the electric window and mirror adjustment switch from the top of the door trim panel, disconnect the switch wiring connector and remove the switch.
23 Refitting is a reversal of removal.

Heating/ventilation/air conditioning system switches

24 The switches are all an integral part of the heating/ventilation control unit, and cannot be individually removed. Should a switch become faulty, the complete control unit assembly must be renewed (see Chapter 3, Section 10).

---

5 Bulbs (exterior lights) – renewal

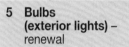

General

1 Whenever a bulb is renewed, note the following points:
 a) *Make sure the switch is in the OFF position, for the respective bulb you are working on.*
 b) *Remember that if the light has just been in use, the bulb may be extremely hot.*
 c) *Always check the bulb contacts and holder, ensuring that there is clean metal-to-metal contact between the bulb and its live(s) and earth. Clean off any corrosion or dirt before fitting a new bulb.*
 d) *Wherever bayonet-type bulbs are fitted, ensure that the live contact(s) bear firmly against the bulb contact.*
 e) *Always ensure that the new bulb is of the correct rating, and that it is completely clean before fitting it; this applies particularly to headlight/foglight bulbs.*

5.4b ...then lift the bulb out of the light unit

4.18a Using two screwdrivers, depress the switch retaining tabs, then pull the switch into the facia

Headlight

Note: *To improve access to the left-hand headlight bulb, remove the battery cover. Alternatively, for better access to the bulbs on both sides, remove the headlight unit as described in Section 7.*
2 Disconnect the headlight bulb wiring connector.
3 Pull off the cover at the rear of the headlight unit (see illustration).
4 Release the legs of the retaining spring clip from their locations in the light unit. Pivot the clip off the bulb, then lift the bulb out of the light unit (see illustrations). When handling the new bulb, use a tissue or clean cloth to avoid touching the glass with the fingers; moisture and grease from the skin can cause blackening and rapid failure of this type of bulb. If the glass is accidentally

5.3 Pull off the cover at the rear of the headlight unit

5.7 Untwist and withdraw the sidelight bulbholder from the rear of the headlight

4.18b Disconnect the wiring connector and remove the switch

touched, wipe it clean using methylated spirit.
5 Fit the new bulb to the headlight unit and secure with the spring clip. Refit the cover to the rear of the headlight unit, then reconnect the wiring connector.
6 Check for satisfactory operation on completion.

Front sidelight

7 Untwist the sidelight bulbholder from the rear of the headlight, and withdraw the bulb and holder (see illustration).
8 The bulb is a bayonet fit in the holder, and can be removed by pressing it and twisting in an anti-clockwise direction (see illustration).
9 Fit the new bulb using a reversal of the removal procedure. Check for satisfactory operation on completion.

5.4a Release the legs of the retaining spring clip...

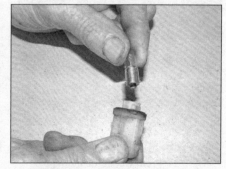

5.8 Remove the bulb by pressing it and twisting in an anti-clockwise direction

5.10a Insert a screwdriver into the gap between the headlight and direction indicator...

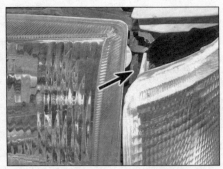

5.10b ...to depress the direction indicator retaining tab (arrowed)

5.12 Disconnect the wiring connector and remove the direction indicator

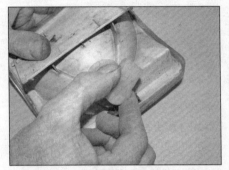

5.13 Twist the indicator bulbholder anti-clockwise, and remove it from the rear of the light unit

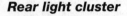

5.14 Remove the bulb by pressing it and twisting in an anti-clockwise direction

Front direction indicator

10 Insert a thin screwdriver into the gap between the headlight and direction indicator, to depress the direction indicator retaining tab **(see illustrations)**.

11 With the tab depressed, pull the direction indicator from its location.

12 Disconnect the wiring connector and remove the direction indicator **(see illustration)**.

13 Twist the indicator bulbholder anti-clockwise, and remove it from the rear of the light unit **(see illustration)**.

14 The bulb is a bayonet fit in the holder, and can be removed by pressing it and twisting in an anti-clockwise direction **(see illustration)**.

15 Fit the new bulb and the light unit using a reversal of the removal procedure. Check for satisfactory operation on completion.

Front foglight

16 From under the front bumper, pull off the cover at the rear of the foglight unit.

17 Disconnect the foglight bulb wiring at the connector and disconnect the foglight unit earth lead.

18 Release the legs of the retaining spring clip from their locations in the foglight unit. Pivot the clip off the bulb, then lift the bulb out of the light unit. When handling the new bulb, use a tissue or clean cloth to avoid touching the glass with the fingers; moisture and grease from the skin can cause blackening and rapid failure of this type of bulb. If the glass is accidentally touched, wipe it clean using methylated spirit.

19 Fit the new bulb to the foglight unit and secure with the spring clip. Reconnect the

wiring, then refit the cover to the rear of the foglight unit.

20 Check for satisfactory operation on completion.

Rear light cluster

Van models

21 From within the luggage compartment, remove the trim cover over the bulb access aperture **(see illustration)**.

22 Reach in through the aperture, depress the two bulbholder retaining tabs and withdraw the bulbholder from the light unit.

23 The bulbs are a bayonet fit in the bulbholder, and can be removed by pressing in and twisting in an anti-clockwise direction **(see illustration)**.

24 Fit the new bulb(s) using a reversal of the removal procedure. Check for satisfactory operation on completion.

Chassis Cab models

25 Undo the retaining screws and lift the lens off the light unit.

26 The bulbs are a bayonet fit in the light unit, and can be removed by pressing in and twisting in an anti-clockwise direction.

27 Fit the new bulb(s) using a reversal of the removal procedure. Check for satisfactory operation on completion.

Rear number plate light

28 Undo the two screws and withdraw the light unit **(see illustration)**.

29 Withdraw the bulbholder from the light

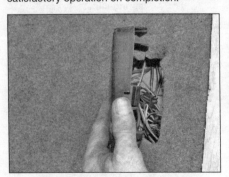

5.21 From within the luggage compartment, remove the trim cover over the bulb access aperture

5.23 Remove the relevant bulb by pressing it and twisting in an anti-clockwise direction

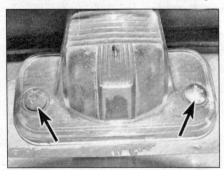

5.28 Undo the two screws (arrowed) and withdraw the number plate light unit

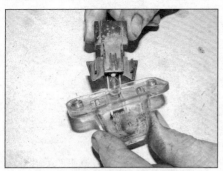

5.29a Withdraw the number plate bulbholder from the light unit...

5.29b ...then remove the push fit bulb from the holder

5.31 Depress the retaining tab and withdraw the light unit from the bumper

unit, then remove the bulb from its holder by pulling it free **(see illustrations)**.

30 Fit the new bulb using a reversal of the removal procedure. Check for satisfactory operation on completion.

Rear foglight

31 Using a small screwdriver, depress the retaining tab and withdraw the light unit from the bumper **(see illustration)**.

32 Twist the foglight bulbholder anti-clockwise, and remove it from the rear of the light unit **(see illustration)**.

33 The bulb is a bayonet fit in the holder, and can be removed by pressing it and twisting in an anti-clockwise direction **(see illustration)**.

34 Fit the new bulb and the light unit using a reversal of the removal procedure. Check for satisfactory operation on completion.

High-level stop-light

35 Depress the tabs on each side of the light unit cover and take off the cover and bulbholder **(see illustration)**.

36 Remove the relevant bulb from the bulbholder by pulling it free **(see illustrations)**.

37 Fit the new bulb using a reversal of the removal procedure. Check for satisfactory operation on completion.

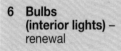

6 Bulbs (interior lights) – renewal

General

1 Refer to Section 5, paragraph 1.

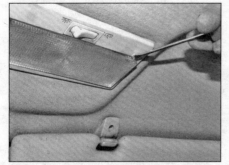

6.2a Carefully release the lens from the courtesy light unit...

5.32 Twist the foglight bulbholder anti-clockwise, and remove it from the light unit

5.35 Depress the tabs and take off the high-level stop-light cover and bulbholder

Courtesy lights

Note: *Various types of light units may be fitted depending on model year and trim level. In general the procedure for bulb renewal is similar for all types. A typical procedure is described here.*

6.2b ...then remove the lens

5.33 Remove the bulb by pressing it and twisting in an anti-clockwise direction

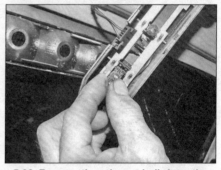

5.36 Remove the relevant bulb from the bulbholder by pulling it free

2 Using a small screwdriver, carefully release the lens from the light unit, then remove the lens **(see illustrations)**.

3 The light has a festoon-type bulb, and this type is simply pulled from its contacts **(see illustration)**.

6.3 Pull the festoon-type bulb from its contacts

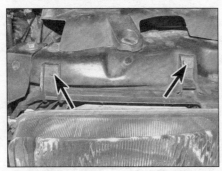

7.3a Undo the two upper screws (arrowed)...

7.3b ...and two lower screws (arrowed) securing the headlight to the body panel

7.4 Withdraw the headlight unit from its location and disconnect the wiring connectors

4 Fit the new bulb using a reversal of the removal procedure. Check for satisfactory operation on completion.

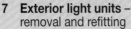
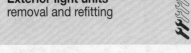

7 Exterior light units – removal and refitting

Note: *Disconnect the battery negative terminal (refer to Disconnecting the battery) before removing any light unit. Reconnect the terminal after refitting.*

Headlight unit

1 Remove the radiator grille as described in Chapter 11, Section 25.
2 On pre-August 1994 models, unscrew the two bolts securing the apron panel below the headlight to the front body panel. Pull the apron forward to disengage the securing clips from the T-studs on the front wing. A suitable hook can be fabricated out of 2 mm diameter rod (ie welding rod) and inserted in the gap between the apron and wing, enabling the apron to be pulled forward off the studs.
3 Undo the four screws securing the headlight to the body panel **(see illustrations)**.
4 Withdraw the headlight unit from its location, disconnect the wiring connectors and remove the unit from the vehicle **(see illustration)**.
5 Refit in the reverse order of removal. Refer to Section 8 for details on headlight beam alignment. Check the headlights, sidelights and indicators for satisfactory operation on completion.

Front direction indicator

6 Removal and refitting of the light unit is part of the bulb renewal procedure. Refer to the procedures contained in Section 5.

Front foglight

7 From under the front bumper, pull off the cover at the rear of the foglight unit.
8 Disconnect the foglight bulb wiring at the connector and disconnect the foglight unit earth lead.
9 Undo the three bolts securing the light unit to the bumper and remove the unit from under the wheel arch.
10 Refit in the reverse order of removal. Check for satisfactory operation on completion, and refer to Section 8 for details on beam alignment.

Rear light cluster

Van models

11 From within the luggage compartment, remove the trim cover over the bulb access aperture **(see illustration 5.21)**.
12 Reach in through the aperture and undo the three nuts securing the light unit to the rear wing.
13 Depress the three retaining tabs and withdraw the light unit from the wing **(see illustrations)**.
14 Disconnect the light unit wiring connector and remove the unit from the vehicle.
15 Refit in the reverse order of removal. Check for satisfactory operation on completion.

Chassis Cab models

16 Disconnect the light unit wiring connector.
17 Undo the two retaining nuts, collect the washers and remove the light unit from the vehicle.
18 Refit in the reverse order of removal. Check for satisfactory operation on completion.

Rear number plate light

19 Undo the two screws and withdraw the light unit **(see illustration 5.28)**.
20 Disconnect the wiring connector and remove the light unit.
21 Refit in the reverse order of removal. Check for satisfactory operation on completion.

Rear foglight

22 Using a small screwdriver, depress the retaining tab and withdraw the light unit from the bumper **(see illustration 5.31)**.
23 Disconnect the wiring connector and remove the light unit.
24 Refit in the reverse order of removal. Check for satisfactory operation on completion.

High-level stop-light

25 Depress the tabs on each side of the light unit cover and take off the cover and bulbholder **(see illustration 5.35)**. Disconnect the wiring connector and remove the bulbholder.
26 Depress the tab at each end of the light unit housing and remove the light unit and remove the housing and lens from the rear window.
27 Refit in the reverse order of removal. Check for satisfactory operation on completion.

8 Headlight beam alignment – general information

1 Accurate adjustment of the headlight/foglight beam is only possible using optical beam-setting equipment, and this work should therefore be carried out by a VW dealer or suitably-equipped workshop.
2 Most models have an electrically-operated headlight beam adjustment system, controlled via a switch in the facia. With the vehicle

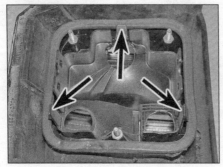

7.13a Depress the three retaining tabs (arrowed) – shown with light unit removed...

7.13b ...and withdraw the light unit from the wing

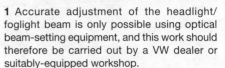

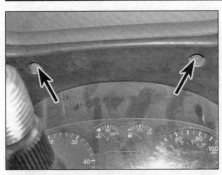

9.3 Undo the two upper screws (arrowed) securing the instrument panel surround to the facia

9.4 Pull the surround away from the facia to release the locating lugs (arrowed) each side

9.5a Undo the right-hand screw (arrowed)...

9.5b ...and left-hand screw (arrowed) securing the instrument panel to the facia

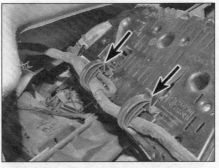

9.6a Release the wiring harness from the clips (arrowed) at the rear of the instrument panel...

9.6b ...then disconnect the wiring connectors

unladen, the switch should be set in position '0'. With the vehicle partially or fully loaded, set the switch position to provide adequate illumination without dazzling oncoming drivers.

9 Instrument panel – removal and refitting

Removal

1 Disconnect the battery negative terminal (refer to *Disconnecting the battery*).
2 Remove the steering column shrouds as described in Chapter 11, Section 29.
3 Undo the two upper screws securing the instrument panel surround to the facia **(see illustration)**.
4 Pull the surround away from the facia to release the locating lugs from the retaining clips each side, then remove the surround **(see illustration)**.
5 Undo the two screws securing the instrument panel to the facia **(see illustrations)**.
6 Withdraw the instrument panel from the facia and, where applicable, disconnect the speedometer cable and vacuum hose. Release the wiring harness from the clips at the rear of the panel, then disconnect the wiring connectors and remove the panel **(see illustrations)**.

Refitting

7 Refitting is a reversal of removal.

10 Headlight levelling motor – removal and refitting

Removal

1 Remove the headlight unit as described in Section 7.
2 Unscrew the bolt securing the levelling motor to the operating arm **(see illustration)**.
3 Release the levelling motor from the headlight unit by rotating it clockwise (right-hand headlight) or anti-clockwise (left-hand headlight) **(see illustration)**.
4 Pull the levelling motor firmly away to release it from the locator and remove the motor from the rear of the headlight.

10.2 Unscrew the bolt (arrowed) securing the headlight levelling motor to the operating arm

Refitting

5 Refit in the reverse order of removal. Check for satisfactory operation on completion.

11 Horn – removal and refitting

Removal

1 The horn is located behind the front bumper on the left-hand side.
2 Firmly apply the handbrake, then jack up the front of the vehicle and support it securely on axle stands (see *Jacking and vehicle support*).
3 Disconnect the wiring connector from the

10.3 Rotate the headlight levelling motor to release it from the light unit

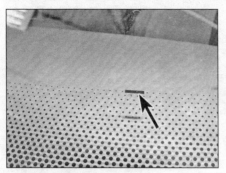

12.1 Lines on the windscreen glass (arrowed) indicate the parked position of the wiper blades

12.2a Lift up the plastic cap from the bottom of the wiper arm...

12.2b ...unscrew the retaining nut...

12.2c ...and remove the washer

12.3 Lift the wiper arm and release it from the taper on the spindle

horn, then unscrew the retaining nut and remove the horn from the mounting bracket. The horn cannot be adjusted or repaired, and therefore if defective, it must be renewed.

Refitting

4 Refit in the reverse order of removal. Check for satisfactory operation on completion.

13.3 Undo the retaining bolts and remove the intercooler upper mounting bracket

13.4a Undo the retaining nut...

13.4b ...and remove the spacer ring securing the wiper linkage frame to the scuttle

13.5 Undo the retaining bolt (arrowed) securing the wiper linkage frame to the engine compartment bulkhead

12 Wiper arms – removal and refitting

Removal

1 With the wipers 'parked' (ie, in the normal at-rest position), check that there are lines on the glass indicating the parked position of the blades (see illustration). If no lines are visible, mark the position of the blades on the windscreen/rear window, using a wax crayon or strips of masking tape.
2 Lift up the plastic cap from the bottom of the wiper arm, unscrew the retaining nut and remove the washer (see illustrations).
3 Lift the wiper arm and release it from the taper on the spindle by easing it from side to side (see illustration). If necessary, use a puller to release it.

Refitting

4 Refitting is a reversal of removal. Make sure the arm is fitted in its previously noted position before tightening the nut to the specified torque.

13 Windscreen wiper motor and linkage – removal and refitting

Removal

1 Disconnect the battery negative terminal (refer to *Disconnecting the battery*).
2 Remove the wiper arms as described in Section 12.
3 Where applicable, remove the intercooler as described in Chapter 4A, Section 14, then undo the retaining bolts and remove the intercooler upper mounting bracket (see illustration).
4 Undo the retaining nut and remove the spacer ring each side securing the ends of the wiper linkage frame to the scuttle (see illustrations).
5 Undo the retaining bolt and recover the spacer and rubber grommet securing the centre of the wiper linkage frame to the underside of the engine compartment bulkhead (see illustration).

6 Disconnect the wiring connector from the wiper motor, then manoeuvre the wiper linkage frame and motor out from the underside of the scuttle **(see illustrations)**.
7 To remove the motor from the linkage, prise the linkage balljoints off the motor crank arm ballpin, using a large screwdriver **(see illustration)**.
8 Undo the three retaining bolts and remove the motor from the linkage frame **(see illustration)**.

Refitting

9 Refitting is a reversal of removal, noting the following points:
a) Switch the wiper motor on then switch it off so that it stops in the 'parked' position before refitting the wiper arms.
b) Refit the wiper arms as described in Section 12.
c) On completion, check the wipers for satisfactory operation.

14 Tailgate/rear door wiper motor – removal and refitting

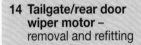

Tailgate wiper motor

Removal

1 Disconnect the battery negative terminal (refer to *Disconnecting the battery*).
2 Remove the wiper arm as described in Section 12.
3 Remove the tailgate trim panel as described in Chapter 11, Section 9
4 Undo the retaining nut and remove the spacer ring securing the wiper linkage to the tailgate **(see illustration)**.
5 Disconnect the wiring connector from the wiper motor **(see illustration)**.
6 Disconnect the washer hose at the plastic connector **(see illustration)**.
7 Undo the two bolts and remove the wiper motor and linkage from the tailgate **(see illustration)**.
8 To remove the motor from the linkage, first make an alignment mark on the motor crank arm and a corresponding mark on the linkage frame.
9 Hold the motor crank arm using an open-ended spanner, then unscrew the crank arm retaining nut with a second spanner.
10 Lift off the crank arm, then undo the three retaining bolts and remove the motor from the linkage frame.

Refitting

11 Refitting is a reversal of removal, aligning the marks made on removal when refitting the crank arm. Check for satisfactory operation on completion.

Rear door wiper motor

Removal

12 Disconnect the battery negative terminal (refer to *Disconnecting the battery*).

13.6a Disconnect the wiring connector from the wiper motor...

13.6b ...then manoeuvre the wiper linkage frame and motor out from the underside of the scuttle

13.7 Prise the linkage balljoints off the wiper motor crank arm ballpin using a large screwdriver

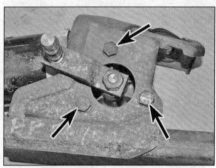

13.8 Undo the three retaining bolts (arrowed) and remove the wiper motor from the linkage frame

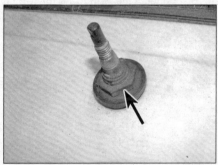

14.4 Undo the retaining nut (arrowed) and remove the spacer ring securing the wiper linkage to the tailgate

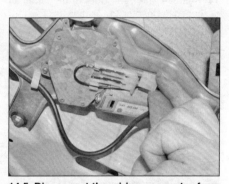

14.5 Disconnect the wiring connector from the tailgate wiper motor

14.6 Disconnect the washer hose at the plastic connector

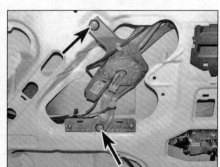

14.7 Undo the two bolts (arrowed) and remove the wiper motor and linkage from the tailgate

14.15 Undo the retaining nut and remove the spacer ring securing the wiper linkage to the door

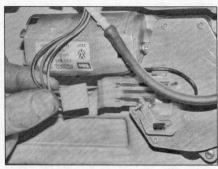

14.16a Disconnect the wiper motor wiring connector...

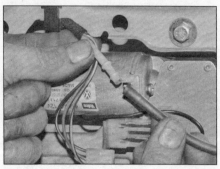

14.16b ...and disconnect the washer hose

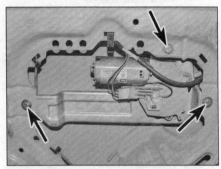

14.17a Undo the three bolts (arrowed)...

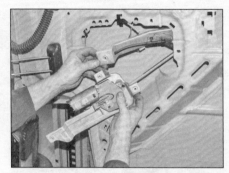

14.17b ...and remove the wiper motor and linkage from the door

13 Remove the wiper arm as described in Section 12.
14 Remove the rear door trim panel as described in Chapter 11, Section 9

15 Undo the retaining nut and remove the spacer ring securing the wiper linkage to the door (see illustration).
16 Disconnect the wiper motor wiring

connector and washer hose (see illustrations).
17 Undo the three bolts and remove the wiper motor and linkage from the door (see illustrations).
18 To remove the motor from the linkage, first make an alignment mark on the motor crank arm and a corresponding mark on the linkage frame.
19 Hold the motor crank arm using an open-ended spanner, then unscrew the crank arm retaining nut with a second spanner (see illustration).
20 Lift off the crank arm, then undo the three retaining bolts and remove the motor from the linkage frame (see illustrations).

Refitting

21 Refitting is a reversal of removal, aligning the marks made on removal when refitting the crank arm. Check for satisfactory operation on completion.

15 Windscreen/tailgate/rear door washer system components – removal and refitting

Washer reservoir

Removal

1 Remove the air cleaner assembly as described in Chapter 4A, Section 2.
2 On vehicles equipped with power steering, lift the power steering fluid reservoir out of its mounting bracket and move it to one side.
3 Disconnect the wiring connector and washer hoses from the washer pump (see illustration).
4 Undo the two retaining nuts and lift the reservoir out of the engine compartment.

Refitting

5 Refitting is a reversal of removal.
6 On completion, top-up the reservoir with the required water/washer solution mix, and check for leaks and satisfactory operation.

Washer pump

Removal

7 On vehicles equipped with power steering, lift the power steering fluid reservoir out of its mounting bracket and move it to one side.

14.19 Hold the motor crank arm using an open-ended spanner, then unscrew the crank arm retaining nut

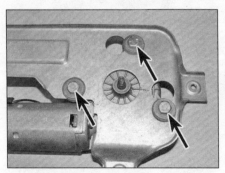

14.20a Lift off the crank arm...

14.20b ...then undo the three bolts (arrowed) and remove the motor from the linkage frame

15.3 Disconnect the wiring connector and washer hoses from the washer pump (arrowed)

15.12 Undo the three screws securing the air intake grille to the bonnet

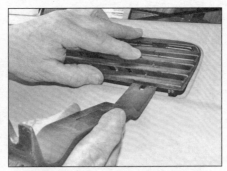

15.13a Carefully release the retaining tabs...

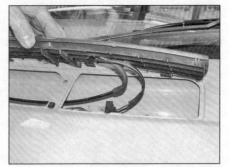

15.13b ...and lift the air intake grille from its location

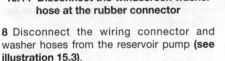

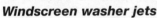

15.14 Disconnect the windscreen washer hose at the rubber connector

15.15a Where applicable, release the washer jet wiring from the retaining clips...

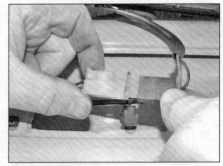

15.15b ...and disconnect the connectors

8 Disconnect the wiring connector and washer hoses from the reservoir pump (see illustration 15.3).
9 Carefully prise the pump out of the seal in the reservoir.

Refitting

10 Refitting is a reversal of removal. Lubricate the pump seal with a little washing-up liquid, to ease fitting of the pump.
11 On completion, top-up the reservoir with the required water/washer solution mix, and check for leaks and satisfactory operation.

Windscreen washer jets

Removal

12 Undo the three screws securing the air intake grille to the bonnet (see illustration).
13 Using a plastic spatula or similar tool carefully release the retaining tabs and lift the air intake grille from its location (see illustrations).
14 Disconnect the windscreen washer hose at the rubber connector (see illustration).
15 If the vehicle is equipped with heated windscreen washer jets, release the washer jet wiring from the retaining clips and disconnect the connectors (see illustrations). Remove the air intake grille.
16 Depress the tab on the end of the jet with a screwdriver and push the jet out of the air intake grille (see illustrations).

Refitting

17 Refitting is a reversal of removal. On completion, check that each nozzle provides a strong jet of washer fluid. The jets should be aimed to spray at a point slightly above

the centre of the windscreen. If necessary, adjust the jets using a pin. Note that on vehicles where the water is sprayed across the windscreen in the shape of a fan, it is not possible to adjust the position of the jets.

Tailgate/rear door washer jets

Removal

18 Remove the tailgate wiper motor or rear door wiper motor as described in Section 14.
19 Pull the jet connecting pipe out of the lower end of the wiper arm shaft, then remove the jet from the upper end of the shaft.

Refitting

20 Refitting is a reversal of removal. On completion, check that the nozzle provides a strong jet of washer fluid. The jet should be aimed to spray at the centre of the wiped area of the glass. If necessary, adjust the jet using a pin.

15.16a Depress the tab on the end of the jet with a screwdriver...

16 Audio unit –
removal and refitting

Removal

Note: This Section applies only to VW standard-fit audio equipment.
1 Removal of the audio unit requires the use of two VW special tools 3316. Equivalent tools are available from car audio specialists. If the audio unit incorporates a navigation system, four of the special tools will be required.
2 Disconnect the battery negative terminal (refer to Disconnecting the battery).
3 Insert the two special tools into the slots on each side of the audio unit. Using the tools, pull the audio unit from the facia.
4 Disconnect the wiring and aerial connections

15.16b ...and push the jet out of the air intake grille

17.1 Carefully lever up the inner facing edge of the speaker grille

17.2 Disengage the lugs on the outer facing edge and remove the speaker grille

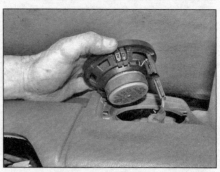

17.3 Lift the loudspeaker out of the facia and disconnect the wiring connector

at the rear of the unit, and remove the unit from the vehicle.

5 Remove the special tools.

Refitting

6 Refitting is a reversal of removal. When the leads are reconnected to the rear of the unit, press it into position to the point where the retaining clips are felt to engage.

17 Loudspeakers – removal and refitting

Facia mounted loudspeakers

Removal

1 Using a small screwdriver, carefully lever up the inner facing edge of the speaker grille (see illustration).

2 Disengage the lugs on the outer facing edge and remove the speaker grille (see illustration).

3 Lift the loudspeaker out of the facia, disconnect the wiring connector and remove the speaker (see illustration).

Refitting

4 Refitting is a reversal of removal.

Loudspeakers in the door trim and side trim panels

Removal

5 Carefully lever off the loudspeaker cover using a small screwdriver.

6 Undo the four screws and remove the loudspeaker from the panel.

7 Disconnect the wiring connector and remove the loudspeaker.

Refitting

8 Refitting is a reversal of removal.

18 Anti-theft alarm system and engine immobiliser – general information

An anti-theft alarm and immobiliser system is fitted as standard or optional equipment. Should the system become faulty, the vehicle should be taken to a VW dealer or specialist for examination. They will have access to a

special diagnostic tester which will quickly trace any fault present in the system.

19 Airbag system – general information and precautions

General information

A driver's airbag, located in the steering wheel centre pad is available as an option on later models. Additionally, a passenger's airbag located in the facia is also optionally available.

The system is armed only when the ignition is switched on however, a reserve power source maintains a power supply to the system in the event of a break in the main electrical supply. The system is activated by a 'g' sensor (deceleration sensor), incorporated in the airbag control unit.

The airbags are inflated by gas generators, which force the bags out from their locations. Although these are safety items, their deployment is violently rapid, and this may cause injury if they are triggered unintentionally.

Precautions

 Warning: The following precautions must be observed when working on vehicles equipped with an airbag system, to prevent the possibility of personal injury.

General precautions

The following precautions must be observed when carrying out work on a vehicle equipped with an airbag:

a) *Do not disconnect the battery with the engine running.*

b) *Before carrying out any work in the vicinity of the airbag, removal of any of the airbag components, or any welding work on the vehicle, de-activate the system as described later in this Section.*

c) *Do not attempt to test any of the airbag system circuits using test meters or any other test equipment.*

d) *If the airbag warning light comes on, or any fault in the system is suspected, consult a VW dealer without delay. Do not attempt to carry out fault diagnosis, or any dismantling of the components.*

Precautions when handling an airbag

a) *Transport the airbag by itself, bag upward.*

b) *Do not put your arms around the airbag.*

c) *Carry the airbag close to the body, bag outward.*

d) *Do not drop the airbag or expose it to impacts.*

e) *Do not attempt to dismantle the airbag unit.*

f) *Do not connect any form of electrical equipment to any part of the airbag circuit.*

Precautions when storing an airbag

a) *Store the unit in a cupboard with the airbag upward.*

b) *Do not expose the airbag to temperatures above 80°C.*

c) *Do not expose the airbag to flames.*

d) *Do not attempt to dispose of the airbag – consult a VW dealer.*

e) *Never refit an airbag which is known to be faulty or damaged.*

De-activation of airbag system

The system must be de-activated before carrying out any work on the airbag components or surrounding area:

a) *Switch on the ignition and check the operation of the airbag warning light on the instrument panel. The light should illuminate when the ignition is switched on, then extinguish.*

b) *Switch off the ignition.*

c) *Remove the ignition key.*

d) *Switch off all electrical equipment.*

e) *Disconnect the battery negative terminal (refer to 'Disconnecting the battery').*

f) *Insulate the battery negative terminal and the end of the battery negative lead to prevent any possibility of contact.*

g) *Wait for at least two minutes before carrying out any further work. Wait at least ten minutes if the airbag warning light did not operate correctly.*

Activation of airbag system

To activate the system on completion of any work, proceed as follows:

a) *Ensure that there are no occupants in the vehicle, and that there are no loose objects around the vicinity of the steering wheel.*

b) *Ensure that the ignition is switched off then reconnect the battery negative terminal.*

c) *Open the driver's door and switch on the*

ignition, without reaching in front of the steering wheel. Check that the airbag warning light illuminates briefly then extinguishes.
d) *Switch off the ignition.*
e) *If the airbag warning light does not operate as described in paragraph c), consult a VW dealer before driving the vehicle.*

20 Airbag system components – removal and refitting

⚠ **Warning: Refer to the precautions given in Section 19 before attempting to carry out work on any of the airbag components.**

Driver's airbag

Removal – pre-August 1998 models

1 De-activate the airbag system as described in Section 19. The airbag unit is an integral part of the steering wheel centre pad.
2 Turn the steering wheel into the centre position (wheels in straight-ahead position).
3 From behind the steering wheel, undo the Torx head airbag retaining screw.
4 Withdraw the airbag from the steering wheel and disconnect the wiring connector.
5 Remove the airbag and store it in a safe place, with reference to the precautions in Section 19.

Removal – August 1998 models onward

6 De-activate the airbag system as described in Section 19. The airbag unit is an integral part of the steering wheel centre pad.
7 Turn the steering wheel 90° to the left so the spokes are uppermost.
8 Insert a screwdriver into the access hole in the back of the steering wheel, with the screwdriver engaged over the airbag retaining wire spring. Move the end of the screwdriver upward to release the wire spring from the lug on the airbag, while at the same time pulling the side of the airbag away from the steering wheel **(see illustrations)**.
9 Turn the steering wheel 180° to the right so the other spokes are uppermost, then repeat the procedure described in paragraph 8.
10 Once the airbag retaining wire springs have been released, withdraw the airbag from the steering wheel and disconnect the wiring connector **(see illustrations)**. Remove the airbag and store it in a safe place, with reference to the precautions in Section 19.

Refitting – all models

11 Refitting is a reversal of removal, noting the following points:
a) *The battery must still be disconnected when reconnecting the airbag wiring.*
b) *Ensure that the airbag wiring connector is securely reconnected.*
c) *On later models the airbag must be firmly pressed into place to secure the retaining wire spring.*

20.8a Move the end of the screwdriver upward (shown with steering wheel removed)...

20.10a Withdraw the airbag from the steering wheel...

Passenger's airbag

Removal

12 De-activate the airbag system as described in Section 19.
13 Remove the passenger's side air vent as described in Chapter 11, Section 29.
14 Remove the audio unit as described in Section 16.
15 Working through the audio unit and air vent apertures, undo the two bolts each side securing the airbag to the facia bracket.
16 Withdraw the airbag from the facia and disconnect the wiring connector.
17 Remove the airbag and store it in a safe place, with reference to the precautions in Section 19.

Refitting

18 Refitting is a reversal of removal, bearing in mind the following points:

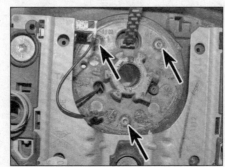

20.21 Airbag contact unit retaining screws (arrowed)

20.8b ...to release the wire spring (arrowed) from the lug on the airbag

20.10b ...and disconnect the wiring connector

a) *The battery must still be disconnected when reconnecting the airbag wiring.*
b) *Make sure that the wiring connector is securely reconnected.*
c) *Tighten the mounting bolts securely.*

Airbag contact unit

Removal

19 De-activate the airbag system as described in Section 19.
20 Remove the steering wheel as described in Chapter 10, Section 20.
21 Undo the three retaining screws and remove the contact unit from the steering wheel **(see illustration)**.

Refitting

22 Refitting is a reversal of removal.
23 Before refitting the steering wheel, the contact unit should be centralised (unless it is known absolutely that the steering wheel was centralised before removal, and that the contact has not been turned during or since its removal).
24 First, turn the contact unit rotor clockwise gently, until resistance is felt.
25 Now turn the contact unit rotor anti-clockwise 3.5 turns.
26 Refit the steering wheel as described in Chapter 10, Section 20.

Airbag control unit

27 The airbag control unit is located beneath the centre of the facia no attempt should be made to remove it. Any suspected problems with the control unit should be referred to a VW dealer.

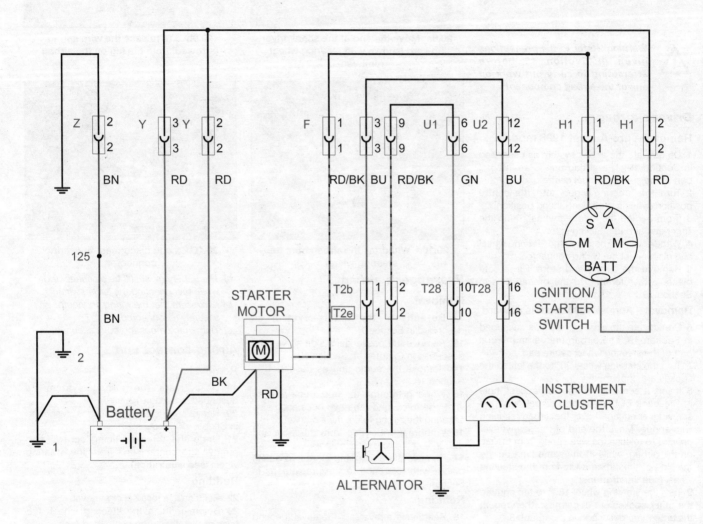

Diagram 1: Starting and charging – 1.9 litre engines

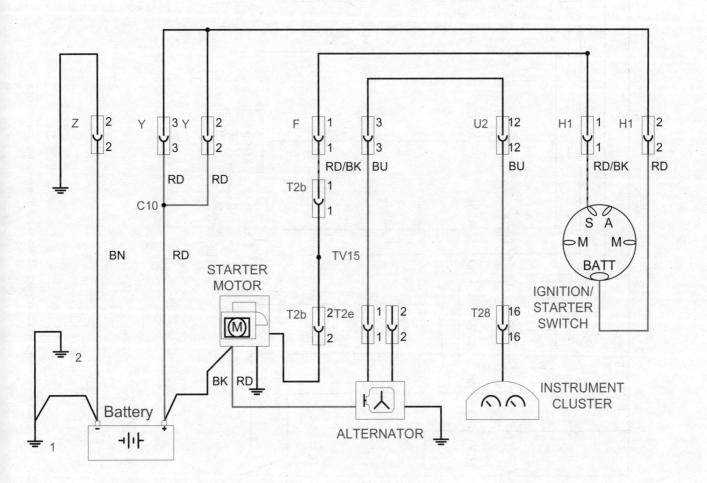

Diagram 2: Starting and charging – 2.5 litre engines from January '96

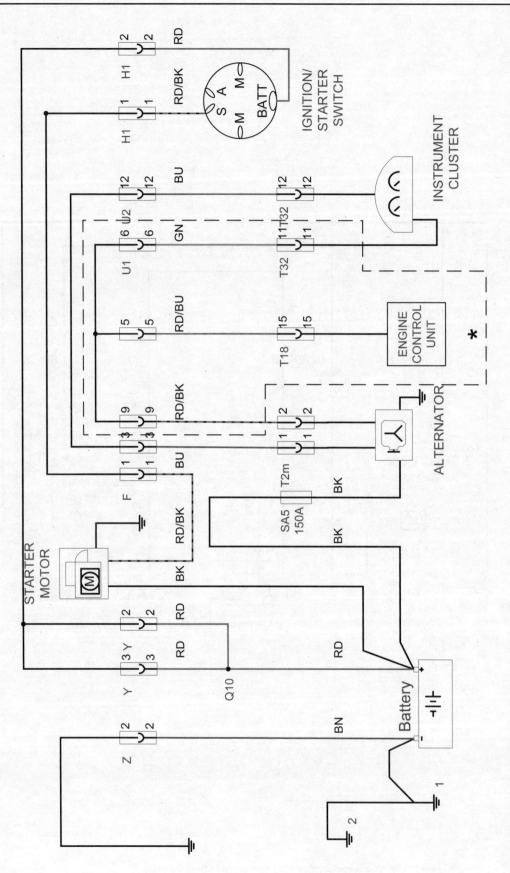

Diagram 3: Starting and charging – 1.9 and 2.5 litre engines from August '98

* Only for vehicles with 1.9 diesel engine

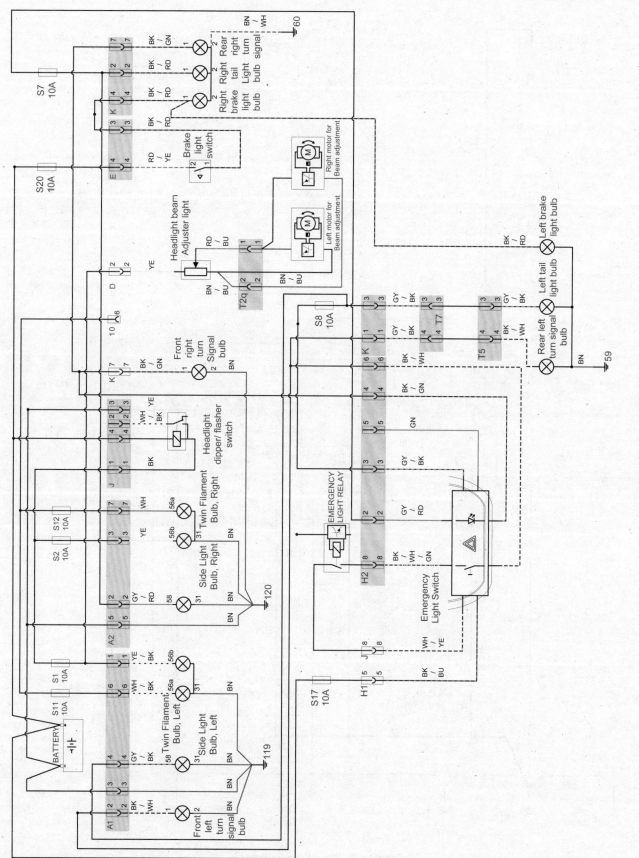

Diagram 4: Typical exterior lights

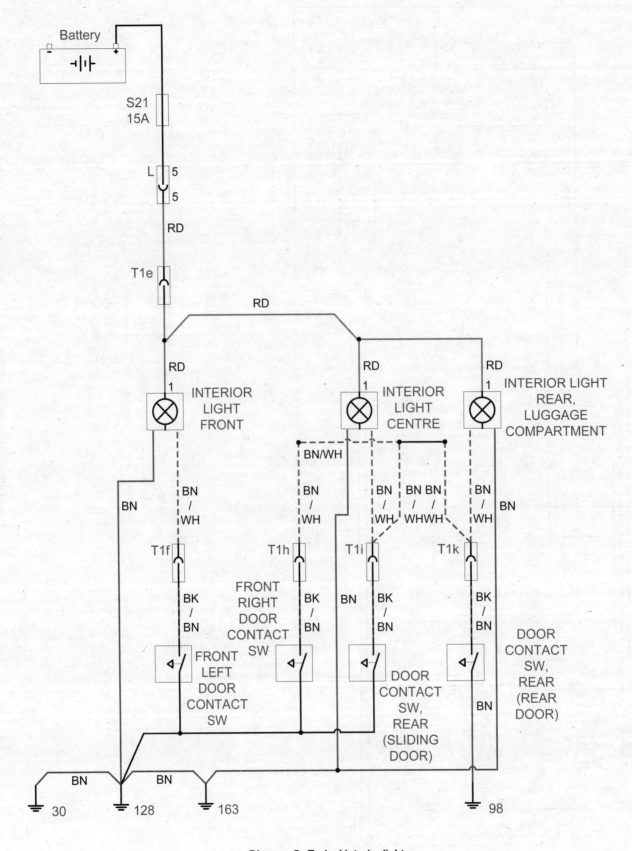

Diagram 5: Typical interior lights

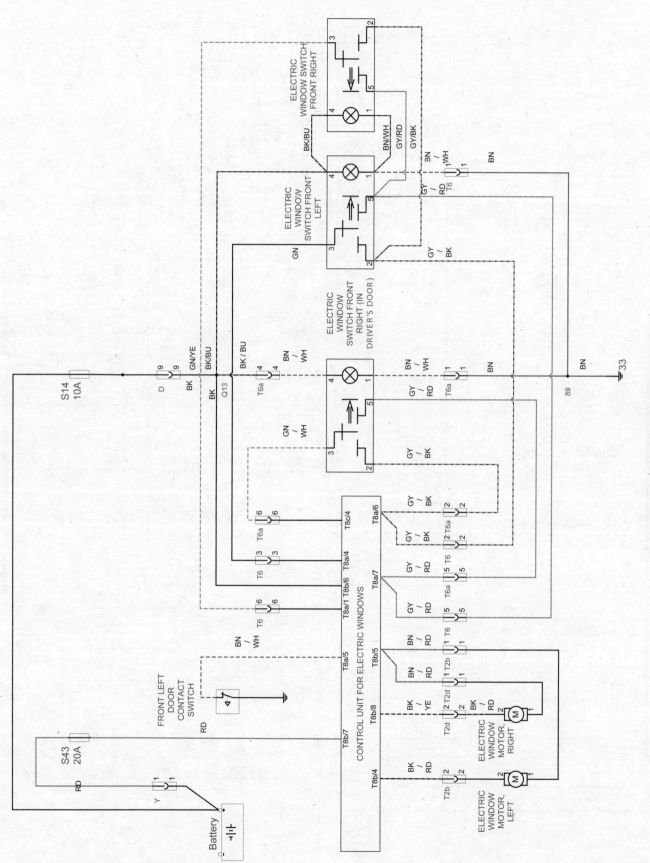

Diagram 6: Electric windows from September '90

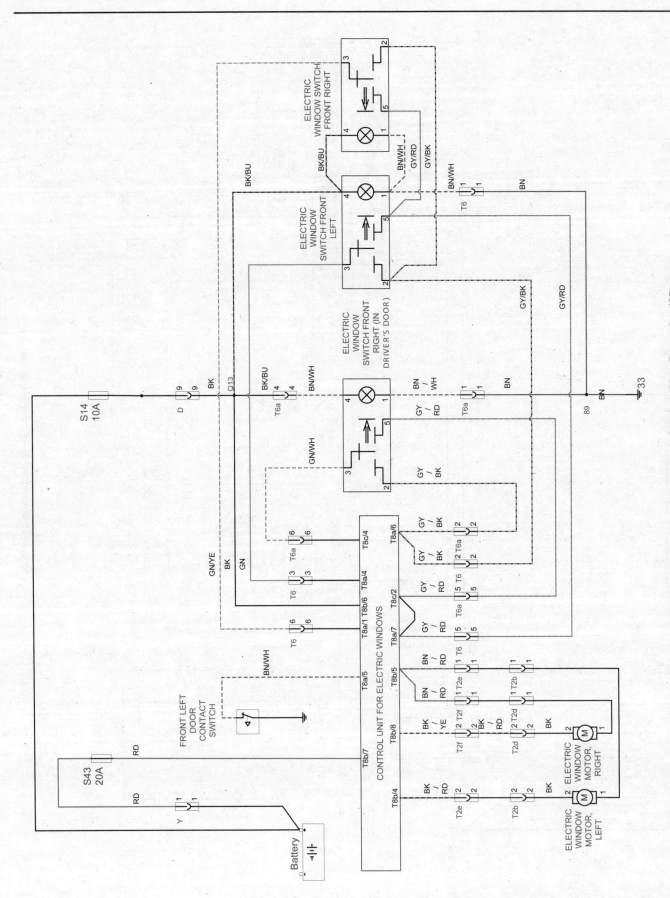

Diagram 7: Electric windows from October '93 to December '95

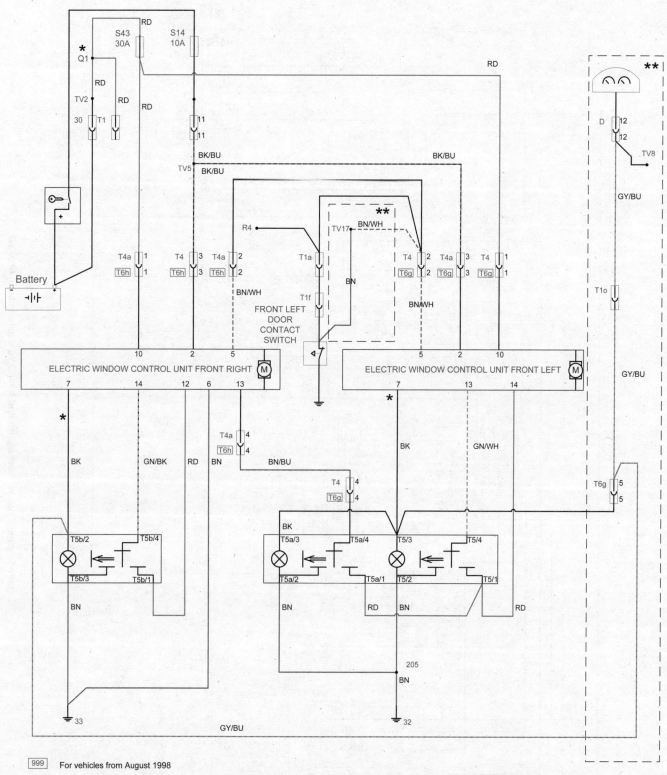

999	For vehicles from August 1998
*	Only for vehicles from January 1996 to June 1998
**	For vehicles from August 1998

Diagram 8: Electric windows from January '96

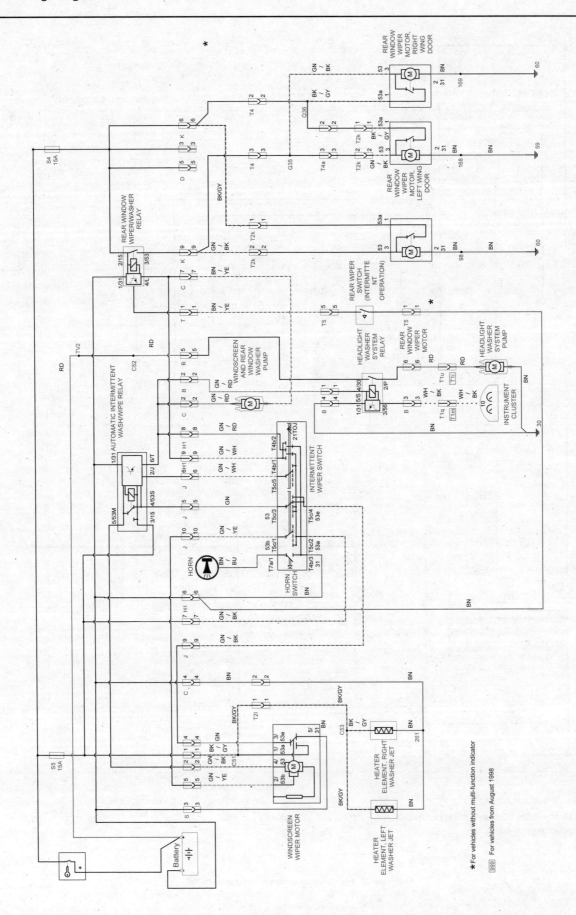

Diagram 9: Windscreen & rear wipers and headlight washers from May '97

★ For vehicles without multi-function indicator

999 For vehicles from August 1998

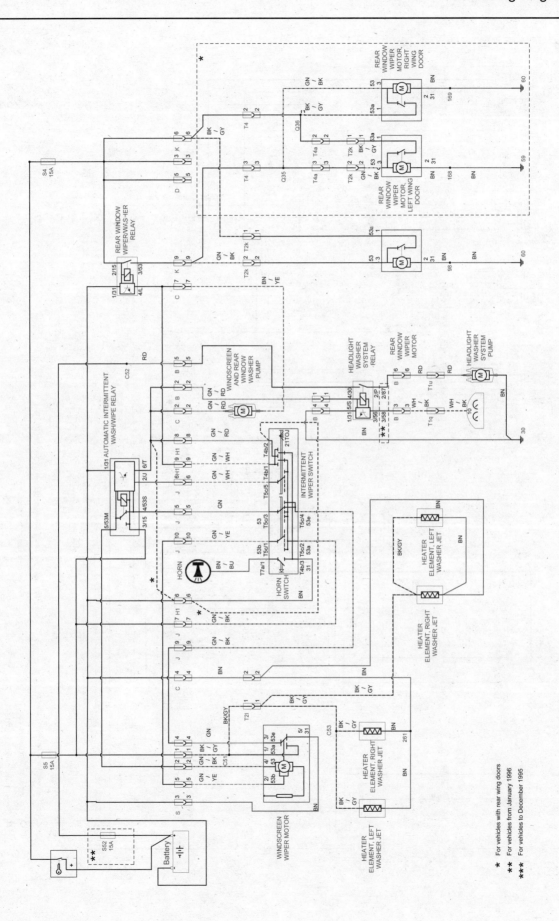

Diagram 10: Windscreen & rear wipers and headlight washers from 2001

* For vehicles with rear wing doors
** For vehicles from January 1996
*** For vehicles to December 1995

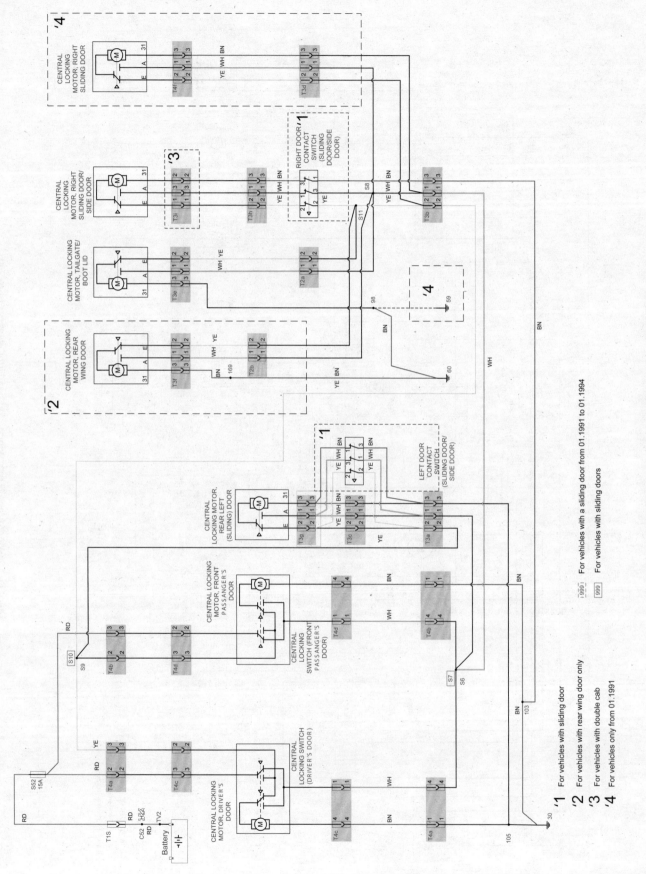

Diagram 11: Typical central locking without remote control

'1 For vehicles with a sliding door from 01.1991 to 01.1994
999 For vehicles with sliding doors

'1 For vehicles with sliding door
'2 For vehicles with rear wing door only
'3 For vehicles with double cab
'4 For vehicles only from 01.1991

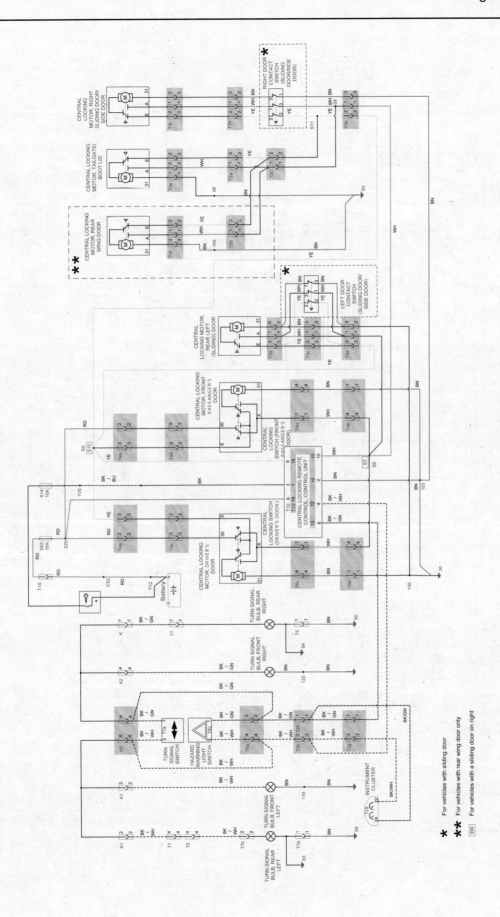

Diagram 12: Typical central locking with remote control

* For vehicles with sliding door

** For vehicles with rear wing door only

*** For vehicles with a sliding door on right

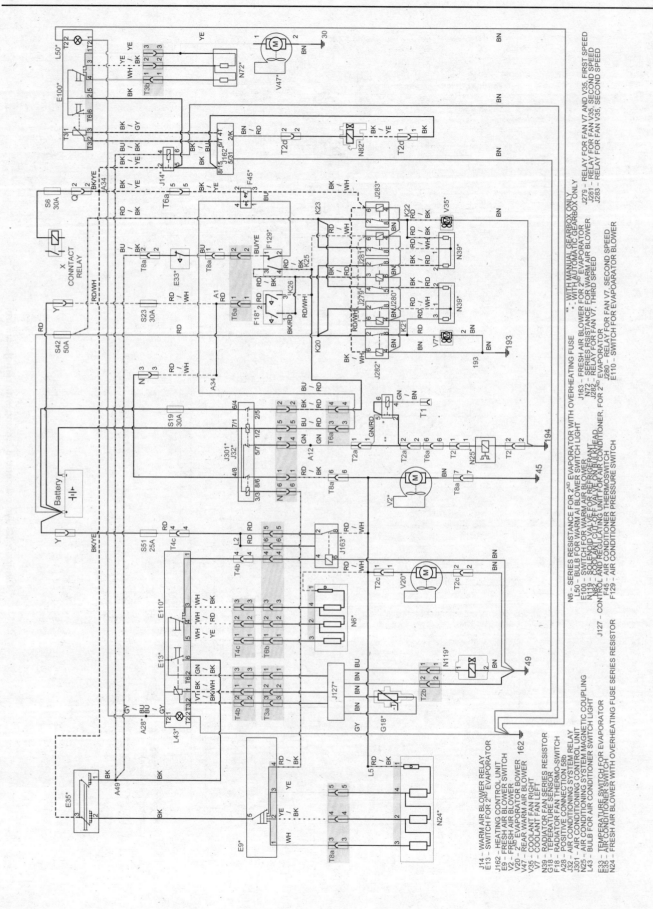

Diagram 13: Typical air conditioning from May '92

J14 – WARM AIR BLOWER RELAY
E13 – SWITCH FOR 2ND EVAPORATOR
J162 – HEATING CONTROL UNIT
E9 – FRESH AIR BLOWER SWITCH
V2 – FRESH AIR BLOWER
V20 – REAR WARM AIR BLOWER
V47 – EVAPORATOR BLOWER 162
V35 – WARM AIR BLOWER
V7 – COOLANT FAN RIGHT
V7 – COOLANT FAN LEFT
N39 – RADIATOR FAN SERIES RESISTOR
G18 – TEPERATURE SENSOR
F18 – RADIATOR FAN THERMO-SWITCH
J301 – POSITIVE CONNECTION 58b
J32 – AIR CONDITIONING SYSTEM RELAY
N25 – AIR CONDITIONING SYSTEM MAGNETIC COUPLING
L43 – BULB FOR AIR CONDITIONER SWITCH LIGHT

E33 – TEMPERATURE SWITCH FOR EVAPORATOR
N24 – FRESH AIR BLOWER WITH OVERHEATING FUSE SERIES RESISTOR

N6 – SERIES RESISTANCE FOR 2ND EVAPORATOR WITH OVERHEATING FUSE
L50 – BULB FOR WARM AI BLOWER SWITCH LIGHT
E100 – SWITCH FOR WARM AIR BLOWER
N72 – SOLENOID VALVE FOR REFRIGERANT
N119 – RELAY FOR RESISTANCE HEAD
J282 – CONTROL AND REGULATING UNIT FOR 2ND AIR CONDITIONER, FOR 2ND
J127 – EVAPORATOR
J280 – RELAY FOR FAN V7, SECOND SPEED
E110 – SWITCH FOR EVAPORATOR BLOWER

* – WITH MANUAL GEARBOX ONLY
** – WITH AUTOMATIC GEARBOX ONLY

J163 – FRESH AIR BLOWER FOR 2 EVAPORATOR
N72 – RELAY FOR FAN V7 AND V35, FIRST SPEED
F45 – AIR CONDITIONER PRESSURE SWITCH
F129 – AIR CONDITIONER THERMO-SWITCH

J279 – RELAY FOR FAN V7 AND V35, FIRST SPEED
J281 – RELAY FOR FAN V35, SECOND SPEED
J283 – RELAY FOR FAN V35, SECOND SPEED

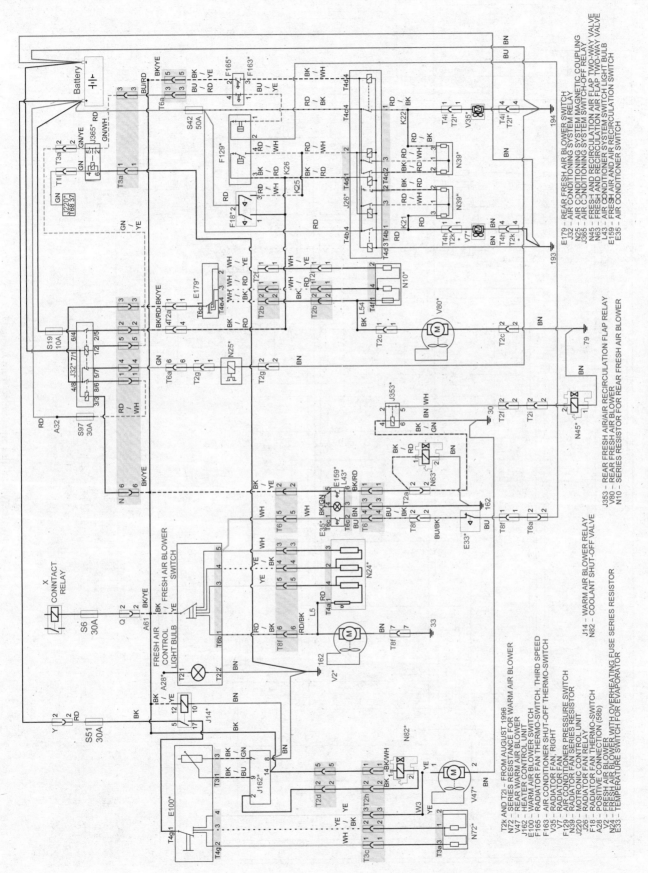

Diagram 14: Typical air conditioning from January '96

T2K AND T2I - FROM AUGUST 1996
N72 - SERIES RESISTANCE FOR WARM AIR BLOWER
V47 - WARM AIR BLOWER
J162 - HEATER/AIR CONTROL UNIT
E100 - WARM AIR BLOWER SWITCH
F163 - RADIATOR FAN THERMO-SWITCH, THIRD SPEED
V35 - RADIATOR FAN, RIGHT
V120 - AIR CONDITIONER SHUT-OFF THERMO-SWITCH
F129 - AIR CONDITIONER PRESSURE SWITCH
J220 - RADIATOR FAN SERIES RESISTOR
J26 - MOTRONIC CONTROL UNIT
F18 - RADIATOR FAN THERMO-SWITCH
A28 - POSITIVE CONNECTION (58b)
V24 - FRESH AIR BLOWER
N39 - FRESH AIR BLOWER WITH OVERHEATING FUSE SERIES RESISTOR
E33 - TEMPERATURE SWITCH FOR EVAPORATOR

E179 - REAR FRESH AIR BLOWER SWITCH
J32 - AIR CONDITIONING SYSTEM RELAY
N25 - AIR CONDITIONING SYSTEM MAGNETIC COUPLING
J365 - AIR CONDITIONING SYSTEM SWITCH-OFF RELAY
N45 - FRESH AND RECIRCULATION AIR FLAP TWO-WAY VALVE
N63 - FRESH AND RECIRCULATION AIR FLAP TWO-WAY VALVE
L43 - AIR CONDITIONER SYSTEM SWITCH LIGHT BULB
E159 - FRESH AIR AND AIR RECIRCULATION SWITCH
E35 - AIR CONDITIONER SWITCH

J353 - REAR FRESH AIR/AIR RECIRCULATION FLAP RELAY
V80 - REAR FRESH AIR BLOWER
N10 - SERIES RESISTOR FOR REAR FRESH AIR BLOWER

J14 - WARM AIR BLOWER RELAY
N82 - COOLANT SHUT-OFF VALVE

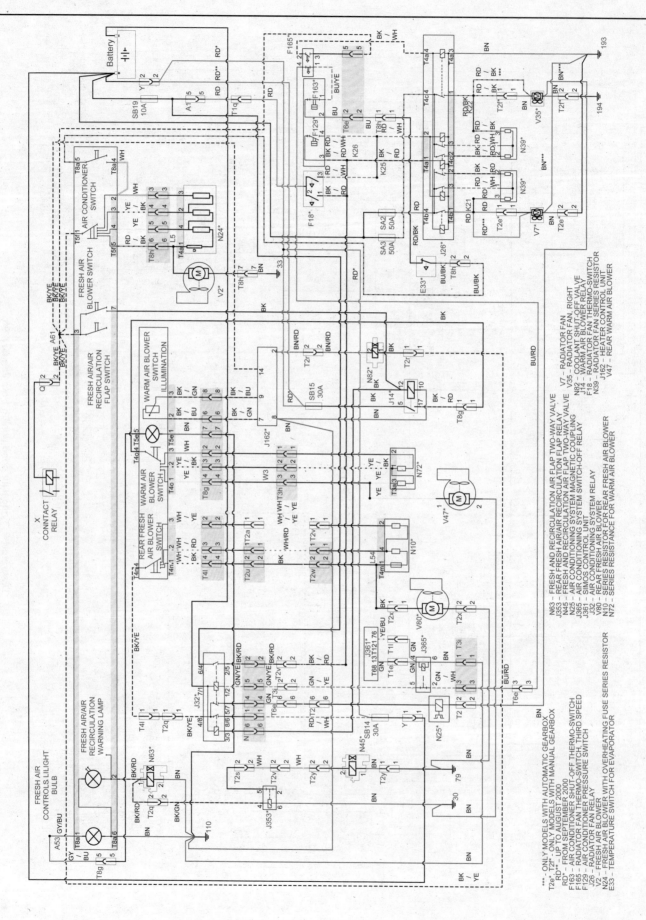

Diagram 15: Typical air conditioning from August '98

*** – ONLY MODELS WITH AUTOMATIC GEARBOX
T2e*, T2f* – ONLY MODELS WITH MANUAL GEARBOX
RD** – UP TO AUGUST 2000
RD* – FROM SEPTEMBER 2000
F163 – AIR CONDITIONER SHUT-OFF THERMO-SWITCH
F165 – RADIATOR FAN THERMO-SWITCH, THIRD SPEED
F129 – AIR CONDITIONER PRESSURE SWITCH
J26 – RADIATOR FAN RELAY
N24 – AIR CONDITIONER PRESSURE SWITCH
E33 – TEMPERATURE SWITCH FOR EVAPORATOR

N63 – FRESH AND RECIRCULATION AIR FLAP TWO-WAY VALVE
J353 – REAR FRESH AIR/AIR RECIRCULATION AIR FLAP FLAP RELAY
N45 – FRESH AND RECIRCULATION AIR FLAP TWO-WAY VALVE
J365 – AIR CONDITIONING SYSTEM MAGNETIC COUPLING
J361 – AIR CONDITIONING SYSTEM SWITCH-OFF RELAY
J32 – SIMOS CONTROL UNIT
J162 – AIR CONDITIONING SYSTEM RELAY
V80 – REAR FRESH AIR BLOWER
V47 – REAR WARM AIR BLOWER

V7 – RADIATOR FAN
V35 – RADIATOR FAN, RIGHT
N82 – COOLANT SHUT-OFF VALVE
J14 – WARM AIR BLOWER RELAY
F18 – RADIATOR FAN SERIES RESISTOR
N39 – RADIATOR FAN SERIES RESISTOR
J162 – HEATER CONTROL
V47 – REAR WARM AIR BLOWER

N10 – SERIES RESISTOR FOR REAR FRESH AIR BLOWER
N72 – SERIES RESISTANCE FOR WARM AIR BLOWER

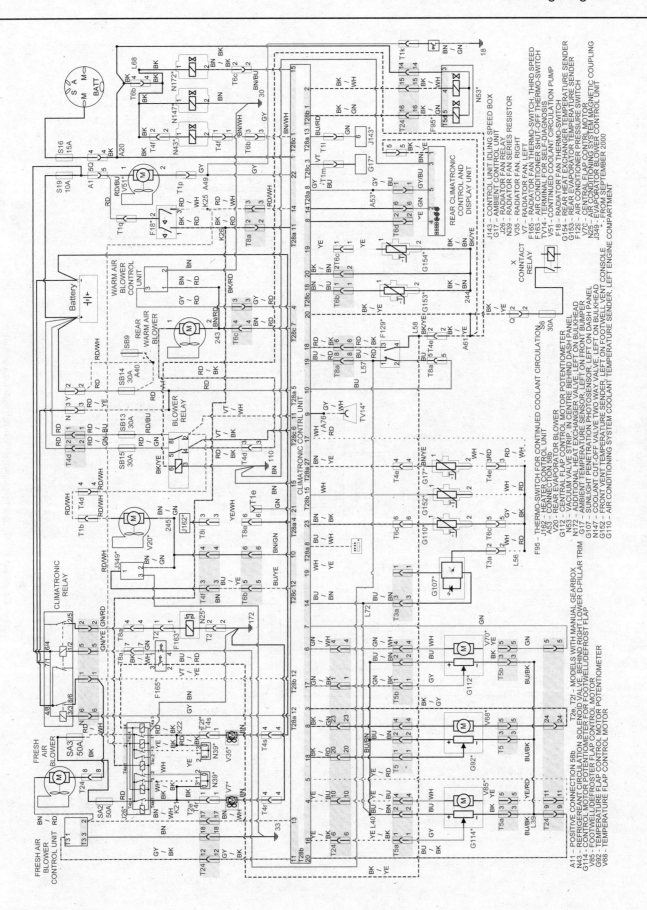

Diagram 16: Typical Climatronic from August '98

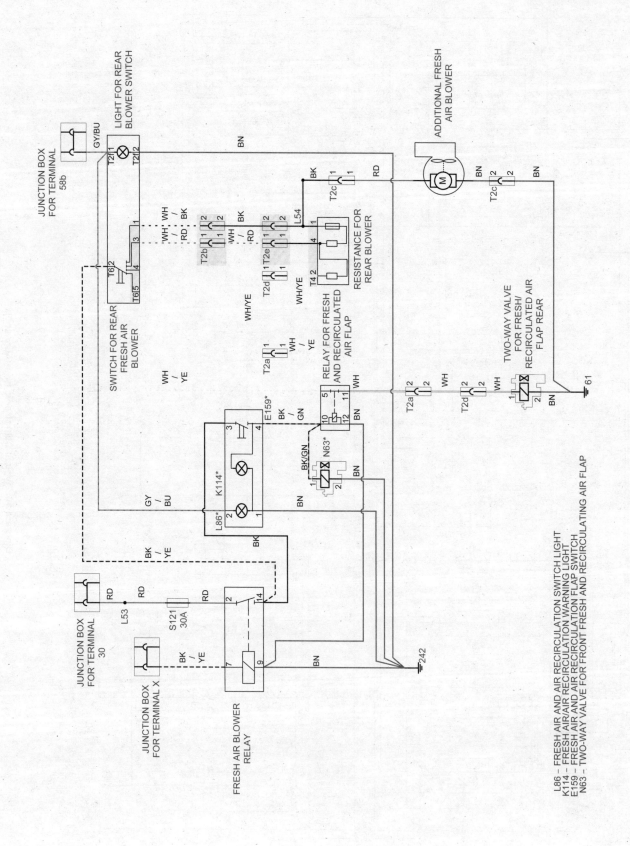

Diagram 17: Typical passenger compartment ventilation

L86 – FRESH AIR AND AIR RECIRCULATION SWITCH LIGHT
K114 – FRESH AIR/AIR RECIRCULATION WARNING LIGHT
E159 – FRESH AIR AND AIR RECIRCULATION FLAP SWITCH
N63 – TWO-WAY VALVE FOR FRONT FRESH AND RECIRCULATING AIR FLAP

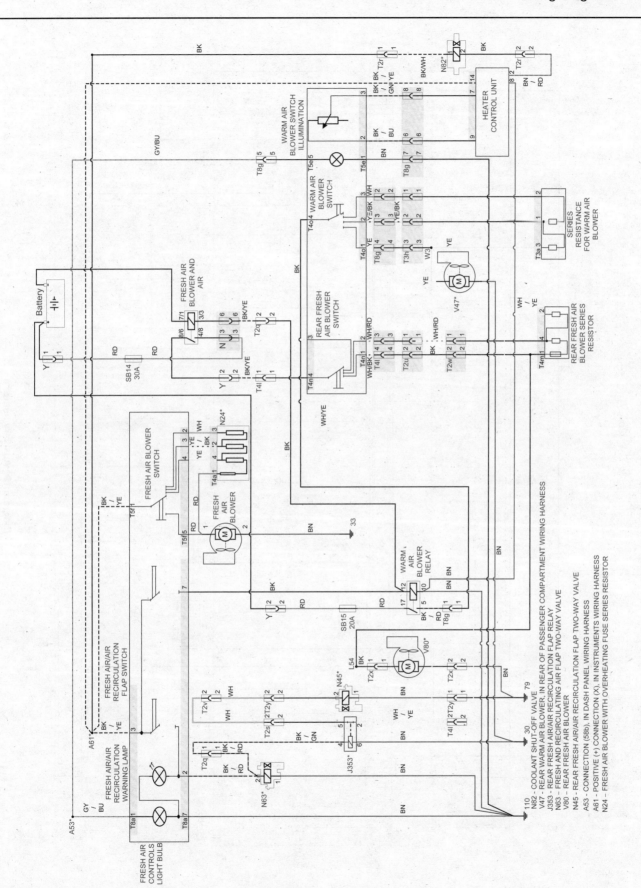

Diagram 18: Typical passenger compartment ventilation with 2nd heat exchanger

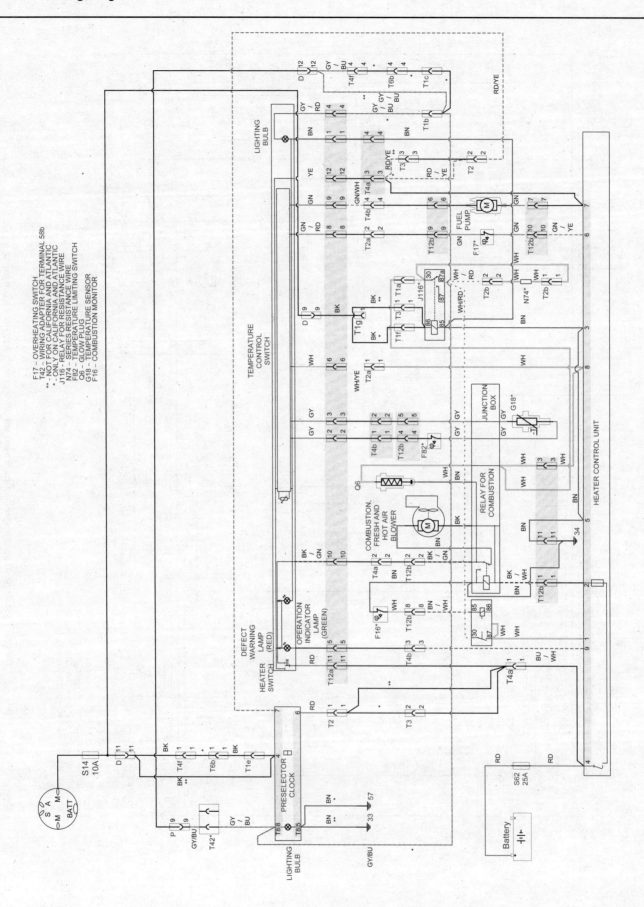

Diagram 19: Auxiliary heater

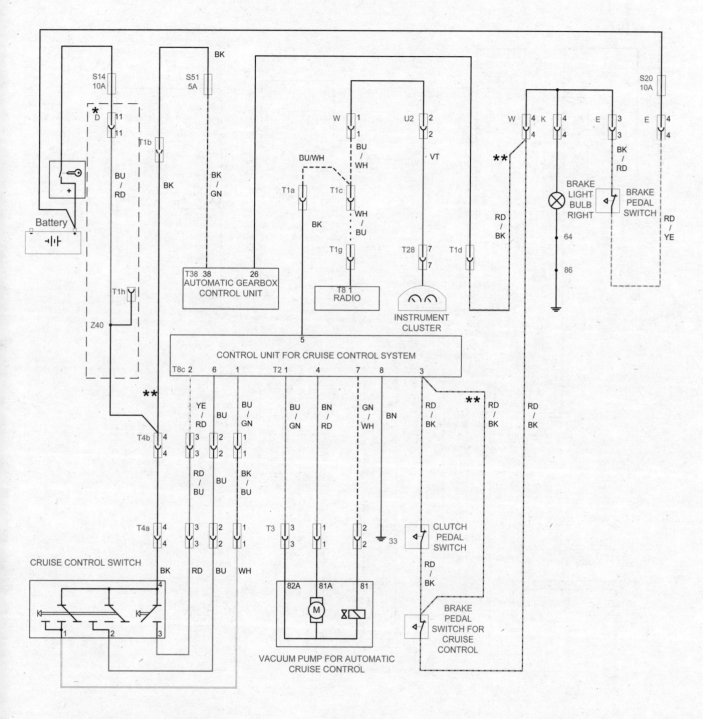

* Only for vehicles with manual transmission

** Only for vehicles with automatic transmission

Diagram 20: Typical cruise control from April '91

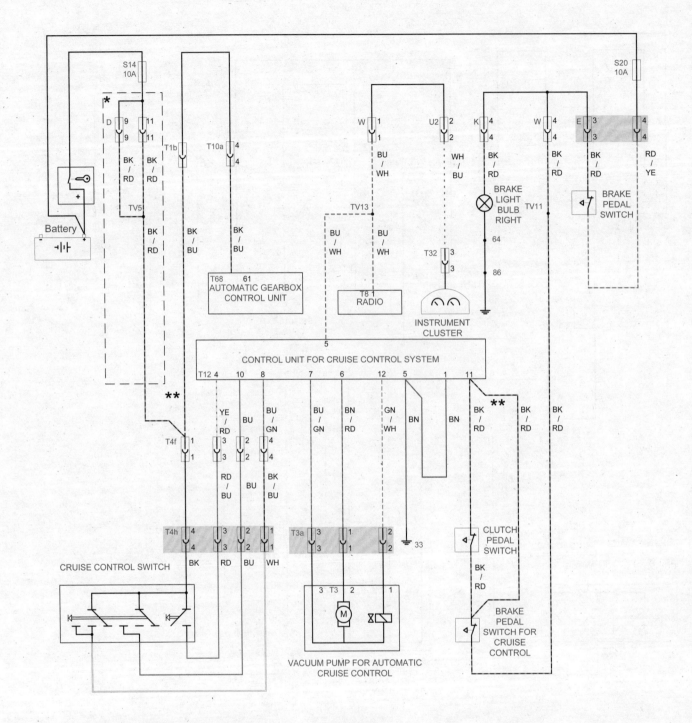

★ Only for vehicles with manual transmission

★★ Only for vehicles with automatic transmission

Diagram 21: Typical cruise control from May '99

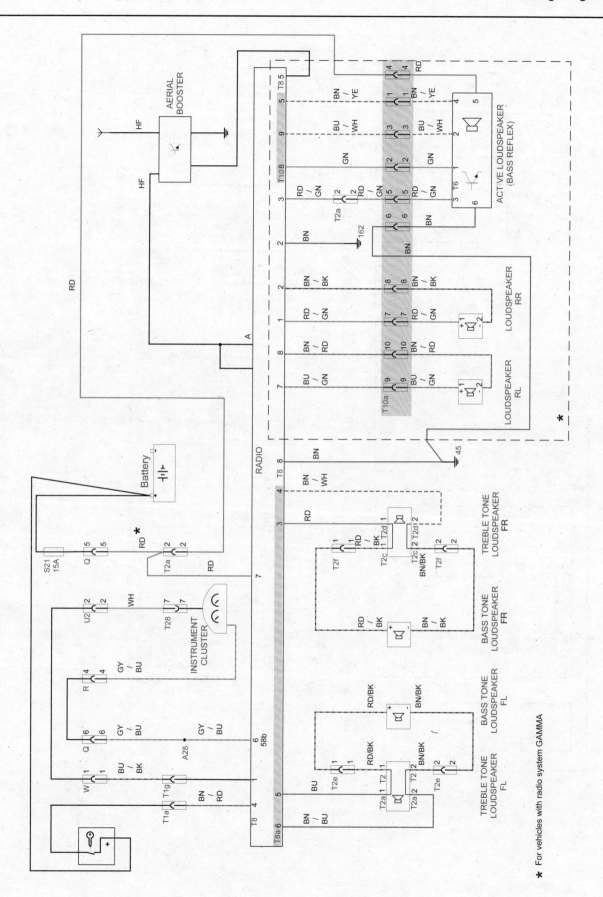

Diagram 22: Radio from September '90

* For vehicles with radio system GAMMA

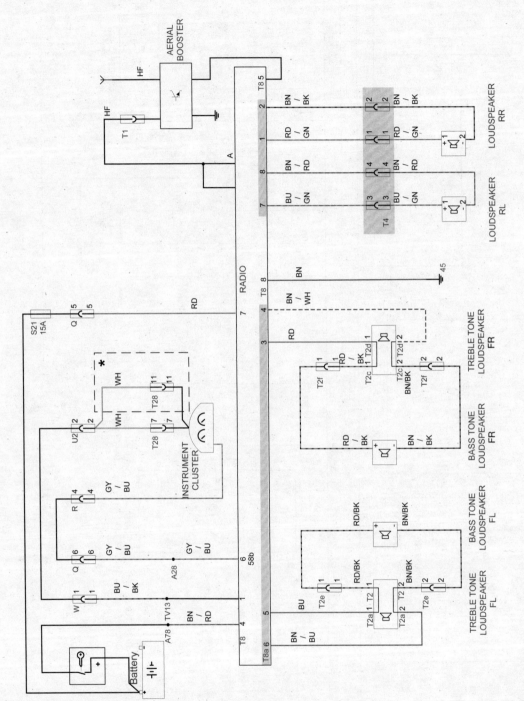

Diagram 23: Radio from January '96

* For vehicles with rod antenna

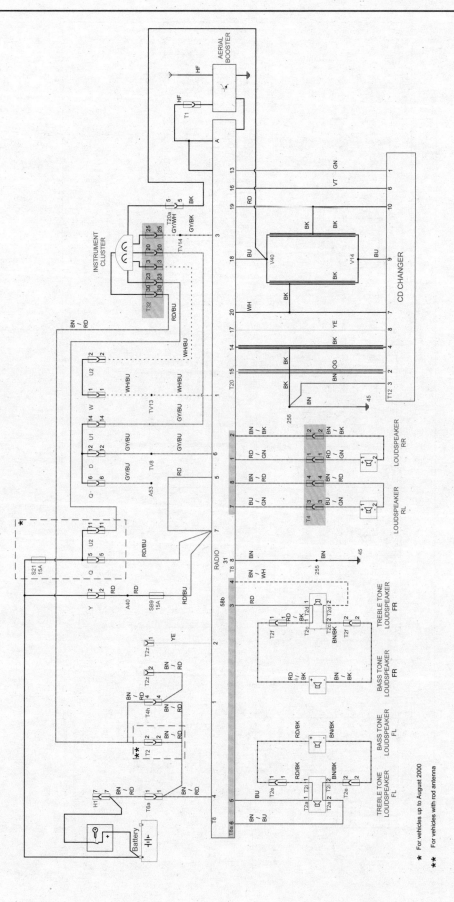

Diagram 24: Radio from May '99

*   For vehicles up to August 2000
** For vehicles with rod antenna

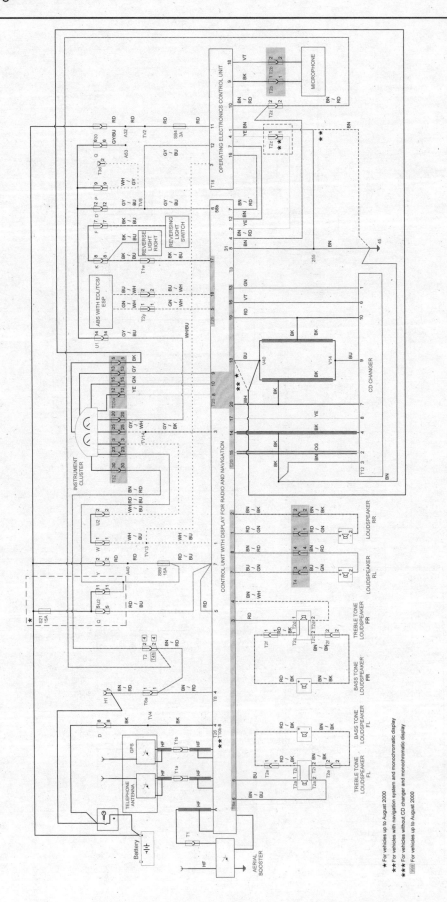

Diagram 25: Navigation system from May '99

★ For vehicles up to August 2000
★★ For vehicles with navigation system and monochromatic display
★★★ For vehicles without CD changer and monochromatic display
999 For vehicles up to August 2000

Reference

Dimensions and weights

Note: *All figures are approximate and may vary according to model. Refer to manufacturer's data for exact figures.*

Dimensions

Overall length:
Van:
    Short wheelbase . . . . 4655 mm
    Long wheelbase . . . . 5055 mm
  Chassis cab . . . . 5111 or 5245 mm
Overall width (excluding door mirrors):
  Van . . . . 1840 mm
  Chassis cab . . . . 1840 or 1979 mm
Overall height (unladen):
Van:
    Standard roof . . . . 1940 mm
    High roof . . . . 2430 mm
  Chassis cab: . . . . 1910 or 1920 mm
Wheelbase:
  Short wheelbase . . . . 2920 mm
  Long wheelbase . . . . 3320 mm
Front track:
  Early models . . . . 1575 mm
  Later models . . . . 1589 mm
Rear track:
  Early models . . . . 1540 mm
  Later models . . . . 1554 mm

Weights

Kerb weight . . . . 1400 to 1710 kg according to specification. Refer to manufacturer's
documentation for latest information.

Conversion factors

Length (distance)

Inches (in)	x 25.4	= Millimetres (mm)	x 0.0394	= Inches (in)
Feet (ft)	x 0.305	= Metres (m)	x 3.281	= Feet (ft)
Miles	x 1.609	= Kilometres (km)	x 0.621	= Miles

Volume (capacity)

Cubic inches (cu in; in^3)	x 16.387	= Cubic centimetres (cc; cm^3)	x 0.061	= Cubic inches (cu in; in^3)
Imperial pints (Imp pt)	x 0.568	= Litres (l)	x 1.76	= Imperial pints (Imp pt)
Imperial quarts (Imp qt)	x 1.137	= Litres (l)	x 0.88	= Imperial quarts (Imp qt)
Imperial quarts (Imp qt)	x 1.201	= US quarts (US qt)	x 0.833	= Imperial quarts (Imp qt)
US quarts (US qt)	x 0.946	= Litres (l)	x 1.057	= US quarts (US qt)
Imperial gallons (Imp gal)	x 4.546	= Litres (l)	x 0.22	= Imperial gallons (Imp gal)
Imperial gallons (Imp gal)	x 1.201	= US gallons (US gal)	x 0.833	= Imperial gallons (Imp gal)
US gallons (US gal)	x 3.785	= Litres (l)	x 0.264	= US gallons (US gal)

Mass (weight)

Ounces (oz)	x 28.35	= Grams (g)	x 0.035	= Ounces (oz)
Pounds (lb)	x 0.454	= Kilograms (kg)	x 2.205	= Pounds (lb)

Force

Ounces-force (ozf; oz)	x 0.278	= Newtons (N)	x 3.6	= Ounces-force (ozf; oz)
Pounds-force (lbf; lb)	x 4.448	= Newtons (N)	x 0.225	= Pounds-force (lbf; lb)
Newtons (N)	x 0.1	= Kilograms-force (kgf; kg)	x 9.81	= Newtons (N)

Pressure

Pounds-force per square inch (psi; lbf/in^2; lb/in^2)	x 0.070	= Kilograms-force per square centimetre (kgf/cm^2; kg/cm^2)	x 14.223	= Pounds-force per square inch (psi; lbf/in^2; lb/in^2)
Pounds-force per square inch (psi; lbf/in^2; lb/in^2)	x 0.068	= Atmospheres (atm)	x 14.696	= Pounds-force per square inch (psi; lbf/in^2; lb/in^2)
Pounds-force per square inch (psi; lbf/in^2; lb/in^2)	x 0.069	= Bars	x 14.5	= Pounds-force per square inch (psi; lbf/in^2; lb/in^2)
Pounds-force per square inch (psi; lbf/in^2; lb/in^2)	x 6.895	= Kilopascals (kPa)	x 0.145	= Pounds-force per square inch (psi; lbf/in^2; lb/in^2)
Kilopascals (kPa)	x 0.01	= Kilograms-force per square centimetre (kgf/cm^2; kg/cm^2)	x 98.1	= Kilopascals (kPa)
Millibar (mbar)	x 100	= Pascals (Pa)	x 0.01	= Millibar (mbar)
Millibar (mbar)	x 0.0145	= Pounds-force per square inch (psi; lbf/in^2; lb/in^2)	x 68.947	= Millibar (mbar)
Millibar (mbar)	x 0.75	= Millimetres of mercury (mmHg)	x 1.333	= Millibar (mbar)
Millibar (mbar)	x 0.401	= Inches of water (inH$_2$O)	x 2.491	= Millibar (mbar)
Millimetres of mercury (mmHg)	x 0.535	= Inches of water (inH$_2$O)	x 1.868	= Millimetres of mercury (mmHg)
Inches of water (inH$_2$O)	x 0.036	= Pounds-force per square inch (psi; lbf/in^2; lb/in^2)	x 27.68	= Inches of water (inH$_2$O)

Torque (moment of force)

Pounds-force inches (lbf in; lb in)	x 1.152	= Kilograms-force centimetre (kgf cm; kg cm)	x 0.868	= Pounds-force inches (lbf in; lb in)
Pounds-force inches (lbf in; lb in)	x 0.113	= Newton metres (Nm)	x 8.85	= Pounds-force inches (lbf in; lb in)
Pounds-force inches (lbf in; lb in)	x 0.083	= Pounds-force feet (lbf ft; lb ft)	x 12	= Pounds-force inches (lbf in; lb in)
Pounds-force feet (lbf ft; lb ft)	x 0.138	= Kilograms-force metres (kgf m; kg m)	x 7.233	= Pounds-force feet (lbf ft; lb ft)
Pounds-force feet (lbf ft; lb ft)	x 1.356	= Newton metres (Nm)	x 0.738	= Pounds-force feet (lbf ft; lb ft)
Newton metres (Nm)	x 0.102	= Kilograms-force metres (kgf m; kg m)	x 9.804	= Newton metres (Nm)

Power

Horsepower (hp)	x 745.7	= Watts (W)	x 0.0013	= Horsepower (hp)

Velocity (speed)

Miles per hour (miles/hr; mph)	x 1.609	= Kilometres per hour (km/hr; kph)	x 0.621	= Miles per hour (miles/hr; mph)

Fuel consumption*

Miles per gallon, Imperial (mpg)	x 0.354	= Kilometres per litre (km/l)	x 2.825	= Miles per gallon, Imperial (mpg)
Miles per gallon, US (mpg)	x 0.425	= Kilometres per litre (km/l)	x 2.352	= Miles per gallon, US (mpg)

Temperature

Degrees Fahrenheit = (°C x 1.8) + 32   Degrees Celsius (Degrees Centigrade; °C) = (°F - 32) x 0.56

It is common practice to convert from miles per gallon (mpg) to litres/100 kilometres (l/100km), where mpg x l/100 km = 282

Spare parts are available from many sources, including maker's appointed garages, accessory shops, and motor factors. To be sure of obtaining the correct parts, it will sometimes be necessary to quote the vehicle identification number. If possible, it can also be useful to take the old parts along for positive identification. Items such as starter motors and alternators may be available under a service exchange scheme – any parts returned should be clean.

Our advice regarding spare parts is as follows.

Officially appointed garages

This is the best source of parts which are peculiar to your car, and which are not otherwise generally available (eg, badges, interior trim, certain body panels, etc). It is also the only place at which you should buy parts if the vehicle is still under warranty.

Accessory shops

These are very good places to buy materials and components needed for the maintenance of your vehicle (oil, air and fuel filters, light bulbs, drivebelts, greases, brake pads/shoes, touch-up paint, etc). Components of this nature sold by a reputable shop are of the same standard as those used by the vehicle manufacturer.

Besides components, these shops also sell tools and general accessories, usually have convenient opening hours, charge lower prices, and can often be found close to home. Some accessory shops have parts counters where components needed for almost any repair job can be purchased or ordered.

Motor factors

Good factors will stock all the more important components which wear out comparatively quickly, and can sometimes supply individual components needed for the overhaul of a larger assembly (eg, brake seals and hydraulic parts, bearing shells, pistons, valves). They may also handle work such as cylinder block reboring, crankshaft regrinding, etc.

Tyre and exhaust specialists

These outlets may be independent, or members of a local or national chain. They frequently offer competitive prices when compared with a main dealer or local garage, but it will pay to obtain several quotes before making a decision. When researching prices, also ask what 'extras' may be added – for instance fitting a new valve and balancing the wheel are both commonly charged on top of the price of a new tyre.

Other sources

Beware of parts or materials obtained from market stalls, car boot sales or similar outlets. Such items are not invariably sub-standard, but there is little chance of compensation if they do prove unsatisfactory. In the case of safety-critical components such as brake pads, there is the risk not only of financial loss, but also of an accident causing injury or death.

Second-hand components or assemblies obtained from a car breaker can be a good buy in some circumstances, but this sort of purchase is best made by the experienced DIY mechanic.

Vehicle identification

Modifications are a continuing and unpublished process in vehicle manufacture, quite apart from major model changes. Spare parts manuals and lists are compiled upon a numerical basis, the individual vehicle numbers being essential to correct identification of the component required.

When ordering spare parts, always give as much information as possible. Quote the vehicle type, year of manufacture and vehicle identification and/or engine numbers as appropriate.

The *Vehicle Identification Number (VIN)* is given on the vehicle data sticker. It is also located on the radiator upper crossmember and stamped on the right-hand side of the body below the windscreen (see illustration).

The *vehicle data sticker* is located either on the underside of the passenger compartment fuse/relay box or at the base of the A-pillar on the driver's side (see illustration). The data sticker includes the Vehicle Identification Number (VIN), engine code, paint and trim colour codes and other additional vehicle information.

The *engine number* is stamped on a horizontal flat located on the front facing side of the cylinder block below the cylinder head joint and is also given on a sticker on the timing belt upper cover. The engine code is also given on the vehicle data sticker.

Vehicle identification number on the radiator upper crossmember

Vehicle data sticker information

1 Production control number
2 Vehicle identification number
3 Model code number
4 Model explanation/engine output
5 Engine and gearbox code letters
6 Paint number/interior trim code
7 Optional extra number

Whenever servicing, repair or overhaul work is carried out on the car or its components, observe the following procedures and instructions. This will assist in carrying out the operation efficiently and to a professional standard of workmanship.

Joint mating faces and gaskets

When separating components at their mating faces, never insert screwdrivers or similar implements into the joint between the faces in order to prise them apart. This can cause severe damage which results in oil leaks, coolant leaks, etc upon reassembly. Separation is usually achieved by tapping along the joint with a soft-faced hammer in order to break the seal. However, note that this method may not be suitable where dowels are used for component location.

Where a gasket is used between the mating faces of two components, a new one must be fitted on reassembly; fit it dry unless otherwise stated in the repair procedure. Make sure that the mating faces are clean and dry, with all traces of old gasket removed. When cleaning a joint face, use a tool which is unlikely to score or damage the face, and remove any burrs or nicks with an oilstone or fine file.

Make sure that tapped holes are cleaned with a pipe cleaner, and keep them free of jointing compound, if this is being used, unless specifically instructed otherwise.

Ensure that all orifices, channels or pipes are clear, and blow through them, preferably using compressed air.

Oil seals

Oil seals can be removed by levering them out with a wide flat-bladed screwdriver or similar implement. Alternatively, a number of self-tapping screws may be screwed into the seal, and these used as a purchase for pliers or some similar device in order to pull the seal free.

Whenever an oil seal is removed from its working location, either individually or as part of an assembly, it should be renewed.

The very fine sealing lip of the seal is easily damaged, and will not seal if the surface it contacts is not completely clean and free from scratches, nicks or grooves. If the original sealing surface of the component cannot be restored, and the manufacturer has not made provision for slight relocation of the seal relative to the sealing surface, the component should be renewed.

Protect the lips of the seal from any surface which may damage them in the course of fitting. Use tape or a conical sleeve where possible. Where indicated, lubricate the seal lips with oil before fitting and, on dual-lipped seals, fill the space between the lips with grease.

Unless otherwise stated, oil seals must be fitted with their sealing lips toward the lubricant to be sealed.

Use a tubular drift or block of wood of the appropriate size to install the seal and, if the seal housing is shouldered, drive the seal down to the shoulder. If the seal housing is unshouldered, the seal should be fitted with its face flush with the housing top face (unless otherwise instructed).

Screw threads and fastenings

Seized nuts, bolts and screws are quite a common occurrence where corrosion has set in, and the use of penetrating oil or releasing fluid will often overcome this problem if the offending item is soaked for a while before attempting to release it. The use of an impact driver may also provide a means of releasing such stubborn fastening devices, when used in conjunction with the appropriate screwdriver bit or socket. If none of these methods works, it may be necessary to resort to the careful application of heat, or the use of a hacksaw or nut splitter device. Before resorting to extreme methods, check that you are not dealing with a left-hand thread!

Studs are usually removed by locking two nuts together on the threaded part, and then using a spanner on the lower nut to unscrew the stud. Studs or bolts which have broken off below the surface of the component in which they are mounted can sometimes be removed using a stud extractor.

Always ensure that a blind tapped hole is completely free from oil, grease, water or other fluid before installing the bolt or stud. Failure to do this could cause the housing to crack due to the hydraulic action of the bolt or stud as it is screwed in.

For some screw fastenings, notably cylinder head bolts or nuts, torque wrench settings are no longer specified for the latter stages of tightening, "angle-tightening" being called up instead. Typically, a fairly low torque wrench setting will be applied to the bolts/nuts in the correct sequence, followed by one or more stages of tightening through specified angles.

When checking or retightening a nut or bolt to a specified torque setting, slacken the nut or bolt by a quarter of a turn, and then retighten to the specified setting. However, this should not be attempted where angular tightening has been used.

Locknuts, locktabs and washers

Any fastening which will rotate against a component or housing during tightening should always have a washer between it and the relevant component or housing.

Spring or split washers should always be renewed when they are used to lock a critical component such as a big-end bearing retaining bolt or nut. Locktabs which are folded over to retain a nut or bolt should always be renewed.

Self-locking nuts can be re-used in non-critical areas, providing resistance can be felt when the locking portion passes over the bolt or stud thread. However, it should be noted that self-locking stiffnuts tend to lose their effectiveness after long periods of use, and should then be renewed as a matter of course.

Split pins must always be replaced with new ones of the correct size for the hole.

When thread-locking compound is found on the threads of a fastener which is to be re-used, it should be cleaned off with a wire brush and solvent, and fresh compound applied on reassembly.

Special tools

Some repair procedures in this manual entail the use of special tools such as a press, two or three-legged pullers, spring compressors, etc. Wherever possible, suitable readily-available alternatives to the manufacturer's special tools are described, and are shown in use. In some instances, where no alternative is possible, it has been necessary to resort to the use of a manufacturer's tool, and this has been done for reasons of safety as well as the efficient completion of the repair operation. Unless you are highly-skilled and have a thorough understanding of the procedures described, never attempt to bypass the use of any special tool when the procedure described specifies its use. Not only is there a very great risk of personal injury, but expensive damage could be caused to the components involved.

Environmental considerations

When disposing of used engine oil, brake fluid, antifreeze, etc, give due consideration to any detrimental environmental effects. Do not, for instance, pour any of the above liquids down drains into the general sewage system, or onto the ground to soak away. Many local council refuse tips provide a facility for waste oil disposal, as do some garages. You can find your nearest disposal point by calling the Environment Agency on 08708 506 506 or by visiting www.oilbankline.org.uk.

Note: It is illegal and anti-social to dump oil down the drain. To find the location of your local oil recycling bank, call 08708 506 506 or visit www.oilbankline.org.uk.

The jack supplied with the vehicle tool kit should only be used for changing roadwheels – see *Wheel changing* at the front of this manual. Ensure the jack head is correctly engaged before attempting to raise the vehicle. When carrying out any other kind of work, raise the vehicle using a hydraulic jack, and always supplement the jack with axle stands positioned under the vehicle jacking points or structural members.

When jacking up the vehicle with a trolley jack, position the jack head under one of the relevant jacking points, front subframe or vehicle structural members. Do not jack the vehicle under the sump or any of the steering or suspension components. Supplement the jack using axle stands.

 Warning: Never work under, around, or near a raised vehicle, unless it is adequately supported in at least two places.

Disconnecting the battery

Numerous systems fitted to the vehicle require battery power to be available at all times, either to ensure their continued operation (such as the clock) or to maintain control unit memories which would be erased if the battery were to be disconnected. Whenever the battery is to be disconnected therefore, first note the following, to ensure that there are no unforeseen consequences of this action:

a) *First, on any vehicle with central locking, it is a wise precaution to remove the key from the ignition, and to keep it with you, so that it does not get locked in, if the central locking should engage accidentally when the battery is reconnected.*

b) *Depending on vehicle and specification, the anti-theft alarm system may be of the type which is automatically activated when the vehicle battery is disconnected and/or reconnected. To prevent the alarm sounding on models so equipped, switch the ignition on, then off, and disconnect the battery within 15 seconds. If the alarm is activated when the battery is reconnected, deactivate the alarm by locking and unlocking one of the front doors.*

c) *If a security-coded audio unit is fitted, and the unit and/or the battery is disconnected, the unit will not function again on reconnection until the correct security code is entered. Details of this procedure, which varies according to the unit fitted, are given in the vehicle audio system operating instructions. Ensure you have the correct code before you disconnect the battery. If you do not have the code or details of the correct procedure, but can supply proof of ownership and a legitimate reason for wanting this information, a VW dealer may be able to help.*

d) *On later models, the engine management electronic control unit is of the 'self-learning' type, meaning that as it operates, it also monitors and stores the settings which give optimum engine performance under all operating conditions. When the battery is disconnected, these settings are lost and the ECU reverts to the base settings programmed into its memory at the factory. On restarting, this may lead to the engine running/idling roughly for a short while, until the ECU has re-learned the optimum settings. This process is best accomplished by taking the vehicle on a road test (for approximately 15 minutes), covering all engine speeds and loads, concentrating mainly in the 2500 to 3500 rpm region.*

e) *On all models, when reconnecting the battery after disconnection, switch on the ignition and wait 10 seconds to allow the electronic vehicle systems to stabilise and re-initialise.*

Introduction

A selection of good tools is a fundamental requirement for anyone contemplating the maintenance and repair of a motor vehicle. For the owner who does not possess any, their purchase will prove a considerable expense, offsetting some of the savings made by doing-it-yourself. However, provided that the tools purchased meet the relevant national safety standards and are of good quality, they will last for many years and prove an extremely worthwhile investment.

To help the average owner to decide which tools are needed to carry out the various tasks detailed in this manual, we have compiled three lists of tools under the following headings: *Maintenance and minor repair*, *Repair and overhaul*, and *Special*. Newcomers to practical mechanics should start off with the *Maintenance and minor repair* tool kit, and confine themselves to the simpler jobs around the vehicle. Then, as confidence and experience grow, more difficult tasks can be undertaken, with extra tools being purchased as, and when, they are needed. In this way, a *Maintenance and minor repair* tool kit can be built up into a *Repair and overhaul* tool kit over a considerable period of time, without any major cash outlays. The experienced do-it-yourselfer will have a tool kit good enough for most repair and overhaul procedures, and will add tools from the *Special* category when it is felt that the expense is justified by the amount of use to which these tools will be put.

Maintenance and minor repair tool kit

The tools given in this list should be considered as a minimum requirement if routine maintenance, servicing and minor repair operations are to be undertaken. We recommend the purchase of combination spanners (ring one end, open-ended the other); although more expensive than open-ended ones, they do give the advantages of both types of spanner.

☐ *Combination spanners:*
  Metric - 8 to 19 mm inclusive
☐ *Adjustable spanner - 35 mm jaw (approx.)*
☐ *Spark plug spanner (with rubber insert) - petrol models*
☐ *Spark plug gap adjustment tool - petrol models*
☐ *Set of feeler gauges*
☐ *Brake bleed nipple spanner*
☐ *Screwdrivers:*
  Flat blade - 100 mm long x 6 mm dia
  Cross blade - 100 mm long x 6 mm dia
  Torx - various sizes (not all vehicles)
☐ *Combination pliers*
☐ *Hacksaw (junior)*
☐ *Tyre pump*
☐ *Tyre pressure gauge*
☐ *Oil can*
☐ *Oil filter removal tool (if applicable)*
☐ *Fine emery cloth*
☐ *Wire brush (small)*
☐ *Funnel (medium size)*
☐ *Sump drain plug key (not all vehicles)*

Repair and overhaul tool kit

These tools are virtually essential for anyone undertaking any major repairs to a motor vehicle, and are additional to those given in the *Maintenance and minor repair* list. Included in this list is a comprehensive set of sockets. Although these are expensive, they will be found invaluable as they are so versatile - particularly if various drives are included in the set. We recommend the half-inch square-drive type, as this can be used with most proprietary torque wrenches.

The tools in this list will sometimes need to be supplemented by tools from the *Special* list:

☐ *Sockets to cover range in previous list (including Torx sockets)*
☐ *Reversible ratchet drive (for use with sockets)*
☐ *Extension piece, 250 mm (for use with sockets)*
☐ *Universal joint (for use with sockets)*
☐ *Flexible handle or sliding T "breaker bar" (for use with sockets)*
☐ *Torque wrench (for use with sockets)*
☐ *Self-locking grips*
☐ *Ball pein hammer*
☐ *Soft-faced mallet (plastic or rubber)*
☐ *Screwdrivers:*
  Flat blade - long & sturdy, short (chubby), and narrow (electrician's) types
  Cross blade – long & sturdy, and short (chubby) types
☐ *Pliers:*
  Long-nosed
  Side cutters (electrician's)
  Circlip (internal and external)
☐ *Cold chisel - 25 mm*
☐ *Scriber*
☐ *Scraper*
☐ *Centre-punch*
☐ *Pin punch*
☐ *Hacksaw*
☐ *Brake hose clamp*
☐ *Brake/clutch bleeding kit*
☐ *Selection of twist drills*
☐ *Steel rule/straight-edge*
☐ *Allen keys (inc. splined/Torx type)*
☐ *Selection of files*
☐ *Wire brush*
☐ *Axle stands*
☐ *Jack (strong trolley or hydraulic type)*
☐ *Light with extension lead*
☐ *Universal electrical multi-meter*

Sockets and reversible ratchet drive

Brake bleeding kit

Torx key, socket and bit

Hose clamp

Angular-tightening gauge

Special tools

The tools in this list are those which are not used regularly, are expensive to buy, or which need to be used in accordance with their manufacturers' instructions. Unless relatively difficult mechanical jobs are undertaken frequently, it will not be economic to buy many of these tools. Where this is the case, you could consider clubbing together with friends (or joining a motorists' club) to make a joint purchase, or borrowing the tools against a deposit from a local garage or tool hire specialist.

The following list contains only those tools and instruments freely available to the public, and not those special tools produced by the vehicle manufacturer specifically for its dealer network. You will find occasional references to these manufacturers' special tools in the text of this manual. Generally, an alternative method of doing the job without the vehicle manufacturers' special tool is given. However, sometimes there is no alternative to using them. Where this is the case and the relevant tool cannot be bought or borrowed, you will have to entrust the work to a dealer.

☐ *Angular-tightening gauge*
☐ *Valve spring compressor*
☐ *Valve grinding tool*
☐ *Piston ring compressor*
☐ *Piston ring removal/installation tool*
☐ *Cylinder bore hone*
☐ *Balljoint separator*
☐ *Coil spring compressors (where applicable)*
☐ *Two/three-legged hub and bearing puller*
☐ *Impact screwdriver*
☐ *Micrometer and/or vernier calipers*
☐ *Dial gauge*
☐ *Tachometer*
☐ *Fault code reader*
☐ *Cylinder compression gauge*
☐ *Hand-operated vacuum pump and gauge*
☐ *Clutch plate alignment set*
☐ *Brake shoe steady spring cup removal tool*
☐ *Bush and bearing removal/installation set*
☐ *Stud extractors*
☐ *Tap and die set*
☐ *Lifting tackle*

Buying tools

Reputable motor accessory shops and superstores often offer excellent quality tools at discount prices, so it pays to shop around.

Remember, you don't have to buy the most expensive items on the shelf, but it is always advisable to steer clear of the very cheap tools. Beware of 'bargains' offered on market stalls, on-line or at car boot sales. There are plenty of good tools around at reasonable prices, but always aim to purchase items which meet the relevant national safety standards. If in doubt, ask the proprietor or manager of the shop for advice before making a purchase.

Care and maintenance of tools

Having purchased a reasonable tool kit, it is necessary to keep the tools in a clean and serviceable condition. After use, always wipe off any dirt, grease and metal particles using a clean, dry cloth, before putting the tools away. Never leave them lying around after they have been used. A simple tool rack on the garage or workshop wall for items such as screwdrivers and pliers is a good idea. Store all normal spanners and sockets in a metal box. Any measuring instruments, gauges, meters, etc, must be carefully stored where they cannot be damaged or become rusty.

Take a little care when tools are used. Hammer heads inevitably become marked, and screwdrivers lose the keen edge on their blades from time to time. A little timely attention with emery cloth or a file will soon restore items like this to a good finish.

Working facilities

Not to be forgotten when discussing tools is the workshop itself. If anything more than routine maintenance is to be carried out, a suitable working area becomes essential.

It is appreciated that many an owner-mechanic is forced by circumstances to remove an engine or similar item without the benefit of a garage or workshop. Having done this, any repairs should always be done under the cover of a roof.

Wherever possible, any dismantling should be done on a clean, flat workbench or table at a suitable working height.

Any workbench needs a vice; one with a jaw opening of 100 mm is suitable for most jobs. As mentioned previously, some clean dry storage space is also required for tools, as well as for any lubricants, cleaning fluids, touch-up paints etc, which become necessary.

Another item which may be required, and which has a much more general usage, is an electric drill with a chuck capacity of at least 8 mm. This, together with a good range of twist drills, is virtually essential for fitting accessories.

Last, but not least, always keep a supply of old newspapers and clean, lint-free rags available, and try to keep any working area as clean as possible.

Micrometers

Dial test indicator ("dial gauge")

Oil filter removal tool (strap wrench type)

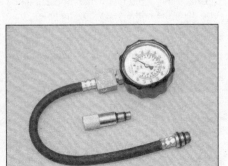
Compression tester

Bearing puller

This is a guide to getting your vehicle through the MOT test. Obviously it will not be possible to examine the vehicle to the same standard as the professional MOT tester. However, working through the following checks will enable you to identify any problem areas before submitting the vehicle for the test.

It has only been possible to summarise the test requirements here, based on the regulations in force at the time of printing. Test standards are becoming increasingly stringent, although there are some exemptions for older vehicles.

An assistant will be needed to help carry out some of these checks.

The checks have been sub-divided into four categories, as follows:

1 Checks carried out **FROM THE DRIVER'S SEAT**

2 Checks carried out **WITH THE VEHICLE ON THE GROUND**

3 Checks carried out **WITH THE VEHICLE RAISED AND THE WHEELS FREE TO TURN**

4 Checks carried out on **YOUR VEHICLE'S EXHAUST EMISSION SYSTEM**

---

1 Checks carried out **FROM THE DRIVER'S SEAT**

Handbrake (parking brake)

☐ Test the operation of the handbrake. Excessive travel (too many clicks) indicates incorrect brake or cable adjustment.
☐ Check that the handbrake cannot be released by tapping the lever sideways. Check the security of the lever mountings.

☐ If the parking brake is foot-operated, check that the pedal is secure and without excessive travel, and that the release mechanism operates correctly.
☐ Where applicable, test the operation of the electronic handbrake. The brake should engage and disengage without excessive delay. If the warning light does not extinguish when the brake is disengaged, this could indicate a fault which will need further investigation.

Footbrake

☐ Depress the brake pedal and check that it does not creep down to the floor, indicating a master cylinder fault. Release the pedal,

wait a few seconds, then depress it again. If the pedal travels nearly to the floor before firm resistance is felt, brake adjustment or repair is necessary. If the pedal feels spongy, there is air in the hydraulic system which must be removed by bleeding.

☐ Check that the brake pedal is secure and in good condition. Check also for signs of fluid leaks on the pedal, floor or carpets, which would indicate failed seals in the brake master cylinder.
☐ Check the servo unit (when applicable) by operating the brake pedal several times, then keeping the pedal depressed and starting the engine. As the engine starts, the pedal will move down slightly. If not, the vacuum hose or the servo itself may be faulty.

Steering wheel and column

☐ Examine the steering wheel for fractures or looseness of the hub, spokes or rim.
☐ Move the steering wheel from side to side and then up and down. Check that the steering wheel is not loose on the column, indicating wear or a loose retaining nut. Continue moving the steering wheel as before, but also turn it slightly from left to right.

☐ Check that the steering wheel is not loose on the column, and that there is no abnormal movement of the steering wheel, indicating wear in the column support bearings or couplings.
☐ Check that the ignition lock (where fitted) engages and disengages correctly.
☐ Steering column adjustment mechanisms (where fitted) must be able to lock the column securely in place with no play evident.

Windscreen, mirrors and sunvisor

☐ The windscreen must be free of cracks or other significant damage within the driver's field of view. (Small stone chips are acceptable.) Rear view mirrors must be secure, intact, and capable of being adjusted.

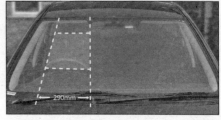

☐ The driver's sunvisor must be capable of being stored in the "up" position.

Seat belts and seats

Note: *The following checks are applicable to all seat belts, front and rear.*

☐ Examine the webbing of all the belts (including rear belts if fitted) for cuts, serious fraying or deterioration. Fasten and unfasten each belt to check the buckles. If applicable, check the retracting mechanism. Check the security of all seat belt mountings accessible from inside the vehicle, ensuring any height adjustable mountings lock securely in place.
☐ Seat belts with pre-tensioners, once activated, have a "flag" or similar showing on the seat belt stalk. This, in itself, is not a reason for test failure.
☐ The front seats themselves must be securely attached and the backrests must lock in the upright position.

Doors

☐ Both front doors must be able to be opened and closed from outside and inside, and must latch securely when closed.

Bonnet and boot/tailgate

☐ The bonnet and boot/tailgate must latch securely when closed.

2 Checks carried out WITH THE VEHICLE ON THE GROUND

Vehicle identification

☐ Number plates must be in good condition, secure and legible, with letters and numbers correctly spaced – spacing at (A) should be 33 mm and at (B) 11 mm. At the front, digits must be black on a white background and at the rear black on a yellow background. Other background designs (such as honeycomb) are not permitted.

☐ The VIN plate and/or homologation plate must be permanently displayed and legible.

Electrical equipment

☐ Switch on the ignition and check the operation of the horn.
☐ Check the windscreen washers and wipers, examining the wiper blades; renew damaged or perished blades. Also check the operation of the stop-lights.

☐ Check the operation of the sidelights and number plate lights. The lenses and reflectors must be secure, clean and undamaged.
☐ Check the operation and alignment of the headlights. The headlight reflectors must not be tarnished and the lenses must be undamaged.
☐ Switch on the ignition and check the operation of the direction indicators (including the instrument panel tell-tale) and the hazard warning lights. Operation of the sidelights and stop-lights must not affect the indicators - if it does, the cause is usually a bad earth at the rear light cluster. Indicators should flash at a rate of between 60 and 120 times per minute – faster or slower than this could indicate a fault with the flasher unit or a bad earth at one of the light units.
☐ Check the operation of the rear foglight(s), including the warning light on the instrument panel or in the switch.
☐ The warning lights must illuminate in accordance with the manufacturer's design. For most vehicles, the ABS and other warning lights should illuminate when the ignition is switched on, and (if the system is operating properly) extinguish after a few seconds. Refer to the owner's handbook.

Footbrake

☐ Examine the master cylinder, brake pipes and servo unit for leaks, loose mountings, corrosion or other damage. If ABS is fitted, this unit should also be examined for signs of leaks or corrosion.

☐ The fluid reservoir must be secure and the fluid level must be between the upper (**A**) and lower (**B**) markings.

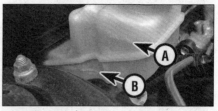

☐ Inspect both front brake flexible hoses for cracks or deterioration of the rubber. Turn the steering from lock to lock, and ensure that the hoses do not contact the wheel, tyre, or any part of the steering or suspension mechanism. With the brake pedal firmly depressed, check the hoses for bulges or leaks under pressure.

Steering and suspension

☐ Have your assistant turn the steering wheel from side to side slightly, up to the point where the steering gear just begins to transmit this movement to the roadwheels. Check for excessive free play between the steering wheel and the steering gear, indicating wear or insecurity of the steering column joints, the column-to-steering gear coupling, or the steering gear itself.
☐ Have your assistant turn the steering wheel more vigorously in each direction, so that the roadwheels just begin to turn. As this is done, examine all the steering joints, linkages, fittings and attachments. Renew any component that shows signs of wear or damage. On vehicles with power steering, check the security and condition of the steering pump, drivebelt and hoses.
☐ Check that the vehicle is standing level, and at approximately the correct ride height.

Shock absorbers

☐ Depress each corner of the vehicle in turn, then release it. The vehicle should rise and then settle in its normal position. If the vehicle continues to rise and fall, the shock absorber is defective. A shock absorber which has seized will also cause the vehicle to fail.

Exhaust system

☐ Start the engine. With your assistant holding a rag over the tailpipe, check the entire system for leaks. Repair or renew leaking sections.

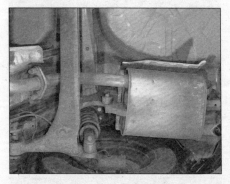

3 Checks carried out **WITH THE VEHICLE RAISED AND THE WHEELS FREE TO TURN**

Jack up the front and rear of the vehicle, and securely support it on axle stands. Position the stands clear of the suspension assemblies. Ensure that the wheels are clear of the ground and that the steering can be turned from lock to lock.

Steering mechanism

☐ Have your assistant turn the steering from lock to lock. Check that the steering turns smoothly, and that no part of the steering mechanism, including a wheel or tyre, fouls any brake hose or pipe or any part of the body structure.

☐ Examine the steering rack rubber gaiters for damage or insecurity of the retaining clips. If power steering is fitted, check for signs of damage or leakage of the fluid hoses, pipes or connections. Also check for excessive stiffness or binding of the steering, a missing split pin or locking device, or severe corrosion of the body structure within 30 cm of any steering component attachment point.

Front and rear suspension and wheel bearings

☐ Starting at the front right-hand side, grasp the roadwheel at the 3 o'clock and 9 o'clock positions and rock gently but firmly. Check for free play or insecurity at the wheel bearings, suspension balljoints, or suspension mount-ings, pivots and attachments.

☐ Now grasp the wheel at the 12 o'clock and 6 o'clock positions and repeat the previous inspection. Spin the wheel, and check for roughness or tightness of the front wheel bearing.

☐ If excess free play is suspected at a component pivot point, this can be confirmed by using a large screwdriver or similar tool and levering between the mounting and the component attachment. This will confirm whether the wear is in the pivot bush, its retaining bolt, or in the mounting itself (the bolt holes can often become elongated).

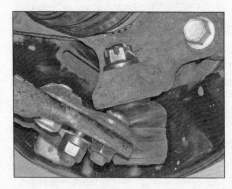

☐ Carry out all the above checks at the other front wheel, and then at both rear wheels.

Springs and shock absorbers

☐ Examine the suspension struts (when applicable) for serious fluid leakage, corrosion, or damage to the casing. Also check the security of the mounting points.

☐ If coil springs are fitted, check that the spring ends locate in their seats, and that the spring is not corroded, cracked or broken.

☐ If leaf springs are fitted, check that all leaves are intact, that the axle is securely attached to each spring, and that there is no deterioration of the spring eye mountings, bushes, and shackles.

☐ The same general checks apply to vehicles fitted with other suspension types, such as torsion bars, hydraulic displacer units, etc. Ensure that all mountings and attachments are secure, that there are no signs of excessive wear, corrosion or damage, and (on hydraulic types) that there are no fluid leaks or damaged pipes.

☐ Inspect the shock absorbers for signs of serious fluid leakage. Check for wear of the mounting bushes or attachments, or damage to the body of the unit.

Driveshafts (fwd vehicles only)

☐ Rotate each front wheel in turn and inspect the constant velocity joint gaiters for splits or damage. Also check that each driveshaft is straight and undamaged.

Braking system

☐ If possible without dismantling, check brake pad wear and disc condition. Ensure that the friction lining material has not worn excessively, (A) and that the discs are not fractured, pitted, scored or badly worn (B).

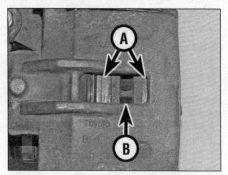

☐ Examine all the rigid brake pipes underneath the vehicle, and the flexible hose(s) at the rear. Look for corrosion, chafing or insecurity of the pipes, and for signs of bulging under pressure, chafing, splits or deterioration of the flexible hoses.

☐ Look for signs of fluid leaks at the brake calipers or on the brake backplates. Repair or renew leaking components.

☐ Slowly spin each wheel, while your assistant depresses and releases the footbrake. Ensure that each brake is operating and does not bind when the pedal is released.

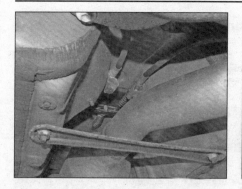

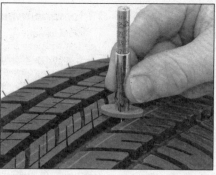

black smoke means unburnt fuel (dirty air cleaner element, or other fuel system fault).

☐ An exhaust gas analyser for measuring carbon monoxide (CO) and hydrocarbons (HC) is now needed. If one cannot be hired or borrowed, have a local garage perform the check.

☐ Examine the handbrake mechanism, checking for frayed or broken cables, excessive corrosion, or wear or insecurity of the linkage. Check that the mechanism works on each relevant wheel, and releases fully, without binding.

☐ It is not possible to test brake efficiency without special equipment, but a road test can be carried out later to check that the vehicle pulls up in a straight line.

Fuel and exhaust systems

☐ Inspect the fuel tank (including the filler cap), fuel pipes, hoses and unions. All components must be secure and free from leaks. Locking fuel caps must lock securely and the key must be provided for the MOT test.

☐ Examine the exhaust system over its entire length, checking for any damaged, broken or missing mountings, security of the retaining clamps and rust or corrosion.

Wheels and tyres

☐ Examine the sidewalls and tread area of each tyre in turn. Check for cuts, tears, lumps, bulges, separation of the tread, and exposure of the ply or cord due to wear or damage. Check that the tyre bead is correctly seated on the wheel rim, that the valve is sound and properly seated, and that the wheel is not distorted or damaged.

☐ Check that the tyres are of the correct size for the vehicle, that they are of the same size and type on each axle, and that the pressures are correct.

☐ Check the tyre tread depth. The legal minimum at the time of writing is 1.6 mm over the central three-quarters of the tread width. Abnormal tread wear may indicate incorrect front wheel alignment or wear in steering or suspension components.

☐ If the spare wheel is fitted externally or in a separate carrier beneath the vehicle, check that mountings are secure and free of excessive corrosion.

Body corrosion

☐ Check the condition of the entire vehicle structure for signs of corrosion in load-bearing areas. (These include chassis box sections, side sills, cross-members, pillars, and all suspension, steering, braking system and seat belt mountings and anchorages.) Any corrosion which has seriously reduced the thickness of a load-bearing area (or is within 30 cm of safety-related components such as steering or suspension) is likely to cause the vehicle to fail. In this case professional repairs are likely to be needed.

☐ Damage or corrosion which causes sharp or otherwise dangerous edges to be exposed will also cause the vehicle to fail.

Towbars

☐ Check the condition of mounting points (both beneath the vehicle and within boot/ hatchback areas) for signs of corrosion, ensuring that all fixings are secure and not worn or damaged. There must be no excessive play in detachable tow ball arms or quick-release mechanisms.

4 Checks carried out on YOUR VEHICLE'S EXHAUST EMISSION SYSTEM

Petrol models

☐ The engine should be warmed up, and running well (ignition system in good order, air filter element clean, etc).

☐ Before testing, run the engine at around 2500 rpm for 20 seconds. Let the engine drop to idle, and watch for smoke from the exhaust. If the idle speed is too high, or if dense blue or black smoke emerges for more than 5 seconds, the vehicle will fail. Typically, blue smoke signifies oil burning (engine wear);

CO emissions (mixture)

☐ The MOT tester has access to the CO limits for all vehicles. The CO level is measured at idle speed, and at 'fast idle' (2500 to 3000 rpm). The following limits are given as a general guide:

At idle speed – Less than 0.5% CO
At 'fast idle' – Less than 0.3% CO
Lambda reading – 0.97 to 1.03

☐ If the CO level is too high, this may point to poor maintenance, a fuel injection system problem, faulty lambda (oxygen) sensor or catalytic converter. Try an injector cleaning treatment, and check the vehicle's ECU for fault codes.

HC emissions

☐ The MOT tester has access to HC limits for all vehicles. The HC level is measured at 'fast idle' (2500 to 3000 rpm). The following limits are given as a general guide:

At 'fast idle' – Less then 200 ppm

☐ Excessive HC emissions are typically caused by oil being burnt (worn engine), or by a blocked crankcase ventilation system ('breather'). If the engine oil is old and thin, an oil change may help. If the engine is running badly, check the vehicle's ECU for fault codes.

Diesel models

☐ The only emission test for diesel engines is measuring exhaust smoke density, using a calibrated smoke meter. The test involves accelerating the engine at least 3 times to its maximum unloaded speed.

Note: *On engines with a timing belt, it is VITAL that the belt is in good condition before the test is carried out.*

☐ With the engine warmed up, it is first purged by running at around 2500 rpm for 20 seconds. A governor check is then carried out, by slowly accelerating the engine to its maximum speed. After this, the smoke meter is connected, and the engine is accelerated quickly to maximum speed three times. If the smoke density is less than the limits given below, the vehicle will pass:

Non-turbo vehicles: 2.5m-1
Turbocharged vehicles: 3.0m-1

☐ If excess smoke is produced, try fitting a new air cleaner element, or using an injector cleaning treatment. If the engine is running badly, where applicable, check the vehicle's ECU for fault codes. Also check the vehicle's EGR system, where applicable. At high mileages, the injectors may require professional attention.

Engine

- ☐ Engine fails to rotate when attempting to start
- ☐ Engine rotates, but will not start
- ☐ Engine difficult to start when cold
- ☐ Engine difficult to start when hot
- ☐ Starter motor noisy or excessively-rough in engagement
- ☐ Engine starts, but stops immediately
- ☐ Engine idles erratically
- ☐ Engine misfires at idle speed
- ☐ Engine misfires throughout the driving speed range
- ☐ Engine hesitates on acceleration
- ☐ Engine stalls
- ☐ Engine lacks power
- ☐ Engine backfires
- ☐ Oil pressure warning light illuminated with engine running
- ☐ Engine runs-on after switching off
- ☐ Engine noises

Cooling system

- ☐ Overheating
- ☐ Overcooling
- ☐ External coolant leakage
- ☐ Internal coolant leakage
- ☐ Corrosion

Fuel and exhaust systems

- ☐ Excessive fuel consumption
- ☐ Fuel leakage and/or fuel odour
- ☐ Excessive noise or fumes from exhaust system

Clutch

- ☐ Pedal travels to floor – no pressure or very little resistance
- ☐ Clutch fails to disengage (unable to select gears)
- ☐ Clutch slips (engine speed increases, with no increase in vehicle speed)
- ☐ Judder as clutch is engaged
- ☐ Noise when depressing or releasing clutch pedal

Manual transmission

- ☐ Noisy in neutral with engine running
- ☐ Noisy in one particular gear
- ☐ Difficulty engaging gears
- ☐ Jumps out of gear
- ☐ Vibration
- ☐ Lubricant leaks

Automatic transmission

- ☐ Fluid leakage
- ☐ Transmission fluid brown, or has burned smell
- ☐ General gear selection problems
- ☐ Transmission will not downshift (kickdown) with accelerator pedal fully depressed
- ☐ Engine will not start in any gear, or starts in gears other than Park or Neutral
- ☐ Transmission slips, shifts roughly, is noisy, or has no drive in forward or reverse gears

Driveshafts

- ☐ Vibration when accelerating or decelerating
- ☐ Clicking or knocking noise on turns (at slow speed on full-lock)

Braking system

- ☐ Vehicle pulls to one side under braking
- ☐ Noise (grinding or high-pitched squeal) when brakes applied
- ☐ Excessive brake pedal travel
- ☐ Brake pedal feels spongy when depressed
- ☐ Excessive brake pedal effort required to stop vehicle
- ☐ Judder felt through brake pedal or steering wheel when braking
- ☐ Brakes binding
- ☐ Rear wheels locking under normal braking

Suspension and steering

- ☐ Vehicle pulls to one side
- ☐ Wheel wobble and vibration
- ☐ Excessive pitching and/or rolling around corners, or during braking
- ☐ Wandering or general instability
- ☐ Excessively-stiff steering
- ☐ Excessive play in steering
- ☐ Lack of power assistance
- ☐ Tyre wear excessive

Electrical system

- ☐ Battery will not hold a charge for more than a few days
- ☐ Ignition/no-charge warning light remains illuminated with engine running
- ☐ Ignition/no-charge warning light fails to come on
- ☐ Lights inoperative
- ☐ Instrument readings inaccurate or erratic
- ☐ Horn inoperative, or unsatisfactory in operation
- ☐ Windscreen wipers inoperative, or unsatisfactory in operation
- ☐ Windscreen washers inoperative, or unsatisfactory in operation
- ☐ Electric windows inoperative, or unsatisfactory in operation
- ☐ Central locking system inoperative, or unsatisfactory in operation

Introduction

The vehicle owner who does his or her own maintenance according to the recommended service schedules should not have to use this section of the manual very often. Modern component reliability is such that, provided those items subject to wear or deterioration are inspected or renewed at the specified intervals, sudden failure is comparatively rare. Faults do not usually just happen as a result of sudden failure, but develop over a period of time. Major mechanical failures in particular are usually preceded by characteristic symptoms over hundreds or even thousands of miles. Those components which do occasionally fail without warning are often small and easily carried in the vehicle.

With any fault-finding, the first step is to decide where to begin investigations. Sometimes this is obvious, but on other occasions, a little detective work will be necessary. The owner who makes half a dozen haphazard adjustments or replacements may be successful in curing a fault (or its symptoms), but will be none the wiser if the fault recurs, and ultimately may have spent more time and money than was necessary. A calm and logical approach will be found to be more satisfactory in the long run. Always take into account any warning signs or abnormalities that may have been noticed in the period preceding the fault – power loss, high or low gauge readings, unusual smells,

etc – and remember that failure of components such as fuses may only be pointers to some underlying fault.

The pages which follow provide an easy-reference guide to the more common problems which may occur during the operation of the vehicle. These problems and their possible causes are grouped under headings denoting various components or systems, such as Engine, Cooling system, etc. The general Chapter which deals with the problem is also shown in brackets; refer to the relevant part of that Chapter for system-specific information. Whatever the fault, certain basic principles apply. These are as follows:

Verify the fault. This is simply a matter of

being sure that you know what the symptoms are before starting work. This is particularly important if you are investigating a fault for someone else, who may not have described it very accurately.

Don't overlook the obvious. For example, if the vehicle won't start, is there fuel in the tank? (Don't take anyone else's word on this particular point, and don't trust the fuel gauge either!) If an electrical fault is indicated, look for loose or broken wires before digging out the test gear.

Cure the disease, not the symptom.

Substituting a flat battery with a fully-charged one will get you off the hard shoulder, but if the underlying cause is not attended to, the new battery will go the same way.

Don't take anything for granted. Particularly, don't forget that a 'new' component may itself be defective (especially if it's been rattling around in the boot for months), and don't leave components out of a fault diagnosis sequence just because they are new or recently-fitted. When you do finally diagnose a difficult fault, you'll probably realise that all the evidence was there from the start.

Consider what work, if any, has recently been carried out. Many faults arise through careless or hurried work. For instance, if any work has been performed under the bonnet, could some of the wiring have been dislodged or incorrectly routed, or a hose trapped? Have all the fasteners been properly tightened? Were new, genuine parts and new gaskets used? There is often a certain amount of detective work to be done in this case, as an apparently-unrelated task can have far-reaching consequences.

Engine

Engine fails to rotate when attempting to start

- [ ] Battery terminal connections loose or corroded (see *Weekly checks*)
- [ ] Battery discharged or faulty (Chapter 5)
- [ ] Broken, loose or disconnected wiring in the starting circuit (Chapter 5)
- [ ] Defective starter solenoid or ignition switch (Chapter 5 or 10)
- [ ] Defective starter motor (Chapter 5)
- [ ] Starter pinion or flywheel ring gear teeth loose or broken (Chapter 2A, 2B or 5)
- [ ] Engine earth strap broken or disconnected (Chapter 5)
- [ ] Engine suffering 'hydraulic lock' (eg from water drawn into the engine after traversing flooded roads, or from a serious internal coolant leak) – consult a main dealer for advice

Engine rotates, but will not start

- [ ] Fuel tank empty
- [ ] Battery discharged (engine rotates slowly) (Chapter 5)
- [ ] Battery terminal connections loose or corroded (see *Weekly checks*)
- [ ] Immobiliser fault, or 'uncoded' ignition key being used (Chapter 12 or Roadside repairs)
- [ ] Preheating system faulty (Chapter 5)
- [ ] Fuel injection/engine management system fault (Chapter 4A)
- [ ] Air in fuel system (Chapter 4A)
- [ ] Major mechanical failure (Chapter 2A, 2B or 2C)

Engine difficult to start when cold

- [ ] Battery discharged (Chapter 5)
- [ ] Battery terminal connections loose or corroded (see *Weekly checks*)
- [ ] Preheating system faulty (Chapter 5)
- [ ] Fuel injection/engine management system fault (Chapter 4A)
- [ ] Wrong grade of engine oil used (*Weekly checks*, Chapter 1)
- [ ] Low cylinder compression (Chapter 2A or 2B)

Engine difficult to start when hot

- [ ] Air filter element dirty or clogged (Chapter 1)
- [ ] Fuel injection/engine management system fault (Chapter 4A)
- [ ] Low cylinder compression (Chapter 2A or 2B)

Starter motor noisy or excessively-rough in engagement

- [ ] Starter pinion or flywheel ring gear teeth loose or broken (2A, 2B or 5)
- [ ] Starter motor mounting bolts loose or missing (Chapter 5)
- [ ] Starter motor internal components worn or damaged (Chapter 5)

Engine starts, but stops immediately

- [ ] Fuel injection/engine management system fault (Chapter 4A)

Engine idles erratically

- [ ] Air filter element clogged (Chapter 1)
- [ ] Uneven or low cylinder compression (Chapter 2A or 2B)
- [ ] Camshaft lobes worn (Chapter 2A or 2B)
- [ ] Fuel injection/engine management system fault (Chapter 4A)
- [ ] Air in fuel system (Chapter 4A)

Engine misfires at idle speed

- [ ] Faulty injector(s) (Chapter 4A)
- [ ] Uneven or low cylinder compression (Chapter 2A or 2B)
- [ ] Disconnected, leaking, or perished crankcase ventilation hoses (Chapter 4B)
- [ ] Fuel injection/engine management system fault (Chapter 4A)

Engine misfires throughout the driving speed range

- [ ] Fuel filter choked (Chapter 1)
- [ ] Fuel tank vent blocked, or fuel pipes restricted (Chapter 4A or 4B)
- [ ] Faulty injector(s) (Chapter 4A)
- [ ] Uneven or low cylinder compression (Chapter 2A or 2B)
- [ ] Blocked catalytic converter (Chapter 4B)
- [ ] Fuel injection/engine management system fault (Chapter 4A)
- [ ] Engine overheating (Chapter 3)

Engine hesitates on acceleration

- [ ] Faulty injector(s) (Chapter 4A)
- [ ] Fuel injection/engine management system fault (Chapter 4A)

Engine stalls

- [ ] Fuel filter choked (Chapter 1)
- [ ] Fuel tank vent blocked, or fuel pipes restricted (Chapter 4A)
- [ ] Faulty injector(s) (Chapter 4A)
- [ ] Fuel injection/engine management system fault (Chapter 4A)

Engine lacks power

- [ ] Air filter element blocked (Chapter 1)
- [ ] Fuel filter choked (Chapter 1)
- [ ] Fuel pipes blocked or restricted (Chapter 4A)
- [ ] Engine overheating (Chapter 3)
- [ ] Accelerator pedal position sensor faulty (Chapter 4A)
- [ ] Faulty injector(s) (Chapter 4A)
- [ ] Uneven or low cylinder compression (Chapter 2A or 2B)
- [ ] Fuel injection/engine management system fault (Chapter 4A)
- [ ] Blocked catalytic converter (Chapter 4B)
- [ ] Brakes binding (Chapter 1 or 9)
- [ ] Clutch slipping (Chapter 6)

Engine backfires

- [ ] Fuel injection/engine management system fault (Chapter 4A or 4B)
- [ ] Blocked catalytic converter (Chapter 4B)

Engine (continued)

Oil pressure warning light illuminated with engine running

- ☐ Low oil level, or incorrect oil grade (see *Weekly checks*)
- ☐ Faulty oil pressure warning light switch, or wiring damaged (Chapter 2A or 2B)
- ☐ Worn engine bearings and/or oil pump (Chapter 2A, 2B or 2C)
- ☐ High engine operating temperature (Chapter 3)
- ☐ Oil pump pressure relief valve defective (Chapter 2A or 2B)
- ☐ Oil pump pick-up strainer clogged (Chapter 2A or 2B)

Engine runs-on after switching off

- ☐ Excessive carbon build-up in engine (Chapter 2A, 2B or 2C)
- ☐ High engine operating temperature (Chapter 3)
- ☐ Fuel injection/engine management system fault (Chapter 4A)

Engine noises

Pre-ignition (pinking) or knocking during acceleration or under load

- ☐ Excessive carbon build-up in engine (Chapter 2A, 2B or 2C)
- ☐ Fuel injection/engine management system fault (Chapter 4A)
- ☐ Faulty injector(s) (Chapter 4A)

Whistling or wheezing noises

- ☐ Leaking exhaust manifold gasket or pipe-to-manifold joint (Chapter 4A)
- ☐ Leaking vacuum hose (Chapter 4A, 4B or 9)
- ☐ Blowing cylinder head gasket (Chapter 2A or 2B)
- ☐ Partially blocked or leaking crankcase ventilation system (Chapter 4B)

Tapping or rattling noises

- ☐ Worn valve gear or camshaft(s) (Chapter 2A, 2B or 2C)
- ☐ Worn or damaged dual-mass flywheel (Chapter 2A or 2B)
- ☐ Ancillary component fault (coolant pump, alternator, etc) (Chapter 3, 5, etc)

Knocking or thumping noises

- ☐ Worn big-end bearings (regular heavy knocking, perhaps less under load) (Chapter 2C)
- ☐ Worn main bearings (rumbling and knocking, perhaps worsening under load) (Chapter 2C)
- ☐ Piston slap – most noticeable when cold, caused by piston/bore wear (Chapter 2C)
- ☐ Ancillary component fault (coolant pump, alternator, etc) (Chapter 3, 5, etc)
- ☐ Engine mountings worn or defective (Chapter 2A or 2B)
- ☐ Front suspension or steering components worn (Chapter 10)

Cooling system

Overheating

- ☐ Insufficient coolant in system (see *Weekly checks*)
- ☐ Thermostat faulty (Chapter 3)
- ☐ Radiator core blocked, or grille restricted (Chapter 3)
- ☐ Cooling fan faulty (Chapter 3)
- ☐ Airlock in cooling system (Chapter 1 or 3)
- ☐ Expansion tank pressure cap faulty (Chapter 1 or 3)
- ☐ Engine management system fault (Chapter 4A)

Overcooling

- ☐ Thermostat faulty (Chapter 3)
- ☐ Cooling fan faulty (Chapter 3)
- ☐ Engine management system fault (Chapter 4A)

External coolant leakage

- ☐ Deteriorated or damaged hoses or hose clips (Chapter 1)
- ☐ Radiator core or heater matrix leaking (Chapter 3)
- ☐ Expansion tank pressure cap faulty (Chapter 1 or 3)
- ☐ Coolant pump internal seal leaking (Chapter 3)
- ☐ Coolant pump gasket leaking (Chapter 3)
- ☐ Boiling due to overheating (Chapter 3)
- ☐ Cylinder block core plug leaking (Chapter 2C)

Internal coolant leakage

- ☐ Leaking cylinder head gasket (Chapter 2A or 2B)
- ☐ Cracked cylinder head or cylinder block (Chapter 2A, 2B or 2C)

Corrosion

- ☐ Infrequent draining and flushing (Chapter 1)
- ☐ Incorrect coolant mixture or inappropriate coolant type (Chapter 1)

Fuel and exhaust systems

Excessive fuel consumption

- ☐ Air filter element dirty or clogged (Chapter 1)
- ☐ Fuel injection system fault (Chapter 4A)
- ☐ Engine management system fault (Chapter 4A)
- ☐ Crankcase ventilation system blocked (Chapter 4B)
- ☐ Tyres under-inflated (see *Weekly checks*)
- ☐ Brakes binding (Chapter 1 or 9)
- ☐ Fuel leak, causing apparent high consumption (Chapter 1, 4A or 4B)

Fuel leakage and/or fuel odour

- ☐ Damaged or corroded fuel tank, pipes or connections (Chapter 4A or 4B)

Excessive noise or fumes from exhaust system

- ☐ Leaking exhaust system or manifold joints (Chapter 1 or 4A)
- ☐ Leaking, corroded or damaged silencers or pipe (Chapter 1 or 4A)
- ☐ Broken mountings causing body or suspension contact (Chapter 1 or 4A)

Clutch

Pedal travels to floor – no pressure or very little resistance

☐ Air in hydraulic system/faulty master or release/slave cylinder (Chapter 6)
☐ Faulty hydraulic release system (Chapter 6)
☐ Broken diaphragm spring in clutch pressure plate (Chapter 6)

Clutch fails to disengage (unable to select gears)

☐ Air in hydraulic system/faulty master or release/slave cylinder (Chapter 6)
☐ Faulty hydraulic release system (Chapter 6)
☐ Clutch disc sticking on transmission input shaft splines (Chapter 6)
☐ Clutch disc sticking to flywheel or pressure plate (Chapter 6)
☐ Faulty pressure plate assembly (Chapter 6)
☐ Clutch release mechanism worn or incorrectly assembled (Chapter 6)

Clutch slips (engine speed increases, with no increase in vehicle speed)

☐ Faulty hydraulic release system (Chapter 6)
☐ Clutch disc linings excessively worn (Chapter 6)
☐ Clutch disc linings contaminated with oil or grease (Chapter 6)
☐ Faulty pressure plate or weak diaphragm spring (Chapter 6)

Judder as clutch is engaged

☐ Clutch disc linings contaminated with oil or grease (Chapter 6)
☐ Clutch disc linings excessively worn (Chapter 6)
☐ Faulty or distorted pressure plate or diaphragm spring (Chapter 6).
☐ Worn or loose engine or transmission mountings (Chapter 2A or 2B)
☐ Clutch disc hub or transmission input shaft splines worn (Chapter 6)

Noise when depressing or releasing clutch pedal

☐ Faulty clutch release/slave cylinder (Chapter 6)
☐ Worn or dry clutch pedal bushes (Chapter 6)
☐ Faulty pressure plate assembly (Chapter 6)
☐ Pressure plate diaphragm spring broken (Chapter 6)
☐ Broken clutch disc cushioning springs (Chapter 6)

Manual transmission

Noisy in neutral with engine running

☐ Lack of oil (Chapter 7A)
☐ Input shaft bearings worn (noise apparent with clutch pedal released, but not when depressed) (Chapter 7A)*
☐ Clutch release/slave cylinder faulty (noise apparent with clutch pedal depressed, possibly less when released) (Chapter 6)

Noisy in one particular gear

☐ Worn, damaged or chipped gear teeth (Chapter 7A)*

Difficulty engaging gears

☐ Clutch fault (Chapter 6)
☐ Worn, damaged, or poorly-adjusted gearchange (Chapter 7A)
☐ Lack of oil (Chapter 7A)
☐ Worn synchroniser units (Chapter 7A)*

Jumps out of gear

☐ Worn, damaged, or poorly-adjusted gearchange (Chapter 7A)
☐ Worn synchroniser units (Chapter 7A)*
☐ Worn selector forks (Chapter 7A)*

Vibration

☐ Lack of oil (Chapter 7A)
☐ Worn bearings (Chapter 7A)*

Lubricant leaks

☐ Leaking driveshaft or selector shaft oil seal (Chapter 7A)
☐ Leaking housing joint (Chapter 7A)*
☐ Leaking input shaft oil seal (Chapter 7A)*

*Although the corrective action necessary to remedy the symptoms described is beyond the scope of the home mechanic, the above information should be helpful in isolating the cause of the condition, so that the owner can communicate clearly with a professional mechanic.

Automatic transmission

Note: *Due to the complexity of the automatic transmission, it is difficult for the home mechanic to properly diagnose and service this unit. For problems other than the following, the vehicle should be taken to a dealer service department or automatic transmission specialist. Do not be too hasty in removing the transmission if a fault is suspected, as most of the testing is carried out with the unit still fitted. Remember that, besides the sensors specific to the transmission, many of the engine management system sensors described in Chapter 4A are essential to the correct operation of the transmission.*

Fluid leakage

☐ Automatic transmission fluid is usually dark red in colour. Fluid leaks should not be confused with engine oil, which can easily be blown onto the transmission by airflow.

☐ To determine the source of a leak, first remove all built-up dirt and grime from the transmission housing and surrounding areas using a degreasing agent, or by steam-cleaning. Drive the vehicle at low speed, so airflow will not blow the leak far from its source. Raise and support the vehicle, and determine where the leak is coming from. The following are common areas of leakage:
  a) *Fluid pan*
  b) *Dipstick tube*
  c) *Transmission-to-fluid cooler unions*

Transmission fluid brown, or has burned smell

☐ Transmission fluid level low (Chapter 1 and 7B)

General gear selection problems

☐ Chapter 7B deals with checking the selector cable on automatic transmissions. The following are common problems which may be caused by a faulty cable or sensor:
  a) *Engine starting in gears other than Park or Neutral.*
  b) *Indicator panel indicating a gear other than the one actually being used.*
  c) *Vehicle moves when in Park or Neutral.*
  d) *Poor gear shift quality or erratic gear changes.*

Transmission will not downshift (kickdown) with accelerator pedal fully depressed

☐ Low transmission fluid level (Chapter 1 or 7B)
☐ Engine management system fault (Chapter 4A)
☐ Faulty transmission sensor or wiring (Chapter 7B)
☐ Incorrect selector cable adjustment (Chapter 7B)

Engine will not start in any gear, or starts in gears other than Park or Neutral

☐ Incorrect selector cable adjustment (Chapter 7B)
☐ Faulty transmission sensor or wiring (Chapter 7B)
☐ Engine management system fault (Chapter 4A)

Transmission slips, shifts roughly, is noisy, or has no drive in forward or reverse gears

☐ Transmission fluid level low (Chapter 1 or 7B)
☐ Faulty transmission sensor or wiring (Chapter 7B)
☐ Engine management system fault (Chapter 4A)

Note: *There are many probable causes for the above problems, but diagnosing and correcting them is considered beyond the scope of this manual. Having checked the fluid level and all the wiring as far as possible, a dealer or transmission specialist should be consulted if the problem persists.*

Driveshafts

Vibration when accelerating or decelerating

☐ Worn inner constant velocity joint (Chapter 8)
☐ Bent or distorted driveshaft (Chapter 8)
☐ Worn intermediate shaft bearing (Chapter 8)

Clicking or knocking noise on turns (at slow speed on full-lock)

☐ Worn outer constant velocity joint (Chapter 8)
☐ Lack of constant velocity joint lubricant, possibly due to damaged gaiter (Chapter 8)

Braking system

Note: *Before assuming that a brake problem exists, make sure that the tyres are in good condition and correctly inflated, that the front wheel alignment is correct, and that the vehicle is not loaded with weight in an unequal manner. Apart from checking the condition of all pipe and hose connections, any faults occurring on the anti-lock braking system should be referred to a VW dealer for diagnosis.*

Vehicle pulls to one side under braking

☐ Worn, defective, damaged or contaminated brake pads/shoes on one side (Chapter 1 or 9)
☐ Seized or partially-seized brake caliper/wheel cylinder piston (Chapter 1 or 9)
☐ A mixture of brake pad/shoe lining materials fitted between sides (Chapter 1 or 9)
☐ Brake caliper mounting bolts loose (Chapter 9)
☐ Worn or damaged steering or suspension components (Chapter 1 or 10)

Noise (grinding or high-pitched squeal) when brakes applied

☐ Brake pad/shoe friction lining material worn down to wear sensor or metal backing (Chapter 1 or 9)
☐ Excessive corrosion of brake disc/drum (may be apparent after the vehicle has been standing for some time (Chapter 1 or 9)
☐ Foreign object (stone chipping, etc) trapped between brake disc and shield (Chapter 1 or 9)

Excessive brake pedal travel

☐ Faulty master cylinder (Chapter 9)
☐ Air in hydraulic system (Chapter 1 or 9)
☐ Faulty vacuum servo unit (Chapter 9)
☐ Faulty vacuum pump (Chapter 9)
☐ Disconnected, damaged or insecure brake servo vacuum hose (Chapter 9)

Braking system (continued)

Brake pedal feels spongy when depressed

- [ ] Air in hydraulic system (Chapter 1 or 9)
- [ ] Deteriorated flexible rubber brake hoses (Chapter 1 or 9)
- [ ] Master cylinder mounting nuts loose (Chapter 9)
- [ ] Faulty master cylinder (Chapter 9)

Excessive brake pedal effort required to stop vehicle

- [ ] Faulty vacuum servo unit (Chapter 9)
- [ ] Faulty vacuum pump (Chapter 9)
- [ ] Disconnected, damaged or insecure brake servo vacuum hose (Chapter 9)
- [ ] Primary or secondary hydraulic circuit failure (Chapter 9)
- [ ] Seized brake caliper/wheel cylinder piston (Chapter 9)
- [ ] Brake pads/shoes incorrectly fitted (Chapter 9)
- [ ] Incorrect grade of brake pads/shoes fitted (Chapter 9)
- [ ] Brake pad/shoe linings contaminated (Chapter 1 or 9)

Judder felt through brake pedal or steering wheel when braking

Note: *Under heavy braking on models equipped with ABS, vibration may be felt through the brake pedal. This is a normal feature of ABS operation, and does not constitute a fault.*

- [ ] Excessive run-out or distortion of discs/drums (Chapter 1 or 9)
- [ ] Brake pad/shoe linings worn (Chapter 1 or 9)
- [ ] Brake caliper mounting bolts loose (Chapter 9)
- [ ] Wear in suspension or steering components or mountings (Chapter 1 or 10)
- [ ] Front wheels out of balance (see *Weekly checks*)

Brakes binding

- [ ] Seized brake caliper/wheel cylinder piston (Chapter 9)
- [ ] Faulty master cylinder (Chapter 9)

Rear wheels locking under normal braking

- [ ] Rear brake pad/shoe linings contaminated or damaged (Chapter 1 or 9)
- [ ] Rear brake disc/drum warped (Chapter 1 or 9)

Suspension and steering

Note: *Before diagnosing suspension or steering faults, be sure that the trouble is not due to incorrect tyre pressures, mixtures of tyre types, or binding brakes.*

Vehicle pulls to one side

- [ ] Defective tyre (see *Weekly checks*)
- [ ] Excessive wear in suspension or steering components (Chapter 1 or 10)
- [ ] Incorrect front wheel alignment (Chapter 10)
- [ ] Accident damage to steering or suspension components (Chapter 1 or 10)

Wheel wobble and vibration

- [ ] Front wheels out of balance (vibration felt mainly through the steering wheel) (see *Weekly checks*)
- [ ] Rear wheels out of balance (vibration felt throughout the vehicle) (see *Weekly checks*)
- [ ] Roadwheels damaged or distorted (see *Weekly checks*)
- [ ] Faulty or damaged tyre (see *Weekly checks*)
- [ ] Worn steering or suspension joints, bushes or components (Chapter 1 or 10)
- [ ] Wheel bolts loose (Chapter 1)

Excessive pitching and/or rolling around corners, or during braking

- [ ] Defective shock absorbers (Chapter 1 or 10)
- [ ] Broken or weak spring and/or suspension component (Chapter 1 or 10)
- [ ] Worn or damaged anti-roll bar or mountings (Chapter 1 or 10)

Wandering or general instability

- [ ] Incorrect front wheel alignment (Chapter 10)
- [ ] Worn steering or suspension joints, bushes or components (Chapter 1 or 10)
- [ ] Roadwheels out of balance (see *Weekly checks*)
- [ ] Faulty or damaged tyre (see *Weekly checks*)
- [ ] Wheel bolts loose (Chapter 1)
- [ ] Defective shock absorbers (Chapter 1 or 10)
- [ ] Power steering system fault (Chapter 10)

Excessively-stiff steering

- [ ] Seized steering linkage balljoint or suspension balljoint (Chapter 1 or 10)
- [ ] Incorrect front wheel alignment (Chapter 10)
- [ ] Steering rack damaged (Chapter 10)
- [ ] Power steering system fault (Chapter 10)

Excessive play in steering

- [ ] Worn steering column/intermediate shaft joints (Chapter 10)
- [ ] Worn track rod balljoints (Chapter 1 or 10)
- [ ] Worn steering rack (Chapter 10)
- [ ] Worn steering or suspension joints, bushes or components (Chapter 1 or 10)

Lack of power assistance

- [ ] Broken power steering pump drivebelt (Chapter 1)
- [ ] Power steering system fault (Chapter 10)
- [ ] Faulty steering rack (Chapter 10)

Tyre wear excessive

Tyres worn on inside or outside edges

- [ ] Tyres under-inflated (wear on both edges) (see *Weekly checks*)
- [ ] Incorrect camber or castor angles (wear on one edge only) (Chapter 10)
- [ ] Worn steering or suspension joints, bushes or components (Chapter 1 or 10)
- [ ] Excessively-hard cornering or braking
- [ ] Accident damage

Tyre treads exhibit feathered edges

- [ ] Incorrect toe-setting (Chapter 10)

Tyres worn in centre of tread

- [ ] Tyres over-inflated (see *Weekly checks*)

Tyres worn on inside and outside edges

- [ ] Tyres under-inflated (see *Weekly checks*)

Tyres worn unevenly

- [ ] Tyres/wheels out of balance (see *Weekly checks*)
- [ ] Excessive wheel or tyre run-out
- [ ] Worn shock absorbers (Chapter 1 or 10)
- [ ] Faulty tyre (see *Weekly checks*)

Electrical system

Note: *For problems associated with the starting system, refer to the faults listed under 'Engine' earlier in this Section.*

Battery will not hold a charge for more than a few days

- [ ] Battery defective internally (Chapter 5)
- [ ] Battery terminal connections loose or corroded (see *Weekly checks*)
- [ ] Auxiliary drivebelt worn, incorrectly adjusted or faulty automatic adjuster (Chapter 1)
- [ ] Alternator not charging at correct output (Chapter 5)
- [ ] Alternator or voltage regulator faulty (Chapter 5)
- [ ] Short-circuit causing continual battery drain (Chapter 5 or 12)

Ignition/no-charge warning light remains illuminated with engine running

- [ ] Auxiliary drivebelt broken, worn, incorrectly adjusted or faulty automatic adjuster (Chapter 1)
- [ ] Internal fault in alternator or voltage regulator (Chapter 5)
- [ ] Broken, disconnected, or loose wiring in charging circuit (Chapter 5 or 12)

Ignition/no-charge warning light fails to come on

- [ ] Faulty instrument panel (Chapter 12)
- [ ] Broken, disconnected, or loose wiring in warning light circuit (Chapter 5 or 12)
- [ ] Alternator faulty (Chapter 5)

Lights inoperative

- [ ] Bulb blown (Chapter 12)
- [ ] Corrosion of bulb or bulbholder contacts (Chapter 12)
- [ ] Blown fuse (Chapter 12)
- [ ] Faulty relay (Chapter 12)
- [ ] Broken, loose, or disconnected wiring (Chapter 12)
- [ ] Faulty switch (Chapter 12)

Instrument readings inaccurate or erratic

Fuel or temperature gauges give no reading

- [ ] Faulty gauge sender unit (Chapter 3 or 4A)
- [ ] Wiring open-circuit (Chapter 12)
- [ ] Faulty instrument panel (Chapter 12)

Fuel or temperature gauges give continuous maximum reading

- [ ] Faulty gauge sender unit (Chapter 3 or 4A)
- [ ] Wiring short-circuit (Chapter 12)
- [ ] Faulty instrument panel (Chapter 12)

Horn inoperative, or unsatisfactory in operation

Horn operates all the time

- [ ] Horn push either earthed or stuck down (Chapter 12)
- [ ] Horn cable-to-horn push earthed (Chapter 12)

Horn fails to operate

- [ ] Blown fuse (Chapter 12)
- [ ] Cable or connections loose, broken or disconnected (Chapter 12)
- [ ] Faulty horn (Chapter 12)

Horn emits intermittent or unsatisfactory sound

- [ ] Cable connections loose (Chapter 12)
- [ ] Horn mountings loose (Chapter 12)
- [ ] Faulty horn (Chapter 12)

Windscreen wipers inoperative, or unsatisfactory in operation

Wipers fail to operate, or operate very slowly

- [ ] Wiper blades stuck to screen, or linkage seized or binding (Chapter 12)
- [ ] Blown fuse (Chapter 12)
- [ ] Battery discharged (Chapter 5)
- [ ] Cable or connections loose, broken or disconnected (Chapter 12)
- [ ] Faulty relay (Chapter 12)
- [ ] Faulty wiper motor (Chapter 12)

Wiper blades sweep over too large or too small an area of the glass

- [ ] Wiper blades incorrectly fitted, or wrong size used (see *Weekly checks*)
- [ ] Wiper arms incorrectly positioned on spindles (Chapter 12)
- [ ] Excessive wear of wiper linkage (Chapter 12)
- [ ] Wiper motor or linkage mountings loose or insecure (Chapter 12)

Wiper blades fail to clean the glass effectively

- [ ] Wiper blade rubbers dirty, worn or perished (see *Weekly checks*)
- [ ] Wiper blades incorrectly fitted, or wrong size used (see *Weekly checks*)
- [ ] Wiper arm tension springs broken, or arm pivots seized (Chapter 12)
- [ ] Insufficient windscreen washer additive to adequately remove road film (see *Weekly checks*)

Windscreen washers inoperative, or unsatisfactory in operation

One or more washer jets inoperative

- [ ] Blocked washer jet
- [ ] Disconnected, kinked or restricted fluid hose (Chapter 12)
- [ ] Insufficient fluid in washer reservoir (see *Weekly checks*)

Washer pump fails to operate

- [ ] Broken or disconnected wiring or connections (Chapter 12)
- [ ] Blown fuse (Chapter 12)
- [ ] Faulty washer switch (Chapter 12)
- [ ] Faulty washer pump (Chapter 12)

Electric windows inoperative, or unsatisfactory in operation

Window glass will only move in one direction

- [ ] Faulty switch (Chapter 12)

Window glass slow to move

- [ ] Battery discharged (Chapter 5)
- [ ] Regulator seized or damaged, or in need of lubrication (Chapter 11)
- [ ] Door internal components or trim fouling regulator (Chapter 11)
- [ ] Faulty motor (Chapter 11)

Window glass fails to move

- [ ] Blown fuse (Chapter 12)
- [ ] Faulty relay (Chapter 12)
- [ ] Broken or disconnected wiring or connections (Chapter 12)
- [ ] Faulty motor (Chapter 11)

Electrical system (continued)

Central locking system inoperative, or unsatisfactory in operation

Complete system failure

☐ Blown fuse (Chapter 12)
☐ Faulty relay (Chapter 12)
☐ Broken or disconnected wiring or connections (Chapter 12)
☐ Faulty motor (Chapter 11)

Latch locks but will not unlock, or unlocks but will not lock

☐ Broken or disconnected latch operating rods or levers (Chapter 11)
☐ Faulty relay (Chapter 12)
☐ Faulty motor (Chapter 11)

One solenoid/motor fails to operate

☐ Broken or disconnected wiring or connections (Chapter 12)
☐ Faulty operating assembly (Chapter 11)
☐ Broken, binding or disconnected latch operating rods or levers (Chapter 11)
☐ Fault in door latch (Chapter 11)

Note: *References throughout this index are in the form* "**Chapter number**" • "**Page number**". *So, for example, 2C•15 refers to page 15 of Chapter 2C.*

Note: *References throughout this index are in the form "**Chapter number**" • "**Page number**". So, for example, 2C•15 refers to page 15 of Chapter 2C.*